THE OFFICIAL 1982 PRICE GUIDE TO COLLECTOR KNIVES

BY
JAMES F. PARKER
AND
J. BRUCE VOYLES

EDITOR
THOMAS E. HUDGEONS, III

FOURTH EDITION
HOUSE OF COLLECTIBLES ORLANDO, FLORIDA 32809

ACKNOWLEDGEMENTS

As any knife historian knows, most of the historical information is usually found through luck more than actual research. An old newspaper report, original catalog, advertisement, or the chance meeting of a former employee or salesman will yield vast amounts of information. Many people have helped us to come in contact with sources of valuable information, and to them we give our heartfelt thanks. Among them are: Purcell Jones, Larry Cook, Bernard Levine, Tommy Shouse, Stan Swanner, Dr. James Golden, Col. Robert Mayes, Dewey and Lavona Ferguson, Howard Rabin, Charlie Genella, M. H. Cole, Ben Kelly, Jr., Allen P. Swayne, Bob Hemmick, Harvey Platts, Mrs. Howard Hillis, W. R. Case & Sons Cutlery Company, Western Cutlery Co., Kabar Knives, Stanley Davenport, Bill Adams, W. W. Williamson and the Library of Sheffield, England.

Published by: The House of Collectibles, Inc.
Orlando Central Park
1900 Premier Row
Orlando, FL 32809
Phone: (305) 857-9095

Printed in the United States of America

Library of Congress Catalog Card Number: 81-81802

ISBN: 0-87637-179-9 / Paperback
ISBN: 0-87637-236-1 / Hardcover

9 8 7 6 5 4 3 2 1

TABLE OF CONTENTS

DEDICATION

When you write a book for knife collectors, you certainly have to stop sometimes and figure who is the leading knife collector in the United States. It only takes a second for you to know who that person is if you have ever attended any major show (or even a minor one that needed a boost with a good display for the show). That collector is Dr. Frank Forsyth. At his own expense and for the advancement of knife collecting he has displayed his fabulous collection from Hartford, CN, to Sacramento, CA, to Tampa, FL and countless points in between. Through it all you can only say one thing about Dr. Forsyth, and that he is a gentleman. That is a title one should not bestow lightly, but Dr. Forsyth fits the bill in every criteria.

So we dedicate this volume four to him. We could think of no individual who deserves it more.

INTRODUCTION

The purpose of this book is to provide answers and information that most collectors need. A serious collector needs to know prices, some history, and where to find them.

We are still the only knife book that answers most of these questions. We back up our prices. When you see a price written by someone who is never at a knife show and not actively in the knife buying and selling business, compare their prices with mail order dealers and others who buy and sell, and then make your choice on whose prices you will go by.

A little note on how these prices will be. When you read this price guide, it is not wise to buy every knife at this price. The knives fluctuate depending on region or a variety of reasons. However, as a general rule either author will pay 75% of the price listed in this book. Naturally, this will not mean we will take 200 of one slow moving pattern, but as long as we are not overloaded on any single knife we will usually take it at that price. We think these prices will be accurate until publication of our next edition. The first few months that this book is out these prices will be slightly high, and the last few months before our next volume comes out they will probably be slightly low, but as a general rule this book is more accurate than any other price guide on the market.

If you are investing in knives, *DO NOT USE THIS BOOK AS YOUR ONLY SOURCE ON PRICING INFORMATION.* If prices never changed, there would be no reason for this book. We recommend you attend as many knife shows as possible, and subscribe to as many knife dealers mail order lists as possible. This, combined with the knife media magazines and newspapers is the true marketplace for knives, and this is where the prices are determined. If you take your time, act wisely and use sound judgement, you can make a lot of money off your knife collecting investment.

HISTORY OF KNIFE COLLECTING

Knife collecting has existed for thousands of years, since the first cave man laid back a well-chipped stone knife of a pretty color rock. Collectors of Bowie knives have collected them since the 1900's, and Chattanooga, Tennessee even had a knife show in the 1930's. These collectors laid the ground work, but the 1960's is when the hobby actually advanced.

During this time gun collecting was in its heyday, and most gun collectors would buy an occasional Remington or Winchester knife, more because it had a firearms manufacturer's name on it than because it was a collectible knife. Even at this time, Bullet Remingtons in good shape would bring $100.

In 1965, W. R. Case changed its logo to comply with government regulations that stated cutlery must have the country of origin stamped on it. Case changed from Case XX to Case XX with U. S. A. stamped underneath. This change did not go unnoticed by the few knife and gun dealers of the time, and soon they were loading up groups of dealers in cars and driving through the country trying to buy the displays with the older Case XX knives. These soon found their way to the gun shows too, and when the Gun Control Act of 1968 put severe restrictions to the trading of guns, particularly across state lines, many of the gun dealers slowly phased out their gun collections and started dealing in knives. A large number of gun collectors started collecting knives instead of guns, and a hobby was born.

A sales manager of a major manufacturer said that during the time he was a salesman, he did his bit to aid collecting by taking rolls of the old bone handled knives and giving one away free whenever he opened a new account.

About this time also some reference works appeared by Dewey Ferguson, Pryce Robinson, Col. Robert Mayes, and more and more people started collecting knives.

It was hard to sell and swap the old knives once your corner of the woods had been gone over, and it was not uncommon for a knife dealer to load his trunk down with knives and drive for weeks winding through the country buying and selling with the collectors of the area. (He usually found them by inquiring at the local Case dealer or hardware store).

To remedy this expenditure of gas and time, several collectors would advertise in Shotgun News and the Antique Trader that they were looking for knives, and in turn would list knives that they had for sale or trade. Jim Parker and W. E. Shockley made it big time, by getting a list of subscribers and mailing out lists of old knives for sale regularly.

When the 1970's arrived, it found Case had again changed its logo, this time adding 10 dots under the Case XX USA. What's more, Case said they were going to take a dot away each year until 1980, when they would change again. (Repaneling all those Case XX boards must have given them some ideas). The dealers who had chased the elusive Case XX boards were now off looking for the USA boards, and many witnesses of these purchases became collectors themselves (including most hardware dealers, who were catching on). In 1980 the stamping was changed. Ten dots were placed between the "Case XX" line and the USA line.

Additionally, Case discontinued its stag handled knives, which were beautiful to start with, and prices on these soon rose to $30 and $40. A boost to this Case interest was the publication of *Romance of Collecting Case Knives,* an illustrated book by Dewey Ferguson that hooked almost everyone who read it.

In 1972 a group of Tennessee and Kentucky collectors at the suggestion of Roy Scott, editor of the only knife publication at the time, *The Blue Mill Blade,* met in Del Rio, Tennessee on June 9, 1972 and formed the National Knife Collectors and Dealers Association for the purpose of advancing knife collecting. The first officers were as follows: James F. Parker, President; John Bengel, Vice President; Roy Scott, Business Manager; and Charter Members Edward Breese, Robert Werner, Herbert Lawson, Maury Shavin,and Morris Young. Board of Director members were Eugene Lampkin, W. E. Shockley, Ed Bruner, and Sanford Overholt. They soon had 300 members, but a dues increase later that year caused some to drop out.

A typical knife show — Cave City, Kentucky.

Then the NKC&DA decided to start sponsoring knife shows, starting with one in Louisville, Kentucky January, 1973. In no time there were shows in Knoxville, Arlington, Texas, Chattanooga, Cincinnati, Greenville, and other places.

In 1974 the association had 600 members, and decided as a service to club members to have a club knife made, with a limited edition available only to members. By 1975 when the knives were available, the club had 1,200 members. Case made the knife in 1976, and there were 3,000 members.

In 1977 5,000 knives were made, for 6,000 members, in October 1980 the membership was 13,500 and in March 1981 the NKCA membership exceeded 15,500 members..

The NKCA began publishing an illustrated newsletter in 1976, and in April of 1977 started the National Knife Collector Magazine, with Bruce Voyles as editor. Bruce Voyles is now the editor of the American Blade Magazine.

In 1978 the project of a National Knife Collectors Museum was begun, and to be more representative the name of the NKC&DA was changed to the National Knife Collectors Association.

Since that first day in 1972, when organized collecting began, over 20 regional cutlery clubs have formed, and shows have been held in California, Oregon, Texas, Ohio, Tennessee, Kentucky, Alabama, Georgia, South and North Carolina, Connecticut, and a hundred places in between.

KNIVES THROUGH THE AGES

Knife cutlery manufacturing started in a sense with the rock chipper in the prehistoric tribes whose rock knives were just a little better than the rock chipper in the next tribe. The extra well-chipped ones or the ones with a pretty color streak of rock no doubt brought a few more saber tooth tiger skins than the plainer ones, and it is here we find our first knife dealer.

When the tribes of this time camped for a prolonged time, the sustained heat eventually smelted a crude form of metal, probably copper, and man, not one usually to let an advance slip by, was soon making bronze, iron, and finally steel.

STONE AGE FLINTS

Of all the instruments made from the discovery of metals, the knife was probably the first thing fashioned, and in time there arose from the tribesmen who became cutlers.

As the finer parts of cutlery became known, it was discovered that certain types of stones, when turned, could be used to shape a knife. By the middle ages, these rocks were powered by water wheels.

QUILL PEN KNIFE

To cut down on the costs of transporting stones, it was natural that areas near water, natural stones for grinding and coal deposits for fueling the fires would soon shine as cutlery centers. Sheffield, England and Solingen, Germany fit this bill, and they remain cutlery centers today.

Solingen and Sheffield later developed different methods of knife manufacturing. The German method was to have each worker make one part of the knife and the parts were assembled in a later step of production.

KNIFE & FORK "FIT-TOGETHER" 18TH CENTURY

The English method was to have one man make one knife at a time, from start to finish. At first this was done at the cutlers home, and once a week he would bring his knives into a central place to sell them to the cutlery manufacturers. This was called "liver & draw", meaning they would deliver their knives they had made in the past week and draw their wages. IXL was one of the first companies to stop this home work, by occupying his Washington Works in 1848. The building was a flatted factory, remaining sections were rented to the cutlers, and the "under-one-roof" scheme hastened production. They later evolved to the German method, after the majority of the skilled Sheffield cutlers were killed in World War I.

BROAD BLADE KNIFE 18TH CENTURY

Early American factories, since they were almost entirely manned by Sheffield cutlers who had emigrated, used the English method, and later switched to the German method.

LIVER & DRAW

DROP FORGING

The first knives were beaten out by hand from a square bar, fresh from the forge. John Russell changed all that when he introduced the use of the drop forge on cutlery.

Today the forging has all but been abandoned in favor of roll steel that is in almost perfect thickness. The general blade shape is blanked out on a stamping press and then ground down to the desired blade shape.

KNIFE NAMES

The origin of knife names is as varied as the knives themselves. The pen knife is mentioned in the Bible, and its name comes from the use of trimming quills for pens. "Barlow" comes from the name of its inventor, an English cutler of that last name. Wharnciffe comes from the title in English nobility (see Joseph Rodgers' story in this book on how this came about). Jaque De Liege reportedly gave the jackknife his name by inventing the folding knife in the 17th century.

Many knives take their name from their uses. A Muskrat knife is used by Muskrat trappers to skin the animals. Same goes for the melon tester, stock man and many others.

PENKNIVES

The penknife was originally designed for just that, cutting and shaping of a quill into a pen. They were first made in Sheffield, England in the early 1700's, continuing until the early 1900's, when the quill gave way to the fountain pen.

Most true penknives have extremely slender blades, one to one and one-half inches long. They're usually handled in stag, metal and ivory.

The first Sheffield directory in 1774 listed 66 penknife cutlers. By the 1820's many penknives were combined with other novelty items, having a penknife fold out from a leg knife, a pair of scissors, and rulers.

Joseph Rodgers made a variety called a library knife, which was a letter opener containing a penknife blade in the handle.

JIM BOWIE

The most famous name comes from its supposed inventor, one Jim Bowie. Bowie has as many legends about him as Paul Bunyan, Mike Fink, or Daniel Boone, and through the colorful journalism of the day and the tall tales it is hard to piece together any truth about the man and his life.

What is agreed to by almost every Bowie scholar is that he owned one heck of a knife, and more than one man died on its steel. He was raised in Louisiana where he began to make his fortune in land speculation and slave running. Disagreement with the competition soon led to a duel that turned into a free-for-all on the Vidalia Sand Bar in 1827. After the bodies were cleared away, Bowie stood as one of the most deadly men in the fight, and every newspaper and rider carried the story over the frontier.

Bowie soon found himself in an area of Mexico known as Texas, where he married a government official's daughter. While back in Louisiana on business a plague swept Texas, killing his entire family.

He returned to Texas, and was soon fighting for Texas independence, which is where we leave him in this narrative, lying on a cot with a brace of pistols and the famous knife at hand, as Mexicans crowd through a door to see who will be the last one to die at the point of the Iron Mistress.

Bowie's knife soon became the only popular fashion in an age when single shot percussion pistols were prone to misfire at critical moments.

The Bowie did not.

By the 1880's many states prohibited the wearing, sale or ownership of Bowie knives, and many of these laws are still on the books.

While the Bowie was at many sides during the opening of the western frontier, more than one or two belts carried Russell Green River knives. Anything "up to Green River" was in the same league with the Hawken rifle. You could depend on it and it would carry you through. A battle cry common at the time, "Give it to em up to Green River" meant to the hilt.

BOWIE KNIVES

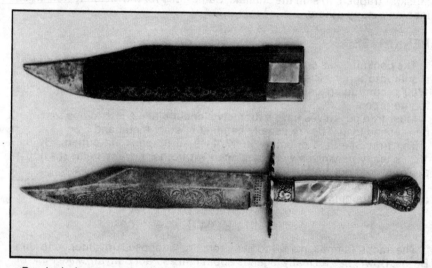

Bowie knives are the highest class of knife collecting in the United States. They bring the highest prices, and they are the oldest. When you hold a Bowie you are not just holding a mere tool, but a tool and a weapon that opened the western frontier, and is as much a part of the western folklore as the Peacemaker Colt or '73 Winchester. It preceded both!

No one knows who actually did invent the knife, but the man who lent his name to it is the one that made it famous.

The majority of Bowies came from Sheffield, England, with a precious few being manufactured in the United States. IXL made more than anyone, but many Sheffield made brands will be encountered

The top grade Bowies command prices of thousands of dollars, and it is not so much a case of how much to pay for one, but instead, whether the owner will let you buy it or not! The prestige Bowie usually has at least some of the following: etched blade with patriotic motto, pearl, ivory, or horn handles, ornate hilt and guard, massive clip blade, and superior workmanship overall, as well as fine condition.

The medium grade Bowies are available at a much reduced price, from $400 down. These are usually plain hilt and guard, smaller, spear pointed sometimes, bone or wood handles, less than fine condition.

What follows is a brief rundown of several Bowie knife makers. No attempt is made to price these because most of those encountered are one of a kind items, and the price will vary greatly on condition, etc.

They are written the way they will be stamped on the knives:

Alexander, Sheffield, NY. This company made a lot of Civil War era knives, and tends to have 8 "blades or less

L. W. Babbitt, Cleveland, OH. 1832-38.

William Bacon, New York City, NY. 1843.

Edward Barnes & Son, Blades up to 12", with patriotic mottos etched on the blades and sometimes "American Hunting Knife."

Louis Bauer, San Francisco, CA. 1872 began, 1879 opened Bauer Bros. and sold out in 1887.

Samuel Bell, Knoxville, TN. Beware of fakes marked "The Gamblers Companion."

Bell & Davis, Atlanta, GA. 1861.

Will Berry. Made knives in 1862 for State of Georgia

Best English Cutlery. 1849-50. Some will be found with cast metal handles and etched, "The Gold Seekers Protection".

C. J. Blitterdorf, Philadelphia, PA. 1849.

Broom & Thomas, Sheffield, NY. Massive style knives, with pearl handles, sheaths sometimes marked, "The Celebrated Arkansas Toothpick."

Brown & Tetley, Pittsburgh, PA 1855-1862.

R. Bunting & Sons, Sheffield, NY. This company also made folding dirks, and is better known for its horsehead pommels. Pre-1840.

Burger & Bros., Richmond, VA. 1861.

W. Butcher. 1836-??? One of the most common names, but good condition knives by this name are hard to find. Commonly counterfeited.

John Chevialier, New York City, NY. 1835-1871. Among the very best, his work covers the golden age of Bowies, and he made them with wood, pearl, or stag handles.

Clarenback & Herder, Philadelphia, PA. 1945.

W. T. Clement, Northampton, MA. 1857. Started business and later bought Bay State Tool Co. It was recognized as Clement Hawks Mfg. Co. in 1866 and in 1882 became Clement Cutlery Co. He was a former employee of Lamson & Goodnow.

Congreve, Sheffield, NY. 1835. Massive style knives. Early.

Simon F. Dodge, Winchester, GA. Civil War Bowie maker.

Enoch Drabble, Royal Cutlers. c. 1855 or earlier. Massive style with horsehead pommels were a specialty.

A. H. Dufilho, New Orleans, LA. 1855-1867. A surgical instrument maker, his knives were exceptional quality. He later made swords for the Confederate army.

J. English & Hubers, Sheffield Works, Philadelphia, PA. c. 1840's.

Fenton & Shore, Sheffield, NY. Made horsehead pommels.

Rees Fitzpatrick, Natches, MA. 1830-1861. One of the various makers credited by some as making Jim Bowie's original knife.

Glitter & Moss, Beal St., Memphis, TN. Civil War makers.

W. R. Goulding New York City, NY. Surgical instrument maker, most of his knives date from 1837-1840's. In 1841 his company became William R. Goulding Co.

Gravely & Wreaks, New York City, NY. 1835. This company was an importer of Sheffield knives, but their names will be marked on the knives.

John D. Gray. Made Bowies for the State of Georgia, 1862.

W. Greaves & Bunting & Sons. c. 1835. Greaves was the New York agent for Bunting.

Hartenstein. San Francisco, CA. c. 1870. In 1868 he went to work for Michael Price, then in 1870 started his own shop with Louis Bauer, which he ran until 1876 when he quit cutlery.

M. J. Hanes, San Francisco, CA. He worked for Michael Price until 1887. His knives are very similar to the M. Price knives.

Hassam, Boston, MA. Civil war era.

R. Heinish, Newark, NJ. c. 1830's.

John Hendrick, Philadelphia, PA. c. 1783-1790.

Andrew Hicks, Cleveland, OH. 1830-1840. Working through the Allegany arsenal he is credited with making the first official U. S. military knives for the U. S. Government. For military knife collectors it all starts with him.

Jph. Holmes, c. 1830's. Made knives marked "Arkansas Toothpick" with half-horse and half-alligator pommels. One of his knives sold from a New York mail order dealer in 1967 for $9.50.

Reinhold Hoppe, San Francisco, CA. Went to work for Will & Finick in 1876, started his own business in 1877, and retired in 1906.

Rudolph Hug, Cincinnati, OH. c. 1853-1882. New York instrument maker.

Alfred Hunder. c. 1840-50.

Ibbotson Peace & Co., Sheffield, NY. They made some horsehead pommels.

Jackson, Baltimore, MD.

W. F. Jackson, Sheffield, NY. Their most famous knife was marked "Rio Grande Camp Knife" and used by John Wilkes Booth to stab Major Rathbone in the President's Box at Ford Theater after shooting Abraham Lincoln.

Benjamin Jones, Tredyffrine, PA. 1775-1881.

Fredrick Kesmodel, San Francisco. CA. One of the most colorful Bowie makers, one of his inventions was the use of dog power to turn his machines. Starting in 1856 he only made knives to order. He hired Fredrick Will in 1861. He went out of business in 1868, but later went to work for Will & Finick until 1870.

Peter W. Krafe, Columbus, SC. c. 1801.

Thomas Lamb, Washington, D. C., c. 1846-50.

Lamphrey. made a small horsehead pommel of carved ivory.

Lan & Sherman, Richmond, VA. c. 1861.

A. Leon, 10 Solly St. Sheffield, NY. c. 1850.

I. Longard. Sheffield, NY.

Manson, Sheffield, NY. Made a large quantity of spear pointed plain dirks for Civil War use.

Mark & Rees, Cincinnati, OH. c. 1845.

McConnell, San Francisco, CA. c. 1852-56. He did not stamp his knives. He worked for all the top name makers in the 1850's.

W. J. McElory, Macon, GA. c. 1860's.

Alexander McKinstrey. c. 1861.

Murdock Morrison, Rockingham, NC. 1862.

Col. Joseph Nathan. San Francisco, CA. Dealer, knives were made by "Queens Own Co. Sheffield."

L. Oppleman, Lynchburg, VA. c. 1860's.

Otto & Koehler, New York City, NY. 1845.

Hiram Peabody, Richmond VA. c. 1850's.

Michael Price. Immigrated to San Francisco because of Ireland's Potato Famine in 1850, and began making knives (he was already a cutler). His knives are among the most prized in the world. He died in 1889.

W. C. Reaves, Sheffield, NY. Made horsehead pommels.

Reinhardt, Baltimore, MD. c. 1840-1868. Started in 1840 by a surgical instrument maker, it became Reinhardt & Bro. in 1865. Charles Reinhardt Jr. took over in 1868 but stayed only one year before closing the business.

Richards Upson & Co., New York City, NY. c. 1808-1816. Makers of Naval dirks, later became Richard & Taylor in 1817.

C. Wester Roby, Chelmsford, MA. c. 1860's.

James Rodgers, Sheffield, NY. Many of their knives were marked "Cast Steel Bowie knife."

Rose, New York City, NY. c. 1833-55. Top of the line in quality and demand by collectors. It is counterfeited a lot.

J. H. Schintz, San Francisco, CA. Started in 1860 after working for McConnell. In 1866 he went to work for Frederick Will, and the following year worked for Michael Price. During that time he made corkscrews with his own name on them. In 1874 he resumed his own knives again.

Schivley, Philadelphia, PA. Top grade knives. Schivley made one knife that was presented by Jim Bowie's brother Rezin to a friend.

Searles, Baton Rouge, LA. He also made a presentation knife for Rezin P. Bowie.

Shirley's OIO Cutlery.

Thomas Short Jr.

J. P. Snow & Company, Hartford, CT. & Chicago, IL. Folding dirks and knives. c. 1860's.

Sommis, Providence, RH. c. 1850.

John J. Staton, Scottsville, VA. c. 1861.

Stenton. c. 1847-67.

Edw. K. Tryon, Philadelphia, PA. 1811 began as a gunsmith by G. W. Tryon. Edward, his son, became a partner in 1836 and two divisions were established — George W. Tryon Co. handling general merchandise, and Tryon & Son, gun manufacturers. In 1841 George retired, and Edward combined everything under the Edw. K. Tryon & Co. name. The company ceased manufacturing in 1872, but continued in business until 1952, when it was purchased by Simmons Hardware. Their pocketknives were made by Utica Cutlery Co. from 1910 until 1952.

Union Car Works, Portsmouth, VA. 1860's.

Unwin & Rodgers, c. 1837's. Early high quality makers.

Silas Walker, Bennington, VT.

William Walker, c. 1851, Salt Lake City. UT.

James Walters & Co., Sheffield, NY.

Fred Watson, San Francisco, CA. c. 1890.

James Westa, Sheffield, NY. c. 1860.

W. H. Whitehead, c. 1860. Many are found etched with patriotic mottos.

W. & H. Whitehead, c. 1860.

H. W. Wilkinson & Co. c. 1855.

H. Wilkinson, Hartford, CT. c. 1860-80.

Will & Finick. Will worked for McConnell 1859-69 when he took over McConnell's business. In 1863 he merged with Finick. The company placed at the St. Louis Fair in 1865, and the American Institute Fair in 1871 (that year they also presented a carving set to U. S. Grant). In 1876 they displayed their knives at the Centennial Exposition and Russell, and Lamson & Goodnow immediately copied their patterns. Will & Finick even bought these copies stamped with their names. (The original Will & Finick carving sets have square tangs while the factory produced knives have round tangs). Will retired in 1883. The company incorporated in 1896 but went bankrupt in 1904. Others continued the name, but when the 1906 earthquake hit San Francisco, they reopened in a poor location. By 1930 their main trade was barber supplies. The company went completely out of business in 1932.

Hawksworth & Ellison Wilson, Sheffield, NY. Ellison was a New York agent in the 1840's.

Wolfe & Clark. Large style knives.

Woodhead & Hartley. Top of the line, particularly the horse head pommel knives.

Samuel C. Wragg. Wragg makes knives under a variety of names and locations, including Wragg & Sons, etc.

John Yeomans. c. 1849-50's.

WHERE TO FIND POCKETKNIVES

Collectible pocketknives can be found anywhere. Although trading has advanced to plush meeting rooms and organized knife shows, there are still groups of old timers gathering on many rural courthouse squares swapping knives.

Although most hardware dealers have long been searched over by collectors, there are still some dealers with discontinued knives in their stock who will still sell the knives at factory prices. Your best bet here is the less popular patterns, because they are likely to have been around longer in the owner's display.

Knives can still be found in attics (this author found a Case Tested in his wife's grandmother's attic, needless to say, every attic in the family got searched soon thereafter, turning up nothing) and in antique stores. One friend bought a Rough Black Case for $6 in September, 1975 and sold it at a knife show in October for $30. They can also be found at flea markets by both the seller and buyer. One trader I know was selling at a flea market and had a Remington on his table. An old man looked at it and told the dealer, "I've got one at home just like that." "Where do you live?" the trader asked, and the old man pointed to a house beside the flea market. At the trader's suggestion the old man took the trader to his house and after rummaging through a tool box came out with an almost mint Remington. The trader saw a similar knife in the box and asked the man what he wanted for that one. The old man said, "Why, that knife's gotta broke backspring. You can have that one for nothing if you give me $5 for the good one." The trader had the knife repaired and sold both Remingtons for $60.

There is no best place to buy pocketknives. Among the best are knife shows, cutlery clubs (usually at cutlery clubs there is a time set aside for knife swapping), and mail-order from reputable dealers. Even asking every person you see, "What kind of knife do you have?" will sometimes turn up an interesting or rare knife.

MAIL ORDER DEALERS

THE FOLLOWING IS A LIST OF MAIL ORDER DEALERS who sell antique and collectible knives, and in our experience with them, have proved to be honest and fair.

James F. Parker Cutlery
6928 Lee Highway
Chattanooga, TN 37421

Jim Sargent
1909 Holiday Drive
Florence, AL 35630

W. E. Shockley
P. O. Box 99151
Jeffersontown, KY 40229

M. C. Matthews Cutlery
P. O. Box 33095
Decatur, GA 30033

Star Sales
1803 N. Central Street
Knoxville, TN 37901

Stan Swanner Cutlery
P. O. Box 432
Fairfield, OH 45014

Smoky Mountain Knife Works
204 Parkway
Sevierville, TN 37862

Atlanta Cutlery Corporation
Box 839 Dept. OPGPK
Conyers, GA 30207

Hixson Knife Shop
5520 Highway 153 N.
Hixson, TN 37343

IF YOU ARE LOOKING FOR EQUIPMENT FOR BUFFING AND POLISHING KNIVES, AS WELL AS SUPPLIES FOR MAKING KNIVES, CONTACT:

Knife & Gun Finishing Supplies
P. O. Box 13522
Arlington, TX 76013

Sheffield Knifemakers Supplies
P. O. Box 141
DeLand, FL 32720

KNIFE PERIODICALS

We heartily recommend a subscription to *American Blade Magazine*. The magazine is owned and published by the authors of this book, James F. Parker and J. Bruce Voyles. It is the official magazine of the Knifemaker's Guild.

The magazine is published six times yearly, and runs between 70 and 100 pages each issue. The subscription rates are $10.00 per year.

Other periodicals available to the knife collector are:

Knife World
P. O. Box 3395
Knoxville, TN 37917

KNIFE BOOKS, OLD AND NEW

A Collection Of U. S. Military Knives by M. H. Cole by the author, Birmingham, AL.

Advertising With A Sharp Edge by Ed Bardy, published by the author.

A Glossary Of The Construction, Decoration And Use Of Arms And Armor, by George Cameron Scott, published by Jack Brussel, New York, 1961.

A Guide To Handmade Knives, by Mel Tappan, ed. The James Press, Box 578 Rouge River, OR, 1977.

A History Of Cutlery In The Connecticut Valley by Martha Van Hoesen Taber, Dept. of History, Smith College, Northhampton, MA, 1955.

A History Of The John Russell Cutlery Co. by Robert L. Merriam et. al. Bete Press, Greenfield, MA, 1976.

American Knives by Harold L. Peterson, Charles E. Scribners & Sons, New York, 1958.

An Old Sheffield Cutlery Firm: P. C. Garlick, the House of Nowell, 1787-1825. Hunter Archeological Society, Transactions, vol. 7, pp 167-179, 1955.

A Royal Record: The Brief History of a Famous Sheffield House. Privately printed, 1930. pp 16.

A Short History Of Sheffield Cutlery And The House Of Wostenhoim by Harold Bexfield.

Associated Cutlery Industries Of America. The cutlery story: a brief history of the romance and manufacture of cutlery from the earliest times to modern methods of manufacture, pocketknives, professional and industrial knives, and household cutlery; with a short summary on the selection and care of knives and minimum requirements of today's kitchen, by Lewis D. Bement. Deerfield, MA, The Associated Cutlery Industries of America, 1950. pp 36.

Bowie Knives by Robert Abels.

British Cut and Thrust Weapons, John Wilkinson-Latham, David & Charles Publishers, LTD, 1971.

Camillus, The Story Of An American Small Business by Alfred Lief, Columbia University Press, New York, 1944.

Case Pocket Knives, by Allen P. Swayne, Etowah, TN.

Collector's Illustrated Price Guide To Pocketknives by Bill Schroeder, 1977.

Committee Of Journeymen Of The Spring Knife Trade. Report of a committee of journeymen of the spring knife trade appointed . . .for the purpose of taking into consideration the propriety of applying to Parliament for an Act for the better protection and welfare of the Incorporated Cutlery Trades. Sheffield, James Montgomery, 1821. pp 16.

Cutlery Products, The U. S. Tariff Commission, 1938.

Cutlery Trades: A Historical Essay in the Economics of Small Scale Production, London and New York by Godfry I. H. Lloyd, 1913.

Discovering Edged Weapons, by Major John Wilkinson-Latham, Shire Publications, Tring, Herts, England, 1972.

Encyclopedia Of Old Pocketknives by Roy Ehrhardt, 1974, by Heart of America Press, Kansas City, MO.

For Knife Lovers Only by Harry McEvoy, from Knife World Books, Knoxville, TN.

Guns And Ammo Guidebook To Knives And Edged Weapons, Jim Woods, Ed., Peterson Publishing Company, Los Angeles 90069.

History Of The Company Of Cutlers In Hallamshire In The County of York. R. E. Leader, Sheffield, Pawson and Brailsford, 1905. 2 vol. pp 328, 412.

How To Make Knives by Richard Barney and Robert Loveless, 1976 by Benefield Publishing Co., Hollywood, CA.

IXL Means I Excel by William R. Williamson, 1974.

Knife Album by Colonel Robert Mayes, P. O. Box 186, Middlesboro, KY 40965.

Knifecraft by Sid Latham, Stackpole Books, 1979.

Knife Digest William L. Cassidy, ed., Knife Digest Publishing Co., 1976.

Knife Digest Volume II by William L. Cassidy, ed., Knife Digest Publishing Co. 1976.

Knifemakers Of Old San Francisco by Bernard L. Levine, Badger Books, San Francisco, CA 94140.

Marbles Knives and Ax's by Konrad F. Schreier, Jr., BeinField Publishing, 1978.

Observations on Swords by Henry Wilkinson, 18th edition.

1000 Razors by Bill Schroder, Paducah, KY.

Pictorial Price Guide to Collecting Cattaraugas, Russell, Robeson & Queen by Mrs. Dewey P. Ferguson, P. O. Box 929, Fairborn, OH 45234. 1978

Pocket Cutlery, The U. S. Tariff Commission, 1939

The Pocketknife Manual by Blackie Collins, Knife World Books, Knoxville, TN.

Pocketknives, Markings, Manufacturers and Dealers by John E. Goins, 1979. Available from the author.

Queen Knives by Mrs. Dewey P. (Lavona) Ferguson, P. O. Box 929, Fairborn, OH 45234. 1978.

Romance Of Collecting Case Knives, Dewey Ferguson, P. O. Box 929, Fairborn, OH 1974. vol. 3, 1976.

Romance Of Knife Collecting by Dewey Ferguson, by the author, address above. 1972. vol. 4,. 1976.

Sheffield Bowie and Pocketknife Makers, 1825-1925 by Richard Washer.

Sheffield Cutlery And The Poll Tax Of 1379. The Journal of the British Archeological Association. New Series, vol. 10, 1904, pp 226-233.

Sheffield, Society For The Preservation Of Old Sheffield Tools, B. R. Dyson. A glossary of words and dialect formerly used in the Sheffield trades, pt. I, 1936, pp. 51.

Sheffield: the Cutlery Capital of the British Empire, Sheffield City Council, Development Committee, Sheffield, Sheffield Independent Press, Ltd., 1918, pp 40.

"Straight Razor Collecting" by Robert A. Doyle Through Collector Books, Paducah, KY.

The Company Of Cutlers In Hallamshire In The County of York, L. du G. Peach, 1906-1956. Sheffield, Pawson & Brailford, Ltd., 1960. pp 6, 306.

The Cutlery Makers Of America: Official directory of the cutlery trade of the United States classified according to the kinds of knives and blades made. New York, Cutlery Publishing Company, 1919 and later editions.

The Cutlery Story, Custom Cutlery Co., Dalton, GA.

The English Illustrated Magazine, H. J. Palmer, Cutlery and cutlers at Sheffield. August, 1884, pp 659-669.

The Old Knife Book by Tracy Tudor, published by the author. Speedway, IN, 1978.

The Practical Book Of Knives by Ken Warner, The Stoeger Publishing Co. South Hackensack, N J, 1977.

The Story of Cutlery, J. B. Himsworth, from flint to stainless steel. London, Benn. 1953, pp 208.

The Knifemakers Who Went West by Harvey Platts, published by Longs Peak Press, 1978.

Under Five Sovereigns, Rogers, Joseph and Sons, Ltd. Privately printed (1918). pp 40.

United States Tariff Commission. Cutlery products, (Report No. 129, 2nd Series). Washington, United States Government Printing Office, 1938, pp 82.

United States Tariff Commission. Pocket cutlery. Washington, United States Government Printing Office, 1939, pp 52.

U. S. Military Knives, Bayonets and Machetes, Book III by M. H. Cole, 501 Ridge Road, Birmingham, AL, 1979.

Victoria And Albert Museum. English cutlery: 16th to 18th century, by J. F. Hayward, London, H. M. Stationery Office, 1956, pp 44.

Western Knives And Knife Nostalgia, by Harvey Platts, published by Western Cutlery Co., Longmont, CO., 1975.

REPRINT CATALOGS:

American Made Pocketknives, Union Cutlery Co. reproduced by Kabar, Cole National, Cleveland, OH.

Case Brothers 1904, reprinted by Bob Cargill. Available from him.

Cattaraugas Cutlery Co. Reproduction by Dewey P. Ferguson, 1971.

1885 IXL Catalog, Atlanta Cutlery Corporation, Decatur, GA.

Napanoch by Rhett C. Stidham, Belpre, OH.

Remington-1929-Available from Parker Frost Cutlery Co. Chattanooga, TN.

Remington-1936-Available from American Reprints, St. Louis, MO.

Remington C-4. Reprinted by J. Bruce Voyles, available through Parker Cutlery Association.

Joseph Rogers & Sons Cutlers.

Russell Green River Works Cutlery by Dewey P. Ferguson, 1972.

Schrade Pocketknives (reprint of 1926 with supplements for 1928, 1930, 1932, 1934, 1936, 1938) Knife Collector's Publishing House, Fayetteville, AR 1971.

E C Simmons & Winchester-American Reprints, St. Louis, MO.

KNIFE ORGANIZATIONS

It is difficult to keep up with the fast growing tide of new knife clubs. The leading club, and the one that you will get the most for your money is the newly formed American Blade Collectors. A membership form can be found on page 23.

AMERICAN BLADE COLLECTORS publishes *Edges,* a knife newspaper, sponsors an annual show each year, awards trophies at every major knife show, offers an annual knife, and many other benefits. Dues are $5.00 yearly.

THE NATIONAL KNIFE COLLECTORS ASSOCIATION publishes *The National Knife Collector* monthly, offers an annual knife, and sponsors 10 shows annually. Dues are $10.00 yearly.

There are now clubs in almost every city of the U.S., consisting of groups of knife makers and collectors who meet regularly to sponsor shows, trade nights, and in most cases offer to members an inexpensive collectors knife, in a quantity less than 300. These knives have in the past been found to be good buys and make a nice collection in themselves. Fightin' Rooster is the major manufacturer of club knives, and a listing of Fightin' Rooster knives made for clubs is listed below. In recent months other manufacturers have entered this market too. Addresses for the clubs are as follows:

ALABAMA
Vulcan Knife Club
Mike Boyd
P. O. Box 11364
Birmingham, AL 35212

Noccalula Knife Club
Ray Keenum
106 Carolyn Lane
Gadsden, AL 35901

CALIFORNIA
Bay Area Knife Collectors
P. O. Box 32631
San Jose, CA 95132

Southern California Blade Collectors
Lowell Shelhart
P. O. Box 1040
Lomita, CA 90717

COLORADO
Rocky Mountain Blade Collectors
Contact Ron Robb
Phone 303-794-0517

FLORIDA
Florida Knife Collectors Association
Dennis Conley
3301 Delaware
Titusville, FL 32780

Gator Cutlery Club
Lamar Baker
1075 Tampa Bay Center
Tampa, FL 33607

GEORGIA
The Chattahoochee Cutlery Club
(Atlanta, GA area)
Box 568
Tucker, GA 30084

Lanier Cutlery Club
Dan Clark
2990 Thompson Mill Road
Gainesville, GA 30501

Three Rivers Knife Club
Jimmy Green
Route 7, Box 783
Rome, GA 30161

INDIANA
Evansville Knife Collectors
Dr. Ken Helm
6700 Darmstadt Road
Evansville, IN 47710

ILLINOIS
American Edge Collectors Association
Contact Louis Jamison
Phone (312) 891-4868

KENTUCKY
Eagle Creek Knife Club
K. F. Ballard, Jr.
Box 278
Owentown, KY 40359

Kentucky Cutlery Association
153 E. Wellington Avenue
Louisville KY 40214

Paducah Knife Collectors
Steve Fowler
215 Longview Drive
Paducah, KY 42001

Yellow Banks Cutlery Club
Jim Neel
2410 Bittel Road
Owenboro, KY 42301

MARYLAND
Chesapeake Bay Area Knife Club
Robert Mayer
545 Woodlyn Terace
Baltimore, MD 21221

MICHIGAN
Wolverine Knife Collectors Club
Gordon O'Leary
P. O. Box 52
Belleville, MI 48111

MINNESOTA
North Star Cutlery Club
Rex L. Rathbone
2013 Maple Street
Hastings, MN 55033

MISSISSIPPI
Rebel Knife Club
Dan Westmorland
1121 Chapman Drive
Tupelo, MS 38801

MISSOURI

St. Louis
Charles A. Carnego
1617 Ray Drive
Arnold, MO 63010

Show Me Cutlery Club
P. O. Box 885
Lebanon, MO 65536

NORTH CAROLINA

Catawba Valley Knife Club
Bud Swink
306 S. Sterling Street
Morganton, NC 28655

Gem Capital Knife Club
P. O. Box 233
Franklin, NC 28734

Kotten Country Knife Collectors
Milton Flowe
5418 Toano Road
Charlotte, NC 28215

Mountain Whittlers Knife Club
P. O. Box 6734
Asheville, NC 28806

North Carolina Cutlery Club
Jim Abernathy
113 Drive
Fuquay Varina, NC 27526

Tarheel Cutlery Club
Clyde Ranson
Tudor Lane
Winston, Salem, NC 27106

OHIO

Western Reserve Cutlery Alliance
J. Nielsen Mayer
2441 Woodmere Drive
Cleveland Heights, OH 44106

OREGON

Oregon Knife Collectors Association
Richard Wagner
P. O. Box 353
Veneta, OR 97487

PENNSYLVANIA

The Delaware Valley Knife Club
Contact Cecila Cheny
Phone (215) 356-1725

Pocono Knife Club
Richard Williamson
Hwy 940
Pocono Lake, PA 18347

SOUTH CAROLINA

The Palmetto Cutlery Club
(Spartanburg, Greenville, SC Area)
James Runyan
Route 3
Taylors, SC 29687

TENNESSEE

Fightin' Rooster Collectors Club
P. O. Box 936
Lebanon, TN 37087

Memphis Knife Collectors
Hales Knives
1795 Dellwood Avenue
Memphis, TN 38127

Middle Tennessee Knife Collectors
1510 Maymont Drive
Murfreesboro, TN 37130

Midsouth Knife Collectors Association
Charles Genella
Hixson Knife Shop
Hwy. 153 N
Chattanooga, TN 37343

Smokey Mountain Knife Collectors
Clines Cafeteria
Alcoa, TN 37701

TEXAS

Texas Knife Collectors Club
P. O. Box 627
Belton, TX 76513

West Texas Knife Club
J. Paul Turner
Star Route
Sweetwater, TX 79556

VIRGINIA

Old Dominion Knife Collectors Association
Bruce Eye
P. O. Box 703
Appomattox, VA 24522

WHAT TO COLLECT

What to collect is one of the first questions anyone asks, and it is the hardest to answer.

First, you need to ask yourself, "What do I want from my collection?" If you want knives for investment purposes, it is a different world from the man who wants a supply of good whittlin' knives to use in his old age.

For the investor, the best rule of thumb is that of the old gun traders, "Don't collect what you like, collect what everyone else likes." Buying what is popular will usually stand the test of time, and will appreciate in value.

For everyone, we recommend to specialize as much as possible. A collection and an accumulation are two different things. The reason we recommend this is as follows: If you want to realize a profit from your collection, you are going to have more markets available when it comes time to sell. If it is something a collector who likes to display knives could put in a display box and win a trophy with, you're a step ahead.

You cannot collect every Case or Remington knife ever made. Remington in 21 years made over 1,200 patterns. The enormity of it would overwhelm anyone after a few shows of finding two or three knives, each priced in the $100 range. A much more logical course would be to collect Remington whittlers, which is still almost 40 knives with a large number of variations, and would represent a large investment for a complete collection.

CONDITION

Used knives in the past were neglected by most collectors, but with the declining availability of mint old knives, the used knives are finally coming into their own. Also, with a used knife, you don't have to worry quite so much about rust getting to it and ruining your investment. Do not confuse the word "used" with broken or worn-out knives. There is quite a difference price wise and demand wise. Many of today's knife repairmen can clean a slightly used knife to almost mint condition, and this type cleaning will not cut down on the price of the knife. At times it will enhance it.

Let us restate here that the prices in this book are for mint knives. **IF YOU SHARPEN A KNIFE ONE TIME, CUT THE MINT PRICE IN HALF AND YOU HAVE THE COLLECTOR'S VALUE.** Mint knives are harder to find and therefore command a much higher price than even an almost mint knife.

No one knows what is going to go up quicker than anything, since there are many factors that affect knife prices. For instance, in 1970 W. R. Case & Sons discontinued all of their stag handled pocketknives. These immediately took a jump in price, but in 1973 special sets were issued using the remaining stag handled knives that had been left in stock at Case in 1970. They also made a few knives just for these sets. Among them a 5111½ called the "Cheetah". There were only 1,200 released, one in each set, and collectors soon discovered a variation in the stamping size, and the price was soon at $210. While the stags discontinued in 1970 and leveled off in price, the pattern that had not been duplicated in the 1973 sets continued to climb.

Then in 1975 Case released 600 more sets. And in most sets they put two Cheetahs. The Cheetahs dropped to around $140, and today they have just started on their climb back up, bottoming for a time at $110.

In 1977 Case came out with a whole new line of stags, and this time put 10,000 knives of each pattern on the market. If you think this does not affect the rising price of stag handled knives, you are mistaken. The older patterns are neglected by the stag collector in order to buy the new sets while the prices are low. While this does not drop the price of the older stags, it does level off the prices since there is a slow down in demand.

It has been a recent trend among newer Case items to get high when they first come out and level out as the larger quantities hit the market. If you are planning on collecting the new Case commemoratives and limited editions, at the present time you are better off waiting for the price to level off. This is not a good idea in every circumstance, but at this writing it is sound advice. However, it will be one year before our next book and we cannot tell you now what will happen in the coming year. We can tell you that if you look close at your market, subscribe to as many dealers' lists as possible, get the major knife publications, and above all, talk to other dealers and collectors, you will be able to keep up with current trends.

At this writing in October of 1980, the winners to collect are: any old bone handled mint knife with etching on the blade, regardless of brand; Case doctors' knives, bone handled Robesons, large factory display knives, pearl handled knives, particularly the larger patterns.

The coming collectibles we predict to be: Ulsters, Uticas and the older bone handled knives with the trend turning to less emphasis on the collector buying a knife only if it is 100% mint. The mint knives are tending to not last long on the market these days.

RESTORED KNIVES

A knife that uses the same original parts as came on that knife is not a counterfeit. If the restoration of a used knife is done properly, with the original parts, it will usually be more valuable than before restoration. A buffed blade will usually be better than a rusted one, but a buffed knife should in no way be confused with a 100% mint knife.

HOW TO GRADE A KNIFE

The different gradings of a knife vary with the individual but most collectors and dealers use the guidelines of the National Knife Collectors Association, which describes the conditions as follows:

MINT-A factory fresh knife, absolutely original as it came from the manufacturer, not carried or sharpened, a perfect knife.

NEAR MINT-A new knife that has seen some time, shows some slight carry or shop wear, blades snap perfectly, handles show no cracks.

EXCELLENT-SHOW NO MORE THAN 10% blade wear, handles are sound, no cracks, blades snap good.

VERY GOOD-About 25% blade wear, slight cracks in handles, may have one lazy blade. Stamping clearly visible to the naked eye, no blades changed or repaired.

FAIR-50% blade wear, blades lazy, cracks and chips in handles, handles replaced with same type, blades repaired, stampings faint, but readable with a glass.

POOR-Blades very worn, handles bad or missing, blades have been replaced with the same type, reading of the stamp is almost impossible even with a glass, good mostly only for parts.

Note: *A tiny hairline crack should not affect the price over 10%, these stress cracks are not to be confused with a broken handle.*

KNIFE REPAIRMEN

Skip Bryan
1852 Albany
Loveland, CO 80537
(Specializes in old knives)

Cecil E. Clark
10903 Sharondale Road
Cincinnati, OH 45241

Charlie Jones
P. O. Box 282
Belton, TX 76513
(Specializes in Case)

Ben Kelley, Jr.
4726 Chamblee-Tucker Road
Tucker, GA 30084

DISPLAYING YOUR COLLECTION

If you want to display your collection, pay special attention to the form used below. It is used to judge every collection at NKCA shows and is considered the standard judging form for knife collection display competition.

NATIONAL KNIFE COLLECTORS ASSOCIATION

EXHIBIT RULES:

(1) No item may be sold, traded and/or removed from the display while on Exhibition.

(2) Any major misrepresentation of any knife on display may disqualify display from award.

(3) Items on display must be owned by the Exhibitor or identified as to who in fact owns the item, if not the Exhibitor.

(4) Exhibitor shall be current member of NKC&DA in order to have his or her display judged for an award.

I. EDUCATIONAL FACTORS   MAXIMUM POINTS
   A. TITLE: Is there a title for the display
      (No title, no points)   (5 points)_____
   B. CONTENTS: How does the display fit
      the title?   (10 points)_____
   C. LABELING:
      1. Is the title adequately explained or
         amplified?   (10 points)_____
      2. Are individual specimens properly and
         adequately identified?   (20 points)_____
   D. RELATED: Are there catalogs, pictures,
      accounterments, or other items to further
      the purpose of the display?   (5 points)_____

II. THE MATERIAL OF THE DISPLAY
   A. COMPLETENESS: Relation of material
      displayed to title. (Quantity)   (10 points)_____
   B. CONDITION: How does condition compare to
      material available?   (10 points)_____
   C. RARITY OF ITEMS DISPLAYED   (15 points)_____
   D. COLLECTOR IMPORTANCE OF ITEMS DISPLAYED
      (Is this popular or less-popular material?)   (5 points)_____

III. GENERAL APPEAL — (ORIGINALITY)
   A. Relative skill evidenced in construction
      and creativity of display.   (5 points)_____
   B. Neatness, general appearance and general
      public appeal. (Is the public interested?)   (5 points)_____

*5 points will be deducted from total if the Exhibitor name is not shown on display.

TOTAL POINTS AWARDED THIS DISPLAY: _____
(Maximum 100)

The fastest growing organization in knife collection is the American Blade Collectors.

This organization was founded as an outgrowth of the American Blade magazine, by the authors of this book.

American Blade Collectors members receive a subscription to *Edges*, the official publication of ABC, a newspaper about knives and knife collecting. Members also receive free appraisals on their collections, consultations in buying and selling on a limited basis, free admission to the annual ABC convention and show, and reduced table rates at that show if they set up.

Current memberships in the American Blade Collectors are $5.00 but subject to change without notice.

To become a member, just fill out the form below: *(To subscribe to the* American Blade *magazine at the same time just add an additional $10.00.)*

(   ) Yes I would like to join the American Blade Collectors. I realize that I may cancel my membership at anytime and receive a prorated refund.

Name: _____

Address: _____

City:_____ State: _____ Zip: _____

If it would be easier to call 615-894-0339 and leave your Mastercharge or Visa number, please feel free to do so.

(   ) Life membership is available which includes a 20-year subscription to *American Blade* and a pearl two-blade trapper for $180.00

THE AMERICAN BLADE COLLECTOR
112 Lee Parkway
Stonewall Bldg., Suite 104
Chattanooga, TN 37421

KNIFE COLLECTING ETIQUETTE

Common courtesy can go a long way, and rudeness is a quick way to make enemies. It should be common practice not to take up space in front of a dealer's table while you try to swap knives with another collector. Move out of the way to trade, don't block the aisles, and everyone will be a lot happier, and you won't get bumped into so much.

A second rude act I've observed of many dealers is ignoring young collectors. Young collectors are the future of the hobby, and a few rude dealers could turn anyone against it. On the other hand, I have seen many collectors get great enjoyment out of showing a six-year-old a Bullet Remington, letting him handle it and watching his eyes get the size of saucers when they tell him the price. One dealer I know, we'll call him George, once told me he didn't waste time with kids because they never had any money and he was in business, not running a knife collectors school. George was forced to change his mind one day. He was showing a handful of Case stags to a collector when a 13-year-old walked up. The collector told George he didn't want the knives, and the young boy asked George how much they were. "They're expensive," George bluntly told him.

"I didn't ask if they were expensive, I asked how much," the boy shot back. George was startled but mumbled out, "Six hundred dollars for all of them." "That sure is a lot," the boy said, as he laid six crisp hundred dollar bills on George's table. George is a lot friendlier to young folks now.

It's also common courtesy to watch a collector's table if you are set up beside him at a knife show and he has to leave for something.

In addition to getting out of the way if you are not conducting business with a dealer, the person not set up at a show has other responsibilities also. If he wants a dealer to hold a knife for him, he should leave a deposit. And even if he does not, he should abide by his word. If he is not sure he will take a knife, he should not obligate the dealer to hold it for him. The dealer might miss a sale while you are making up your mind!

Some collectors buy their knives, then go over every nook and cranny of a knife, and if they find one bit of rust or a chip they go running back to the dealer demanding their money back. This return policy is a good one on counterfeits or misrepresented knives, but the dealer should know the knife well enough to tell the buyer if it is not 100% mint, and even if not, the buyer should examine the knife *before* he buys it. It saves a lot of time and wasted effort.

The most important courtesy in knife collecting is not to sell a knife at an outrageous price. I know that at the last knife show I went to, a dealer sold a knife for $80 that I had paid $25 for and sold to him for $30. (The knife was going for around $35, and several other dealers had the same knife for $35.) When the person who bought that knife discovers the shaft, he might become soured on collecting, and then that hurts us all. Make a profit, but it is better to sell many knives to a collector than trying to retire off the profit of one knife sale.

Many of the old-time courthouse traders operated under the premise "Do it to me first, 'cause I'm gonna do it to you if I get the chance." That premise is the best way to destroy a hobby and take the hobby back from the motel convention centers to the old courthouses. I don't think anyone really wants that.

Mail order dealers have a hard problem when describing their knives. The section on how to grade a knife may seem cut and dried, but when a knife is described less than mint, there are fine lines between excellent and near mint condition. Courtesy here goes both ways. The mail order dealer should describe his knives as closely as possible, and the buyer should not order a knife described as excellent expecting a mint or near mint one.

Mail order dealers will refund within a certain time for any reason, but if you have ordered 10 knives on 10 occasions, and every knife he described as near mint and you thought was excellent and returned them, *DO NOT ORDER AN 11th KNIFE DESCRIBED AS NEAR MINT FROM THE SAME DEALER AND EXPECT IT TO MEET YOUR STANDARDS.* While the knife is being examined by you the dealer could be losing a sale, not to mention the time it took to wrap and record each shipment.

THE STORING OF POCKETKNIVES

The storing of pocketknives is a tricky situation at best, for rust can ruin the value of a valuable collection, and most collectors will be quick to say there is no foolproof method of storing knives over a period of time and keeping them rust-free.

Most collectors first clean the knife with a polishing paste to remove impurities and remove some tiny scratches. Then a thin layer of oil or vaseline will be put on the knife to prevent corrosion, but a thin oil will not cover the knife over time, and a thick coat of vaseline will let moisture under the layer of vaseline and cause rust. The best method I have found to date is to store them in a dry place, spreading a thin coat of machine oil over the entire knife, and repeating this at least once a month.

If knives are stored in direct sunlight, the sun will fade bone handles, and uneven colored handles detract from the value of a pocketknife.

The old knife company salesmen carried their samples in rolls of oilcloth and felt, or sometimes specially treated leather rolls (the tanning acids of common tanned leather will rust knives).

Today, vinyl rolls lined with crushed velvet holding 60, 90, and 125 knives are popular for carrying knives, but if knives are stored in them, rolled up, moisture will collect and rust the knives. If knives are carried in a vinyl roll, it is best to unroll it when storing knives for a period of time. Some collectors put a coat hanger through the handle of these rolls and hang them in a closet under a long coat to hide them from thieves.

A less expensive roll that is made of cloth-backed paper with a flannel lining will not hold moisture, but will fade on white and yellow composition handled knives. It comes in 12, 24, and 36 knife sizes.

Felt-lined boxes with elastic strips are preferred by some collectors, and are convenient if you set up at knife shows since it is easy to put a plexiglass cover over the knives to prevent pilferage. The drawback is that boxes are bulky and sometimes hard to carry.

In any type of transporter for your knives, when they are brought from a cold area to a warm area they will usually condense, leaving a layer of moisture on the knives, and if not cleaned, a layer of rust.

There are many different ways to carry a knife, but to store it, rust-free, is very difficult. One of the main things to remember is to keep the temperature as constant as possible. This, combined with wiping the knives with a silicone cloth prior to storage will keep them as rust free as anything. But always check them. It is easy to miss a spot, and nothing is foolproof.

PROTECTING YOUR COLLECTION

There have been some drastic changes in the knife collecting field in this department. To be blunt, the interest and rising values of knives have caught many collectors flat-footed. The knives that many old-time collectors bought in 1965 for $5 could easily bring $300 or $400. Multiply that by a full 150 knife roll and you see that while you may have had a low initial investment, as time goes by it will appreciate to a large sum. This is fine. It is one of the reasons most people collect. But while you are collecting, bear in mind that the more valuable things become, the more thieves desire them also.

I originally wrote the following paragraph in July 1978. Since that time nothing has changed, and even more collections have been stolen.

Treat knives like you treat anything of value, make an effort to protect or conceal it. Safe deposit boxes, burglar alarms, and insurance are all good.

It seems that anything worth having to you is worth stealing to someone else. Keep this in mind when you decide on a place to keep your collection. We don't want to scare you off from knife collecting. It is no different than coins, valuable stamps, or anything else, but you should keep the thought of theft in mind.

Knives are a thief's dream. They are small, hard to trace, and if found in someone else's possession, it's hard to prove that they are yours. In 1965, these knives would have been hard to sell, bringing only $3 or $4 each, and then it would have been hard to find someone willing to buy 100 knives.

Today it is different. With over 45,000 knife collectors in the U. S., some of them are greedy and will buy stolen knives. A local store near me was burglarized recently and the thieves took only pocketknives and cigarettes. They left a gun, because if a gun is stolen, the Alcohol, Tobacco and Firearms agents will investigate. If it cannot be proven that the thieves crossed a state line or stole guns, it is almost impossible for a federal enforcement agency to find your knives.

There are few major dealers who cannot relate one instance that either they or someone they know was subjected to burglary or theft.

I HOPE I HAVEN'T SCARED ANYONE OFF. It is no different than collecting anything else of value, and with the problems there are also remedies.

Insurance is a touch and go business when it comes to pocketknives. When living in Atlanta, Georgia I had a knife collector friend that sold insurance and he could not furnish me with a reasonable policy. In general you can always get an insurance policy, but the premium might be more than the value of your collection over a five year period. Upon moving to North Carolina I finally found one company that would write a decent policy, but it was similar to the one the company issued for diamond salesmen.

This is a roundabout way of saying you can get insurance on your pocketknife collection, but you will no doubt run into people who say you cannot. Shop around, for price as well as coverage. If you want to attach your knife collection to your homeowners insurance, it will probably require that you list or photograph each knife and file a copy with them. It will usually mean an appraisal by a bona fide knife expert. Always check with your individual agent, for the particulars of insurance vary with each circumstance.

A common sense approach to your collecting will make you less likely to lose your knives to thieves. If you advertise in knife publications and magazines, rent a post office box, do not use your street address. This is one of the main reasons most cutlery clubs guard their mailing lists. They don't want a directory for thieves.

Don't leave your knives out in plain sight. A few mounted in plaques on the wall are fine, but do not put a 500 knife collection on the wall where it can be seen by anyone walking down the street.

If you have a large investment in knives, don't overlook the possibility of a safe deposit box. It will cut down on your being able to enjoy them as much as having them at home, but they are much safer there. If you don't like safe deposit boxes, be sure to check into a good alarm system. We might add here that if you keep your knives in a safe or safe deposit box, special care should be taken to prevent rust.

One nice thing about knives that are kept in rolls is that they can be hung under a long coat in the closet and hidden from thieves. Their compact size enables you to hide them almost anywhere. (If you think knives are hidden when you put them under the bed or mattress, you are wrong.)

TRAVELING WITH YOUR KNIVES

With the trend in shows beginning to spread out, more and more collectors are flying with their knives. At this writing, the airlines will only insure a bag up to $750 per bag. Additional insurance may be bought up to $5,000 per bag at the rate of $1 per thousand. They will require that they inspect the knives and they will not insure "Antique" knives. Further, they will insure knives only at your invoice price, so you only get your money back, not what the knife may actually be worth.

You cannot take your knives on the plane with you. Airline people still think that if you board a plane with 150 knives, you will arm 150 of the passengers and hijack the plane to Bradford, Pennsylvania.

If you fly on two different airlines, the knives will only be insured as long as you fly with the first airline. For instance, if you are going to Los Angeles from Atlanta, and flew to Dallas on Delta, continued to Los Angeles on United, you would have to have the knives insured and inspected in Atlanta. Then in Dallas you have to pick up your bags, carry them to the United counter and have them reinsured and reinspected. For $5,000 worth of knives this runs into $20 insurance alone, not to mention the time and trouble to lug the bags around getting them inspected.

It is such a problem that many of the dealers who regularly fly to shows do not insure their bags at all, saying that if anyone knows something valuable is in one of the bags it will be the one that they steal. It is gambling, but if you want to fly with mostly old knives, it is about all you can do.

BONE HANDLES

Of all the knife handle materials, the most popular has to be bone. It comes in hundreds of jigging patterns, sometimes even slick. It will be dyed red, green, brown, black, and every color in between. It has been used by every major manufacturer in the past. In short, it is one of the first things you look for in a collector's knife.

Bone was first used in its natural color and without jigging, but when cutlers began to dye and jig patterns on the bone, it phased out the older style. Almost every company had its own style of jigging and some companies such as Rogers (Handle Material Company (not Joseph Rodgers), specialized in supplying their own style of bone jigging to the industry. (This is where the Rogers Bone and Rogers Stag names come from).

By the 1950's almost every major American manufacturer had discontinued bone except *W. R. CASE & SONS.* Some German knives were still handled in bone, but even Boker, Solingen had changed from bone to a black composition.

Case's bone in the mid '20's was dyed brown, and then from the 1940's until the mid '50's the dye began affecting the bone differently, and it started coming out green. In the later '50's Case still used the same dye, bought from the same company, but now when they pulled the bone from the dye it had the deep red appearance, and red bone was born. (Thus the reason for the higher prices on green bones, they are older knives.)

Case gradually began following the trail of the other companies by discontinuing bone patterns. The problem with the bone was that it was all imported from South America. It seems that it is more economical for U. S. Packers to sell the bone unstripped to fertilizer producers, while the South Americans can strip out the bone, boil off the residue and ship it to the U. S. and still make a profit!

On top of that, Eastman Kodak uses the bone in part of their film production, and they usually outbid everyone for the bone. Case has its bone handles available today much through the courtesy of Eastman Kodak. Delrin is a better handle material. It doesn't crack, it doesn't have deep luster, and can hold up but it does not have the variation and beauty found in bone handled knives. However, the collector's market had enough of an effect on Case that it was worthwhile to continue making bone handled knives. At one time in the early '70's Case had to limit their dealers to the number of knives each one could order, because they were the only manufacturer at the time with bone handled knives.

At this writing, the collector's market has had an impact on other companies too. Queen Cutlery and Boker Germany have come out with bone handles on limited edition knives. And Schrade is reintroducing IXL knives with genuine bone handles.

As a twist, Parker-Frost began making a line of regular production bone handled knives in 1978. Their bone is processed overseas which does not make it as difficult as if they imported it in bulk unprocessed. The fact that they do make bone handled knives makes Parker-Frost and W. R. Case & Sons the only two U. S. manufacturers that make a bone handled knife for regular production. Both companies stamp their knives so it is possible for any collector to know what year the knife was made.

A quick means of identifying knives and their manufacturers are the styles of bone they used. Although the bone is the same, each company had its own jigging machines and each company's bone comes out with a distinctive jigging pattern.

All of the factories have done contract work, and sometimes identifying the bone can be the only key to who manufactured the knife, since the contract knife will have the name of the contractor stamped on the tang.

It is sometimes possible to determine who made a knife just by the way the bone is jigged. Jigging is the cutting of the design on the bone.

Bone naturally is white, smooth substance, and when first used on cutlery it was used in that fashion, but then cutlers discovered that it could be dyed and, if cut in certain patterns, could be held better or sometimes could resemble genuine stag. Each company had its own jigging pattern, and this is very helpful in determining what factory made certain contract knives for obscure contractors.

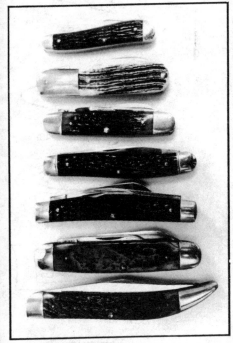

Illustrated top to bottom:

Peach Seed bone (early version). This was used by Schrade Cutlery in the late 1940's and early 1950's.

Winterbottom bone. This was used exclusively by Queen Cutlery Co., and was furnished by the Winterbottom Cutlery Co. Even today the Queen delrin handles are formed to resemble this handle.

Cattarraugas used its unique style of bone jigging, as shown on this knife.

This muskrat made by Schrade utilizes the latter version of Peach Seed bone. This was used just prior to the conversion to plastic handles for their knives.

Case jigs its own bone in this distinctive pattern, but this Case XX jigging (1940-1965) will vary slightly from the jigging on currently made Case knives.

This style jigging is on a W. R. Case and Sons Cutlery Co. knife, which demonstrates the very earliest style of case bone jigging.

The bottom knife shows the most famous bone jigging, that of the Roger Cutlery Handle Material Co. They made it for everyone, in various colors including Queen, Case, Utica, Kutmaster, and dozens of smaller factories.

Smooth Bone, not pictured, is fast becoming the leading collectible handle material.

POCKET KNIFE SHIELDS

There is no way to date the period of time different shields were used on knives in general, however, the approximate period of time each shield was used on Case knives is stated with the first eleven shields in the list.

Shield #CS3 was predominatly used from about 1942 to 1974. Case designed shield #CS2 to be used on all pocket knives handled in Delrin and Laminated Wood. Because some beginning collectors were having some difficulty in identifying Bone Stag from the handle material mentioned above especially Delrin. The difference between the two shields is the circle immediately surrounding the word CASE has been deleted.

CS1
(about 1920-1940)

CS2
(first used in 1974)

*CS3
(first used about 1935)

CS4
(about 1903-1940)

CS5
(about 1900-1940)

CS6
(about 1903-1920)

CS7
(about 1910-1940)

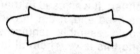

CS8
(about 1920-1940)

CS9
(about 1935-1941)

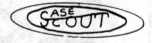

CS9A
(about 1905-1950)

CS9B
(about 1910-1930)

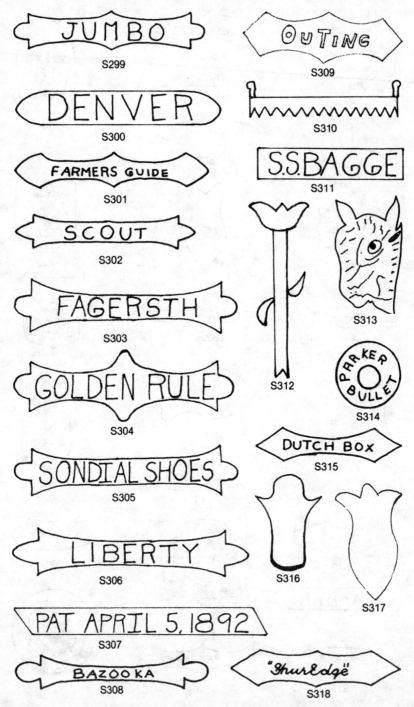

JUMBO
S299

OUTING
S309

DENVER
S300

S310

FARMERS GUIDE
S301

S.S.BAGGE
S311

SCOUT
S302

FAGERSTH
S303

S313

GOLDEN RULE
S304

PARKER BULLET
S314

SONDIAL SHOES
S305

S312

DUTCH BOX
S315

LIBERTY
S306

S316

PAT APRIL 5, 1892
S307

S317

BAZOOKA
S308

"ShurEdge"
S318

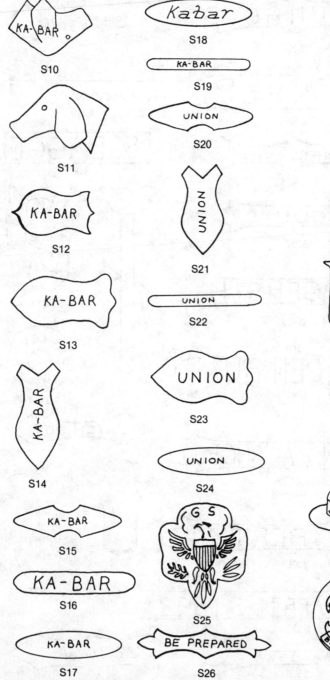

KA-BAR

S10

S11

KA-BAR

S12

KA-BAR

S13

KA-BAR

S14

KA-BAR

S15

KA-BAR

S16

KA-BAR

S17

Kabar

S18

KA-BAR

S19

UNION

S20

UNION

S21

UNION

S22

UNION

S23

UNION

S24

S25

BE PREPARED

S26

S27

S28

S29

S30

SCOUT

S31

S32

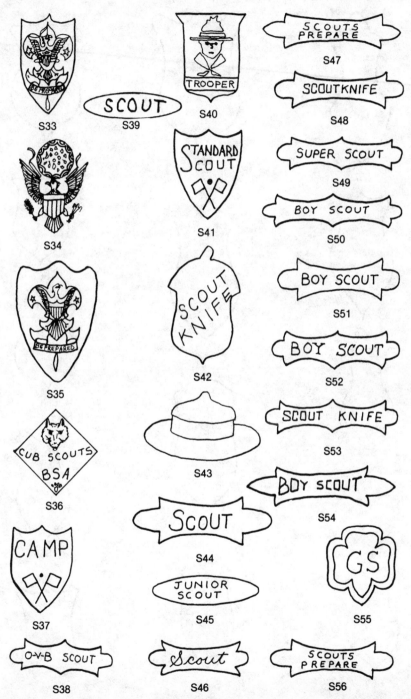

S33

SCOUT
S39

TROOPER
S40

SCOUTS
PREPARE
S47

SCOUTKNIFE
S48

S34

STANDARD
SCOUT
S41

SUPER SCOUT
S49

BOY SCOUT
S50

S35

SCOUT
KNIFE
S42

BOY SCOUT
S51

BOY SCOUT
S52

CUB SCOUTS
BSA
S36

S43

SCOUT KNIFE
S53

CAMP
S37

SCOUT
S44

JUNIOR
SCOUT
S45

BOY SCOUT
S54

GS
S55

O-V-B SCOUT
S38

Scout
S46

SCOUTS
PREPARE
S56

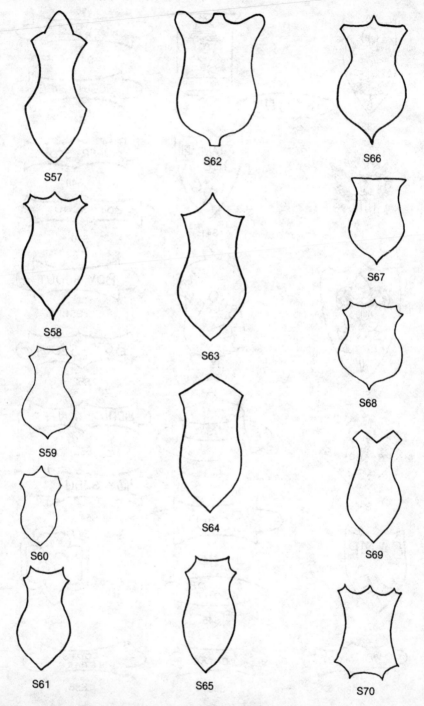

S57

S62

S66

S58

S63

S67

S59

S64

S68

S60

S69

S61

S65

S70

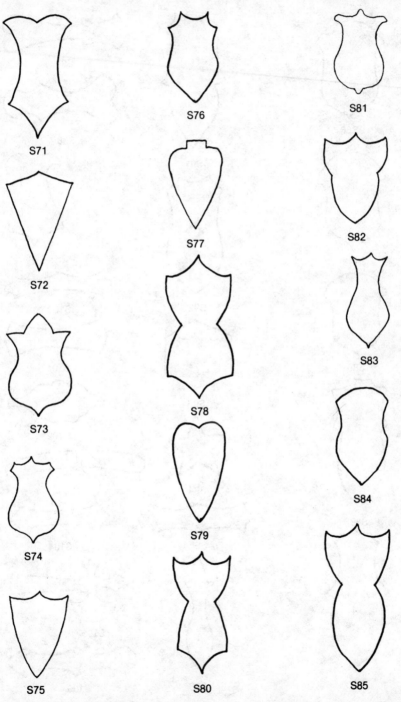

S71

S72

S73

S74

S75

S76

S77

S78

S79

S80

S81

S82

S83

S84

S85

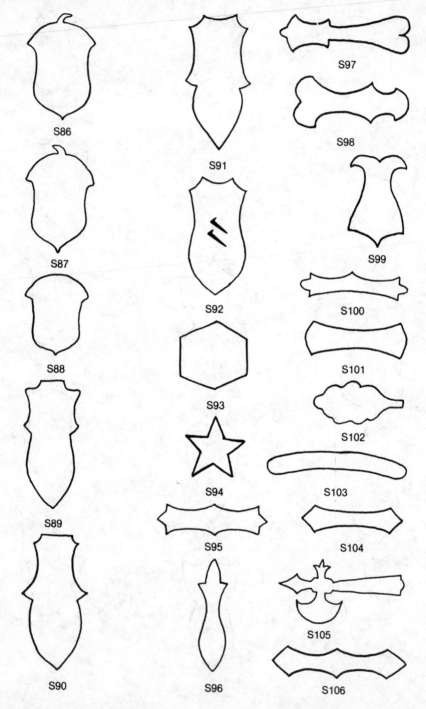

S86

S87

S88

S89

S90

S91

S92

S93

S94

S95

S96

S97

S98

S99

S100

S101

S102

S103

S104

S105

S106

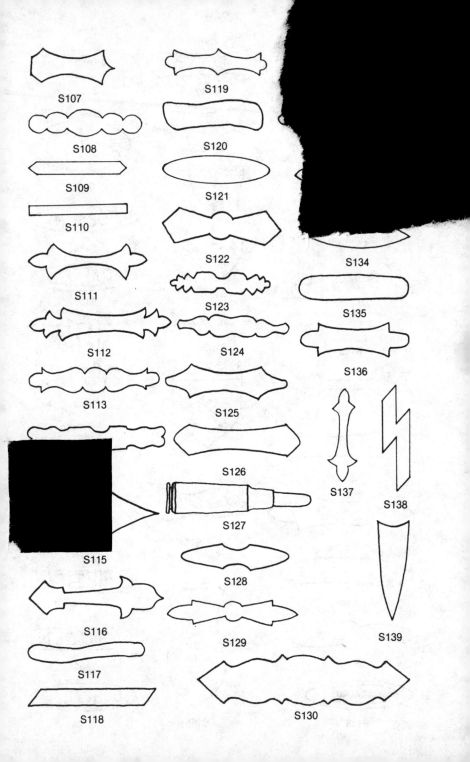

S107

S119

S108

S120

S109

S121

S110

S122

S111

S123

S134

S112

S124

S135

S113

S125

S136

S115

S126

S137

S138

S116

S127

S139

S117

S128

S118

S129

S130

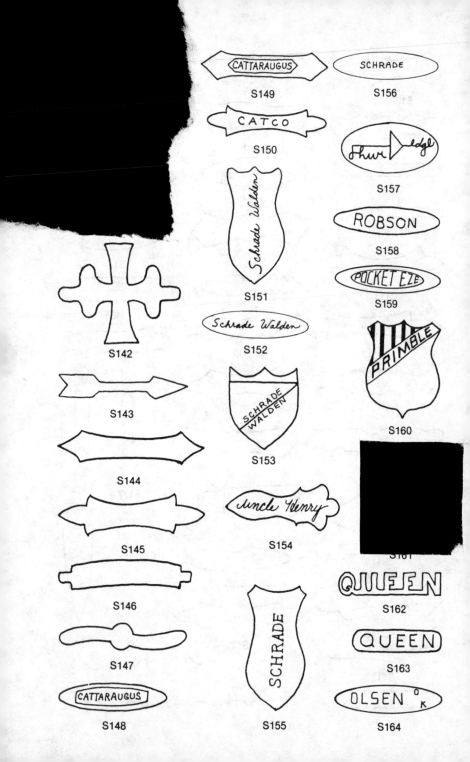

CATTARAUGUS
S149

SCHRADE
S156

CATCO
S150

Shur edge
S157

Schrade Walden
S151

ROBSON
S158

Schrade Walden
S152

POCKET EZE
S159

SCHRADE WALDEN
S153

PRIMBLE
S160

Uncle Henry
S154

S161

S142

S143

S144

S145

S146

S147

CATTARAUGUS
S148

SCHRADE
S155

QUEEN
S162

QUEEN
S163

OLSEN O K
S164

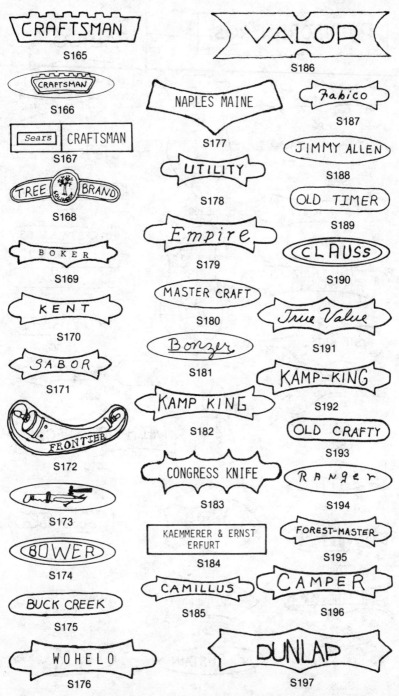

CRAFTSMAN
S165

CRAFTSMAN
S166

Sears | CRAFTSMAN
S167

TREE SOLINGEN BRAND
S168

BOKER
S169

KENT
S170

SABOR
S171

FRONTIER
S172

S173

BOWER
S174

BUCK CREEK
S175

WOHELO
S176

VALOR
S186

NAPLES MAINE
S177

UTILITY
S178

Empire
S179

MASTER CRAFT
S180

Bonzer
S181

KAMP KING
S182

CONGRESS KNIFE
S183

KAEMMERER & ERNST
ERFURT
S184

CAMILLUS
S185

Fabico
S187

JIMMY ALLEN
S188

OLD TIMER
S189

CLAUSS
S190

True Value
S191

KAMP-KING
S192

OLD CRAFTY
S193

Ranger
S194

FOREST-MASTER
S195

CAMPER
S196

DUNLAP
S197

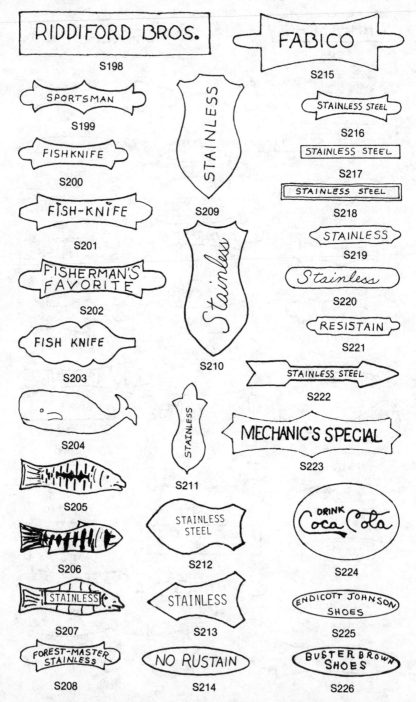

RIDDIFORD BROS.
S198

FABICO
S215

SPORTSMAN
S199

STAINLESS
S209

STAINLESS STEEL
S216

FISHKNIFE
S200

STAINLESS STEEL
S217

FISH-KNIFE
S201

STAINLESS STEEL
S218

FISHERMAN'S FAVORITE
S202

Stainless
S210

STAINLESS
S219

Stainless
S220

FISH KNIFE
S203

RESISTAIN
S221

S204

STAINLESS STEEL
S222

STAINLESS
S211

MECHANIC'S SPECIAL
S223

S205

S206

STAINLESS STEEL
S212

DRINK Coca Cola
S224

STAINLESS
S207

STAINLESS
S213

ENDICOTT JOHNSON SHOES
S225

FOREST-MASTER STAINLESS
S208

NO RUSTAIN
S214

BUSTER BROWN SHOES
S226

STAR BRAND SHOES
ARE "BETTER"

S227

Premier
LIFE TIME

S228

WESTERN
ELECTRIC

S229

CURTISS
BABY RUTH
CANDY & GUM

S230

THE FVERSTICK ANCHOR CO

S231

PETERS SHOES

S232

RADIO TOOL

S233

AUTO & RADIO

S234

ENDICOTT JOHNSON
SHOES

S235

MECHANIC'S SPECIAL

S236

JIM DANDY
COLLARS

S237

BROWN SHOE
COMPANY

S238

W.L. DOUGLAS
SHOE CO.

S239

FLOUR

S240

SHAPLEIGH'S
KEEN
KUTTER

S241

KEEN KUTTER
KROME·PLATE

S242

KEEN KUTTER

S243

KEENKUTTER

S244

KEEN KUTTER

S245

S246

KEEN
KUTTER

S247

S248

S249

Solingen

S250

Solingen

S251

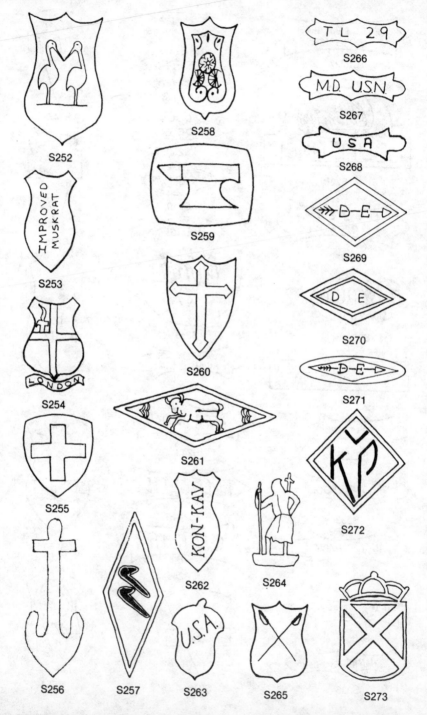

S252

S253

S254

S255

S256

S257

S258

S259

S260

S261

S262

S263

S264

S265

S266

S267

S268

S269

S270

S271

S272

S273

S274

S281

S287

S293

S275

S282

S288

S294

S276

S283

S289

S295

S277

S284

S290

S296

S278

S285

S291

S297

S279

S280

S286

S292

S298

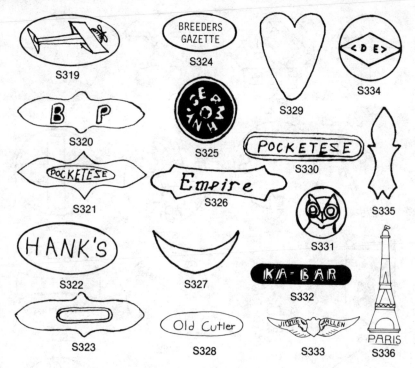

S319

BREEDERS GAZETTE
S324

S329

< D E >
S334

B   P
S320

GERMAN HAND
S325

POCKETESE
S330

POCKETESE
S321

Empire
S326

S335

HANK'S
S322

S327

S331

S323

KA-BAR
S332

Old Cutler
S328

JIMMIE ALLEN
S333

PARIS
S336

BLADE PATTERNS

Most manufacturers produced similar patterns, and it is almost impossible to determine the maker of a knife without a logo stamped somewhere on the knife. Most logos are stamped on the tang of the master blade.

Not illustrated is a long pull. A long pull is a nail mark that runs from the swage to the tang.

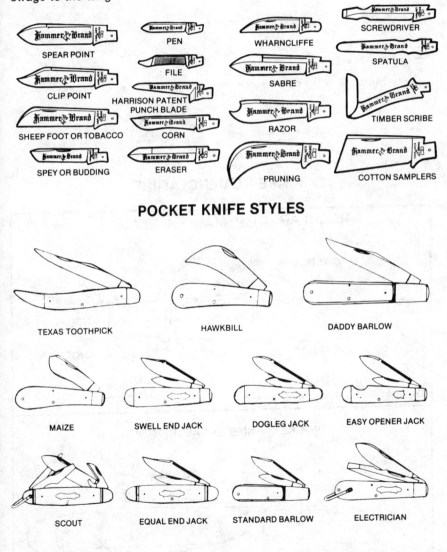

SPEAR POINT

PEN

WHARNCLIFFE

SCREWDRIVER

CLIP POINT

FILE

SABRE

SPATULA

SHEEP FOOT OR TOBACCO

HARRISON PATENT PUNCH BLADE

RAZOR

TIMBER SCRIBE

SPEY OR BUDDING

CORN

ERASER

PRUNING

COTTON SAMPLERS

POCKET KNIFE STYLES

TEXAS TOOTHPICK

HAWKBILL

DADDY BARLOW

MAIZE

SWELL END JACK

DOGLEG JACK

EASY OPENER JACK

SCOUT

EQUAL END JACK

STANDARD BARLOW

ELECTRICIAN

MOOSE

PREMIUM STOCK

SERPENTINE JACK

CATTLE

SWELL CENTER

CONGRESS PEN

MUSKRAT

SLEEVEBOARD PEN

SENATOR PEN

LOBSTER PEN

KNIFE NOMENCLATURE

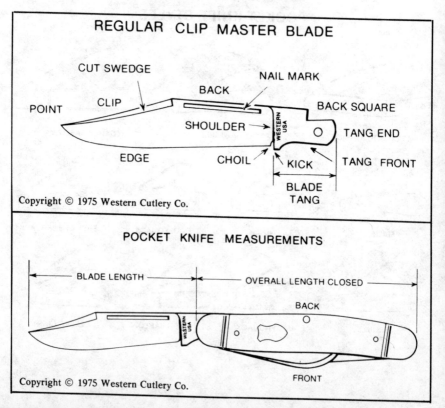

REGULAR CLIP MASTER BLADE

CUT SWEDGE

NAIL MARK

BACK

POINT

CLIP

BACK SQUARE

SHOULDER

WESTERN USA

TANG END

EDGE

CHOIL

KICK

TANG FRONT

BLADE TANG

POCKET KNIFE MEASUREMENTS

BLADE LENGTH

OVERALL LENGTH CLOSED

BACK

WESTERN USA

FRONT

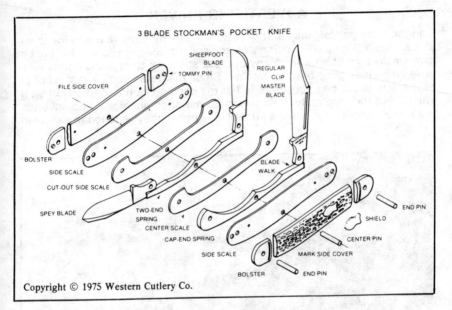

3 BLADE STOCKMAN'S POCKET KNIFE

SWITCHBLADES

Switchblades were common in America until Congress passed a law in 1958 regulating the sale, possession, and manufacture of switchblades. Despite this, switchblades are a part of the cutler's art and are popular among many collectors. The laws regarding the ownership of such weapons depend upon the state and local laws and should be checked before buying or collecting switchblades.

Most major companies made switchblades. A popular one was the Press-Button Knife Company, Walden, New York which had the button in the bolster, but there were other variations. Lever knives, button knives, and out-the-end were a few of the popular methods of triggering the knives.

Schrade Walden was the major American manufacturer of switchblades, using both the Schrade Cutlery Company logo and the Schrade-Walden logo. Too, the George Schrade Knife Company had an extensive line of switches under the "Presto" logo. Schrade-Walden made a top line (Keen Kutter), and a cheaper line (Edgemaster) of switchblades.

Remington switches are identical to Schrade except the stamping and were probably made by Schrade.

W. R. Case & Sons made some switchblades using the lever release method, but their pushbutton switches were made by Schrade on contract.

Imperial Knife Company made switchblades under "Hammer Brand" and "Jackmaster", as well as Imperial.

Most well-known European firms made switches, with Bonsas being more common than most.

Switchblades are still made today for use by paratroopers to cut their lines if caught in a tree and one arm is injured. Most of these are made by Schrade and Camillus.

ADVERTISING KNIVES

In the early part of this century there were many firms that had inexpensive knives made up with their name and some slogan or address on it to be given away as a promotion. Many of these still exist though the companies have long since gone out of business. Since there was such a vast number of these it would be impossible to list the companies that had advertising knives, but they are collectible and most major companies made advertising knives, some even using switchblades (when they were legal) as advertising knives.

Note all the knives pictured above are reproductions. Beware when purchasing originals.

HANDMADE AND CUSTOM KNIVES

Some of the nicest pocketknives around are coming from the one man workshops of custom makers. The knives from these craftsmen are just like a fine painting or sculpture. They are works of art, a form of metal sculpture, with adornments such as engraving, etched blades, ivory scrimshawed handles, and much more. As any knife that is collected today, they are going up in price, and when you buy one there are two ways you can go.

The first is to buy from a relatively unknown knifemaker who produces a superior knife but has not had the publicity and achieved the fame of some of the better known makers. If his knives are truly superior, they will soon become the object of many collectors, and he will soon raise his prices as demand increases, thereby increasing your investment. Too, some collectors look only for the early cruder work of custom makers. The bad point is if he loses interest and drops his quality, you will not gain on your investment.

The second way is to buy the knives only from well-known makers. This has the advantage of a ready market when you decide to sell, and probably increasing your investment. However, the drawback is that many of the makers are years behind in orders, and when you buy their knives it will require a more substantial investment than that of an unknown maker.

We recommend that you never buy a knife of shoddy workmanship or a handmade knife with no name stamped on it. True, there are some famous maker's knives floating around in the market with no name stamped on them, but it takes an experienced hand to identify them.

When you buy a custom folder, some of the things to look for are as follows:

Fit: The handles fit flush and tight with the bolsters or are they filled with epoxy to take up the space?

Nailmark: Is the nailmark as good as that of most factory knives? This is where most custom makers blow it.

Bolsters: If the liners and bolster are the same material, can you tell where the bolster and liner join? If you can, beware.

Pivot Rivet: Can you tell where it is? On a good knife it should not be visible.

Lock: Does the knife lock and unlock easily?

Evenness: Does the backspring come back level with the liners in both the open and closed position?

Polish: Is the polish good or are waves visible? Is the inside polished?

Grind Lines: Are both sides of the blade ground even?

This is a starting guideline for the buyer of a custom folder. The best advice was given to us by Wayne Goddard, a knifemaker of the first rank from Oregon. He said, "I can tell you what to look for a hundred times, but the only way to really tell is to go to a well-known maker who makes top quality knives, look his folders over and then go look at the one you are considering buying. There is where the difference will show." Following are some custom knives from the files of the National Knife Collector magazine. (Used with permission.)

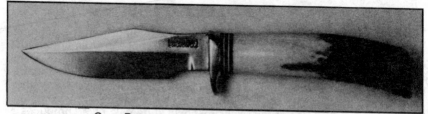

Gary Barnes, one of the rising knifemakers.

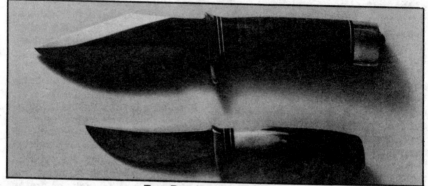

Two Randall made knives.

Paul Fox, made this fine one-blade.

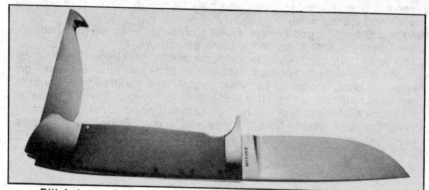

Bill Ankrom, Cody, WY, made this fold out gut hook drop point.

A stone handled kris by Ted Dowell. This knife was stolen at the Houston gun show in 1979.

W. T. Fuller Fixed blade, Gasden Alabama knifemaker.

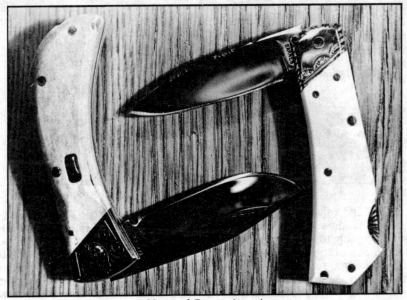

More of Barnes' work.

Four functional hunting knives by Pass of Florida.

"CUSTOM knives" has become a field of knife collecting in itself. The majority of handmade knife collectors collect only handmade knives, and collect as much for the artistic work as for the collectibility of the knife. Regardless of the reason, it is a field still reasonably small (less than 500 knifemakers are in the "Knifemakers Guild"). Many of those are part-time makers, so the overall output of handmade knives is limited to a great degree. The thing the collector needs to look for is whether the maker is well-known now or his talent is destined to become well known.

Handmade knife collecting began about the same time modern handmade knives started being made. The term "Handmade Knives" in knife collecting circles denotes roughly the 1930's to the present. World War II seemed to be the thing that prompted most of the pioneers in the handmade knifemaking field. Bo Randall, Rudy Ruana, and Bill Scagel are credited with being among the first to offer the sportsman a handmade knife. The idea was a fine one. In a society where a sportsman could ill afford a rifle or car built to his specific requirements, for a reasonable sum he could design a knife just the way he wanted it, and the maker would come up with a similar knife. A few sportswriters caught on, and through their publicity made names like Bob Loveless and D. E. Henry famous in knifemaking circles. Their work warranted the attention it was given, but it is a recent trend that for every maker in the United States there are three people wanting to write his life's story. That's not to say his story is not worth telling, but it is to remind the collector that publicity is not the way to make a choice of knives for your collection. Look to the quality of the knives for your collection. Unless you plan to collect the early work of knifemakers, you should only buy a good quality knife for your collection. We cannot describe in these pages what a "quality" handmade knife is, but its craftsmanship should be better than that of a factory produced knife of a similar style.

The knife factories have recently turned a listening ear to the voices of the custom makers. In the early '60's most factory knives were inferior quality when compared with handmade knives by the top makers. Sure, there was a large price difference too, but the influence of the makers can be seen today in every major factory. The factories have improved their quality of their hunting knives, and the main reason is because the handmade makers have shown the factories how it's supposed to be done.

Prices for collector's knives in the handmade field can range from a few dollars to several thousand. Handmade knives are works of art, and the stature of the artist plays as much a part in the pricing as the knife itself. Therefore, we have not included a price guide to the knifemakers. However, we have listed a large number of those in the Knifemakers Guild, and through personal correspondence with them you can learn more about them and their knives. Most offer catalogs, and the price of the catalogs vary with each maker.

As with all things, the knives no longer produced bring high prices, and though only in operation for a few years, the Knifemakers Guild has said good-bye to some fine gentlemen: Pete Heath, Red Watson, and Ron Little, who have all died in recent years. As you might suspect, knives made by these makers are among the fast rising in price.

Following is a list of some knifemakers:

ALABAMA

Dick Dorough
Rt. 1, Box 130
Gadsden, AL 35901

Fain E. Edwards
209 E. Mountain Avenue
Jacksonville, AL 36265

Fuller & Hall
F & H Knives
P. O. Box 734
Livingston, AL 35470

W. T. Fuller
One Hander
400 South 8th Street
East Gadsden, AL 35903

Jim Hammond
P. O. Box 486
Arab, AL 35010

J. B. Hodge
1100 Woodmont Avenue SE
Huntsville, AL 35801

D. M. Howard
Rt. 5, Box 77
Gadsden, AL 35903

Norman Levine
915 Tascosa Drive S.E.
Huntsville, AL 35802

Harvey McBurnette
Rt. 4, Box 337
Piedmont, AL 36272

Melvin Pardue
Rt. 1, Box 130
Ripton, AL 36475

ALASKA
A. W. Amoureux
2311 Barrow
Anchorage, AK 99503

ARIZONA
William D. Cheatham
2930 W. Marlette
Phoenix, AZ 85017

Gerald Click
5611 S. Doubloon Ct.
Tempe, AZ 85283

Lorenzo (Larry) Hendricks
9919 East Apache Trail
Mesa, AZ 85207

Steve Hoel
P. O. Box 283
Pine, AZ 85544

Dan Rafferty
P. O. Box 1415
Apache Junction, AZ 85220

Charles L. Weiss
18847 N. 13th Avenue
Phoenix, AZ 85027

ARKANSAS
Pat Crawford
205 North Center
West Memphis, AR 72301

Joe Flournoy
P. O. Box 895
El Dorado, AR 71730

Vernon Hicks
Route 1, Box 387
Bauxite, AR 72011

Jon Kirk
600 N. Olive Street
Fayetteville, AR 72701

James B. Lile
Route 1
Russellville, AR 72801

Tom Maringer
2306 S. Powell Street
Springdale, AR 72764

Robert Ogg
Route 1, Box 230
Paris, AR 72855

Clifton Polk
3526 Eller
Ft. Smith, AR 72904

A. G. Russell
1705 Highway 71 North
Sprindale, AR 72764

Art Wiman
P. O. Box 92
Plummerville, AR 72127

CALIFORNIA
Leslie Berryman
39885 San Murout Court
Fremont, CA 94538

Rick Browne
265 East 7th Street
Upland, CA 91786

Joe Funderburg
P. O. Box 6193
Los Osos, CA 93402

Frank Gamble
20533 Blossom Lane
Cupertino, CA 95014

Donald B. Hoffman
P. O. Box 174
San Miguel, CA 93451

Jess Horn
P. O. Box 1274
Redding, CA 96099

R. W. Loveless
P. O. Box 7836
Riverside, CA 92503

Robert Lum
1714½ Grand Avenue
Santa Barbara, CA 93103

Mickey Maddox
63 Spring Circle
Ringgold, CA 30736

Robert Oleson
800 Keokuk Street
Petaluma, CA 94952

Lloyd Pendleton
2116 Broadmore Avenue
San Pablo, CA 94806

Ron Richard
4873 Colaveras Avenue
Fremont, CA 94538

Herman Schneider
24296 Via Aquara
Leguna Niguel, CA 92677

Jim Sornberger
5675 Meridian Avenue
San Jose, CA 95118

Stephen Terrill
908 S. Magnolia, Box 669
Lindsay, CA 93247

Carolyn Tinker
1699 N. Marengo Avenue
Pasadena, CA 91103

Mike Wesolowski
902A Lohrman Lane
Petaluma, CA 94952

Barry Wood
650½ S. Venice Boulevard
Venice, CA 90291

COLORADO
Richard Campbell
365 W. Oxford Avenue
Englewood, CO 80110

Roy E. Genge
P. O. Box 57
Eastlake, CO 80614

Rick Genovese
2838 E. Prospect Street
Colorado Springs, CO 80908

Jim Hardenbrook
17988 RD G
Cortez, CO 81321

Hanford Miller
5105 South LeMaster Road
Evergreen, CO 80439

R. D. Nolen
P. O. Box 2895
Estes Park, CO 80517

Don Puterbaugh-Bob Schultz
4062 Templeton Gap
Colorado Springs, CO 80907

Jim Sasser
1811 Sante Fe Drive
Pueblo, CO 81006

T. J. Yancey
P. O. Box 943
Estes Park, CO 80517

CONNECTICUT
Arthur J. Hubbard
574 Cutlers Farm Road
Monroe, CT 06468

Gerry Jean
25B Clifford Drive
Manchester, CT 06040

FLORIDA
Bill Bagwell
Rt. 2, Box 72-C
DeFuniak Springs, FL 32433

Frank Centofante
P. O. Box 17587
Tampa, FL 33612

Brad Embry
7137 N. 50th Street
Tampa, FL 33617

Tom Enos
Rt. 1, Box 66
Winter Garden, FL 32787

Ernest L. Lyle, III
4501 Meadowbrook Avenue
Orlando, FL 32808

Clinton Manley
Rt. 1, Box 28
Zolfo Springs, FL 33890

Chris Miller
1961 Southwest 36 Avenue
Fort Lauderdale, FL 33312

John Owens
8755 S.W. 96th Street
Miami, FL 33156

W. C. Pass
P. O. Box 307
Merritt Island, FL 32952

Dean Roath
5959 Fort Caroline Road
Apt. #605
Jacksonville, FL 32211

GEORGIA
Jack Barrett
2133 Peach Orchard Road
Augusta, GA 30906

Michael Collins
Rt. 4, Battesville Road
Woodstock, GA 30188

Leonard Corlee
P. O. Box 143
Georgetown, GA 31754

John Fuller
6156 Ridgeway
Douglasville, GA 30135

Rade Hawkins
P. O. Box H
Red Oak, GA 30272

Wayne G. Hensley
469 Hilltop Road, S.W.
Conyers, GA 30207

Lance Kelly
4226 Lamar Street
Decatur, GA 30035

Leon Pittman
Route 2
Pendergrass, GA 30567

James L. Poplin
P. O. Box 947
Washington, GA 30673

E. W. (Bubba) Schulenburg
406 Sunset Boulevard
Carrollton, GA 30117

A. F. Walters
609 East 20th Street
Tifton, GA 31794

IDAHO
Ivan Nealey
Anderson Dam
Mountain Home, ID 83647

Barr Quarton
P. O. Box 984
Sun Valley, ID 83353

Clifton Schenck
P. O. Box 1017
Bonners Ferry, ID 83805

Bernard Sparks
P. O. Box 32
Dingle, ID 83233

Dwight Towell
Rt. 1
Midvale, ID 83645

ILLINOIS
Dick Atkinson
2524 S. 34th Street
Decatur, IL 62521

E. D. Brignardello
Rt. 2, Box 152A
Beecher, IL 60401

Bob Cargill
14401 136th Avenue
Lock Port, IL 60441

Jim Corrado
1032 N. Columbian
Oak Park, IL 60302

William Heath
P. O. Box 131
Bondville, IL 61815

Ron Lake
123 East Park
Taylorville, IL 63568

Paul Myers
128 12th Street
Wood River, IL 62095

Maurice and Alan Schrock
1708 S. Plum Street
Pontiac, IL 61764

Ralph Turnbull
5722 Newburg Road
Roackford, IL 61108

Tim Wright
5831 S. Blackstone
Chicago, IL 60637

INDIANA
Sid Birt
P. O. Box 544
Bunker Hill, IN 46914

W. W. Cronk
511 Boyd Avenue
Greenfield, IN 46140

Billy Mace Imel
1616 Bundy Avenue
New Castle, IN 47362

Jim Minnick
144 N. 7th Street
Middletown, IN 47356

William Welch
3220 Lafayette
Fort Wayne, IN 46806

IOWA
Dennis B. Brooker
1526 Walnut
Des Moines, IA 50309

KANSAS
Elton Courtney
2718 Bullinger
Wichita, KS 67204

Michael Ray
347 N. Fern
Wichita, KS 67203

Jim Smith
1608 Joann
Wichita, KS 67203

KENTUCKY
Larry Brandstetter
827 North 25th
Paducah, KY 42001

J. D. Clay
4 A Graysbranch Road
Lloyd, KY 41156

William Keeton
4234 Lynnbrook Dr.
Louisville, KY 40220

LOUISIANA
John Culpepper
2102 Spencer Avenue
Monroe, LA 71202

Howard Fauchezux
P. O. Box 206
Loreauville, LA 70552

Cary Smith
946 Marigney
Mandeville, LA 70448

Frank Vought
Rt. 2, Box 60
Hammond, LA 70401

Horace Wiggins
P. O. Box 152
Mansfield, LA 71502

MAINE
Murad Sayen
P. O. Box 109
Norway, ME 04268

MARYLAND
Ray Beers
9 Manorbrook Road
Monkton, MD 21111

C. R. Hudson
R.R. 1, Box 128B
Rock Hall, MD 21661

Robert H. Keller
Sam's Lane
Ijamsville, MD 21754

William F. Moran, Jr.
P. O. Box 68
Braddock Heights, MD 21714

MASSACHUSETTS
Jimmy Fikes
215 North Main Street
Orange, MA 01364

Jot Khalsa
54 Kenwood Street
Dorchester, MA 02124

MICHIGAN
Andrew "Andy" Blackton
39501 Lakeshore Drive
Mt. Clemens, MI 48045

Don Ellison
670 Browning
Ypsilanti, MI 48197

Mike Leach
5377 W. Grand Blanc Road
Swartz Creek, MI 48473

James Serven
6153 Third Street
Mayville, MI 48744

MISSISSIPPI
Jesse W. Davis
5810 Highway 301
Walls, MS 38680

Glen David Messer
RFD E-1
Sumrall, MS 39482

John T. Smith
8404 Cedar Crest Drive
Southaven, MS 38671

MISSOURI
Raymond Cover
Rt. 1, Box 101
Mineral Point, MO 63660

James H. Craig
334 Novara
Manchester, MO 63011

W. C. Davis
Route 2, S. Madison
Raymore, MO 64083

Charles W. Graham
Box 111
Eolia, MO 63344

Paul Rizal
2643 Sidney
Blue Springs, MO 64015

MONTANA
Henry Frank
210 Meadows Road
Whitefish, MT 59937

Dennis Friedly
Star Route
Belfry, MT 59005

Russ Moyer
915 2nd Avenue
Haure, MT 59501

Eldon Peterson
260 Haugen Heights
Whitefish, MT 59937

Aaron Pursley
Bear Paw Route, Box 6A
Big Sandy, MT 59520

NEBRASKA
Terry Miller
450 South 1st Street
Seward, NB 68434

NEVADA
Bill Duff
P. O. Box 694
Virginia City, NV 89440

NEW HAMPSHIRE
Don Fogg
Rt. 152
Nottingham, NH 03290

NEW JERSEY
Charles A. Doak
P. O. Box 143
Saddle River, NJ 07458

Fredrick Weber
401 W. Clinton Street
Haledon, NJ 07508

Howard J. Viele
99 Lexington Avenue
Westwood, NJ 07657

NEW MEXICO
Joseph G. Cordova
1450 Lillie Drive
Bosque Farms, NM 87068

Don Hethcoat
Rt. 1, Box 412
Belen, NM 87002

Bob Jones
6219 Aztec N.E.
Albuquerque, NM 87110

Don Karlin
P. O. Box 668
Aztec, NM 87410

Roger J. Russell
P. O. Box 27
Peralto, NM 87042

Weldon Whitley
P. O. Box 746
Jal, NM 88252

NEW YORK
Frank D'Elia
2050 Hillside Avenue
New Hyde Park, NY 11040

Thomas G. Down
195 River Road
Grandview, NY 10960

Dan Maragni
47 Fifth Avenue
Northport, NY 11768

Michael Sampogna
43 E. Argyle Street
Valley Stream, NY 11040

Murad Sayen
Black Oak Knives
City of Ithaca, Youth Bureau
1701 North Cayuga Street
Ithaca, NY 14850

James A. Schmidt
Rt. 3 - Eastern Avenue
Ballston Lake, NY 12019

NORTH CAROLINA
G. M. (Tim) Britton
Rt. 2, Box 271B
Kingston, NC 28501

Paul E. Compton
108 Overbrook Road
Goldsboro, NC 27530

Paul Fox
Box 2130 Hog Hill
Hickory, NC 28601

Mickey Tedder
Rt. 2, Box 13A
Conover, NC 28613

NORTH DAKOTA
Dr. Philip Hagen
702 28th Avenue North
Fargo, ND 58102

OHIO
Dan Dagget
Route 1
Stewart, OH 45778

Mike Franklin
P. O. Box 88
Aberdeen, OH 45101

Mike Koval
P. O. Box 14130
Columbus, OH 43214

Michael Manrow
6093 Saddlewood
Toledo, OH 43613

Robert Papp
331 Winckles Street
Elyria, OH 44035

W. D. Pease
5415 Mt. Aire Road
Ripley, OH 45167

Harold Rollins
662 Breathitt Avenue
Columbus, OH 43207

David Sites
2665 Atwood Terrace
Columbus, OH 43211

Dale Warther
c/o Warther Museum, Inc.
331 Karl Avenue
Dover, OH 44622

OKLAHOMA
Mike England
608 West 4th
Cordell, OK 73632

John McCormick
32 East 26th Street
Tulsa, OK 74129

Ted Miller
4333 S.E. 17th Street
Del City, OK 73115

Woody Naifeh
Rt. 13, Box 380
Tulsa, OK 74107

Harold Phillips
Rt. #1, Box 37
Waukomis, OK 73773

OREGON
Ted M. Dowell
130 NW St. Helens
Bend, OR 97701

Wayne Goddard
473 Durham Avenue
Eugene, OR 97404

R. H. Hanson
1977 S.W. Burdette Drive
Roseburg, OR 97470

Gary Kelley
17485 S.W. Pheasant Lane
Aloha, OR 97005

Leon Thompson
1735 Leon Drive
Forest Grove, OR 97116

PENNSYLVANIA
D. E. (Lucky) Clark
Box 216 Woodlawn Street., Rt. 1
Mineral Point, PA 15942

Vince Feragotti
Rt. 1, Beechwood Drive
Industry, PA 15052

SOUTH CAROLINA
P. F. Beck
1504 Haggod Avenue
Barnwell, SC 29812

Richard Bridwell
Rt. 2
Taylors, SC 29687

Walter "Blackie" Collins
P. O. Box 508
Clover, SC 29710

Davis Brothers Knives
P. O. Box 793
Camden, SC 29010

William G. DeFreest
P. O. Box 573
Barnwell, SC 29812

E. E. Gillenwater
921 Dougherty Road
Aiken, SC 29801

George Herron
920 Murrah Avenue
Aiken, SC 29801

Tommy Lee
Rt. 2, Box 463
Gaffney, SC 29340

James (Danny) Thornton
P. O. Box 334
Fort Mill, SC 29715

E. A. Wheman, Jr.
104 Drive Avenue
Summerville, SC 29483

TENNESSEE
Ronald Canter
96 Bon Air Circle
Jackson, TN 38301

Vernon W. Coleman
141 Lakeside Park Drive
Hendersonville, TN 37075

Harold Corby
1714 Brandonwood Drive
Johnson City, TN 37601

Jim Cunningham
519 Madison Avenue
Memphis, TN 38104

Joe Hales
1742 Corning Avenue
Memphis, TN 38127

C. Gray Taylor
134 Lana View Drive
Kingsport, TN 37664

TEXAS
James Barbee
P. O. Box 1702
Fort Stockton, TX 79753

Fred Carter
2303 Dorothy
Wichita Falls, TX 76306

John E. Chase
P. O. Drawer H
Aledo, TX 76008

Mike Connor
P. O. Box 1205
Winters, TX 70567

Don Couchmann
Knife Shop
El Paso International Airport
El Paso, TX 79925

Steve Davenport
301 Meyer
Alvin, TX 77511

L. C. Finger
Rt. 5, Box 97B
Wetherford, TX 76086

Clay Gault
Rt. 1, Box 184
Lexington, TX 78947

Rendon and Mark Griffin
9706 Cedardale
Houston, TX 77055

Robert Hajovsky
P. O. Box 21
Scotland, TX 76379

Don Hastings
P. O. Box 181
Palestine, TX 75801

D'Alton Holder
7102 Gainsborough
Amarillo, TX 79106

David M. Howie
P. O. Box 1662
Bay City, TX 77414

Chubby Hueske
4808 Tamarisk
Bellaire, TX 77401

Gorden W. Johnson
5426 Sweetbriar
Houston, TX 77060

Ruffin Johnson
215 La Fonda
Houston, TX 77060

Joe Kious
Rt. 1, Box 232
Alamo, TX 78516

Don Laughlin
190 Laughlin Drive
Vidor, TX 77662

Loyd McConnell
P. O. Box 7162
Odessa, TX 79760

Jim Nolen
P. O. Box 6216
Corpus Christi, TX 78411

Jim Pugh
P. O. Box 711
Azle, TX 76020

Martin Pullen
Rt. 1, Box 22
Rio Vista, TX 76093

Norman Simons
12006 Newbrook
Houston, TX 77072

G. W. Stone
610 N. Glenville Drive
Richardson, TX 75081

George A. Walker
7703 Miller Glen Lane
Houston, TX 77072

W. C. Williams
Rt. 2, Box 452
Atlanta, TX 75551

Bill Winn
Star Route
Gruver, TX 79040

W. W. Wood
731 Wood Ridge Drive
Cedar Hill, TX 75104

UTAH
Jim Ence
145 South 200 East
Richfield, UT 84701

Steve Johnson
P. O. Box S
Manti, UT 84642

David Shaw
2009 North 450 East
Ogden, UT 84404

Buster Warenski
P. O. Box 214
Richfield, UT 84701

Richard Worthen
834 Carnation Drive
Sandy, UT 84070

VIRGINIA
Ron Frazier
Rt. 6, Box 217
Powhatan, VA 23139

Ben A. Shelor
Rt. 14, Box 318B
Richmond, VA 23231

Major Jack R. Smith
1404 Deerfield Lane
Woodbridge, VA 22191

Pat Tomes
41 Greenbriar Avenue
Hampton, VA 23661

WEST VIRGINIA
Don Cantini
3933 Claremont Place
Weirton, WV 26062

Douglas Dent
1208 Chestnut Street
S. Charleston, WV 25309

Charles McConnell
158 Genteel Ridge
Wellsburg, WV 26070

Corbet R. Sigman
Rt. 1, Box 212A
Liberty, WV 25124

R. W. Wilson
P. O. Box 2012
Weirton, WV 26062

WISCONSIN
John Bassney
Rt. 3, Box 277A
Lodi, WI 53555

WYOMING
W. E. Ankrom
Rt. 2, Box 3506
Cody, WY 82414

Scott Barry
P. O. Box 354
Laramie, WY 82070

FOREIGN COUNTRIES

CANADA
Matthew A. Schoenfeld
RR 3
Nelson, B.C.
V1L 5P6 Canada

Adam Smith
92 Monsheen Drive
Woodbridge, Ontario
Canada L4L 2E7

ENGLAND
J. Niall Heywood
17 Stamford Road
Bowdon, Altricham England

GERMANY
Matthias E. Holze
D 6740 Landau/pfalz
Postfach 1451 Germany

Team KSK
Kressler . Kuhne . Sachse
SpichernstraBe 48
D-5000 Kohn 1
Germany

GUATEMALA
Robert Terzuola
Apartado 213
Antiqua, Guatemala, C.A.

JAPAN
Tak Fukuta
c/o Kazuo Kishida
4-1-26 Enokimoto Machi
Sakai City Osaka-Pref
Japan 0722

COUNTERFEITING

The counterfeit knife is the topic of a great many knife collectors, and in the course of the conversation they do a lot of swearing about it, but precious little is told to beginning collectors about how to detect them. It seems that the knowledge of what to look for in a counterfeit should be a secret, told only after the beginner has the trust of the old sage collector and is deserving. While interviewing collectors and dealers for this article most expressed concern that an article on how to detect counterfeits could easily be an article on how to counterfeit, and then they would clam up. All the while, beginners were buying counterfeits, discovering it, and quitting knife collecting. If the information below tells how to counterfeit but still stops some beginning collector from dropping out of the hobby, it will be worth it.

Fortunately, most counterfeiters don't have the equipment or parts necessary to make a foolproof counterfeit, and there are certain things to look for in detecting a counterfeit.

The most important thing is to know your knife. There are few Case Canoe collectors who would not look extra close at a 62131 XX with bone handles, or a Rough Black collector who would buy a Rough Black 6111 ½ Lockback. This familiarity with a knife will sometimes ring a bell in your head when one "just doesn't look right".

I have noticed that most counterfeits are around the $50.00 price range. Cheaper priced knives are not worth the effort, and more expensive knives usually mean the buyer wants return privileges and will have the knive inspected by several knowledgeable collectors.

Case stags are popular among many collectors, and are popular among counterfeiters as well. The thing to look for first is to be sure that a Case stag has a 5 as the first pattern number digit. If it is a 5, then look for signs of etching and buffing. The 5 denotes genuine stag handles, and was discontinued in 1970, but some bone handled knives, with a 6 as the first pattern number digit, are counterfeited by buffing off the 6 and engraving the 5 with a jeweler's engraver. Look to see if the number 5 is stamped the same size and spaced the same as the other numbers. The dots on knives made in 1970 should be evenly spaced and have 10 of them. (Some knives were made by Case in collector's sets in 1973 and some of these had 8 and 9 dots under the logo. The collector should be familiar with which ones were so stamped. The information is in most Case collector's guides.)

Some counterfeits glue the shield on the stag. The genuine article has two rivets attaching the shield and are visible inside the knife where they attach to the liner.

On any knife, look for sign of work, be suspicious of one almost new blade or handle and the rest of the knife well-worn. Look for hammer marks on the inside of the knife. Few battered knives leave the factory in a hammered up condition.

Check the thickness of the tang as compared with the backspring to see if the old logo has been buffed off completely and be careful of light stamped knives. Compare the stamping of a known good knife.

Use a match or toothpick and try to scratch the black from around the logo. If the black comes out easily and it is shiny underneath, beware, because blades are stamped before they are heat treated and the black is hard to come off on a good knife.

On a Case knife the main backspring rivets are spun. A Case knife without spin rivets was probably tampered with.

Brass rivets are usually used with brass liners, as are nickel silver rivets used with nickel silver liners.

One time rusty blades that have been buffed will be dull and have a slick edge, while a good genuine knife will be sharp.

A major thing is to *TAKE YOUR TIME* and look over the knife carefully, later will usually be too late.

Beware of bargains. Quality knives demand quality prices, and most counterfeiters don't want to keep bad knives around.

The most important thing is to deal with a reputable dealer you can trust and who will refund your money if a counterfeit knife slips by him. Members of the National Knife Collectors Association have sworn to do this, and are subject to expulsion if they don't.

Know your dealer, know your prices, and know your knife. Read every knife book you can get your hands on, and eventually the counterfeiter may be forced to go out of business, when everyone knows what to look for.

I realize that it is frustrating for some people to keep hearing *"COUNTER-FEIT"*, but it frustrates me when I see a new collector that has been hung with a counterfeit piece. As long as there are things of value, there will be unscrupulous people who will try to imitate the valued thing, pass their imitation to the unwary, and make the quick buck. We have counterfeit coins, stamps, guns, antiques of all descriptions and knives. Permit me to delve into the subject of counterfeit pocketknives. Maybe I can save you some embarrassment and some hard earned money.

Mr. Webster defines counterfeit as an imitation made of the genuine with intent to defraud. I define counterfeiting a pocketknife as taking a knife that is a particular cheap John Doe knife and converting it to appear to be a different more expensive John Doe knife in order or with intent to defraud.

Counterfeiting a knife can be accomplished in a variety of ways. The most common means are as follows: *1.* Grinding original name off and restamping with another name. *2.* Removing original handles and replacing them with different handles. *3.* Removing current master blade from knife and replacing with older period of time blade marked differently. *4.* Taking old knife that has blades worn out but still retains sharp stamping and handles and welding new blades onto the old worn out blades. *6.* Taking old knife parts (usually of second quality) and making into complete knife. *7.* Re-etching blades after cleaning or refinishing of blades. *8.* Adding older shield to handle. *9.* Aging a knife to make it appear older than it is. *10.* Taking old knives or new knives that got out of factory unstamped and stamping them with rare or old marking.

There are two classes of counterfeit knives. Number one is the low quality or inferior workmanship quality of counterfeit. In this group are the knives that have the tang or one side of the tang ground down to where it does not fill out the space between the liners, knives that have handles that do not fit up even with the bolsters or level with the bolsters and knives that have off color rivets. These types are relatively easy to spot just by comparing and being observant.

Number two I will call the professional counterfeit knife. These are the ones that are made by the fellows who have factory quality equipment to work with, old handle materials, old parts and blades, etc. Some of these are really hard or next to impossible to spot. Here we have to get into comparing beveling of blades, handle jigging, location of thumb pull on blade, etc.

You are probably thinking by now, how do I recognize a counterfeit knife and keep from getting burned? Follow a few simple rules. Carry a magnifying glass to examine stampings. An engraved stamp or cold-stamped stamp stands out like a sore thumb from a factory stamp when put under a ten power glass. Study the old handles on knives. Ninety-nine percent of the time Remington, Winchester, Case and most other popular brands have their own distinct jigging pattern on the bone or bone stag handles. Compare the liners on old knives against liners on new ones. You will notice that many of the old knives had iron liners and bolsters; whereas, many later production knives have brass liners and nickel silver bolsters. This does not always hold true but is so in many cases. Don't be gullible. There are still some good buys to be found but when a knife dealer offers a $100 item for $30 or $40, watch out. Get a bill of sale or guarantee on the knife. Any reputable dealer will stand behind what he sells. Deal with the man that you know will back up what he sells.

Last, but not least important, if you get stuck with a counterfeit knife and can't find the seller, be man enough to take your loss and don't try to pass it off on someone else. Of course, if you buy a counterfeit and the seller won't take it back and if you have proof that he sold it to you, you can initiate legal action.

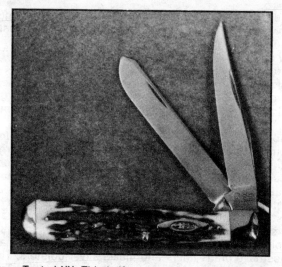

Engraved Case Tested XX. This knife appears to have been a Kabar frame and handles to which a Case shield has been added. The shield is not correct for a Circle C Shield, as the C on the Circle C Shield is more of a square block type where the C is round like on the later shields. The tang on this knife has been cut down before the Case Tested XX was applied.

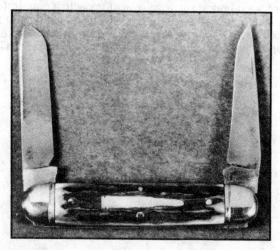

This is a Cattaraugas knife. Someone has added the bullet shield. Cattaraugas never made a bullet knife.

This was a Kent knife. Someone has engraved Napanoch Knife Company, Napanoch, New York on it. These original Kents are very hard to find now, as so many of them were ground down at the tang to make up other knives. They ground this tang a little too deep and the tang doesn't come all the way up to the side of the blade.

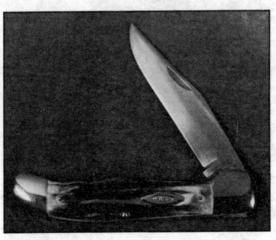

This knife has had Case Tested XX stamped on the blade. This was probably a blade that left the factory unmarked and someone got hold of it and stamped it. The blades in this knife should be flat ground with the bevel on the top. Note that they are all hollow ground.

PROTOTYPE KNIVES

Many of the cutlery companies have made huge knives either for exhibition purposes or as prototypes. The Case ones having black or blue composition handles are about 12 inches long and run about $700 with "W. R. Case & Sons, Bradford, PA" stampings. I have seen one four blade Boker about 2½ feet long owned by Frank Buster, and Dr. Frank Forsyth of Winston-Salem owns several by various companies. The knives are extremely rare and command a premium price.

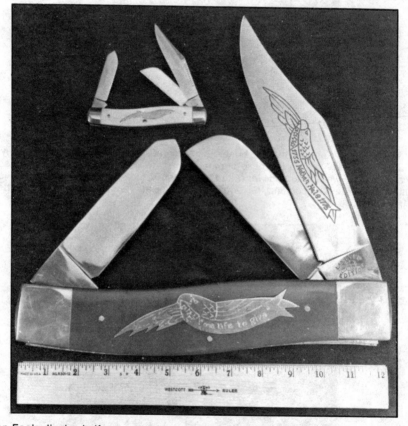

An Eagle display knife compared to a standard 4" Eagle knife. There were 25 Eagle display knives made and sold in sets of five for $2,500 per set.

NOTES ON TRADEMARKS

We recently came across a number of trademark registrations and wanted to list these separately from our knives around the world. We are presently researching more about some of these companies, but at present all we have is these dates, which tells the time they had used the trademark and the time of the registration.

Note: *Many of these trademarks were blade etchings only.*

TRADEMARK REGISTRATION	DATES
Valley Forge, N. J.	4-24-16
J. Dunlap & Co.	1866 (Owned by Schrantenberg Bros.)
St. Lawrence Cutlery Co.	5-18-16
Flex O	8-19-15 (Owned by Cattaraugas)
John Chatillion & Sons "American Maid"	1-9-14
Clean Cut	1884 (Owned by Dunham, Carrigan & Hayden Co.) San Francisco Hardware Firm
Pocketeze	12-1-14 (Owned by Robeson)
Hike	5-1-23
Gilt Edge	1-1-1886 (Owned by Flagg Cutlery Co.)
Canton Cutlery Co.	1-1-1889
Eagle	1883 (Owned by Eagle Pencil Co.)
Tip Top	1904 (A. Kaston & Bros. [later Camillus])
Keen Kutter	1868 (Owned by Simmons Hardware Co.)
Challenge	1867 (Owned by Challenge Cutlery, Bridgeport, CT)
Marble's	4-1-11
UTK Supreme	5-1-24 (Owned by Utica Cutlery Co.)
Topsy	1937 (Owned by Imperial)
Tom Thumb	1933 (Owned by Imperial)
Tiny Champ	1939 (Owned by Colonial Knife Co., Providence, RI)
Cub Hunter	1939 (Owned by Colonial)
Flip Knife	1946 (Owned by Lectrolite Corp., NY)
Ruf 'n Tuf	1924 (Owned by Union Cutlery Co.)
Camillus	1902 (Still in use in 1949)
Shorty	1948 Imperial
Sport Topper	1939 Colonial (Still in use as of 1950)
Junior Topper	1940 Colonial (Still in use as of 1950)
ToppeR	1938 Colonial (Still in use as of 1950)
I. O. A.	1907 Brown Camp Hardware, Des Moines, IA (Still in use in 1938)
Trail Blazer	1936 George Worthington Co., Cleveland, (Still in use in 1949)
Koinife	1937 Hickhock Mfg., Rochester, NY (Still in use in 1949)
Featherweight	1933 Utica
Kamp King	1935 Imperial

Paremaster	1937 Imperial
Sportsmaster	1937 Imperial
Harlen	1942 Geneder Sales, Chicago
America Veterans	1945 National Allied Co., NY
Gits	1941 Gits Molding Co., Chicago (Still used 1950)
Blitzknife	1946 Wilbur Harwell, Charlotte, NC
Academy Award	1946 Academy Award Products, NY
Poppo	1945 Oscar Galter, Chicago
Manna	1946
G. F.	1921 Giesen & Forsthoff, Solingen
Alco	1926 Alexander Coppel, Solingen
Jack-O-Matic	1943 Imperial
Ben Hur	1943 Hugo Herkenrath, Merscheid, Germany 1927
Tiffany & Co.	1900
Pocket Pard	1929 Utica
Esemco	1921 Shiman Mfg. Co., N. Y. (Still used 1949)
Unitas	1906 Pape-Thiebes Cutlery Co., St. Louis (Still used 1954)
Dollar Knife Corp., **Titusville, PA.**	1926 (C. B. Morgan of Schratt & Morgan was Vice President)
Edward Fiddler	1878 Landars Frary & Clark
Crown	1878 Frary Cutlery Co., James D. Frary, President
Union Cutlery, Chicago, Ill.	1887
Hammer Brand	1882 (Filed by Thomas W. Bradley, President) New York Knife Co.
(Design of Arm and Hammer by itself)	1878 New York Knife Co.
Adolph Kastor (4 leaf clover)	1893 (Still in use)
Aim Well (Drawing of arrow in target)	1899
Diamond Edge	1870 R. J. Roberts
B4 ANY	1867 Frederick Ward & Co., Sheffield
CAR-VAN	6-9-11 Canton Cutlery Co.
R with an arrow through it	1879 Russell Cutlery Co.
W. G. Clark & Co.	1914
Charles C. Stieff, Baltimore	10-1-10
Remington	6-30-20
Remington UMC	6-30-20

AERIAL MANUFACTURING COMPANY
MARINETTE, WISCONSIN

The Aerial Cutlery Company began in Duluth, Minnesota in 1909, and was one of the early pioneers of the picture handles. The company was started by Thomas Madden and Chris, Richard and Fred Jaeger, who took the company's name for the bridge over St. Louis Bay, linking Park Point and Duluth. The bridge was the first suspension bridge of its kind and quality, and they hoped that this would be associated with their cutlery.

Between 1909 and 1912 the company had 186 full-time employees and 220 part-time employees and salesmen.

In 1912 the company moved to Marinette, Wisconsin. Soon after World War I the company began distributing barber supplies, and was gradually increasing this distribution by 1925. In 1932 the company added a line of beauty supplies and from that time eventually phased out their knives completely, becoming a distributor that still serves over 5,000 barber and beauty shops.

In 1973, 2300 of the old Aerials were discovered and dumped on the market. The prices on the fine old knives dropped for a while, but now are in line with similar knives produced in that time.

The most popular Aerials are the picture handled knives, which they made in a large variety of sizes, from a lockback folding hunter down. Their knives will also be found with various composition handles.

ALLEN CUTLERY COMPANY
NEWBURGH, NEW YORK

Allen Cutlery Company was founded by Benjamin Allen in 1917 to manufacture knives like those illustrated. The company went out of business in 1925. Knives with this same construction and the Jan. 23-17 patent date will be found with "Ulery" and "Shapleigh Hdw." stampings.

☐**01**—BOYS PATTERN (3⅛") Allen patent handle, Spear **15.00**

☐**02**—BOYS PATTERN (3⅛") Allen patent handle, Clip **15.00**
☐**03**—BOYS PATTERN (3⅛") Allen patent handle, Sheep **15.00**
☐**04**—BOYS PATTERN (3⅛") Allen patent handle, Spay **15.00**
☐**01**—Spear and 02 clip pattern made with chain and shackle.
☐**10**—BARLOW (3½") Allen patent handle, one blade, Spear **15.00**

☐**11**—BARLOW (3½") Allen patent handle, one blade, Clip **15.00**
☐**12**—BARLOW (3½") Allen patent handle, one blade, Sheep **15.00**
☐**14**—BARLOW (3½") Allen patent handle, one blade, Spey **15.00**

☐**20**—NIGGER CHASER (4¾") Allen patent handle **20.00**

☐40—JACK KNIFE PATTERN (3½″) oxidized
black rustless handle, two blades spring backs
.................................18.00
☐41—JACK KNIFE PATTERN (3½″) oxidized
black rustless handle, 2 blades spring backs
.................................18.00

☐30—PRUNER PATTERN (4″) Allen patent
handle 15.00

AMES MANUFACTURING COMPANY
CHICOPEE FALLS, MASSACHUSETTS

Nathan and James Ames were the sons of a blacksmith in Chelmsford, Massachusetts, where they learned how to work metals. It is said that Edmund Dwight, one of a group of Boston textile promoters, met Nathan on a stagecoach journey and was so impressed by the bright young man that he offered him the use of some old repair shops in Chicopee Falls. There the brothers began to make items for the textile industry and made axes, hammers, farm implements and knives. By 1832 the output of the brothers' company was 56,000 knives. In 1833 the English reportedly shipped into the U. S. a cheap counterfeit of the Ames sword. (Evidently counterfeiting is not a new problem in the cutlery business.) In 1834 the company was incorporated as the Ames Manufacturtng Company.

BATTLE AX KNIVES
SOLINGEN, GERMANY

Battle Ax knives revitalized a long discontinued trademark placing it on well made line of German made sets. Started by Tommy Shouse of Winston-Salem, North Carolina and George T. Smith of Kenova, West Virginia, most of the sets are limited editions of 300-600 knives, usually handled in natural handle materials such as genuine bone, genuine pearl, genuine stag.

BAYONNE KNIFE COMPANY BAYONNE
BAYONNE, NEW JERSEY

Importers and jobbers of a general line of cutlery. C. B. Morgan who later started Schatt & Morgan worked for them from 1890-95.

BENNETT CUTLERY WORKS
CANTON, NEW YORK

Bennett had worked for various cutlery companies for 15 years prior to his opening his own company in Canton, New York in 1922.

BELKNAP HARDWARE COMPANY, INC.
LOUISVILLE, KENTUCKY

Belknap Hardware Company was founded in 1840 by W. B. Belknap, dealing in carriage supplies, horseshoes, and blacksmith supplies. The company sold Russell, I*XL, and LF&C in addition to its own brands. Some of Belknap's own brands were:

PINE KNOT—Probably made by Robeson, the Pine Knot was stamped "Pine Knot" and "Pine Knot, J. W. Price," and handled in bone, redwood, and celluloid. Produced only for 15 to 20 years, the knife was discontinued in the 1930's.

BLUEGRASS—One of the oldest trademarks in American cutlery, the Bluegrass is still made, but only in the Barlow pattern. Any pattern other than this or a bone handled Bluegrass Barlow is collectible. The line (except the Barlow) was discontinued in the 1950's.

JOHN PRIMBLE—Although the John Primble is still made, some of the older stampings are collectible. At one time the knife was made using a British steel exported from India. These knives are stamped "John Primble, India Steel Works." A second older pattern is one stamped "John Primble, Germany," made in Solingen. Camillus or Boker USA probably made the Primble with a star stamped under the logo, and Schrade-Walden makes the current John Primble. The knife will also be found stamped, "Primble" and "J. Primble."

Today Belknap is one of the largest hardware companies in the world, occupying over 36 acres of floor space.

☐**4904S**—(3¾") Stag handle; with chain; brass lining; steel bolster; half polished; chain 21 inches long **80.00**

☐**4812S**—3⅞") Stag handle; steel lining and bolster; nickel silver shield; half polished **50.00**

☐**5008S**—(3⁷⁄₁₆") Stag handle; steel lining; nickel silver bolster; half polished **130.00**

☐**5010S**—(3⁷⁄₁₆") Stag handle; steel lining; nickel silver bolster; half polished **130.00**

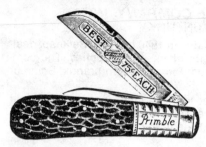

☐**5012S**—(3⁷⁄₁₆″) Stag handle; steel lining; nickel silver bolster; half polished **130.00**

☐**5014S**—(3⁷⁄₁₆″) Stag handle; steel lining; nickel silver bolster; half polished **150.00**

☐**5018S**—(3⁹⁄₁₆″) Stag handle; steel lining; nickel silver bolster; half polished **150.00**

☐**5322S**—(3″) Stag handle; congress; brass lining; nickel silver bolster; half polished .....
...........................**125.00**

☐**5324GS**—(3¼″) Genuine stag handle; congress; brass handle; nickel silver bolsters and shield; half polished **175.00**

☐**5325GS**—(3¾″) Genuine stag handle; congress; nickel silver lined; flat nickel silver bolsters and shield; half polished; half sunk joing...........................**175.00**

☐**5331GS**—(3¼″) Genuine stag handle; congress; nickel silver lined; flat nickel silver bolsters and shield; half polished; half sunk joing...........................**175.00**

☐**5369GS**—(3⅛″) Genuine stag handle; congress; pen blade instead of tobacco blade; brass lining; hollow steel bolsters; nickel silver shield; half polished **175.00**

☐**5009S**—(3¼″) Stag handle; congress; with tobacco blade, as illustrated; half polished; brass lining; steel bolsters; nickel silver shield; highly glazed **175.00**

☐**5516S**—(4¼″) Stag handle; congress; brass lining; steel bolsters; nickel silver shield; half polished **300.00**

☐**5512S**—(3⅞″) Stag handle; congress; with tobacco blade, as illustrated; brass lining; steel bolsters; nickel silver shield; half polished **$200.00**

BINGHAM, W. W. AND COMPANY
CLEVELAND, OHIO

This company was a hardware firm that was in business from 1841 to the late 1940's. Some of their stampings were, "W. Bingham and Co.," "B.B.B." (Bingham's best brand), "Excelsior", and "EXCR". The Excelsior and EXCR logos have an arrow through the stamping. The company also carried Winchester and other popular brands of cutlery.

BOKER, HEINR & COMPANY
SOLINGEN, GERMANY

Founded in Remscheid, Germany by Heinrich Boker and Herman Heauser in 1869, Heinr Boker & Company grew out of the Boker family's need for a reliable cutlery manufacturer for their export business.

Using Solingen steel, the company has stamped its knives "H. Boker & Co.'s Cutlery," "H. Boker, Improved Cutlery, H. Boker & Co.", "Heinr Boker & Co.", and currently, "Boker Solingen, Germany". Some of the older patterns will have Alemania stamped on them. This is due to the large export business to Spain (The Spanish name for Germany is Alemania), but recent imports to the United States do not have this stamping.

The company has never made contract knives, but has handled its knives with bone, stag, hard rubber and mother of pearl. They currently handle their knives in wood.

BOKER MANUFACTURING COMPANY
MAPLEWOOD, NEW JERSEY

Boker started at the export of Heinrich Boker in Remscheid, Germany. He had bought and sold cutlery in Solingen since 1812. In 1869, H. Boker and Herman Heuser founded Heinrich Boker & Company in Solingen. It is reported that Boker was the first company to use the steam hammer in stamping out blades. In the 1880's the company's main interest was razors, making the Red Injun, King Kutter, Rastus, Imperial, Radium and others.

Until 1921 the company had operated three different manufacturing plants in the U. S.: two produced H. Boker U.S.A. knives and the third made Valley Forge knives. In 1921 all the factories were combined under one roof in Maplewood, New Jersey. In 1930 the company added 35,000 square feet to their building, giving it a total of 150,000 square feet.

Boker was also the exclusive importing agent for John Wilson Sheffield knives.

Boker U. S. A. was bought by J. Wiss and Sons in 1969, a shear manufacturer since 1847. Boker originally used the usual handle materials (bone, celluloid, etc.) but today uses plastic. The only stamping Boker has ever used as far as known, is "Boker, U. S. A."

BROWNING
GUNNISON, UTAH

Browning knives, a part of the Browning line of guns and other sportsman goods, introduced their knives in 1968 with four patterns. These four patterns were and still are made in Gunnison, Utah. In 1970, two pocketknives were added, and made in the U. S. for one year, then switched to a German factory in 1971. (The original four were still being made in Utah, only the two patterns introduced in 1970 were changed to Germany.) New "Made in U. S." patterns were added, and in 1975 three patterns made in Japan were introduced. In all today, there are four factories producing Browning knives in three different countries.

The number of patterns were increased as follows:

1968-70 4 patterns   1970-71 6 patterns
1971-73 8 patterns   1973-75 15 patterns
1975-76 20 patterns

The following patterns are made in the respective countries:

Japan	Germany	United States	
3018F2	3218F	5518	6018
3018F1	2718FO	4518	4018F
2718F2	2518*	35181	2018F2
3718	3018*	40181	2018F3
		37181	2518F2

*These knives were only made for one year with a U.S.A. stamping, and are the most collectible Browning knives at present.

The number 2518 is currently selling for $30 and the 3018 sells for $35.

BUCK KNIVES, INC.
EL CAJON, CALIFORNIA

Buck, originated by H. H. Buck, the son of a blacksmith, built a good reputation on sheath knives, selling them through outdoor magazines. His son, Alfred, carried on the business with his two sons after H. H. Buck's death in 1949. Buck incorporated in 1961 and produced its first folding knife in 1965, their Folding Hunter model. In 1968 Buck added a three-blade stockman and today have a full line of pocket cutlery. It is possible that H. H. Buck himself made pocketknives, but probably only as an experiment. The current trademark is "Buck, Made in U. S. A.

☐**102**—WOODSMAN (4") **24.00**

☐**103**—SKINNER (4") **29.00**

☐**104**—TWIN SET, WOODSMAN AND SKINNER
in double sheath **50.00**

☐**105**—PATHFINDER (5″) **27.00**

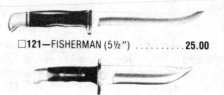

☐**121**—FISHERMAN (5½″) **25.00**

☐**124**—FRONTIERSMAN (7″) **58.00**
☐**301**—STOCKMAN (3⅞″) Black delrin handles **22.00**
☐**303**—CADET (3¼″) Black delrin handles . . .
. . . .**20.00**
☐**305**—LANCER (2⅝″) Black delrin handles, two blades **13.00**
☐**307**—WRANGLER (4¼″) Black delrin handles, three blades **25.00**

☐**106**—HUNTERS AX (2½″) Head ax . . .**50.00**
☐**107**—SCOUT (4″) **27.00**

☐**309**—COMPANION (3″) Black delrin handles, two blades **15.00**

☐**110**—FOLDING HUNTER (4⅞″) Ebony wood handle **35.00**
☐**111**—CLASSIC (4⅞″) Aluminum handles . . .
. . . .**47.00**

☐**112**—RANGER (4¼″) Ebonywood handles . .
. . . .**33.00**
☐**115**—SPORTSMAN SET, BUCK PERSONAL AND SKINNER in double sheath **51.00**

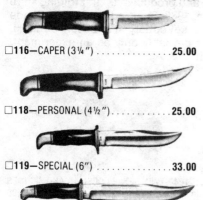

☐**116**—CAPER (3¼″) **25.00**

☐**311**—TRAPPER (4″) Black delrin handles, two blades **18.00**
☐**313**—MUSKRAT (3⅞″) Black delrin handles, two blades **18.00**
☐**315**—YACHTSMAN (4⅜″) Black delrin handles, marlin spike **25.00**
☐**317**—TRAILBLAZER (5¼″) Black delrin handles, folding hunter **34.00**
☐**319**—RANCHER (3⅞″) Black delrin handles, same as 301 but with punch blade **22.00**
☐**321**—BIRD KNIFE—(3⅞″) Black delrin handles, with gutting hook for feathered game**20.00**
☐**401**—KALINGA (5″) **70.00**
☐**402**—AKONUA (5″) **65.00**
☐**500**—DUKE (4¼″) Buckarta handles . .**35.00**

☐**118**—PERSONAL (4½″) **25.00**

☐**119**—SPECIAL (6″) **33.00**

☐**120**—GENERAL (7½″) **35.00**

☐**501**—ESQUIRE (3¾″) Buckarta handles . . . .
. . . .**29.00**
☐**503**—PRINCE (3⅜″) Buckarta handle . .**26.00**
☐**505**—KNIGHT (2¾″) Buckarta handle .**25.00**
☐**506**—WHITE KNIGHT. Same as 505 Knight
but with white micarta handles **26.00**

☐**701**—MUSTANG (3⅞″) Laminated wood
handles **28.00**
☐**703**—COLT (3¼″) Laminated wood handles .
. . . .**26.00**

BUCKCREEK
LONDON, KENTUCKY

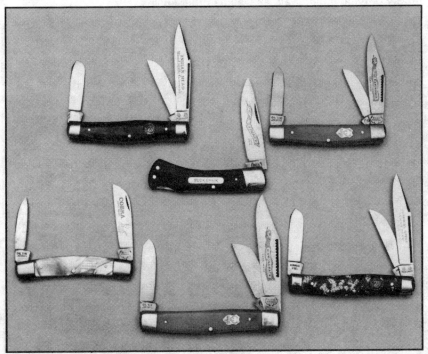

☐COBRA (3½″) Cracked Ice handle **10.00**
☐DIAMONDBACK (4¼″) Various celluloid handles available **15.00**
☐INDIANHEAD (4″) Various handles available, including bone and stag as well as various celluloid
handles **12.00-18.00**
☐INDIANHEAD SURGICAL STEEL (4″) Various handles **15.00-20.00**
☐LITTLE DIAMONDBACK (3⅜″) Various handles available **12.00**
☐SKINNER (4″) Various handles available. **16.00**

BULLDOG BRAND
SOLINGEN, GERMANY

A Pit Bulldog fighting another Pit Bulldog is the trademark for one of the newest line of consumer German-made knives.

Started by Charles Dorton of Kingsport, Tennessee in 1980, the knives immediately met acceptance by the critical knife buyers on the NKCA show circuit. While several commemoratives have been manufacturer, he specialized in a high quality knife for use, offering a 4″ stock knife in a variety of handle materials as well as other knives.

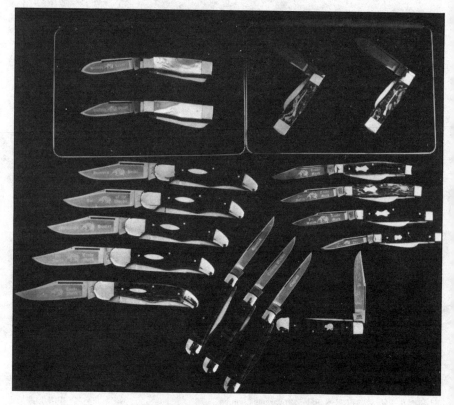

BURKINSHAW CUTLERY
PEPPERELL, MASSACHUSETTS

Arron Burkinshaw established the company in 1853 after coming to the United States from Sheffield, England. His sons followed in the business, but the company ceased operation in the early 1920's.

CAMILLUS CUTLERY COMPANY
CAMILLUS, NEW YORK

The Camillus Cutlery Company is named for Camillus, New York, the home of the first factory. Started by Charles Sherwood in 1894, the company was small scale, facing strong competition from Solingen and Sheffield cutlery. With the Dingly Tariff of 1897 raising the tariff on imported cutlery 98%, many importers had to turn to U. S. manufacturers for goods. One of these importers was Adolf Kastor, who had been importing cutlery since 1876 and in 1902, he bought the Camillus Cutlery Company. By 1912 the company was producing 75,248 dozen knives per year.

Camillus has done contract work for almost every contracting company. The company has made such knives as "Henry Sears, 1865," " OVB", "Hibbard, Spencer and Bartlett," "Keen Kutter," "Diamond Edge," "Circle Van Camp," "America's Best," and "Case".

Some of the stampings that Camillus used in the past were "Camillus Cutlery Company, Camillus New York, U. S. A." (this logo used four lines for the above information and is called a "four-line"); "TIP TOP Mumbly Peg" (this knife came with instructions on how to play the game); "Sword Brand" (introduced in 1908, it had "streamline" stamped vertically on the master blade and the four-line logo on the other side of the tang.)

The current Camillus stampings are "Camillus, New York, U. S. A.", "Camco", and "Sword Brand" (two swords etched on the master blade and the current stamping on the tang).

During World War II Camillus made over 15 million knives for the Armed Forces.

After the death of Kastor, leadership of Camillus fell to John and Bess Kaufman, Dr. Miles and Margey Schwartz. Nilo Miori became president.

□**1**—(4") Rosewood handle, with hole for cord, one blade, standard pruner; steel lining, with lock to keep blade from closing while in use; steel bolster **10.00**

□**5**—(5") Maize pyroxylin handle, one blade; chrome plated sabre clip with scaler and caplifter; brass linings with lock to keep blade open when in use; nickel silver bolsters with disgorger **12.00**

□**14**—(3⅜") Stagged handle, two blades, 1 clip, 1 pen; brass linings, nickel silver trim **20.00**

☐**15**—(3⅝″) Red horn pyroxylin handle, two blades, 1 clip, 1 pen; brass llinings; nickel silver trim........................**15.00**

☐**23**—(3″) Nu-pearl handle, two blades; 1 clip and 1 pen; brass linings; nickel silver bolsters **12.00**

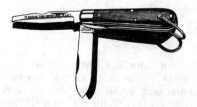

☐**16**—(3⅝″) Stagged handle, two blades, 1 clip, 1 pen; brass llinings; nickel silver trim **30.00**

☐**27**—(3¾″) Rosewood handle, two blades, 1 spear, 1 screw driver, with sharp edge for scraping insulation; brass linings with lock to keep screw driver from closing; nickel silver bolster and shackle, for electricians.....**15.00**

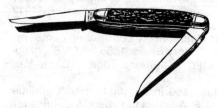

☐**20**—(3⅞″) Stagged handle, two skinning clip blades; brass linings, nickel silver trim, for muskrat skinning...................**50.00**

☐**33**—(3⅜″) Stagged handle, two blades, 1 spear, 1 pen; brass linings; nickel silver trim **38.00**

☐**21**—(2¹³⁄₁₆″) Stagged handle, two blades, 1 sabre clip, 1 pen; brass linings, nickel silver trim **20.00**

☐**40**—(3⁷⁄₁₆″) Stagged handle, two blades, 1 pen; 1 sheepfoot, brass linings; nickel silver trim **15.00**

☐**41**—(3⅛″) Stagged handle, two blades, 1 spear, 1 pen; brass linings; nickel silver trim **15.00**

☐**22**—(2³⁄₁₆″) Maize pryoxylin handle, two blades, 1 sabre clip, 1 pen; brass linings; nickel silver trim **12.00**

☐**42**—(3⅛″)Nu-Pearl handle, two blades, 1 spear, 1 pen; brass linings; nickel silver trim **12.00**

□**43**—(2¹³⁄₁₆″) Nu-Pearl handle, two blades, 1 spear, 1 file; brass linings, nickel silver tips and shackle **12.00**

□**45**—(2¹³⁄₁₆″) Plastag handle, two blades; 1 spear and 1 pen; brass linings; nickel silver bolsters **15.00**

□**51**—(3⅜″) Brown bone handle, two blades; 1 clip and 1 pen; brass linings; nickel silver bolsters **39.00**
□**52**—(3⁵⁄₁₆″) Plastag handle, two blades, 1 clip and 1 pen; brass linings; nickelsilver bolsters **35.00**
□**53**—(2⁵⁄₁₆″) Plastag handle, two blades, 1 spear and 1 pen; brass linings; nickel silver bolsters **40.00**
□**54**—(2¹³⁄₁₆″) Brown agate pyroxylin handle, two blades, 1 sabre clip and 1 pen; brass linings, nickel silver bolsters **28.00**

□**60**—(3⅛″) Bone stag handle, three blades; 1 pen, 1 spear and 1 file; nickel silver milled linings; nickel silver tips **65.00**

□**62**—(2¾″) Genuine pearl handle, three blades; 1 pen, 1 spear and 1 long file; nickel silver milled linings **45.00**

□**64**—(3⅜″) Stagged handle, three blades, 1 clip, 1 spey, 1 spiral punch; brass linings; nickel silver trim **50.00**

□**65**—(3⅜″) Brown horn pyroxylin handle, three blades; 1 clip, 1 sheepfoot, 1 spey; brass linings; nickel silver bolsters **65.00**

□**66**—(3⅞″) Grain white pyroxylin handle, three blades; 1 clip, 1 sheepfoot, 1 spey; brass linings; nickel silver trim **38.00**

□**67**—(3⅞″) Stagged handle, three blades; 1 clip, 1 sheepfoot, 1 spey; brass linings; nickel silver trim **65.00**

□**68**—(3⅞″) Stagged handle, three blades, 1 clip, 1 spey, 1 spiral punch; brass linings; nickel silver trim **55.00**

□**69**—(4″) Bone stag handle, three blades, 1 Turkish clip, 1 sheepfoot, 1 spey; milled nickel silver linings; nickel silver trim **90.00**

□**70**—(3⅝″) Stagged handle, three blades, 1 clip, 1 sheepfoot, 1 spey; brass linings, nickel silver trim **90.00**

□**72**—(3⅝″) Stagged handle, three blades; 1 sabre clip, 2 pen clip, 1 coping; brass linings, nickel silver trim **35.00**

□**74**—(3⅝″) Maize pyroxylin handle, three blades, 1 clip, 1 spey and 1 spiral punch; brass linings; nickel silver bolsters **25.00**

□**75**—(¾″) Plastag handle, three blades; 1 pen, 1 sheepfoot and 1 clip; brass linings; nickel silver bolsters **45.00**

□**76**—(3″) Plastag handle, three blades; 1 clip, 1 spey and 1 pen; brass linings; nickel silver bolsters **40.00**

□**99**—(3⅝″) Stagged handle, four blades; 1 spear, 1 can opener, 1 punch and 1 screwdriver - caplifter; brass linings; nickel silver trim and shackle **3.00**
□**295**—(3⁵⁄₁₆″) Grain white proxylin handle, two blades; 1 spear and 1 spey; brass linings **35.00**

CANTON CUTLERY COMPANY
CANTON, OHIO

Canton Cutlery Company was the originator of the transparent cutlery handle. Started around 1879, W. Stuart Carnes became president in 1910 (he had previously sold surgical and dental equipment for the Harvard Company of Canton, Ohio). At first he bought an interest in the company, but by 1925 was the sole owner.

The company ceased making pocketknives in the 1930's, but continued making other products until the 1940's. Among the stampings used were CCC, Canton Cutlery Co. and Car-Van.

☐ **41**—BUTTERCUP, Two blades **60.00**
☐ **43**—(One blade and glove hook) **60.00**
☐ **35**—(Three blades) **85.00**
☐ **33**—(Four blades) **110.00**
☐ **31**—(Three blades and file) **100.00**

☐ **172**—BABY NOVELTY, Two Blades . . **50.00**
☐ **173**—(Three blades) **80.00**
☐ **174**—(Four blades) **100.00**

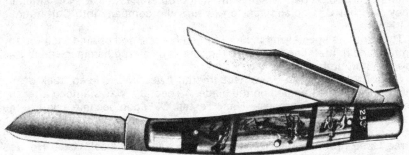

☐ **233**—STOCKMAN, Three blades as shown **125.00**

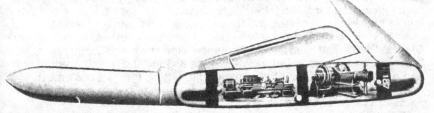

☐ **186**—CARPENTER, Two large and a small spear blade **175.00**
☐ **187**—Two large and a coping blade **150.00**

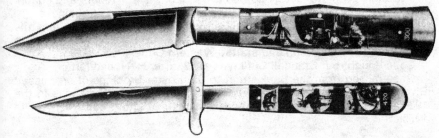

☐ **300**—HUNTER, Large clip or spear blade **200.00**
☐ **470**—LOCK KNIFE, Clip or spear point **175.00**

W. R. CASE & SONS
BRADFORD, PENNSYLVANIA

Any history of W. R. Case & Sons starts with Job Russell Case. While many people quickly associate Job Russell Case with the origins of the American knife industry, the truth is that old man Job never made a knife! However, as far as the cutlery historian, is concerned, the interesting aspect is the unique ability of Job's descendants to get involved in the cutlery business, sometimes by no more than marrying a cutler, but that was being involved just the same.

Job's sons, Andrew, John, and Jean became interested in cutlery and entered into a brief partnership with their brother-in-law, J. B. F. Champlain. They left, but Champlain went on to turn the company into Cattaraugus Cutlery.

The brothers specialized in hand forged blades, and offered $100 for any knife found in their line that had been forged by a drop hammer, which was the popular method of the day.

Case Brothers knives were heat treated twice and to keep track of the blades, an X was stamped on the blade. A second X was stamped after the second heat treating process. This "Tested XX" soon became a part of the trademark.

Among the salesmen employed by Case Brothers was the nephew of the three Case brothers that owned the company, J. Russell Case. He was working on commission of sales, and was burning the woods up in sales. His uncles wanted him to switch to salary instead, so he quit and he began jobbing his line of knives made by another factory from space over Sweetland's Grocery store in Bradford, Pennsylvania. By 1905 he graduated to his own factory on Bank Street in Bradford, making knives for use in the oil boom at Bradford. His father W. R. Case and brother-in-law, H. N. Platts joined him in the business. W. R. was not a cutler but an investor in the business. H. N. came from a long line of Sheffield cutlers. N. N.'s father, Charles Platts, had been superintendent of Northfield and Cattaraugus. The business was incorporated as W. R. Case & Sons. J. Russell was the only son of W. R. so they bent the rules a little, letting the "& Sons" mean son and son-in-law. (For a brief time the company was in business under the name of W. R. Case & Son).

H. N. bought out his brother's factory "C. Platts & Sons"and merged the plant operations with Case.

The Case brothers factory burned in 1905, but it was rebuilt and continued manufacturing knives until 1912, when they went out of business.

In 1911, H. N., who was suffering grinder's consumption from his knifemaking, was forced to go west for his health. He sold his interest in Case, moved to Colorado and started Western Cutlery Co.

Case bought out Crandall Cutlery in 1912, after H. N. had left.

Case moved from the Bank street to the Foster Brook plant on Russell Blvd. in 1929. A shear factory was started in Nashville, Arkansas in the 1930's, and new factories were added in both Bradford and Nashville in 1975.

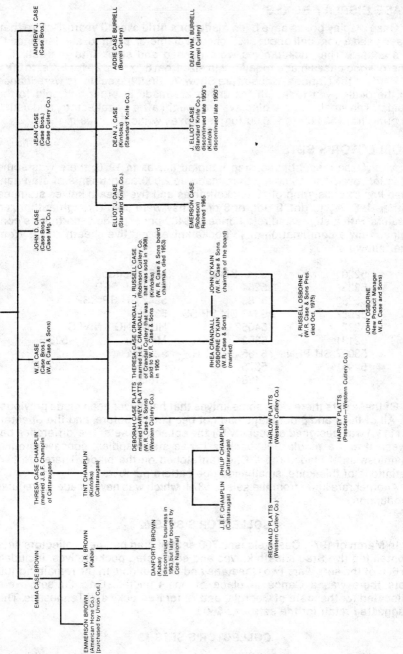

JOB RUSSELL CASE

ANDREW J. CASE
(Case Bros.)

JEAN CASE
(Case Bros.)
(Case Cutlery Co.)

JOHN D. CASE
(Case Bros.)
(Case Mfg. Co.)

W.R. CASE
(Case Bros.)
(W.R. Case & Sons)

THRESA CASE CHAMPLIN
(married J.B.F. Champlin
of Cattaraugas)

EMMA CASE BROWN

ADDIE CASE BURRELL
(Burrell Cutlery)

DEAN WM. BURRELL
(Burrell Cutlery)

DEAN J. CASE
(Kinfolks) (Standard Knife Co.)

J. ELLIOT CASE
(Standard Knife Co.)
discontinued late 1950's
(Kinfolk)
discontinued late 1950's

ELLIOT J. CASE
(Standard Knife Co.)

EMERSON CASE
(Robeson)
Retired 1965

DEBORAH CASE PLATTS
married HARVY PLATTS
(W.R. Case & Sons)
(Western Cutlery Co.)

THERESA CASE CRANDALL
married H. E. CRANDALL
of Crandall Cutlery that was
sold to W. R. Case & Sons

J. RUSSELL CASE
(Robinson Cutlery Co.
that was sold in 1908)
(Kinfolks)
(W. R. Case & Sons board
chairman, died 1953)

RHEA CRANDALL
OSBORNE O'KAIN
(W.R. Case & Sons)
(married)

JOHN O'KAIN
(W. R. Case & Sons
chairman of the board)

J. RUSSELL OSBORNE
(W.R. Case & Sons Pres
died Oct. 1975)

JOHN OSBORNE
(New Product Manager
W.R. Case and Sons)

TINT CHAMPLIN
(Kinfolks)
(Cattaraugas)

DANFORTH BROWN
(Kabar)
[discontinued business in
1963 but later bought by
Cole National]

W.R. BROWN
(Kabar)

EMMERSON BROWN
(American Hone Co.)
[purchased by Union Cut.]

J.B.F. CHAMPLIN
(Cattaraugas)

PHILIP CHAMPLIN
(Cattaraugas)

REGINALD PLATTS
(Western Cutlery Co.)

HARLOW PLATTS
(Western Cutlery Co.)

HARVEY PLATTS
(President—Western Cutlery Co.)

CASE DISPLAY BOXES

Case display boxes have been made for a little over 40 years. Before that, Case used a cork ball about six inches in diameter, painted, and fastened to a standard. The pocketknives were opened and stuck into the ball. The cherrywood cases made today run in size from 8″ x 6″ x 2″ for PX's, to 30′ x 8′ x 10′ for the National Houseware Show. At first, the cabinets were loaned to the dealer, but today all the cases are made to order and sold to the dealer. The small counter displays are sought after by collectors, and usually bring from $35.00 to $50.00 for just boxes without knives in them.

COLLECTOR'S SETS

After Case discontinued stag handled knives in 1970, there was some stag left over. The company then made up 2,000 assortments of stag handled knives consisting of 18 pocketknives and five sheath knives stamped either U. S. A., 10 dot, 9 dot, or 8 dot. They were sold through authorized dealers with a suggested retail price of $400 per set. The assortments contained only a combination of 18 pocketknives and five sheath knives from the following:

5220	5347 SHSP	5172 Bulldog	
5233	5254	5111½ L SSP	
05263	5383	5347 SH SP SSP	
52087	5347 SH SP SS	53047	
5232	54052	HUNTING KNIVES	
52131	5392	M5Finn	523-5
53087 SH PEN	5265 SAB DR	523 3¼	523-6
5299½	5375	5361	5325-6
5332	5488	516-5	

Of these sets there were some knives that had never been made previously. All of the 9 and 8 dot stags had not been made before, and the Cheetah (5111½) was designed especially for the collector's sets. The difference between it and a regular lockback is it has stag handles, concave ground stainless steel blade, and a Cheetah etched on the blade. There are two variations of this knife, small and large pattern numbers.

Another rare knife from the sets is 5374, which was never made for regular production.

COLLECTOR'S SETS #2

In March of 1976, Case released 700 sets of stag handled collectors sets containing five Stag sheath knives and seven stag pocketknives. Included in 600 of the sets were two Cheetahs and one bulldog. In the remaining 100 sets there was a Canoe in place of one Cheetah. Only 20 sets were allocated for the state of Georgia, and 70 for Kentucky and Tennessee. The suggested retail for the sets was $600.

COLLECTOR'S SETS #3

In 1977 Case announced they would be producing an annual edition of stag handled knives, depending entirely upon the availability of stag for the handles.

The first of these sets issued in 1977 contained seven pocketknives and five sheath knives with a suggested retail of $237 on the pocketknives and $77 on the sheath knives. On January 1, 1978 the suggested retail on these 1977 sets remaining in stock was raised approximately 10%.

This set featured several knives made for the first time in stainless steel. The pocketknives were listed as follows. 5111½ LSSP, 5265SAB SSP, 5172 SSP (these did not have boxes), 5254SS, 5347 SHSPSSP, 52087 SSP, 5233 SSP. Blades on all these were etched with **CASE XX RAZOR EDGE.**

COLLECTOR'S SETS #4

The successful sets of 1977 were followed by a second set in 1978 containing the same patterns as the 1977 sets, but with the addition of a 52131SSP. This is the first time a stainless steel canoe had been made by Case, making a total of eight pocketknives in the sets. These differ from the 1977 sets in that these blades all contain a blue swirl etching.

An added plus to the Blue Scroll collector's set is that many salesmen required their dealers to order the sets only as complete sets. 15,000 of most knives were made, except for the 5233. 12,600 of the 5233 were made. In order to complete the sets, Case went back a few months later and resumed production of the 33 pattern to fill out the sets (all the other knives had been shipped to the dealers without the 33's included). The good thing for collectors is that in the meantime Case had changed its regular 6233 pattern by shortening it and changing the blade shape. This new modification was a 62033. Since the dies were set up, the remaining 33's run to fill out the last sets were 52033's. Only 2,400 of these were made and have a collector's value of $65.

COLLECTOR'S SET #5

In 1979 Case again made a set of stag handled knives. This time with a red scroll etching on the blades. These were made with a number of newer patterns. They were S254SSP, S347SSP, S220SSP, S279SSP, Muskrat SSP, 52087SSP, 52032SSP.

CASE STAG INVESTING

Quite often I hear the statement, "Genuine stag handled knives are my favorite to collect." The other ear hears at the same time, "I'm laying these back for the grandkids or the boys (this is just another way of saying, "I'm buying these for a rainy day). Are Case stag handled knives a sound investment? Without a doubt, they are a favorite of collectors.

The wide variety of different categories in stags are one of the things that make them so popular. I won't get into Case Tested stags because they are so few and far between that only the most dedicated collector will ever assemble many of them together. However Case XX stags are still plentiful enough in dealers inventories if not in complete collections.

See Chart A that shows the increases in Case XX stags over the past five years.

You will notice in Chart A that I did not get into the different categories of handles such as red stag or green stag. A few of the patterns will be found in red stag only, and some of them will appear in both red stag and the common yellow or orange stag handles.

From my studies, I believe that red stag was used from 1945 to 1955. Most often a knife with fine color and matched handles will bring a premium of 10-20% more than the current 1980 price (one must bear in mind that these knives have just, with usual handling, passed through a lot of hands, knife rolls, dealers' drawers, and pockets in a 15 to 40 year span). A fine red stag specimen will command a premium of 40% to 50% over the average handle.

Case XX USA stags were made from 1965 to 1970. That was the year Case started their dating system and began placing 10 dots under the USA to identify the year the knives were made. In the USA group you will find three key knives. They are the 5165SAB, 5279ss, and 05247. These three patterns were discontinued in 1965 so there were few of them that were shipped to dealers.

The overall Case XX USA picture can be seen in Chart B.

Case manufactured stag handled knives for only six months in 1970, due to an embargo on India stag exports and the difficulty in obtaining a steady supply of stag. In 1973 stag became available again, and Case still had many 10 dot blades of some patterns left in stock. They made a large quantity of stag handled knives in sets of 18 pocketknives and five hunting knives to their dealers. Case listed 22 different pocketknives on the packing sheet. Of these 22 listed, the 5111½ is an eight dot knife, the 5347hsp is a nine dot and the 5172 is marked Case XX USA, so there are only 19 different 10 dot knives. The rarest 10 dot is the 5347ss with polished blade (it was made for the six months in 1970, but never released in the 1973 sets).

Other rare ones are the 52087, 5299½, 5383, 5347hp, 53047, and 5488.

In 1976 Case again sold some stag collectors sets. These sets consisted of seven pocketknives and five hunting knives. All the pocketknives were 10 dots except the 5111½ eight dot again, the 5347hsp nine dot and the USA 5172. Most of these sets that were shipped contained only four different patterns. See Fergurson's *Romance of Collecting Case Knives* 4th edition, page 23 and 24, for more information on the stag collectors sets.

A breakdown on the Case 10 dots is listed in Chart C.

In addition to the 5347 nine dot, the eight dot 5111½, and the USA 5172, there were three other nine dot knives shipped in the 1976 sets. They were: 5232, 5332, 53087. I think the 5232, 5332, and 53087 are sleepers and will increase rapidly in the future. The 5347hps was made in great quantity, so I think it will increase moderately.

In 1977, Case sold approximately 10,000 stag collectors sets. There were seven knives in each set. All seven were stainless steel, all had four dots and all had the long tail "Case Tested XX Razor edge" etched on the blade. See Chart D.

Most of these four dot knives were shipped to dealers in full sets and a lot of them were sold in full sets. You could usually pick up a set of them a little cheaper than you could if you bought one knife at a time. As you can see the lower priced knives have increased much more percentage wise than the higher priced knives.

In 1978 Case produced approximately 15,000 Case collectors sets. Once again these were sold to dealers mostly in sets. Again they were stainless and were supposed to be all three dot stampings. Case did let a few of the 52087's get out with two dots and some of 52087 two dots were restruck with another dot before they left the factory. Also, they had advertised that this set would contain a 52033ssp. Approximately 12,500 5233ssp were shipped and about 2,500 52033ssp were shipped, hence you have 10 different three dot blue scroll etched stags.

In 1979 Case produced approximately 25,000 stag collectors sets. They were marked with two dots and were etched in red on the blade with the long tailed C Case trademark. All seven patterns in the sets were stainless steel. Also later in the year Case released a set of four stag hunting knives to go with the stag sets. The pocketknives were started shipping in November 1979, and were still being shipped as late at June, 1980.

The knives in the 1979 sets and their suggested retail are as follows: 5220ssp-$30, 5279ssp-$30, 5254ssp-$45, 5347ssp-$40, 52032ssp-$40, 52087ssp-$35, Muskrat ssp-$40.

Most of these knives can be bought a little cheaper than retail but no doubt they will increase in value as stags have in the past. The biggest problem with the Case stag is that in some sections dealers don't get many sets so they will not discount them off list; however, in another section of the country, one dealer may end up with 200-400 sets of the knives. Usually he is interested in moving them so he sells them out cheap and thus depresses the market. A customer soon gets price conscious and is slower in buying when something new comes out.

Collectors and investors, the figures and percentages tell the story. Stag knives by W. R. Case have beat inflation over the past five years. The main thing, especially on the later sets is to ship shop around. As long as dealers have plenty on hand you can buy at the right price. As you can see the older knives (Case XX) have increased the most and I think this will continue to be true as there are fewer available than the USA, 10 dot, and later stags.

This article leaves out several Case stags that will be included in Part II. These include Case Mako, Hammerhead, Sharkstooth, Bicentennial Knives, 5165ssp, Case hunting knives, the Gators, and several others.

Case XX Stags (1945-1965)
CHART A

Pattern No.	Value 1975	1976	1977	1978	1979	1980	% of Increase 5 years
#5165 SAB	75.00	80.00	85.00	110.00	130.00	175.00	133%
5165 Flat Ground	100.00	110.00	125.00	160.00	200.00	275.00	175%
5172	85.00	95.00	110.00	140.00	160.00	195.00	129%
5220	20.00	22.00	27.00	32.00	45.00	55.00	175%
5232	27.00	31.00	35.00	40.00	45.00	55.00	104%
5233	20.00	20.00	25.00	38.00	47.00	60.00	200%
05247	50.00	50.00	55.00	65.00	75.00	90.00	80%
#5254	40.00	45.00	50.00	65.00	85.00	100.00	150%
5260	80.00	90.00	95.00	140.00	175.00	200.00	150%
05263 XX	75.00	75.00	75.00	80.00	85.00	90.00	20%
05263 SS	18.00	22.00	25.00	32.00	40.00	45.00	150%
5265 SAB	65.00	70.00	80.00	95.00	115.00	130.00	100%
5265 FLAT	80.00	90.00	100.00	145.00	175.00	200.00	150%
5279 XX	35.00	45.00	55.00	90.00	125.00	150.00	329%
5279 SS	25.00	27.00	30.00	40.00	45.00	50.00	100%
52087	32.00	32.00	35.00	42.00	50.00	60.00	88%
5299½	40.00	42.00	45.00	60.00	70.00	85.00	113%
5299½ A/Blade	45.00	50.00	55.00	75.00	95.00	120.00	167%
52131	60.00	60.00	65.00	80.00	90.00	100.00	67%
52131 Long Pull	110.00	120.00	135.00	175.00	200.00	225.00	105%
5332	40.00	44.00	48.00	65.00	75.00	90.00	125%
5347 HP	42.00	45.00	50.00	60.00	75.00	85.00	102%
5347 HP LP	45.00	55.00	65.00	85.00	115.00	140.00	211%
5347 SS	50.00	55.00	70.00	75.00	85.00	95.00	90%
53047	40.00	40.00	45.00	60.00	70.00	85.00	113%
5375	55.00	60.00	65.00	80.00	90.00	105.00	91%
5375 LP	65.00	75.00	85.00	125.00	160.00	200.00	207%
5375 Second Cut	85.00	100.00	120.00	200.00	300.00	400.00	371%
5383	45.00	50.00	55.00	70.00	85.00	100.00	122%
5383 Sabre	75.00	85.00	95.00	125.00	150.00	175.00	133%
53087	28.00	32.00	37.00	45.00	50.00	60.00	114%
5391	600.00	650.00	700.00	850.00	1000.00	1200.00	100%
5392	50.00	50.00	50.00	65.00	80.00	90.00	80%
54052	45.00	45.00	50.00	65.00	80.00	95.00	111%
54052 XX-USA Trans.	55.00	55.00	55.00	80.00	95.00	120.00	118%
5488	50.00	55.00	60.00	80.00	95.00	130.00	160%
5488 Trans. XX-USA	55.00	60.00	60.00	90.00	125.00	150.00	173%
5488 Long Pull	65.00	75.00	85.00	125.00	175.00	225.00	246%
5488 2nd Cut	95.00	100.00	120.00	175.00	225.00	300.00	216%
5488 2nd Cut Trans.	95.00	110.00	125.00	175.00	225.00	300.00	216%

Average increase for all knives for 5 years 145%.

Case XX USA'S 1965-1970
CHART B

Pattern No.	Value 1975	1976	1977	1978	1979	1980	% of Increase 5 years
#5165 SAB Small Pattern #	225.00	240.00	260.00	275.00	290.00	325.00	44%
5165 SAB Large Pattern #	225.00	240.00	260.00	275.00	290.00	325.00	44%
5172	80.00	90.00	100.00	110.00	125.00	135.00	69%
5172 Transition	90.00	105.00	120.00	135.00	145.00	160.00	78%
5220	20.00	25.00	30.00	35.00	40.00	45.00	125%
5232	16.00	22.00	28.00	35.00	38.00	50.00	212%
5233	20.00	25.00	30.00	35.00	40.00	45.00	125%
05247	125.00	140.00	175.00	150.00	150.00	150.00	20%
5254	35.00	40.00	45.00	50.00	55.00	65.00	86%
5254 Muskrat Blade	40.00	50.00	55.00	60.00	65.00	75.00	88%
5254 Second Cut	65.00	75.00	100.00	150.00	225.00	300.00	362%
5254 2nd Cut Muskrat Bl.	75.00	100.00	125.00	175.00	225.00	300.00	300%
05263	18.00	22.00	25.00	30.00	35.00	40.00	122%
5265 SAB Dr.	50.00	55.00	60.00	60.00	65.00	65.00	30%
5265 SAB Not Drilled XX Frame	75.00	85.00	90.00	100.00	115.00	125.00	67%
5265 SAB Drilled XX Frame	55.00	65.00	75.00	90.00	100.00	110.00	100%
5279 SS	125.00	130.00	140.00	140.00	140.00	140.00	12%
52087	30.00	30.00	35.00	40.00	40.00	45.00	50%
5299½	35.00	40.00	45.00	50.00	55.00	60.00	71%
5332	35.00	40.00	40.00	45.00	50.00	55.00	57%
5347 HP	40.00	40.00	40.00	45.00	50.00	55.00	38%
5347 SS	50.00	50.00	55.00	65.00	65.00	65.00	30%
53047	40.00	40.00	40.00	45.00	50.00	55.00	38%
5375	45.00	50.00	55.00	60.00	60.00	65.00	44%
5375 2nd Cut	90.00	125.00	200.00	250.00	350.00	450.00	400%
5383	40.00	45.00	50.00	55.00	60.00	60.00	50%
53087	30.00	32.00	35.00	40.00	45.00	45.00	50%
5392	45.00	45.00	50.00	55.00	60.00	60.00	33%
54052	40.00	45.00	50.00	50.00	55.00	60.00	50%
54052 Trans. USA 10 Dots	50.00	55.00	60.00	65.00	70.00	75.00	50%
5488	40.00	40.00	45.00	50.00	60.00	70.00	75%
5488 Trans. USA 10 Dots	150.00	150.00	140.00	150.00	160.00	175.00	17%
5488 2nd Cut	75.00	100.00	125.00	175.00	225.00	275.00	267%

Average increase all USA stags for 5 years 97%.

Case XX USA 10 Dots (1970)
CHART C

Pattern No.	Value 1975	1976	1977	1978	1979	1980	% of Increase 5 years
#5220	18.00	22.00	25.00	30.00	40.00	45.00	150%
5232	32.00	35.00	40.00	42.00	45.00	50.00	56%
5233	25.00	30.00	30.00	35.00	40.00	45.00	80%
5254	42.00	45.00	45.00	50.00	55.00	60.00	43%
05263 SS	18.00	25.00	30.00	30.00	35.00	40.00	122%
5265 DR	45.00	45.00	50.00	55.00	65.00	60.00	33%
52087	50.00	50.00	55.00	60.00	60.00	60.00	20%
5299½	60.00	65.00	65.00	65.00	65.00	70.00	17%
52131	50.00	60.00	65.00	70.00	75.00	80.00	60%
5332	45.00	45.00	50.00	55.00	60.00	60.00	33%
5347 HP	40.00	55.00	55.00	60.00	60.00	65.00	63%
5347 SS	60.00	80.00	110.00	130.00	150.00	165.00	175%
53047	40.00	50.00	55.00	60.00	65.00	65.00	63%
5375	50.00	50.00	50.00	55.00	65.00	65.00	30%
5383	40.00	55.00	65.00	65.00	65.00	65.00	63%
53087	30.00	40.00	40.00	45.00	45.00	50.00	67%
5392	40.00	40.00	50.00	50.00	60.00	65.00	63%
54052	40.00	50.00	50.00	65.00	65.00	65.00	63%
5488	130.00	70.00	80.00	90.00	110.00	140.00	8%

Average increase — 5 years — 64%.

1977 Collector Set Knives
CHART D

Pattern No.	Collector Price 1977	Value 1980	%Increase 3 Years
5111½ SSP	35.00	50.00	43%
5172 SSP	35.00	55.00	57%
5233 SSP	15.00	30.00	100%
52087 SSP	15.00	35.00	133%
5254 SSP	25.00	45.00	80%
5265 SSP	30.00	47.00	57%
5347 SSP	30.00	40.00	33%
PHLC of Set of 7	170.00	290.00	71%

1978 Collector Set Knives
CHART E

Pattern No.	1978 Value	1980 Value	% Increase
5233 SSP	20.00	30.00	50%
52033 SSP (Shipped June 1979)	25.00	45.00	80%
52087 SSP	20.00	35.00	75%
52087 SSP 2nd Cut or Restrike	25.00	45.00	80%
5111½ LSSP	35.00	50.00	43%
5265 SAB SSP	32.00	45.00	41%
5172 SSP	35.00	50.00	43%
5254 SSP	25.00	40.00	60%
5347 SSP	27.00	42.00	56%
52131 SSP	30.00	45.00	60%

OLDER CASE KNIVES

The one thing to remember about collecting older Case knives is that few will ever be found in mint condition. A much higher value is placed on these knives since they are so rare. An older Case knive in less than mint condition will not bring near the mint prices listed in this guide.

You will find some pattern numbers that are duplicated today in different patterns (such as the '51 pattern). The bone pattern willb e different in color as well as jigging pattern. And you will find a variety of stampings.

In fact, Mr. Allen Swayne has a collection of rare Case stampings on about twenty different knives.

The older Case knives are a world apart from the collecting of Case Tested, XX, USA, and 10 dot knives, but it is a field that right now has a limited number of collectors. In future years we expect it to be one of the fastest growing segments of knife collecting.

DISCONTINUED GERMAN IMPORTS

In the late 1970's W. R. Case & Sons trial marketed a line of knives from Germany. The attempt failed. The knives were sold by the Case salesmen through the Case company, but the knives were not marked with any Case trademark.

However, in 1979, James F. Parker bought the remaining stock of the German imports, with the stipulation that all of the knives remaining in stock be etched with the Case trademark.

The blades of each knife were etched "Case German Import". Only the knives bought by Parker have the "Case German Import" blade etching. The quantities ranged from 144 of some patterns to 1200 of others.

W. R. Case & Sons imported these knives from one of the finest firms in Soligen, Germany.

After test marketing, the knives were discontinued.

Parker Cutlery has bought the remaining stock of these discontinued imports.

These are the only knives ever made with a Case imprint. Blades on these knives are etched XX German import. Quantities are as low as 144 of some patterns.

HOW TO USE THE CASE SECTION OF THIS PRICE GUIDE

This guide contains more on Case than any other brand because it is the most popular among collectors, and the beginning collector will see more of these than any other brand.

You will note that the price guide to Tested knives is shown right along with Case XX, U.S.A. and Dot knives. In the stamping section, Tested means the Case Tested XX stamping, XX means Case XX stamping, U.S.A. means Case XX U.S.A. stamping, and DOTS means Case XX U.S.A. with dots underneath the stamping. A price guide for knives stamped W. R. Case & Sons, Bradford, PA. (last used around 1920) are not included. Very few W. R. Case stamped knives will be encountered so it is hard to build a reliable price structure on them, but on most patterns, a W. R. Case or Bradford stamped knife will bring 15 to 20% more than the same pattern in Case Tested.

Also, please note the pricing structure of Dot knives. From our experience in dealing with collectors we find that 99% of them collect the 10 dot only, or the 9, 8, 7, 6, 5, dots only as a group. A 5 dot knife with bone handles will not bring any less than a 9 dot of the same handle and pattern. As of this writing, only Delrin handled knives are not popular among collectors. The prices you find on many of the knives will not sell at the retail price to a collector, while a person wanting to use a knife would be happy at the retail price.

It is impossible to tell when The Case company will or will not use bone handles. The bone handled barlows were thought to have changed completely to Delrin in the 10 dot knives, 6233, 6227, 06244, 6333, 6327, 6214, 6214½ and 62087. Also, these patterns have not been seen in bone since 9 dots, 6220, 6244, 6344.

Keep in mind that these prices are printed as a guide, but that both of the authors, sell at these prices and will buy at 75% of the published price. They do, however, reserve the right to limit quantities. Demand and market considerations create a price (i.e. some XX knives command more than Tested due to there being more XX collectors than Tested collectors.)

All Tested knives are priced as green bone handles because 95% of bone handled tested knives were green bone. The other 5% is split between red bone and rough black. Red bone will bring about 2% less than green bone, and rough black handled knives will be 20-30% below green bone tested knives.

A note to you collectors, the authors would appreciate a picture of any knives that do not appear in this guide so that they might be included in a more complete later edition.

LININGS ON CASE KNIVES

Case lined its knives with iron until the late 1920's, when it changed to nickel silver, which was better even than brass. In some times, nickel silver has been in short supply and Case substituted brass. There is one exception to this, the Big Daddy Barlow was lined with iron until 1973, when the pattern was changed to delrin handles with brass liners.

PATTERN NUMBERS

The pattern number system of W. R. Case & Sons allows the collector to tell if a knife has the proper handle, number of blades, and if the proper handles and blades are on the proper pattern knife. However, these pattern numbers can only help on Case knives made after 1949, when the pattern numbers started appearing on each knife.

The pattern number is usually four digits. The first digit is a code for the type of handle material, the second digit is the number of blades, and the last two digits are the factory pattern numbers and "O" between the second and third digits represents a variation of an existing pattern.

When asking for a knife by a pattern number, most collectors learn them by groups of two. Example: They say, on asking to se a stag trapper (5254), "I would like to see a fifty-two, fifty-four." They do not say, "I would like to see a five-two-five-four.

THE FIRST DIGIT

The handle material numbers and letters are listed below. An "*" will be used to show a handle material found only on Case Tested XX knives (1920-50). *(See color section)*

P-Pakkawood

1—Walnut   M-Metal
2—Black Composition   S-Silver
3—Yellow Composition   R-Red Striped Celluloid* (candy striped)
4—White Composition   B-Imitation Onyx*
5—Genuine Stag   G-Green and Red Metal flake under clear celluloid
    (this is called Christmas Tree handles)*
6—Bone Stag   W-Wire*
7—*   H-Mottled Brown and Cream Composition*
8—Genuine Mother of   HA-A bathing beauty under clear celluloid*
      Pearl   GS-Gold Stone (Gold Metal Flake)
9—Imitation Pearl

* The 7 denoted imitation tortise shell in Tested XX days, but when Case introduced its Sharkstooth they originally planned to use Curly Maple and use a 7 to denote it. A few blades were stamped 7, but then the company decided to use Pakkawood dyed black instead, then instead of a 7 a P was used, but the blades stamped 7 were put into the Pakkawood handled knives and will sometimes be found in a Sharkstooth.

Following is an explanation of each handle material, its origin, and current usage.

Walnut-has been used on Case knives since 1920.

Black Composition-was used since before 1940 and has a smooth glossy texture. It is made by a chemical process.

Yellow Composition-has two variations, one being a white line around the outer edge and is sometimes referred to as having a white liner. The handle with a white liner has a deep glossy yellow, and is usually found only on XX or older knives. The other variation is yellow without a white liner and can be found on knives today. At present there is no price difference between the two variations.

White Composition-is the same as black composition, only a different color. At present, there are no regular production knives handled in White composition. It was discontinued around 1974.

Genuine and Second Cut Stag-was made from the remaining antler after cutting for Genuine stag. It was jigged, and also used. It will be found on knives stamped both 5 and 6, and this type handle has been used only on patterns 5254, 6254, 5375, 6375, 6488, and 5488.

The red and white candy striped, Christmas tree, metal flake, and other Tested material are in most cases a celluloid based material.

Genuine Stag comes from antlers of Indian deer and has been used since the first days of Case. It was temporarily discontinued in 1971, but the company still puts stag handles on its Kodiak Sheath knife and they have twice issued collector's sets of stag handled knives, once in 1973 and once in 1976, and started limited production use again in 1977.

Genuine Mother of Pearl-comes from the shell of an Oyster, not a pearl itself. The industrialization of Japan, where most pearl comes from, caused many of the men pearl divers to go to work in the factories. The women cannot dive to the depth that the men could, and the larger pieces of mother of pearl are deep. Consequently, Case has had to cut back on its pearl handled knives. The first cutback came in 1967, and their 1968 catalog listed no pearl handled knives at all, but in 1970 they brought back the 8261, 8279½, 82053 SC SS, and the 8364 SC SS. Case again discontinued all pearl handled knives in 1975 (except 82079½).

Imitation Pearl-There are several variations of imitation pearl, the most well-known being cracked ice, which has a flaky look.

THE FOLLOWING HANDLE MATERIALS ARE DENOTED BY A (6)

Appaloosa-is a smooth brown bone not jigged. Case first used this material in 1979.

Bone Stag-importation is stopped from time to time due to outbreaks of Hoof and Mouth disease in South America where most of the bone comes from. The material comes from a cow's shin bone, and at one-time, almost every knife manufacturer used bone to handle its knives. Today, in the U.S. only Case handles its knives in bone stag, but it is becoming harder to get. Although the company uses bone as it is available, shortages sometimes force the company to use Delrin, a plastic imitation of bone stag. It would be safe to predict that in a few years bone stag will be discontinued.

Delrin-is a chemical process made handle material first used in 1967. It looks much like genuine bone. The way to distinguish between bone and Delrin handles is to look closely at the handles under a strong magnifying glass. With a glass it is possible to see tiny blood channels and pores in genuine bone stag, while Delrin will have no pores. Too, there is usually a bit of discoloration on the edges of bone handles. Since 1974, the shield of a genuine bone stag handled knife will have a circle around the CASE on the shield, while a Delrin or laminated wood handle will not have a circle. Prior to 1974, all shields had the circle around the CASE.

Green Bone-is bone stag with a deep green or brownish green tint. It is quite common on Tested knives, and is found on the older XX knives. It was used between 1940 and 1955. It is fast becoming one of the most collectible hand materials.

High Art-is a handle material similar to the handle made famous by Canton Cutlery Company. It features a photo under a transparent plastic cover. It is found on the extremely old Case knives and a 1980 commemorative, the HA199½.

Red Bone-in its true form is found only on XX or Tested knives. It was probably caused by a particular dye Case was using at the time. A true redbone should have the front handle the same tint as the back handle. Knives that have been displayed on dealer's boards in the sun sometimes fade to a red color, but this is usually a dull finish and will not match the back handle. This isn't a true redbone. Many USA's and Dot knives have beautiful red handles that would be redbone if they were a XX. They bring from $3 to $5 more than the price of regular bone in the same pattern.

Rough Black-was used as a substitute for bone stag during and following World War II. It has a rubber-like base and is called Plastag by W. R. Case & Sons. The design has no set pattern of jigging as most handles do.

Smooth Rose-is a red bone handle that is not jigged. Case introduced it on their knives in 1979.

THE SECOND DIGIT

The second digit of the Case pattern numbers tells the number of blades. W. R. Case & Sons made a few patterns with five blades in the Tested XX and Bradford days, but since that time has only made 1, 2, 3, and 4 bladed knives.

THE REMAINING DIGITS IN THE CASE PATTERN NUMBERS

The remaining digits of a Case pattern number denote the factory pattern number. An "O" denoted a variation from an existing pattern. For example, 06247 is a variation of the 6347, only it has two blades.

On a few knives, the handle material and blade numbers are omitted, leaving only the factory pattern number. Example: 6225½ will be stamped 25½.

BLADE ABBREVIATIONS

After many pattern numbers there are abbreviations for the various blades or a description of the knife. They are:

DR- Drilled through bolster for lanyard
EO- Easy Open
F- File blade
I- Iron liners
L- Blade locks open
½- Clip master blade
P- Punch blade
PEN- Pen blade
R- Bail in handle
RAZ- One arm man blade or razor blade

SAB- Saber ground master blade
SH- Sheepfoot blade
SHAD OR S- No bolsters (shadow)
SICS OR SC- Scissors
SP- Spray blade
SS- Stainless steel blades and springs
SSP- Stainless steel blade and springs, polished edge or blade
T- Tip bolsters
¾- Saber ground like a dagger

 NOTE-*These abbreviations are sometimes abbreviated further. For example H will sometimes denote SH and E will sometimes denote PEN.*

COLLECTORS' INFORMATION

According to W. R. Case & Sons, the following patterns never had rough black handles: 6249, 6380, 6111 ½ L, 61011, 62131.

Case has never produced a folding hunter with "American Tobacco" etched on the blade.

Case has never made a Case XXX.

Occasionally a knife will have a slipped stamp and appear double stamped. Too, this author has seen a shield upside down on a knife, and two knives with Case shields and pattern numbers but without logos. At present these are not more valuable than a regular Case knife of the same pattern, but they may appreciate in the future.

THE FOLLOWING POCKETKNIVES WERE DISCONTINUED FROM 1970:

13031 L	9333	3185
M1270 SC SS	M3102 R SS	82079½
31048 SP	3201	6380
61048 SP	6214½	2231½
06263 F SS	6232	62042 Delrin
9201	6333	6332
9261	62055	6208 Delrin
4100 SS	6202½	62052
4200 SS	6235½ Delrin	6185
Fly Fish	SR63047	6229
61093	6225½ Delrin	11031SH
6445 R	62009½ Delrin	6244
6220 Delrin	62009	3299½
63047 Bone	2220	33044
62027 Delrin	3220	6488
6244 Delrin	3233	62009 RAZ
92042R	8364 SC SS	6205 RAZ
4318 SH SP	8233	6244 Delrin
6347 PU	8261	6232
6347 SPPEN	82053 SR SS	62009½ Delrin

NOTE: The following pattern numbers were discontinued as of August 1981. The individual listings under each of these pattern numbers do not indicate this recent change.

6111½ L	6165
61011	P172 BUFFALO
6318 PEN	6383
3318	33092
6318 SH P	32095 F
6231½	64052
12031 LR	6279 SS
6143	SR62027
6250	63027

KNIVES WITHOUT PATTERN NUMBERS

There are many knives in the collecting field that were started and discontinued by Case between the times they finished their last catalog and had begun work on the next catalog. When the workers died, there was no record of their knives other than the knives themselves. Too, many contract knives were not carried in their general catalogs at all and records got lost over periods of time.

SHEATH KNIVES

There are several things that should be fully understood before beginning to collect sheath knives. First, they do not trade or sell as well as pocketknives. Second, because of their slowness in selling, they are priced quite a bit under pocketknives of the same time period. For example, when Case issued its collector's sets, there were five sheath knives with stag in each set. While many of the pocketknives were selling for $30, the sheath knives were going for $15. However, with the growing scarcity of the older pocketknives, we would recommend that the investor pick up an occasional sheath knife as long as the price is reasonable.

Case did stamp its sheath knives with "Case Tested XX" but when they changed the logo on their pocketknives to Case XX around 1940, the stamping on the sheath knives was changed from "Case XX" to "Case". When the logo was changed from "Case XX" to "Case XX, U. S. A." in 1965, the sheath knive stamping was changed to "Case XX Made in U.S.A." and when the pocketknife stamping was changed to the dots system, the sheath knife stamping was not changed. At present, there is no way to tell the difference between a sheath knife made in 1965 and 1975.

STAMPINGS ON CASE KNIVES

W. R. Case & Sons have used a variety of stampings, some of which are illustrated below with the dates they were used. The Case XX stamping was used from 1940-65 with pattern numbers added to the reverse side of the tang in 1949, and in 1965 the comany began stamping their knives "Case XX U. S. A." At the time there were rumors that the Case XX was made in Germany. Case did have some file blades made in Germany and the blades were stamped on them, but these were the only ones. In 1970 the logo was again changed, this time to Case XX U. S. A. with 10 dots under the logo. Each year after that, a dot is removed. A 1975 knife will have five dots and a 1979 knife will have one dot, and in 1980 the stamping will be changed again. At each of these logo changes there were large numbers of collectors that bought store displays of the old logo knives. Some can still be found at knife shows, etc., intact as they were bought, but individual knives that have been on those boards usually fade on one side and do not bring as much as knives of the same stamping that were not on a board.

TRANSITIONS

With each logo change there were some knives such as the 6488 and the 64052 that have two blades stamped with the logo. Sometimes one blade with the old logo and one blade with the new logo were used in the same knife. These knives are called transitions and can be found in XX to USA, USA to 10 dots, and various combinations of dots, with eight to 10 dots being most common for the 6488. The knife is considered a USA, XX, 10 dot, etc., by the master blade stamping. The master blade is the closest to the shield.

CASE BROS
SPRINGVILLE
N.Y.

1889 — 1903

CASE BROS
CUT
CO
1889 — 1903

Prior to 1915

CASE
BRADFORD
PA.

1903 — 1920

CASES SONS
BRADFORD, PA.

1903 — 1920

W.R.CASE
&SONS
BRADFORD, PA.

1903 — 1920

W. R. CASE
& SONS
BRADFORD, PA.

Prior to 1920

CASE BROS & CO
GOWANDA, N.Y.

1889 — 1903

CASE BROS
LITTLE VALLEY
N.Y.
1889 — 1903

Prior to 1915

CASE'S
BRADFORD

1903 — 1920

CASE
BRADFORD, PA.

1903 — 1920

CASE & SONS
BRADFORD
PA
1903 — 1920

CASE XX

Prior to 1920

STANDARD
KNIFE CO.

1920 — 1923

1920 — 1940

1920 — 1940

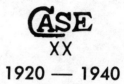
XX

1920 — 1940

TESTED XX

1920 — 1940

TESTED XX

1920 — 1940

CASE
Pat.
9-21-26

1926 — 1940

CASE XX
METAL STAMPINGS
L.T.D.

1942 — 1945

CASE'
TESTED XX

1940 — 1950

CASE'S
TESTED XX

1940 — 1950

CASE XX
STAINLESS

1940 — 1965

CASE
XX

1940 — 1965

CASE XX

1940 — 1965

CASE XX
U.S.A.

1965 — 1970

CASE XX
STAINLESS
U.S.A.
1965 — 1970

CASE XX
STAINLESS
U.S.A.
• • • • • • • • • •
1970

CASE XX
U.S.A.
• • • • • • • • • •
1970

W. R. CASE & SONS
CUTLERY CO.
BRADFORD, PA.

NOTE: NEW MARKING DISCOVERED.
JUNE, 1976. PROBABLY USED
1903-1920

CASE SHEATH KNIVES

Case sheath knives have come into their own in recent years. The steady rise in pocketknife prices left collectors looking for a less expensive route with the same potential. The sheath knives were a natural.

Handles in the same material, the same age, and cheaper! But at current rates of increase they won't be cheaper much longer.

They are a steady increase investment, and can make an extraordinary knife collection.

W.R. CASE & SONS
BRADFORD, PA.

(Until 1932)

(A)

CASE
BRADFORD, PA.

(Until 1932)

(B)

STAINLESS

(Mid 1930s)

(C)

CASE

(About 1932 - 1940)

(D)

CASE
TESTED XX

(About 1932 - 1940)

(E)

CASE'S
TESTED XX

(About 1932 - 1940)

(F)

CASE

(About 1932 - 1940)

(G)

CASE'S
STAINLESS

(About 1945 - 1955)

(H)

CASE

(About 1940 - 1965)

(I)

CASE

(About 1940 - 1965)

(J)

CASE XX

(About 1940 - 1965)

(K)

CASE XX
U.S.A.

(1965 to Date)

(L)

CASE XX
· · · · · · · · ·
U.S.A.

(1980)

(M)

CASE SHEATH KNIVES
(BLADE LENGTH ?)
NO PHOTO AVAILABLE

PATTERN	STAMPING CODE	YEARS MADE	HANDLE	VARIATION/BLADE	MINT PRICE
☐ M-15	D	1934-1940			60.00
☐	I	1940-1965			30.00
☐	J	1940-1965			50.00
☐	K	1940-1965			30.00

(BLADE LENGTH 3¾″)

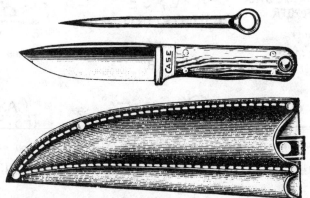

PATTERN	STAMPING CODE	YEARS MADE	HANDLE	VARIATION/BLADE	MINT PRICE
☐ 147	D	1937-1940	Walnut	Chrome Plated	50.00
☐	E	1937-1940	Walnut	Chrome Plated	50.00
☐	F	1937-1940	Walnut	Chrome Plated	50.00
☐	G	1937-1940	Walnut	Chrome Plated	50.00
☐	H	1945-1955	Walnut	Chrome Plated	40.00
☐	I	1940-1965	Walnut	Chrome Plated	40.00
☐	J	1940-1965	Walnut	Chrome Plated	40.00
☐	K	1940-1965	Walnut	Chrome Plated	40.00
☐	L	1965-1975	Walnut	Chrome Plated	30.00

(BLADE LENGTH 4½″)

PATTERN	STAMPING CODE	YEARS MADE	HANDLE	VARIATION/BLADE	MINT PRICE
☐ 161	D	1934-1940	Bone Stag	Chromium Plated	70.00
☐	E	1934-1940	Bone Stag	Chromium Plated	70.00
☐	F	1934-1940	Bone Stag	Chromium Plated	70.00
☐	G	1934-1940	Bone Stag	Chromium Plated	70.00
☐	I	1940-1949	Bone Stag	Chromium Plated	55.00
☐	J	1940-1949	Bone Stag	Chromium Plated	55.00
☐	K	1940-1949	Bone Stag	Chromium Plated	55.00

(BLADE LENGTH 4½")

PATTERN	STAMPING CODE	YEARS MADE	HANDLE	VARIATION/BLADE	MINT PRICE
☐2 FINN	L	1968-DATE	Black Plastic	Chrome Plated	**15.00**

(BLADE LENGTH ?)
NO PHOTO AVAILABLE

PATTERN	STAMPING CODE	YEARS MADE	HANDLE	VARIATION/BLADE	MINT PRICE
☐E-22-5	D	1937-1940			**60.00**
☐	E	1937-1940			**60.00**

(BLADE LENGTH 5")

PATTERN	STAMPING CODE	YEARS MADE	HANDLE	VARIATION/BLADE	MINT PRICE
☐E-23-5	D	1937-1940	Mottled Pearl, Black and Red Composition	Chromium Plated	**90.00**
☐	E	1937-1940	Mottled Pearl, Black and Red Composition	Chromium Plated	**90.00**
☐	F	1937-1940	Mottled Pearl, Black and Red Composition	Chromium Plated	**90.00**
☐	G	1937-1940	Mottled Pearl, Black and Red Composition	Chromium Plated	**90.00**
☐	H	1945-1949	Mottled Pearl, Black and Red Composition	Chromium Plated	**90.00**

(BLADE LENGTH ?)
NO PHOTO AVAILABLE

PATTERN	STAMPING CODE	YEARS MADE	HANDLE	VARIATION/BLADE	MINT PRICE
☐C-23-5	D	1937-1940			**90.00**
☐	E	1932-1942			**90.00**

(BLADE LENGTH ?)
NO PHOTO AVAILABLE

PATTERN	STAMPING CODE	YEARS MADE	HANDLE	VARIATION/BLADE	MINT PRICE
☐206	I	1940-1949			**55.00**
☐	J	1940-1949			**55.00**

(BLADE LENGTH 5″)

PATTERN	STAMPING CODE	YEARS MADE	HANDLE	VARIATION/BLADE	MINT PRICE
☐208-5	E	1934-1940	Black Rubber	Chromium Plated	**60.00**
☐	I	1940-1949	Black Rubber	Chromium Plated	**45.00**

(BLADE LENGTH 5″)
PHOTO SAME AS NO. NO. 208-5

PATTERN	STAMPING CODE	YEARS MADE	HANDLE	VARIATION/BLADE	MINT PRICE
☐209	H	1942-1949	Mottled Brown and Black Rubber	Chromium Plated Saber	**55.00**
☐	J	1942-1949	Mottle Brown and Black Rubber	Chromium Plated Saber	**40.00**

(BLADE LENGTH 5″)

PATTERN	STAMPING CODE	YEARS MADE	HANDLE	VARIATION/BLADE	MINT PRICE
☐216-5	L	1972-DATE	Black Plastic	Chrome Plated	**16.00**

(BLADE LENGTH 5″)
PHOTO SAME AS NO. 223-6

PATTERN	STAMPING CODE	YEARS MADE	HANDLE	VARIATION/BLADE	MINT PRICE
☐223-5	L	1965-DATE	Black Plastic	Chrome Plated Saber	**19.00**

(BLADE LENGTH 6″)

PATTERN	STAMPING CODE	YEARS MADE	HANDLE	VARIATION/BLADE	MINT PRICE
☐223-6	L	1968-DATE	Black Plastic	Chrome Plate Saber	**24.00**

(KNIFE BLADE LENGTH 5″)
(AXE BLADE LENGTH 4½ ″)

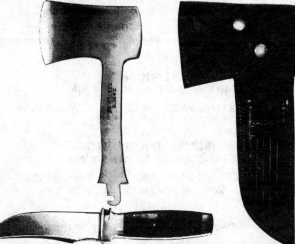

PATTERN	STAMPING CODE	YEARS MADE	HANDLE	VARIATION/BLADE	MINT PRICE
☐261-KINFAX	E	1934-1940	Walnut	Chromium Plated	**225.00**
☐	F	1934-1940	Walnut		**225.00**
☐	K	1940-1965	Walnut		**150.00**
☐	L	1965-1968	Walnut		**125.00**

(BLADE LENGTH 5″)
NO PHOTO AVAILABLE

PATTERN	STAMPING CODE	YEARS MADE	HANDLE	VARIATION/BLADE	MINT PRICE
☐261 Deluxe	J	1940-1964	Walnut	Chromium Plated Large Axe Head	**175.00**
☐	K	1960-1964	Walnut	Chromium Plated Large Axe Head	**125.00**

(BLADE LENGTH 4½ ″)
PHOTO SAME AS NO. 5362

PATTERN	STAMPING CODE	YEARS MADE	HANDLE	VARIATION/BLADE	MINT PRICE
☐262	D	1932-1940	Rubber	Chrome Plated Skinning	**60.00**

(BLADE LENGTH 4¼ ″)
(description on following page)

PATTERN	STAMPING CODE	YEARS MADE	HANDLE	VARIATION/BLADE	MINT PRICE
☐3-FINN	D	1937-1940	Leather	Chromium Plated Saber	25.00
☐	I	1940-1965	Leather	Chromium Plated Saber	20.00
☐	L	1965-DATE	Leather	Chromium Plated Saber	15.00

(BLADE LENGTH 4¼ ")
PHOTO SAME AS NO. 3 FINN

PATTERN	STAMPING CODE	YEARS MADE	HANDLE	VARIATION/BLADE	MINT PRICE
☐3-FINN CC SS H		1949-1955	Leather	Carbon Steel	20.00

(BLADE LENGTH 4¼ ")
PHOTO SAME AS NO. 3 FINN

PATTERN	STAMPING CODE	YEARS MADE	HANDLE	VARIATION/BLADE	MINT PRICE
☐3-FINN SS	H	1949-1955	Leather	Carbon Steel	25.00

(BLADE LENGTH 4¼ ")
PHOTO SAME AS NO. 3 FINN

PATTERN	STAMPING CODE	YEARS MADE	HANDLE	VARIATION/BLADE	MINT PRICE
☐3-FINN SSP	L	1966-DATE	Leather	Carbon Steel	18.00

(BLADE LENGTH 4¼ ")
PHOTO SAME AS TWIN FINN

PATTERN	STAMPING CODE	YEARS MADE	HANDLE	VARIATION/BLADE	MINT PRICE
☐3-TWIN FINN	I	1942-1965	Leather	Carbon Steel	40.00
☐	L	1965-1977	Leather	Carbon Steel	30.00

(BLADE LENGTH 3")
PHOTO SAME AS NO. 3 FINN

PATTERN	STAMPING CODE	YEARS MADE	HANDLE	VARIATION/BLADE	MINT PRICE
☐M3-FINN	I	1942-1965	Leather	Chrome Plated Saber	15.00
☐	L	1965-DATE	Leather	Chrome Plated Saber	12.00

(BLADE LENGTH ?)
NO PHOTO AVAILABLE

PATTERN	STAMPING CODE	YEARS MADE	HANDLE	VARIATION/BLADE	MINT PRICE
☐M3-FINN	H	1949-1955			15.00

(BLADE LENGTH ?)
NO PHOTO AVAILABLE

PATTERN	STAMPING CODE	YEARS MADE	HANDLE	VARIATION/BLADE	MINT PRICE
☐M3-FINN SSP	L	1966-DATE			15.00

(BLADE LENGTH ?)
NO PHOTO AVAILABLE

PATTERN	STAMPING CODE	YEARS MADE	HANDLE	VARIATION/BLADE	MINT PRICE
☐34	D	1937-1940			**50.00**
☐	E	1937-1942			**50.00**
☐	F	1937-1942			**50.00**

(BLADE LENGTH 4¼ ")

PATTERN	STAMPING CODE	YEARS MADE	HANDLE	VARIATION/BLADE	MINT PRICE
☐303	D	1934-1940	Fiber	Chromium Plated	**25.00**
☐	K	1940-DATE	Fiber	Chromium Plated	**15.00**

(BLADE LENGTH 5")

PATTERN	STAMPING CODE	YEARS MADE	HANDLE	VARIATION/BLADE	MINT PRICE
☐309	D	1932-1940	Leather Over Aluminum	Chromium Plated Saber	**75.00**
☐	G	1937-1949	Leather Over Aluminum	Chromium Plated Saber	**75.00**

(BLADE LENGTH 4")

PATTERN	STAMPING CODE	YEARS MADE	HANDLE	VARIATION/BLADE	MINT PRICE
☐315-4	D	1934-1940	Leather and Fiber	Chromium Plated	**35.00**
☐	K	1940-1965	Leather and Fiber	Chromium Plated	**25.00**
☐	L	1965-1974	Leather and Fiber	Chromium Plated	**20.00**

(BLADE LENGTH 4¼ ")
(description on following page)

PATTERN	STAMPING CODE	YEARS MADE	HANDLE	VARIATION/BLADE	MINT PRICE
☐315-4¼	I	1942-1949	Leather and Fiber	Chromium Plated	**35.00**
☐	K	1940-1949	Leather and Fiber	Chromium Plated	**35.00**

(BLADE LENGTH 4½ ")
PHOTO SAME AS NO. 315-4¼

PATTERN	STAMPING CODE	YEARS MADE	HANDLE	VARIATION/BLADE	MINT PRICE
☐315-4½	I	1955-1965	Leather and Fiber	Chromium Plated	**30.00**
☐	L	1965-DATE	Leather and Fiber	Chromium Plated	**18.00**

(BLADE LENGTH 5")
PHOTO SAME AS NO. 315-4¼

PATTERN	STAMPING CODE	YEARS MADE	HANDLE	VARIATION/BLADE	MINT PRICE
☐316-5	I	1942-1965	Leather and Fiber	Chromium Plated	**25.00**
☐	J	1940-1965	Leather and Fiber	Chromium Plated	**25.00**
☐	K	1940-1965	Leather and Fiber	Chromium Plated	**15.00**
☐	L	1965-DATE	Leather and Fiber	Chromium Plated	**15.00**

(BLADE LENGTH 5")
PHOTO SAME AS NO. 316-5

PATTERN	STAMPING CODE	YEARS MADE	HANDLE	VARIATION/BLADE	MINT PRICE
☐316-5 SSP	L	1966-DATE	Leather and Fiber	Stainless Steel	**20.00**

(BLADE LENGTH ?)
NO PHOTO AVAILABLE

PATTERN	STAMPING CODE	YEARS MADE	HANDLE	VARIATION/BLADE	MINT PRICE
☐317	D	1932-1940			**70.00**
☐	E	1932-1940			**70.00**
☐	F	1932-1940			**70.00**
☐	G	1932-1940			**70.00**

(BLADE LENGTH 5")
(description on following page)

PATTERN	STAMPING CODE	YEARS MADE	HANDLE	VARIATION/BLADE	MINT PRICE
☐322-5	D	1937-1940	Leather and Fiber	Chromium Plated	70.00
☐	E	1937-1940	Leather and Fiber	Chromium Plated	70.00
☐	F	1937-1949	Leather and Fiber	Chromium Plated	70.00
☐	G	1937-1949	Leather and Fiber	Chromium Plated	70.00

(BLADE LENGTH ?)
NO PHOTO AVAILABLE

PATTERN	STAMPING CODE	YEARS MADE	HANDLE	VARIATION/BLADE	MINT PRICE
☐322½-5	I	1942-1949			40.00
☐	J	1942-1949			40.00
☐	K	1942-1949			40.00

(BLADE LENGTH 3¼")
PHOTO SAME AS NO. 523-3¼

PATTERN	STAMPING CODE	YEARS MADE	HANDLE	VARIATION/BLADE	MINT PRICE
☐323-3¼	I	1959-1965	Leather		15.00
☐	J	1959-1965	Leather		15.00
☐	K	1959-1965	Leather		15.00
☐	L	1965-DATE	Leather		12.00

(BLADE LENGTH 5")
PHOTO SAME AS NO. 523-6

PATTERN	STAMPING CODE	YEARS MADE	HANDLE	VARIATION/BLADE	MINT PRICE
☐323-5	D	1934-1940	Leather		30.00
☐	E	1934-1940	Leather		30.00
☐	F	1934-1940	Leather		30.00
☐	G	1934-1940	Leather		30.00
☐	I	1940-1965	Leather		25.00
☐	J	1940-1965	Leather		30.00
☐	K	1940-1965	Leather		20.00
☐	L	1965-DATE	Leather		15.00

(BLADE LENGTH 6")

PATTERN	STAMPING CODE	YEARS MADE	HANDLE	VARIATION/BLADE	MINT PRICE
☐323-6	D	1934-1940	Leather and Fiber		35.00
☐	E	1934-1940	Leather and Fiber		35.00
☐	F	1934-1940	Leather and Fiber		35.00
☐	G	1934-1940	Leather and Fiber		35.00

PATTERN	STAMPING CODE	YEARS MADE	HANDLE	VARIATION/BLADE	MINT PRICE
☐	I	1940-1965	Leather and Fiber		25.00
☐	J	1940-1965	Leather and Fiber		35.00
☐	K	1940-1965	Leather and Fiber		25.00
☐	L	1965-DATE	Leather and Fiber		20.00

(BLADE LENGTH 4⅝″)

PATTERN	STAMPING CODE	YEARS MADE	HANDLE	VARIATION/BLADE	MINT PRICE
☐324	D	1934-1940	Leather and Fiber	Skinning	35.00
☐	E	1934-1940	Leather and Fiber	Skinning	35.00
☐	F	1934-1940	Leather and Fiber	Skinning	35.00
☐	G	1934-1940	Leather and Fiber	Skinning	35.00

(BLADE LENGTH 4″)

PATTERN	STAMPING CODE	YEARS MADE	HANDLE	VARIATION/BLADE	MINT PRICE
☐325-4	D	1934-1940	Leather, Fiber and Brass	Chromium Plated	35.00
☐	E	1934-1940	Leather, Fiber and Brass	Chromium Plated	35.00
☐	F	1934-1940	Leather, Fiber and Brass	Chromium Plated	35.00
☐	G	1934-1940	Leather, Fiber and Brass	Chromium Plated	35.00
☐	I	1940-1965	Leather, Fiber and Brass	Chromium Plated	25.00
☐	J	1940-1965	Leather, Fiber and Brass	Chromium Plated	35.00
☐	K	1940-1965	Leather, Fiber and Brass	Chromium Plated	25.00
☐	L	1965-1974	Leather, Fiber and Brass	Chromium Plated	18.00

(BLADE LENGTH 5″)

PATTERN	STAMPING CODE	YEARS MADE	HANDLE	VARIATION/BLADE	MINT PRICE
☐3025-5	C	1932-1938	Leather, Fiber and Brass	Chromium Plated	**75.00**
☐	D	1932-1940	Leather, Fiber and Brass	Chromium Plated	**65.00**
☐	E	1932-1940	Leather, Fiber and Brass	Chromium Plated	**65.00**
☐	F	1932-1940	Leather, Fiber and Brass	Chromium Plated	**65.00**
☐	K	1940-1959	Leather, Fiber and Brass	Chromium Plated	**40.00**

PHOTO SAME AS NO. 3025-5

PATTERN	STAMPING CODE	YEARS MADE	HANDLE	VARIATION/BLADE	MINT PRICE
☐3025-6	D	1937-1940	Leather, Fiber and Brass	Chromium Plated	**50.00**
☐	K	1940-1965	Leather, Fiber and Brass	Chromium Plated	**30.00**
☐	L	1965-1966	Leather, Fiber and Brass	Chromium Plated	**45.00**

(BLADE LENGTH 4½″)

PATTERN	STAMPING CODE	YEARS MADE	HANDLE	VARIATION/BLADE	MINT PRICE
☐326	D	1937-1940	Leather, Fiber and Brass	Chromium Plated	**40.00**
☐	E	1937-1940	Leather, Fiber and Brass	Chromium Plated	**40.00**
☐	F	1937-1940	Leather, Fiber and Brass	Chromium Plated	**40.00**
☐	G	1937-1949	Leather, Fiber and Brass	Chromium Plated	**40.00**

(BLADE LENGTH 5″)
PHOTO SAME AS NO. 652

PATTERN	STAMPING CODE	YEARS MADE	HANDLE	VARIATION/BLADE	MINT PRICE
☐352	D	1934-1940	Cream Composition	Chromium Plated Saber	**40.00**
☐	E	1934-1949	Cream Composition	Chromium Plated Saber	**40.00**

PATTERN	STAMPING CODE	YEARS MADE	HANDLE	VARIATION/BLADE	MINT PRICE
☐	F	1934-1949	Cream Composition	Chromium Plated Saber	40.00
☐	G	1934-1939	Cream Composition	Chromium Plated Saber	40.00

(BLADE LENGTH 4½ ")
PHOTO SAME AS NO. 5361

PATTERN	STAMPING CODE	YEARS MADE	HANDLE	VARIATION/BLADE	MINT PRICE
☐0361	D	1937-1942	Leather and Fiber	Stainless Steel	45.00

(BLADE LENGTH 4½ ")
PHOTO SAME AS NO. 5361

PATTERN	STAMPING CODE	YEARS MADE	HANDLE	VARIATION/BLADE	MINT PRICE
☐361	D	1934-1937	Leather and Fiber	Chromium Plated Skinning	45.00
☐	E	1934-1937	Leather and	Chromium Plated ▮▮▮kinning	45.00
☐	F	1934-1937	Leather and Fiber	Chromium Plated Skinning	45.00
☐	G	1934-1937	Leather and Fiber	Chromium Plated Skinning	45.00

(BLADE LENGTH 4½ ")

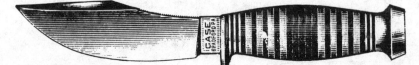

PATTERN	STAMPING CODE	YEARS MADE	HANDLE	VARIATION/BLADE	MINT PRICE
☐362	D	1934-1940	Leather, Fiber and Brass	Chromium Plated	45.00
☐	J	1940-1965	Leather, Fiber and Brass	Chromium Plated	45.00
☐	L	1965-1974	Leather, Fiber and Brass	Chromium Plated	25.00

(BLADE LENGTH 4½ ")

PATTERN	STAMPING CODE	YEARS MADE	HANDLE	VARIATION/BLADE	MINT PRICE
☐364 SAB	D	1937-1940	Leather and Fiber	Chromium Plated Saber	25.00
☐	I	1940-1965	Leather and Fiber	Chromium Plated Saber	25.00
☐	L	1965-DATE	Leather and Fiber	Chromium Plated Saber	15.00

(BLADE LENGTH 5″)

PATTERN	STAMPING CODE	YEARS MADE	HANDLE	VARIATION/BLADE	MINT PRICE
☐365	D	1934-1940	Leather, Fiber and Brass	Chromium Plated	25.00
☐	I	1940-1965	Leather, Fiber and Brass	Chromium Plated	25.00
☐	L	1965-1974	Leather, Fiber and Brass	Chromium Plated	15.00

(BLADE LENGTH 5″)
PHOTO SAME AS NO. 365

PATTERN	STAMPING CODE	YEARS MADE	HANDLE	VARIATION/BLADE	MINT PRICE
☐365 SAB	I	1942-1965	Leather, Fiber and Brass	Chromium Plated Saber	20.00
☐	J	1942-1965	Leather, Fiber and Brass	Chromium Plated Saber	20.00
☐	L	1965-DATE	Leather, Fiber and Brass	Chromium Plated Saber	15.00

(BLADE LENGTH 4″)

PATTERN	STAMPING CODE	YEARS MADE	HANDLE	VARIATION/BLADE	MINT PRICE
☐366	D	1937-1940	Leather, Fiber and Brass	Chromium Plated	25.00
☐	I	1940-1965	Leather, Fiber and Brass	Chromium Plated	20.00
☐	L	1965-DATE	Leather, Fiber and Brass	Chromium Plated	15.00

(BLADE LENGTH 4½ ″)
(description on following page)

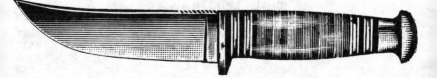

PATTERN	STAMPING CODE	YEARS MADE	HANDLE	VARIATION/BLADE	MINT PRICE
☐378	D	1934-1940	Leather and Fiber	Chromium Plated	**35.00**
☐	I	1940-1959	Leather and Fiber	Chromium Plated	**25.00**
☐	J	1940-1959	Leather and Fiber	Chromium Plated	**35.00**
☐	K	1940-1959	Leather and Fiber	Chromium Plated	**25.00**

(BLADE LENGTH 4½ ")

PATTERN	STAMPING CODE	YEARS MADE	HANDLE	VARIATION/BLADE	MINT PRICE
☐392	D	1934-1940	Ivory	Chrome Plated Skinning	**60.00**
☐	E	1934-1940	Ivory	Chrome Plated Skinning	**60.00**
☐	F	1934-1940	Ivory	Chrome Plated Skinning	**60.00**
☐	G	1934-1940	Ivory	Chrome Plated Skinning	**60.00**

(BLADE LENGTH 4½ ")
PHOTO SAME AS NO. 5361

PATTERN	STAMPING CODE	YEARS MADE	HANDLE	VARIATION/BLADE	MINT PRICE
☐3361	D	1934-1942	Ivory	Chrome Plated Skinning	**65.00**
☐	J	1940-1942		Chrome Plated Skinning	**60.00**

(BLADE LENGTH 3¾ ")

PATTERN	STAMPING CODE	YEARS MADE	HANDLE	VARIATION/BLADE	MINT PRICE
☐457	D	1934-1940	Ivory Composition	Chrome Plate Saber	**55.00**
☐	E	1934-1940	Ivory Composition	Chrome Plated Saber	**55.00**

(BLADE LENGTH 4¼ ")
PHOTO SAME AS NO. 3 FINN

PATTERN	STAMPING CODE	YEARS MADE	HANDLE	VARIATION/BLADE	MINT PRICE
☐5-FINN	D	1937-1940	Stag	Chromium Plated Saber	**55.00**
☐	I	1940-1965	Stag		**35.00**
☐	L	1965-DATE	Stag		**30.00**

(BLADE LENGTH 4¼")
PHOTO SAME AS NO. 3 FINN

PATTERN	STAMPING CODE	YEARS MADE	HANDLE	VARIATION/BLADE	MINT PRICE
☐5-FINN	I	1962-1975	Second Cut Stag	Chromium Plated Saber	**85.00**

(BLADE LENGTH ?)
NO PHOTO AVAILABLE

PATTERN	STAMPING CODE	YEARS MADE	HANDLE	VARIATION/BLADE	MINT PRICE
☐5-FINN CC SS	H	1949-1955			**45.00**
☐	I	1949-1955			**35.00**

(BLADE LENGTH ?)
NO PHOTO AVAILABLE

PATTERN	STAMPING CODE	YEARS MADE	HANDLE	VARIATION/BLADE	MINT PRICE
☐5-FINN SS	H	1949-1955			**45.00**
☐	I	1949-1955			**35.00**

(BLADE LENGTH 5")

PATTERN	STAMPING CODE	YEARS MADE	HANDLE	VARIATION/BLADE	MINT PRICE
☐M-5-FINN	G	1940-	Stag		**35.00**
☐	I	1940-1965	Stag		**25.00**
☐	L	1965-DATE	Stag		**20.00**

(BLADE LENGTH 5")

PATTERN	STAMPING CODE	YEARS MADE	HANDLE	VARIATION/BLADE	MINT PRICE
☐523-5	D	1934-1940	Stag	Chromium Plated	**75.00**
☐	E	1934-1940	Stag	Chromium Plated	**75.00**
☐	I	1940-1965	Stag	Chromium Plated	**45.00**
☐	L	1965-1974	Stag	Chromium Plated	**35.00**

(BLADE LENGTH 5")
PHOTO SAME AS NO. M-5-FINN

PATTERN	STAMPING CODE	YEARS MADE	HANDLE	VARIATION/BLADE	MINT PRICE
☐M-5-FINN SS	I	1949-1955	Stag	Stainless Steel	**35.00**
☐	J	1949-1955	Stag	Stainless Steel	**35.00**

(BLADE LENGTH ?)
NO PHOTO AVAILABLE

PATTERN	STAMPING CODE	YEARS MADE	HANDLE	VARIATION/BLADE	MINT PRICE
☐F52	D	1934-1940			60.00
☐	E	1934-1940			60.00
☐	F	1934-1940			60.00
☐	G	1934-1940			60.00

(BLADE LENGTH ?)
NO PHOTO AVAILABLE

PATTERN	STAMPING CODE	YEARS MADE	HANDLE	VARIATION/BLADE	MINT PRICE
☐501	D	1937-1940			60.00
☐	E	1937-1940			60.00
☐	F	1937-1949			60.00
☐	G	1937-1949			60.00

(BLADE LENGTH 4″)

PATTERN	STAMPING CODE	YEARS MADE	HANDLE	VARIATION/BLADE	MINT PRICE
☐515	D	1934-1940	Stag	Chromium Plated	45.00
☐	E	1934-1940	Stag	Chromium Plated	45.00
☐	F	1934-1940	Stag	Chromium Plated	45.00
☐	G	1934-1940	Stag	Chromium Plated	45.00
☐	I	1940-1965	Stag	Chromium Plated	35.00

(BLADE LENGTH 5″)

PATTERN	STAMPING CODE	YEARS MADE	HANDLE	VARIATION/BLADE	MINT PRICE
☐516-5	I	1940-1965	Stag	Chrome Plated Saber	35.00
☐	J	1940-1965	Stag	Chrome Plated Saber	40.00
☐	K	1940-1965	Stag	Chrome Plated Saber	35.00
☐	L	1965-DATE	Stag	Chrome Plated Saber	30.00

(BLADE LENGTH 3¼″)

PATTERN	STAMPING CODE	YEARS MADE	HANDLE	VARIATION/BLADE	MINT PRICE
☐523-3¼	I	1959-1965	Leather		25.00
☐	J	1959-1965	Leather		35.00
☐	K	1959-1965	Leather		25.00
☐	L	1965-DATE	Leather		25.00

PATTERN	STAMPING CODE	YEARS MADE	HANDLE	VARIATION/BLADE	MINT PRICE
☐523-6	D	1934-1940	Stag		75.00
☐	I	1940-1965	Stag		50.00
☐	K	1965-1974	Stag		35.00

(BLADE LENGTH 5″)
PHOTO SAME AS NO. 3025-5

PATTERN	STAMPING CODE	YEARS MADE	HANDLE	VARIATION/BLADE	MINT PRICE
☐5025-5	D	1934-1940	Stag	Chromium Plated	85.00
☐	E	1934-1940	Stag	Chromium Plated	85.00
☐	F	1934-1940	Stag	Chromium Plated	85.00
☐	G	1934-1940	Stag	Chromium Plated	85.00
☐	K	1940-1962	Stag	Chromium Plated	75.00

(BLADE LENGTH 6″)
PHOTO SAME AS NO. 3025-5

PATTERN	STAMPING CODE	YEARS MADE	HANDLE	VARIATION/BLADE	MINT PRICE
☐5026-6	K	1964	Stag	Chromium Plated	100.00
☐	L	1965-1968	Stag	Chromium Plated	125.00

(BLADE LENGTH 5¾″)

PATTERN	STAMPING CODE	YEARS MADE	HANDLE	VARIATION/BLADE	MINT PRICE
☐551	I	1940-1941	Stag		450.00

(BLADE LENGTH ?)
NO PHOTO AVAILABLE

PATTERN	STAMPING CODE	YEARS MADE	HANDLE	VARIATION/BLADE	MINT PRICE
☐552	I	1959-1962			45.00
☐	J	1959-1962			60.00
☐	K	1959-1962			45.00

PATTERN	STAMPING CODE	YEARS MADE	HANDLE	VARIATION/BLADE	MINT PRICE
☐557	D	1934-1940	Stag	Chromium Plated	**65.00**
☐	E	1934-1940	Stag	Chromium Plated	**65.00**
☐	I	1940-1965	Stag	Chromium Plated	**50.00**
☐	L	1965-1968	Stag	Chromium Plated	**75.00**

(BLADE LENGTH 3¾″)
PHOTO SAME AS NO. 557

PATTERN	STAMPING CODE	YEARS MADE	HANDLE	VARIATION/BLADE	MINT PRICE
☐557 SAB	D	1937-1940	Stag	Chromium Plated Saber	**60.00**
☐	E	1937-1940	Stag	Chromium Plated Saber	**60.00**
☐	I	1940-1949	Stag	Chromium Plated Saber	**50.00**
☐	J	1940-1949	Stag	Chromium Plated Saber	**60.00**
☐	K	1940-1949	Stag	Chromium Plated	**50.00**

(KNIFE BLADE LENGTH 5″)
(AXE BLADE LENGTH 4½″)
(description on following page)

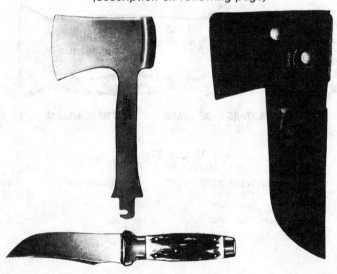

PATTERN	STAMPING CODE	YEARS MADE	HANDLE	VARIATION/BLADE	MINT PRICE
☐561 Deluxe	E	1937-1940	Stag	Chrome Plated Large Axe Head	400.00
☐	F	1937-1940	Stag	Chrome Plated Large Axe Head	400.00
☐	K	1940-1965	Stag	Chrome Plated Large Axe Head	325.00
☐	L	1965-1974	Stag	Chrome Plated Large Axe Head	275.00

(BLADE LENGTH ?)
NO PHOTO AVAILABLE

PATTERN	STAMPING CODE	YEARS MADE	HANDLE	VARIATION/BLADE	MINT PRICE
☐578	D	1934-1940	Deer Horn		65.00
☐	E	1934-1940	Deer Horn		65.00
☐	J	1940-1959	Deer Horn		60.00
☐	K	1940-1959	Deer Horn		35.00

(BLADE LENGTH 4⅝″)
PHOTO SAME AS NO. 324

PATTERN	STAMPING CODE	YEARS MADE	HANDLE	VARIATION/BLADE	MINT PRICE
☐5324	D	1934-1940	Stag	Skinning	85.00
☐	E	1934-1940	Stag	Skinning	85.00
☐	I	1940-1941	Stag	Skinning	75.00
☐	J	1940-1941	Stag	Skinning	75.00
☐	K	1940-1941	Stag	Skinning	75.00

(BLADE LENGTH 5″)
PHOTO SAME AS NO. 325

PATTERN	STAMPING CODE	YEARS MADE	HANDLE	VARIATION/BLADE	MINT PRICE
☐5325-5	D	1934-1940	Stag	Chromium Plated	100.00
☐	E	1934-1940	Stag	Chromium Plated	100.00
☐	I	1940-1965	Stag	Chromium Plated	75.00
☐	K	1940-1965	Stag	Chromium Plated	75.00
☐	L	1965-1966	Stag	Chromium Plated	125.00

(BLADE LENGTH 6″)
PHOTO SAME AS NO. 325

PATTERN	STAMPING CODE	YEARS MADE	HANDLE	VARIATION/BLADE	MINT PRICE
☐5325-6	D	1934-1940			100.00
☐	E	1934-1940			100.00
☐	I	1940-1965			75.00
☐	K	1940-1965			75.00
☐	L	1965-1968			125.00

(BLADE LENGTH 4½″)
(description on following page)

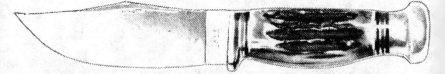

PATTERN	STAMPING CODE	YEARS MADE	HANDLE	VARIATION/BLADE	MINT PRICE
☐5361	D	1934-1940	Deer Horn	Chrome Plated Skinning	100.00
☐	J	1940-1965	Deer Horn	Chrome Plated Skinning	80.00
☐	K	1940-1965	Deer Horn	Chrome Plated Skinning	75.00
☐	L	1965-1974	Deer Horn	Chrome Plated Skinning	95.00

(BLADE LENGTH 4½ ")

PATTERN	STAMPING CODE	YEARS MADE	HANDLE	VARIATION/BLADE	MINT PRICE
☐5362	D	1934-1940	Deer Horn	Chrome Plated Skinning	90.00
☐	I	1940-1949	Deer Horn		75.00

(BLADE LENGTH ?)
NO PHOTO AVAILABLE

PATTERN	STAMPING CODE	YEARS MADE	HANDLE	VARIATION/BLADE	MINT PRICE
☐E62	F	1937-1942			110.00

(BLADE LENGTH ?)
NO PHOTO AVAILABLE

PATTERN	STAMPING CODE	YEARS MADE	HANDLE	VARIATION/BLADE	MINT PRICE
☐RE-62	F	1937-1940			90.00

(BLADE LENGTH 5")

PATTERN	STAMPING CODE	YEARS MADE	HANDLE	VARIATION/BLADE	MINT PRICE
☐62-5	F	1934-1949	Bone Stag	Chromium Plated	120.00

(BLADE LENGTH 6")
PHOTO SAME AS NO. 62-5

PATTERN	STAMPING CODE	YEARS MADE	HANDLE	VARIATION/BLADE	MINT PRICE
☐62-6	F	1934-1949			125.00

(BLADE LENGTH 5″)

PATTERN	STAMPING CODE	YEARS MADE	HANDLE	VARIATION/BLADE	MINT PRICE
☐ 63-5	D	1934-1940	Bone Stag	Chrome Plated Saber	**140.00**
☐	J	1940-1942	Bone Stag	Chrome Plated Saber	**110.00**

(BLADE LENGTH 6″)
PHOTO SAME AS NO. 63-5

PATTERN	STAMPING CODE	YEARS MADE	HANDLE	VARIATION/BLADE	MINT PRICE
☐ 63-6	B	1926-1934	Bone Stag	Chrome Plated	**150.00**
☐	D	1934-1940	Bone Stag	Chrome Plated	**125.00**
☐	I	1940-1942	Bone Stag	Chrome Plated	**95.00**

(BLADE LENGTH 4″)

PATTERN	STAMPING CODE	YEARS MADE	HANDLE	VARIATION/BLADE	MINT PRICE
☐ 64	F	1934-1940	Bone Stag	Chrome Plated Straight	**90.00**
☐	H	1940-1949	Bone Stag	Chrome Plated Straight	**90.00**
☐	K	1940-1949	Bone Stag	Chrome Plated Straight	**60.00**

(BLADE LENGTH ?)
NO PHOTO AVAILABLE

PATTERN	STAMPING CODE	YEARS MADE	HANDLE	VARIATION/BLADE	MINT PRICE
☐ E66	F	1934-1940			**90.00**
☐	I	1940-1941			**90.00**

(BLADE LENGTH 4″)

PATTERN	STAMPING CODE	YEARS MADE	HANDLE	VARIATION/BLADE	MINT PRICE
☐ RE66	F	1934-1940	Mottled Pearl and Brown	Chromium Plated	**75.00**
☐	I	1940-1941	Mottled Pearl and Brown		**65.00**

(BLADE LENGTH ?)

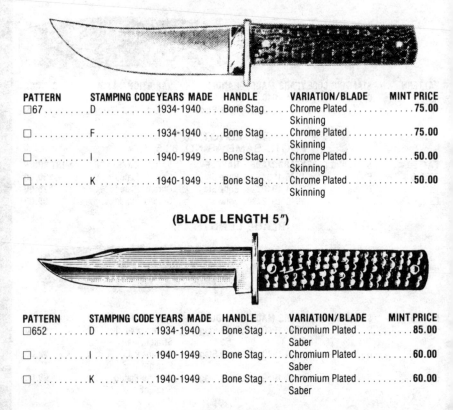

PATTERN	STAMPING CODE	YEARS MADE	HANDLE	VARIATION/BLADE	MINT PRICE
☐67	D	1934-1940	Bone Stag	Chrome Plated Skinning	75.00
☐	F	1934-1940	Bone Stag	Chrome Plated Skinning	75.00
☐	I	1940-1949	Bone Stag	Chrome Plated Skinning	50.00
☐	K	1940-1949	Bone Stag	Chrome Plated Skinning	50.00

(BLADE LENGTH 5″)

PATTERN	STAMPING CODE	YEARS MADE	HANDLE	VARIATION/BLADE	MINT PRICE
☐652	D	1934-1940	Bone Stag	Chromium Plated Saber	85.00
☐	I	1940-1949	Bone Stag	Chromium Plated Saber	60.00
☐	K	1940-1949	Bone Stag	Chromium Plated Saber	60.00

(BLADE LENGTH 5″)

PATTERN	STAMPING CODE	YEARS MADE	HANDLE	VARIATION/BLADE	MINT PRICE
☐652-5	I	1962-1965	Bone Stag	Chrome Plated Saber	65.00
☐	K	1962-1965	Bone Stag	Chrome Plated Saber	65.00
☐	L	1965-1968	Bone Stag	Chrome Plated Saber	25.00

(KNIFE LENGTH 5″)
(AXE BLADE LENGTH 4½″)
(picture on following page)

PATTERN	STAMPING CODE	YEARS MADE	HANDLE	VARIATION/BLADE	MINT PRICE
☐661-KINFAX	D	1934-1942	Bone Stag	Chromium Plated	450.00
☐	E	1934-1942	Bone Stag	Chromium Plated	450.00
☐	F	1934-1942	Bone Stag	Chromium Plated	450.00
☐	G	1934-1942	Bone Stag	Chromium Plated	400.00

(KNIFE LENGTH 5″)
(AXE BLADE LENGTH 4½ ″)

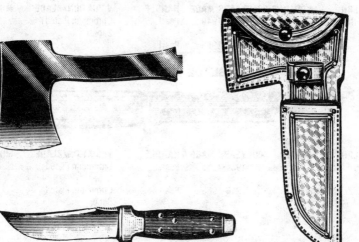

(BLADE LENGTH ?)
NO PHOTO AVAILABLE

PATTERN	STAMPING CODE	YEARS MADE	HANDLE	VARIATION/BLADE	MINT PRICE
☐F78	E	1934-1937			80.00
☐	G	1934-1937			80.00

(BLADE LENGTH ?)
NO PHOTO AVAILABLE

PATTERN	STAMPING CODE	YEARS MADE	HANDLE	VARIATION/BLADE	MINT PRICE
☐PS78	E	1934-1937			85.00
☐	G	1934-1937			85.00

(BLADE LENGTH 5″)

PATTERN	STAMPING CODE	YEARS MADE	HANDLE	VARIATION/BLADE	MINT PRICE
☐709	E	1934-1942	Metal	Chrome Plated Saber	125.00

(BLADE LENGTH ?)
NO PHOTO AVAILABLE

PATTERN	STAMPING CODE	YEARS MADE	HANDLE	VARIATION/BLADE	MINT PRICE
☐M-8-FINN	I	1940-1949			40.00
☐	K	1940-1949			40.00

(BLADE LENGTH 4¼")
PHOTO SAME AS NO. 3-FINN

PATTERN	STAMPING CODE	YEARS MADE	HANDLE	VARIATION/BLADE	MINT PRICE
☐9-FINN	F	1934-1940	Pearl	Chromium Plated Saber	40.00
☐	K	1940-1955	Pearl		30.00

(BLADE LENGTH 3")

PATTERN	STAMPING CODE	YEARS MADE	HANDLE	VARIATION/BLADE	MINT PRICE
☐M-9-FINN	E	1934-1955	Pearl	Chromium Plated Saber	40.00
☐	K	1940-1955	Pearl	Chromium Plated Saber	30.00

(BLADE LENGTH 4½")

PATTERN	STAMPING CODE	YEARS MADE	HANDLE	VARIATION/BLADE	MINT PRICE
☐92	D	1934-1940	Leather and Fiber	Chromium Plated	60.00
☐	E	1934-1940	Leather and Fiber	Chromium Plated	60.00
☐	F	1934-1940	Leather and Fiber	Chromium Plated	60.00
☐	G	1934-1940	Leather and Fiber	Chromium Plated	60.00
☐	I	1940-1949	Leather and Fiber	Chromium Plated	50.00
☐	J	1940-1949	Leather and Fiber	Chromium Plated	60.00
☐	K	1940-1949	Leather and Fiber	Chromium Plated	50.00

(BLADE LENGTH ?)
NO PHOTO AVAILABLE

PATTERN	STAMPING CODE	YEARS MADE	HANDLE	VARIATION/BLADE	MINT PRICE
☐PS97	D	1934-1937			90.00
☐	E	1934-1937			90.00

(BLADE LENGTH ?)
NO PHOTO AVAILABLE

PATTERN	STAMPING CODE	YEARS MADE	HANDLE	VARIATION/BLADE	MINT PRICE
☐903	E	1934-1937			80.00

(BLADE LENGTH 5")
PHOTO SAME AS NO. 323-3¼

PATTERN	STAMPING CODE	YEARS MADE	HANDLE	VARIATION/BLADE	MINT PRICE
☐923-5	D	1934-1940	Leather		85.00
☐	I	1940-1949	Leather		70.00
☐	J	1940-1949	Leather		85.00
☐	K	1940-1949	Leather		70.00

(BLADE LENGTH 6")
PHOTO SAME AS NO. 323-6

PATTERN	STAMPING CODE	YEARS MADE	HANDLE	VARIATION/BLADE	MINT PRICE
☐923-6	D	1934-1940	Leather		85.00
☐	I	1940-1949	Leather		65.00
☐	J	1940-1949	Leather		85.00
☐	K	1940-1949	Leather		65.00

(BLADE LENGTH ?)
NO PHOTO AVAILABLE

PATTERN	STAMPING CODE	YEARS MADE	HANDLE	VARIATION/BLADE	MINT PRICE
☐952	D	1934-1940			65.00
☐	E	1934-1942			65.00
☐	G	1934-1943			65.00

(BLADE LENGTH ?)
NO PHOTO AVAILABLE

PATTERN	STAMPING CODE	YEARS MADE	HANDLE	VARIATION/BLADE	MINT PRICE
☐957	D	1934-1940			85.00
☐	E	1934-1940			85.00
☐	G	1934-1940			85.00
☐	I	1940-1942			65.00
☐	J	1940-1942			85.00

(BLADE LENGTH ?)
NO PHOTO AVAILABLE

PATTERN	STAMPING CODE	YEARS MADE	HANDLE	VARIATION/BLADE	MINT PRICE
☐957-SAB	D	1937-1940			70.00
☐	E	1937-1940			70.00
☐	G	1937-1940			70.00
☐	I	1940-1949			60.00

(BLADE LENGTH ?)
NO PHOTO AVAILABLE

PATTERN	STAMPING CODE	YEARS MADE	HANDLE	VARIATION/BLADE	MINT PRICE
☐961	E	1934-1940	Imitation Pearl		400.00
☐	F	1934-1940	Imitation Pearl		400.00
☐	K	1940-1959	Imitation Pearl		300.00

(BLADE LENGTH 5")
NO PHOTO AVAILABLE

PATTERN	STAMPING CODE	YEARS MADE	HANDLE	VARIATION/BLADE	MINT PRICE
☐961-DELUXE	E	1932-1940	Imitation Pearl		400.00
☐	F	1932-1940	Imitation Pearl		400.00

(BLADE LENGTH 4″)
PHOTO SAME AS NO. 64

PATTERN	STAMPING CODE	YEARS MADE	HANDLE	VARIATION/BLADE	MINT PRICE
☐964	F	1932-1940	Fancy Composition	Chrome Plated Straight	95.00
☐	I	1940-1965	Fancy Composition	Chrome Plated Straight	70.00
☐	K	1940-1965	Fancy Composition	Chrome Plated Straight	70.00

(BLADE LENGTH 4½″)
PHOTO SAME AS NO. 378

PATTERN	STAMPING CODE	YEARS MADE	HANDLE	VARIATION/BLADE	MINT PRICE
☐978	F	1932-1940	Pearl Composition	Chromium Plated	75.00

(BLADE LENGTH 5″)
NO PHOTO AVAILABLE

PATTERN	STAMPING CODE	YEARS MADE	HANDLE	VARIATION/BLADE	MINT PRICE
☐9325-5	F	1932-1940			75.00
☐	I	1940-1965			75.00

(BLADE LENGTH 4½″)
PHOTO SAME AS NO. 5362

PATTERN	STAMPING CODE	YEARS MADE	HANDLE	VARIATION/BLADE	MINT PRICE
☐9362	F	1932-1940	Deer Horn	Chrome Plated Skinning	75.00
☐	I	1940-1965	Deer Horn	Chrome Plated Skinning	75.00

(BLADE LENGTH 5¼″)

PATTERN	STAMPING CODE	YEARS MADE	HANDLE	VARIATION/BLADE	MINT PRICE
☐APACHE 300	L	1966-1980	Stag	Stainless Steel	30.00
☐	M	1981	Stag	Stainless Steel	65.00

(BLADE LENGTH ?″)
(picture on following page)

PATTERN	STAMPING CODE	YEARS MADE	HANDLE	VARIATION/BLADE	MINT PRICE
☐BOWIE	L	1967-DATE	Stag		60.00
☐	M	1980	Stag	2500 made	200.00

(BLADE LENGTH ?)

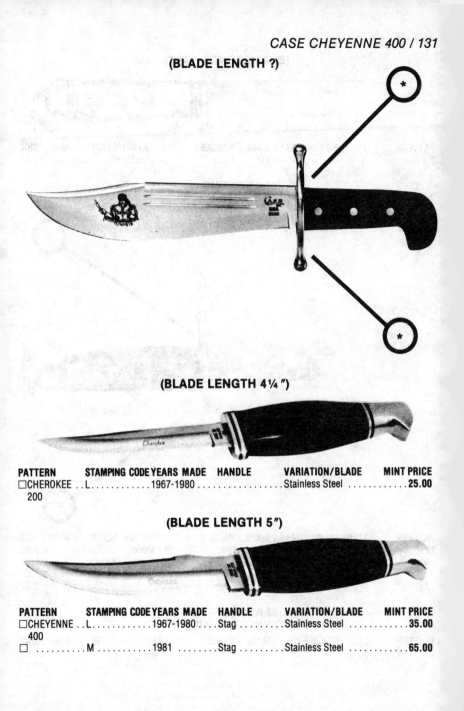

(BLADE LENGTH 4¼ ″)

PATTERN	STAMPING CODE	YEARS MADE	HANDLE	VARIATION/BLADE	MINT PRICE
☐CHEROKEE 200	L	1967-1980		Stainless Steel	25.00

(BLADE LENGTH 5″)

PATTERN	STAMPING CODE	YEARS MADE	HANDLE	VARIATION/BLADE	MINT PRICE
☐CHEYENNE 400	L	1967-1980	Stag	Stainless Steel	35.00
☐	M	1981	Stag	Stainless Steel	65.00

(BLADE LENGTH 4⅜")

PATTERN	STAMPING CODE	YEARS MADE	HANDLE	VARIATION/BLADE	MINT PRICE
☐FINN	D	1934-1937	Pearl	Chrome Plated	50.00

(BLADE LENGTH ?)

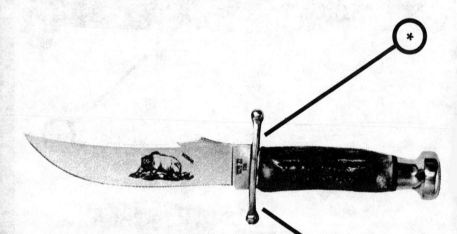

PATTERN	STAMPING CODE	YEARS MADE	HANDLE	VARIATION/BLADE	MINT PRICE
☐KODIAK	I	1964-1966	Stag	XX Model	125.00
☐	K	1966-1967	Stag	Transitional Model	100.00
☐	L	1967-1973	Stag	No Stars Model	80.00
☐	M	1973-DATE	Stag		70.00

(BLADE LENGTH ?)
NO PHOTO AVAILABLE

PATTERN	STAMPING CODE	YEARS MADE	HANDLE	VARIATION/BLADE	MINT PRICE
☐MACHETE	K	1942		Military	60.00

PATTERN	STAMPING CODE	YEARS MADE	HANDLE	VARIATION/BLADE	MINT PRICE
☐380 COMBO	.L	1968-1974		Chromium Plated Axe and Hunter	.50.00

PATTERN	STAMPING CODE	YEARS MADE	HANDLE	VARIATION/BLADE	MINT PRICE EACH
☐CRUISER and SPORTSMAN AXE	E	1937-1949	Hardwood		50.00
☐	K	1949-1960	Hardwood		35.00

(NO. 380 BLADE LENGTH 2⅝″)
(NO. 580 BLADE LENGTH 2⅝″)
(picture on following page)

PATTERN	STAMPING CODE	YEARS MADE	HANDLE	VARIATION/BLADE	MINT PRICE EACH
☐380 AXE and 580	F	1934-1940	Metal		25.00
☐	G	1934-1940	Metal		25.00
☐	K	1940-1965	Metal		20.00
☐	L	1965-1966	Metal		20.00

(BLADE LENGTH 11½ ")
(description on following page)

ICE
.00

.00
.00
.00
of
ed
ng
he
ng.
ur-
SA

NO PHOTO AVAILABLE

PATTERN	STAMPING CODE	YEARS MADE	HANDLE	VARIATION/BLADE	MINT PRICE
3-TWIN FINN SET SSP	L	1965-DATE		USA Model Discontinued	35.00

(BLADE LENGTH ?)
NO PHOTO AVAILABLE

PATTERN	STAMPING CODE	YEARS MADE	HANDLE	VARIATION/BLADE	MINT PRICE
3-TWIN FINN SET	L	1965-DATE		USA Model Discontinued	30.00

(BLADE LENGTH ?)
NO PHOTO AVAILABLE

PATTERN	STAMPING CODE	YEARS MADE	HANDLE	VARIATION/BLADE	MINT PRICE
162	I	1940-1950			55.00

(BLADE LENGTH 3″)

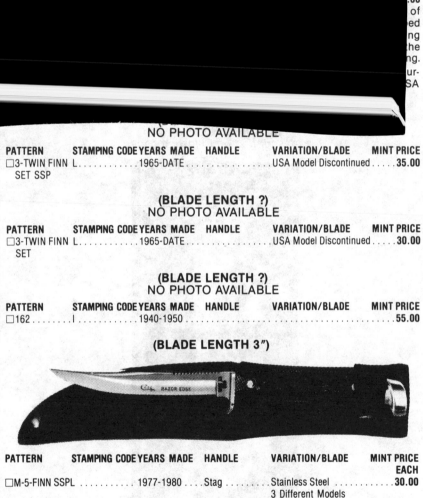

PATTERN	STAMPING CODE	YEARS MADE	HANDLE	VARIATION/BLADE	MINT PRICE EACH
M-5-FINN SSPL		1977-1980	Stag	Stainless Steel 3 Different Models	30.00

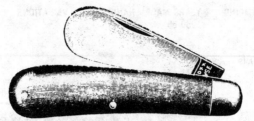

(LENGTH 3¼ ")

PATTERN	STAMPING	YEARS MADE	HANDLE	VARIATIONS	MINT PRICE
☐Maize No. 1	Tested	Prior 1940	Cocobola	3⅝"	85.00
☐Maize No. 2	Tested	Prior 1940	Cocobola	4"	85.00

(LENGTH 4½ ")

PATTERN	STAMPING	YEARS MADE	HANDLE	VARIATIONS	MINT PRICE
☐3100	Tested	Prior 1940	Yellow Composition		175.00
☐6100	Tested	Prior 1940	Green Bone		600.00

(LENGTH 3¼ " CLOSED)

PATTERN	STAMPING	YEARS MADE	HANDLE	VARIATIONS	MINT PRICE
☐M100	Tested	Prior 1940	Cracked Ice		90.00
☐	Tested	Prior 1940	Green Bone		90.00
☐	Tested	Prior 1940	Royal Blue	Celluloid	90.00
☐	XX	1940's	Nickel Plated		90.00
☐	XX	1940's	Gold Plated		135.00

**MELON TESTER, CITRUS
(LENGTH 5½ " CLOSED)**

PATTERN	STAMPING	YEARS MADE	HANDLE	VARIATIONS	MINT PRICE
☐4100	XX	1960-65	White Composition		50.00
☐	USA	1965-70			45.00
☐	10 Dots	1970-71			40.00
☐	Dots	1971-74	White Composition	Discontinued	35.00

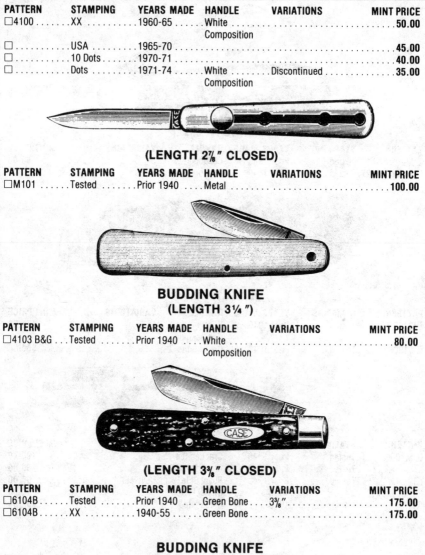

(LENGTH 2⅞" CLOSED)

PATTERN	STAMPING	YEARS MADE	HANDLE	VARIATIONS	MINT PRICE
☐M101	Tested	Prior 1940	Metal		100.00

BUDDING KNIFE
(LENGTH 3¼ ")

PATTERN	STAMPING	YEARS MADE	HANDLE	VARIATIONS	MINT PRICE
☐4103 B&G	Tested	Prior 1940	White Composition		80.00

(LENGTH 3⅜" CLOSED)

PATTERN	STAMPING	YEARS MADE	HANDLE	VARIATIONS	MINT PRICE
☐6104B	Tested	Prior 1940	Green Bone	3⅜"	175.00
☐6104B	XX	1940-55	Green Bone		175.00

BUDDING KNIFE
(LENGTH 3¼ " CLOSED)

PATTERN	STAMPING	YEARS MADE	HANDLE	VARIATIONS	MINT PRICE
☐2109B	Tested	Prior 1950	Black Composition		90.00
☐2109B	XX	1950-65	Black Composition		85.00
☐2109B	USA	1965-68	Black Composition		85.00

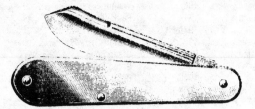

SPAYING KNIFE
(LENGTH 3⅛″)

PATTERN	STAMPING	YEARS MADE	HANDLE	VARIATIONS	MINT PRICE
☐M110	Tested	Prior 1940	Nickel Silver		100.00
☐M110	XX	1940's	Nickel Silver		100.00

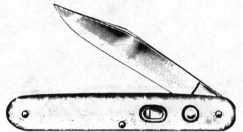

SWITCHBLADE
(LENGTH 3⅜″ CLOSED)

PATTERN	STAMPING	YEARS MADE	HANDLE	VARIATIONS	MINT PRICE
☐91210½	Tested	Prior 1940	White Onyx		165.00

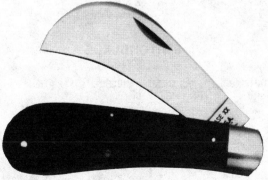

HAWKBILL
(LENGTH 4″ CLOSED)

PATTERN	STAMPING	YEARS MADE	HANDLE	VARIATIONS	MINT PRICE
☐11011	Tested	Prior 1950	Walnut		50.00
☐	XX	1950-65	Walnut		30.00

☐	USA	1965-70	Walnut		**20.00**
☐	5 Dots	1974	Pakkawood		**30.00**
☐	10 Dots	1970-71	Walnut		**18.00**
☐	Dots	1970's	Walnut		**16.00**
☐61011	Tested	Prior 1940	Green Bone		**70.00**
☐	XX	1940's	Green Bone		**70.00**
☐	XX	1940's-65	Bone		**35.00**
☐	XX	1964-65	Laminated Wood		**25.00**
☐	USA	1965	Bone		**25.00**
☐	USA	1965-70	Laminated Wood		**16.00**
☐	10 Dots	1970-71	Laminated Wood		**15.00**
☐	Dots	1970's	Laminated Wood		**10.00**
☐	Lightning S. 10 Dots	1980	Laminated Wood		**12.00**

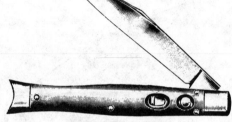

SWITCHBLADE
(LENGTH 4″ CLOSED)

PATTERN	STAMPING	YEARS MADE	HANDLE	VARIATIONS	MINT PRICE
☐31211½	Tested	Prior 1940	Cream Composition		**165.00**
☐H1211½	Tested	Prior 1940	Mottled Brown & Cream Composition		**165.00**

SWITCHBLADE
(LENGTH 4″)

PATTERN	STAMPING	YEARS MADE	HANDLE	VARIATIONS	MINT PRICE
☐31212½	Tested	Prior 1940	Cream Composition	4″	**165.00**
☐1212½	Tested	Prior 1940	Red and white Striped Celluloid		**165.00**

LOCKBACK
(LENGTH 4⅜″ CLOSED)

PATTERN	STAMPING	YEARS MADE	HANDLE	VARIATIONS	MINT PRICE
☐5111½	8 Dots	1973	Stag	Small Stamp	200.00
☐5111½	8 Dots	1973	Stag	Large Stamp	175.00
☐5111½	4 Dots	1977	Stag	Case Razor Edge Etched	60.00
☐5111½	3 Dots	1978	Stag	Blue Scroll	50.00

THE CHEETAH'S WERE MADE ONLY FOR THE CASE COLLECTOR'S SET ISSUED IN 1973

PATTERN	STAMPING	YEARS MADE	HANDLE	VARIATIONS	MINT PRICE
☐3111½	Tested	Prior 1940	Yellow Comp.		325.00
☐6111½	Tested	Prior 1940	Green Bone		400.00
☐6111½	Tested	Prior 1940	Green Bone	Long Pull	450.00
☐6111½L	Tested	Prior 1940	Green Bone		400.00
☐6111½L	XX	1940-45	Green Bone		300.00
☐6111½L	XX	1955-65	Bone		75.00
☐6111½L	USA	1965	Bone	Extra one in pattern was a factory error	95.00
☐6111½L	USA	1965-70	Bone		45.00
☐L	10 Dots	1970-71	Bone		45.00
☐L	Dots	1970's	Bone		35.00
☐L	Dots	1970's	Delrin		20.00
☐L					
☐6111½L	Lightning S 10 Dots	1980	Bone		25.00

(LENGTH 4" CLOSED)

PATTERN	STAMPING	YEARS MADE	HANDLE	VARIATIONS	MINT PRICE
☐61013	Tested	Prior 1940	Green Bone		100.00

(LENGTH 4″ CLOSED)

PATTERN	STAMPING	YEARS MADE	HANDLE	VARIATIONS	MINT PRICE
☐61213½	Tested	Prior 1940	Green Bone		325.00

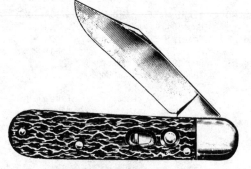

SWITCHBLADE
(LENGTH 4⅛″ CLOSED)

PATTERN	STAMPING	YEARS MADE	HANDLE	VARIATIONS	MINT PRICE
☐61214½	Tested	Prior 1940	Bone		300.00
☐61215½	Tested	Prior 1940	Bone	Same as above pattern except 5″ long	475.00

SWITCHBLADE
(LENGTH 5″ CLOSED)

PATTERN	STAMPING	YEARS MADE	HANDLE	VARIATIONS	MINT PRICE
□51215 G	Tested	Prior 1940	Bone stag horn		425.00
□51215½ F	Tested	Prior 1940	Bone stag horn	Fish Scaler on back	425.00

BUDDING KNIFE
(LENGTH 3½ ″ CLOSED)

PATTERN	STAMPING	YEARS MADE	HANDLE	VARIATIONS	MINT PRICE
□1116 SP	XX	1960's-65	Walnut		35.00
□	USA	1965-70			30.00
□	10 Dots	1070-71			30.00
□	9 Dots	1971-72		Discontinued in Sept.	25.00

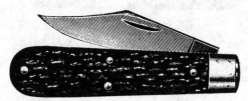

(LENGTH 3⅜″ CLOSED)

PATTERN	STAMPING	YEARS MADE	HANDLE	VARIATIONS	MINT PRICE
☐6116½	Tested	Prior 1950	Green Bone		90.00
☐6116 SP	Tested	Prior 1950	Green Bone		90.00

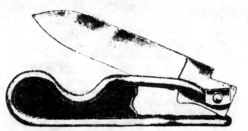

(LENGTH 3⅛" CLOSED)

PATTERN	STAMPING	YEARS MADE	HANDLE	VARIATIONS	MINT PRICE
☐W1216	Tested	Prior 1940	Wire	Backspring and handle are 1 piece	65.00
☐W1216 K	Tested	Prior 1940	Wire	Cap lifter in blade	65.00
☐W1216 Pr	Tested	Prior 1940	Wire	Pruner Blade	65.00

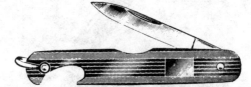

(LENGTH 3" CLOSED)

PATTERN	STAMPING	YEARS MADE	HANDLE	VARIATIONS	MINT PRICE
☐M1218K	Tested	Prior 1940	Metal		65.00

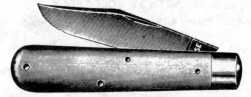

(LENGTH 3" CLOSED)

PATTERN	STAMPING	YEARS MADE	HANDLE	VARIATIONS	MINT PRICE
☐3124	Tested	Prior 1950	Yellow Comp.		65.00
☐6124	Tested	Prior 1950	Green Bone		110.00
☐61024	Tested	Prior 1950	Green Bone		125.00
☐31024	Tested	Prior 1950	Yellow Comp.		70.00
☐31024½	XX	1955-65	Yellow Comp.	(Also found in white lined yellow)	45.00
☐61024½	XX	1955-65	Bone		40.00
☐61024½	USA	1965-67	Bone		40.00

(LENGTH 3¹¹⁄₁₆″ CLOSED)

PATTERN	STAMPING	YEARS MADE	HANDLE	VARIATIONS	MINT PRICE
☐11031 SH	Tested	Prior 1950	Walnut		55.00
☐11031 SH CC	Tested	Prior 1950	Walnut	Blade Concave Grd.	70.00
☐11031 SH CC	XX	1950-52	Walnut	Blade Concave Grd.	60.00
☐11031 SH	XX	1950-65	Walnut		25.00
☐	USA	1965-70	Walnut		19.00
☐	10 Dots	1970-71	Walnut		22.00
☐	Dots	1970's	Walnut	Discontinued	13.00

BUDDING KNIFE
(LENGTH 4⅛″ CLOSED)

PATTERN	STAMPING	YEARS MADE	HANDLE	VARIATIONS	MINT PRICE
☐2136	Tested	Prior 1940	Black Composition	Not made in XX	55.00

SODBUSTER, JR.

PATTERN	STAMPING	YEARS MADE	HANDLE	VARIATIONS	MINT PRICE
☐2137 SS	10 Dots	1970-71	Black Composition		20.00
☐2137 SS	Dots	1970's			13.95
☐2137 SS	Lightning S. 10 Dots	1980			15.00
☐2137	10 Dots	1970-71			35.00
☐2137	Dots	1970's			13.50
☐2137	Lightning S. 10 Dots	1980			14.00
☐P13755		1970's	Pakkawood	Kentucky Bic	30.00
☐G13755		1970's	Green Delrin	Kentucky Bic	30.00
☐5137SS			Stag	Kentucky Bic	35.00
☐5137SS		1970's	Stag	Kentucky Bic	50.00

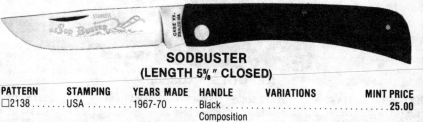

SODBUSTER
(LENGTH 5⅝″ CLOSED)

PATTERN	STAMPING	YEARS MADE	HANDLE	VARIATIONS	MINT PRICE
☐2138	USA	1967-70	Black Composition		25.00

☐2138	10 Dots	1970-71			**18.00**
☐2138	Lightning S. 10 Dots	1980			**15.00**
☐2138	Dots	1970's			**11.50**
☐2138 SS	10 Dots	1970-71			**18.00**
☐2138 SS	Lightning S. 10 Dots	1980			**14.00**
☐2138 SS	Dots	1970's			**15.50**
☐2138 SS L	10 Dots	1970-71		Blade locks open	**30.00**
☐2138 SS L	Dots	1970's		Blade locks open	**20.95**
☐2138L SS	Lightning S 10 Dots	1980			**20.00**
☐P138L SS	Dots	1970's		Alyeska	**110.00**

BANANA KNIFE
(LENGTH 4¼ " CLOSED)

PATTERN	STAMPING	YEARS MADE	HANDLE	VARIATIONS	MINT PRICE
☐1139	XX	1955-65	Walnut	Not made in USA stamping	110.00
☐1139	Tested XX	Prior 1940			125.00

The Case Founders knife is a 5143 in a special presentation box. The knife has a stainless steel blade etched with the likeness of Job Russell Case, W. R. Case, and J. Russell Case.

The knife has genuine stag handles. 5,000 knives were made and serial numbered with a C prefix, 5,000 with an "A" prefix, 5,000 with a "S" prefix, and 5,000 with an "E" prefix. Total run of 20,000 knives. The matching number sets of four are the rarest and go for $400. Suggested retail on the knife at time of release was $80. Current collector's value is $75.

(LENGTH 5″ CLOSED)

PATTERN	STAMPING	YEARS MADE	HANDLE	VARIATIONS	MINT PRICE
☐6143	Tested	Prior 1940	Brown Bone		175.00
☐6143	XX	1940's	Smooth Black	Iron liners	75.00

☐6143	XX	1940's	Green Bone	Iron liners	**100.00**
☐6143	XX	1950-65	Bone	Iron liners	**45.00**
☐6143	USA	1965-70	Bone	Iron liners	**25.00**
☐6143	10 Dots	1970-71	Bone	Iron liners	**30.00**
☐6143	Dots	1970's	Bone	Iron liners	**18.00**
☐6143	Dots	1970's	Delrin	Brass liners	**11.00**
☐6143	Lightning S. 10 Dots	1980	Delrin	Brass liner	**12.00**

(LENGTH 4⅛" CLOSED)

PATTERN	STAMPING	YEARS MADE	HANDLE	VARIATIONS	MINT PRICE
☐31048 SHR	XX	1950's-65	Yellow Composition	"Florists Knife"	**50.00**
☐31048	XX	1950's-65			**18.00**
☐	USA	1965-70			**22.00**
☐	10 Dots	1970-71			**22.00**
☐	Dots	1970's			**10.00**
☐	Lightning S. 10 Dots	1980			**10.00**
☐31048SP	XX	1958-65			**22.00**
☐	USA	1965-70			**21.00**
☐	10 Dots	1970-71			**22.00**
☐	Dot	1971-Oct. 1972		Discontinued	**15.00**
☐B1048	Tested	Prior 1940	Imitation Onyx		**110.00**
☐61048	Tested	Prior 1940	Green Bone		**125.00**
☐	XX	1940-55	Green Bone		**110.00**
☐	XX	1950-65	Red Bone		**45.00**
☐	XX	1950-65	Bone		**25.00**
☐	USA	1965-70	Bone		**22.00**
☐	USA	1965-70	Delrin		**16.00**
☐	10 Dots	1970-71	Delrin		**16.00**
☐	Dots	1970's	Delrin		**10.00**
☐	Lightning S. 10 Dots	1980			**10.00**
☐61048 SP	XX	1957-63	Bone		**30.00**
☐61048 SP	XX	1963-65	Delrin		**20.00**
☐61048 SP	USA	1965-70	Bone		**35.00**
☐61048 SP	USA	1965-70	Delrin		**18.00**
☐61048 SP	10 Dots	1970-71	Delrin	Discontinued	**19.00**
☐61048 SSP	USA	1966-69	Bone	Blade marked "Tested XX Stainless"	**35.00**
☐61048 SSP	USA	1966-69	Bone		**25.00**
☐61048 SSP	USA	1965-70	Bone	Blade polished	**35.00**
☐61048 SSP	10 Dots	1970-71	Delrin		**17.00**
☐61048 SSP	Dots	1970's	Delrin		**11.50**

(LENGTH 4¹/₁₆" CLOSED)

PATTERN	STAMPING	YEARS MADE	HANDLE	VARIATIONS	MINT PRICE
☐61049	Tested	Prior 1940	Green Bone		**140.00**

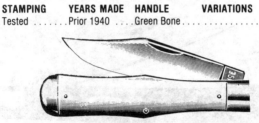

(LENGTH 5¹/₈" CLOSED)

PATTERN	STAMPING	YEARS MADE	HANDLE	VARIATIONS	MINT PRICE
☐310050	Tested	Prior 1940	Cream Composition		**300.00**
☐610050	Tested	Prior 1940	Green Bone Stag		**425.00**

(LENGTH 5³/₈" CLOSED)

PATTERN	STAMPING	YEARS MADE	HANDLE	VARIATIONS	MINT PRICE
☐C51050 SAB	Tested	Prior 1940	Genuine Stag		**600.00**
☐C61050 SAB	Tested	Prior 1950	Green Bone		**375.00**
☐C61050 SAB	Tested	Prior 1950	Red Bone		**325.00**
☐C61050 SAB	XX	1940's	Green Bone		**325.00**
☐C61050 SAB	XX	1950-65	Red Bone		**175.00**
☐C61050 SAB	XX	1950-65	Bone		**130.00**
☐C61050 SAB	XX	1964-65	Laminated Wood		**70.00**
☐C61050 SAB	USA	1965-70	Laminated Wood		**40.00**
☐C61050 SAB	10 Dots	1970-71	Laminated Wood		**35.00**
☐C61050 SAB	Dots	1970's	Laminated Wood	Discontinued	**30.00**

(LENGTH 5½″ CLOSED)

PATTERN	STAMPING	YEARS MADE	HANDLE	VARIATIONS	MINT PRICE
☐C61050 L	Tested	Prior 1940	Green Bone		1,400.00

(LENGTH 5⅜″ CLOSED)

PATTERN	STAMPING	YEARS MADE	HANDLE	VARIATIONS	MINT PRICE
☐61050	Tested	Prior 1950	Green Bone		425.00

(LENGTH 5⅜″ CLOSED)

PATTERN	STAMPING	YEARS MADE	HANDLE	VARIATIONS	MINT PRICE
☐PBB1050	Tested	Prior 1940	Imitation Onyx		225.00
☐PB31050 F	Tested	Prior 1940	Cream Composition	Fish scaler on back of blade	190.00

(LENGTH 5¼″ CLOSED)

PATTERN	STAMPING	YEARS MADE	HANDLE	VARIATIONS	MINT PRICE
☐6151	Tested	Prior 1940	Green Bone		425.00
☐6151 L	Tested	Prior 1940	Green Bone		500.00
☐9151	Tested	Prior 1940	Imitation Pearl		300.00

(LENGTH 3⅞" CLOSED)

PATTERN	STAMPING	YEARS MADE	HANDLE	VARIATIONS	MINT PRICE
☐61051	Tested	Prior 1950	Green Bone		185.00

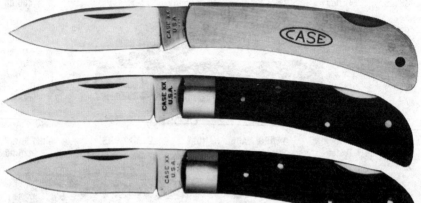

PATTERN	STAMPING	YEARS MADE	HANDLE	VARIATIONS	MINT PRICE
☐M1051L	4 Dots		Metal		17.00
☐21051L	4 Dots		Black Composition		18.00
☐61051L	4 Dots		Jigged Laminated Wood		18.00

☐All 3 made in Lightning S 10 Dots

MAKO

PATTERN	STAMPING	YEARS MADE	HANDLE	VARIATIONS	MINT PRICE
☐P158LSSP	3 Dots	1977	Black Pakkawood		30.00
☐5158LSSP	1 Dot	1979	Stag		95.00
☐P158LSSP	Lightning S 10 Dots	1980			30.00
☐5158LSSP	Lightning S 10 Dots	1980	Stag		65.00

HAMMERHEAD

PATTERN	STAMPING	YEARS MADE	HANDLE	VARIATIONS	MINT PRICE
☐P159LSSP	3 Dots	1977	Black Pakkawood		35.00
☐P159LSSP	Lightning S. 3 Dots	1977	Black Pakkawood		35.00
☐5159LSSP	1 Dot	1979	Stag		95.00
☐5159LSSP	Lightning S 1 Dot	1979	Stag		70.00

SWITCHBLADE
(LENGTH 4⅜" CLOSED)

PATTERN	STAMPING	YEARS MADE	HANDLE	VARIATIONS	MINT PRICE
☐5161 L	Tested	Prior 1940	Stag	4⅜"	550.00
☐6161L	Tested	Prior 1940	Green Bone		550.00

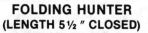

FOLDING HUNTER
(LENGTH 5½" CLOSED)

PATTERN	STAMPING	YEARS MADE	HANDLE	VARIATIONS	MINT PRICE
☐Moby Dick	1978	White Bone			200.00
☐Bicentennial	1976	Stag			200.00
☐Nantucket Sleigh Ride	1980	White Bone	not yet released		200.00
☐3165	Tested	Prior 1940	Yellow Composition		225.00
☐5165	Tested	Prior 1940	Stag		450.00

☐ 6165	Tested		Green Bone		**400.00**
☐ 9165	Tested		Imitation Pearl		**275.00**
☐ 5165	XX	1940's	Stag	Flat Ground Blade	**350.00**
☐ 5165 SAB	XX	1950-65	Stag	Bolster Drilled	**175.00**
☐ 5165 SAB	XX	1964-65	Stag	Bolster Not Drilled	**175.00**
☐ 5165 SAB	USA	1965-66	Stag	Small pattern #	**290.00**
☐ 5165 SAB	USA	1965-66	Stag	Big pattern #	**290.00**
☐ 6165	XX	1940's-55	Green Bone	Flat Ground Master Blade	**325.00**
☐ 6165SAB	XX	1940-55	Green Bone		**275.00**
☐ 6165SAB	XX	1940's	Rough Black		**175.00**
☐ 6165SAB	XX	1950-60	Red Bone		**175.00**
☐ 6165	XX	1940's	Bone	Flat Ground Master Blade	**225.00**
☐ 6165SAB	USA		Bone		**150.00**
☐ 6165SAB	XX	1950-65	Bone		**135.00**
☐ 6165SAB	XX	1964-65	Laminated Wood		**70.00**
☐ 6165SAB	USA	1965-66	Laminated Wood	XX Frame Bolster Not Drilled	**85.00**
☐	USA	1965-66	Laminated Wood	XX Frame	**65.00**
☐	USA	1965-70	Laminated Wood		**32.00**
☐	10 Dots	1970-71	Laminated Wood		**25.00**
☐	Dots	1970's	Laminated Wood		**17.50**
☐	Lightning S. 10 Dots				**20.00**

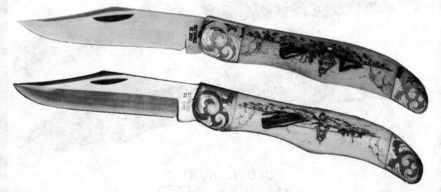

(LENGTH 5½ ")

PATTERN	STAMPING	YEARS MADE	HANDLE	VARIATIONS	MINT PRICE
☐ 6165LSSP	2 Dots	1978	Laminated Wood		27.00
☐ 6165LSSP	Lightning S 2 Dots	1978	Laminated Wood		27.00

SWITCHBLADE
(LENGTH 5½ ")

PATTERN	STAMPING	YEARS MADE	HANDLE	VARIATIONS	MINT PRICE
☐5171 L	Tested	Prior 1940	Stag	5⅜"	700.00
☐6171 L	Tested	Prior 1940	Green Bone		700.00

BULLDOG OR CLASP KNIFE
(LENGTH 5½ " CLOSED)

PATTERN	STAMPING	YEARS MADE	HANDLE	VARIATIONS	MINT PRICE
☐5172	Tested	Prior 1940	Stag		1,400.00
☐7172	Tested	Prior 1940	Imitation Tortoise Shell		800.00
☐3172	Tested	Prior 1940	Yellow Comp.	(Most of the tested knives won't have	600.00
☐6172	Tested	Prior 1940	Green Bone	the box, but XX and later are price as complete with box.	1,100.00
☐5172	XX	1950's	Stag	No Handmade in USA on Blade	300.00
☐5172	XX	1957-65	Stag	"Handmade in U.S.A." stamped on tang.)	250.00
☐5172	USA	1965-70	Stag		150.00
☐5172	Transition	1964-65	Stag		200.00
☐5172	4 Dots	1978	Stag	Part of 1978 Set	75.00
☐5172	3 Dots	1979	Stag	Blue Scroll	70.00

A transition bulldog is identifiable because it has the stamping and pattern number on the same side of the blade.

BUFFALO
(LENGTH 5½ " CLOSED)

PATTERN	STAMPING	YEARS MADE	HANDLE	VARIATIONS	MINT PRICE
☐P172	USA	1969-70	Pakkawood		50.00
☐	9 Dots	1971-72	Pakkawood	There were no 10 dot Buffalos	35.00
☐	Dots	1970's			35.00
☐	Lightning S. 10 Dots				35.00

DOCTOR'S KNIFE
(LENGTH 3⅝" CLOSED)

This knife is so called because the blunt end was used by doctors years ago to crush pills in order to mix medicines. It is common to find this knife with and without a shield.

PATTERN	STAMPING	YEARS MADE	HANDLE	VARIATIONS	MINT PRICE
☐3185	Tested	Prior 1949	Yellow Composition		90.00
☐	XX	1950-65	Yellow Composition		45.00
☐	USA	1965-70	Yellow Composition		35.00
☐	10 Dots	1970-71	Yellow Composition		35.00
☐	Dots	1971-1975	Yellow Composition	Discontinued	30.00
☐	Tested	Prior 1949	Green Bone		140.00
☐6185	Tested	Prior 1949	Red Bone		125.00
☐	XX	1950-65	Red Bone		65.00
☐	XX	1950-65	Bone		55.00
☐	USA	1965-70	Bone		40.00
☐	10 Dots	1970-71	Bone		35.00
☐	Dots	1971-1976	Bone	Discontinued	30.00
☐	Dots	1971-1976	Delrin	Discontinued	22.00

TEXAS TOOTHPICK
(LENGTH 5" CLOSED)

PATTERN	STAMPING	YEARS MADE	HANDLE	VARIATIONS	MINT PRICE
☐61093	Tested	Prior 1940	Green Bone		225.00
☐R1093	Tested	Prior 1940	Candy Stripe Celluloid		185.00
☐61093	XX	1940's	Green Bone		175.00
☐	XX	1949-53	Red Bone		65.00
☐	XX	1949-65	Bone		75.00
☐31093	XX	1960-65	Yellow Composition		65.00
☐61093	USA	1965-70	Bone		65.00
☐61093	10 Dots	1970-71	Bone		60.00
☐61093	Dots	1970-75	Bone	Discontinued	50.00
☐	Dots	1973-75	Delrin	Discontinued	35.00
☐61093	7 Dots		Bone		35.00

Please examine any 7 Dot 61093 very closely as they are questionable.

PATTERN	STAMPING	YEARS MADE	HANDLE	VARIATIONS	MINT PRICE
☐4100 SS	USA	1965	White Composition	Serrated blade	90.00

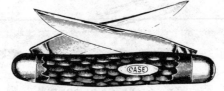

MUSKRAT
(LENGTH 3⅞" CLOSED)

PATTERN	STAMPING	YEARS MADE	HANDLE	VARIATIONS	MINT PRICE
☐Muskrat	Tested	Prior 1940	Green Bone		500.00
☐	XX	1940's	Green Bone		300.00
☐	XX	1940's	Rough Black		150.00
☐	XX	1950's-65	Red Bone		85.00
☐	XX	1950's-65	Bone		60.00
☐	USA	1965-70	Bone		40.00
☐	10 Dots	1970-71	Bone		35.00
☐	Dots	1970's	Bone		20.00
☐	2 Dots	1979	Stag	Collector's Set	40.00
☐	Lightning S 10 Dots		Bone		20.00

MUSKRAT HAWBAKER SPECIAL
(LENGTH 3⅞")

PATTERN	STAMPING	YEARS MADE	HANDLE	VARIATIONS	MINT PRICE
☐	XX	1950-60's	Bone		150.00
☐	USA	1965-70	Bone		90.00
☐	10 Dots	1970-71	Bone		60.00
☐	Dots	1970	Bone		50.00
☐	Dots	1970-73	Delrin		20.00
☐	2 to 3 Dots	1978	Bone	1,000 made in 1978	40.00

CITRUS, MELON TESTER
(LENGTH 5½ " CLOSED)

PATTERN	STAMPING	YEARS MADE	HANDLE	VARIATIONS	MINT PRICE
☐4200 SS	XX	1964-65	White Composition		125.00
☐	USA	1965-70	White Composition		70.00
☐	10 Dots	1970-71	White Composition		60.00
☐	Dots	1971-73	White Composition		50.00

CITRUS, MELON TESTER
CONTRACT KNIFE, MADE AS A PROTOTYPE AND ISSUED
ONLY TO CASE SALEMAN'S SAMPLES
(LENGTH 5½ " CLOSED)

PATTERN	STAMPING	YEARS MADE	HANDLE	VARIATIONS	MINT PRICE
☐4200 SS	USA	Approx. 65	White Composition	Serrated blades	125.00

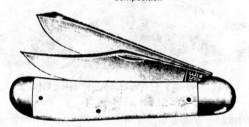

(LENGTH 3¹⁵⁄₁₆ " CLOSED)

PATTERN	STAMPING	YEARS MADE	HANDLE	VARIATIONS	MINT PRICE
☐9200	Tested	Prior 1940	Imitation Pearl		250.00
☐6200	Tested	Prior 1940	Greenbone		350.00

(LENGTH 4⅝ " CLOSED)

PATTERN	STAMPING	YEARS MADE	HANDLE	VARIATIONS	MINT PRICE
☐62100	Tested	Prior 1940	Green Bone		550.00

(LENGTH 2⅝″ CLOSED)

PATTERN	STAMPING	YEARS MADE	HANDLE	VARIATIONS	MINT PRICE
☐3201	Tested	Prior 1950	Yellow Composition		45.00
☐	XX	1950-65	Yellow Composition		25.00
☐	USA	1965-70	Yellow Composition		18.00
☐	10 Dots	1970-71	Yellow Composition		20.00
☐	Dots	1971-75	Yellow Composition	Discontinued	15.00
☐6201	Tested	Prior 1950	Green Bone		75.00
☐	XX	1964-65	Bone		35.00
☐	USA	1965-70	Bone		25.00
☐	10 Dots	1970-71	Bone		25.00
☐	Dots	1970's	Bone		20.00
☐		1970's	Delrin	Discontinued	12.00
☐9201	Tested	Prior 1950	Cracked Ice		50.00
☐	XX	1950-65	Imitation Pearl		25.00
☐	XX	1950-65	Cracked Ice		24.00
☐9201 R	XX	1950-65	Imitation Pearl	Bail in Handle	35.00
☐9201 R	XX	1950-65	Cracked Ice	Bail in Handle	35.00
☐9201	USA	1965-70	Imitation Pearl		15.00
☐9201	10 Dots	1970-71	Imitation Pearl		20.00
☐9201	Dots	1970-75	Imitation Pearl	Discontinued	14.00

(LENGTH 2⅝″ CLOSED)

PATTERN	STAMPING	YEARS MADE	HANDLE	VARIATIONS	MINT PRICE
☐22001 R	Tested	Prior 1940	Black Composition		50.00
☐62001	Tested	Prior 1940	Green Bone		80.00
☐82001	Tested	Prior 1940	Pearl		100.00
☐82001 R	Tested	Prior 1940	Pearl		100.00

(LENGTH 2¼ ″ CLOSED)

PATTERN	STAMPING	YEARS MADE	HANDLE	VARIATIONS	MINT PRICE
☐S2	XX	1963-65	Sterling Silver	Long Pull	100.00
☐	XX	1963-65	Sterling Silver		100.00
☐	USA	1965-68	Sterling Silver		90.00

(LENGTH 2¼ ″ CLOSED)

PATTERN	STAMPING	YEARS MADE	HANDLE	VARIATIONS	MINT PRICE
☐82101 R	Tested	Prior 1940	Pearl		100.00
☐92101 R	Tested	Prior 1940	Imitation Pearl		50.00

(LENGTH 3⅜ ″ CLOSED)

PATTERN	STAMPING	YEARS MADE	HANDLE	VARIATIONS	MINT PRICE
☐1202 D&B	Tested	Prior 1940	Cocobola		325.00

(LENGTH 3⅜ ″ CLOSED)

PATTERN	STAMPING	YEARS MADE	HANDLE	VARIATIONS	MINT PRICE
☐5202 RAZ	Tested	Prior 1940	Stag		250.00
☐5202½	Tested	Prior 1940	Stag		200.00
☐6202	Tested	Prior 1940	Green Bone		125.00
☐6202½	Tested	Prior 1940	Green Bone		125.00
☐6202½	XX	1940-65	Green Bone		70.00
☐2202½	XX	1940's	Black Composition		75.00
☐6202½	XX	1940-55	Bone		35.00
☐6202½	USA	1965-70	Bone		22.00

☐6202½	10 Dots	1970-71	Bone		**20.00**
☐6202½	10 Dots	1970-71	Delrin		**16.00**
☐6202½	Dots	1970's	Delrin	Discontinued	**9.00**

(LENGTH 1¾″ CLOSED)

PATTERN	STAMPING	YEARS MADE	HANDLE	VARIATIONS	MINT PRICE
☐82103	Tested	Prior 1940	Pearl		**100.00**
☐82103 R	Tested	Prior 1940	Pearl		**100.00**

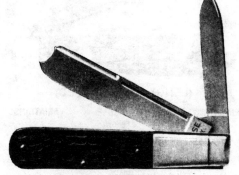

(LENGTH 3¾″ CLOSED)

PATTERN	STAMPING	YEARS MADE	HANDLE	VARIATIONS	MINT PRICE
☐6205	Tested	Prior 1950	Green Bone		**275.00**
☐5205	Tested	Prior 1950	Stag		**300.00**
☐6205½	Tested	Prior 1950	Green Bone		**275.00**
☐5205½	Tested	Prior 1950	Stag		**300.00**
☐6205 RAZ	Tested	Prior 1950	Green Bone		**275.00**
☐6205	XX	1950's	Green Bone		**125.00**
☐6205	XX	1950's	Bone		**80.00**
☐6205 RAZ	XX	1950's	Green Bone		**150.00**
☐6205 RAZ	XX	1950-65	Bone		**80.00**
☐6205 RAZ	USA	1965-70	Bone		**60.00**
☐6205 RAZ	10 Dots	1970-71	Bone		**50.00**
☐6205 RAZ	Dots	1970's	Bone		**45.00**
☐6205 RAZ	Dots	1970's	Delrin	Discontinued	**30.00**

(LENGTH 2⅝" CLOSED)

PATTERN	STAMPING	YEARS MADE	HANDLE	VARIATIONS	MINT PRICE
☐ 5206½	Tested	Prior 1940	Stag		130.00
☐ 6206½	Tested	Prior 1940	Green Bone		90.00
☐ 6206½	Tested	1940's	Rough Black		65.00
☐ 6206½	XX	Early 1950's	Rough Black		75.00

(LENGTH 3½" CLOSED)

PATTERN	STAMPING	YEARS MADE	HANDLE	VARIATIONS	MINT PRICE
☐ 3207	Tested	Prior 1940	Yellow Composition		100.00
☐ 5207	Tested	Prior 1940	Stag		165.00
☐ 6207	Tested	Prior 1940	Green Bone		140.00
☐ 2207	XX	1940's	Black Composition		110.00
☐ 6207	XX	1940's	Green Bone		120.00
☐	XX	1940's	Rough Black		70.00
☐	XX	1940-55	Red Bone		55.00
☐	XX	1950-65	Bone		35.00
☐	USA	1965-70	Bone		30.00
☐	10 Dots	1970-71	Bone		25.00
☐	Dots	1970's	Bone	Discontinued	20.00
☐	Dots	1970's	Delrin	Discontinued	14.00
☐ 6207SSP	Lightning S 10 Dot	1980	Bone	Mini Trapper	21.50

HALF WHITTLER
(LENGTH 3¼" CLOSED)

PATTERN	STAMPING	YEARS MADE	HANDLE	VARIATIONS	MINT PRICE
☐5208	Tested	Prior 1940	Stag		**140.00**
☐6208	Tested	Prior 1940	Green Bone		**85.00**
☐6208	XX	1950-53	Green Bone		**65.00**
☐	XX	1950-55	Rough Black		**45.00**
☐	XX	1950-65	Bone		**25.00**
☐	USA	1965-70	Bone		**19.00**
☐	10 Dots	1970-71	Bone		**20.00**
☐	Dots	1970-79	Bone	Discontinued	**15.00**
☐	Dots	1970-79	Delrin	Discontinued	**12.00**
☐A6208	1 Dot	1979	Bone		**20.00**
☐A6208	Lightning S 10 Dots	1980	Bone		**15.00**

BABY COPPERHEAD
(LENGTH 3⅛" CLOSED)

PATTERN	STAMPING	YEARS MADE	HANDLE	VARIATIONS	MINT PRICE
☐62109X	XX	1940-51	Rough Black		**60.00**
☐	XX	1940-55	Green Bone		**90.00**
☐	XX	1950-65	Bone		**40.00**
☐	USA	1965-70	Bone		**30.00**
☐	10 Dots	1970	Bone		**25.00**
☐	Dots	1971	Bone		**15.00**
☐	Dots		Delrin		**10.00**
☐	Lightning S 10 Dots	1980	Bone		**15.00**

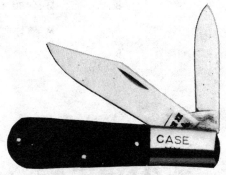

BARLOW
(LENGTH 3⁹⁄₁₆" CLOSED)

PATTERN	STAMPING	YEARS MADE	HANDLE	VARIATIONS	MINT PRICE
☐62009 SH	Tested	Prior 1940	Brown Bone		**120.00**
☐62009 SH	XX	1940-45	Black Composition	3⁹⁄₁₆ in.	**90.00**
☐62009 SP	Tested	Prior 1940	Brown Bone		**120.00**
☐62009	Tested	Prior 1940	Brown Bone		**120.00**

Pattern	Stamping	Years Made	Handle	Variations	Mint Price
☐62009	XX	1940-45	Black Composition	3⁵⁄₁₆ in.	90.00
☐62009	XX	Early 1950's	Green Bone		90.00
☐	XX	1940-65	Red Bone		40.00
☐	XX	1940-65	Bone		35.00
☐	USA	1965-70	Bone	Master Blade in Front	23.00
☐	USA	1965-70	Bone	Master Blade in Back	23.00
☐	10 Dots	1970-71	Bone		25.00
☐	10 Dots	1970-71	Delrin		15.00
☐	Dots	1970-76	Delrin	Discontinued	10.00
☐62009½	Tested	Prior 1940	Green Bone		105.00
☐	XX	1940's	Black Composition	3⁵⁄₁₆ in.	90.00
☐	XX	1950-55	Green Bone		90.00
☐	XX	1945-55	Red Bone		40.00
☐	XX	1950-65	Bone		30.00
☐	USA	1965-70	Bone	Master Blade in Front	20.00
☐	USA	1965-70	Bone	Master Blade in Back	20.00
☐	10 Dots	1970-71	Bone		25.00
☐	5 Dots		Bone		30.00
☐	10 Dots	1970-71	Delrin	62009½	13.00
☐	Dots	1970's	Delrin		8.00
☐A62009½	1 Dot	1979	Slick Bone		20.00
☐A62009½	Lightning S 10 Dots		Slick Bone		18.00
☐62009 RAZ	Tested	Prior 1940	Green Bone		130.00
☐	XX	1940-55	Green Bone		100.00
☐	XX	1955-65	Bone	Long Pull	60.00
☐	XX	1955-65	Bone		45.00
☐	USA	1965-70	Bone	Master Blade in Front	35.00
☐	USA	1965-70	Bone	Master Blade in Back	35.00
☐	10 Dots	1970-71	Bone		35.00
☐	10 Dots	1970-71	Delrin		20.00
☐	Dots	1970's	Delrin	Discontinued	9.00

SWITCHBLADE
(LENGTH 3⅜" CLOSED)

PATTERN	STAMPING	YEARS MADE	HANDLE	VARIATIONS	MINT PRICE
☐62210	Tested	Prior 1940	Green Bone		180.00
☐92210	Tested	Prior 1940	Imitation Pearl		150.00

☐H2210	Tested	Prior 1940	Mottled Brown and Cream Composition		**150.00**
☐T2210	Tested	Prior 1940	Tortoise Shell Composition		**150.00**

(LENGTH 3⅛" CLOSED)

PATTERN	STAMPING	YEARS MADE	HANDLE	VARIATIONS	MINT PRICE
☐5210½	Tested	Prior 1940	Stag		**150.00**
☐6210½	Tested	Prior 1940	Green Bone		**150.00**

(LENGTH 4⅜" CLOSED)

PATTERN	STAMPING	YEARS MADE	HANDLE	VARIATIONS	MINT PRICE
☐6211	Tested	Prior 1940	Green Bone		**400.00**
☐6211½	Tested	Prior 1940	Green Bone		**400.00**

ELECTRICIAN'S KNIFE
(LENGTH 3⅝" CLOSED)

PATTERN	STAMPING	YEARS MADE	HANDLE	VARIATIONS	MINT PRICE
☐2212 L	Tested	Prior 1940	Walnut		**70.00**

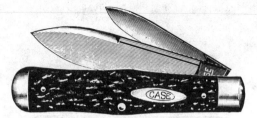

(LENGTH 4″ CLOSED)

PATTERN	STAMPING	YEARS MADE	HANDLE	VARIATIONS	MINT PRICE
☐6213	Tested	Prior 1940	Green Bone		350.00

(LENGTH 3⅜″ CLOSED)

PATTERN	STAMPING	YEARS MADE	HANDLE	VARIATIONS	MINT PRICE
☐6214	Tested	Prior 1940	Green Bone		120.00
☐6214	XX	1940-55	Green Bone		105.00
☐	XX	1940's	Rough Black	With Shield	45.00
☐	XX	1040's	Rough Black	Without Shield	40.00
☐	XX	1950-65	Bone		40.00
☐	USA	1965-70	Bone		35.00
☐	10 Dots	1970-71	Bone	Bone discontinued in '71	35.00
☐	10 Dots	1970-71	Delrin		15.00
☐	Dots	1970's	Delrin	Discontinued	11.00
☐5214½	Tested	Prior 1940	Stag		150.00
☐6214½	Tested	Prior 1940	Green Bone		120.00
☐	XX	1940-55	Green Bone		85.00
☐	XX	1940's	Rough Black		40.00
☐	XX	1955-65	Bone		35.00
☐	USA	1965-70	Bone		25.00
☐	10 Dots	1970-71	Bone		30.00
☐	10 Dots	1970-71	Delrin		20.00
☐	Dots	1970's	Delrin	Discontinued	12.00

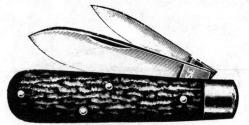

(LENGTH 3⅜" CLOSED)

PATTERN	STAMPING	YEARS MADE	HANDLE	VARIATIONS	MINT PRICE
☐6216	Tested	Prior 1950	Green Bone		110.00
☐6216	XX	1964-65	Bone		50.00
☐6216½	Tested	Prior 1950	Green Bone		110.00
☐6216½	XX	1964-65	Bone		40.00
☐6216½	USA	1965-67	Bone		35.00

(LENGTH 4" CLOSED)

PATTERN	STAMPING	YEARS MADE	HANDLE	VARIATIONS	MINT PRICE
☐2217	Tested	Prior 1940	Black Composition		130.00
☐6217	Tested	Prior 1940	Green Bone		190.00
☐2217	XX	1940's	Black Composition		125.00
☐6217	XX	1940-55	Green Bone		135.00
☐	XX	1950-65	Red Bone		75.00
☐	XX	1950-55	Bone		45.00
☐	USA	1965-70	Bone		35.00
☐	10 Dots	1970-71	Laminated Wood	(Wood Introduced in 1971)	30.00
☐	10 Dots	1970-71	Bone		45.00
☐	Dots	1970's	Laminated Wood	Discontinued	18.00

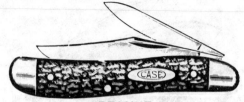

PEANUT
(LENGTH 2¾ " CLOSED)

PATTERN	STAMPING	YEARS MADE	HANDLE	VARIATIONS	MINT PRICE
2220	Tested	Prior 1950	Black Composition		90.00
	XX	1950-65	Black Composition		45.00
	USA	1965-70	Black Composition		24.00
	10 Dots	1970-71	Black Composition		25.00
	Dots	1970-75	Black Composition	Discontinued	20.00
3220	Tested	Prior 1950	Yellow Composition		90.00
	XX	1950-65	Yellow Composition		45.00
	USA	1965-70	Yellow Composition		25.00
	10 Dots	1970-71	Yellow Composition		25.00
	Dots	1971-75	Yellow	Discontinued	20.00
5220	Tested	Prior 1950	Stag		150.00
	XX	1950-65	Stag		75.00
	USA	1965-70	Stag		60.00
	10 Dots	1970-71	Stag	Discontinued	50.00
	2 Dots	1979	Red Scroll		35.00
6220	Tested	Prior 1950	Green Bone	LP, Saber Ground	200.00
	XX	1950-65	Green Bone		150.00
	XX	1940's	Rough Black		85.00
	XX	1950-65	Red Bone		75.00
	XX	1950-65	Bone		55.00
	USA	1965-70	Bone		35.00
	10 Dots	1970-71	Bone		35.00
	10 Dots	1970-71	Delrin		25.00
	9 Dots	1971-72	Bone	Limited # in bone	30.00
	Dots	1970's	Delrin	Discontinued	15.00
A6620	Dots	1979	Bone Appaloosa''		35.00
SR6220	1 Dot	1979	Red Bone ''Slick Bone''		30.00
SR6220	Lightning S. 10 Dots				20.00
8220	Tested	Prior 1950	Pearl		150.00
9220	Tested	Prior 1950	Imitation Pearl		90.00
	XX	1950-65	Cracked Ice		85.00
	XX	1950-65	Imitation Pearl		85.00

(LENGTH 4⅛" CLOSED)

PATTERN	STAMPING	YEARS MADE	HANDLE	VARIATIONS	MINT PRICE
☐62019	Tested	Prior 1940	Green Bone		325.00

(LENGTH 3¼" CLOSED)

PATTERN	STAMPING	YEARS MADE	HANDLE	VARIATIONS	MINT PRICE
☐0221½	Tested	Prior 1940	Black Composition		120.00
☐06221½	Tested	Prior 1940	Green Bone		190.00

(LENGTH 3" CLOSED)

PATTERN	STAMPING	YEARS MADE	HANDLE	VARIATIONS	MINT PRICE
☐220024 SP	XX	1959-60	Black Composition		1,000.00

This is an extremely rare knife. In fact, there are only five known specimens in the original wood block. The price quoted for the above knife is with the original wood block.

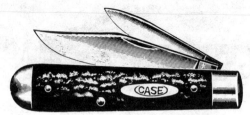

(LENGTH 3″ CLOSED)

PATTERN	STAMPING	YEARS MADE	HANDLE	VARIATIONS	MINT PRICE
☐2224SH	Tested	Prior 1940	Black Composition		90.00
☐2224RAZ	Tested	Prior 1940	Black Composition		110.00
☐2224SP	XX	1940's	Black Composition		130.00
☐2224SH	XX	1940's	Black Composition		130.00
☐2224RAZ	XX	1940's	Black Composition		130.00
☐3224	Tested	Prior 1940	Yellow Composition		65.00
☐3224½	Tested	Prior 1940	Yellow Composition		60.00
☐5224½	Tested	Prior 1940	Stag		140.00
☐32024½	XX	1957-65	Yellow Composition		30.00
☐32024½	USA	1965-68	Yellow Composition		35.00
☐52024½	Tested	Prior 1940	Stag		135.00
☐62024	Tested	Prior 1940	Green Bone		100.00
☐62024 RAZ	Tested	Prior 1940	Green Bone		95.00
☐62024½	Tested	Prior 1940	Green Bone		85.00
☐62024½	XX	1940-55	Green Bone		45.00
☐62024½	XX	1955-65	Bone		35.00
☐62024½	USA	1965-68	Bone		30.00

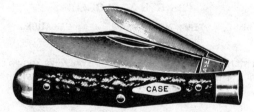

COKE BOTTLE
(LENGTH 3″ CLOSED)

PATTERN	STAMPING	YEARS MADE	HANDLE	VARIATIONS	MINT PRICE
☐5225½	Tested	Prior 1940	Stag		200.00
☐6225½	Tested	Prior 1940	Green Bone		160.00
☐6225½	XX	1940-55	Green Bone		125.00

☐6225½	XX	1942-50	Rough Black		**65.00**
☐6225½	XX	1950-65	Bone		**45.00**
☐6225½	USA	1965-70	Bone		**35.00**
☐6225½	10 Dots	1970-71	Bone		**30.00**
☐6225½	Dots	1970's	Bone	Discontinued	**20.00**
☐6225½	Dots	1970's	Delrin	Discontinued	**15.00**
☐SR6225½	1 Dot	1979	S. Bone		**25.00**
☐SR6225½	Lightning S. 10 Dots	1980	S. Bone		**20.00**
☐32025½	Tested	Prior 1940	Yellow Composition	No bolster on 1 end	**70.00**
☐62025½	Tested	Prior 1940	Green Bone	No bolster on 1 end	**175.00**

The Case 2226½. Similar to the 6225½. Case one dot. Dots 1979. Special edition of 5,000 honoring the 75th anniversary of Coca-Cola, featured a coffin shaped bolster that enabled the knife to sit up like a coke bottle.

A Coke bottle is etched on both sides of the knife and the Coke emblem of "1 of 5,000" is etched on the master blade. Collector's value $75.

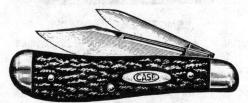

(LENGTH 3″ CLOSED)

PATTERN	STAMPING	YEARS MADE	HANDLE	VARIATIONS	MINT PRICE
☐6226½	Tested	Prior 1940	Green Bone		**150.00**

(LENGTH 2¾″ CLOSED)

PATTERN	STAMPING	YEARS MADE	HANDLE	VARIATIONS	MINT PRICE
☐6227	XX	1955-65	Bone		**30.00**
☐	USA	1965-70	Bone		**20.00**
☐	10 Dots	1970-71	Bone		**20.00**
☐	10 Dots	1970-71	Delrin		**12.00**
☐	Dots	1970's	Delrin		**9.00**
☐62027	Dots	1978-79	Delrin		**10.00**
☐SR62027	1 Dot	1979	Red Bone		**20.00**
☐SR62027	Lightning S. 10 Dots				**15.00**

(LENGTH 2¾″ CLOSED)

PATTERN	STAMPING	YEARS MADE	HANDLE	VARIATIONS	MINT PRICE
☐62027	Tested	Prior 1950	Green Bone		**100.00**
☐62027½	Tested	Prior 1950	Green Bone		**90.00**
☐62027½	XX	1960-65	Bone		**45.00**
☐92027	Tested	Prior 1950	Imitation Pearl		**60.00**
☐92027½	Tested	Prior 1950	Imitation Pearl		**60.00**
☐92027½	XX	1950	Cracked Ice		**65.00**

(LENGTH 3½″ CLOSED)

PATTERN	STAMPING	YEARS MADE	HANDLE	VARIATIONS	MINT PRICE
☐6228EO	Tested	Prior 1950	Green Bone		**200.00**
☐2228EO	Tested	Prior 1950	Black Composition		**130.00**
☐6228EO	XX	Early 1950	Red Bone		**160.00**

(LENGTH 3½″ CLOSED)

PATTERN	STAMPING	YEARS MADE	HANDLE	VARIATIONS	MINT PRICE
☐22028	Tested	Prior 1940	Black Composition		**95.00**
☐62028	Tested	Prior 1940	Green Bone		**175.00**
☐62028½	Tested	Prior 1940	Green Bone		**140.00**
☐22028½	XX	1950-65	Black Composition		**80.00**
☐62028½	XX	1940's	Rough Black		**85.00**

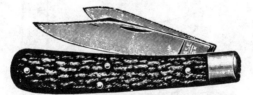

(LENGTH 2½″ CLOSED)

PATTERN	STAMPING	YEARS MADE	HANDLE	VARIATIONS	MINT PRICE
☐6229½	Tested	Prior 1940	Green Bone		**100.00**
☐9229½	Tested	Prior 1940	Imitation Pearl		**85.00**
☐9229½	XX	1940-55	Imitation Pearl		**70.00**
☐2229½	XX	1958-65	Black Composition		**55.00**
☐6229½	XX	1960-65	Bone		**50.00**
☐6229½	USA	1965-67	Bone		**40.00**
☐8229½	Tested	Prior 1940	Mother of Pearl		**125.00**

(LENGTH 3¼″ CLOSED)

PATTERN	STAMPING	YEARS MADE	HANDLE	VARIATIONS	MINT PRICE
☐02230	Tested	Prior 1940	Black Composition		**70.00**
☐2230½	Tested	Prior 1940			**70.00**
☐05230½	Tested	Prior 1940	Stag		**200.00**
☐06230	Tested	Prior 1940	Green Bone		**170.00**
☐06230½	Tested	Prior 1940	Green Bone		**170.00**
☐06230 SP	Tested	Prior 1940	Green Bone		**170.00**
☐06230 SH	Tested	Prior 1940	Green Bone		**170.00**
☐09230	Tested	Prior 1940	Green Bone		**110.00**

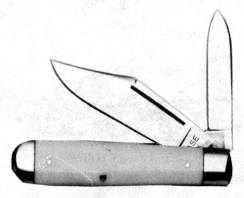

(LENGTH 3¾″ CLOSED)

PATTERN	STAMPING	YEARS MADE	HANDLE	VARIATIONS	MINT PRICE
☐6231	Tested	Prior 1940	Green Bone	Long Pull	**170.00**
☐6231	XX	1940-55	Green Bone		**140.00**
☐	XX	1940's	Green Bone	Long Pull	**150.00**
☐	XX	1950-65	Red Bone		**85.00**
☐	XX	1940's	Rough Black		**50.00**
☐	XX	1950-65	Bone	Not made in "USA" stamping	**45.00**
☐62031	XX	1940-55	Green Bone		**140.00**
☐	XX	1940's	Green Bone	Long Pull	**155.00**
☐	XX	1950-65	Red Bone		**85.00**
☐	XX	1940's	Rough Black		**60.00**
☐	XX	1940's	Rough Black	Long Pull	**60.00**
☐22031½	Tested	Prior 1940	Black Composition		**80.00**

☐22031½	XX	Prior 1940	Black Composition		**55.00**
☐52031	Tested	Prior 1940	Stag		**180.00**
☐52031½	Tested	Prior 1940	Stag		**180.00**
☐62031	Tested	Prior 1940	Green Bone		**160.00**
☐62031½	Tested	Prior 1940	Green Bone		**160.00**
☐62031½	XX	1940-55	Green Bone		**150.00**
☐62031½	XX	1940's	Rough Black		**60.00**
☐62031½	XX	1950-60	Bone		**70.00**
☐2231½	Tested	Prior 1940	Black Composition		**70.00**
☐2231½	XX	1940-54	Black Composition		**50.00**
☐2231½ SAB	Tested	Prior 1940	Black Composition		**70.00**
☐2231½ SAB	XX	1940-65	Black Composition		**30.00**
☐2231½ SAB	USA	1965-70	Black Composition		**20.00**
☐2231½ SAB	10 Dots	1970-71	Black Composition		**20.00**
☐2231½ SAB	Dots	1970's	Black Composition	Discontinued	**15.00**
☐4231½	XX	1948-49	White Composition		**110.00**
☐6231½	XX	1940-55	Green Bone		**120.00**
☐	XX	1950-65	Red Bone		**85.00**
☐	XX	1940's	Rough Black		**45.00**
☐	XX	1950-65	Bone		**50.00**
☐	USA	1965-70	Bone		**30.00**
☐	10 Dots	1970-71	Bone		**25.00**
☐	Dots	1970's	Bone		**20.00**
☐	Lightning S. 10 Dots	1980			

ELECTRICIAN'S KNIFE
(LENGTH 3¹¹⁄₁₆″ CLOSED)

PATTERN	STAMPING	YEARS MADE	HANDLE	VARIATIONS	MINT PRICE
☐12031	Tested	Prior 1950	Walnut		60.00
☐	XX	1950-65	Walnut		30.00
☐	USA	1965-70			20.00
☐	10 Dots	1970-71			17.00
☐	Dots	1970's			13.95
☐12031LHR	Dots	1978	Hawkbill blade		18.00

CANOE
(LENGTH 3⅝" CLOSED)

PATTERN	STAMPING	YEARS MADE	HANDLE	VARIATIONS	MINT PRICE
☐52131	Tested	Prior 1940	Stag		450.00
☐52131	XX	1940-50	Stag	Long Pull	350.00
☐52131	XX	1950-65	Stag		110.00
☐52131	USA	1965-70	Stag		85.00
☐52131	10 Dots	1970-71	Stag	Discontinued	85.00
☐52131SS	3 Dots	1978	Genuine Stag	In the Blue Scroll Sets	45.00

CAUTION: The canoe in bone handles was not produced until 1966, but a few XX blades were made. This is one of the most common counterfeits. *BEWARE!!!*

PATTERN	STAMPING	YEARS MADE	HANDLE	VARIATIONS	MINT PRICE
☐62131	XX	1966	Bone		165.00
☐62131	USA	1966-70	Bone		50.00
☐62131	10 Dots	1970-71	Bone		40.00
☐62131	Dots	1970's	Bone	Blade not etched is discontinued	35.00
☐62131	Dots	1970's	Bone	Canoe etched on the master blade	30.00
☐	Lightning S. 10 Dots	1980	Bone		30.00

(LENGTH 3⅝" CLOSED)

PATTERN	STAMPING	YEARS MADE	HANDLE	VARIATIONS	MINT PRICE
☐3232	Tested	Prior 1940	Yellow Composition		65.00
☐5232	XX	1960-65	Stag		75.00
☐	USA	1965-70	Stag		50.00

PATTERN	STAMPING	YEARS MADE	HANDLE	VARIATIONS	MINT PRICE
☐	10 Dots	1970-71	Stag		**50.00**
☐	9 Dots	1973	Stag	From the collector's sets	**65.00**
☐5232	2 Dots	1979	Stag	From the collector's sets	**30.00**
☐6232	Tested	Prior 1940	Green Bone		**130.00**
☐	XX	1940-55	Green Bone		**95.00**
☐	XX	1950-65	Red Bone		**65.00**
☐	XX	1940's	Rough Black		**50.00**
☐	XX	1950-65	Bone		**40.00**
☐	USA	1965-70	Bone		**27.00**
☐	10 Dots	1970-71	Bone		**22.00**
☐	Dots	1970's	Bone		**18.00**
☐	Dots	1970's	Delrin	Discontinued Changed to 62032	**14.00**
☐	Lightning S. 10 Dots	1980	Bone		**18.00**

PATTERN	STAMPING	YEARS MADE	HANDLE	VARIATIONS	MINT PRICE
☐5234	Tested	Prior 1940	Stag		**160.00**

(LENGTH 2⅝" CLOSED)

PATTERN	STAMPING	YEARS MADE	HANDLE	VARIATIONS	MINT PRICE
☐G5233	Tested	Prior 1950	Gold Metal Flake		**135.00**

PATTERN	STAMPING	YEARS MADE	HANDLE	VARIATIONS	MINT PRICE
☐3233	Tested	Prior 1950	Yellow Composition		**75.00**
☐	XX	1950-65			**30.00**
☐	USA	1965-70			**18.00**
☐	10 Dots	1970-71			**17.00**
☐	Dots	1971-75		Discontinued	**15.00**
☐5233	XX	1960-65	Stag		**65.00**
☐	USA	1965-70	Stag		**50.00**
☐	10 Dots	1970-71	Stag		**50.00**
☐5233 SSP	4 Dots	1977	Stag		**40.00**
☐5233SSP	3 Dots	1978	Stag		**38.00**
☐52033SSP	3 Dots	1978	Stag		**55.00**

☐6233	Tested	Prior 1940	Rough Black		75.00
☐6233	XX	1940's	Rough Black		50.00
☐	XX	1940's	Rough Black	Long Pull	55.00
☐	Tested	Prior 1940	Green Bone		120.00
☐	XX	1940-55	Green Bone		100.00
☐	XX	1940-55	Green Bone	Long Pull	110.00
☐	XX	1950-65	Bone		35.00
☐	USA	1965-70	Bone		28.00
☐	10 Dots	1070-71	Bone		25.00
☐	10 Dots	1970-71	Delrin		15.00
☐	Dots	1970's	Delrin	Discontinued	10.00
☐62033	Dots	1976	Delrin		8.00
☐62033	Dots	1976-79	Delrin Disc		15.00
☐A62033	1 Dot	1979	Smooth Bone		18.00
☐A62033	Lightning S 10 Dot		Smooth Bone		15.00
☐8233	Tested	Prior 1940	Pearl		120.00
☐	XX	1960-65	Pearl		50.00
☐	USA	1965-70	Pearl		40.00
☐	10 Dots	1970-71	Pearl		35.00
☐	Dots	1970-75	Pearl	Discontinued	35.00
☐9233	Tested	Prior 1950	Imitation Pearl		70.00
☐	XX	1950-65	Cracked Ice	(Shad, no bolsters)	50.00
☐	XX	1950-65	Imitation Pearl	Bolsters on these below	20.00
☐	XX	1950-65	Cracked Ice		30.00
☐	XX	1950-65	Cracked Ice	Long Pull	40.00
☐	USA	1965-70	Pearl		20.00
☐	10 Dots	1970-71	Imitation Pearl		15.00
☐	Dots	1970's	Imitation Pearl		10.00
☐92033	Dots	1976	Cracked Ice		10.00

(LENGTH 3¼ " CLOSED)

PATTERN	STAMPING	YEARS MADE	HANDLE	VARIATIONS	MINT PRICE
☐6235 EO	Tested	Prior 1940	Green Bone	Easy Open	125.00
☐6235 EO	XX	1940-50	Bone	Easy Open	95.00
☐6235 EO	XX	1940's	Rough Black	Easy Open	85.00
☐6235	Tested	Prior 1940	Green Bone		85.00
☐	XX	1940-55	Green Bone		60.00
☐	XX	1940's	Rough Black	With Shield	30.00
☐	XX	1940's	Rough Black	Without Shield	25.00

☐	XX	1950-65	Bone		40.00
☐6235 SH	Tested	Prior 1940	Green Bone		125.00
☐3235½	Tested	Prior 1940	Yellow Composition		80.00
☐5235½	Tested	Prior 1940	Stag		140.00
☐6235½ P	Tested	Prior 1940	Green Bone		120.00
☐6235½	Tested	Prior 1940	Green Bone		95.00
☐	XX	1940-55	Green Bone		65.00
☐	XX	1940's	Rough Black	With Shield	30.00
☐	XX	1940's	Rough Black	Without Shield	25.00
☐	XX	1950-65	Bone		30.00
☐	USA	1965-70	Bone		20.00
☐	10 Dots	1970-71	Bone		22.00
☐	Dots	1970's	Bone		15.00
☐62035½	Tested	Prior 1940	Green Bone		95.00
☐A6235½	1 Dot	1979	Smooth Bone		18.00
☐A6235½	Lightning S. 10 Dots	1980	Smooth Bone		15.00

☐620035	XX	1950-60	Black Plastic	Standard Long Pull	15.00
☐620035½	XX	1950-60	Black Plastic	Standard Long Pull	20.00
☐620035 EO	XX	1945-50	Black Plastic	Standard Long Pull	20.00

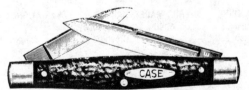

(LENGTH 3" CLOSED)

PATTERN	STAMPING	YEARS MADE	HANDLE	VARIATIONS	MINT PRICE
☐52042	Tested	Prior 1940	Stag		120.00
☐62042	Tested	Prior 1940	Green Bone		95.00
☐62042	XX	1940-55	Green Bone		50.00
☐	XX	1940's	Rough Black		25.00
☐	XX	1950-65	Bone		25.00
☐	USA	1965-70	Bone		20.00
☐	10 Dots	1970-71	Bone		18.00

☐	Dots	1970's	Bone	Discontinued	**15.00**
☐	Dots	1970's	Delrin		**8.00**
☐62042 R	XX	1957-65	Bone	Bail in Handle	**35.00**
☐	USA	1965-70	Bone		**25.00**
☐	10 Dots	1070-Oct. 70	Bone	Discontinued	**25.00**
☐82042	Tested	Prior 1940	Pearl		**95.00**
☐92042	Tested	Prior 1940	Imitation Pearl		**60.00**
☐92042	XX	1940-65	Imitation Pearl		**18.00**
☐	XX	1940-65	Cracked Ice		**20.00**
☐	USA	1965-70	Imitation Pearl		**16.00**
☐	10 Dots	1970-71	Imitation Pearl		**15.00**
☐	Dots	1970's	Imitation		**8.00**
☐92024 R	XX	1957-65	Imitation Pearl	Bail in Handle	**30.00**
☐	XX	1957-65	Cracked Ice	Bail in Handle	**35.00**
☐	USA	1965-70	Imitation Pearl	Bail in Handle	**20.00**
☐	10 Dots	1970-Oct. 70	Imitation Pearl	Discontinued	**25.00**
☐A62042	1 Dot	1979	Smooth bone		**20.00**
☐A62042	Lightning S 10 Dots	1980	Smooth bone		**15.00**

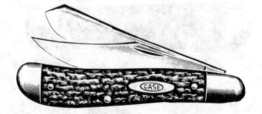

(LENGTH 4⁷⁄₁₆″ CLOSED)

PATTERN	STAMPING	YEARS MADE	HANDLE	VARIATIONS	MINT PRICE
☐6240	Tested	Prior 1940	Green Bone		400.00
☐6240 SP	Tested	Prior 1940	Green Bone		400.00

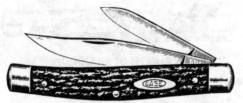

(LENGTH 3¼″ CLOSED)

PATTERN	STAMPING	YEARS MADE	HANDLE	VARIATIONS	MINT PRICE
☐3244	Tested	Prior 1940	Yellow Composition		80.00
☐3244	5 Dot	1976	Acorn Shop		40.00

☐5244	Tested	Prior 1940	Stag		**140.00**
☐6244	Tested	Prior 1940	Green Bone		**120.00**
☐9244	Tested	Prior 1940	Imitation Pearl		**70.00**
☐6244	XX	1955-65	Bone		**30.00**
☐6244	USA	1965-70	Bone		**25.00**
☐6244	10 Dots	1970-71	Bone		**22.00**
☐6244	10 Dots	1970-71	Delrin	Delrin intro-duced in 1971	**13.00**
☐6244	Dots	1970's	Delrin		**10.00**
☐SR-6244	1 Dot	1979	Smooth Base		**25.00**
☐SR-6244	Lightning S. 10 Dots	1980	Smooth Bone		**20.00**

(LENGTH 3¼ " CLOSED)

PATTERN	STAMPING	YEARS MADE	HANDLE	VARIATIONS	MINT PRICE
☐06244	Tested	Prior 1940	Green Bone		**80.00**
☐06244	XX	1940-55	Green Bone		**50.00**
☐06244	XX	1950-65	Red Bone		**35.00**
☐06244	XX	1950-65	Bone		**25.00**
☐06244	USA	1965-70	Bone		**16.00**
☐06244	10 Dots	1970-71	Bone		**22.00**
☐	10 Dots	1070-71	Delrin	Delrin intro-duced in 1971	**13.00**
☐	9 Dots	1971-72	Bone Limited		**20.00**
☐	Dots	1970's	Delrin	Discontinued	**12.50**

(LENGTH 3¼ ")

PATTERN	STAMPING	YEARS MADE	HANDLE	VARIATIONS	MINT PRICE
☐82044	Tested	Prior 1940	Pearl		**120.00**

GRAFTING KNIFE
(LENGTH 3¼ " CLOSED)

PATTERN	STAMPING	YEARS MADE	HANDLE	VARIATIONS	MINT PRICE
☐2245 SH SP	XX	1960-65	Black Composition		**70.00**

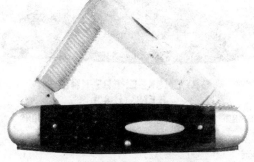

(LENGTH 3¼ " CLOSED)

PATTERN	STAMPING	YEARS MADE	HANDLE	VARIATIONS	MINT PRICE
☐6245DG	Tested	Prior 1940	Green Bone	Dog Grooming Knife	250.00

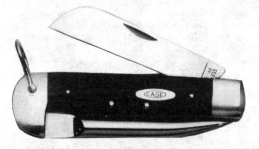

RIGGERS KNIFE, MARLIN SPIKE
(LENGTH 4⅜″ CLOSED)

PATTERN	STAMPING	YEARS MADE	HANDLE	VARIATIONS	MINT PRICE
☐3246	Tested	Prior 1940	Yellow Composition		100.00
☐3246 R	XX	1940-52	Yellow Composition	Blade not stamped ''Stain-less''	75.00
☐3246 RSS	XX	1950-65	Yellow Composition		55.00
☐3246 RSS	USA		Yellow Composition		110.00
☐6246 RSS	Tested	Prior 1940	Green Bone		140.00
☐6246 RSS	XX	1963-65	Bone		55.00
☐6246 RSS	USA	1965-70	Bone		40.00
☐6246 RSS	10 Dots	1970-71	Bone		30.00
☐6246 RSS	Dots	1970's	Bone	Discontinued	25.00
☐6246L RSS	Lightning S. 10 Dots		Delrin		18.00

GREENSKEEPERS KNIFE
(LENGTH 4″)

PATTERN	STAMPING	YEARS MADE	HANDLE	VARIATIONS	MINT PRICE
☐4247K	Dots	1970	White Composition	V-shaped 2 edge blade	75.00
☐	10 Dots				100.00
☐4247K	USA Standing	1965-70			135.00
☐4247K	XX	Prior 1965			200.00

(LENGTH 3⁷⁄₈" CLOSED)

PATTERN	STAMPING	YEARS MADE	HANDLE	VARIATIONS	MINT PRICE
☐6247J	Tested	Prior 1940	Green Bone		350.00
☐5247J	Tested	Prior 1940	Stag		350.00

(LENGTH 3⁷⁄₈" CLOSED)

PATTERN	STAMPING	YEARS MADE	HANDLE	VARIATIONS	MINT PRICE
☐04247SP	Tested	Prior 1940	White Composition		90.00
☐05247SP	Tested	Prior 1940	Stag		170.00
☐06247SP	Tested	Prior 1940	Green Bone		145.00
☐06247 PEN	Tested	Prior 1940	Green Bone		145.00
☐05247 SP	XX	1940-65	Stag		100.00
☐05247 SP	USA	1965-66	Stag		150.00
☐04247 SP	XX	1940-65	White Composition		60.00
☐04247 SP	USA	1965-66	White Composition		60.00
☐06247 PEN	XX	1940-55	Green Bone		95.00
☐	XX	1040's	Rough Black		70.00
☐	XX	1940-65	Bone		40.00
☐	USA	1965-70	Bone		30.00
☐	10 Dots	1970-71	Bone		25.00
☐	Dots	1970's	Bone		15.00
☐	Dots	1970's	Delrin		12.00
☐	Lightning S. 10 Dots	1980	Bone		15.00

(LENGTH 4" CLOSED)

PATTERN	STAMPING	YEARS MADE	aANDLE	VARIATIONS	MINT PRICE
☐32048 SP	XX	1949-65	Yellow Composition		25.00
☐	USA	1965-70	Yellow Composition		20.00
☐	10 Dots	1970-71	Yellow Composition		18.00
☐	Dots	1970's	Yellow Composition		12.00
☐62048	Tested	Prior 1940	Green Bone		125.00
☐62048 SP	Tested	Prior 1940	Imitation Onyx		90.00
☐62048 SP	Tested	Prior 1940	Green Bone		125.00
☐	XX	1940-55	Green Bone		95.00
☐	XX	1950-65	Bone		30.00
☐	USA	1965-69	Bone		25.00
☐	USA	1969-70	Delrin		15.00
☐	10 Dots	1970-71	Delrin		20.00
☐	Dots	1970's	Delrin		10.50
☐62048 SP SSP	USA	1966-67	Bone	Blade etched "Tested XX stainless"	45.00
☐62048 SP SSP	USA	1967-69	Bone	Blade polished and etched, "Tested XX Razor Edge"	35.00
☐62048 SP SSP	USA	1967-69	Bone	Brushed Blade and etched, "Tested XX Razor Edge"	35.00
☐62048 SP SSP	USA	1966-70	Delrin		20.00
☐62048 SP SSP	10 Dots	1970-71	Delrin		17.00
☐62048 SP SSP	Dots	1970's	Delrin		15.00
☐62048 SP SSP	Lightning S. 10 Dots	1980	Delrin		15.00

COPPERHEAD
(LENGTH 3¹⁵⁄₁₆″ CLOSED)

PATTERN	STAMPING	YEARS MADE	HANDLE	VARIATIONS	MINT PRICE
☐6249	Tested	Prior 1940	Green Bone		225.00
☐	XX	1940-55	Green Bone		175.00
☐	XX	1950's-65	Bone		55.00
☐	USA	1965-70	Bone		35.00

☐	10 Dots	1970-71	Bone		**28.00**
☐	Dots	1970's	Bone		**20.00**
☐	Dots	1970's	Delrin		**15.00**
☐	Lightning S		Bone		**16.00**
☐5249	1 Dot		Stag		**30.00**

(LENGTH 6¾" CLOSED)

PATTERN	STAMPING	YEARS MADE	HANDLE	VARIATIONS	MINT PRICE
☐6251 CLASP	Tested	Prior 1940	Green Bone	Knife & fork can be separated	**400.00**
☐9251	Tested	Prior 1940	Imitation Pearl	Knife & fork can be separated	**300.00**

(LENGTH 4⅝" CLOSED)

PATTERN	STAMPING	YEARS MADE	HANDLE	VARIATIONS	MINT PRICE
☐6250	Tested	Prior 1940	Green Bone		**450.00**
☐	XX	1940-55	Green Bone		**400.00**
☐	XX	1940-65	Red Bone		**240.00**
☐	XX	1940-65	Bone		**170.00**
☐	XX	1964-65	Laminated Wood		**80.00**
☐	USA	1964-65	Bone		**160.00**
☐	USA	1965-70	Laminated Wood		**45.00**
☐	10 Dots	1970-71	Laminated Wood		**40.00**
☐	Dots	1970's	Laminated Wood	Blade not etched Discontinued	**30.00**
☐	Dots	1970's	Laminated Wood	Elephant etched on master blade	**30.00**
☐	1 Dot	1979	Laminated Wood	Bradford Bonanza	**40.00**
☐	Lightning S 10 Dots		Laminated Wood		**30.00**

(LENGTH 3¾" CLOSED)

PATTERN	STAMPING	YEARS MADE	HANDLE	VARIATIONS	MINT PRICE
☐6452	Tested	Prior 1940	Green Bone		**190.00**
☐3452	Tested	Prior 1940	Composition Ivory handles		**165.00**

(LENGTH 3½" CLOSED)

PATTERN	STAMPING	YEARS MADE	HANDLE	VARIATIONS	MINT PRICE
☐62052	Tested	Prior 1950	Green Bone		**120.00**
☐	XX	1950-56	Green Bone		**85.00**
☐	XX	1950-65	Bone		**30.00**
☐	USA	1965-70	Bone		**24.00**
☐	10 Dots	1970-71	Bone		**20.00**
☐	Dots	1971-76	Bone	Discontinued	**18.00**
☐	Dots	1971-76	Delrin	Discontinued	**12.00**

(LENGTH 3¼" CLOSED)

PATTERN	STAMPING	YEARS MADE	HANDLE	VARIATIONS	MINT PRICE
☐5253	Tested	Prior 1950	Stag		**120.00**
☐	XX	Approx. 1950	Stag		**80.00**
☐6253	Tested	Prior 1950	Green Bone		**90.00**
☐6253	XX	1940-50	Green Bone		**95.00**
☐6253	XX	Approx. 1950	Rough Black		**65.00**

☐9253	Tested	Prior 1950	Imitation Pearl		**70.00**
☐9253	XX	Approx. 1950	Imitation Pearl		**60.00**

(LENGTH 2¹³⁄₁₆" CLOSED)

PATTERN	STAMPING	YEARS MADE	HANDLE	VARIATIONS	MINT PRICE
☐62053SS	XX	1950-65	Bone		**40.00**
☐62053SS	USA	1965-69	Bone	Discontinued	**60.00**
☐82053 SR	Tested	Prior 1940	Pearl		**90.00**
☐82053	XX	1950-64	Pearl		**40.00**
☐82053 SS	XX	1949-64	Pearl	Bolsters	**45.00**
☐82053 SR SS	XX	1949-64	Pearl	Bail in handle and no bolsters	**35.00**
☐	USA	1965-70	Pearl		**28.00**
☐	10 Dots	1970-71	Pearl	Not sure if ever made in 10 dots, if so worth 35.00	**35.00**
☐82053 SRSS	Dots	1970's	Pearl		**30.00**

TRAPPER
(LENGTH 4⅛" CLOSED)

PATTERN	STAMPING	YEARS MADE	HANDLE	VARIATIONS	MINT PRICE
☐3254	XX	1950-65	Yellow Composition		**75.00**
☐	USA	1965-70	Yellow Composition		**50.00**
☐	USA	1965-67	Yellow Composition	Muskrat Blade	**65.00**
☐	10 Dots	1970-71			**40.00**
☐	Dots	1970's			**20.00**
☐3254	Lightning S 10 Dots	1980			**15.00**
☐5254	Tested	Prior 1950	Stag		**900.00**
☐5254	XX	About 1950	Stag	Tested Frame	**225.00**
☐	XX	1950-65	Stag		**140.00**
☐	USA	1965-70	Stag		**80.00**
☐	USA	1965-67	Stag	Muskrat Blade	**80.00**
☐	USA	1965-70	Stag (second cut)		**400.00**

☐	USA	1965-67	Stag (second cut)	Muskrat Blade	**400.00**
☐	10 Dots	1970-71	Stag		**70.00**
☐5254SS	4 Dots	1978	Stag	Part of 1978 Set	**50.00**
☐5254SSP	3 Dots	1978	Stag	Part of 1978 Set	**50.00**
☐6254	Tested	Prior 1940	Green Bone		**900.00**
☐	XX	1941-53	Green Bone		**700.00**
☐	XX	1958-65	Bone		**100.00**
☐	USA	1965-70	Stag (second cut)		**250.00**
☐	USA	1965-67	Bone	Muskrat Blade	**60.00**
☐	USA	1965-70	Bone		**50.00**
☐	10 Dots	1970-71	Bone		**40.00**
☐	Dots	1970's	Bone		**25.00**
☐	Dots	1970's	Delrin		**40.00**
☐	Lightning S 10 Dots	1980	Bone		**20.00**

TRAPPER

MUSKRAT

PATTERN	STAMPING	YEARS MADE	HANDLE	VARIATIONS	MINT PRICE
☐6254 SSP	USA	1965-66	Bone	Glazed finish, etched ''Tested XX Stainless''	**80.00**
☐	USA	1965-67	Bone	Muskrat Blade Polished Edge	**70.00**
☐	USA	1965-67	Bone	Muskrat Blade Polished Blade	**70.00**
☐	USA	1965-67	Bone	Polished Blade etched ''Tested XX Razor edge''	**60.00**
☐	USA	1965-70	Bone		**55.00**
☐	10 Dots	1970-71	Bone		**50.00**
☐	Dots	1970's	Bone		**30.00**
☐	Dots	1970's	Delrin		**40.00**
☐	Lightning S 10 Dots		Bone		**24.00**

(LENGTH 3½ " CLOSED)

PATTERN	STAMPING	YEARS MADE	HANDLE	VARIATIONS	MINT PRICE
□32055	Tested	Prior 1940	Yellow Composition		85.00
□92055	Tested	Prior 1940	Imitation Pearl		85.00
□22055	Tested	Prior 1940	Black Composition		85.00
□22055	XX	1940-65	Black Composition		45.00
□22055	XX	1940's	Black Composition	Long Pull	75.00
□22055	USA	1965-67	Black Composition		130.00
□62055	Tested	Prior 1940	Green Bone		145.00
□62055	XX	1940-55	Green Bone	Long Pull	100.00
□62055	XX	1940-55	Green Bone		95.00
□62055	XX	1940's	Rough Black	Long Pull	85.00
□62055	XX	1940's	Rough Black		65.00
□62055	XX	1950-65	Bone		40.00
□62055	USA	1965-70	Bone		30.00
□62055	10 Dots	1970-71	Bone		25.00
□62055	Dots	1970's	Bone	Discontinued	20.00
□62055	Dots	1970's	Delrin	Discontinued	11.00

OFFICE KNIFE
(LENGTH 3⁵⁄₁₆" CLOSED)

PATTERN	STAMPING	YEARS MADE	HANDLE	VARIATIONS	MINT PRICE
□92057	Tested	Prior 1940			80.00
□42057	Tested	Prior 1940			70.00
□4257	Tested	Prior 1940			70.00

☐42057	XX	1940-50	Imitation Ivory		**75.00**
☐42057	XX	1950-55	Imitation Ivory	"Office knife" not etched on handle	**45.00**
☐4257	XX	1940-50	Imitation Ivory		**75.00**
☐4257	XX	1950-60	Imitation Ivory	"Office knife" not etched on handle	**40.00**

(LENGTH 3¼ " CLOSED)

PATTERN	STAMPING	YEARS MADE	HANDLE	VARIATIONS	MINT PRICE
☐92058	Tested	Prior 1940	Imitation Pearl		**80.00**

(LENGTH 3¼ " CLOSED)

PATTERN	STAMPING	YEARS MADE	HANDLE	VARIATIONS	MINT PRICE
☐62059	Tested	Prior 1940	Green Bone		**110.00**
☐62059 SP	Tested	Prior 1940	Green Bone		**110.00**

(LENGTH 3⁷⁄₁₆" CLOSED)

PATTERN	STAMPING	YEARS MADE	HANDLE	VARIATIONS	MINT PRICE
☐5260	Tested	Prior 1950	Stag		**250.00**
☐5260	XX	1950-52	Stag		**225.00**

(LENGTH 2⅞" CLOSED)

PATTERN	STAMPING	YEARS MADE	HANDLE	VARIATIONS	MINT PRICE
☐2261	Tested	Prior 1940	Black Composition		50.00
☐6261F	Tested	Prior 1940	Green Bone		85.00
☐6261	Tested	Prior 1940	Green Bone		90.00
☐8261F	Tested	Prior 1940	Pearl		95.00
☐8261	Tested	Prior 1940	Pearl		95.00
☐	XX	1950-65	Pearl		45.00
☐	USA	1965-70	Pearl		40.00
☐	10 Dots	1970-71	Pearl		35.00
☐	Dots	1970-76	Pearl	Discontinued	30.00
☐9261F	Tested	Prior 1940	Imitation Pearl		55.00
☐9261	Tested	Prior 1940	Imitation Pearl		55.00
☐	XX	1950-65	Imitation Pearl		24.00
☐	XX	1945-50	Cracked Ice		28.00
☐	USA	1965-70	Imitation Pearl		18.00
☐	10 Dots	1970-71	Imitation Pearl		16.00
☐	Dots	1970-75	Imitation Pearl	Discontinued	14.00

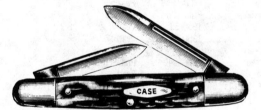

(LENGTH 3⅛" CLOSED)

PATTERN	STAMPING	YEARS MADE	HANDLE	VARIATIONS	MINT PRICE
☐05263	Tested	Prior 1940	Stag		135.00
☐05263	XX	1950-52	Stag		90.00
☐05263 SS	XX	1940-65	Stag		50.00
☐05263 SS	USA	1965-70	Stag		35.00
☐05263 SS	10 Dots	1970-71	Stag	Discontinued	45.00
☐06263	Tested	Prior 1950	Green Bone		95.00
☐06263	XX	1945-50	Green Bone		70.00
☐06263 SS	XX	1945-55	Green Bone		50.00
☐06263	XX	1945-55	Bone		40.00
☐06263 SS	XX	1950-65	Bone		30.00
☐06263 SS	USA	1965-70	Bone		20.00
☐06263 SS	10 Dots	1970	Bone	Discontinued	20.00
☐06263 F	XX	1940-45	Bone		40.00
☐06263 F SS	XX	1950-65	Bone		22.00
☐	USA	1965-70	Bone		18.00
☐	10 Dots	1970-71	Bone	Discontinued	22.00

☐06263 SSP	USA	1965-66	Bone	Flat Ground etched ''Tested XX Stainless''	35.00
☐	USA	1965-70		Hollow Ground etched ''Tested XX Razor Edge''	32.00
☐	10 Dots	1960-71			20.00
☐	Dots	1970's	Bone		18.00
☐	Dots	1970's	Delrin		15.00
☐	Lightning S. 10 Dots		Delrin		12.00

(LENGTH 3¹/₁₆″ CLOSED)

PATTERN	STAMPING	YEARS MADE	HANDLE	VARIATIONS	MINT PRICE
☐62063½ SS	XX	1950-60	Bone		25.00
☐62063½ SS	XX	1950-55	Green Bone		45.00
☐62063½	XX	1940-55	Green Bone		50.00
☐82063 SHAD	Tested	Prior 1940	Pearl		90.00
☐82063½	Tested	Prior 1940	Pearl		120.00
☐82063	Tested	Prior 1940	Pearl		120.00
☐82063 SHAD	XX	1950-55	Pearl		60.00
☐82063 SHAD SS	XX	1950-65	Pearl		50.00
☐90063½	Tested	Prior 1940	Imitation Pearl		70.00
☐	XX	1940-42	Imitation Pearl		60.00

(LENGTH 3¹/₈″ CLOSED)

PATTERN	STAMPING	YEARS MADE	HANDLE	VARIATIONS	MINT PRICE
☐8264 T	Tested	Prior 1940	Pearl		100.00
☐9264 TF	Tested	Prior 1940	Imitation Pearl		70.00
☐6264 TG	Tested	Prior 1940	Green Bone		110.00
☐6264 T	Tested	Prior 1940	Green Bone		110.00

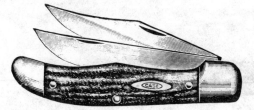

(LENGTH 5¼ " CLOSED)

PATTERN	STAMPING	YEARS MADE	HANDLE	VARIATIONS	MINT PRICE
☐5265	XX	1940-50	Stag	Master Blade Flat Ground	300.00
☐5265 SAB	Tested	Prior 1940	Stag		375.00
☐	XX	1940-65	Stag		150.00
☐	XX	1964-65	Stag	Drilled Bolster	150.00
☐	USA	1965-66	Stag	XX frame, not drilled	135.00
☐	USA	1965-66	Stag	XX frame, drilled bolster	120.00
☐	USA	1965-70	Stag	Drilled	70.00
☐	10 Dots	1970-71	Stag	Discontinued	70.00
☐5265SS	4 Dots	1978	Stag	From 1978 Sets	55.00
☐5265SSP	3 Dots	1978	Stag		50.00
☐6265	Tested	Prior 1940	Green Bone		400.00
☐	XX	1940-55	Green Bone	Master Blade flat ground	325.00
☐	XX	1940's	Green Bone		275.00
☐6265 SAB	Tested	Prior 1940	Green Bone		400.00
☐	XX	1940-55	Green Bone		275.00
☐	XX	1940's	Rough Black		140.00
☐	XX	1950-65	Red Bone		180.00
☐	XX	1950-65	Bone		120.00
☐	XX	1964-65	Laminated Wood		65.00
☐	USA	1965-66	Bone	XX frame, not drilled	160.00
☐	USA	1965-66	Bone	XX frame, drilled bolster	160.00
☐	USA	1965-66	Laminated Wood	XX frame, not drilled	60.00
☐	USA	1965-70	Laminated Wood		40.00
☐	10 Dots	1960-71	Laminated Wood		30.00
☐	Dots	1970's	Laminated Wood		22.00
☐6265 SAB	Lightning S	1980	Laminated Wood		20.00
☐6265 SAB SS	Dots	1970's	Laminated Wood		20.00
☐6265 SAB SS	Lightning S 10 Dots	1980	Laminated Wood		25.00

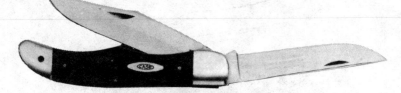

(Contract Knife)
BILL BOATMAN SPECIAL
(LENGTH 5¼ " CLOSED)

PATTERN	STAMPING	YEARS MADE	HANDLE	VARIATIONS	MINT PRICE
☐6265 SAB	XX	1960-65	Bone	Serrated Skinner Blade	250.00
☐6265 SAB	XX	1964-65	Laminated Wood	Serrated Skinner Blade	150.00
☐	USA	1965-66	Bone	Serrated Skinner Blade	175.00
☐	USA	1965-70	Laminated Wood		75.00
☐	10 Dots				45.00
☐	Dots				35.00

(LENGTH 3¼ " CLOSED)

PATTERN	STAMPING	YEARS MADE	HANDLE	VARIATIONS	MINT PRICE
☐06267	Tested	Prior 1940	Green Bone		150.00
☐	XX	1940-65	Bone	Long Pull	70.00
☐	USA	1965-67	Bone		90.00

(LENGTH 3¼ " CLOSED)

PATTERN	STAMPING	YEARS MADE	HANDLE	VARIATIONS	MINT PRICE
☐6268	Tested	Prior 1940	Green Bone		110.00

(LENGTH 3" CLOSED)

PATTERN	STAMPING	YEARS MADE	HANDLE	VARIATIONS	MINT PRICE
☐6269	Tested	Prior 1940	Green Bone		**95.00**
☐8269	Tested	Prior 1940	Pearl		**120.00**
☐9269	Tested	Prior 1940	Imitation Pearl		**75.00**
☐6269	XX	1940's	Rough Black		**40.00**
☐	XX	1940-55	Green Bone		**80.00**
☐	XX	1940-65	Red Bone		**50.00**
☐	XX	1940-65	Bone		**30.00**
☐	USA	1965-70	Bone		**24.00**
☐	10 Dots	1970-71	Bone		**18.00**
☐	Dots	1970's	Bone	Discontinued	**16.00**
☐	Dots	1970's	Delrin	Discontinued	**10.00**

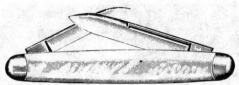

(LENGTH 3¼ " CLOSED)

PATTERN	STAMPING	YEARS MADE	HANDLE	VARIATIONS	MINT PRICE
☐8271	Tested	Prior 1950	Pearl		**180.00**
☐8271 F	Tested	Prior 1950	Pearl		**180.00**
☐8271	XX	1950-58	Pearl	Long Pull	**150.00**
☐8271 F	XX	1950-58	Pearl		**140.00**
☐8271 SS	XX	1950-60	Pearl	Long Pull	**150.00**
☐8271 SS	XX	1950-60	Pearl		**140.00**
☐6271 SS	XX	1963-65	Bone		**70.00**

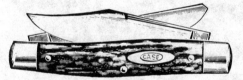

MOOSE
(LENGTH 4¼ " CLOSED)

PATTERN	STAMPING	YEARS MADE	HANDLE	VARIATIONS	MINT PRICE
☐6275 SP	Tested	Prior 1940	Green Bone		**300.00**
☐5275 SP	Tested	Prior 1940	Stag		**300.00**
☐6275 SP	XX	1940-55	Green Bone	Long Pull	**250.00**
☐	XX	1940's	Rough Black	Long Pull	**120.00**
☐	XX	1950-65	Red Bone	Long Pull	**200.00**
☐	XX	1950-65	Red Bone		**120.00**
☐	XX	1950-65	Bone		**70.00**
☐	USA	1965-70	Bone		**40.00**
☐	10 Dots	1970-71	Bone		**30.00**
☐	Dots	1970's	Bone		**22.00**
☐	Dots	1970's	Delrin		**18.00**
☐	Lightning S. 10 Dots	1980	Bone		**24.00**
☐5275 SSP	1 Dot	1979	Stag		**40.00**

(LENGTH 3⅝″ CLOSED)

PATTERN	STAMPING	YEARS MADE	HANDLE	VARIATIONS	MINT PRICE
☐6276½	Tested	Prior 1940	Green Bone		225.00

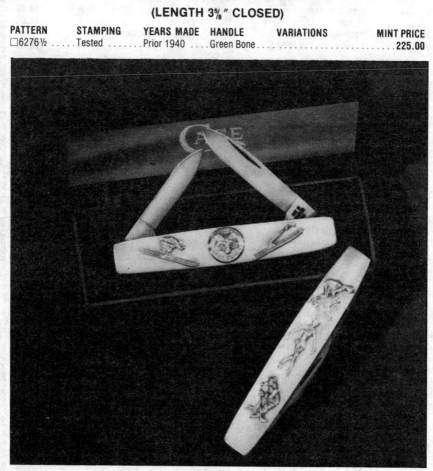

Case Olympic Knife

OL278 — This knife was a limited edition of 1,000 beginning with #1000 — 1999. It was the official knife of the 1980 Winter Olympics in Lake Placid, New York   Value $325.00

The I278ss is a new pattern for Case, introduced in 1979. The knife has no bolsters, and a white plastic handle. The first ones were stamped with a gold seal on the front handle commemorating the centennial of Bradford, Pennsylvania. The knives were a limited production run, and discontinued January 1, 1980.

The knife will still be made in different configurations. Suggested retail on the Bradford knives was $16, and they currently bring $20 on the collector's market. It is also being offered in a variety of different handles for regular production.

I278
S278

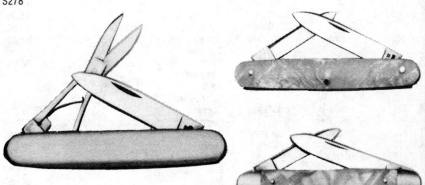

(LENGTH 3⅛" CLOSED)

PATTERN	STAMPING	YEARS MADE	HANDLE	VARIATIONS	MINT PRICE
☐M-279	Tested	Prior 1940	Metal		50.00
☐M279 R	Tested	Prior 1940	Metal		50.00
☐GM279	Tested	Prior 1940	Gun metal		70.00
☐M-279 SS	XX	1940-65	Stainless Steel		24.00
☐	USA	1965-70	Stainless Steel		18.00
☐	10 Dots	1970-71	Stainless Steel		12.00
☐	Dots	1970's	Stainless Steel		15.00
☐	Lightning S. 10 Dots	1980	Stainless Steel		15.00
☐M279 F SS	XX	1962-65	Stainless Steel		24.00
☐	USA	1965-70	Stainless Steel		20.00
☐	10 Dots	1970-71	Stainless Steel		18.00
☐	Dots	1970's	Stainless Steel		15.00

(LENGTH 3⅛" CLOSED)

PATTERN	STAMPING	YEARS MADE	HANDLE	VARIATIONS	MINT PRICE
☐ M279SC SS	XX	1958-64	Stainless Steel	Special Order Knife	70.00
☐	USA	1965-70			45.00
☐	10 Dots	1970-71			40.00
☐	Dots	1970's		Discontinued	30.00
☐ R279	Tested	Prior 1940	Red Stripped Celluloid		80.00
☐ 2279 SHAD SS	Tested	Prior 1940	Black Composition	No bolster	60.00
☐ 3279 R	Tested	Prior 1940	Yellow Composition		55.00
☐ 3279	Tested	Prior 1940	Yellow Composition		55.00
☐ 5279	Tested	Prior 1940	Stag		140.00
☐ 5279	XX	1940-50	Stag		90.00
☐ 5279 SS	XX	1950-65	Stag		55.00
☐ 5279 SS	USA	1965-66	Stag		150.00
☐ 52799SSP	2 Dots	1979	Stag		30.00
☐ 6279	Tested	Prior 1940	Green Bone		95.00
☐ 6279	XX	1940-55	Green Bone		60.00
☐ 6279	XX	1940's	Rough Black		50.00
☐ 6279 SS	XX	1940's	Rough Black		35.00
☐ 6279	XX	1950-65	Bone		30.00
☐ 6279 SS	USA	1965-70	Bone		24.00
☐ 6279 SS	10 Dots	1970-71	Bone		24.00
☐	Dots	1970's	Bone		18.00
☐	Dots	1970's	Delrin		12.00
☐	Lightning S 10 Dots	1980	Delrin		10.00
☐ 8279	Tested	Prior 1940	Pearl		120.00
☐ 8279	XX	1940's	Pearl		75.00
☐ 8279 SS	XX	1950-60	Pearl		60.00
☐ 9279	XX	1945-55	Imitation		50.00
☐ 9279 SHAD SS	XX	1962-63	Cracked Ice	No bolsters	28.00

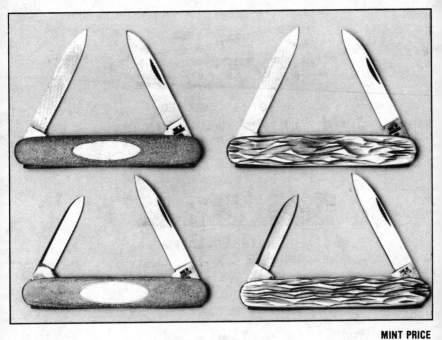

MINT PRICE

☐M279 CASE Prototypes - Only 12 Sets Sent to each CASE salesman . . . . **150.00 per set**

(LENGTH 3¼ " CLOSED)

PATTERN	STAMPING	YEARS MADE	HANDLE	VARIATIONS	MINT PRICE
☐62079½ F	Tested	Prior 1940	Green Bone		150.00
☐62079	Tested	Prior 1940	Green Bone		150.00
☐92079½	Tested	Prior 1940	Imitation Pearl		75.00
☐92079½	XX	Late 1940	Imitation Pearl		75.00
☐82079½	Tested	Prior 1940	Pearl		125.00
☐82079	Tested	Prior 1940	Pearl		125.00
☐82079½	XX	1940-65	Pearl		55.00
☐82079½	XX	1940-65	Pearl		45.00
☐82079½ SS	XX USA	1965-70	Pearl		35.00
☐82079½	USA	1965-70	Pearl		35.00
☐82079½ SS	XX 10 Dots	1970-71	Pearl		30.00
☐82079½	Dots	1970-71	Pearl		30.00

(LENGTH 2¾" CLOSED)

PATTERN	STAMPING	YEARS MADE	HANDLE	VARIATIONS	MINT PRICE
☐6282	Tested	Prior 1940	Green Bone		290.00

(LENGTH 3⅝" CLOSED)

PATTERN	STAMPING	YEARS MADE	HANDLE	VARIATIONS	MINT PRICE
☐6285	Tested	Prior 1940	Green Bone		290.00
☐7285	Tested	Prior 1940	Imitation Tortoise Shell		325.00
☐7285	Tested	Prior 1940	Christmas Tree Handles		325.00
☐5285	Tested	Prior 1940	Stag		325.00

(LENGTH 3¼" CLOSED)

PATTERN	STAMPING	YEARS MADE	HANDLE	VARIATIONS	MINT PRICE
☐52086	Tested	Prior 1940	Stag		275.00
☐62086	Tested	Prior 1940	Green Bone		250.00
☐82086	Tested	Prior 1940	Pearl		300.00

CASE GUNSTOCK
(LENGTH 3½" CLOSED)

PATTERN	STAMPING	YEARS MADE	HANDLE	VARIATIONS	MINT PRICE
☐5287	Tested	Prior 1940	Stag		300.00

(LENGTH 4⅛" CLOSED)

PATTERN	STAMPING	YEARS MADE	HANDLE	VARIATIONS	MINT PRICE
☐6288	Tested	Prior 1940	Green Bone		400.00

(LENGTH 3⅜" CLOSED)

PATTERN	STAMPING	YEARS MADE	HANDLE	VARIATIONS	MINT PRICE
☐22087	Tested	Prior 1940	Black Composition		65.00
☐	XX	1940-65	Black Composition		25.00
☐	USA	1965-70	Black Composition		22.00
☐	10 Dots	1970-71	Black Composition		18.00
☐	Dots	1970's	Black Composition		14.00
☐22087	Lightning S 10 Dot	1980	Black Composition		12.00
☐42087	Tested	Prior 1940	White Composition		60.00
☐52087	XX	1955-65	Stag		65.00
☐	USA	1965-70	Stag		45.00
☐	10 Dots	1970-71	Stag	Discontinued	65.00
☐62087	Tested	Prior 1940	Green Bone		75.00
☐	XX	1940-55	Green Bone		50.00
☐	XX	1940's	Rough Black		40.00
☐	XX	1940-55	Red Bone		40.00
☐	XX	1950-65	Bone		30.00
☐	USA	1965-70	Bone		20.00
☐	10 Dots	1970-71	Bone		23.00
☐	10 Dots	1970-71	Delrin		16.00
☐	Dots	1970's	Delrin		12.50
☐52087 SS	4 Dots	1978	Stag	1978 Sets	35.00
☐52087SSP	3 Dots	1979	Stag	1979 Sets	35.00
☐52087SSP	2 Dots	1979	Stag	1979 Sets	40.00

TEXAS JACK
(LENGTH 4" CLOSED)

PATTERN	STAMPING	YEARS MADE	HANDLE	VARIATIONS	MINT PRICE
☐3292	Tested	Prior 1940	Yellow Composition		120.00
☐6292	Tested	Prior 1940	Green Bone		200.00
☐6292	XX	1940-55	Green Bone		150.00
☐6292	XX	1940's	Rough Black		70.00
☐	XX	1950-65	Red Bone		75.00
☐	XX	1950-65	Bone		50.00
☐	USA	1965-70	Bone		30.00
☐	10 Dots	1970-71	Bone		25.00
☐	Dots	1970's	Bone		20.00
☐	Lightning S 10 Dots	1980	Bone		18.00
☐5292SSP	1 Dot	1979	Genuine Stag		40.00

(LENGTH 5″ CLOSED)

PATTERN	STAMPING	YEARS MADE	HANDLE	VARIATIONS	MINT PRICE
☐32093 F	Tested	Prior 1940	Yellow Composition		90.00
☐62093 F	Tested	Prior 1940	Green Bone		165.00

(LENGTH 3⅛″ CLOSED)
NEW TOLEDO SCALE

(LENGTH 3⅛″ CLOSED)
OLD TOLEDO SCALE

TOLEDO SCALE
(LENGTH 3⅛″)

PATTERN	STAMPING	YEARS MADE	HANDLE	VARIATIONS	MINT PRICE
☐T3105SS	XX	1950-53	Brass		160.00
☐T3105SS	XX	1973	Brass		80.00

Illustrated here are the two Toledo Scale (T3105SS) knives. They are named Toledo Scale because the first ones were made for the Toledo Scale Company. The original knives were made in early 1950's but Case had some blades left over from this issuance and they made 2,000 more, releasing them in June, 1973. The space in the design surrounding the areas finished in black has little dots on the new covers, while the old covers do not.

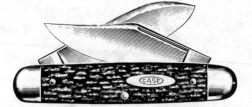

(LENGTH 4¼" CLOSED)

PATTERN	STAMPING	YEARS MADE	HANDLE	VARIATIONS	MINT PRICE
☐6294J	Tested	Prior 1950	Green Bone		500.00

(LENGTH 4¼" CLOSED)

PATTERN	STAMPING	YEARS MADE	HANDLE	VARIATIONS	MINT PRICE
☐6294	Tested	Prior 1950	Green Bone	Long Pull	500.00
☐	XX	1950-55	Green Bone	Long Pull	400.00
☐	XX	1950-55	Red Bone	Long Pull	250.00
☐	XX	1950-65	Red Bone		200.00
☐	XX	1950-55	Bone	Long Pull	175.00
☐	XX	1950-65	Bone		160.00

CITRUS
(LENGTH 4¼" CLOSED)

PATTERN	STAMPING	YEARS MADE	HANDLE	VARIATIONS	MINT PRICE
☐6296X	Tested	Prior 1950	Green Bone		400.00
☐6296X SS	XX	1950-55	Green Bone		250.00
☐6296X SS	XX	1950-65	Bone		120.00
☐6296X SS	USA	1965	Bone		220.00

FISHERMAN'S KNIFE
(LENGTH 4⅞″ CLOSED)

PATTERN	STAMPING	YEARS MADE	HANDLE	VARIATIONS	MINT PRICE
☐32095 F SS	Tested	Prior 1950	Yellow Composition		70.00
☐B2095 F SS	Tested	Prior 1950	Imitation Onyx		85.00
☐32095 F SS	XX	1950-65	Yellow Composition		25.00
☐	USA	1965-70	Yellow Composition		20.00
☐	10 Dots	1970-71	Yellow Composition		20.00
☐	Dots	1970's	Yellow Composition		17.00
☐	Lightning S 10 Dots	1980	Yellow Composition		15.00

(LENGTH 4½″)

PATTERN	STAMPING	YEARS MADE	HANDLE	VARIATIONS	MINT PRICE
☐3297	Tested	Prior 1940	Yellow Composition	This is not the same pattern as a sharkstooth	95.00

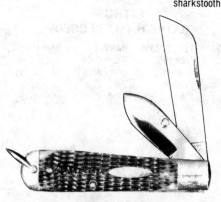

(LENGTH 4⅛″)

(LENGTH 4⅛")

PATTERN	STAMPING	YEARS MADE	HANDLE	VARIATIONS	MINT PRICES
☐6299 SH OP R	Tested	Prior 1940	Green Bone		**225.00**

(LENGTH 2⅞" CLOSED)

PATTERN	STAMPING	YEARS MADE	HANDLE	VARIATIONS	MINT PRICE
☐82099 R	Tested	Prior 1940	Pearl		**140.00**

(LENGTH 4⅛" CLOSED)

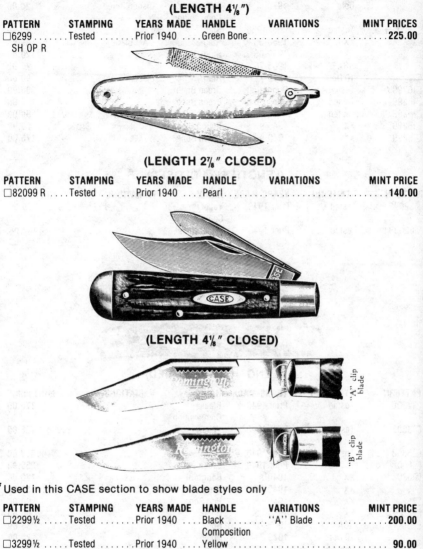

"A" clip blade

"B" clip blade

* Used in this CASE section to show blade styles only

PATTERN	STAMPING	YEARS MADE	HANDLE	VARIATIONS	MINT PRICE
☐2299½	Tested	Prior 1940	Black Composition	"A" Blade	**200.00**
☐3299½	Tested	Prior 1940	Yellow Composition		**90.00**
☐3299½	XX	1950-65	Yellow Composition	"A" Blade	**60.00**
☐	XX	1950-65	Yellow Composition		**40.00**
☐	USA	1965-70	Yellow Composition		**30.00**
☐	10 Dots	1970-71	Yellow Composition		**30.00**

☐	Dots	1970's	Yellow Composition	Discontinued	**20.00**
☐5299½	Tested	Prior 1950	Stag		**300.00**
☐	XX	1950-65	Stag	''A'' Blade	**140.00**
☐	XX	1950-65	Stag		**120.00**
☐	USA	1965-70	Stag		**75.00**
☐	10 Dots	1970-71	Stag	Discontinued	**90.00**
☐6299½	Tested	Prior 1950	Green Bone		**300.00**
☐6299	Tested	Prior 1950	Green Bone		**190.00**
☐6299	Tested		Rough Black		**80.00**
☐6299	XX	1940's	Rough Black		**90.00**
☐6299	XX	1940's	Green Bone		**175.00**

(LENGTH 5½ " CLOSED)

PATTERN	STAMPING	YEARS MADE	HANDLE	VARIATIONS	MINT PRICE
☐32098 F	Tested	Prior 1940	Yellow Composition		**70.00**
☐62098 F	Tested	Prior 1940	Green Bone		**180.00**

(LENGTH 3¼ " CLOSED)

PATTERN	STAMPING	YEARS MADE	HANDLE	VARIATIONS	MINT PRICE
☐2308	Tested	Prior 1940	Black Composition		**175.00**
☐3308	Tested	Prior 1940	Yellow Composition		**175.00**
☐5308	Tested	Prior 1940	Stag		**300.00**
☐6308	Tested	Prior 1940	Green Bone		**250.00**
☐6308	XX	1940's	Rough Black		**120.00**
☐	XX	1940-55	Green Bone		**150.00**
☐	XX	1940-55	Red Bone		**90.00**
☐	XX	1950-65	Bone		**60.00**
☐	USA	1965-70	Bone		**30.00**
☐	10 Dots	1970-71	Bone		**25.00**
☐	Dots	1970's	Bone		**20.00**
☐	Dots	1970's	Delrin		**18.00**
☐	Lightning S 10 Dots	1980	Bone		**18.00**

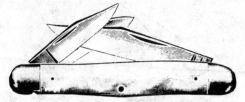

(LENGTH 3¼ " CLOSED)

PATTERN	STAMPING	YEARS MADE	HANDLE	VARIATIONS	MINT PRICE
☐8308	Tested	Prior 1940	Pearl		300.00

(LENGTH 3½ " CLOSED)

PATTERN	STAMPING	YEARS MADE	HANDLE	VARIATIONS	MINT PRICE
☐3318 SH SP	Tested	Prior 1940	Yellow Composition		75.00
☐3318 SH PEN	Tested	Prior 1940	Yellow Composition		75.00
☐3318 SH PEN	XX	1940-65	Yellow Composition		40.00
☐	USA	1965-70			25.00
☐	10 Dots	1970-71			17.00
☐3318	Lightning S 10 Dots				15.00
☐	Dots	1970's			15.00
☐4318 SP P	XX	1950-57	White Composition		90.00
☐4318 SH SP	XX	1957-65			45.00
☐	XX	1957-65		Calif. Clip blade	45.00
☐	USA	1965-70			40.00
☐	10 Dots	1970-71		Discontinued	40.00
☐	Dots	1970's			16.00
☐5318 SH SP	Tested	Prior 1940	Stag		190.00
☐6318 SH P	Tested	Prior 1940	Green Bone		150.00

(LENGTH 3½ " CLOSED)

PATTERN	STAMPING	YEARS MADE	HANDLE	VARIATIONS	MINT PRICE
☐6318 SP P	Tested	Prior 1940	Green Bone		150.00
☐	XX	1940-55	Green Bone		130.00
☐	XX	1940's	Rough Black		70.00
☐	XX	1950-65	Red Bone		55.00
☐	XX	1962-65	Bone		45.00
☐	USA	1965-70	Bone		24.00
☐	10 Dots	1970-71	Bone		22.00
☐	Dots	1970's	Bone		20.00
☐	Lightning S 10 Dots	1980	Bone		18.00
☐6318 SH SP	Tested	Prior 1940	Green Bone		150.00
☐	XX	1940-55	Green Bone	Long Pull	175.00
☐	XX	1940-55	Green Bone		120.00
☐	XX	1940's	Rough Black		50.00
☐	XX	1950-65	Red Bone		60.00
☐	XX	1950-65	Bone		40.00
☐	USA	1965-70	Bone		30.00
☐	10 Dots	1970-71	Bone		25.00
☐	Dots	1970's	Bone		20.00
☐	Dots	1970's	Delrin		16.00
☐	Lightning S 10 Dots	1980	Bone		18.00
☐6318 SP PEN	Tested	Prior 1940	Green Bone		150.00
☐6318 SH PEN	Tested	Prior 1940	Green Bone		150.00
☐	XX	1940-55	Green Bone		120.00
☐	XX	1940's	Rough Black		50.00
☐	XX	1950-65	Red Bone		60.00
☐	XX	1950-65	Bone		40.00
☐	USA	1965-70	Bone		30.00
☐	10 Dots	1970-71	Bone		25.00
☐	Dots	1970's	Bone		20.00
☐	Dots	1970's	Delrin		18.00
☐	Lightning S 10 Dots	1980	Bone		18.00
☐6318 SH SP SSP	USA	1965-66	Bone	Flat Ground, etched ''Tested XX Stainless''	50.00

☐	USA	1965-67	Bone	Concave Ground, polished blade, etched "Tested XX Razor edge"	**40.00**
☐	10 Dots	1970-71	Bone		**35.00**
☐	10 Dots	1970-71	Bone	Entire Blade polished	**45.00**
☐	Dots	1970's	Bone		**25.00**
☐	Lightning S 10 Dots	1980	Bone		**22.00**
☐5318 SSP	1 Dot 10 Dots	1979	Genuine Stag		**45.00**
☐	Dots	1970's	Delrin		**12.00**
☐8318	Tested	Prior 1940	Pearl		**200.00**
☐9318 SH PEN	Tested	Prior 1940	Imitation Pearl		**120.00**

CANOE
(LENGTH 3⅝" CLOSED)

PATTERN	STAMPING	YEARS MADE	HANDLE	VARIATIONS	MINT PRICE
☐53131	Tested	Prior 1940	Stag		950.00

(LENGTH 2¾" CLOSED)

PATTERN	STAMPING	YEARS MADE	HANDLE	VARIATIONS	MINT PRICE
☐6327 SH SP	XX	1957-65	Bone		35.00
☐	USA	1965-70	Bone		24.00
☐	10 Dots	1970-71	Bone		25.00
☐	10 Dots	1970-71	Delrin		16.00
☐	Dots	1970's	Delrin	Discontinued	15.00
☐9327 SH SP	XX	1957-65	Imitation Pearl		30.00
☐	USA	1965-70	Imitation Pearl		20.00
☐	10 Dots	1970-71	Imitation Pearl		17.00
☐	Dots	1971-74	Imitation Pearl	Discontinued	15.00
☐63027	3 Dots	1978	Delrin		12.00
☐	Lightning S 10 Dots	1980	Delrin		12.00

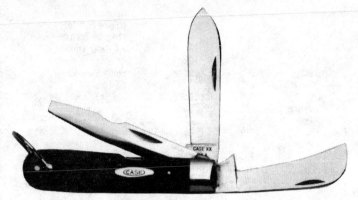

ELECTRICIAN'S KNIFE
(LENGTH 3¾ " CLOSED)

PATTERN	STAMPING	YEARS MADE	HANDLE	VARIATIONS	MINT PRICE
☐13031 L R	XX	1964-65	Walnut		38.00
☐	USA	1965-70			30.00
☐	10 Dots				25.00
☐	Dots	1970-74		Discontinued	20.00
☐	8 Dots	1970-74			20.00

(LENGTH 3⅝" CLOSED)

PATTERN	STAMPING	YEARS MADE	HANDLE	VARIATIONS	MINT PRICE
☐5332	Tested	Prior 1940	Stag		200.00
☐	XX	1960-65	Stag		110.00
☐	USA	1965-70	Stag		65.00
☐	10 Dots	1970-71	Stag	Discontinued in '70	65.00
☐	9 Dots	1973	Stag	From the Collector's Sets	75.00
☐6332	Tested	Prior 1940	Green Bone		200.00
☐	XX	1940-55	Green Bone		150.00
☐	XX	1940's	Rough Black		90.00
☐	XX	1950-55	Red Bone		85.00
☐	XX	1950-65	Bone		50.00
☐	USA	1965-70	Bone		35.00
☐	10 Dots	1970-71	Bone		30.00
☐	Dots	1970's	Bone		20.00
☐	Dots	1970's	Delrin	Discontinued after 2 Dots-Changed to 63032	18.00
☐	Lightning S 10 Dots	1980	Bone		20.00

(LENGTH 2⅝" CLOSED)

PATTERN	STAMPING	YEARS MADE	HANDLE	VARIATIONS	MINT PRICE
☐6333	Tested	Prior 1940	Green Bone		150.00
☐	XX	1940-55	Green Bone		110.00
☐	XX	1940's	Rough Black		50.00
☐	XX	1940's	Rough Black	Long Pull	65.00
☐	XX	1950-65	Bone		40.00

☐	USA	1965-70	Bone		**30.00**
☐	10 Dots	1970-71	Bone		**25.00**
☐	10 Dots	1970-71	Delrin		**20.00**
☐	Dots	1970's	Delrin	Discontinued	**14.00**
☐9333	Tested	Prior 1950	Imitation Pearl		**85.00**
☐	XX	1950-65	Imitation Pearl	Long Pull	**40.00**
☐	XX	1950-65	Imitation Pearl		**28.00**
☐	USA	1965-70	Imitation Pearl		**20.00**
☐	10 Dots	1970-71	Imitation Pearl		**20.00**
☐	Dots	1970-74	Imitation Pearl	Discontinued	**15.00**
☐63033	1 Dot	1979	Delrin		**12.00**
☐93033	1 Dot	1979	Imitation Pearl	C. Ice	**15.00**
☐63033	Lightning S 10 Dots		Delrin		**12.00**

(LENGTH 3¼″ CLOSED)

PATTERN	STAMPING	YEARS MADE	HANDLE	VARIATIONS	MINT PRICE
☐3344 SP P	Tested	Prior 1940	Imitation Onyx		**80.00**
☐3344 SH P	Tested	Prior 1940	Yellow Composition		**80.00**
☐3344 SP P	Tested	Prior 1940	Yellow Composition		**80.00**
☐3344 SH SP	Tested	Prior 1940			**80.00**
☐3344 SH PEN	Tested	Prior 1940			**80.00**
☐5344 SHSP	Tested	Prior 1940	Stag		**125.00**
☐5344 SH PEN	Tested	Prior 1940	Stag		**125.00**
☐6344 SH P	Tested	Prior 1940	Green Bone		**110.00**
☐6344 SP P	Tested	Prior 1940	Green Bone		**110.00**
☐6344 SP PEN	Tested	Prior 1940	Green Bone		**110.00**
☐6344 SH SP	Tested	Prior 1940	Green Bone		**110.00**
☐	XX	1940-55	Green Bone		**110.00**
☐	XX	1950-65	Red Bone		**50.00**
☐	XX	1960-65	Bone		**35.00**
☐	USA	1965-70	Bone		**25.00**

☐	10 Dots	1970-71	Bone		**25.00**
☐	10 Dots	1970-71	Delrin		**20.00**
☐	9 Dots	1971-72	Bone	Limited # in bone	**30.00**
☐	Dots	1970's	Delrin		**15.00**
☐	Lightning S 10 Dots	1980	Delrin		**12.00**
☐6344 SH PEN	Tested	Prior 1940	Green Bone		**110.00**
☐	XX	1940-55	Green Bone		**90.00**
☐	XX	1950-65	Red Bone		**50.00**
☐	XX	1950-65	Bone		**35.00**
☐	USA	1965-70	Bone		**22.00**
☐	10 Dots	1970-71	Bone		**25.00**
☐	10 Dots	1970-71	Delrin		**20.00**
☐	Dots	1970's	Delrin		**13.95**
☐9344 SH PEN	Tested	Prior 1940	Imitation Pearl		**90.00**
☐9344 SH SP	Tested	Prior 1940	Imitation Pearl		**90.00**

BIRDSEYE
(LENGTH 3¼ " CLOSED)

PATTERN	STAMPING	YEARS MADE	HANDLE	VARIATIONS	MINT PRICE
☐33044 SH SP	XX	1964-65	Yellow Composition		**70.00**
☐	USA	1965-70			**45.00**
☐	10 Dots	1970-71			**40.00**
☐	Dots	1970's		Discontinued 1978	**25.00**

(LENGTH 3⅝" CLOSED)

PATTERN	STAMPING	YEARS MADE	HANDLE	VARIATIONS	MINT PRICE
☐2345½ SP PEN	Tested	Prior 1940	Black Composition		**110.00**

□2345½ P	Tested	Prior 1940	Black Composition		**135.00**
□2345½ P	XX	1940's	Black Composition	Long Pull	**120.00**
□2345½ SH	XX	1950-65	Black Composition		**60.00**
□2345½ SH	USA	1965-67	Black Composition		**135.00**
□6345½ SH	Tested	Prior 1940	Green Bone		**230.00**
□	XX	1940-55	Green Bone		**175.00**
□	XX	1950-65	Red Bone		**110.00**
□	XX	1950-65	Bone		**70.00**

(LENGTH 3⅞" CLOSED)

PATTERN	STAMPING	YEARS MADE	HANDLE	VARIATIONS	MINT PRICE
□3347 SH P	Tested	Prior 1940	Yellow Composition		**85.00**
□3347 SH SP	Tested	Prior 1940	Yellow Composition		**90.00**
□3347 SP PEN	Tested	Prior 1940	Yellow Composition		**90.00**
□3347 SH SP	XX	1940-53		Long Pull	**60.00**
□	XX	1950-65			**30.00**
□	USA	1965-65			**25.00**
□	10 Dots	1970-71			**20.00**
□	Dots	1970's			**15.00**
□	Lightning S 10 Dots	1980			**15.00**
□5347 SH PEN	Tested	Prior 1940	Stag		**215.00**
□5347 SH SP	Tested	Prior 1940	Stag		**200.00**
□	XX	1950-65	Stag	Long Pull	**190.00**
□	XX	1950-65	Stag		**110.00**
□	USA	1965-70	Stag		**60.00**
□	10 Dots	1970-71	Stag	Discontinued	**70.00**
□5347 SSP	4 Dots	1977	Stag		**50.00**
□5347 SS	3 Dots	1978	Stag	1978 Sets	**45.00**
□5347 SSP	2 Dots	1979	Stag		**40.00**
□5347 SH SP SS	XX	1950-65	Stag		**140.00**
□	USA	1965-70	Stag		**80.00**
□	10 Dots	1970-71	Stag	Discontinued	**175.00**

☐5347 SH SP SSP	9 Dots	1973	Stag	From the Collector's Sets	70.00
☐6347 J	Tested	Prior 1940	Green Bone		275.00
☐6347 PJ	Tested	Prior 1940	Green Bone		275.00
☐6347 SH P	Tested	Prior 1940 P	Green Bone		275.00
☐	XX	1940-55	Green Bone	Long Pull	225.00
☐	XX	1940-55	Green Bone		150.00
☐	XX	1940's	Rough Black	Long Pull	110.00
☐	XX	1950-65	Bone		50.00
☐	USA	1965-66	Bone		30.00
☐6347 SP P	Tested	Prior 1940	Green Bone		275.00
☐	XX	1940-55	Green Bone	Long Pull	225.00
☐	XX	1940-55	Green Bone		150.00
☐	XX	1950-65	Red Bone		75.00
☐	XX	1950-65	Bone		50.00
☐	USA	1965-70	Bone		40.00
☐	10 Dots	1970-71	Bone		35.00
☐	Dots	1970-75	Bone	Discontinued	35.00
☐6347 SP PEN	Tested	Prior 1940	Green Bone		250.00
☐6347 SH PEN	Tested	Prior 1940	Green Bone		250.00
☐	XX	1955-65	Bone		45.00
☐	XX	1940-55	Green Bone		170.00
☐	XX	1940's	Rough Black		75.00
☐	XX	1950-65	Red Bone		85.00
☐	XX	1950-65	Bone		45.00
☐	USA	1965-70	Bone		38.00
☐	10 Dots	1970-71	Bone		25.00
☐	Dots	1970-76	Bone	Discontinued	22.00
☐6347 SH SP	Tested	Prior 1940	Green Bone		225.00
☐	XX	Prior 1940	Green Bone	Long Pull	275.00
☐	XX		Green Bone		170.00
☐	XX	1940's	Rough Black	Long Pull	90.00
☐	XX	1940's	Rough Black		60.00
☐	XX	1950-65	Red Bone		75.00
☐	XX	1950-65	Bone		45.00
☐	USA	1965-70	Bone		30.00
☐	Lightning S. 10 Dots	1980	Bone		20.00

(LENGTH 3⅞″ CLOSED)

PATTERN	STAMPING	YEARS MADE	HANDLE	VARIATIONS	MINT PRICE
☐6347 SH SP SSP	10 Dots	1970-71	Bone		35.00
☐	Dots	1970's	Bone		22.00
☐	Dots	1970's	Delrin		20.00
☐6347 SH SP SS	XX	1950-55	Green Bone		150.00
☐	XX	1950-65	Bone		70.00
☐	XX	1955-65	Red Bone		85.00
☐6347 SH SP SSP	USA	1965-70	Bone		40.00
☐	Lightning S. 10 Dots	1980	Bone		22.00

☐	USA	1965		Blade etched Tested XX Stainless (1st Model)	70.00
☐	USA	1965-70	Bone	Polished Blade	45.00
☐	10 Dots				30.00
☐53047	XX	1955-65	Stag		100.00
☐	USA	1965-70	Stag		60.00
☐	10 Dots	1970-	Stag		70.00
☐63047	XX	1955-65	Bone		50.00
☐	USA	1965-70	Bone		40.00
☐	10 Dots	1970-71	Bone		35.00
☐	Dots	1970's	Bone	Discontinued	30.00
☐	Dots	1970's	Delrin		20.00
☐SR63047	1 Dot		Smooth Rose Bone		35.00
☐SR63047	1 Dot		Smooth Green Bone		40.00
☐93047	XX	1950-56	Imitation Pearl		165.00

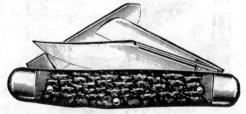

(LENGTH 4″ CLOSED)

PATTERN	STAMPING	YEARS MADE	HANDLE	VARIATIONS	MINT PRICE
☐630047	Tested	Prior 1940	Green Bone		**170.00**
☐630047 P	Tested	Prior 1940	Green Bone		**170.00**
☐630047 SH PEN	Tested	Prior 1940	Green Bone		**170.00**

(LENGTH 3½″ CLOSED)

PATTERN	STAMPING	YEARS MADE	HANDLE	VARIATIONS	MINT PRICE
☐63052	Tested	Prior 1940	Green Bone		**325.00**

No photo was available, but is very similar to the 62055 and 64055, differing only in the number of blades, one which is a punch blade.

PATTERN	STAMPING	YEARS MADE	HANDLE	VARIATIONS	MINT PRICE
☐33055 P	Tested	Prior 1940	Yellow Composition		**200.00**
☐23055	XX	1942	Black Composition	Long Pull	**200.00**
☐23055	XX	1942	Black Composition	Long Pull	**200.00**

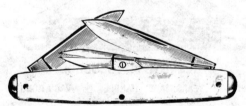

(LENGTH 3⁷⁄₁₆″ CLOSED)

PATTERN	STAMPING	YEARS MADE	HANDLE	VARIATIONS	MINT PRICE
☐8360 SCI	Tested	Prior 1940	Pearl		**175.00**

(LENGTH 3⅛″ CLOSED)

PATTERN	STAMPING	YEARS MADE	HANDLE	VARIATIONS	MINT PRICE
☐5364 T	Tested	Prior 1940	Stag		**200.00**
☐8364 SCIS	Tested	Prior 1940	Pearl		**175.00**
☐8364 T	Tested	Prior 1940	Pearl		**175.00**

☐8364 T SS	XX	1950-60	Pearl			**85.00**
☐8364	XX	1950-65	Pearl			**85.00**
SCIS SS						
☐	USA	1965-70	Pearl			**75.00**
☐	10 Dots	1970-71	Pearl	Discontinued		**70.00**
☐	Dots			Discontinued		**65.00**

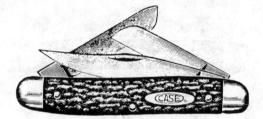

(LENGTH 3⅛" CLOSED)

PATTERN	STAMPING	YEARS MADE	HANDLE	VARIATIONS	MINT PRICE
☐6366	Tested	Prior 1940	Green Bone		**190.00**
☐6366 PEN	Tested	Prior 1940	Green Bone		**190.00**

(LENGTH 3⅛" CLOSED)

PATTERN	STAMPING	YEARS MADE	HANDLE	VARIATIONS	MINT PRICE
☐6370	Tested	Prior 1940	Green Bone		**290.00**

(LENGTH 4⁵⁄₁₆" CLOSED)

PATTERN	STAMPING	YEARS MADE	HANDLE	VARIATIONS	MINT PRICE
☐5375	Tested	Prior 1940	Stag		**300.00**
☐	XX	1940-54	Stag	Long Pull	**225.00**
☐	XX	1950-65	Stag		**110.00**
☐	XX	1960-65	Stag (second cut)		**500.00**
☐	USA	1965-70	Stag (second cut)		**500.00**

☐	USA	1965-70	Stag		**75.00**
☐	10 Dots	1970	Stag		**75.00**
☐6375	Tested	Prior 1940	Green Bone		**400.00**
☐	XX	1940-55	Green Bone	Long Pull	**300.00**
☐	XX	1940's	Rough Black	Long Pull	**140.00**
☐	XX	1940-55	Red Bone	Long Pull	**225.00**
☐	XX	1950-65	Red Bone		**90.00**
☐	XX	1950-55	Bone	Long Pull	**160.00**
☐	XX	1950-65	Bone		**60.00**
☐	USA	1965-70	Bone		**40.00**
☐	10 Dots	1970-71	Bone		**35.00**
☐	Dots	1970's	Bone		**24.00**
☐	Dots	1970's	Delrin		**15.00**
☐	Lightning S. 10 Dots	1980	Bone		**20.00**

(LENGTH 4″ CLOSED)

PATTERN	STAMPING	YEARS MADE	HANDLE	VARIATIONS	MINT PRICE
☐2376	Tested	Prior 1940	Black Composition		**190.00**

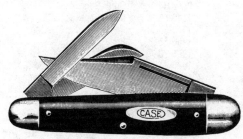

(LENGTH 3⅝″ CLOSED)

PATTERN	STAMPING	YEARS MADE	HANDLE	VARIATIONS	MINT PRICE
☐2376½	Tested	Prior 1940	Black Composition		**175.00**
☐5376½	Tested	Prior 1940	Stag		**400.00**
☐6376½	Tested	Prior 1940	Green Bone		**400.00**

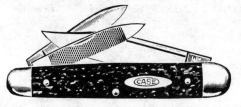

(LENGTH 3¼″ CLOSED)

PATTERN	STAMPING	YEARS MADE	HANDLE	VARIATIONS	MINT PRICE
☐63079½F	Tested	Prior 1940	Green Bone		**275.00**

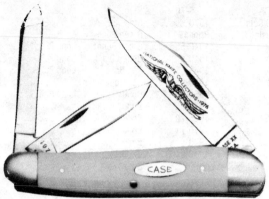

WHITTLER
(LENGTH 3⅞" CLOSED)

PATTERN	STAMPING	YEARS MADE	HANDLE	VARIATIONS	MINT PRICE
☐4380	Dots	1976	White Comp.	NKCA Club Knife	200.00
☐6380	Tested	Prior 1940	Green Bone		425.00
☐	XX	1940-55	Green Bone		350.00
☐	XX	1940-55	Red Bone		125.00
☐	XX	1955-65	Bone		80.00
☐	USA	1965-70	Bone		45.00
☐	10 Dots	1970-71	Bone		40.00
☐	Dots	1970's	Bone	Discontinued	30.00
☐	Dots	1970's	Delrin	Discontinued	21.00

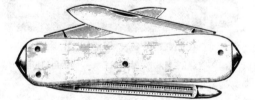

(LENGTH 3" CLOSED)

PATTERN	STAMPING	YEARS MADE	HANDLE	VARIATIONS	MINT PRICE
☐83081	Tested	Prior 1940	Pearl		150.00

(LENGTH 3³⁄₁₆" CLOSED)

PATTERN	STAMPING	YEARS MADE	HANDLE	VARIATIONS	MINT PRICE
☐83083	Tested	Prior 1940	Pearl		200.00

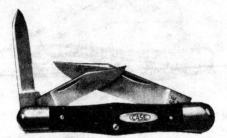

(LENGTH 3½ " CLOSED)

PATTERN	STAMPING	YEARS MADE	HANDLE	VARIATIONS	MINT PRICE
☐2383	Tested	Prior 1940	Black Composition		150.00
☐2383 SAB	XX	1940's	Black Composition		165.00
☐2383	XX	1950-65	Black Composition		75.00
☐2383	USA	1965-66	Black Composition		90.00
☐5383	Tested	Prior 1950	Stag		325.00
☐	XX	1950-65	Stag		110.00
☐	USA	1965-70	Stag		75.00
☐	10 Dots	1970-71	Stag		85.00
☐6383 SAB	Tested	Prior 1940	Green Bone		450.00
☐6383 SAB	XX	1940-42	Bone		150.00
☐6383 SAB	XX	1940's	Rough Black		165.00
☐6383	Tested	Prior 1940	Green Bone		400.00
☐6383	XX	1940's	Rough Black		150.00
☐6383	XX	1940-55	Red Bone		100.00
☐6383	XX	1955-65	Bone		80.00
☐6383	USA	1965-70	Bone		45.00
☐6383	10 Dots	1970-71	Bone		35.00
☐6383	Dots	1970's	Bone		24.00
☐6383	Dots	1970's	Delrin		15.00
☐6383	Lightning S. 10 Dots	1980	Bone		20.00
☐9383 SAB	Tested	Prior 1940	Imitation Pearl		200.00
☐9383 SAB	Tested	1940-42	Imitation Pearl		170.00
☐	XX	1940-42	Imitation Pearl		145.00

(LENGTH 3¼ " CLOSED)

PATTERN	STAMPING	YEARS MADE	HANDLE	VARIATIONS	MINT PRICE
☐23087 SH PEN	Tested	Prior 1940	Black Composition		60.00
☐	XX	1950-65			22.00
☐	USA	1965-70			22.00
☐	10 Dots	1970-71			18.00
☐	Dots	1970's			13.95
☐23087	Lightning S 10 Dots	1980	Bone		12.00
☐43087 SH SP	Tested	Prior 1950	White Composition		70.00
☐63087 SP PEN	Tested	Prior 1950	Green Bone		90.00
☐53087 SH PEN	XX	1940-65	Stag		65.00
☐	USA	1965-70	Stag		60.00
☐	10 Dots	1970-71	Stag		65.00
☐	9 Dots	1973	Stag	Made Only for the 1st Collector's Sets	60.00
☐63087 SH PEN	XX	1940-55	Green Bone		75.00
☐	XX	1940's	Rough Black		50.00
☐	XX	1950-65	Red Bone		50.00
☐	XX	1950-65	Bone		30.00
☐	USA	1965-70	Bone		21.00
☐	10 Dots	1970-71	Bone		25.00
☐	10 Dots	1970-71	Delrin		15.00
☐	Dots	1970's	Delrin		13.95
☐63087	Lightning S 10 Dots	1980	Bone		18.00

(LENGTH 3⅛" CLOSED)

PATTERN	STAMPING	YEARS MADE	HANDLE	VARIATIONS	MINT PRICE
☐83088 SS	Tested	Prior 1950	Pearl		165.00
☐83088 SS	XX	1950-64	Pearl		110.00

(LENGTH 3¹⁄₁₆″ CLOSED)

PATTERN	STAMPING	YEARS MADE	HANDLE	VARIATIONS	MINT PRICE
☐83089	Tested	Prior 1950	Pearl		**165.00**
☐83089 SC F SS	XX	1950-65	Pearl		**135.00**
☐83089 SC F SS	USA	1965-66	Pearl		**200.00**

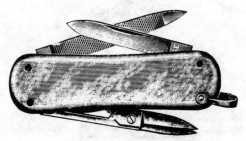

(LENGTH 2¼″ CLOSED)

PATTERN	STAMPING	YEARS MADE	HANDLE	VARIATIONS	MINT PRICE
☐83090 SC R SS	Tested	Prior 1940	Pearl		**165.00**
☐83090 SC R SS	XX	1940-65	Pearl		**135.00**

WHITTLER
(LENGTH 4½″ CLOSED)

PATTERN	STAMPING	YEARS MADE	HANDLE	VARIATIONS	MINT PRICE
☐3391	Tested	Prior 1940	Yellow Composition		**1000.00**
☐5391	Tested	Prior 1940	Stag		**1500.00**

☐5391	Tested	Prior 1940	Stag (second cut)	**1500.00**
☐	XX	1940-42	Stag	**1200.00**
☐6391	Tested	Prior 1940	Green Bone	**2000.00**

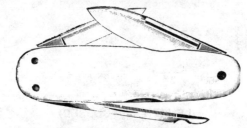

(LENGTH 2¼″ CLOSED)

PATTERN	STAMPING	YEARS MADE	HANDLE	VARIATIONS	MINT PRICE
☐83091	Tested	Prior 1940	Pearl		**160.00**

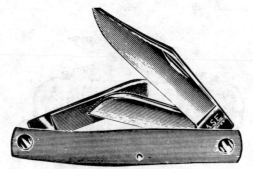

BIRDS EYE
(LENGTH 4″ CLOSED)

PATTERN	STAMPING	YEARS MADE	HANDLE	VARIATIONS	MINT PRICE
☐33092	Tested	Prior 1950	Yellow Composition		**150.00**
☐	XX	1950-65	Yellow Composition	Without shield	**45.00**
☐	XX	1950-65	Yellow Composition	With shield	**58.00**
☐	USA	1965-70	Yellow Composition		**35.00**
☐	10 Dots	1970-71	Yellow Composition		**30.00**
☐	Dots	1970's	Yellow Composition		**21.00**

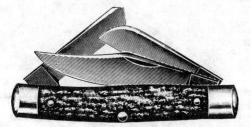

(LENGTH 4″ CLOSED)

PATTERN	STAMPING	YEARS MADE	HANDLE	VARIATIONS	MINT PRICE
☐630092	Tested	Prior 1940	Green Bone		225.00
☐630092 P	Tested	Prior 1940	Green Bone		225.00

(LENGTH 4″ CLOSED)

PATTERN	STAMPING	YEARS MADE	HANDLE	VARIATIONS	MINT PRICE
☐5392	Tested	Prior 1950	Stag		250.00
☐	XX	1950-65	Stag		100.00
☐	USA	1965-70	Stag		60.00
☐	10 Dots	1970	Stag	Discontinued	65.00
☐6392P	Tested	Prior 1950	Green Bone	Punch Blade	325.00
☐6392	Tested	Prior 1950	Green Bone		300.00
☐6392	XX	1940's	Rough Black		80.00
☐6392	XX	1940-50's	Green Bone		175.00
☐6392	XX	1940-50's	Red Bone		75.00
☐6392	XX	1950-65	Bone		50.00
☐6392	USA	1965-70	Bone		35.00
☐6392	10 Dots	1970-71	Bone		30.00
☐6392	Dots	1970's	Bone		24.25
☐	Lightning S. 10 Dots	1980	Bone		21.00

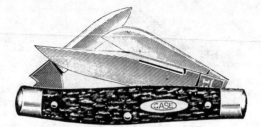

(LENGTH 3¹⁵⁄₁₆" CLOSED)

PATTERN	STAMPING	YEARS MADE	HANDLE	VARIATIONS	MINT PRICE
☐6393 PEN	Tested	Prior 1940	Green Bone		250.00
☐6393	Tested	Prior 1940	Green Bone		250.00
☐5393	Tested	Prior 1940	Stag		275.00
☐9393	Tested	Prior 1940	Imitation Pearl		150.00

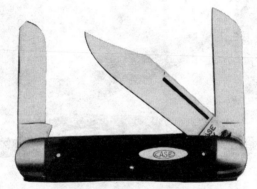

(LENGTH 4¼" CLOSED)

PATTERN	STAMPING	YEARS MADE	HANDLE	VARIATIONS	MINT PRICE
☐6394½	Tested	Prior 1940	Green Bone		600.00
☐5394	Tested	Prior 1940	Stag		1250.00
☐6394½	XX	1940's	Green Bone	Long Pull	500.00
☐6394½	XX	1940's	Red Bone		500.00

GUNBOAT
(LENGTH 4¼" CLOSED)

PATTERN	STAMPING	YEARS MADE	HANDLE	VARIATIONS	MINT PRICE
☐5394	Tested	Prior 1940	Stag		**1250.00**

NAVY KNIFE
(LENGTH 4¹³⁄₁₆″ CLOSED)

PATTERN	STAMPING	YEARS MADE	HANDLE	VARIATIONS	MINT PRICE
☐CASE	XX	42-45	METAL		**75.00**
☐CASE	XX	42-45	METAL	British Ordmarks	**75.00**

FLY FISHERMAN
(LENGTH 3⅞″ CLOSED)

PATTERN	STAMPING	YEARS MADE	HANDLE	VARIATIONS	MINT PRICE
☐Fly Fisherman	Tested	Prior 1950	Stainless Steel		**175.00**
☐Fly Fisherman	XX	1950-55	Stainless Steel	Not Stainless Blades	**130.00**
☐Case Fly Fisherman	XX SS	1950-65			**125.00**
☐Case Fly Fisherman	Transition SS	1964-65		XX to US	**110.00**
☐Case Fly Fisherman	USA SS	1965-70			**110.00**
☐Case Fly Fisherman	Transition SS	1969-70		USA to 10 Dots	**100.00**
☐Case Fly Fisherman	10 Dots SS	1970-71			**100.00**
☐	Dots	1970's		Discontinued	**95.00**

SCOUT KNIFE
(LENGTH ⅝″ CLOSED)

PATTERN	STAMPING	YEARS MADE	HANDLE	VARIATIONS	MINT PRICE
☐640045R	Tested	Prior 1940	Black Composition		**45.00**
☐	XX	1950-65	Black Composition		**18.00**

☐	XX	1950-65	Brown Composition		**18.00**
☐	USA	1965-70	Brown Composition		**14.00**
☐	10 Dots	1970-71	Brown Composition		**15.00**
☐	Dots	1970's	Brown Composition		**12.00**

(LENGTH 3¾" CLOSED)

PATTERN	STAMPING	YEARS MADE	HANDLE	VARIATIONS	MINT PRICE
☐6445 R	Tested	Prior 1940	Green Bone		**140.00**
☐6445 R	Tested	Prior 1940	Black Composition		**80.00**
☐6445 R	Tested	Prior 1940	Rough Black		**80.00**
☐6445 R	XX	1940-50	Rough Black		**50.00**
☐	XX	1942-50	Black Composition		**35.00**
☐	XX	1940-55	Red Bone		**55.00**
☐	XX	1940-65	Bone		**45.00**
☐	USA	1965-70	Bone		**35.00**
☐	10 Dots	1970-71	Bone		**30.00**
☐	Dots	1970's	Bone	Discontinued	**25.00**
☐	Dots	1970's	Delrin	Discontinued	**15.00**

(LENGTH 4" CLOSED)

PATTERN	STAMPING	YEARS MADE	HANDLE	VARIATIONS	MINT PRICE
☐64047 P	Tested	Prior 1940	Green Bone		**250.00**
☐94047 P	Tested	Prior 1940	Imitation Pearl		**180.00**
☐64047 P	XX	1940-55	Green Bone		**180.00**
☐	XX	1942-55	Rough Black		**120.00**
☐	XX	1950-65	Bone		**45.00**
☐	USA	1965-70	Bone		**35.00**

☐	10 Dots	1970-71	Bone		**30.00**
☐	Dots	1970's	Bone		**27.00**
☐	Dots	1970's	Delrin		**14.00**
☐	Dots 10 Dot	1979	Bone	Discontinued	**27.00**

(LENGTH 4″ CLOSED)

PATTERN	STAMPING	YEARS MADE	HANDLE	VARIATIONS	MINT PRICE
☐3452	Tested	Prior 1940	Yellow Composition		165.00
☐6452	Tested	Prior 1940	Green Bone		190.00

(LENGTH 3½ ″ CLOSED)

PATTERN	STAMPING	YEARS MADE	HANDLE	VARIATIONS	MINT PRICE
☐54052	Tested	Prior 1950	Stag		275.00
☐	XX	1950-65	Stag		120.00
☐	Transition	1964-65	Stag	XX to USA	140.00
☐	USA	1965-70	Stag		70.00
☐	Transition	1969-70	Stag	USA to 10 Dots	90.00
☐	10 Dots	1970-71	Stag	Discontinued	75.00
☐64052	Tested	Prior 1940	Green Bone		300.00
☐	XX	1940-55	Green Bone		200.00
☐	XX	1940-55	Red Bone		110.00
☐	XX	1955-65	Bone		65.00
☐	Transition	1964-65	Bone	XX to USA	50.00
☐	USA	1965-70	Bone		45.00
☐	Transition	1969-70	Bone	USA to 10 Dots	40.00
☐	10 Dots	1970-71	Bone		40.00
☐	Dots	1970's	Bone		25.00
☐	Dots	1970's	Delrin		20.00
☐	Lightning S. 10 Dots	1980	Bone		20.00

(LENGTH 3⁷⁄₁₆″ CLOSED)

PATTERN	STAMPING	YEARS MADE	HANDLE	VARIATIONS	MINT PRICE
☐ 64055 P	Tested	1940-42	Green Bone		500.00

(LENGTH 3⅜″ CLOSED)

PATTERN	STAMPING	YEARS MADE	HANDLE	VARIATIONS	MINT PRICE
☐ 5460	Tested	Prior 1940	Stag		325.00

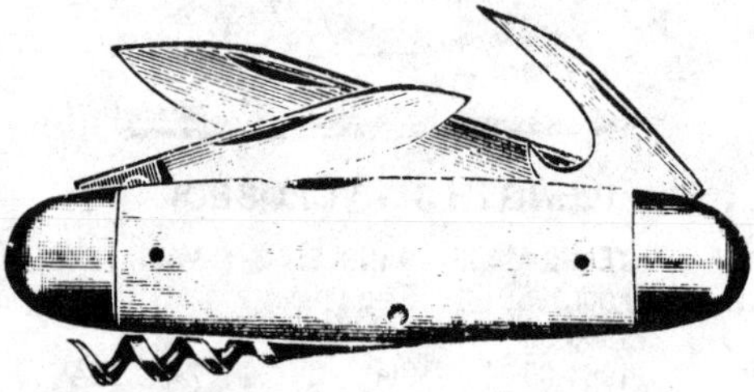

(LENGTH 3⁵⁄₁₆″ CLOSED)

PATTERN	STAMPING	YEARS MADE	HANDLE	VARIATIONS	MINT PRICE
☐ 84062 K	Tested	Prior 1940	Pearl		350.00

FOLDING HUNTER
(LENGTH 5¼″ CLOSED)

PATTERN	STAMPING	YEARS MADE	HANDLE	VARIATIONS	MINT PRICE
☐ 6465 CLASP	Tested	Prior 1940	Green Bone		1850.00

(LENGTH 3⅛″ CLOSED)

PATTERN	STAMPING	YEARS MADE	HANDLE	VARIATIONS	MINT PRICE
☐ 6470	Tested	Prior 1940	Green Bone		350.00

BABY SCOUT KNIFE
(LENGTH 3⅜″ CLOSED)

PATTERN	STAMPING	YEARS MADE	HANDLE	VARIATIONS	MINT PRICE
☐640090	Tested	Prior 1940	Green Bone		120.00

(LENGTH 4″ CLOSED)

PATTERN	STAMPING	YEARS MADE	HANDLE	VARIATIONS	MINT PRICE
☐6592	Tested	Prior 1940	Green Bone		1600.00

(LENGTH 4⅛″ CLOSED)

PATTERN	STAMPING	YEARS MADE	HANDLE	VARIATIONS	MINT PRICE
☐5488	Tested	Prior 1940	Stag		400.00
☐5488	XX	1940-54	Stag	Long Pull	350.00
☐5488	XX	1950-65	Stag		160.00
☐5488	XX	1960-65	Stag (second cut)		350.00
☐5488	Transition	1964-65	Stag	XX to USA	175.00
☐5488	Transition	1964-65	Stag (second cut)	XX togUSA	350.00
☐	USA	1965-70	Stag		110.00
☐	USA	1965-70	Stag (second cut)		350.00
☐	10 Dots	1970-July	70 Stag	Discontinued	155.00
☐6488	XX	1940-55	Green Bone	Long Pull	400.00
☐	XX	1940-55	Rough Black	Long Pull	200.00
☐	XX	1940-55	Red Bone	Long Pull	285.00
☐	XX	1940-55	Red Bone		120.00
☐	XX	1940-55	Bone	Long Pull	150.00
☐	Transition	1964-65	Bone	XX to USA	100.00
☐	USA	1965-70	Bone		70.00
☐	USA	1965-70	Stag (second cut)	This No. was stamped with both a 5″ and 6″	350.00
☐	Transition	1969-70	Bone	USA to 10 Dots	60.00
☐	10 Dots	1970-71	Bone		50.00
☐	Dots	1970's	Bone	Discontinued	35.00
☐	Dots	1970's	Delrin	Discontinued	20.00
☐	Transitions	1970's	Bone	8 to 10 Dots	45.00

OLDER CASE KNIVES

PATTERN NO.	MINT PRICE	PATTERN NO.	MINT PRICE	PATTERN NO.	MINT PRICE
6100	400.00	5308	200.00	6217	135.00
P200	300.00	6208	200.00	B318 SH SP	100.00
5200	300.00	8308	300.00	3318 SH SP	100.00
6200	450.00	6209	125.00	3318 SH PEN	100.00
9200	450.00	62009	125.00	5318 SH SP	150.00
3201	60.00	62009 RAZ	200.00	6318 SH SP	115.00
3201 R	60.00	62009 SH	125.00	6318 SH P	115.00
6201	60.00	62009 SP	140.00	6318 SH PEN	115.00
62001	60.00	62009½	125.00	8318 SH SP	200.00
8201	80.00	83109	125.00	5318 SH SP	130.00
82001	75.00	3210½	150.00	9318 SP PEN	130.00
9201	65.00	5210½	175.00	6219	200.00
9201 R	65.00	6210	165.00	62019	210.00
P202	135.00	6210 S	180.00	Y220	140.00
R202	135.00	62010	165.00	3220	140.00
1202 D&B	400.00	6210½	165.00	5220	150.00
5202 RAZ	275.00	B1011	85.00	66220	150.00
5202½	180.00	R111½	400.00	62200	75.00
6202	185.00	11011	95.00	62020 S	75.00
6202 I	185.00	3111½	400.00	62020½	75.00
6202 S	185.00	6111½	400.00	8220	170.00
6202½	186.00	6111½	300.00	9220	150.00
6202½	185.00	61011	95.00	B221	150.00
B3102	125.00	6211	315.00	0B221	150.00
63102	175.00	6211½	315.00	6221	150.00
83102	190.00	1212L	100.00	06221	105.00
6103 B&G	65.00	62012	95.00	06221½	105.00
6203	65.00	61013	100.00	08221	160.00
2104	100.00	6213	225.00	6321	175.00
6104 BUD	190.00	5214½	150.00	G222	90.00
M204	80.00	6214	100.00	6222	90.00
6204½	190.00	6214½	100.00	8222	110.00
5205	300.00	P215	115.00	P223	125.00
5205 RAZ	250.00	6215	115.00	6223	125.00
5205½	250.00	8215	150.00	9223	125.00
6205	265.00	6116	90.00	3124	80.00
6205 RAZ	300.00	6116½	90.00	3124½	80.00
6205½	250.00	61016½	80.00	6124	80.00
6106	100.00	22016	95.00	6124½	80.00
5206½	115.00	22016½	95.00	B224	90.00
6206	125.00	6216	115.00	3224	80.00
6206½	125.00	6216 I	115.00	3224½	80.00
62006½	125.00	6216 S	115.00	5224	150.00
8206	200.00	6216 EO	125.00	52024	150.00
3207	190.00	62016	80.00	5224½	150.00
5207	175.00	62016½	115.00	52024½	150.00
6207	175.00	62016 S	115.00	6224	85.00
8407	400.00	6216½	115.00	62024	110.00
5208	175.00	6216½ I	115.00	62024 RAZ	125.00
6208	150.00	62116	80.00	62024 SH	125.00
3308	200.00	2217	125.00	62024½	110.00

PATTERN NO.	MINT PRICE	PATTERN NO.	MINT PRICE	PATTERN NO.	MINT PRICE
8224	150.00	G232	125.00	B224	110.00
32025½	100.00	3232	125.00	3244	100.00
5225½	165.00	6232	125.00	5224	125.00
6225	125.00	5332	160.00	05244	125.00
6225½	125.00	6332	130.00	6224	125.00
62025½	100.00	3233	60.00	06244	90.00
8225	175.00	6233	60.00	62044	95.00
B226	150.00	62033	60.00	62044 FILE	95.00
6226	150.00	8233	90.00	8244	125.00
62026	100.00	9233	60.00	82044	100.00
6226½	135.00	6333	65.00	72044 FILE	125.00
82026	125.00	9333	65.00	08244	125.00
62027	90.00	5234	250.00	9244	100.00
62027½	90.00	G2035	110.00	B334 SH SP	135.00
82027	125.00	5235½	110.00	3344 SH SP	115.00
92027	90.00	5235½	135.00	5344 SH SP	225.00
92027½	90.00	6235	90.00	6344 SH SP	125.00
P228 EO	150.00	6235 EO	115.00	6344 SH PEN	125.00
2228	150.00	62035	110.00	8344	200.00
2228 EO	160.00	6235½	90.00	9344 SH PEN	110.00
2228 P	150.00	62035½	120.00	02245	95.00
6228	150.00	2237	165.00	02245½	95.00
6228 EO	175.00	2237½	165.00	04245 B&G	180.00
6228 P	150.00	6237	165.00	05245	200.00
62028	150.00	6237½	175.00	05245½	200.00
82028	175.00	5238	150.00	06245	140.00
6229½	65.00	5438	250.00	06245½	140.00
9229½	65.00	8438	300.00	2345½	125.00
P0230	115.00	1139	130.00	5345	110.00
02230	80.00	B239	225.00	5345 P	110.00
02230½	80.00	G2039	250.00	5345½	110.00
05230½	190.00	6239	150.00	6345	190.00
06230	125.00	B339	250.00	6345 P	190.00
06230½	125.00	G3039	230.00	6345½	190.00
09230	125.00	6339	275.00	6345½ P	190.00
09230½	125.00	63039	225.00	6345½ SH	90.00
6230 SH	125.00	6539	700.00	B445 R	115.00
1131 SH	80.00	11040	95.00	6445 R	110.00
2231	125.00	3240 SP	300.00	640045 R	75.00
22031	125.00	6240	275.00	G2046	100.00
2231½	125.00	6240 SP	325.00	3246	135.00
2231½ SAB	125.00	6241	95.00	6246	140.00
22031½	125.00	G242	120.00	62046	100.00
52031	190.00	52042	125.00	B346 P	130.00
52031½	190.00	6242	125.00	G3046	110.00
52131	300.00	62042	80.00	6346	130.00
6231	125.00	82042	95.00	63046	110.00
62031	125.00	92042	80.00	04247 SP	110.00
6231½	125.00	63042	150.00	5247 J	500.00
62031½	125.00	83042	225.00	05247 SP	150.00
53131	700.00	6143	175.00	6247 J	450.00
		5343	200.00		

PATTERN NO.	MINT PRICE	PATTERN NO.	MINT PRICE	PATTERN NO.	MINT PRICE
06247	110.00	610050	500.00	64055 P	425.00
06247 PEN	100.00	61050	440.00	62056	90.00
06247 SP	100.00	C61050	560.00	82056	85.00
B3047	125.00	C61050 SAB	560.00	63056	125.00
P347 SH SP	125.00	C61050 L	800.00	83056	180.00
3347 SH SP	125.00	C91050 SAB	500.00	4257	80.00
3347 SP PEN	125.00	6250	450.00	42057	75.00
43047	135.00	8250	550.00	8257	85.00
5347 SH PEN	160.00	B1051	200.00	92057	75.00
53047	200.00	G1051	200.00	32058	75.00
6347 SH PEN	200.00	R1051	200.00	6258	75.00
6347 SH P	200.00	R1051 L	300.00	8258	90.00
6347 P PEN	200.00	6151	400.00	92058	75.00
6347 PJ	400.00	6151 L	600.00	8358	110.00
6347 SH SP	200.00	61051	225.00	P259	100.00
63047	200.00	61051 L	300.00	62059	75.00
630047	200.00	81051	280.00	62059 SP	80.00
630047 P	200.00	9151	500.00	8259	100.00
8347 SH SP	250.00	6251	500.00	5260	200.00
83047	300.00	P2052	100.00	8260	225.00
9347 SH SP	200.00	3252	240.00	8360 SCI	200.00
9347 PJ	325.00	32052	100.00	5460	260.00
93047	210.00	52052	110.00	8460	250.00
5447 SH SP	150.00	6252	250.00	5161 L	600.00
5447 SP P	150.00	62052	125.00	6161 L	550.00
64047 P	250.00	63052	275.00	82062 K	100.00
94047 P	250.00	3452	280.00	83062 K	175.00
B1048	175.00	54052	200.00	84062 K	235.00
G1048	175.00	6452	285.00	94062	180.00
R1048	190.00	64052	175.00	B2063	100.00
61048	110.00	HA253	135.00	P263	115.00
B2048	200.00	5253	115.00	05263	110.00
B2048 SP	200.00	6253	85.00	62063	85.00
G2048	200.00	62053	80.00	06263	85.00
G2048 S	200.00	8253	130.00	61063½	85.00
R2048	215.00	82053	80.00	82063	100.00
R2048 S	200.00	82053 SR	80.00	08263	90.00
62048	150.00	9253	80.00	82063½	90.00
62048 SP	125.00	6353	90.00	92063½	90.00
R1049 L	250.00	6353 P	90.00	B3063	110.00
61049	175.00	P254	180.00	63063	95.00
61049 L	250.00	3254	180.00	83063	100.00
B249	150.00	5254	200.00	6264	100.00
R2049	200.00	6245	190.00	6264 FILE	100.00
6249	150.00	8254	300.00	62064	100.00
62049	175.00	9254	225.00	8264 T	130.00
B10050	500.00	22055	90.00	8264 T FILE	130.00
CB1050 SAB	500.00	32055	100.00	82064	110.00
C31050 SAB	500.00	62055	100.00	9264 T FILE	110.00
310050	500.00	82055	125.00	B165	250.00
C51050 SAB	700.00	92055	125.00	3165 SAB*	275.00

*Made with flat ground blade same price as SAB blade.

PATTERN NO.	MINT PRICE	PATTERN NO.	MINT PRICE	PATTERN NO.	MINT PRICE
5165 SAB*	300.00	5275 SP	250.00	9383	200.00
6165 SAB*	250.00	6275 SP	210.00	3185	150.00
8165	1200.00	0627½	175.00	6185	150.00
9165 SAB	350.00	G375	225.00	B285	175.00
G265	350.00	5375	275.00	G285	175.00
3265 SAB	250.00	6375	210.00	R185	175.00
5265 SAB*	350.00	6276½	140.00	3285	200.00
6265 SAB	300.00	06276	190.00	6285	225.00
8265	1200.00	06276½	190.00	G2086	200.00
9265 SAB	400.00	2376½	350.00	52806	175.00
6366	125.00	5376½	400.00	62086	200.00
6366 PEN	125.00	6376	350.00	82086	235.00
8366 PEN	190.00	6376½	350.00	5287	350.00
62067	80.00	4277	130.00	5387	400.00
06267	90.00	8277	160.00	6288	150.00
82067	85.00	6278 T	160.00	6388	250.00
08267	95.00	GM279	75.00	83088	185.00
B3067	110.00	M279 R	75.00	5488	275.00
6367	100.00	3279	75.00	6488	290.00
63067	95.00	3279 R	75.00	83089	175.00
8367	110.00	5279	115.00	M2090 R	75.00
83067	100.00	6279	75.00	83090 SCI	175.00
9367	110.00	62079	100.00	B490 R	100.00
6268	100.00	62079½	100.00	6490 R	100.00
8268	150.00	8279	110.00	640090 R	90.00
6368	200.00	8279 SHAD	110.00	GM3091	125.00
8368	280.00	82079	125.00	GM3091 R	125.00
G2069	110.00	82079½	125.00	5391	1500.00
6269	95.00	92079½	110.00	83091	180.00
8269	115.00	B3079	275.00	3292	150.00
9269	100.00	63079	275.00	5292	185.00
6369	175.00	63079½ FILE	250.00	6292	150.00
8369	300.00	83079	275.00	33092	150.00
6370 FILE	275.00	P280	140.00	5392	200.00
8370 FILE	300.00	6280	140.00	6392	150.00
6470 FILE	210.00	G281	125.00	6392 P	190.00
5171 L	800.00	6281	120.00	630092	160.00
8271	190.00	9281	115.00	63092 IP	175.00
8371	375.00	83081	130.00	6592	1200.00
6172	600.00	64081	190.00	B1093	165.00
22074½ P	200.00	84081	230.00	G1093	165.00
62074½	225.00	6282	110.00	R1093	165.00
62074½	225.00	8282	130.00	61093	165.00
B3074	275.00	P383	325.00	32093 F	80.00
B3074½	275.00	2838	190.00	6293	110.00
B3074½ P	275.00	5383	210.00	62093 F	100.00
5374	300.00	6383	210.00	B393	225.00
63074	250.00	6383 SAB	210.00	H393	200.00
63074½	250.00	63083	185.00	4393	225.00
63074½ P	250.00	8383	300.00	5393	225.00
830,4	300.00	83083	200.00	6393	200.00

*Made with flat ground blade same price as SAB blade.

PATTERN NO.	MINT PRICE	PATTERN NO.	MINT PRICE	PATTERN NO.	MINT PRICE
6393 S	200.00	6396	95.00	31100	375.00
6393 PEN	175.00	B1097*	200.00	61100	400.00
9393	240.00	G1097*	200.00	62100	450.00
93093	120.00	GS1097*	200.00	82101 R	90.00
05294	250.00	R1097*	200.00	92101 R	65.00
6294	200.00	P297**	200.00	M3102 R	75.00
6294 J	500.00	R297**	200.00	83102 R	110.00
5394	800.00	3297**	200.00	63109 K	110.00
6394	550.00	8297**	210.00	31113	250.00
B1095	200.00	61098	100.00	61113	260.00
G1095	200.00	32098 F	125.00	32113	300.00
HA1095	250.00	62098 F	110.00	62113	315.00
R1095	200.00	6199	125.00	MAIZE #1	95.00
31095	200.00	GM2099 R	85.00	MAIZE #2	95.00
61095	225.00	3299	125.00	MUSKRAT	200.00
B2095 F	90.00	3299½	125.00	FLYFISHERMAN	150.00
32095 F	90.00	5299½	200.00	1502 SCOUT	80.00
B296	100.00	6299	200.00	1503 JUNIOR SCOUT	80.00
6296	100.00	6299½	200.00		
B396	100.00	82099 R	90.00		

*Large Leg Knife　　　　　　　　　　　　　　　　　　　　　　**Small Leg Knife

CATTARAUGUS CUTLERY COMPANY
LITTLE VALLEY, NEW YORK

Cattaraugus Cutlery Company
Little Valley, New York

J. B. F. Champlin first became associated with Cutlery at the age of 25, when be became a cutlery salesman for importers Friedman and Lauterjung.

When he was 41 he left Friedman and Lauterjung to start his own jobbing operation with his son Tint. Their business was named J. B. F. Champlin & Son.

In 1886 four of Champlin's brothers-in-law came to work in the jobbing business with him. They were W. R. Jean, John, and Andrew Case. When they entered into the business the name was changed to Cattaraugus Cutlery Company.

The Case brothers soon dropped out, but this was the first of a long association of the Case family with cutlery. This is also the first time (1886) any of the Case family had anything to do with cutlery, other than the daughters of Job Russell marrying cutlers.

The Champlins bought the equipment of the Beaver Falls Cutlery Company of Beaver Falls, Pennsylvania. in 1890, and built their factory in that year.

The company went out of business in 1963.

Cattaraugus made knives for the Armed Forces and the Byrd Polar expeditions. Too, the company also sponsored whittling compeition, offering $50,000 in prizes.

The company seemed to favor bone-handled, large pattern knives, but also produced some knives with plastic handles. Going out of business in the mid-1950's, Cattaraugus stamped its knives "Whittle Craft," "3" and a "C" inside a circle, and "Cattaraugus Cutlery Company, Little Valley, New York.

More Cattaraugus knives were stamped with pattern numbers. The first digit indicates the number of blades (up to 5-blade knives were made by Cattaraugus), and the second digit indicates the type of bolsters as follows:

0-bolsters
1-1 bolster or front bolsters only
2-2 bolsters
3-tip bolsters
4-unknown
5-slant bolsters

The third and fourth digits are the factory pattern numbers. The rule that knives be arranged by factory pattern number is of little or no value to the Cattaraugus collector. The 20224 pattern will be a different knife than a 22223 pattern, although both knives will be 22 patterns. Cattaraugus made so many patterns (over 100) that the factory pattern number is not the reliable reference that you find in Case and other brands.

Few collectors, if any, have memorized the pattern numbers of the Cattaraugus knives. There are so many different knives that it would be impossible. What we recommend is when buying a Cattaraugus, find the pattern number, and then look up the price in this book by *numerical order of the first three digits of the pattern number. We have found this to be a more reasonable organization of the Cattaraugus number system.* The last digit of the pattern number stands for the handle material. The handle materials numbers were:

1-White fiberloid
2-Pearl (French)
3-Mother of Pearl
4-Fiberloid
5-Genuine Stag
6-Ebony
7-Cocobola, fancy fiberloid, burnt bone
8-White bone
9-Stag bone

PATTERN NO.	MINT PRICE
☐P-1	60.00
☐1-W	130.00
☐3-W	130.00
☐10101	35.00
☐10484	50.00
☐10851	35.00
☐1159 (BW)	80.00
☐11067-S	65.00
☐11079	130.00
☐11227	50.00
☐11247	40.00
☐11404	35.00
☐11486	90.00
☐11704 (L)	90.00

☐**11709**—SMALL HUNTER (4") Long clip blade. Brass lined. Nickel silver bolsters. Glaze finish. Stag handle. Shielded. This knife has a spring lock which holds the blade in position when open. **70.00**

☐11709 (L)	95.00
☐11804	30.00
☐11827	80.00
☐11844	80.00
☐11839	100.00
☐11996-S	50.00

☐**12099-L**—"THE DEER SLAYER" (4½") A great favorite with deer hunters. Long clip blade with spring lock. Brass lined. Nickel silver bolsters. Glaze finish. Stag handle Shielded. **200.00**

☐12099 (L)	200.00
☐12099	100.00
☐12114	100.00
☐12134 (Y)	35.00
☐12144	45.00

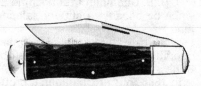

☐**12819**—"KING OF THE WOODS" (5⅜") This knife is made especially for big game hunting. Blade has a clip point and 3¾" cutting surface. Built exceptionally strong. Brass lined. Long nickel silver bolsters on one end and round nickel silver bolsters on other. Hole drilled for ring or thong. Glaze finish. Stag handle. **200.00**

☐12819	300.00

☐**12829**—"KING OF THE WOODS" (5⅜") This knife is identical in appearance with No. 12819 with the exception that it has a spring lock, which holds the blade in position when open. **300.00**

☐12829 (L)	400.00
☐12839 (L)	700.00
☐200-OP	45.00
☐200-PP	45.00
☐2000	30.00
☐2013	50.00
☐2022	25.00
☐2022-OP	50.00
☐2022-PP	65.00
☐20223	90.00
☐20224	40.00

☐20228	175.00
☐20232	35.00
☐20233	45.00
☐20234	30.00
☐203-G	30.00
☐203-Ori	45.00
☐203-O	30.00
☐203-OP	30.00

☐20371	40.00
☐2059-Ori	70.00
☐2059-OP	70.00
☐2059-PP	70.00

☐20594—(3¼") Fine office knife. One medium size pocket blade in one end and one ink erasing blade in the other end. Brass lined. Fine glazed finish. Amber celluloid handle 50.00

☐20594	50.00
☐206-Shrine	45.00
☐206-32nd	45.00
☐206-O	30.00
☐206-K of P	50.00
☐206-IOOF	30.00
☐2066-Ori	30.00
☐2066-G	30.00
☐2066-OP	30.00
☐2066-O	30.00
☐2066-PP	30.00
☐20664	30.00
☐20673	40.00
☐20677	40.00
☐20701	30.00
☐20853	40.00
☐B2109	85.00
☐21046	65.00
☐21049	75.00
☐21087	35.00
☐21089	40.00
☐21169	50.00
☐21169-G	50.00
☐21229	60.00
☐21246	35.00
☐21249	50.00
☐21259	75.00
☐21266	60.00
☐21269	85.00
☐21269-C	85.00
☐21269-CC	85.00
☐2139 (BW)	125.00
☐21356	70.00
☐21359	65.00
☐21411	110.00
☐21419	25.00
☐21476	40.00
☐21479	50.00
☐21484	30.00

☐21486	40.00
☐21489	50.00
☐2149	110.00
☐2159 (BW)	100.00

☐21079—(4") Small hunter. Long clip blade. Brass lined. Nickel silver bolsters. Glaze finish. Stag handle. Shielded. This knife has a spring lock which holds the blade in position when open 90.00

☐21709	50.00
☐11804	30.00
☐21816	50.00
☐21819	85.00
☐21826	50.00
☐21829	85.00
☐21839	65.00
☐21899-C	40.00
☐21899-S	40.00
☐22029	55.00
☐22039	80.00
☐22053	45.00
☐22069	65.00
☐22079	60.00
☐22084	65.00
☐22099	150.00
☐22099-F	150.00
☐22104	55.00
☐22109	150.00
☐22109-F	150.00
☐22119	45.00
☐22139	45.00
☐22149	125.00
☐22153	55.00
☐22159	50.00
☐22162	50.00
☐22163	75.00
☐22169	80.00
☐22182	50.00
☐22182 (SS)	50.00
☐22186	50.00
☐22187	45.00
☐22104	55.00
☐2219	100.00
☐221039	60.00
☐221049	130.00
☐22199	125.00
☐22209	30.00
☐22213	75.00

☐22219 . . . . 50.00
☐22223 . . . . 55.00

☐22226 . . . . 60.00
☐22229 . . . . 55.00
☐22233 . . . . 60.00
☐22239 . . . . 55.00
☐2224B 50.00
☐22246 . . . . 50.00
☐22248 . . . . 75.00
☐22249 . . . . 60.00
☐22256 . . . . 50.00
☐22258 . . . . 75.00
☐22259 . . . . 60.00
☐22269 . . . . 65.00
☐22219 . . . . 400.00
☐2227 . . . . 50.00
☐22276 . . . . 50.00
☐22278 . . . . 65.00
☐22279 . . . . 60.00
☐22286 . . . . 55.00
☐22289 . . . . 65.00
☐22292 . . . . 40.00
☐22299 . . . . 50.00
☐22329 (SS) 30.00
☐22336 . . . . 150.00

☐**2239**—(4½″) Long spear point and long pen blades. Brass lined. Nickle silver bolsters. Glaze finish. Stag handle. Shielded. . . . **140.00**

☐2239 . . . . 140.00
☐22339 . . . . 200.00
☐22349 . . . . 75.00
☐22356 . . . . 75.00
☐22359 . . . . 90.00
☐22366 . . . . 130.00
☐22369 . . . . 150.00
☐22376 . . . . 70.00

☐22378 . . . . 100.00
☐22379 . . . . 80.00
☐22389 . . . . 55.00
☐22389 (SS) 55.00
☐22396 . . . . 80.00
☐22399 . . . . 75.00
☐22406 . . . . 50.00
☐22419 . . . . 90.00

☐**22429**—(3⅝″) Gun stock pattern. Large spear point and pen blades. Brass lined. Flat nickel silver bolsters. Glaze finish. Stag handle. Shielded. **125.00**

☐22429 . . . . 125.00

☐**22439**—(3⅝″) Two blades. Iron lined. Iron bolsters. Glaze finish. Stag handle. Shielded **80.00**

☐22439 . . . . 80.00

☐**22449**—(3⅝″) Large spear point, long pen blades. Brass lined. Flat nickel silver bolsters. Glaze finish. Stag handle. Shielded. **75.00**

☐22449 . . . . 75.00
☐22459 . . . . 45.00
☐22463 . . . . 40.00
☐22469 . . . . 30.00
☐22474 . . . . 45.00
☐22476 . . . . 40.00
☐22479 . . . . 65.00
☐22486 . . . . 50.00
☐22489 . . . . 60.00

☐**2249**—(4") Long spear point and long pen blades. Brass lined. Nickel silver bolsters. Glaze finish. Stag handle. Shielded. **45.00**

☐2249	45.00
☐2259	95.00
☐2259	95.00
☐22509	50.00
☐22519	50.00

☐**22526**—(3⁷⁄₁₆") Two blades. Brass lined. Iron bolsters. Glaze finish. Ebony handle. Shielded. **50.00**
☐**22529**—Same with stag handle **65.00**

☐22526	50.00
☐22529	65.00

☐**22536**—(3⁷⁄₁₆") Two blades. Brass lined. Iron bolsters. Glaze finish. Ebony handle. Shielded. **60.00**
☐**22539**—Same with stag handle.......**75.00**

☐22536	60.00
☐22539	75.00
☐22549	50.00

☐**22554**—(3⅜") Medium pen knife blade in either end. Brass lined. Nickel silver bolsters. Glaze finish. Celluloid handle. **40.00**
☐**22559**—Same with stag handle.......**50.00**

☐22554	40.00
☐22556	50.00

☐22557	45.00
☐22559	50.00
☐22559	50.00
☐22569	65.00
☐22576	50.00
☐22579	60.00

☐**22586**—(3⅜") Two blades. Brass lined. Nickel silver bolsters. Glaze finish. Ebony handle. Shielded. **60.00**

☐22586	60.00
☐22589	90.00
☐33594 (SS)	30.00
☐22599 (SS)	30.00
☐22599	30.00
☐22609	35.00
☐22612	30.00

☐**22614**—(2¾") Small pen knife with blade in either end. Brass lined. Nickel silver bolsters. Crocus finish. Celluloid handle. **35.00**

☐22614	35.00
☐22622	45.00
☐22624-Y	45.00
☐22628 (SS)	40.00
☐22629 (SS)	55.00
☐22629	55.00
☐22633 (SS)	40.00
☐22639	40.00
☐22642	45.00
☐22643 (SS)	75.00
☐22649	50.00
☐22652	30.00
☐22653	50.00

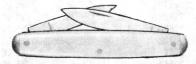

☐**22654**-(2¾") Clip and pen blades in same end. Brass lined. Nickel silver bolsters. Crocus finish. Celluloid handle. **40.00**

☐22654	40.00
☐22659 (SS)	30.00
☐22659	30.00
☐22663	45.00
☐22664	35.00
☐22679	40.00

☐**2269**—(4") Large spear point and long pen blades. Brass lined. Nickel silver bolsters. Glaze finish. Stag handle. Shielded. . . . **120.00**

☐2269	120.00
☐22682 (SS)	35.00
☐22683	75.00
☐22684	50.00
☐22686	50.00
☐22689	55.00
☐22689 (SS)	55.00
☐22729	100.00
☐22739	75.00
☐22749	50.00
☐22753	75.00
☐22754	50.00
☐22759	50.00
☐22762	60.00
☐22763	130.00
☐22766	50.00
☐22769	80.00
☐22772	55.00
☐22773	80.00
☐22779	60.00
☐22783	35.00
☐2279	55.00
☐2279-P	55.00
☐22793	75.00
☐22793 (SS)	75.00
☐22794	45.00
☐22796	45.00
☐22799	55.00
☐22799-N	45.00
☐22183	30.00
☐22184	35.00
☐22819	30.00
☐22822	35.00
☐22823	35.00
☐22833	30.00
☐2284	60.00
☐22849	45.00
☐22859	65.00
☐22869	45.00
☐22874	55.00

☐22877	50.00
☐B2879	55.00
☐22879	55.00
☐22879 (SS)	55.00
☐22882	55.00
☐22883	50.00
☐22884	45.00
☐22886	45.00
☐22889	60.00
☐22893	65.00
☐22894	60.00
☐22896	50.00
☐22899	60.00
☐22899-Jr	55.00
☐B2909	45.00
☐22909 (SS)	50.00
☐22911	100.00
☐B2919	60.00
☐22919	150.00
☐22929	300.00
☐22936	75.00
☐22939	75.00
☐22949	150.00
☐22952	50.00
☐22959	65.00
☐22963	55.00
☐22964	45.00
☐22967	50.00
☐22969	45.00
☐22979	60.00
☐2319	40.00
☐23009	95.00
☐23224	40.00
☐23229	40.00
☐23232	35.00
☐23232 C-SS	35.00
☐23234	35.00
☐2342	35.00
☐2343	50.00
☐2344	30.00
☐2349	40.00
☐2379	60.00
☐2389	55.00
☐23642 (SS)	45.00
☐23649	45.00
☐23662	45.00
☐23663	50.00
☐23669	30.00
☐23669-N	35.00
☐23672	40.00

☐**23673**—(3") Two blades. Brass lined. Nickel silver tips. Crocus finish. Mother of pearl handle. **50.00**

☐23673	50.00
☐23679	45.00
☐23689	55.00
☐24376	60.00
☐24337	60.00
☐24379	75.00
☐24396	75.00
☐24399	80.00
☐24409	55.00
☐24889	70.00
☐C2589	135.00
☐D2589	135.00
☐B2672	45.00
☐B2874-Y	70.00
☐B2879	80.00
☐B2909 (SS)	50.00
☐B2919 (SS)	45.00
☐2929	175.00
☐300-Ori	40.00
☐300-G	45.00
☐300-OP	65.00
☐3003	50.00
☐3009	50.00
☐301	30.00
☐301-IOOF	25.00
☐301-BPOE	25.00
☐301-F & AM	25.00
☐301-Shrine	25.00
☐301-Ori	40.00
☐303-G	30.00
☐303-D-Ori	40.00
☐304-Ori	50.00
☐304-G	50.00
☐305-F & AM	40.00
☐305-FOE	40.00
☐305-KT	40.00
☐305-Shrine	40.00
☐305-K of P	45.00
☐305-IOCF	35.00
☐305-32nd	40.00
☐305-BPOE	40.00
☐3013	40.00
☐30673	50.00
☐309-Ori	40.00
☐309-OP	45.00
☐32009	100.00

☐32019	90.00
☐32019-S	90.00
☐32019-C	90.00
☐32029	90.00
☐32039	90.00
☐32053 (WH)	75.00
☐32059 (WH)	90.00
☐32099 (WH)	90.00
☐32125	60.00
☐32126 (WH)	80.00
☐32139 (WH)	140.00
☐32141	60.00
☐32144	95.00
☐32145	130.00
☐32149	100.00
☐32149-G	100.00
☐32149-SH & G	100.00
☐32149-P & SH	100.00
☐32164 (WH)	90.00

☐**32173**—(3⅞") Fine stock pattern. Large clip, Sheepfoot and spey blades. Brass lined. Nickel silver bolsters. Crocus finish. Mother of pearl handle. **165.00**

☐32173	165.00
☐32174	100.00
☐32175	90.00
☐32179	85.00
☐32183	160.00
☐32184	130.00
☐32189	100.00
☐32189-S	125.00
☐32189-G	125.00
☐32189-S & G	125.00

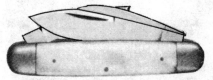

☐**32203**—(3⅝") Fine stock pattern. Large spear, sheepfoot and pen blades. Brass lined. Nickel silver bolsters. Crocus finish. Mother of pearl handle. **165.00**

☐32203	175.00

☐32204	90.00
☐32204-G	90.00
☐32204-C & G	90.00
☐32205	130.00
☐32206-G	80.00
☐32206-C & G	90.00
☐32206	80.00
☐32209	115.00
☐32209-G	90.00
☐32209-G & P	90.00
☐32209-C & G	90.00
☐32233 (WH)	130.00
☐32243	130.00
☐32244	70.00
☐32245	80.00
☐32249	75.00
☐3229	75.00
☐3233	75.00
☐3239-H	50.00
☐3299	55.00
☐32389	90.00
☐32403 (WH)	100.00
☐32404 (WH)	100.00
☐32406 (WH)	85.00
☐32409 (WH)	115.00
☐32443	85.00
☐32449 (WH)	90.00
☐32566 (WH)	125.00
☐32569 (WH)	160.00
☐32575 (WH)	155.00
☐32576 (WH)	125.00
☐32579 (WH)	130.00
☐32586 (WH)	100.00
☐32589 (WH)	130.00
☐32599 (WH)	120.00
☐32643 (WH)	120.00
☐32644 (WH)	115.00
☐32646 (WH)	120.00
☐32649 (WH)	200.00

☐32734 (WH)	150.00
☐32739 (WH)	165.00
☐32779 (WH)	160.00
☐32793 (WH)	165.00
☐32794 (WH)	125.00
☐32799 (WH)	140.00
☐32866 (WH)	125.00
☐32969 (WH)	175.00
☐32876 (WH)	110.00
☐32879 (WH)	175.00
☐3289 (WH)	130.00
☐32889 (WH)	175.00
☐32916 (WH)	275.00
☐32919 (WH)	325.00
☐3293	75.00
☐32956 (WH)	130.00
☐32959 (WH)	150.00
☐32973 (WH)	100.00
☐32976 (WH)	90.00
☐32979 (WH)	100.00
☐3299	60.00
☐33073	75.00
☐33079	70.00
☐3343	90.00
☐3349	80.00
☐33637 (WH)	155.00
☐33674 (WH)	140.00
☐33679 (WH)	150.00
☐33683 (WH)	180.00
☐33689 (WH)	150.00
☐35141	65.00
☐35144	65.00
☐35151	60.00
☐3913	60.00
☐4003	90.00
☐4059-Ori	120.00
☐4059-OP	120.00

☐**32653**—(3½″) Large clip, one clip pen and one small pen blade. Brass lined. Nickel silver bolsters. Crocus finish. Mother of pearl handle.
☐**32659**—Same with stag handle......**175.00**

☐32656 (WH)	175.00
☐32659 (WH)	175.00
☐32683 (WH)	175.00
☐32689 (WH)	150.00

☐**40503**—(3½″) One large, two pen and one flexible file blade. Brass lined. Full crocus finish. Mother of pearl handle. Shielded. **130.00**
☐**4053** **130.00**

☐ **40593**—(3¼") One large, two pen and one flexible file blade. Brass lined. Milled. Full crocus finish. Mother of pearl handle. . .**120.00**
☐ **4059-OP**—Same with opal pearl handle. . . . .
. . . .**120.00**

☐ **40593** **120.00**
☐ **40673** **165.00**
☐ **40683** **180.00**
☐ **42049** **110.00**

☐ **42469**	**65.00**
☐ **42509**	**115.00**
☐ **42519**	**115.00**
☐ **42559**	**120.00**
☐ **42689**	**125.00**
☐ **42793**	**130.00**
☐ **42795**	**110.00**
☐ **4303**	**155.00**
☐ **4309**	**130.00**
☐ **43559**	**115.00**
☐ **43593**	**130.00**
☐ **43673**	**120.00**
☐ **43679**	**110.00**
☐ **43683**	**130.00**
☐ **43689**	**110.00**
☐ **4503 (WE)**	**95.00**
☐ **4509 (WE)**	**90.00**

☐ **42053**—(3¼") Large sheepfoot blade, two pen and one flexible file blade. Brass lined. Nickel silver bolsters. Crocus finish. Mother of pearl handle. **140.00**
☐ **42059**—Same with stag handle. **100.00**

☐ **42053** **140.00**
☐ **42059** **100.00**
☐ **42069** **175.00**
☐ **42070** **120.00**
☐ **42099** **165.00**
☐ **42109** **150.00**
☐ **42172** **90.00**
☐ **42179** **100.00**
☐ **42209-B** **75.00**

☐ **5003**—(3¼") One large, one pen blade, scissors with cork-screw and manicure blade in back. Silver lined. Full crocus finish. Mother of pearl handle **130.00**
☐ **5009**—Same as stag handle. **100.00**

☐ **5003** **130.00**
☐ **5009** **100.00**

☐ **42363**—(3⁹⁄₁₆") One large and one pen blade, cap lifter and cork-screw. Brass lined. Nickel silver bolsters. Crocus finish. Mother of pearl handle. **120.00**
☐ **42369**—Same with stag handle.

☐ **42363** **120.00**
☐ **42369** **110.00**
☐ **42459** **85.00**

CENTRAL CITY KNIFE COMPANY
PHOENIX, NEW YORK

The Central City Knife Company operated from 1880 until 1892 when it became the Phoenix Knife Company. The Phoenix Knife Company burned in 1916.

CENTRAL CUTLERY COMPANY
ELIZABETH, NEW JERSEY

This company was incorporated with $25,000 capital in October 1925 by Benjamin Gordon at Elizabeth, New Jersey for the manufacture of cutlery. (Not related to Central City Knife Company)

CHALLENGE CUTLERY COMPANY
BRIDGEPORT, CONNECTICUT

Originally the trademark of the B. J. Eyre, Sheffield Company The Frederick Wiebusch Co. of New York obtained the trademark when it purchased Eyre in 1877. This company later became Wiebusch and Hilger Company The first factory in the U. S. for Challenge was opened in 1891 in Bridgeport, Connecticut. Earlier imported made knives were marked "Challenge Cutlery Company" while U. S. produced knives were marked "Challenge Cutlery Corp."

The Challenge factory had been originally owned by the Hatch Cutlery Company and later the Griffon Cutlery Works. Challenge obtained the building in 1905, although it had been contracting knives from the factory since 1891.

In February 1921 the company introduced the Flylock knife in two sizes. The smaller size was a two blade pen knife offered in pearl, shell rosewood, smoked pearl, nickel silver with a beaded edge and sterling silver. The larger pattern was the same pattern as the Schrade "Hunters Pride."

A new factory was built prior to 1930, and in 1930 the original factory burned.

CLAUSS SHEAR COMPANY
FREMONT, OHIO

The Clauss Shear Company is a scissor manufacturer that had a line of pocketknives for a short time in the mid-twenties. Schatt & Morgan Cutlery Company made some for them and it is possible that Clauss made some of their own. The knives came in an assortment of patterns, using both bone and celluloid. Some knives were made by W. R. Case & Sons.

CLEVELAND CUTLERY COMPANY
CLEVELAND, OHIO

The Cleveland Cutlery Company was incorporated by J. H. Nancy in July 1925 in Cleveland, Ohio.

CLYDE CUTLERY COMPANY.
CLYDE, OHIO

The August 1925 American Cutler Magazine reported Clyde Cutlery Company holding a 75th anniversary party, making the company being established in 1850.

COL. COON KNIVES
COLUMBIA, TENNESSEE

Adrian Harris formed this company in 1978, and currently manufactures a barlow, muskrat, stock knife, and congress. He offers his knives with a choice of either bone or genuine stag handles.

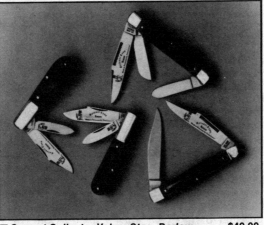

☐ *Current Collector Value: Stag, Barlow* $40.00
☐   *Bone, Barlow* 30.00
☐   *Stag, Muskrat* 45.00
☐   *Stag, Stockman* 50.00

COLONIAL CUTLERY COMPANY
PROVIDENCE, RHODE ISLAND

Frederick Paolantonio, the founder of Colonial, first was trained in the cutlers art in his home town of Frosolone, Italy.

He arrived in the United States in 1903, working briefly in a Rhode Island cutlery shop, when he went to work for Empire Knife Company, where he worked for five years.

He became production foreman in 1914 when he went to work for Miller Brothers Cutlery Company

While there he met Edward Oefinger, and together they started their own company named "Meriden" to make skeleton knives for Miller Brothers. (These knives were not stamped Meriden, and should not be confused with the older Meriden Cutlery Company)

In 1920 they started P. & S. Cutlery Company in Meriden, which they sold the following year to Imperial, a company also started by former Empire employees. Paolantonio's brothers, Dominick and Anthony had immigrated in 1910, also going to work for Empire until 1917, when they started the Providence Cutlery Company, making skeleton knives. Anthony joined the Army during World War I, leaving the business to his brother, Dominick.

In 1920 Anthony started the A. Paolantonio Cutlery Company in Providence, making gold and pearl handled knives.

Dominick sold the Providence Cutlery Company in 1925, joining Anthony in his business. The three brothers got together in 1926 and organized the Colonial Cutlery Company.

The president today is Al D. Paolantonio, son of Dominick. Among the knives they produce are the Anvil, Ranger brands and the old Cutler brand introduced in 1978.

COLT KNIVES
HARTFORD, CONNECTICUT

"If God didn't make all men equal, then Samuel Colt sure did". Oft quoted, studied, and collected, the romance around the name Colt stirs the imagination with a smoke filled bar, harsh words at the poker table, and stabs of flame leaping out to claim another victim for Boot Hill. Only the quick and the dead existed in such times, and the Colt proved to be an able companion for both good and bad during the western expansion.

For the knife collector, there is another kind of romance, for like gun manufacturers Remington and Winchester, Colt too made collectible knives. The only difference is that Colt made the knives late in the game, starting in 1969 and discontinuing them in 1973.

During that time they made one folder and several sheath knives, with assorted variations that can leave the knife collector with a collection of 15 or so different Colt knives.

The most unusual of the Colt knives is the Colt "tuckaway" folder, designed by Knifemaker Barry Wood of Venice, California.

According to Wood, he had been using the patented design since 1967 on his own knives, and was approached by Colt about making the knives for them in 1968. Production on the first knives was completed in October of 1969.

Wood had the blades for the knives made by Russell Harrington Company of Southbridge, Massachusetts, and contracted for several other of the components with different manufacturers. Wood then assembled and finished the knives in his California shop.

Over the next four years Wood was to make 15,300 of the Colt folders, with four distinct variations.

The first 500 knives featured the Colt "Rampant Colt" (a rearing horse) trademark on the face side of the pivot pin. (The face side of the knife is the side with the pivot pin on the right and the blade opening upward.) On the reverse side of the knife the Colt "serpentine" name is etched on the blade. These "first models" have a handle shaped like a rectangle with rounded edges. The knives all have canvas micarta handles and these are probably the rarest of the Colt knife variations.

The second model is similar to the first with the same shape and canvas micarta handle, but his variation has the rampant Colt on the face side of the pivot pin, the Colt serpentine trademark etched on the face side of the blade, and on the liner the "Colt, Hartford, Conn." mark is stamped in large letters. With the knife half open, it is possible to see all three marks at one time. 2,000 of these knives were made.

The most common is the third model, and this model has a changed shape, which Wood calls a "four arch contour". The shape is slightly curved, with a few knives still using the canvas micarta handles. The majority used a burgundy micarta handle. When production was begun on this new shape, the stamping on the liner was deleted because of the difficulty of getting buffing compound out of the letters in the final polish stage.

Some collectors pay a premium for various color sheaths, but the sheath is not a factor in determining age or scarcity of the Colt folder. The sheaths were all made by a North Hollywood, California manufacturer, and he shipped various colors at different times throughout the production of the knives. A black sheath may be found with any of the four variations mentioned above.

The knives with the burgundy handle and "four arch contour" start at $150 from most dealers. The sheath will add $10 to the price, and the sheath and original box will add $25 to the price. Rarer variations go up from there.

Although collectors will likely never see them, there are two other variations. Twelve of the Colt knives were made with black micarta handles for salesmen's samples, and two were made with sambar stag handles for Colt executives. We recommend you obtain a letter of verification before buying either of these extra rare variations.

When the knives were first marketed they retailed for $29.95, and were selling at $31.97 when discontinued. Distributors and dealers got their usual discounts from that price.

Although Wood terminated his agreement with Colt in 1978, he continues to make a similar knife. Today his knives are all 100% handmade, using 154CM steel and a variety of handle materials. There is a heavy collector demand for his knives, with prices starting at $200 for a metal handled folder. He told the author that if he ordered a knife the day they talked that it would be 1984 before he could expect delivery.

Sheath Knives, Made in Sheffield

The Colt sheath knives were packaged as attractively as any knife ever made. Inside the wood grain paper box, each knife is carried inside a red velvet drawstring pouch, with the rampant Colt emblem on each pouch.

These knives were made by two different manufacturers. The knives marked "Sheffield" were all made by J. A. and F. H. Hopkins & Sons of Sheffield, England, on designs by Dale Edwards of Indian Ridge Traders. The knive were imported through Indian Ridge. Approximately 2,500 of each knife was made.

There were four variations of the Sheffield made knives, each with sweeping clip blades. The three larger patterns each have a snap that closes over the bottom of the guard. The smallest skinner utilizes a pouch sheath. Each variation of the English knives is illustrated with this article.

Sheath Knives, Made in U. S. A.

The American made knives are all stamped with the Colt Serpentine trademark and "Hartford Conn." They were made by the Olsen Knife Company of Howard City, Michigan, and most of the Colt patterns have similar patterns currently made in the Olsen line.

Owner Fred Olsen said his company made a total of 20,000 knives for Colt, in 2,500 in each of six patterns.

We were able to obtain only one of the Olsen knives for this article, but Olsen said there were 2,500 of each of the following (name and pattern number are for the same knife in the Olsen line.)

Model 500—Bird Knife, Model 501 Trout Knife, Model 504 All Purpose, Model 505 Pro Skinner with a 4½″ blade, Model 505 Pro Skinner with 5½″blade, and a 508 Alaskan Skinner.

Most of these will have black leather sheaths while the Sheffield knives will have brown leather sheaths. Both came in the red velvet pouches.

Prices on most of the hunting knives ranged from $29 to $49 in 1973. Current collector's value on each of the Colt hunting knives ranges around $75, slightly more for the larger patterns, slightly less for the smaller ones.

As with anything, there are countless minor variations on every knife, it only takes looking at a lot of Colt knives to determine the variations.

Unfortunately, they are not common. Their scarcity makes them subject to a quick gain in price, and their limited number of variations make it within the financial reach of most collectors to assemble a near-complete collection of Colt knives.

□U-1010—TRAILBLAZER (7″) Resin impregnated rosewood handles, forged guard, handles have brass cap with thong holder, with heavy duty leather scabbard. Original retail 54.40 . . . .**25.00**

□U1020—MOUNTAINEER (6″) Resin impregnated rosewood handles, brass guard and end cap with heavy duty leather scabbard. Original retail 47.50 . . . .**47.50**

□U1030—PLAINSMAN (5½″) Resin impregnated rosewood handles, stainless steel handle cap with thong holder. With heavy duty leather scabbard, nickel silver bolsters and shield; brass lining **35.00**

□U1040—TRAPPER (3½″) Skinning knife, brass guard and end cap with thong holder. Heavy-duty leather scabbard **100.00**

□U1050—TUCKAWAY HUNTER (3½″) Folding knife with heavy-duty blade. Heavy leather carrying case with flap and snap fastener . .**300.00**

□U1130—(4″) Trout and bird knife **90.00**

□U1120—(4½″) All-purpose knife **90.00**

□U1110—(5½″) All-purpose knife **90.00**

CRANDALL CUTLERY COMPANY
BRADFORD, PENNSYLVANIA

Herbert Crandall married Theresa Case, who was the daughter of W. R. Case. Crandall Cutlery was started in 1902 in Bradford and merged with W. R. Case & Sons in 1912, stamping its knives "Crandall, Bradford, Pa." Most of their knives had bone handles.

CUSSIN AND FERN

Cussin and Fern knives were probably made by Schatt & Morgan and were given away to contest winners by the Cussin & Fern chain of stores. There were not a large number of these knives and they are scarce.

E. C. B.

Knives stamped "E. C. B." were made by a Sheffield, England manufacturer for E. C. Boughton in New York City, a firm that dealt in furs.

The information we have is dated 1888, and it states they were established in 1845, although it is not sure they handled knives since that time.

All their knives were stamped "E C B" on the tang, and their straight razors carried the full name, E. C. Boughton, 44 Bond St., N. Y. N. Y.

ELECTRIC CUTLERY COMPANY
NEWARK, NEW JERSEY AND WALDEN, NEW YORK

The Electric Cutlery Company knife, handled in bone, celluloid, and rosewood, was made on contract by Walden Knife Company, Walden, New York. The knives were stamped "Electric Cutlery Company, Walden, New York" and "Electric Cutlery Company Newark, New Jersey".

ELLIOT, JOSEPH AND SONS
SHEFFIELD, ENGLAND

Joseph Elliot and Sons was established in 1795. Over the years they have incorporated many other companies into the largest producer of real stag and horn handled pocketknives in Sheffield. They presently produce James Barber, Lockwood Brothers and Elliot knives. In the past they made knives with the James Allen trademark as well as Wigfall and Thomas Ellin. This company still produces pocketknives in the old way and their knives show this. They do not use precision parts such as Schrade and Case do, and the demand is still great for their products, since most are sold in the British Isles. One of the pleasures of owning one of the above marked knives is knowing that more "man" went into the knife than "machine".

EMPIRE KNIFE COMPANY
WINSTEAD, CONNECTICUT

Two brothers named Alvord started the Empire Knife Company in Winstead, Connecticut in 1856.

In 1920 the brothers sold the company to a group of investors headed by George Brill, a mechanical and electrical engineer.

Upon Brill's takeover, the company changed their power source from water to motors, but the advance did not stop the low tariff on German cutlery and the beginning of the depression from forcing the company out of business in 1929.

A highlight of the Empire story is the existence of a factory display collection. In 1858 the company made a sample board of every pocketknife they were currently making, wiring it into a dark oak box with a felt back. There were approximately 100 of these knives.

At the company's demise in 1929, the collection was still intact, and loaned to the Winstead museum. When George Brill died, his son Elliot discovered that 15 of the knives had been stolen while at the museum. He removed them and kept them himself until 1972, when he sold them to a resident of West Liberty, Kentucky. In the set at the time were 23 ivory handled knives, 23 horn handled, 19 ebonywood, 11 genuine tortoiseshell, six mother of pearl and one stag handled knife.

Six of the knives were congress patterns, 19 were whittlers and the rest, one and two blades of various styles.

H. G. Workman managed to buy one of the whittlers for his collection. The West Liberty owner kept eight of the knives and the remainder were sold to a Corbin, Kentucky resident in 1975. In 1978 he still owned the knives and would not show or sell them to this author. In 1980 the knives were broken up and sold individually. Most of the Whittlers sold for $300.00 each.

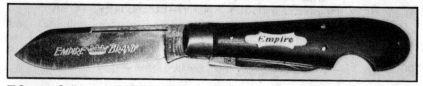

☐ *Current Collector Value* **$65.00**

EXCELSIOR KNIFE COMPANY
TORRINGTON, CONNECTICUT

Excelsior Knife Company, started in 1880. They expanded into steel bits in 1883. In 1884 the company was auctioned because of bankruptcy proceedings. The Northfield Knife Company bought the company at this auction.

FIGHTIN' ROOSTER
SOLINGEN, GERMANY

The Fightin' Rooster brand belongs to Frank Buster Cutlery Company, a product of Frank Buster, a Tennessee knife dealer who has built the brand into one of the largest in the collectors market.

Frank began his trading at a central Tennessee store that hosted a rook game weekly. Then one day he noticed that old knives were getting hard to find, and he thought there might be some more at the site of some of the old factories. So he loaded up on a plane and went to Solingen, Germany.

Once there, he found a few old knives, but in his door knocking he made a connection with some German cutlery factories to make knives for him, and in the early 1970's he began making his Fightin' Rooster brand. The idea for the brand came from an old print in his antique shop showing two fighting roosters.

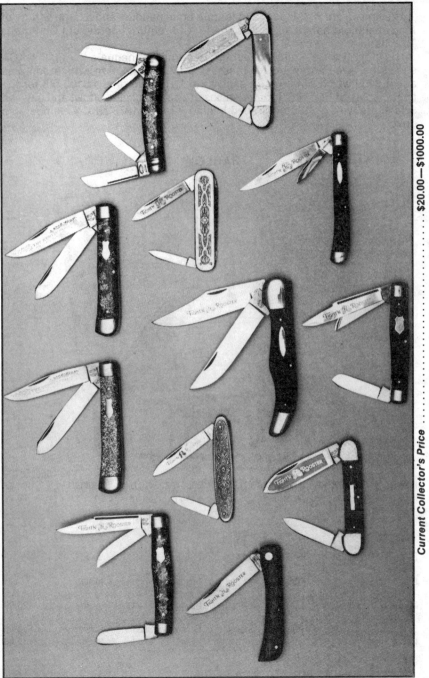

His knives are well-made, and feature bone handles and a large variety of fancy celluloid handles. He was the first to reintroduce the old Christmas Tree handle.

His donation to knife collecting is perhaps unequaled. At all NKCA shows he gives an award for the best Ladies' Collection, which contains about $100 worth of knives in each award. He also give a $100 bill for the best display of Fightin' Rooster knives at each Knoxville show, and gave an $800 knife with a $100 bill folded behind it in the 1978 NKCA membership drive.

BARLOW

HANDLE	SERIES	NUMBER PRODUCED	ETCH	BOLSTER	PULL	SHIELD	COLLECTOR VALUE
☐Butter & Molasses	Master Blade	Very Rare Approx. 12		1 Long	Short		80.00
☐Pearl	Middle Tennessee 1978	200	Gold Etching	1 Long	Short		175.00
☐Red & Black	Country Gentleman	300	Etched	1 Long	Short	Inlaid	
☐Butter & Molasses	Country Gentleman	300	Etched	1 Long	Short	Inlaid	Set of 3
☐Pearl & Black	Country Gentleman	300	Etched	1 Long	Short	Inlaid	125.00
☐Bone		300	Etched	1 Long	Short	Shield	35.00
☐New Xmas		300	Etched	1 Long	Short	Inlaid	35.00

BICENTENNIAL

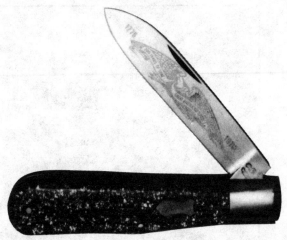

HANDLE	SERIES	NUMBER PRODUCED	ETCH	BOLSTER	PULL	SHIELD	COLLECTOR VALUE
☐Old Christmas	Bicentennial	1200	Gold Etched	1 Smooth	Short	Crest	55.00
☐Old Christmas Pink & Green Checked	Bicentennial	1200	Gold Etched	1 Smooth	Short	Crest	55.00

BUDDING

HANDLE	SERIES	NUMBER PRODUCED	ETCH	BOLSTER	PULL	SHIELD	COLLECTOR VALUE
☐Comp		100	Etched	No	Short		15.00
☐Roswood	Clip Blade	100	Etched	One	Short		15.00
☐Rosewood		100	Etched	One	Short		15.00
☐Horn		3 Doz.	Etched	No	Short		65.00

CANOES

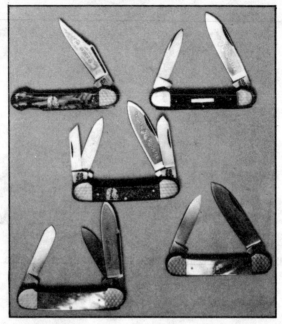

HANDLE	SERIES	NUMBER PRODUCED	ETCH	BOLSTER	PULL	SHIELD	COLLECTOR VALUE
☐Old Christmas		300	Etched	Fancy	Long	Inlaid	**30.00**
☐Red & Black		300	Etched	Fancy	Long	Inlaid	**30.00**
☐Pearl & Black		300	Etched	Fancy	Long	Inlaid	**30.00**
☐Bone		300	Etched	Fancy	Long	Bar	**30.00**
☐Pearl & Black		300	Reversed Etched	Fancy	Long	Inlaid	**30.00**
☐Old Christmas		300	Reversed Etched	Fancy	Long	Bar	**30.00**
☐Tortoise Shell		300	Reversed Etched	Fancy	Long	Bar	**30.00**
☐Pearl	C. Rooster	250	Gold Etching	Fancy	Long		Set of 4
☐Brown & Pearl	C. Rooster	250	Gold Etching	Fancy	Long	Bar	
☐Pearl & Black	C. Rooster	250	Gold Etching	Fancy	Long	Bar	**250.00**
☐Gold & Black	C. Rooster	250	Gold Etching	Fancy	Long	Bar	
☐Old Christmas	Canittler	300	Reversed Etching	Fancy	Long	Bar	**35.00**
☐Red & Black	Canittler	300	Reversed Etched	Fancy	Long	Inlaid	**35.00**

HANDLE	SERIES	NUMBER PRODUCED	ETCH	BOLSTER	PULL	SHIELD	COLLECTOR VALUE
☐ Pearl & Black	Canittler	300	Reversed Etched	Fancy	Long	Inlaid	35.00
☐ Goldflake	Canittler	300	Reversed Etched	Fancy	Long	Inlaid	35.00
☐ Butter & Molasses	Canittler	300	Etched	Fancy	Long	Inlaid	35.00
☐ Old Christmas	Canittler	300	Etched	Fancy	Long	Inlaid	35.00
☐ Old Christmas	Very Rare	Approx. 12 made	Etched	Fancy	Short	Inlay	100.00
☐ Pearl & Black		600	Etched	Fancy	Short	Inlaid	25.00
☐ Red & Black		600	Etched	Fancy	Short	Inlaid	25.00
☐ Black & Pearl	"Ohio"	300	Gold Etching	Fancy	Long	Inlaid	42.00
☐ New Christmas	"Indiana"	300	Gold Etching	Fancy	Long	Inlaid	42.00
☐ Butter & Molasses	"Georgia"	300	Gold Etching	Fancy	Long	Inlaid	42.00
☐ Red & Black	"Alabama"	300	Gold Etching	Fancy	Long	Inlaid	42.00
☐ Pearl	1977 Tar Heel Club	200	Gold Etching	Fancy	Short	Inlaid	100.00
☐ Pearl	Captain Rooster	1200	Gold Etching	Fancy	Short	Inlaid	70.00
☐ Pearl	CR Scrimshaw	1200	Gold Etching	Fancy	Short	Scrimshaw	120.00
☐ Pearl & Brown		300	Reversed Etching	Fancy	Short	Inlaid	35.00
☐ Old Christmas		600	Reversed Etching	Fancy	Long	Inlaid	30.00
☐ Old Christmas		600	Reversed Etching	Fancy	Short	Inlaid	30.00
☐ Tortoise Shell	1979 Eagle Creek	100	Reversed Etching	Fancy	Long	Inlaid	50.00
☐ Tortoise Shell	TarHeel 1979 Albemarle		Reversed Etching	Fancy	Long	Inlaid	50.00
☐ Tortoise Shell		600	Reversed Etching	Fancy	Long	Inlaid	30.00
☐ Tortoise Shell		600	Reversed Etching	Fancy	Short	Inlaid	30.00
☐ Bone		300	Reversed Etching	Fancy	Short	Bar	35.00
☐ Old Christmas	One of the First Made	300	Reversed Etching	Smooth	Long	Inlaid	45.00
☐ Tortoise Shell		300	Reversed Etching	Smooth	Long	Inlaid	45.00
☐ Pearl & Brown		300	Reversed Etching	Smooth	Long	Inlaid	45.00
☐ Pearl	C. R.	300	Gold Etching	Smooth	Short		100.00
☐ Horn		100	Red Etching	Smooth	Short	Horn	150.00

CANOES — (FOUR BLADE)
NO PHOTO AVAILABLE

HANDLE	SERIES	NUMBER PRODUCED	ETCH	BOLSTER	PULL	SHIELD	COLLECTOR VALUE
☐New Christmas		300	Reverse Etching	Fancy	Short	Inlaid	40.00
☐Red & Black		300	Reverse Etching	Fancy	Short	Inlaid	40.00
☐Pearl & Black		300	Reverse Etching	Fancy	Short	Inlaid	40.00
☐Goldflake		300	Reverse Etching	Fancy	Short	Inlaid	40.00

CHICKEN FIGHTIN'
NO PHOTO AVAILABLE

HANDLE	SERIES	NUMBER PRODUCED	ETCH	BOLSTER	PULL	SHIELD	COLLECTOR VALUE
☐Bone	Very Rare	40	Old Style Stamp	Smooth	Short	Oval	60.00

CONGRESS

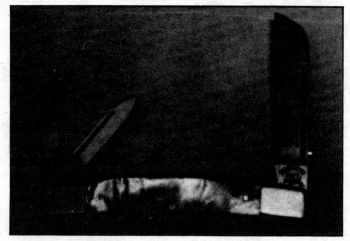

HANDLE	SERIES	NUMBER PRODUCED	ETCH	BOLSTER	PULL	SHIELD	COLLECTOR VALUE
☐Pearl	C. Rooster	600	Gold Etching	Smooth	Long		50.00
☐Pearl	C. Rooster	600	Gold Etching	Smooth	Long	4 Roses (Scrimshaw)	100.00
☐Red & Black			Etched	Grooved	Long	Bar	30.00
☐Pearl	C. Rooster	100	Gold C. Rooster	Grooved	Long		75.00
☐Pearl	Kentucky Club 1979	600	Gold Etching	Long Smooth	Long		75.00

HANDLE	SERIES	NUMBER PRODUCED	ETCH	BOLSTER	PULL	SHIELD	COLLECTOR VALUE
☐Old Christmas		300	No Etching	Grooved	Long	Bar	**40.00**
☐Old Christmas		1200	Etching	Grooved	Long	Bar	**40.00**
☐Pearl	C. Rooster	600	Gold Etching	Grooved	Long	Scrimshaw	**170.00**
☐Pearl	C. Rooster	600	Gold Etching	Long Smooth	Long		**70.00**
☐Stag		300	Etched	Smooth	Long	Bar	**60.00**
☐Bone		600	Etched	Smooth	Long	Bar	**40.00**
☐Red & Black		600	Etched	Smooth	Long	Bar	**35.00**
☐Pearl	C. Rooster	600	Gold Etching	Grooved	Long		**85.00**
☐Pearl	C. Rooster	600	Gold Etching	Grooved	Long	2 Roosters Scrimshaw	**135.00**

COPPERHEAD
NO PHOTO AVAILABLE

HANDLE	SERIES	NUMBER PRODUCED	ETCH	BOLSTER	PULL	SHIELD	COLLECTOR VALUE
☐Pearl	Tar Heel Club 1979	400	Gold Etching	Smooth	Short		**100.00**
☐Red & Black		300	Etched	Smooth	Short	Inlaid	**35.00**
☐Pearl & Black		300	Etched	Smooth	Short	Inlaid	**35.00**
☐Old Christmas		300	Etched	Smooth	Short	Inlaid	**35.00**
☐Butter & Molassas		300	Etched	Smooth	Short	Inlaid	**35.00**

CROWBAR
(description on following page)

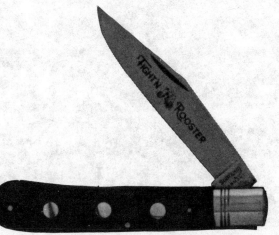

CROWBAR

HANDLE	SERIES	NUMBER PRODUCED	ETCH	BOLSTER	PULL	SHIELD	COLLECTOR VALUE
☐Rosewood		100	Etched	Pinched	Short		20.00
☐Rosewood		100	Etched	Smooth	Short	Oval	20.00

DISPLAY

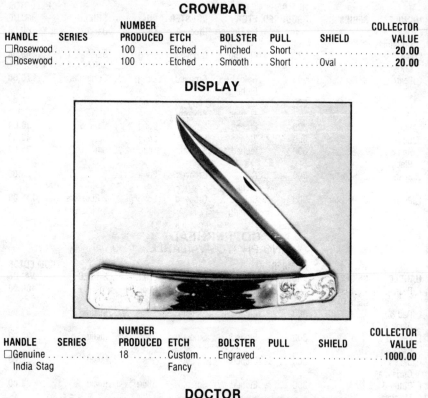

HANDLE	SERIES	NUMBER PRODUCED	ETCH	BOLSTER	PULL	SHIELD	COLLECTOR VALUE
☐Genuine India Stag		18	Custom Fancy	Engraved			1000.00

DOCTOR
(description on following page)

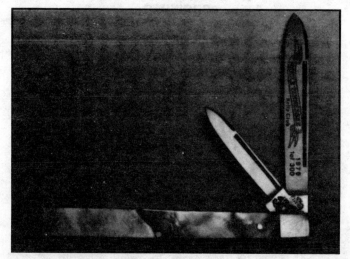

DOCTOR

HANDLE	SERIES	NUMBER PRODUCED	ETCH	BOLSTER	PULL	SHIELD	COLLECTOR VALUE
☐Pearl	82	600	Gold Etching	Smooth	Long		Set of
☐Pearl	82	600	Gold Etching	Smooth	Long		2 **200.00**
☐Pearl	500	300	Gold Etching	Smooth	Long	Crest	Set of
☐Stag	500	300	Gold Etching	Smooth	Long	Crest	2 **110.00**
☐Pearl	1979 Middle Tennessee Club		Gold Etching	Smooth	Long		**110.00**
☐Red & Black		300	Etched	Smooth	Long	Crest	Set of
☐New Christmas		300	Etched	Smooth	Long	Crest	2 **75.00**

DOCTORS ONE ARM

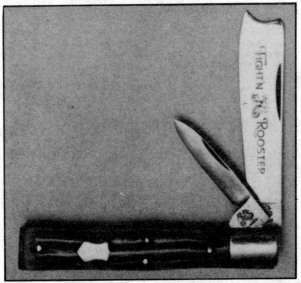

HANDLE	SERIES	NUMBER PRODUCED	ETCH	BOLSTER	PULL	SHIELD	COLLECTOR VALUE
☐Pearl	Very very rare	One arm man 2 doz.	Etch	Smooth	Short		**95.00**
☐Pearl	Tar Heel Club 1980	400	Gold Etched	Smooth	Short		**80.00**
☐Pearl	C. Rooster	600	Gold Etched	Smooth	Short		**75.00**
☐Stag		300	Etched	Smooth	Short	Crest	**35.00**
☐Brown Bone		300	Etched	Smooth	Short	Crest	**35.00**

HANDLE	SERIES	NUMBER PRODUCED	ETCH	BOLSTER	PULL	SHIELD	COLLECTOR VALUE
☐Butter & Molasses		300	Etched	Smooth	Short	Crest	28.00
☐Tortoise Shell		300	Etched	Smooth	Short	Crest	28.00
☐Old Christmas		300	Etched	Smooth	Short	Crest	28.00
☐Pearl & Black		300	Etched	Smooth	Short	Crest	28.00
☐Red & Black		300	Etched	Smooth	Short	Crest	28.00

ELECTRICIAN
NO PHOTO AVAILABLE

HANDLE	SERIES	NUMBER PRODUCED	ETCH	BOLSTER	PULL	SHIELD	COLLECTOR VALUE
☐Rosewood	Notch for Wire	100	Etched	One	Short		15.00

FOLDING HUNTER

HANDLE	SERIES	NUMBER PRODUCED	ETCH	BOLSTER	PULL	SHIELD	COLLECTOR VALUE
☐Pearl & Black	Cock of the Walk	600	Etched	Smooth	Short	Inlaid	Set of 2
☐New Christmas	Cock of the Walk	600	Etched	Smooth	Short	Inlaid	100.00
☐Bone		100	Etched	Smooth	Short	Oval	45.00
☐Bone		100	Etched	Smooth	Short	Crest	45.00

GUNSTOCKS

HANDLE	SERIES	NUMBER PRODUCED	ETCH	BOLSTER	PULL	SHIELD	COLLECTOR VALUE
Pearl & Black	Tar Heel Show 1979	200	Etched	Smooth	Short	Inlaid	40.00
Red & Black	Tar Heel Show 1979	200	Etched	Smooth	Short	Inlaid	40.00
Pearl & Black		600	Etched	Smooth	Short	Inlaid	Set of 2
Red & Black		600	Etched	Smooth	Short	Inlaid	60.00
New Christmas	C. Rooster	150	Gold Etching	Smooth	Short	Inlaid	45.00
Pearl	1979 Palmetto Club	200	Gold	Smooth	Short	Inlaid	85.00
Bone	½ Whittler	Very Rare	Etched	Smooth	Short	Crest	75.00
Stag	C. Rooster	150	Gold Etched	Smooth	Short	Crest	45.00
New Christmas	C. Rooster		Gold Etching	Smooth	Short	Inlaid	40.00
Pearl	C. Rooster	300	Gold Etched				50.00
Pearl	1978 Kentucky Club	300	Gold Etched	Smooth	Short	Scrimshaw	95.00
Pearl	Tar Heel Club	350	Gold Etching	Smooth	Short		95.00
Bone		300	Etched	Smooth	Short	Crest	45.00
Old Christmas		300	Etched	Smooth	Short	Inlaid	45.00
Brown & Pearl		300	Etched	Smooth	Short	Inlaid	45.00

HANDLE	SERIES	NUMBER PRODUCED	ETCH	BOLSTER	PULL	SHIELD	COLLECTOR VALUE
☐Goldflake		300	Etched	Smooth	Short	Inlaid	45.00
☐Red & Black		300	Etched	Smooth	Short	Inlaid	45.00
☐Butter & Molasses		300	Etched	Smooth	Short	Inlaid	45.00

GUNSTOCKS — (LOCKBACK)

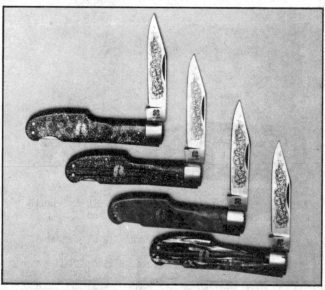

HANDLE	SERIES	NUMBER PRODUCED	ETCH	BOLSTER	PULL	SHIELD	COLLECTOR VALUE
☐Butter & Molasses	King of the Woods	300	Etched	1 Smooth	Short	Inlaid	45.00
☐Red & Black	King of the Woods	300	Etched	1 Smooth	Short	Inlaid	45.00
☐Pearl & Black	King of the Woods	300	Etched	1 Smooth	Short	Inlaid	45.00
☐Old Christmas	King of the Woods	300	Etched	1 Smooth	Short	Inlaid	45.00
☐Pearl & Abalone	King of the Woods	200	Gold Etch	1 Smooth	Short	Inlaid	100.00

HAWKBILL
NO PHOTO AVAILABLE

HANDLE	SERIES	NUMBER PRODUCED	ETCH	BOLSTER	PULL	SHIELD	COLLECTOR VALUE
☐Rosewood	Large	100	Etched	No	Short	Large Solingen	20.00
☐Rosewood	Large	100	Etched	No	Short	Small Solingen	20.00

JACKS — (TEARDROP)

HANDLE	SERIES	NUMBER PRODUCED	ETCH	BOLSTER	PULL	SHIELD	COLLECTOR VALUE
☐ Old Christmas	Southern Belle	600	Gold Etching	Smooth	Long	Crest	Set of 3
☐ Old Christmas	Tennessean	600	Gold Etching	Smooth	Long	Crest	
☐ Old Christmas	Kentuckian	600	Gold Etching	Smooth	Long	Crest	**150.00**
☐ Black	Kentuckian	Very Rare	Gold Etching	Smooth	Long	Crest	**70.00**

LADIES — (BANTY)
(description on following page)

LADIES — (BANTY)

HANDLE	SERIES	NUMBER PRODUCED	ETCH	BOLSTER	PULL	SHIELD	COLLECTOR VALUE
☐Pearl		300		Engraving Smooth (2)	Short		30.00
☐Amber		300		Engraving	Short		15.00
☐Goldflake		300		Engraving Bolster (1)	Short		15.00
☐Old Christmas		300		Engraving Bolster (1)	Short		15.00

LOCKBACKS

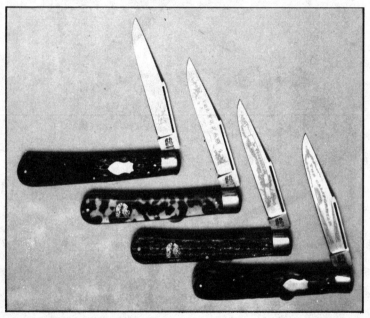

HANDLE	SERIES	NUMBER PRODUCED	ETCH	BOLSTER	PULL	SHIELD	COLLECTOR VALUE
☐Bone	Kentuckian	300	Gold Etched	1 Smooth	Long	Crest	50.00
☐Tortoise Shell	Texan	300	Gold Etched	1 Smooth	Long	Inlaid	50.00
☐Stag	Calforian	300	Gold Etched	1 Smooth	Long	Crest	65.00
☐New Christmas	Tennessean	300	Gold Etched	1 Smooth	Long	Inlaid	50.00
☐Rosewood	4¾ in. long	100	Etched	1 Smooth	Short	Fancy	45.00

MELON TESTER
NO PHOTO AVAILABLE

HANDLE	SERIES	NUMBER PRODUCED	ETCH	BOLSTER	PULL	SHIELD	COLLECTOR VALUE
☐White Comp		24	Etch	Long	Long		40.00
☐Black Comp		24	Etch	Long	Long		40.00

MUSKRAT

HANDLE	SERIES	NUMBER PRODUCED	ETCH	BOLSTER	PULL	SHIELD	COLLECTOR VALUE
☐Bone	Very Rare		Etched	Smooth	Short	Crest	40.00
☐Red & Black Checked	Tennessean	250	Gold & Etching	Pinched	Short	Crest	Set of 2
☐Gold & Black Checked	Kentuckian	250	Gold Etching	Pinched	Short	Crest	70.00
☐Blue & Black	Tennessean	250	Gold Etching	Pinched	Short	Crest	Set of 2
☐Gold & Black Checked	Kentuckian	250	Gold Etching	Pinched	Short	Crest	70.00
☐Butter & Molasses	Tennessean	250	Gold Etching	Pinched	Short	Crest	Set of 2
☐Old Christmas	Kentuckian	250	Gold Etching	Pinched	Short	Crest	65.00
☐Old Christmas	Kentuckian	250	Gold Etching	Pinched	Short	Crest	Set of 2
☐Pearl & Black	Tennessean	250	Gold Etching	Pinched	Short	Crest	65.00
☐Pearl	Captain Rooster	600	Gold Etching	Pinched	Short		85.00
☐Pearl	Captain Rooster	600	Gold Etching	Smooth	Short		70.00

HANDLE	SERIES	NUMBER PRODUCED	ETCH	BOLSTER	PULL	SHIELD	COLLECTOR VALUE
☐Pearl	1978 Palmetto Club	200	Gold Etching	Smooth	Short		**85.00**
☐Bone			Old Style Lamp	Smooth	Short	Crest	**45.00**
☐Pearl	Swanner	600	Gold Etch	Smooth	Short		**70.00**

PEANUTS

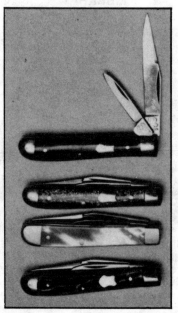

HANDLE	SERIES	NUMBER PRODUCED	ETCH	BOLSTER	PULL	SHIELD	COLLECTOR VALUE
☐Bone		100	No	Short	Short	Crest	**25.00**
☐Old Christmas		600	No	Short	Short	Crest	
☐Red & Black		600	No	Short	Short	Crest	Set
☐Pearl & Black		600	No	Short	Short	Crest	of 4
☐Butter & Molasses		600	No	Short	Short	Crest	**110.00**
☐Horn		300	No	Short	Short	Crest	Set
☐Pearl		300	No	Short	Short	Crest	of
☐New Xmas		300	No	Short	Short	Crest	4
☐Stag		300	No	Short	Short	Crest	**125.00**

PENKNIFE
NO PHOTO AVAILABLE

HANDLE	SERIES	NUMBER PRODUCED	ETCH	BOLSTER	PULL	SHIELD	COLLECTOR VALUE
☐ Brass	2 Blades & 1 File	300 or less made	Etched		Short		20.00

PENKNIVES — (BRASS)

HANDLE	SERIES	NUMBER PRODUCED	ETCH	BOLSTER	PULL	SHIELD	COLLECTOR VALUE
☐ Brass	"The Miner"	300	(Logo on Tang)		Short		30.00
☐ Brass	"Blacksmith"	300	(Logo on Tang)		Short		30.00
☐ Brass	"AC"	300	(Logo on Tang)		Short		20.00
☐ Brass	"Delco"	300	(Logo on Tang)		Short		20.00

PENKNIVES — (LADIES)
(description on following page)

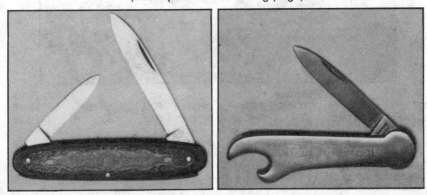

PENKNIVES — (LADIES)

HANDLE	SERIES	NUMBER PRODUCED	ETCH	BOLSTER	PULL	SHIELD	COLLECTOR VALUE
☐ Brown Celluloid	Very Very Rare	2 Dozen Each	Also A Block Made		Short		30.00
☐ Simulated Pearl Xmas & Silver Inlaid	"Ladies"	300			Short		25.00
☐ Tortoise Simulated Pearl & Silver Inlaid	"Gentlemen"	300			Short		25.00
☐ All Metal		300	Fighting Rooster	None	Short	4 color	30.00
☐ All Metal	Bottle Opener	400	Fighting Rooster	None	Short	None	15.00

POWDER HORNS

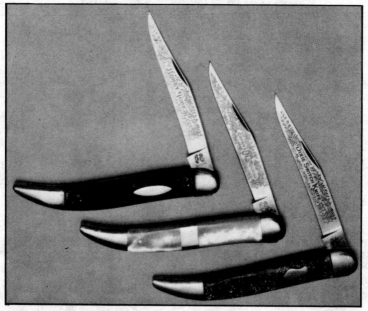

HANDLE	SERIES	NUMBER PRODUCED	ETCH	BOLSTER	PULL	SHIELD	COLLECTOR VALUE
☐ Stag	Gator Club 1979	300	Gold Etching	Smooth	Short	Bar	110.00
☐ Black & Red	Dixie Switch	600	Etched	Smooth	Short	Crest	30.00
☐ Old Christmas	Dixie Switch	600	Etched	Smooth	Short	Crest	35.00

HANDLE	SERIES	NUMBER PRODUCED	ETCH	BOLSTER	PULL	SHIELD	COLLECTOR VALUE
☐Bone	Honky Tonk	600	Etched	Smooth	Short	Oval	**35.00**
☐Bone	New Orleans	300	Gold Etch	Fancy Old	Short	Bar	**40.00**
☐Stag	Cajun Queen	300	Gold Etch	Fancy Old	Short	Bar	**45.00**
☐Pearl	Captain Rooster	300	Gold Etch	Smooth	Short		**65.00**
☐Pearl with Rubies	Gem Capital	150	Fancy Etch	Smooth	Short	None	**275.00**

SEMI-HAWK

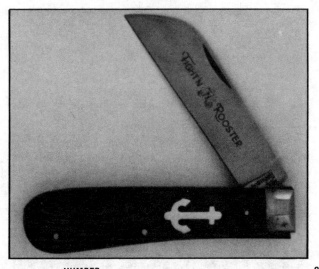

HANDLE	SERIES	NUMBER PRODUCED	ETCH	BOLSTER	PULL	SHIELD	COLLECTOR VALUE
☐Rosewood	Semi-Hawkbill	Small 100 Blade	Etched	Pinched	Short	Anchor	**15.00**
☐Rosewood		Large 100 Blade	Etched	Pinched	Short	Anchor	**15.00**

SHORT BOWIES
(description on following page)

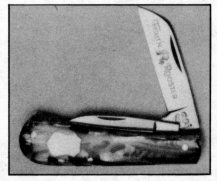

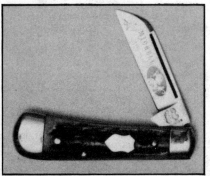

SHORT BOWIES

HANDLE	SERIES	NUMBER PRODUCED	ETCH	BOLSTER	PULL	SHIELD	COLLECTOR VALUE
☐ Butter-Scotch		200	Etched	None	Short	Crest	**25.00**
☐ Black & Pearl		200	Etched	None	Short	Crest	**25.00**
☐ Red & Black		200	Etched	None	Short	Crest	**25.00**
☐ New Xmas		200	Etched	None	Short	Crest	**25.00**
☐ Tortoise		200	Etched	None	Short	Crest	**25.00**
☐ Butter & Molasses		200	Etched	None	Short	Crest	**25.00**
☐ Stag	Michell	300	Etched	Fancy	Short	Crest	**35.00**

SOD BUSTERS

HANDLE	SERIES	NUMBER PRODUCED	ETCH	BOLSTER	PULL	SHIELD	COLLECTOR VALUE
☐ Pearl	C. Rooster	600	Gold Etched	Smooth	Short		**55.00**
☐ Pearl	Albemarle Club 1980	200	Gold Etched	Smooth	Short		**90.00**
☐ Pearl & Black	Southern Style Part 2	300	Etched		Short	Inlaid	**30.00**
☐ Pearl & Black	Southern Style Part 2	300	Etched		Short	Inlaid	**30.00**
☐ Old Christmas	Southern Style Part 1	300	Etched		Short	Inlaid	**30.00**
☐ Butter & Molasses	Southern Style Part 1	300	Etched		Short	Inlaid	**30.00**

HANDLE	SERIES	NUMBER PRODUCED	ETCH	BOLSTER	PULL	SHIELD	COLLECTOR VALUE
☐Rosewood	3¾" long	300	Old Style Stamp		Short	Only Stamp Soligen, Germ	20.00
☐Rosewood	4¾" long	300 or less	Old Style Stamp		Short	Only Stamp Soligen, Germ	20.00
☐Rosewood	3¾" long	300 or less	Old Style Stamp		Short		20.00
☐Rosewood	4¾" long	300 or less	Old Style Stamp		Short		20.00
☐Black	4¾" long	300 or less	Etched		Short		20.00
☐Black	3¾" long	200	Etched		Short		25.00
☐Yellow Comp	3¾" long	Very Rare	Etched		Short		25.00
☐Black	4¾" long	100	Large Stamp		Short		25.00
☐Green	House of Coutel Workback	16	Gold Etch		Short	Gold Scroll	145.00
☐Rosewood	3" long	100	Large Stamp		Short		20.00
☐Rosewood	3" long	100	Small Stamp		Short		20.00

STOCK

HANDLE	SERIES	NUMBER PRODUCED	ETCH	BOLSTER	PULL	SHIELD	COLLECTOR VALUE
☐Crystal White	Rare Approx. 12 Dozen	TN Highway Patrol Mistake 1 of 100	Etched	Short	Long		55.00
☐Horn	Rare Approx. 12 Dozen	Tennessee Patrol	Etched	Long	Long	Crest	60.00

HANDLE	SERIES	NUMBER PRODUCED	ETCH	BOLSTER	PULL	SHIELD	COLLECTOR VALUE
Black & Orange	Grit & Steele	1200	Etched	Long	Long	Crest	30.00
Old Xmas		Rare	Reverse Etching	Short	Long	Shield	30.00
Horn		150		Long	Long	Shield	45.00
Pearl	Captain & Rooster Scrimshaw	2 Dozen	Gold-Red Etching	Long	Long	Shield	120.00
Pearl	Knife City	100	Etch	Long	Long	Fightin' Rooster	90.00
Golden Fluff		400	Etch	Long	Long	Shield	25.00
Butter-Scotch		400	Etch	Long	Long	Shield	25.00
Mint Green		400	Etch	Long	Long	Shield	25.00
Smokey Grey		400	Etch	Long	Long	Shield	25.00
Black Comp	Has Tweezers & Toothpick	24 Made	Etch	No	Short		60.00
Bone	1 of 700	TN. Highway Patrol 1 Dozen	Etch	Short	Long	Shield	60.00
Crystal White	''Moonshine''	1200	Gold Etching	Long	Long	Crest	40.00
Black	Black Diamond	1200	Gold Etching	Short	Long	Crest	50.00
Gold & Black Stripe	Kentuckian	600	Reverse Etching	Long	Long	Crest	30.00
Brown & Black Stripe	Tennessean	300	Reverse Etching	Short	Long	Crest	30.00
Blue & Black Stripe	Virginian	300	Reverse Etching	Short	Long	Crest	30.00
Gold & Black Stripe	Kentuckian	300	Reverse Etching	Short	Long	Crest	30.00
Green & Black Stripe	Carolinian	150	Reverse Etching	Short	Long	Crest	40.00
Feather White	Carolinian	150	Reverse Etching	Short	Long	Crest	40.00
New Christmas	Easy Money	1200	Etched	Short	Long	Crest	35.00
Tortoise Shell	Easy Money	Rare 12 Made	Etched	Long	Long	Crest	60.00
Tortoise Shell	Black Widow	1200	Etched	Short	Long	Crest	30.00
Tortoise Shell	Black Widow	Not Limited	Etched	Long	Long	Crest	35.00

HANDLE	SERIES	NUMBER PRODUCED	ETCH	BOLSTER	PULL	SHIELD	COLLECTOR VALUE
☐Tortoise Shell	Black Widow	Rare 24 Made	Etched	Long	Long	Circle	30.00
☐Goldflake	Twenty Dollar Gold Piece	Not Limited	Gold Etching	Long	Long	Crest	30.00
☐Goldflake	Twenty Dollar Gold Piece	500	Gold Etching	Short	Long	Crest	35.00
☐Pearl & Black	Nice & Easy	300	Etched	Short	Long	Crest	30.00
☐Red & Black	Wildfire	300	Etched	Short	Long	Crest	30.00
☐Red & Black	Till Death do us Apart	1200	Gold Etched	Long	Long	Crest	25.00
☐Gold & Black Stripe	Kentuckian	Rare	Reverse Etching	Long	Long	No Shield	50.00
☐Crystal White	Moonshiner Still	100	Gold	Long	Long	Crest	300.00
☐Bone	Very Rare	100	Etched	Short	Long	Crest	70.00
☐Pearl & Black	Coal Miner Daughters	600	Etched	Short	Long	Crest	Set of 2
☐Goldflake	Coal Miner	600	Etched	Short	Long	Crest	270.00
☐Horn	Very Rare	132 a Dozen	Reverse Etching	Short	Long	Crest	70.00
☐Pearl	Captain Rooster	900	Gold Etching	Long	Long		65.00
☐Crystal White	Rare	300	Etched	Short	Long	Crest	50.00
☐Yellow Comp	Very Rare		Etched	Short	Long	Crest	50.00
☐Yellow Comp	Very Rare	100	Etched	Short	Long	Crest	50.00
☐Feather White	Rare	300	Reverse Etched	Short	Long	Crest	65.00
☐Stag	Very Very Rare	5 or 7 Approx.	Etched	Short	Long	Circle	100.00
☐Stag		600	Etched	Long	Long	Crest	45.00
☐Bone		300	Etched	Short	Long	Crest	30.00
☐Bone		600	Etched	Long	Long	Crest	30.00
☐Bone		100	Etched	Round	Long	Crest	30.00
☐Goldflake		300	Etched	Short	Long	Crest	30.00
☐Tortoise Shell		2400	Etched	Short	Long	Crest	30.00
☐Pearl & Black		300	Etched	Short	Long	Crest	30.00
☐Butter & Molasses		300	Etched	Short	Long	Crest	30.00
☐Old Christmas	300 Made	300	Etched	Short	Long	Crest	30.00
☐Stag	Florida Club 1979	200	Gold Etching	Long Smooth	Long	Crest	80.00
☐Smooth Bone	TN Highway Patrol	600	Gold Etching	Long	Long	Crest (THP)	100.00

HANDLE	SERIES	NUMBER PRODUCED	ETCH	BOLSTER	PULL	SHIELD	COLLECTOR VALUE
☐Red & Black		300	Etched	Short	Long	Crest	**30.00**
☐Pearl	Capt. Rooster	100	Gold	Short	Long		**100.00**

TOLEDO SCALE

HANDLE	SERIES	NUMBER PRODUCED	ETCH	BOLSTER	PULL	SHIELD	COLLECTOR VALUE
☐Brass	2 bl.	Office Pen Knife	Etch		Short		**45.00**

TRAPPERS

HANDLE	SERIES	NUMBER PRODUCED	ETCH	BOLSTER	PULL	SHIELD	COLLECTOR VALUE
☐Bone		300	Etched	Smooth	Short	Crest	**45.00**
☐Old Christmas	Tennessean	600	Etched	Smooth	Short	Crest	Set of 2
☐Old Christmas	Kentuckian	600	Etched	Smooth	Short	Crest	**95.00**
☐Bone		100	Old Style Stamp	Smooth	Short	Crest	**35.00**

HANDLE	SERIES	NUMBER PRODUCED	ETCH	BOLSTER	PULL	SHIELD	COLLECTOR VALUE
☐Bone	Frank Buster Cutlery on Tang	100	Old Style Stamp	Smooth	Short	Crest	30.00
☐Bone	One Short Blade	100	Etched	Smooth	Short	Oval	30.00
☐Bone		100	Etched	Fancy Bolster	Short	Oval	30.00

WHITTLERS

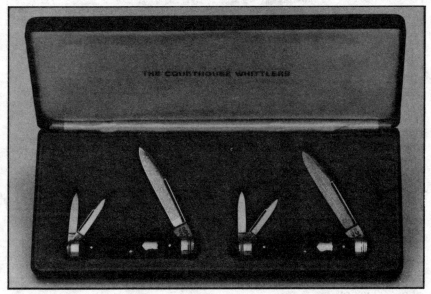

HANDLE	SERIES	NUMBER PRODUCED	ETCH	BOLSTER	PULL	SHIELD	COLLECTOR VALUE
☐White Bone	Kentuckian	15	Gold Etching	Smooth	Long	Bar	100.00
☐White Bone		300	Etched	Smooth	Long	Bar	35.00
☐Red & Black Checked	Court House	600	Gold Etching	Sculpture	Lone	Crest	Set of 2
☐Blue & Black	Court House	600	Gold Etching	Sculpture	Long	Crest	95.00 95.00
☐Stag		300	Etched	Smooth	Long	Bar	35.00
☐Pearl & Black		300	Etched	Smooth	Long	Bar	30.00
☐Old Christmas		300	Etched	Smooth	Long	Bar	30.00

FROST CUTLERY COMPANY

Frost Cutlery Company was formed by James A. Frost in 1979. A partner in the Parker-Frost Cutlery Company, he branched out on his own in 1978, importing his own line of knives from Japan.

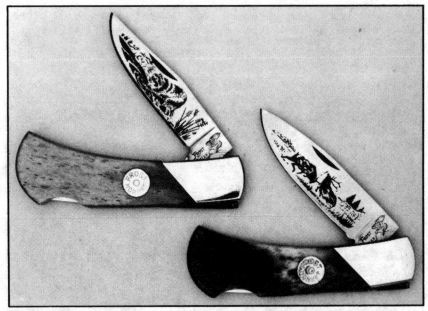

☐ *Current Collector Value* . . . . **$14.00 each**

G-96 BRAND

G-96 knives are produced by the Jet Aer Corporation, a company that has produced a broad line of chemicals for sportsmen under the G-96 Brand for about 20 years.

Around 1971, the company introduced the Titan line, then the mariner fishing knives, the G-96 customline knives, and the Appollo line of teflon coated knives. Other lines are planned.

The current catalog shows several lockback folding hunters, including two teflon coated folding hunters.

GERBER LEGENDARY BLADES
PORTLAND, OREGON

Gerber has produced home cutlery since 1940 and introduced their line of hunting and camping knives in 1950, including several versions of folding hunter lockbacks. Their knives are stamped "GERBER" with "Portland, OR 97223 U.S.A." on the reverse of the tang.

THE PAUL KNIFE

Copyright 1979, National Knife Collector Magazine, Compliments National Knife Collector Association

The Paul/Gerber knife already has become an important collector's item on the west coast where the knife is produced at the Gerber factory in Portland, Oregon.

The first Paul knives were manufactured by Gerber in October 1978. "From October through December 1978 we made 1,891 knives," reports Joseph R. (Pete) Gerber Jr., president of the company.

"These are indicated by no markigs on the bottom side of the spacer," explains Gerber. "All knives produced on or after January 2, 1979 have the number "1" etched on the bottom side of the spacer. This number will be used during the entire calendar year of 1979. The number "2" will be used beginning January 2, 1980."

Three different types of handles were produced in the 1,891 "no-numbers" of 1978 — ivory micarta, cocobola, and stainless steel.

Of these 1,891 knives, Gerber reports that 250 with cocobola handles were etched at the factory with the Abercrombie & Fitch logo on the blade, and merchandised in an A&F mail order catalog revived for the 1978 season.

The Abercrombie & Fitch knife was sold with a Gerber-produced leather belt sheath which also carried the A&F logo stamped on its face.

The original retail price of the 1978 Paul/Gerber was $55 for the 2P steel handled knife, and 160 for the 2PM micarta handle or the 2PW wood handle. The knives now retail at $60 for the 2P, and $70 for the 2PM and 2PW. The belt sheath first went for $5 retail, and now costs $7.

At the February 1979 Sahara Knife Show in Las Vegas, the very few 1978 "no-numbers" sold for $90 to $120. The few available of the A&F "no-numbers" 2PWs with the A&F embossed sheath accompanying have sold

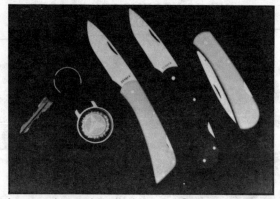

A new micarta handled line by Gerber.
☐ *Current Collector Value* . . . . **$25.00 each**

The Gerber Guardian.
☐ *Current Collector Value* . . . **$49.50**

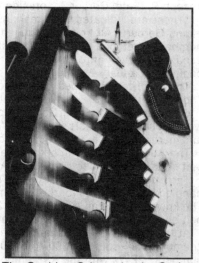

The Cushion Grip series by Gerber.

for $150. It is easily predictable that the values on these already rare knives will soar as those remaining at large disappear into collector's cases.

Patents for the Paul knives made by Gerber are held by Paul W. Poehlmann, a brilliant California design and production engineer who first came on the handmade knife scene in 1975.

Because of the stimulus of the Paul/Gerber, interest is growing in collecting other earlier Gerber folding knives no longer on the market. Particularly collectible is the early "Folding Hunter" with checkered handles of delrin, walnut, or Macassar ebony. This knife was produced in the three above handle materials with blades of either stainless steel or of "tool steel", so marked on the tang.

Another interesting aspect of collecting early Gerbers is the relatively few "FS" (for Folding Sportsman) knives which had blades made in Germany and were so marked on the tang. A total of 20,094 of these were produced by Helmut Giesen from 1971 through 1973, and are very rare.

The patented Paul Knife by Gerber Blades of Portland, Oregon: Three models, each featuring an exclusive axial locking mechanism. Offered with handles of brushed stainless steel, tropical hardwood or white Micarta. Genuine leather belt scabbard optional.

☐ *Current Collector Value* **$60.00-75.00**

GERMAN EYE — CARL SCHLIEPER
SOLINGEN, GERMANY

Eye Brand was started in the 1880's and at one time was quite scarce. Today they are readily available and are stamped with both one and two eyes on the tang. The company also has two other lines, "El Gallo" and "Jim Bowie".

Forest Cruse & Son of Austin, Texas is the exclusive importer of Eye Brand knives, and they are available from most mail-order dealers.

H & B
NEW BRITTON, CONNECTICUT

Although Humason and Beckley had made knives since 1852, the trademark was not registered until 1864. The trademark was registered by Landers, Frary and Clark in December of 1916.

Three hen and roosters made for the Acorn Shop.

☐ *Current Collector Value: Stag handle, large* $75.00
☐   *Stag handle, small* 65.00
☐   *Genuine pearl handle* 120.00

Three late model hens and roosters — Ron Lake model.

☐ *Current Collector Value* . . . . $105.00 each

HEN AND ROOSTER
SOLINGEN GERMANY

The Hen and Rooster knife is produced by the C. Bertram Company of Siligen, Germany and takes its trademark from the company's founder, Carl Bertram, who was a well-known chicken breeder. When the company was founded in 1872, most of their knives were the four blade congress pattern with first cut stag handles and a few with genuine pearl handles. In recent years the company has introduced some stainless steel two blade knives and bone handled three blade stockman knives.

C. Bertram has made a large number of contract knives with the customer's name and the Hen and Rooster trademark on the same knife (i.e. Fife Cutlery Co.) or with only the customer's name or the Hen and Rooster trademark.

The company ceased production and closed out the Solingen facilities in 1980, although the trademark will continue to be used.

HENCKELS, J. A.
SOLINGEN, GERMANY

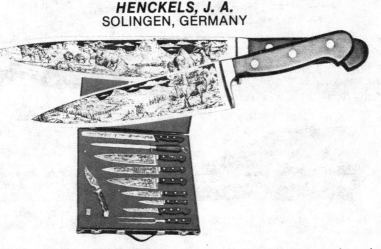

One of the best known trademarks in cutlery is the Henckels trademark, registered in Solingen since 1731.

Johann Abraham Henckels established his second showroom of Henckels cutlery in Berlin in 1816, a three week journey from Solingen. This was a drastic step for cutlery manufacturers of that time, but it soon paid off. Henckels was also one of the first to change from water power to steam power (they made the change in 1839).

The first American showroom was opened in New York City in 1883, and Henckels also maintains showrooms that are tourist attractions in Dresden, Vienna, Paris, and other major cities of the world.

The Henckels plant, covering 26 acres and employing 2,500 workers, produces over 2,300 different patterns of cutlery, including a line of cutlery that is produced only for United States markets.

HIBBARD, SPENCER AND BARTLETT
CHICAGO, ILLINOIS

Hibbard and Spencer originally formed HS&B, later bringing in Bartlett as a junior partner. They sold knives under the OVB (Our Very Best) Brand. The company was a large hardware distributor. These knives were made primarily by Schrade, and are a popular collectible.

The company closed out in the 1960's to Cotter & Co. of Chicago (Tru-Value Hardware).

☐**1H**—(3⅜") Black bone handle, one blade; iron lined **120.00**

☐**2H**—(3⅜") Black bone handle, two blades; iron lined **120.00**

☐**144**—(5¾") Cocoa handle, one blade; iron lined **150.00**

☐**145**—(5⅝") Cocoa handle, one blade; iron lined **150.00**

☐**146**—(5⅝") Stag handle, one blade; iron lined **150.00**

☐**156**—(5⅜") Stag handle, one blade; "OUR VERY BEST", brass lined, lock back . . . **150.00**

☐**375**—PHYSICIANS' KNIFE (3¾") two blades, highly finished; brass lined, nickel silver bolster and cap **125.00**

☐**379**—(3⅜") Stag handle, two blades, highly finished; brass linings, nickel silver bolsters, plain without shield **75.00**

☐**548**—(3½") Stag handle, two blades, highly finished; brass linings, nickel silver bolsters, nickel silver shield **75.00**

☐**589**—OFFICE KNIFE (3¾") White ivoroid handle, two blades, highly finished; brass lined **40.00**

☐**738**—CARPENTERS' KNIFE (3⅝") Stag handle, three blades, highly finished; brass linings, nickel silver bolsters, nickel silver shield **175.00**

☐**785**—CARPENTERS' KNIFE (3⅝") Pearl handle of finest quality, three blades, highly finished; brass linings, nickel silver bolsters, plain without shield **175.00**

☐**798**—CARPENTERS' KNIFE (3⅝") Ebony handle, three blades, large blade extra heavy and extra strong, sabre pattern, highly finished; brass lined, nickel silver bolsters and shield **140.00**

☐**827**—(3⅜″) Stag handle, four blades including finger nail blade; brass linings, nickel silver bolsters, nickel silver shield **150.00**

☐**839**—(3″) Stag handle, plain without shield, four blades, including finger nail blade; brass linings, nickel silver bolsters **150.00**

☐**839**—(3″) Stag handle, plain without shield, four blades, including finger nail blade; brass linings, nickel silver bolsters **150.00**

☐**844**—(3¾″) Stag handle, four blades, not including finger nail blade; brass linings, nickel silver bolsters, nickel silver shield **150.00**

☐**845**—(3½″) Stag handle, four blades, highly finished; brass linings, steel bolsters and nickel silver shields **150.00**

☐**1041**—(3⅜″) Black fubbaly horn handle, two blades, highly finished; brass linings, nickel silver bolsters and shields **65.00**

☐**1042**—(3⅜″) Stag handle, two blades, highly finished; brass linings, nickel silver bolsters and shields **65.00**

☐**51036D**—(3½″) Stag handle, two blades, glazed; nickel silver bolster, brass lined **125.00**

☐**51046D**—(3½″) Stag handle, three blades, polished; brass lined **160.00**

☐**51047D**—(3⅞″) Stag handle, two blades, large clip and large spear, glazed; brass lined **90.00**

☐**51073D**—''OFFICE KNIFE,'' (3¾″) White celluloid handle stamped in blacke, two blades, highly finished; brass lined **65.00**

☐**51014D**—(3½″) Cocobola handle, two blades, glazed; brass lined **65.00**

☐**51085D**—(3⅛″) Stag handle, two blades, polished; brass lined, nickel silver cap, bolster and shield **65.00**

☐**51086D**—(3½″) Stag handle, two blades, one large spear point blade, glazed, one leather punch blade; brass lined, steel bolster, nickel silver shield **65.00**

☐**51015D**—(3½″) Stag handle, two blades, glazed; brass lined.................**60.00**

☐**51025D**—(3⅛″) Stag handle, three blades, polished; brass lined **90.00**

☐**518087D**—(3½") Cocobola handle, two blades, one large spear point blade, glazed, one leather punch blade; brass lined, steel bolster, nickel silver shield **65.00**

☐**51088D**—(3½") Stag handle, two blades, one large spear point blade and one leather punch blade or gouge, glazed; brass lined, nickel silver bolsters and shield **60.00**

☐**51089D**—(3½") Cocobola handle, two blades, one large spear point blade and one leather punch blade or gouge, glazed; brass lined, nickel silver bolsters and shield **60.00**

☐**51091D**—(3⅜") Stag handle, three blades, one large spear point blade, one spey blade and one leather punch blade, glazed; brass lined, nickel silver bolsters and shield **100.00**

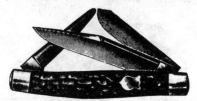

☐**5190D**—(3¼") Stag handle, three blades, one large clip point blade, one spey blade, and one leather punch blade or gouge, glazed; brass lined, nickel silver bolsters and shield . . **100.00**

HOLLEY MANUFACTURING COMPANY
LAKEVILLE, CONNECTICUT

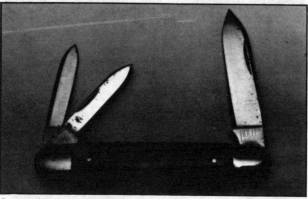

A rare Holley whittler.
☐ *Current Collector Value* **$150.00**

The Holley Manufacturing Company of Lakeville, Connecticut is reputed to have been the oldest pocketknife manufacturer. Built on the site of patriot Ethan Allen's blast furnace, the company imported skilled cutlers from Sheffield and in 1844 Alexander Holley, son of the founders, built a new factory and started nationwide distribution, but due to slower methods used by Holley lost most of its national sales markets by 1904.

A second thing that added to the downfall of Holley Manufacturing Company was the Holley guarantee. The guarantee said that Holley would replace any worn-out Holley knife with a brand new Holley knife. Some salesmen misunderstood this guarantee and gave a new Holley knife for any brand worn-out knife.

At one time Holley made a 24 blade knife for the Philadelphia Exposition and was "commended as excellent in styles and finish" by the judges.

The company handled its knives in horn, bone, ivory, metal, and wood, always using brass liners. The factory was converted into a ski factory during World War II.

HONK FALLS KNIFE COMPANY
NAPANOCH, NEW YORK

Four employees of Napanoch were hired by Winchester when Winchester bought the old Napanoch factory from Winchester in 1921 and began to make knives under the Honk Falls Knife Company trademark. The factory burned in 1929 and the company did not manufacture knives under the Honk Falls trademark again. The knives were stamped, "Honk Falls, Napanoch, New York, U. S. A."

HORNET
ST. LOUIS, MISSOURI

"Hornet," a brand of E. C. Simmons Hardware was discontinued around 1915. "Hornet" was etched on the master blade and "E. C. Simmons Company" was stamped on the tang.

HOWARD CUTLERY COMPANY
NEW YORK, NEW YORK

"Howard" was a house brand name for the C. B. Barker Co., Ltd., 40 E. 12th St., New York. The line was introduced to the company that before had been distributing sewing machine parts sometime after 1881, and prior to 1890.

The knives were made by the old Canastota Knife Company, Canastota, New York

IBBERSON, GEORGE & COMPANY
SHEFFIELD, ENGLAND

This Company's current trademark is the Violin. They were founded in 1700 and received their first mark in 1716 which was an S over a T. The Violin mark was first used in 1880 when it was granted to George Ibberson. It is interesting to note that the Ibberson firm has recorded 33 different trademarks with Cutlers' Hall since 1716.

Ibberson's current production covers the cutlery field. They make scissors which are used extensively in the textile trades as well as table cutlery and even letter openers. Now these cutlery items are useful and some of them are even interesting, but nothing to match their fine pocket-knives. Besides a fine range of matching knives sold worldwide, they produce beautiful workback knives. These are called chased knives in Sheffield. The backsprings and blade tops are cut and designed with fine files and wheels to produce a truly premium knife.

IDEAL KNIFE COMPANY
PROVIDENCE, RHODE ISLAND

In 1931 Ideal introduced a two blades brass lined two bolster fancy handled knife. It was available with and without a shackle.

Ideal was owned by Dominick and Michael Marseli and Phillip Magioni.

IMPERIAL KNIFE ASSOCIATED COMPANIES INCORPORATED
NEW YORK, NEW YORK

Ulster Knife Company, Imperial Knife Company, and Schrade are all divisions of Imperial Knife Associated Companies Incorporated, making it one of the largest cutlery concerns in the United States. The company was incorporated in 1947, and began manufacturing knives for the United States government.

IMPERIAL KNIFE COMPANY, INC.
PROVIDENCE, RHODE ISLAND

The Imperial Knife Company was started by the Mirando brothers, Felix and Michael, in 1916. The descendants of Italian knifemakers from Frosilona, Felix made his first knife at age eight.

The brothers worked at Empire until 1916, when they moved to Providence, Rhode Island to make knives for the jewelry industry centered in Providence.

They first began to make Waldemar knives (watch chain knives) and in six months had eight employees turning out 100 dozen knives per week.

By the 1930's they were turning out 10,000 knives per day, and the 1940's found them the largest cutlery concern in the world.

Bought in 1947 by the Imperial Knife Associated Companies Incorporated, the company has produced such brands as "Imperial, Providence, Rhode Island," "Jack Master," "Hammer Brand," "I.K. CO." In 1967 Imperial introduced a Diamond Edge stainless steel stamping it "Diamond Edge." Although currently made knives have plastic handles, the older knives were handled in bone and celluloid. Imperial is known to have made many contract knives.

INTERNATIONAL CUTLERY COMPANY
FREEMONT, OHIO

According to a news release in American Cutler magazine in 1922, the company was incorporated by LC Anna, A. W. Harold and Carl M. Haaser in 1922.

KA-BAR CUTLERY COMPANY, INC.
OLEAN, NEW YORK

Wallace Brown started his knife business in Tidioute, Pennsylvania with a company called Union Razor Company, which operated in Tidioute for 14 years, specializing in straight razors but also making pocketknives and other lines of cutlery.

Olean, New York, a nearby town, offered several enticements to Union Razor Company, if they would bring their industry to the small town. For the next two years the company moved, and by 1912 were in full operation at the Olean facility. The knives made at this time were stamped Union Cutlery Company, Olean New York (the Razor Company trademark had been dropped on Jan. 15, 1909).

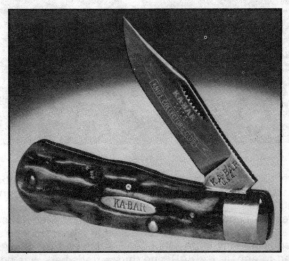

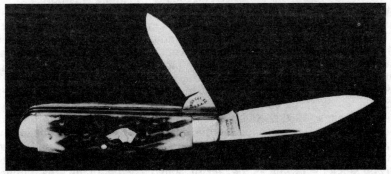

The two knives pictured above are sold exclusively to members of the Kabar Knife Collectors Club.

☐ *Current Collector Value (each)* . . . . **40.00 — 60.00**

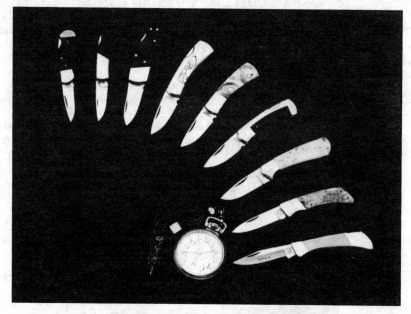

A Japanese import "Khyber" distributed by Kabar.

They were soon making an extensive line of pocketknives bearing such stamping as O/cut, Keenwell, and a trademark that was popular on their large folding hunter patterns, the KA-BAR.

This trademark came from a testimonial letter, the legend says, written by an old trapper whose life had been saved in a bear fight by a well-made Union Cutlery Company knife. His poor English had the Kill A-Bear statement shorted to appear KA-BAR, and thus a trademark was born.

Union Cutlery also added to many of their folding hunters a Dogshead shaped shield (dealt with later in this book in a complete chapter).

The Kabar name soon became more popular than the Union Cutlerytrademark, and in 1951 the board of directors changed the corporate name to the KA-BAR Cutlery Company, Inc. The tang stamping was changed from KA-BAR to Kabar.

Wallace Brown died in 1956, but by this time the company had been in the capable hands of his son Danforth Brown for a number of years.

In the early 1950's Kabar tried to move the production of their pocketknives to Dawsonville, Georgia, hoping to cash in on the cheap labor supply in the North Georgia mountains. The Kabar people did not reckon with the area residents taking off completely for much of the planting and harvest seasons as well as the lack of skilled workers in the area. Within a year the company was moving back to Olean.

After Danforth Brown's death the company changed hands several times, and for a brief while in the 1960's, stopped knife production. Then in 1966 Cole National Corporation purchased the company and started national distribution again, moving into many large discount stores.

By 1977, Kabar had ceased all knife production by their own employees. Instead many of their knives are made across town from the original Kabar factory at the Alcas knife factory. Many of the old Kabar employees are still there working on the Kabar knives. The old factory is still used for storage and shipping purposes.

Kabar has also recently taken on the importation of a line of Japanese cutlery under the Khyber trademark.

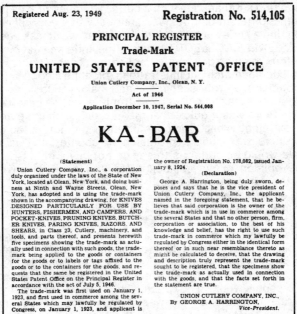

Registered Aug. 23, 1949

Registration No. 514,105

PRINCIPAL REGISTER
Trade-Mark

UNITED STATES PATENT OFFICE

Union Cutlery Company, Inc., Olean, N. Y.

Act of 1946

Application December 10, 1947, Serial No. 544,008

KA-BAR

(Statement)

Union Cutlery Company, Inc., a corporation duly organized under the laws of the State of New York, located at Olean, New York, and doing business at Ninth and Wayne Streets, Olean, New York, has adopted and is using the trade-mark shown in the accompanying drawing, for KNIVES DESIGNED PARTICULARLY FOR USE BY HUNTERS, FISHERMEN, AND CAMPERS, AND POCKET-KNIVES, PRUNING KNIVES, BUTCHER KNIVES, PARING KNIVES, RAZORS, AND SHEARS, in Class 23, Cutlery, machinery, and tools, and parts thereof, and presents herewith five specimens showing the trade-mark as actually used in connection with such goods, the trade-mark being applied to the goods or containers for the goods or to labels or tags affixed to the goods or to the containers for the goods, and requests that the same be registered in the United States Patent Office on the Principal Register in accordance with the act of July 5, 1946.

The trade-mark was first used on January 1, 1923, and first used in commerce among the several States which may lawfully be regulated by Congress, on January 1, 1923, and applicant is the owner of Registration No. 178,082, issued January 8, 1924.

(Declaration)

George A. Harrington, being duly sworn, deposes and says that he is the vice president of Union Cutlery Company, Inc., the applicant named in the foregoing statement, that he believes that said corporation is the owner of the trade-mark which is in use in commerce among the several States and that no other person, firm, corporation or association, to the best of his knowledge and belief, has the right to use such trade-mark in commerce which my lawfully be regulated by Congress either in the identical form thereof or in such near resemblance thereto as might be calculated to deceive, that the drawing and description truly represent the trade-mark sought to be registered, that the specimens show the trade-mark as actually used in connection with the goods, and that the facts set forth in the statement are true.

UNION CUTLERY COMPANY, INC.,
By GEORGE A. HARRINGTON,
Vice-President.

HOW TO USE THE KABAR SECTION

We are not listing the small variations, such as the different shields, or a price difference between a saber ground blade or a flat ground one. The variations are there, but we have not seen enough of them to start listing them. At this time the different variations will not make a great difference in price.

In this price guide we have also not listed Union Razor Tideoute, Pennsylvania or the Union shield stamping. These are so seldom encountered that we did not feel it necessary. As a general guide, however, if the knife is priced with a Union Cutlery Company stamping and you run across a Union Razor in the same pattern, the knife should be worth double the price of the Union Cutlery stamping. The same goes for the Union Shield. If a Union Cutlery stamping is listed at $50, the same knife with a Union Razor or Union Shield stamp would bring $100.

Many of the patterns will be handled in both bone stag and rough black composition. The rough blacks should bring half the price of the same knive in bone. For instance, a bone handled trapper priced at $60 would be worth $30 with the same stamping but with rough black composition handles.

Please note that Ka-Bar Olean New York and Ka-Bar USA are two different stampings. We are not listing them separate because we have insufficient dating on the two. However, the KA-BAR Olean New York with all capital letters will bring 50% more than a Ka-Bar USA stamping.

Unlike many other companies, Kabar on several occasions duplicated their pattern numbers on different style knifes. Therefore, it is not entirely impossible to find a Kabar knife with a pattern number already listed in this book but with a different picture. We cannot say that you will not find this, but if you do find a knife such as I have described, we do ask one thing. LET A KNOWLEDGEABLE COLLECTOR look at the knife and get his opinion on the knife before you plop down your hard earned cash. A knife with pattern numbers that do not match our illustrations might be a good knife, but even if it is, it should arouse your suspicions and make you look more carefully.

Soon after Kabar started giving away trophies for the best Kabar collections in 1975, there was a quick upsurge in Kabar collecting and in Kabar prices. As you might expect, the counterfeiters did not let the opportunity go by, and there was soon a profusion of counterfeit Dogsheads and Grizzleys. We would go so far as to say do not buy a mint Grizzley unless you get the opinion of several collectors and a return privilege. (Mint Dogsheads the same way, especially the switchblade model.) This is the same frame as an Aerial, and a large number of Aerials were discovered a few years back, so many fakers restamped the blades and rehandled the knives.

As for the prices, they are for 100% mint knives. If they have been sharpened or near mint deduct 15% of the mint price. In excellent condition, the price you pay should be 25% of the mint price. Below excellent, you should use your own judgement, for when a knife gets in worse shape excellent the people who will buy such a knife are a minority. If you plan on building a Kabar collection as an investment, we suggest you try to collect only excellent or better. If you trade for the knives the condition will probably not matter that much, as long as you get them at a decent price.

As a collector you should expect to pay full book price. Sometimes in quantity buying you might be able to buy the knives at 10% the book price. Dealers who plan on reselling the knives should give no more than 25% off of book price. A note to you collectors: Please don't think that any dealer in Kabar knives can make a living on 15% profit. Offering someone less than 25% off of book price is bordering on an insult. Dealers have to make money, so don't begrudge them if they try to make an honest profit.

PATTERN NUMBERS

The pattern numbers on the Kabar line can tell you much about the knives once you become familiar with them.

The FIRST NUMBER in the pattern number is the Handle Material. Following are the handle material keys.

1-Ebony

2-Natural Stag

3-Redwood

4-White Imitation Ivory

5-Black Celluloid

6-Bone Stag

7-Mother of Pearl
8-Unknown
9-Silver Pyraline Handle
0-Pyraline (candy striped)
  and fancy celluloid
P-Imitation Pearl Handle

H-Horn
C-Unknown
T-Fancy Pearl Handles (early use)
  Cream celluloid in later years.
R-Rainbow celluloid

The second digit in the pattern number told the number of blades, and they make up to a seven blade knife. The four blades are not common, but any seven blade is a rare Kabar.

The remaining digits made up the factory pattern number. Let us stress here that the knives in this guide are arranged by the factory pattern number. A 6234 is not followed by a 62134, because the pattern number on the first one is "34" and the pattern number on the second one is "134". Also, a 531 would mean the knife has a factory pattern number of "1". What this means is take off the first two numbers no matter what. What is left is your factory pattern number.

The knives are in order of Dogsheads first, followed by one blades, two blades, three blades, four blades, six blades, and seven blades.

There is one major drawback, and if you have had any experience with Kabars you already know what it is. Unlike many of the other manufacturers of the time, few Kabars had the pattern numbers stamped on them, therefore to use this guide effectively it is important that you study the styles of knives more than the pattern numbers.

TANG STAMPINGS

Kabar has reported that they have over 200 different tang stampings over the years, but through our research so far we have uncovered the following.

U-R Co. Tidioute PA
Union Razor Co. Tidioute, Pa
Union Cutlery Co. Tidioute Pa
Union Cut. Co. Tidioute
Union inside a North American
shield
(The Union Cut. Co.) stamping
was
adopted in 1909.
Union Cut. Co. Olean N. Y.
Union Cut. Co.

KA-BAR
KA-BAR, Olean N. Y.
Ka-Bar Stainless
Ka-Bar Olean N. Y.
Kabar Stainless
Kabar (pattern no.) USA (current
stamping
Olcut
Keenwell
VikingU-C Co. Olean, N. Y. USA
John Jay Made in USA

RARE KABAR KNIVES

While any Kabars of the older stampings are rare, as well as the Dogsheads, there are several things you should be on the lookout for.

First, Kabar made very few four blade knives. Most of the people who bought a four blade knife did so because they needed it to use. If they did not plan to use all four blades they would have settled for a three or two blade. Its heavy construction did not lend itself to vest pocket wear, so most of the four blades you find will be in well-used condition. The author of this section has collected Kabars for five years, and in that time he has only been able to buy a very few of these knives. Anyone having any of these to sell, or photos of them to lend for next year's edition of this book is urged to contact James F. Parker, 615-894-1782.

Other rare Kabars are any Kabar USA stamped knife with bone handles. Rarer still is the Kabar stamping, since by this time almost all the knives were made with plastic handles.

For price difference, the Kabars with every blade stamped will bring 10 to 15% more than a knife with just the master blade stamped.

Most of the Kabars will be found with brass liners, nickel silver bolsters, although a few early knives were made with iron liners.

We have not seen any Kabars made with nickel silver liners.

Sheath knives are not listed in this book, and you should not expect these knives to bring the prices of pocketknives. They will not. The stampings were changed at the same times as the pocketknife stampings.

EVERY DOGSHEAD...has its day.

(Copyright 1977, by the National Knife Collector Magazine)

by James F. Parker

Kabar, being in business since 1898, has made many varied types of knives throughout the last 80 years. Probably their most famous knife or knives ever made have been the Ka-Bar Dogsheads. As most of you knowledgeable collectors know, Ka-Bar was founded in 1898 by Mr. Wallace Brown as the Union Razor Company of Tidioute, Pennsylvania. In 1909, according to company records, the name was changed to Union Cutlery Company, and in 1912 the company moved to Olean, New York. The company was changed to Ka-Bar about 1950, but Union Cutlery Company has used the Ka-Bar logo since 1920. The hyphen was dropped from the Ka-Bar logo approximately 1950 to 1951.

Going back to the statement of the Kabar Dogsheads being the most collectible of the Kabar or Union Cutlery Company knives, the question is raised: "What makes them so collectible?" First, from the author's viewings and from the knives in my collection, I find that there are probably 55 or 60 different Kabar Dogshead knives. At the present time I have 53 different Kabar Dogshead knives in my collection. This is counting the different stamping variations, the different styles, etc. These range all the way from a 4½ inch switchblade to the beautiful 5¼ inch Folding Hunters. Evidently Kabar made Dogshead knives all the way from inception of using the North America Shaped Shield. This North America Shaped Shield with Union inside was started when they changed their name to Union Cutlery Company. (See the accompanying photo.) This marking has been viewed on both the knife and fork combination and also the Folding Hunter or Fiddle Back knife. Records do not indicate that this North American Shield was made in Tidioute, Pennsylvania, but was started when they adopted the North American Shield as a trademark. Probably after that Union Shield, they started using either the circular Union Cutlery Company markings, which are shown at the right, or the Union Cutlery Company, Olean, New York USA in the straight line markings, also shown at the right. The author feels sure that these markings were used up until 1925, when they adopted the Ka-Bar logo. All total there are six different tang stampings on the Dogshead knives: The Union Shield, Union Cutlery Co. Olean, New York USA, Circle marking, Union Cutlery Company Olean, New York USA straight line markings, Ka-Bar Olean, New York in small letters and Ka-Bar in large capital letters, USA underneath, also Ka-Bar with the patent date underneath, Union Cutlery Co. Olean, New York on the second blade or on rear tang. None of the knife patterns have been found with all six different markings, but several have been found with three different markings on the same pattern. For instance, the 1920 style Fiddle Back Hunter is located with the Union in a shield, the large Ka-Bar USA, and also straight Union Cutlery Co. All these markings appear on the front of the tang. Of course the Ka-Bar USA Union Cutlery Company Olean, New York appears on the back of the tang also. From the many different tang stampings, you can readily see for just the one reason, why Kabar Dogsheads or Union Cutlery Company Dogheads, as you may have it, are so collectible. The second thing that makes them so collectible the many varieties of patterns the Dogshead Shield was used on. From extensive research and viewing other knife collections, as well as my own, I find that the following patterns have the Ka-Bar Dogsheads emblem on them:

5¼" single blade Fiddle Back Folding Hunter.
This same style in the lockback pattern with the thumb release.
5¼" single blade Folding Hunter with the extended bolster, available in bone stag handles.
Same as the 65 pattern in Case, is available in genuine stag handle.
Drilled bolster as 65 pattern in Case.
Single blade Folding Hunter, 5¼" lockback with the extended bolster, same as the two blade #65 pattern in Case, is available in bone stag handles.
Same as #8 in genuine stag handles.
Genuine stag handles drilled frame.
5¼" single blade Fiddle Back Folding Hunter pattern in cracked ice handles.
4½" two blade Trapper style, available with bone stag handles.
4½" single blade Switchblade, with the release in the bolster, this is available in bone stag handles.
5¼" two blade knife-fork combination.
5¼" three blade knife, fork, spoon combination.
The 5¼" single blade Lockback, shown in accompanying photo, with the finger guard.
5" knife hatchet combination.

If one would observe the different picks or cuts of the bone, it is readily seen that the very deep worm groove type pick was used on the early Union in the Shield Dogsheads and the Union Cutlery Co. Olean, New York USA Dogsheads. The finer pick bone seems to have been used on the Ka-Bar Dogsheads with the master blade marked Ka-Bar in large capitals, Union Cutlery Co. either on the rear of the tang or the second blade. This pick closely resembles the pick used by Remington, W.R. Case and Winchester. It is a much finer cut than the early Ka-Bar Dogsheads. (Different handles on the Dogsheads for comparison.)

In studying the Dogsheads it is noted in every instance that the Dogshead knives with Ka-Bar USA on the master blade and either Union Cutlery Co. Olean, New York on the rear tang or on the secondary blade have Ka-Bar in small letters on the Ka-Bar Shield. In the Ka-Bar Dogshead knives where the master blade is stamped Union Cutlery Co. Olean, New York or Union in the Shield on the tang, the Dogshead is smooth without this Ka-Bar in small letters on it.

There are probably more varieties of Dogsheads than the ones listed, but did not want to list knives that had only heard of or knives that thought were not 100% authentic. These knives that I have listed are either in his collection or in collections where I have ready access to them. If anyone has other Dogsheads not listed here that are completely authentic I would be very much interested in buying or trading for these Dogsheads, or to have the information on them to add to files.

Another interesting feature of Dogsheads is that there are other companies that use the Dogshead emblem. You will note the Photo #16-A&B at the right showing the Western States and the Union Cutlery Company together. These two knives are identical down to the match striker pull, the swedge of the blade, the cut of the bone, the locking mechanism, etc. Possibly Union Cutlery made this knife on a contract basis for Western States or possibly it was a copy. The Napanoch Catalogue shows a Dogshead in their catalogue. I have never observed one of these and I don't know of anyone who has one, but if one is out there it will probably turn up some day. I would sure be interested in it. Also, you will observe, in the accompanying photo #17, the Stilletto Dogshead. Note that the Dogshead on this knife points the other way from the Ka-Bar knives. Also note that this knife is identical to the two blade, the match striker emblem, handles, etc. Possibly this knife was made by Ka-Bar, but they show no records of ever making any knives for Stilletto Cutlery Company. But remember back in the 1910's, '20's and early '30's, many knife companies made parts and sold them to other companies for assembly, so this could explain the blades. Possibly Stilletto or some other company bought blades from Ka-Bar and then assembled the knives and stamped their tang stamp for them. The last Ka-Bar Dogshead made by Ka-Bar is the two blade Trapper, shown at right photo #18, for the 1976 Bi-Centennial. They combine their most famous markings and their most famous trademarks to make this knife up to celebrate the Nation's 200th birthday. These are beautiful knives and have proved to be very popular with the collectors.

The only two knives found by the author with the small Ka-Bar Olean, New York stamping with no stamping on the second blade, have been the two blade Folding Hunter patterns #22107 and #62107. These are available with the bone stag handles and genuine stag handles. Both these knives are in mint condition and have not been sharpened I have not located any other Ka-Bar Dogsheads with this tang stamping.

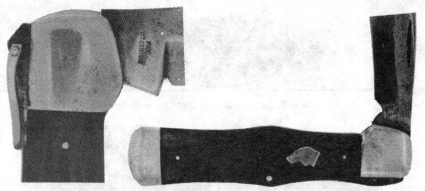

A 61106 LG model with Union in shield and marked "Patented Oct. 23, 1916 on rear of tang.

An extremely rare Dogshead showing the Patent 70342 and date Aug. 31, 1926 on the tang. This is the only knife that bears this tang stamping.

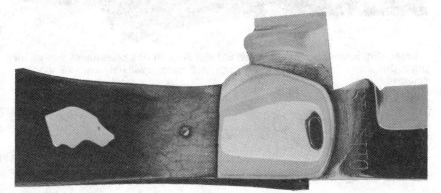

Stilletto Dogshead
Identical to Ka-Bar knives in every respect. Probably a contract knife.

Early Dogshead with straight-up emblem.

Kabar, Olean, New York — Small letter markings, only two knives found to this date, Pattern Nos. 22107 and 62107.

Union Cut. circle marking on Model 61126L. *Note:* It has been found that on all Union Cut. marked master blades, the dogshead emblem will not have Ka-Bar on the emblem.

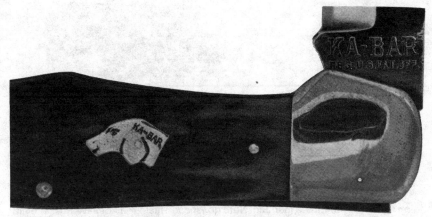

STANDARD KABAR MARKING. Not that Ka-Bar marking will also appear in the dogshead emblem on all knives with this marking.

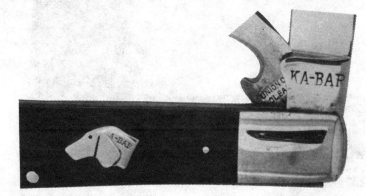

STANDARD KABAR mark with Union Cut. straightline on second blade.

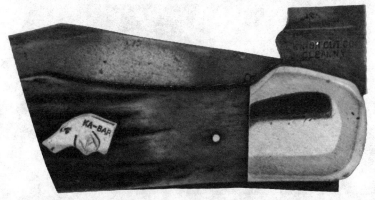

Union Cut. Co. straightline marking, this will also appear on the master blade of some of the earlier models made before 1925.

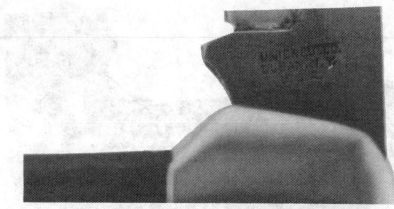

Union Cut. Co. straightline marking. Note dogshead shield will not have Ka-Bar on it.

Early Union Dogshead marking.

KA-BAR USA Union Cut. Co. on second blade or on rear of tang in single blade knives.

(LENGTH 5⅜" CLOSED)

PATTERN	STAMPING	HANDLE	
☐61106 LG	Union in North American Shield	Bone Stag	
☐61106 LG	Union Cut Co. Circle Marking	Bone Stag	
☐61106 LG	Union Cut Co. Straightline Mark	Bone Stag	725.00
☐61106 LG	KA-BAR Union Cut on Rear Tang or on Second Blade	Bone Stag	

(LENGTH 5⅜" CLOSED)
(Same as above but without lock)

PATTERN	STAMPING	HANDLE	MINT PRICE
☐61106	Union in North American Shield	Bone Stag	850.00
☐61106	Union Cut Co. Circle Marking	Bone Stag	700.00
☐61106	Union Cut Co. Straightline Mark	Bone Stag	700.00
☐21106	KA-BAR Union Cut on Rear Tang or on Second Blade	Genuine Stag	800.00
☐61106	KA-BAR Union Cut on Rear Tang or on Second Blade	Bone Stag	650.00
☐P1106	KA-BAR Union Cut on Rear Tang or on Second Blade	Pearl Celluloid	465.00

(LENGTH 5¼″ CLOSED)

PATTERN	STAMPING	HANDLE	MINT PRICE
☐21107	Union Cut Co. Straightline Mark	Genuine Stag	600.00
☐21107	KA-BAR Union Cut on Rear Tang or on Second Blade	Genuine Stag	500.00
☐21107	Current Model Dated	Genuine Stag	80.00

(LENGTH 5¼″ CLOSED)

PATTERN	STAMPING	HANDLE	MINT PRICE
☐22107	Union Cut Co. Straightline Mark	Genuine Stag	550.00
☐22107	KA-BAR Union Cut on Rear Tang or on Second Blade	Genuine Stag	500.00
☐22107	KA-BAR OLEAN, N.Y. in small letters	Genuine Stag	450.00
☐22107	Current Model Dated	Genuine Stag	80.00

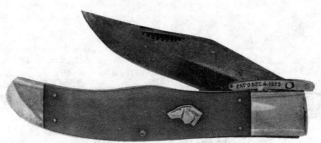

(LENGTH 5¼ " CLOSED)

PATTERN	STAMPING	HANDLE	MINT PRICE
☐61107 LG	KA-BAR Union Cut on Rear Tang or on Second Blade	Bone Stag	850.00
☐21107 LG	KA-BAR Union Cut on Rear Tang or on Second Blade	Genuine Stag	900.00
☐T1107 LG	KA-BAR Union Cut on Rear Tang or on Second Blade	Cream Celluloid	650.00

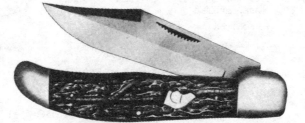

(LENGTH 5¼ " CLOSED)

PATTERN	STAMPING	HANDLE	MINT PRICE
☐61107	Union in North American Shield	Bone Stag	800.00
☐61107	Union Cut Co. Straightline Mark	Bone Stag	575.00
☐61107	KA-BAR Union Cut on Rear Tang or on Second Blade	Bone Stag	475.00

Note: *Very early model shown with upside down Dogshead*

(LENGTH 5¼″ CLOSED)

PATTERN	STAMPING	HANDLE	MINT PRICE
☐62107	Union Cut Co. Straightline Mark	Bone Stag	550.00
☐62107	KA-BAR Union Cut on Rear Tang or on Second Blade	Bone Stag	475.00
☐62107	KA-BAR OLEAN, N.Y. in small letters	Bone Stag	425.00

(LENGTH 4⅝″ CLOSED)

PATTERN	STAMPING	HANDLE	MINT PRICE
☐61110	Union in North American Shield	Bone Stag	650.00

(LENGTH 4″ CLOSED)

PATTERN	STAMPING	HANDLE	MINT PRICE
☐02118	Bicentennial Model	Red, White & Blue Overlay Celluloid	75.00

(LENGTH 4⅝" CLOSED)

PATTERN	STAMPING	HANDLE	MINT PRICE
☐61126 L	Union Cut Co. Circle Marking	Bone Stag	1000.00

(LENGTH 5¼" CLOSED)

PATTERN	STAMPING	HANDLE	MINT PRICE
☐22156	Union in North American Shield	Genuine Stag	800.00
☐22156	UNION CUT CO. Straightline Mark	Genuine Stag	600.00

(LENGTH 5¼" CLOSED)

PATTERN	STAMPING	HANDLE	MINT PRICE
☐62156	Union in North American Shield	Bone Stag	700.00
☐62156	UNION CUT CO. Straightline Mark	Bone Stag	550.00

KA-BAR ONE-BLADE SECTION

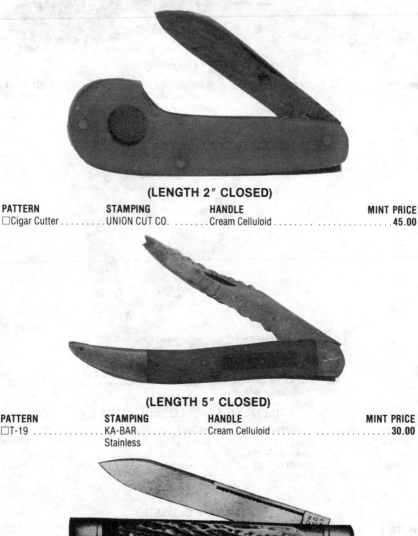

(LENGTH 2″ CLOSED)

PATTERN	STAMPING	HANDLE	MINT PRICE
☐Cigar Cutter	UNION CUT CO.	Cream Celluloid	45.00

(LENGTH 5″ CLOSED)

PATTERN	STAMPING	HANDLE	MINT PRICE
☐T-19	KA-BAR Stainless	Cream Celluloid	30.00

(LENGTH 3⅞″ CLOSED)

PATTERN	STAMPING	HANDLE	MINT PRICE
☐6111	UNION CUT CO.	Bone Stag	100.00
☐0111	UNION CUT CO.	Pyraline	75.00

(LENGTH 4" CLOSED)

PATTERN	STAMPING	HANDLE	MINT PRICE
☐6112	UNION CUT CO.	Bone Stag	70.00
☐0112	UNION CUT CO.	Pyraline	60.00
☐6112	KA-BAR	Bone Stag	60.00
☐0112	KA-BAR	Pyraline	55.00
☐6112	kabar	Rough Black	35.00
☐T112	kabar	Cream Celluloid	30.00

(LENGTH 3" CLOSED)

PATTERN	STAMPING	HANDLE	MINT PRICE
☐T118	KA-BAR	Cream Celluloid	30.00

(LENGTH 3½" CLOSED)

PATTERN	STAMPING	HANDLE	MINT PRICE
☐3163	UNION CUT CO.	Redwood	35.00
☐6163	UNION CUT CO.	Bone Stag	55.00

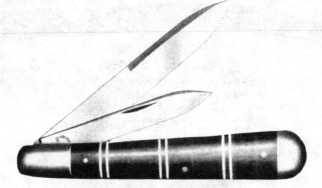

(LENGTH 4½ " CLOSED)

PATTERN	STAMPING	HANDLE	MINT PRICE
☐6165	UNION CUT CO.	Bone Stag	90.00
☐0165	UNION CUT CO.	Fancy Celluloid	80.00

(LENGTH 4⅜" CLOSED)

PATTERN	STAMPING	HANDLE	MINT PRICE
☐6165 LG	UNION CUT CO.	Bone Stag	175.00
☐6165 LG	KA-BAR	Bone Stag	140.00
☐2165 LG	kabar	Genuine Stag	85.00
☐6165 LG	kabar	Rough Black Composition	50.00
☐6165 LG	kabar	Imitation Bone Delrin	10.00
	computer number USA		

(LENGTH 4" CLOSED)

PATTERN	STAMPING	HANDLE	MINT PRICE
☐3170	UNION CUT CO.	Redwood	90.00

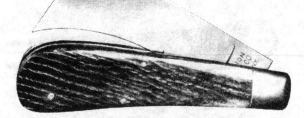

(LENGTH 3¾″ CLOSED)

PATTERN	STAMPING	HANDLE	MINT PRICE
☐3174	UNION CUT CO.	Redwood	**30.00**
☐6174	UNION CUT CO.	Bone Stag	**45.00**
☐3174	KA-BAR	Redwood	**25.00**
☐6174	KA-BAR	Bone Stag	**40.00**

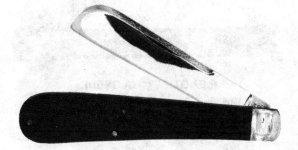

(LENGTH 4½″ CLOSED)

PATTERN	STAMPING	HANDLE	MINT PRICE
☐6175 RG	UNION CUT CO.	Bone Stag	**50.00**

(LENGTH 5½″ CLOSED)

PATTERN	STAMPING	HANDLE	MINT PRICE
☐2179-L Grizzley	KA-BAR	Genuine Stag	**1500.00**
☐T179	KA-BAR	Cream Celluloid	**400.00**
☐9179	KA-BAR	Silver Pyraline	**600.00**

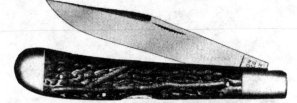

(LENGTH 5½″ CLOSED)

PATTERN	STAMPING	HANDLE	MINT PRICE
☐6191 L	UNION CUT CO.	Bone Stag	600.00
☐6191 L	UNION CUT CO.	Genuine Stag	750.00

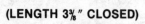

(LENGTH 3⅜″ CLOSED)

PATTERN	STAMPING	HANDLE	MINT PRICE
☐61103	UNION CUT CO.	Bone Stag	70.00
☐01103	UNION CUT CO.	Fancy Celluloid	55.00
☐71103	UNION CUT CO.	Pearl	85.00
☐61103	KA-BAR	Bone Stag	70.00
☐01103	KA-BAR	Fancy Celluloid	50.00

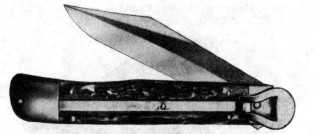

(LENGTH 4½″ CLOSED)

PATTERN	STAMPING	HANDLE	MINT PRICE
☐21105	UNION CUT CO.	Genuine Stag	500.00
☐21105	KA-BAR	Genuine Stag	400.00
☐61105	KA-BAR	Bone Stag	400.00
☐T1105	KA-BAR	Cream Celluloid	350.00

(LENGTH 5⅜″ CLOSED)

PATTERN	STAMPING	HANDLE	MINT PRICE
☐61106	UNION CUT CO.	Bone Stag	**300.00**
☐61106	KA-BAR	Bone Stag	**250.00**
☐T1106	KA-BAR	Cream Celluloid	**175.00**

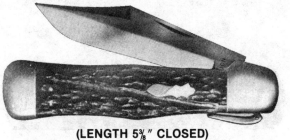

(LENGTH 5⅜″ CLOSED)

PATTERN	STAMPING	HANDLE	MINT PRICE
☐61106 L	UNION CUT CO.	Bone Stag	**450.00**

(LENGTH 5¼ ″ CLOSED)

PATTERN	STAMPING	HANDLE	MINT PRICE
☐21107 LG Little Grizzly KA-BAR		Genuine Stag	**1500.00**

(LENGTH 5¼ ″ CLOSED)

PATTERN	STAMPING	HANDLE	MINT PRICE
☐61107	UNION CUT CO.	Bone Stag	300.00
☐61107	KA-BAR	Bone Stag	250.00
☐61107	KA-BAR	Rough Black	125.00
☐P-1107	KA-BAR	Imitation Pearl	150.00
☐61107	kabar	Rough Black	75.00

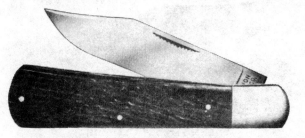

(LENGTH 5¼ ″ CLOSED)

PATTERN	STAMPING	HANDLE	MINT PRICE
☐31108	kabar	Redwood	30.00
☐31108	kabar	Redwood	15.00
	computer number USA		

(LENGTH 4½ ″ CLOSED)

PATTERN	STAMPING	HANDLE	MINT PRICE
☐61110	UNION CUT CO.	Bone Stag	95.00

(LENGTH 4¼ ″ CLOSED)

PATTERN	STAMPING	HANDLE	MINT PRICE
☐61118	UNION CUT CO.	Bone Stag	200.00
☐01118	UNION CUT CO.	Fancy Celluloid	140.00

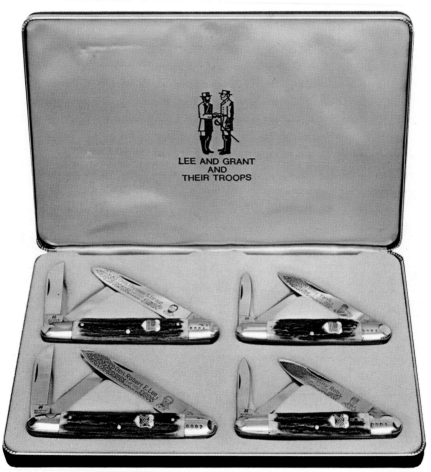

NORTH SOUTH WHITTLER SET, *by Parker-Frost, set of 4* **$250.00**

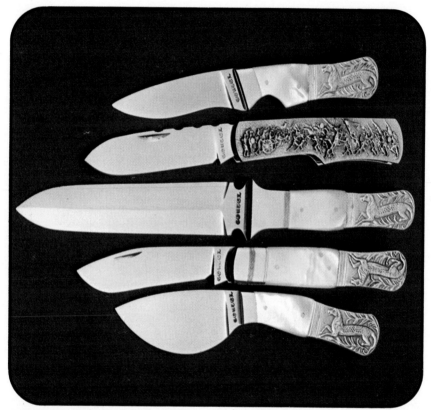

COUTEL KNIVES *(top to bottom)*

Skinner **$100.00**
Civil War Scene Folder **210.00**
Boot Knife **125.00**
Folding Horse / Alligator Folder **225.00**
Moon Skinner **100.00**

COUTEL KNIVES *(top to bottom)*

Coutel Whittler, one of six made **$300.00**
Display Knife, first display knife made **900.00**
Bicentennial Knife, red, white and blue handle **150.00**

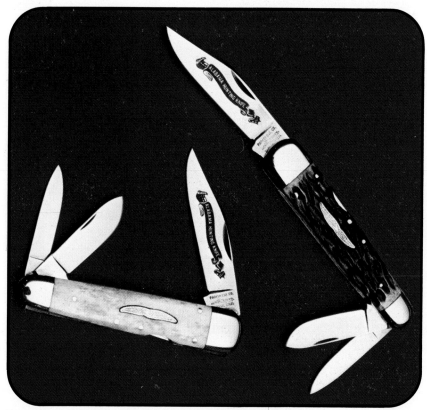

PARKER CUTLERY LOCKBACK WHITTLER, *12 different blade etchings, soon to become a rare collectors' item* . . . . . **$45.00 each**

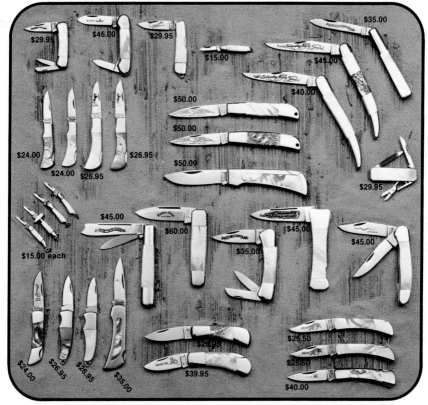

$29.95 $45.00 $29.95 $35.00

$15.00 $45.00

$40.00

$50.00

$50.00

$24.00 $50.00

$24.00 $26.95 $26.95 $29.95

$15.00 each $45.00 $60.00 $45.00 $45.00

$35.00

$24.00 $26.95 $26.95 $35.00 $29.95 $25.50 $25.60 $39.95 $40.00

1980 MOTHER OF PEARL HANDLE KNIVES PARKER CUTLERY

EAGLE BRAND KNIVES *manufactured by Parker Cutlery.*

PARKER – FROST KNIVES, *manufactured by Schrade Cutlery for Parker -Frost in 1978. This series was the first bone handled knives made by Schrade in the last 25 years. They have been discountinued and are prized by collectors.*

13 COLONY BICENTENNIAL SERIES, *manufactured by Schrade Cutlery for Parker-Frost, set of 14* .... **$400.00 - 700.00**

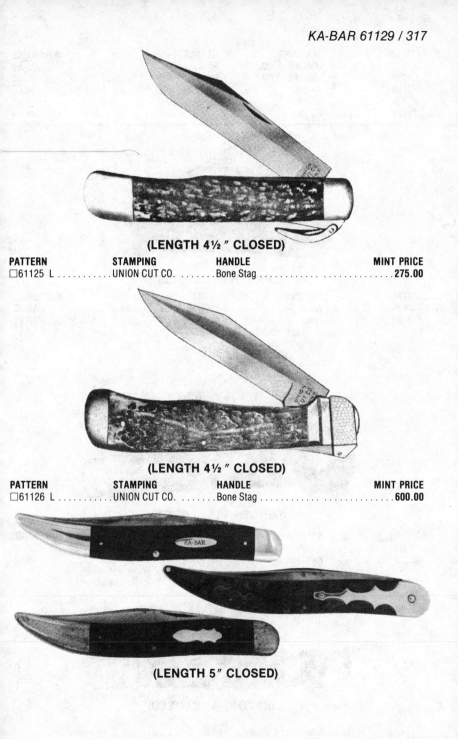

(LENGTH 4½ " CLOSED)

PATTERN	STAMPING	HANDLE	MINT PRICE
☐61125 L	UNION CUT CO.	Bone Stag	275.00

(LENGTH 4½ " CLOSED)

PATTERN	STAMPING	HANDLE	MINT PRICE
☐61126 L	UNION CUT CO.	Bone Stag	600.00

(LENGTH 5″ CLOSED)

PATTERN	STAMPING	HANDLE	MINT PRICE
☐61129	UNION CUT CO.	Bone Stag	125.00
☐G1129	UNION CUT CO.	Pyraline	90.00
☐61129	KA-BAR	Bone Stag	90.00
☐K1129	KA-BAR	Fancy Celluloid	90.00
☐T1129	KA-BAR	Cream Celluloid	75.00

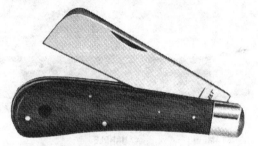

(LENGTH 4″ CLOSED)

PATTERN	STAMPING	HANDLE	MINT PRICE
☐31130	kabar	Redwood	15.00
☐31130	kabar	Redwood	10.00
	computer number USA		

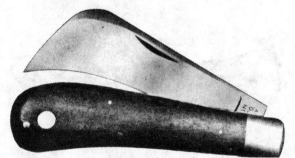

(LENGTH 4⅝″ CLOSED)

PATTERN	STAMPING	HANDLE	MINT PRICE
☐31131	UNION CUT CO.	Redwood	50.00
☐31131	KA-BAR	Redwood	40.00

(LENGTH 5½ ″ CLOSED)

PATTERN	STAMPING	HANDLE	MINT PRICE
☐61132	UNION CUT CO.	Bone Stag	**250.00**
☐11132	UNION CUT CO.	Ebony	**150.00**
☐91132	UNION CUT CO.	Silver Pyraline	**200.00**
☐61132	KA-BAR	Bone Stag	**200.00**

(LENGTH 4½ " CLOSED)

PATTERN	STAMPING	HANDLE	MINT PRICE
☐P-1147	KA-BAR	Imitation Pearl	**50.00**
☐T-1147	KA-BAR	Cream Celluloid	**50.00**

(LENGTH 4¾ " CLOSED)

PATTERN	STAMPING	HANDLE	MINT PRICE
☐P 1154	UNION CUT CO.	Fancy Celluloid	**175.00**
☐P-1154	KA-BAR	Fancy Celluloid	**140.00**

(LENGTH 1½ " CLOSED)

PATTERN	STAMPING	HANDLE	MINT PRICE
☐71155	UNION CUT CO.	Genuine Pearl	**75.00**

(LENGTH 5¾" CLOSED)

PATTERN	STAMPING	HANDLE	MINT PRICE
☐X 1157	UNION CUT CO.	Metal	125.00
☐X 1157	KA-BAR	Metal	100.00

(LENGTH 4¼" CLOSED)

PATTERN	STAMPING	HANDLE	MINT PRICE
☐R-1160	UNION CUT CO.	Fancy Celluloid	50.00

(LENGTH 4½" CLOSED)

PATTERN	STAMPING	HANDLE	MINT PRICE
☐61161	UNION CUT CO.	Bone Stag	200.00
☐61161-BAIL	KA-BAR	Bone Stag	175.00
☐T-1161	KA-BAR	Cream Celluloid	225.00

(LENGTH 4½ " CLOSED)

PATTERN	STAMPING	HANDLE	MINT PRICE
☐61169	KA-BAR	Bone Stag	150.00

(LENGTH 4½ " CLOSED)

PATTERN	STAMPING	HANDLE	MINT PRICE
☐T-1175	KA-BAR	Cream Celluloid	45.00

(LENGTH 5¼ " CLOSED)

PATTERN	STAMPING	HANDLE	MINT PRICE
☐21187	KA-BAR	Genuine Stag	350.00
☐61187	KA-BAR	Bone Stag	290.00
☐31187	KA-BAR	Red Wood	175.00

(LENGTH 5¼ " CLOSED)

PATTERN	STAMPING	HANDLE	MINT PRICE
☐61187	UNION CUT CO.	Smooth Bone	125.00
☐61187	KA-BAR	Smooth Bone	100.00
☐51187	kabar	Slick Black Composition	40.00
☐51187	kabar	Black Celluloid	10.00
	computer number USA		

NO PHOTO AVAILABLE

See 52198 in 2 Blade Section. Same Knife Only Single Blade.

(LENGTH 4″ CLOSED)

PATTERN	STAMPING	HANDLE	MINT PRICE
☐51198	kabar	Black Celluloid	20.00
☐51198	kabar	Black Celluloid	10.00
	computer number USA		

KA-BAR TWO-BLADE SECTION

(LENGTH 3½ ″ CLOSED)

PATTERN	STAMPING	HANDLE	MINT PRICE
☐42027 S	UNION CUT CO.	Imitation Ivory	80.00
☐42027 S(3 inch)	UNION CUT CO.	Imitation Ivory	70.00

(LENGTH 5″ CLOSED)

PATTERN	STAMPING	HANDLE	MINT PRICE
☐5-29	KA-BAR	Black Celluloid	35.00
☐T-29	KA-BAR	Cream Celluloid	25.00
☐R-29	KA-BAR	Red Celluloid	25.00
☐T-29	kabar	Cream Celluloid	12.00
☐R-29	kabar	Red Celluloid	12.00
☐T-29	kabar	Cream Celluloid	8.00
	computer number USA		

(LENGTH 2½ " CLOSED)

PATTERN	STAMPING	HANDLE	MINT PRICE
☐6200	UNION CUT CO.	Bone Stag	45.00
☐T 200	UNION CUT CO.	Cream Celluloid	25.00
☐T 200 RG	UNION CUT CO.	Cream Celluloid	25.00
☐T 200 RG	UNION CUT CO.	Genuine Pearl	50.00
☐R 200 RG	KA-BAR	Rainbow Celluloid	30.00
☐6200	KA-BAR	Bone Stag	50.00

(LENGTH 2⅞ " CLOSED)

PATTERN	STAMPING	HANDLE	MINT PRICE
☐6201 T	UNION CUT CO.	Bone Stag	45.00
☐7201 T	UNION CUT CO.	Genuine Pearl	70.00
☐6201	KA-BAR	Bone Stag	40.00

(LENGTH 3″ CLOSED)

PATTERN	STAMPING	HANDLE	MINT PRICE
☐6202	UNION CUT CO.	Bone Stag	45.00
☐7202	UNION CUT CO.	Genuine Pearl	45.00
☐6202	KA-BAR	Bone Stag	40.00
☐7202	KA-BAR	Genuine Pearl	70.00

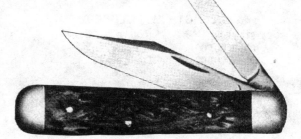

(LENGTH 3″ CLOSED)

PATTERN	STAMPING	HANDLE	MINT PRICE
☐6203½	UNION CUT CO.	Bone Stag	40.00
☐0203½	UNION CUT CO.	Fancy Pyraline	45.00
☐7203½	UNION CUT CO.	Genuine Pearl	70.00

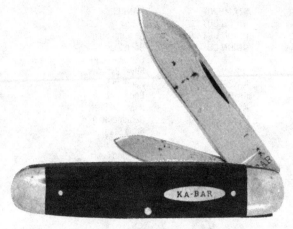

(LENGTH 3″ CLOSED)

PATTERN	STAMPING	HANDLE	MINT PRICE
☐6204	UNION CUT CO.	Bone Stag	50.00
☐7204	UNION CUT CO.	Genuine Pearl	70.00
☐6204	KA-BAR	Bone Stag	45.00
☐6204	KA-BAR	Rough Black	25.00

(LENGTH 3⅛″ CLOSED)

PATTERN	STAMPING	HANDLE	MINT PRICE
☐6205	UNION CUT CO.	Bone Stag	50.00
☐6205	KA-BAR	Bone Stag	40.00

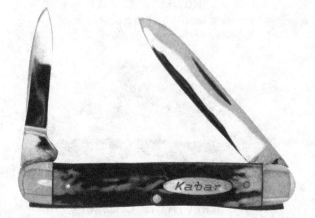

(LENGTH 3¼″ CLOSED)

PATTERN	STAMPING	HANDLE	MINT PRICE
☐1206	UNION CUT CO.	Ebony	30.00
☐2206	UNION CUT CO.	Genuine Stag	45.00
☐6206	UNION CUT CO.	Bone Stag	40.00
☐7206	UNION CUT CO.	Genuine Pearl	65.00
☐9206	UNION CUT CO.	Silver Pyraline	35.00
☐2206	KA-BAR	Genuine Stag	40.00
☐6206	KA-BAR	Bone Stag	40.00
☐P206	KA-BAR	Imitation Pearl	35.00
☐2206	kabar	Genuine Stag	30.00
☐6206	kabar	Bone Stag	25.00
☐P206	kabar	Pearl Celluloid	20.00
☐7206	kabar	Genuine Pearl	40.00
☐6206	kabar	Delrin	5.00

computer number USA

(LENGTH 3¾″ CLOSED)

PATTERN	STAMPING	HANDLE	MINT PRICE
☐6209¼	UNION CUT CO.	Bone Stag	125.00

(LENGTH 3½″ CLOSED)

PATTERN	STAMPING	HANDLE	MINT PRICE
☐6210	UNION CUT CO.	Bone Stag	120.00
☐6210	KA-BAR	Bone Stag	95.00

(LENGTH 4⅛" CLOSED)

PATTERN	STAMPING	HANDLE	MINT PRICE
☐6212 J	UNION CUT CO.	Bone Stag	75.00
☐0212 J	UNION CUT CO.	Pyraline	55.00
☐6212 J	KA-BAR	Bone Stag	65.00
☐6212 J	kabar	Bone Stag	50.00
☐5212 J	kabar	Black Celluloid	25.00

(LENGTH 3⅞" CLOSED)

PATTERN	STAMPING	HANDLE	MINT PRICE
☐6213 J	UNION CUT CO.	Bone Stag	135.00
☐2213 J	KA-BAR	Genuine Stag	145.00
☐6213 J	KA-BAR	Bone Stag	120.00

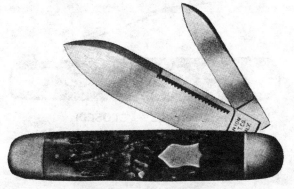

(LENGTH 3⅝" CLOSED)

PATTERN	STAMPING	HANDLE	MINT PRICE
☐ 1215	UNION CUT CO.	Ebony	**80.00**
☐ 6215	UNION CUT CO.	Bone Stag	**140.00**
☐ 6215 PU	UNION CUT CO.	Bone Stag	**130.00**
☐ 6215	KA-BAR	Bone Stag	**110.00**
☐ 6215½	KA-BAR	Bone Stag	**110.00**
☐ 6215 & 15½	kabar	Bone Stag	**80.00**
☐ 6215 & 15½	kabar	Rough Black	**40.00**
☐ 6215	kabar	Delrin	**10.00**

computer number USA

(LENGTH 3¼″ CLOSED)

PATTERN	STAMPING	HANDLE	MINT PRICE
☐ 1218	UNION CUT CO.	Ebony	**50.00**
☐ 2218	UNION CUT CO.	Genuine Stag	**90.00**
☐ 6218	UNION CUT CO.	Bone Stag	**75.00**
☐ 7218	UNION CUT CO.	Pearl	**120.00**
☐ 1218	KA-BAR	Ebony	**40.00**
☐ 6218	KA-BAR	Bone Stag	**75.00**

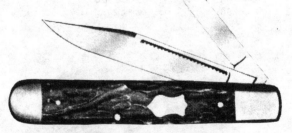

(LENGTH 3¼″ CLOSED)

PATTERN	STAMPING	HANDLE	MINT PRICE
☐ 6219½	UNION CUT CO.	Bone Stag	**65.00**

(LENGTH 3½ " CLOSED)

PATTERN	STAMPING	HANDLE	MINT PRICE
☐6220 J	UNION CUT CO.	Bone Stag	95.00
☐2220 J	KA-BAR	Genuine Stag	100.00
☐6220 J	KA-BAR	Bone Stag	85.00
☐7220 J	KA-BAR	Genuine Pearl	135.00

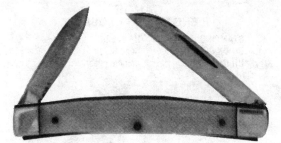

(LENGTH 3¼ " CLOSED)

PATTERN	STAMPING	HANDLE	MINT PRICE
☐6221	UNION CUT CO.	Bone Stag	65.00
☐6221	KA-BAR	Bone Stag	50.00
☐6221	kabar	Rough Black	25.00
☐T 221	kabar	Cream Composition	20.00

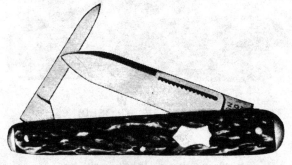

(LENGTH 3⅜ " CLOSED)

PATTERN	STAMPING	HANDLE	MINT PRICE
☐1222 T	UNION CUT CO.	Ebony	**40.00**
☐6222 T	UNION CUT CO.	Bone Stag	**65.00**
☐7222 T	UNION CUT CO.	Genuine Pearl	**90.00**
☐9222 T	UNION CUT CO.	Silver Pyraline	**60.00**

CANOE
(LENGTH 3¼" CLOSED)

PATTERN	STAMPING	HANDLE	MINT PRICE
☐6223 EX	UNION CUT CO.	Bone Stag	**175.00**
☐P223 EX	UNION CUT CO.	Imitation Pearl	**140.00**

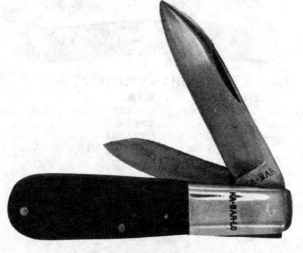

BARLOW
(LENGTH 3¼" CLOSED)

PATTERN	STAMPING	HANDLE	MINT PRICE
☐5223	KA-BAR	Black Composition	**60.00**
☐6223	KA-BAR	Smooth Bone	**90.00**
☐6223½	KA-BAR	Smooth Bone	**90.00**

☐ 5223 SH	kabar	Black Composition	**40.00**
☐ 5223	kabar	Black Composition	**30.00**
☐ 5223½	kabar	Black Composition	**30.00**
☐ 6223	kabar	Delrin	**10.00**
	computer number USA		
☐ 6223½	kabar	Delrin	**10.00**
	computer number USA		

(LENGTH 2¾″ CLOSED)

PATTERN	STAMPING	HANDLE	MINT PRICE
☐ 6224	UNION CUT CO.	Bone Stag	**55.00**
☐ 6224	KA-BAR	Bone Stag	**45.00**

(LENGTH 3¾″ CLOSED)

PATTERN	STAMPING	HANDLE	MINT PRICE
☐ P 225	UNION CUT CO.	Imitation Pearl	**70.00**
☐ 6225½	KA-BAR	Bone Stag	**125.00**
☐ 6225	KA-BAR	Bone Stag	**125.00**

(LENGTH 3″ CLOSED).

PATTERN	STAMPING	HANDLE	MINT PRICE
☐5226 Emb	UNION CUT CO.	Black Pyraline	**35.00**
☐7226 Emb	UNION CUT CO.	Genuine Pearl	**65.00**
☐6226	KA-BAR	Bone Stag	**50.00**
☐7226	KA-BAR	Genuine Pearl	**60.00**

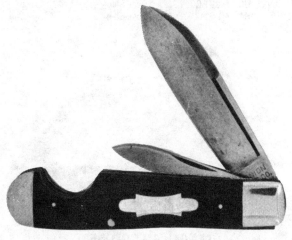

(LENGTH 3⅝″ CLOSED)

PATTERN	STAMPING	HANDLE	MINT PRICE
☐1228 EO	UNION CUT CO.	Ebony	**90.00**
☐2228 EO	UNION CUT CO.	Genuine Stag	**150.00**
☐6228 EO	UNION CUT CO.	Bone Stag	**110.00**
☐6228 EO	UNION CUT CO.	Bone Stag	**130.00**
☐9228 EO	UNION CUT CO.	Silver Pyraline	**115.00**

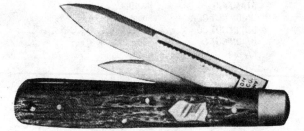

(LENGTH 3¼ ″ CLOSED)

PATTERN	STAMPING	HANDLE	MINT PRICE
☐6229	UNION CUT CO.	Bone Stag	55.00
☐6229½	UNION CUT CO.	Bone Stag	55.00
☐6229	KA-BAR	Bone Stag	50.00
☐6229½	kabar	Rough Black	25.00
☐6229½	kabar	Delrin	8.00
	computer number USA		

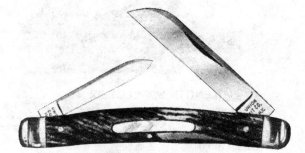

(LENGTH 3¼ ″ CLOSED)

PATTERN	STAMPING	HANDLE	MINT PRICE
☐6230	UNION CUT CO.	Bone Stag	60.00
☐7230	UNION CUT CO.	Genuine Pearl	100.00

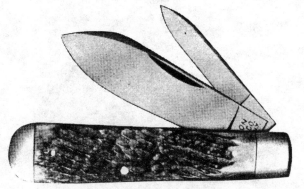

(LENGTH 3⅜ ″ CLOSED)

PATTERN	STAMPING	HANDLE	MINT PRICE
☐1232	UNION CUT CO.	Ebony	50.00
☐6232 & 32½	UNION CUT CO.	Bone Stag	90.00
☐9232	UNION CUT CO.	Silver Pyraline	70.00
☐1232	KA-BAR	Ebony	35.00
☐6232 & 32½	KA-BAR		75.00
☐6232 & 32½	kabar	Rough Black	30.00
☐6232½	kabar	Delrin	8.00
	computer number USA		

(LENGTH 3⅝" CLOSED)

PATTERN	STAMPING	HANDLE	MINT PRICE
☐1233	UNION CUT CO.	Ebony	90.00
☐2233	UNION CUT CO.	Genuine Stag	130.00
☐6233	UNION CUT CO.	Bone Stag	120.00
☐9233	UNION CUT CO.	Silver Pyraline	105.00
☐2233	KA-BAR	Genuine Stag	115.00
☐6233	KA-BAR	Bone Stag	100.00

(LENGTH 3⅜" CLOSED)

PATTERN	STAMPING	HANDLE	MINT PRICE
☐6236 LL	KA-BAR	Bone Stag	**60.00**
☐6236 LL	kabar	Rough Black	**25.00**

(LENGTH 3⅛″ CLOSED)

PATTERN	STAMPING	HANDLE	MINT PRICE
☐Gunstock 6237	UNION CUT CO.	Bone Stag	**135.00**
☐Gunstock P237	UNION CUT CO.	Imitation Pearl	**110.00**
☐Gunstock 6237	KA-BAR	Bone Stag	**115.00**
☐Gunstock 2237	KA-BAR	Genuine Stag	**135.00**
☐Gunstock 7237	KA-BAR	Genuine Pearl	**160.00**
☐Gunstock P237	KA-BAR	Imitation Pearl	**100.00**

(LENGTH 3″ CLOSED)

PATTERN	STAMPING	HANDLE	MINT PRICE
☐6239	UNION CUT CO.	Bone Stag	**45.00**
☐9239	UNION CUT CO.	Fancy Celluloid	**40.00**

(LENGTH 3¼″ CLOSED)

PATTERN	STAMPING	HANDLE	MINT PRICE
☐6240 J	UNION CUT CO.	Bone Stag	120.00
☐6240 J	KA-BAR	Bone Stag	95.00

(LENGTH 2¾″ CLOSED)

PATTERN	STAMPING	HANDLE	MINT PRICE
☐6241	UNION CUT CO.	Bone Stag	40.00
☐7241	UNION CUT CO.	Genuine Pearl	50.00
☐P-241	KA-BAR	Pearl Celluloid	20.00
☐6241	KA-BAR	Bone Stag	30.00
☐7241 RG	KA-BAR	Genuine Pearl	35.00
☐P-241	kabar	Pearl Celluloid	15.00
☐2241	kabar	Genuine Stag	30.00

(LENGTH 3½ " CLOSED)

PATTERN	STAMPING	HANDLE	MINT PRICE
☐6242	UNION CUT CO.	Bone Stag	55.00

(LENGTH 3⅛ " CLOSED)

PATTERN	STAMPING	HANDLE	MINT PRICE
☐6242	KA-BAR	Bone Stag	65.00
☐T 242	KA-BAR	Cream Celluloid	50.00
☐6242	kabar	Bone Stag	50.00

(LENGTH 3⅝ " CLOSED)

PATTERN	STAMPING	HANDLE	MINT PRICE
☐6244	UNION CUT CO.	Bone Stag	150.00
☐7244	UNION CUT CO.	Genuine Pearl	175.00

(LENGTH 3½ " CLOSED)

PATTERN	STAMPING	HANDLE	MINT PRICE
☐1246	UNION CUT CO.	Ebony	80.00
☐2246	UNION CUT CO.	Genuine Stag	150.00
☐6246	UNION CUT CO.	Bone Stag	140.00
☐P246	UNION CUT CO.	Imitation Pearl	110.00
☐2246	KA-BAR.	Genuine Stag	135.00
☐6246	KA-BAR.	Bone Stag	120.00

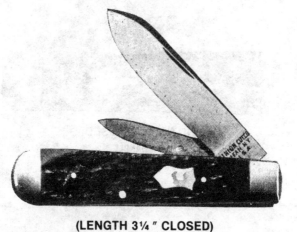

(LENGTH 3¼ " CLOSED)

PATTERN	STAMPING	HANDLE	MINT PRICE
☐6247	UNION CUT CO.	Bone Stag	65.00
		Iron Bolsters	

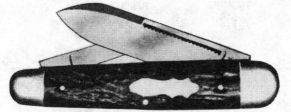

(LENGTH 3⅝" CLOSED)

PATTERN	STAMPING	HANDLE	MINT PRICE
☐6249	UNION CUT CO.	Bone Stag	**120.00**

(LENGTH 4¼" CLOSED)

PATTERN	STAMPING	HANDLE	MINT PRICE
☐6250	UNION CUT CO.	Bone Stag	**350.00**
☐R250	UNION CUT CO.	Rainbow Celluloid	**275.00**
☐6250	KA-BAR	Bone Stag	**275.00**

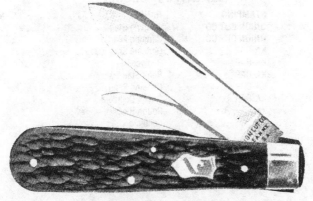

(LENGTH 4" CLOSED)

PATTERN	STAMPING	HANDLE	MINT PRICE
☐6251	KA-BAR	Bone Stag	135.00
☐6251½	KA-BAR	Bone Stag	135.00

(LENGTH 3¾" CLOSED)

PATTERN	STAMPING	HANDLE	MINT PRICE
☐1252	UNION CUT CO.	Ebony	65.00
☐2252½	UNION CUT CO.	Genuine Stag	130.00
☐6252 & 52½	UNION CUT CO.	Bone Stag	110.00
☐6252 Saber	UNION CUT CO.	Bone Stag	125.00

(LENGTH 3⅛" CLOSED)

PATTERN	STAMPING	HANDLE	MINT PRICE
☐2253	UNION CUT CO.	Genuine Stag	60.00
☐7253	UNION CUT CO.	Genuine Pearl	75.00
☐2253	KA-BAR	Genuine Stag	65.00
☐3253	KA-BAR	Redwood	35.00
☐6253	KA-BAR	Bone Stag	55.00
☐7253	KA-BAR	Genuine Pearl	75.00
☐T253	KA-BAR	Cream Celluloid	40.00
☐6253	kabar	Rough Black	25.00
☐T253	kabar	Celluloid	20.00

(LENGTH 3⅛″ CLOSED)

PATTERN	STAMPING	HANDLE	MINT PRICE
☐2255	UNION CUT CO.	Genuine Stag	85.00
☐6255	UNION CUT CO.	Bone Stag	80.00
☐7255	UNION CUT CO.	Genuine Pearl	120.00
☐9255	UNION CUT CO.	Fancy Celluloid	60.00
☐6255	KA-BAR	Bone Stag	70.00
☐7255	KA-BAR	Genuine Pearl	100.00
☐6255	kabar	Rough Black	30.00
☐T255	kabar	Cream Celluloid	25.00

(LENGTH 3¼″ CLOSED)

PATTERN	STAMPING	HANDLE	MINT PRICE
☐6256 J	UNION CUT CO.	Bone Stag	75.00
☐7256 J	UNION CUT CO.	Genuine Pearl	110.00
☐R256 J	UNION CUT CO.	Imitation Pearl	60.00
☐6256 J	KA-BAR	Bone Stag	65.00
☐2256 J	KA-BAR	Genuine Stag	75.00
☐7256 J	KA-BAR	Genuine Pearl	100.00
☐P256 J	KA-BAR	Imitation Pearl	50.00
☐6256 J	kabar	Bone Stag	45.00
☐2256 J	kabar	Genuine Stag	50.00
☐T256 J	kabar	Cream Celluloid	25.00
☐6256	kabar	Delrin	9.00

computer number USA

(LENGTH 3⅝" CLOSED)

PATTERN	STAMPING	HANDLE	MINT PRICE
☐6257 mu	KA-BAR	Bone Stag	120.00
☐6257 mu	kabar	Imitation Bone	60.00
		Rough Black	
☐2257 mu	kabar	Genuine Stag	85.00

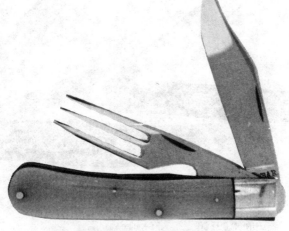

No. 493

(LENGTH 3⅞" CLOSED)

PATTERN	STAMPING	HANDLE	MINT PRICE
☐2260 K&F	UNION CUT CO.	Genuine Stag	145.00
☐6260 K&F	UNION CUT CO.	Bone Stag	130.00
☐6260 K&F	KA-BAR	Bone Stag	100.00
☐T260 K&F	KA-BAR	Cream Celluloid	80.00

(LENGTH 4″ CLOSED)

PATTERN	STAMPING	HANDLE	MINT PRICE
☐6261	UNION CUT CO.	Bone Stag	150.00
☐6261	KA-BAR	Bone Stag	120.00
☐6261	KA-BAR	Rough Blace	60.00
☐6261	kabar	Rough Black	40.00

(LENGTH 3⅜″ CLOSED)

PATTERN	STAMPING	HANDLE	MINT PRICE
☐6263	UNION CUT CO.	Bone Stag	60.00
☐6263 PU	UNION CUT CO.	Bone Stag	60.00
☐6263	KA-BAR	Bone Stag	50.00
☐6263	kabar	Rough Black	20.00
☐6263	kabar	Delrin	7.00
	computer number USA		

(LENGTH 4½″ CLOSED)

PATTERN	STAMPING	HANDLE	MINT PRICE
☐6265	UNION CUT CO.	Bone Stag	200.00
☐0265	UNION CUT CO.	Fancy Celluloid	160.00
☐6265 & 65½	KA-BAR	Bone Stag	170.00

(LENGTH 4⅜″ CLOSED)

PATTERN	STAMPING	HANDLE	MINT PRICE
☐2266 J	UNION CUT CO.	Genuine Stag	275.00
☐6266 J	UNION CUT CO.	Bone Stag	250.00
☐2266 J	KA-BAR	Genuine Stag	240.00
☐6266 J	KA-BAR	Bone Stag	210.00

(LENGTH 4″ CLOSED)

PATTERN	STAMPING	HANDLE	MINT PRICE
☐6267	UNION CUT CO.	Bone Stag	250.00
☐6267	KA-BAR	Bone Stag	210.00

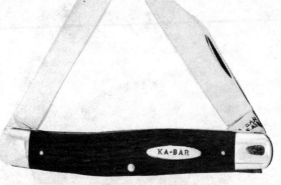

(LENGTH 4″ CLOSED)

PATTERN	STAMPING	HANDLE	MINT PRICE
☐P269 J	UNION CUT CO.	Imitation Pearl	80.00
☐2269 J	UNION CUT CO.	Genuine Stag	140.00
☐6269 J	UNION CUT CO.	Bone Stag	120.00
☐P269 J	KA-BAR	Imitation Pearl	60.00
☐2269 J	KA-BAR	Genuine Stag	110.00
☐6269 J	KA-BAR	Bone Stag	95.00
☐5269 J	KA-BAR	Black Celluloid	35.00

(LENGTH 4½″ CLOSED)

PATTERN	STAMPING	HANDLE	MINT PRICE
☐6270	UNION CUT CO.	Bone Stag	150.00
☐2270½	KA-BAR	Genuine Stag	130.00
☐6270½	KA-BAR	Bone Stag	110.00
☐2270½	kabar	Second Cut Stag	85.00
☐2270½	kabar	Genuine Stag	70.00
☐6270½	kabar	Delrin	30.00

(LENGTH 4¼″ CLOSED)

PATTERN	STAMPING	HANDLE	MINT PRICE
☐6271 J	UNION CUT CO.	Bone Stag	110.00
☐2271 J	UNION CUT CO.	Genuine Stag	135.00
☐6271 (Blade each end)	UNION CUT CO.	Bone Stag	130.00
☐6271 J	KA-BAR	Bone Stag	95.00
☐2271 J	KA-BAR	Genuine Stag	115.00

(LENGTH 3⅝″ CLOSED)

PATTERN	STAMPING	HANDLE	MINT PRICE
☐3273	UNION CUT CO.	Redwood	30.00
☐3273	KA-BAR	Redwood	35.00
☐TL-29 Model	KA-BAR	Redwood	35.00
☐5273	kabar	Black Celluloid	8.00
	computer number USA		

(LENGTH 4¼″ CLOSED)

PATTERN	STAMPING	HANDLE	MINT PRICE
☐T275	KA-BAR	Cream Celluloid	20.00
☐T275	kabar	Cream Celluloid	15.00

(LENGTH 2⅝″ CLOSED)

PATTERN	STAMPING	HANDLE	MINT PRICE
☐7285 and 86	UNION CUT CO.	Genuine Pearl	75.00
☐7285 Emblem	UNION CUT CO.	Genuine Pearl	95.00

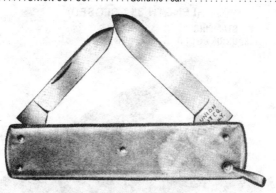

(LENGTH 2½″ CLOSED)

PATTERN	STAMPING	HANDLE	MINT PRICE
☐7286 RG	UNION CUT CO.	Genuine Pearl	75.00

NO PHOTO AVAILABLE

Same size as 6488 picture with 4 blades.

(LENGTH 4¼ " CLOSED)

PATTERN	STAMPING	HANDLE	MINT PRICE
☐6288	UNION CUT CO.	Bone Stag	175.00
☐6288	KA-BAR	Bone Stag	150.00

(LENGTH 2¼ " CLOSED)

PATTERN	STAMPING	HANDLE	MINT PRICE
☐7289 R	KA-BAR	Genuine Pearl	120.00

(LENGTH 3⅛" CLOSED)

PATTERN	STAMPING	HANDLE	MINT PRICE
☐6290	UNION CUT CO.	Bone Stag	70.00

(LENGTH 5¼ " CLOSED)

PATTERN	STAMPING	HANDLE	MINT PRICE
☐2291 K&F	UNION CUT CO.	Genuine Stag	350.00
☐6291 K&F	UNION CUT CO.	Bone Stag	300.00
☐7291 K&F	UNION CUT CO.	Genuine Pearl	450.00
☐0291 K&F	UNION CUT CO.	Fancy Celluloid	250.00
☐6291 K&F	KA-BAR	Bone Stag	225.00

(LENGTH 3½ " CLOSED)

PATTERN	STAMPING	HANDLE	MINT PRICE
☐6295 EX	UNION CUT CO.	Bone Stag	140.00
☐9295 EX	UNION CUT CO.	Silver Pyraline	105.00
☐6295 EX	KA-BAR	Bone Stag	110.00
☐9295 EX	KA-BAR	Silver Pyraline	80.00

(LENGTH 3¼ " CLOSED)

PATTERN	STAMPING	HANDLE	MINT PRICE
☐6296	UNION CUT CO.	Bone Stag	90.00
☐7296	UNION CUT CO.	Genuine Pearl	130.00
☐2296	KA-BAR	Genuine Stag	120.00
☐6296	KA-BAR	Bone Stag	90.00

(LENGTH 3″ CLOSED)

PATTERN	STAMPING	HANDLE	MINT PRICE
☐T-298	UNION CUT CO.	Fancy Pearl	**125.00**
☐7298	UNION CUT CO.	Genuine Pearl	**90.00**
☐6298	UNION CUT CO.	Bone Stag	**60.00**
☐6298	KA-BAR	Bone Stag	**45.00**

(LENGTH 2⅞″ CLOSED)

PATTERN	STAMPING	HANDLE	MINT PRICE
☐6299	UNION CUT CO.	Bone Stag	**80.00**
☐7299	UNION CUT CO.	Genuine Pearl	**110.00**

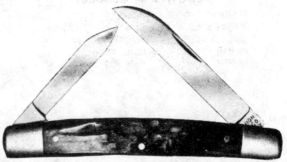

(LENGTH 3⁹⁄₁₆″ CLOSED)

PATTERN	STAMPING	HANDLE	MINT PRICE
☐22100	UNION CUT CO.	Genuine Stag	110.00
☐62100	UNION CUT CO.	Bone Stag	90.00
☐62100	KA-BAR	Bone Stag	80.00

(LENGTH 5¼ " CLOSED)

PATTERN	STAMPING	HANDLE	MINT PRICE
☐22106-Cleaver	KA-BAR	Genuine Stag	475.00

(LENGTH 5¼ " CLOSED)

PATTERN	STAMPING	HANDLE	MINT PRICE
☐62107	UNION CUT CO.	Bone Stag	275.00
☐62107	KA-BAR	Bone Stag	225.00
☐62107	KA-BAR	Rough Black	125.00
☐P2107	KA-BAR	Imitation Pearl	125.00
☐22107	kabar	Genuine Stag	80.00
☐62107	kabar	Rough Black	45.00
☐62107	kabar	Aster Felts Model	100.00
☐22107	kabar computer number USA	Imitation Stag	15.00
☐22107	kabar computer number USA	Imitation Stag Serrated	15.00

(LENGTH 3⅛" CLOSED)

PATTERN	STAMPING	HANDLE	MINT PRICE
☐P-2109	UNION CUT CO.	Imitation Pearl	45.00
☐52109	UNION CUT CO.	Black Celluloid	45.00
☐72109	UNION CUT CO.	Genuine Pearl	95.00
☐52109	KA-BAR	Black Celluloid	35.00
☐02109	KA-BAR	Fancy Celluloid (Gold Metalic or Christmas Tree)	75.00

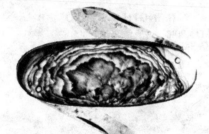

(LENGTH 2" CLOSED)

PATTERN	STAMPING	HANDLE	MINT PRICE
☐72110	UNION CUT CO.	Abalone Pearl	175.00

(LENGTH 2" CLOSED)

PATTERN	STAMPING	HANDLE	MINT PRICE
☐72111	UNION CUT CO.	Abalone Pearl	175.00

(LENGTH 4¼″ CLOSED)

PATTERN	STAMPING	HANDLE	MINT PRICE
☐62118	UNION CUT CO.	Bone Stag	250.00
☐22118	KA-BAR	Genuine Stag	225.00
☐62118	KA-BAR	Bone Stag	200.00
☐P2118	KA-BAR	Imitation Pearl	200.00
☐R2118	KA-BAR	Rainbow Celluloid	200.00
☐22118	kabar	Genuine Stag	80.00
☐62118	kabar	Bone Stag	120.00
☐62118	kabar	Rough Black	60.00
☐T2118	kabar	Cream Composition	45.00
☐62118	kabar	Delrin	12.00
	computer number USA		
☐T2118	kabar	Cream Composition	15.00
	computer number USA		
☐52118	kabar	Chattahoochee Knife	50.00
	computer number USA		

(LENGTH 2¼″ CLOSED)

PATTERN	STAMPING	HANDLE	MINT PRICE
☐72124 RG	UNION CUT CO.	Genuine Pearl	60.00

(LENGTH 3¼″ CLOSED)

PATTERN	STAMPING	HANDLE	MINT PRICE
☐P2127	UNION CUT CO.	Imitation pearl	60.00
☐R2127	UNION CUT CO.	Rainbow Celluloid	70.00
☐52127	KA-BAR	Black Celluloid	55.00
☐P-2127	KA-BAR	Imitation Pearl	55.00

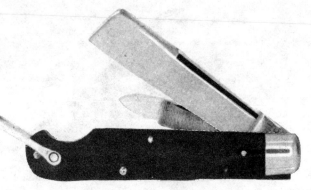

(LENGTH 3¼ " CLOSED)

PATTERN	STAMPING	HANDLE	MINT PRICE
☐62128-F	UNION CUT CO.	Bone Stag	75.00
☐62128 Boy Scout	UNION CUT CO.	Bone Stag	100.00
☐62128 Boy Scout	KA-BAR	Bone Stag	75.00

(LENGTH 5¼ " CLOSED)

PATTERN	STAMPING	HANDLE	MINT PRICE
☐62132	UNION CUT CO.	Bone Stag	225.00
☐62132	KA-BAR	Bone Stag	180.00
☐T2132	KA-BAR	Cream Celluloid	150.00

(LENGTH 2¾ " CLOSED)

PATTERN	STAMPING	HANDLE	MINT PRICE
☐62133	UNION CUT CO.	Bone Stag	**50.00**
☐72133	UNION CUT CO.	Genuine Pearl	**70.00**
☐R2133	UNION CUT CO.	Rainbow Celluloid	**40.00**
☐62133	KA-BAR	Bone Stag	**45.00**
☐72133	KA-BAR	Genuine Pearl	**65.00**
☐62133	kabar	Bone Stag	**30.00**
☐T2133	kabar	Cream Composition	**20.00**
☐P2133	kabar	Pearl Celluloid	**20.00**

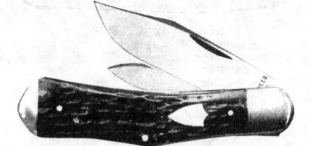

(LENGTH 3⅜″ CLOSED)

PATTERN	STAMPING	HANDLE	MINT PRICE
☐62134	UNION CUT CO.	Bone Stag	**175.00**
☐62134	KA-BAR	Bone Stag	**160.00**

(LENGTH 3⅞″ CLOSED)

PATTERN	STAMPING	HANDLE	MINT PRICE
☐62135	UNION CUT CO.	Bone Stag	**60.00**
☐B2135	UNION CUT CO.	Goldstone Celluloid	**50.00**
☐72135	KA-BAR	Genuine Pearl	**90.00**

(LENGTH 3⅛″ CLOSED)

PATTERN	STAMPING	HANDLE	MINT PRICE
☐62140	UNION CUT CO.	Bone Stag	80.00
☐72140	UNION CUT CO.	Genuine Pearl	110.00
☐H2140	UNION CUT CO.	Horn	65.00
☐62140	KA-BAR	Bone Stag	65.00

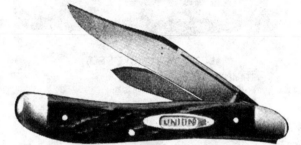

PEANUT
(LENGTH 3″ CLOSED)

PATTERN	STAMPING	HANDLE	MINT PRICE
☐62141	UNION CUT CO.	Bone Stag	80.00
☐72141	UNION CUT CO.	Genuine Pearl	110.00
☐62141	KA-BAR	Bone Stag	75.00
☐T2141	KA-BAR	Cream Celluloid	45.00
☐62141	kabar	Rough Black	30.00
☐T2141	kabar	Cream Celluloid	30.00
☐62141	kabar	Delrin	8.00
	computer number USA		

(LENGTH 3″ CLOSED)

PATTERN	STAMPING	HANDLE	MINT PRICE
☐62142	UNION CUT CO.	Bone Stag	70.00
☐72142	UNION CUT CO.	Genuine Pearl	95.00
☐62142	KA-BAR	Bone Stag	60.00
☐72142	KA-BAR	Genuine Pearl	85.00

(LENGTH 3″ CLOSED)

PATTERN	STAMPING	HANDLE	MINT PRICE
☐62143	UNION CUT CO.	Bone Stag	75.00
☐72143	UNION CUT CO.	Genuine Pearl	120.00
☐62143	KA-BAR	Bone Stag	70.00
☐72143	KA-BAR	Pearl	110.00
☐92143	KA-BAR	Silver Pyraline	80.00

(LENGTH 2⅞″ CLOSED)

PATTERN	STAMPING	HANDLE	MINT PRICE
☐22144	UNION CUT CO.	Genuine Stag	150.00
☐62144	UNION CUT CO.	Bone Stag	150.00
☐72144	UNION CUT CO.	Genuine Pearl	200.00
☐22144	KA-BAR	Genuine Stag	150.00
☐62144	KA-BAR	Bone Stag	150.00
☐72144	KA-BAR	Genuine Pearl	200.00

(LENGTH 2⅝" CLOSED)

PATTERN	STAMPING	HANDLE	MINT PRICE
☐62145	UNION CUT CO.	Bone Stag	50.00
☐72145	UNION CUT CO.	Genuine Pearl	90.00
☐62145	KA-BAR.	Bone Stag	45.00
☐72145	KA-BAR.	Genuine Pearl	80.00
☐92145	KA-BAR.	Fancy Celluloid	75.00

(LENGTH 3¼" CLOSED)

PATTERN	STAMPING	HANDLE	MINT PRICE
☐22146	UNION CUT CO.	Genuine Stag	65.00
☐62146	UNION CUT CO.	Bone Stag	55.00
☐72146 and 46 EX	UNION CUT CO.	Genuine Pearl	90.00
☐P2146 EX (No Bolster)	UNION CUT CO.	Fancy Celluloid	60.00

(LENGTH 2⅞" CLOSED)

PATTERN	STAMPING	HANDLE	MINT PRICE
☐H2147	UNION CUT CO.	Horn Celluloid	35.00
☐62147	UNION CUT CO.	Bone Stag	50.00
☐72147	UNION CUT CO.	Genuine Pearl	75.00

(LENGTH 4¾″ CLOSED)

PATTERN	STAMPING	HANDLE	MINT PRICE
☐62147	KA-BAR	Bone Stag	**75.00**
☐M2147	KA-BAR	Metal Handle	**50.00**
☐P2147	kabar	Pearl Celluloid	**30.00**
☐T2147	kabar	Cream Celluloid	**30.00**

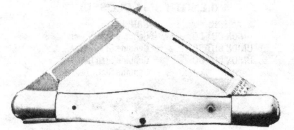

(LENGTH 3¼″ CLOSED)

PATTERN	STAMPING	HANDLE	MINT PRICE
☐62148	UNION CUT CO.	Bone Stag	**85.00**
☐72148	UNION CUT CO.	Genuine Pearl	**120.00**
☐62148	KA-BAR	Bone Stag	**70.00**
☐72148	KA-BAR	Genuine Pearl	**100.00**

(LENGTH 3″ CLOSED)

PATTERN	STAMPING	HANDLE	MINT PRICE
☐62149	UNION CUT CO.	Bone Stag	70.00
☐72149	UNION CUT CO.	Genuine Pearl	90.00
☐P2149	KA-BAR	Imitation Pearl	45.00

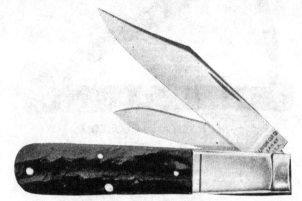

(LENGTH 3¾″ CLOSED)

PATTERN	STAMPING	HANDLE	MINT PRICE
☐22150	UNION CUT CO.	Genuine Stag Spear	140.00
☐22150 R	UNION CUT CO.	Genuine Stag Razor	160.00
☐22150½	UNION CUT CO.	Genuine Stag Clip	120.00
☐22150	KA-BAR	Genuine Stag	115.00

(LENGTH 3¼″ CLOSED)

PATTERN	STAMPING	HANDLE	MINT PRICE
☐220151	UNION CUT CO.	Genuine Stag	175.00
☐620151	UNION CUT CO.	Bone Stag	150.00

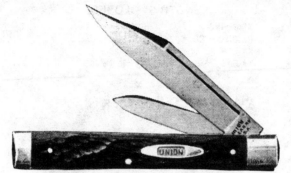

(LENGTH 3¼ " CLOSED)

PATTERN	STAMPING	HANDLE	MINT PRICE
☐22151	UNION CUT CO.	Stag	200.00
☐62151	UNION CUT CO.	Bone Stag	175.00
☐02151	UNION CUT CO.	Fancy Celluloid	150.00
☐22151	KA-BAR	Stag	175.00
☐62151	KA-BAR	Bone Stag	150.00
☐72151	KA-BAR	Genuine Pearl	200.00

(LENGTH 3½ " CLOSED)

PATTERN	STAMPING	HANDLE	MINT PRICE
☐62152	UNION CUT CO.	Bone Stag	150.00
☐62152	KA-BAR	Bone Stag	135.00

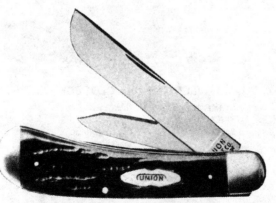

(LENGTH 3⅝" CLOSED)

PATTERN	STAMPING	HANDLE	MINT PRICE
☐62153	UNION CUT CO.	Bone Stag	160.00
☐62153	KA-BAR	Bone Stag	150.00

(LENGTH 5″ CLOSED)

PATTERN	STAMPING	HANDLE	MINT PRICE
☐62156	UNION CUT CO.	Bone Stag	175.00
☐62156	KA-BAR	Bone Stag	150.00
☐62156	KA-BAR	Boy Scout Model	190.00

(LENGTH 4″ CLOSED)

PATTERN	STAMPING	HANDLE	MINT PRICE
☐52198	KA-BAR	Black Celluloid	40.00
☐52198	kabar	Black Celluloid	25.00

(LENGTH 4½″ CLOSED)

PATTERN	STAMPING	HANDLE	MINT PRICE
☐T2217	KA-BAR	Cream Celluloid	75.00
☐T2217	kabar	Cream Celluloid	55.00
☐52217	kabar	Black Composition	30.00
☐52217	kabar	Black Composition	15.00
	computer number USA		

KA-BAR THREE-BLADE SECTION

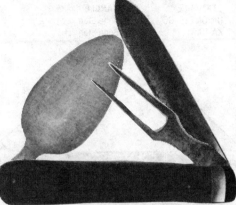

(LENGTH 5″ CLOSED)

PATTERN	STAMPING	HANDLE	MINT PRICE
☐Army Knife	UNION CUT CO.	Ebony	125.00

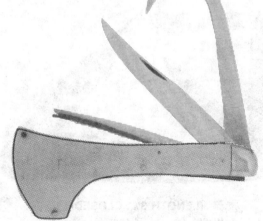

(LENGTH 5″ CLOSED)

PATTERN	STAMPING	HANDLE	MINT PRICE
☐T-33	KA-BAR	Cream Celluloid	75.00
☐T-33	kabar	Cream Celluloid	60.00

WHITTLER
(LENGTH 3¼ " CLOSED)

PATTERN	STAMPING	HANDLE	MINT PRICE
☐6306	UNION CUT CO.	Bone Stag	200.00
☐6306	KA-BAR	Bone Stag	180.00

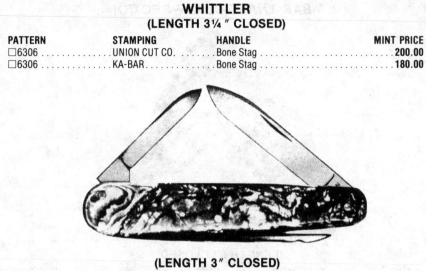

(LENGTH 3" CLOSED)

PATTERN	STAMPING	HANDLE	MINT PRICE
☐2307	UNION CUT CO.	Genuine Stag	70.00
☐7307	UNION CUT CO.	Genuine Pearl	120.00
☐T 307	UNION CUT CO.	Abalone Pearl	175.00

(LENGTH 3⅞" CLOSED)

PATTERN	STAMPING	HANDLE	MINT PRICE
☐1309½	UNION CUT CO.	Ebony	200.00
☐6309 (Wharnc Life Blade)	UNION CUT CO.	Bone Stag	300.00

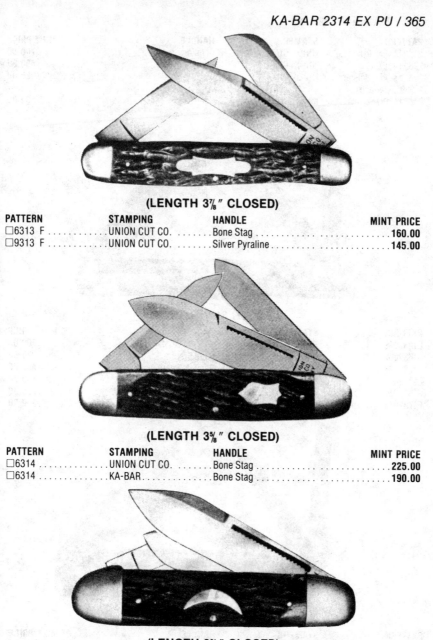

(LENGTH 3⅞" CLOSED)

PATTERN	STAMPING	HANDLE	MINT PRICE
☐6313 F	UNION CUT CO.	Bone Stag	160.00
☐9313 F	UNION CUT CO.	Silver Pyraline	145.00

(LENGTH 3⅝" CLOSED)

PATTERN	STAMPING	HANDLE	MINT PRICE
☐6314	UNION CUT CO.	Bone Stag	225.00
☐6314	KA-BAR	Bone Stag	190.00

(LENGTH 3⅝" CLOSED)

PATTERN	STAMPING	HANDLE	MINT PRICE
☐2314 EX PU	UNION CUT CO.	Genuine Stag	700.00
☐6314 EX	UNION CUT CO.	Bone Stag	600.00
☐6314 PU (Bolsters Not Extended)	UNION CUT CO.		225.00
☐6314 PU	KA-BAR	Bone Stag	200.00

(LENGTH 3½ " CLOSED)

PATTERN	STAMPING	HANDLE	MINT PRICE
☐2320½	UNION CUT CO.	Genuine Stag	300.00
☐6320½	UNION CUT CO.	Bone Stag	275.00
☐7320½	UNION CUT CO.	Genuine Pearl	400.00
☐2320½	KA-BAR	Genuine Stag	250.00
☐6320½	KA-BAR	Bone Stag	225.00
☐7320½	KA-BAR	Genuine Pearl	350.00

(LENGTH 3⅜" CLOSED)

PATTERN	STAMPING	HANDLE	MINT PRICE
☐6322 T	UNION CUT CO.	Bone Stag	275.00

(LENGTH 3½ " CLOSED)

PATTERN	STAMPING	HANDLE	MINT PRICE
☐6324 RG	KA-BAR	Bone Stag	80.00

(LENGTH 3" CLOSED)

PATTERN	STAMPING	HANDLE	MINT PRICE
☐6326	KA-BAR	Bone Stag	180.00
☐P326	kabar	Imitation Pearl	125.00

(LENGTH 3¼ " CLOSED)

PATTERN	STAMPING	HANDLE	MINT PRICE
☐6331 EX PU	UNION CUT CO.	Bone Stag	600.00
☐7331 EX PU	UNION CUT CO.	Genuine Pearl	900.00
☐6331 EX PU	KA-BAR	Bone Stag	600.00

WHITTLER
(LENGTH 3¼ " CLOSED)

PATTERN	STAMPING	HANDLE	MINT PRICE
☐6340½	UNION CUT CO.	Bone Stag	250.00
☐7340½	KA-BAR	Genuine Pearl	300.00

(LENGTH 3⅜″ CLOSED)

PATTERN	STAMPING	HANDLE	MINT PRICE
☐2345	UNION CUT CO.	Genuine Stag	110.00
☐7345	UNION CUT CO.	Genuine Pearl	140.00

(LENGTH 3⅝″ CLOSED)

PATTERN	STAMPING	HANDLE	MINT PRICE
☐6349	UNION CUT CO.	Bone Stag	375.00
☐6349½	KA-BAR	Bone Stag	325.00

(LENGTH 3⅜" CLOSED)

PATTERN	STAMPING	HANDLE	MINT PRICE
☐T3256 CC	KA-BAR	Cream Celluloid	**90.00**
☐T3256 CC	kabar	Cream Celluloid	**50.00**

(LENGTH 3¼" CLOSED)

PATTERN	STAMPING	HANDLE	MINT PRICE
☐6356	UNION CUT CO.	Bone Stag	**135.00**
☐7356	UNION CUT CO.	Genuine Pearl	**175.00**
☐6356	KA-BAR	Bone Stag	**120.00**
☐2356	kabar	Genuine Stag	**60.00**
☐6356	kabar	Bone Stag	**50.00**
☐P356	kabar	Imitation Pearl	**35.00**
☐6356	kabar	Delrin	**10.00**
	computer number USA		

(LENGTH 3⅝″ CLOSED)

PATTERN	STAMPING	HANDLE	MINT PRICE
☐T3257 CC	KA-BAR	Cream Celluloid	120.00
☐T3257 CC	kabar	Cream Celluloid	60.00

(LENGTH 3⅝″ CLOSED)

PATTERN	STAMPING	HANDLE	MINT PRICE
☐2357	UNION CUT CO.	Genuine Stag	160.00
☐6357	UNION CUT CO.	Bone Stag	150.00
☐9357	UNION CUT CO.	Fancy Celluloid	125.00
☐2357	KA-BAR	Genuine Stag	135.00
☐6357	KA-BAR	Bone Stag	120.00
☐9357	KA-BAR	Fancy Celluloid	110.00
☐2357	kabar	Genuine Stag	60.00
☐6357	kabar	Rough Black	40.00
☐P357	kabar	Imitation Pearl	40.00
☐6357	kabar	Delrin	8.00
	computer number USA		

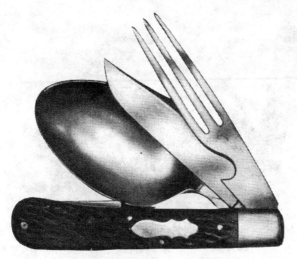

(LENGTH 3⅞" CLOSED)

PATTERN	STAMPING	HANDLE	MINT PRICE
☐6360	UNION CUT CO.	Bone Stag	**140.00**
☐9360	UNION CUT CO.	Rainbow Stag	**120.00**
☐6360	KA-BAR	Bone Stag	**120.00**

(LENGTH 4½" CLOSED)

PATTERN	STAMPING	HANDLE	MINT PRICE
☐2366 EX	UNION CUT CO.	Genuine Stag	**750.00**
☐6366 EX	UNION CUT CO.	Bone Stag	**700.00**
☐2366 EX	KA-BAR	Genuine Stag	**650.00**
☐6366 EX	KA-BAR	Bone Stag	**600.00**

(LENGTH 4″ CLOSED)

PATTERN	STAMPING	HANDLE	MINT PRICE
☐2367	UNION CUT CO.	Genuine Stag	700.00
☐6367	UNION CUT CO.	Bone Stag	600.00

No. 544

(LENGTH 3⅞″ CLOSED)

PATTERN	STAMPING	HANDLE	MINT PRICE
☐2369	UNION CUT CO.	Genuine Stag	175.00
☐6369	UNION CUT CO.	Bone Stag	160.00
☐6369 PU	UNION CUT CO.	Bone Stag	165.00
☐P367 PU	UNION CUT CO.	Imitation Pearl	130.00
☐2369	KA-BAR	Genuine Stag	150.00
☐2369	KA-BAR	Second Cut Stag	175.00
☐6369	KA-BAR	Bone Stag	135.00
☐P369	KA-BAR	Imitation Pearl	100.00
☐2369	kabar	Genuine Stag	75.00
☐6369	kabar	Bone Stag	70.00
☐6369	kabar	Rough Black	45.00
☐P369	kabar	Imitation Pearl	40.00
☐6369	kabar	Delrin	10.00

computer number USA

(LENGTH 4¼ " CLOSED)

PATTERN	STAMPING	HANDLE	MINT PRICE
☐2371	UNION CUT CO.	Genuine Stag	250.00
☐6371	UNION CUT CO.	Bone Stag	225.00
☐2371	KA-BAR	Genuine Stag	225.00
☐6371	KA-BAR	Bone Stag	200.00
☐9371	KA-BAR	Fancy Celluloid	180.00
☐T371	kabar	Cream Celluloid	45.00

(LENGTH 2¾ " CLOSED)

PATTERN	STAMPING	HANDLE	MINT PRICE
☐2381	UNION CUT CO.	Genuine Stag	95.00
☐7381	UNION CUT CO.	Genuine Pearl	125.00
☐7381	KA-BAR	Genuine Pearl	110.00
☐P381	KA-BAR	Imitation Pearl	60.00

(LENGTH 2⅝" CLOSED)

PATTERN	STAMPING	HANDLE	MINT PRICE
☐6390	KA-BAR	Bone Stag	70.00
☐P390	KA-BAR	Cream Celluloid	45.00
☐6390	kabar	Rough Black	30.00
☐P390	kabar	Cream Celluloid	30.00
☐6390	kabar	Delrin	6.00
	computer number USA		

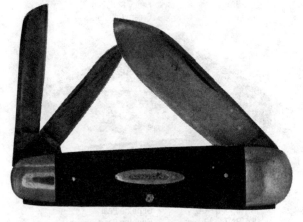

(LENGTH 3⅝" CLOSED)

PATTERN	STAMPING	HANDLE	MINT PRICE
☐6397	UNION CUT CO.	Bone Stag	400.00
☐6397	KA-BAR	Bone Stag	300.00

(LENGTH 2⅝" CLOSED)

PATTERN	STAMPING	HANDLE	MINT PRICE
☐23101	UNION CUT CO.	Genuine Stag	**55.00**
☐73101	UNION CUT CO.	Genuine Pearl	**100.00**
☐73101	KA-BAR	Genuine Pearl	**90.00**

(LENGTH 3" CLOSED)

PATTERN	STAMPING	HANDLE	MINT PRICE
☐73101	UNION CUT CO.	Abalone Pearl	**190.00**

(LENGTH 4¼" CLOSED)

PATTERN	STAMPING	HANDLE	MINT PRICE
☐63104	UNION CUT CO.	Bone Stag	**800.00**
☐73104	UNION CUT CO.	Genuine Pearl	**1200.00**
☐P3104	UNION CUT CO.	Imitation Pearl	**650.00**

(LENGTH 4¼" CLOSED)

PATTERN	STAMPING	HANDLE	MINT PRICE
☐63111	UNION CUT CO.	Bone Stag	190.00
☐P3111	UNION CUT CO.	Imitation Pearl	150.00
☐P3111 PU	UNION CUT CO.	Imitation Pearl	150.00
☐63111	KA-BAR	Bone Stag	160.00
☐P3111	KA-BAR	Imitation Pearl	120.00
☐P3111 PU	KA-BAR	Imitation Pearl	120.00

(LENGTH 4″ CLOSED)

PATTERN	STAMPING	HANDLE	MINT PRICE
☐23116	UNION CUT CO.	Genuine Stag	175.00
☐63116	UNION CUT CO.	Bone Stag	160.00
☐P3116	UNION CUT CO.	Imitation Pearl	110.00
☐23116	KA-BAR	Genuine Stag	150.00
☐63116	KA-BAR	Bone Stag	130.00
☐P3116	KA-BAR	Imitation Pearl	90.00
☐23116	kabar	Genuine Stag	65.00
☐63116	kabar	Rough Black	45.00
☐63116	kabar	Delrin	10.00

computer number USA

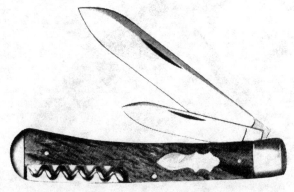

(LENGTH 4¼″ CLOSED)

PATTERN	STAMPING	HANDLE	MINT PRICE
☐63118	UNION CUT CO.	Bone Stag	300.00

(LENGTH 3½ " CLOSED)

PATTERN	STAMPING	HANDLE	MINT PRICE
☐63152	UNION CUT CO.	Bone Stag	**200.00**
☐W3152	UNION CUT CO.	Golden Celluloid	**180.00**
☐63152	KA-BAR	Bone Stag	**175.00**

(LENGTH 3¼ " CLOSED)

PATTERN	STAMPING	HANDLE	MINT PRICE
☐62163	KA-BAR	Bone Stag	**120.00**

Photo Same as No. 63198
(LENGTH 4" CLOSED)

PATTERN	STAMPING	HANDLE	MINT PRICE
☐62195 TJ	KA-BAR	Bone Stag	**90.00**
☐62195 TJ	KA-BAR	Rough Black	**45.00**
☐T2195 TJ	KA-BAR	Cream Celluloid	**40.00**
☐62195 TJ	kabar	Rough Black	**35.00**
☐T2195 TJ	kabar	Cream Celluloid	**30.00**
☐62195 TJ	kabar	Delrin	**12.00**

computer number USA

(LENGTH 4" CLOSED)

PATTERN	STAMPING	HANDLE	MINT PRICE
☐63195	KA-BAR	Bone Stag	150.00
☐23195	kabar	Genuine Stag	75.00
☐63195	kabar	Bone Stag	70.00
☐63195	kabar	Rough Black	40.00
☐63195	kabar	Delrin	10.00
	computer number USA		

KA-BAR MULTI-BLADE SECTION

PHOTO SEE NO. 6201
(LENGTH 2⅞″ CLOSED)

PATTERN	STAMPING	HANDLE	MINT PRICE
☐6401 T	UNION CUT CO.	Bone Stag	200.00
☐7401 T	UNION CUT CO.	Genuine Pearl	275.00

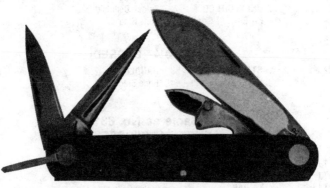

(LENGTH 4″ CLOSED)

PATTERN	STAMPING	HANDLE	MINT PRICE
☐R466 Kamp Knife	KA-BAR	Fibroid Handle	125.00

(LENGTH 5¼″ CLOSED)

PATTERN	STAMPING	HANDLE	MINT PRICE
☐T4107	KA-BAR	Cream Celluloid	**1,000.00**
☐64107	KA-BAR	Green Bone	**1,500.00**
☐24107	KA-BAR	Genuine Stag	**2,000.00**

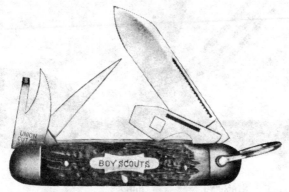

(LENGTH 3⅝″ CLOSED)

PATTERN	STAMPING	HANDLE	MINT PRICE
☐6415 RG	UNION CUT CO.	Bone Stag	**100.00**
☐6415 RG	KA-BAR	Bone Stag	**80.00**
☐P415 RG	KA-BAR	Imitation Pearl	**90.00**
☐6415 RG	kabar	Rough Black	**20.00**
☐6415 RG	kabar	Rough Black	**8.00**
	computer number USA		

(LENGTH 3¼″ CLOSED)

PATTERN	STAMPING	HANDLE	MINT PRICE
☐6421	UNION CUT CO.	Bone Stag	**250.00**
☐6421	KA-BAR	Bone Stag	**225.00**

(LENGTH 3″ CLOSED)

PATTERN	STAMPING	HANDLE	MINT PRICE
☐6426	UNION CUT CO.	Bone Stag	**140.00**
☐7426	UNION CUT CO.	Genuine Pearl	**180.00**
☐7426	KA-BAR	Genuine Pearl	**160.00**

(LENGTH 3⅛″ CLOSED)

PATTERN	STAMPING	HANDLE	MINT PRICE
☐7455	UNION CUT CO.	Genuine Pearl	**225.00**
☐7455	KA-BAR	Genuine Pearl	**225.00**

(LENGTH 3⅞″ CLOSED)

PATTERN	STAMPING	HANDLE	MINT PRICE
☐6460	UNION CUT CO.	Bone Stag	150.00
☐6460	KA-BAR	Bone Stag	135.00

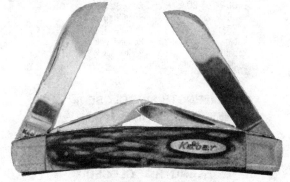

(LENGTH 4″ CLOSED)

PATTERN	STAMPING	HANDLE	MINT PRICE
☐2461 PU	UNION CUT CO.	Genuine Stag	250.00
☐6461 PU	UNION CUT CO.	Bone Stag	240.00
☐6461 PU	KA-BAR	Bone Stag	225.00
☐2461	kabar	Genuine Stag	100.00
☐6461	kabar	Rough Black	75.00

(LENGTH 4⅛″ CLOSED)

PATTERN	STAMPING	HANDLE	MINT PRICE
☐2462	UNION CUT CO.	Genuine Stag	200.00

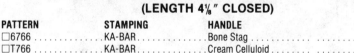

(LENGTH 4⅛″ CLOSED)

PATTERN	STAMPING	HANDLE	MINT PRICE
☐6766	KA-BAR	Bone Stag	2,500.00
☐T766	KA-BAR	Cream Celluloid	2,000.00

PHOTO SEE NO. 6369
(LENGTH 4″ CLOSED)

PATTERN	STAMPING	HANDLE	MINT PRICE
☐6469 PU	UNION CUT CO.	Bone Stag	250.00

(LENGTH 3⅛″ CLOSED)

PATTERN	STAMPING	HANDLE	MINT PRICE
□5480	UNION CUT CO.	Black Celluloid	125.00
□P480	UNION CUT CO.	Imitation Pearl	125.00
□P480	KA-BAR	Imitation Pearl	110.00

(LENGTH 3″ CLOSED)

PATTERN	STAMPING	HANDLE	MINT PRICE
□7487	UNION CUT CO.	Genuine Pearl	150.00
□T487	UNION CUT CO.	Abalone Pearl	175.00

(LENGTH 4¼″ CLOSED)

PATTERN	STAMPING	HANDLE	MINT PRICE
□2488	UNION CUT CO.	Genuine Stag	325.00
□6488	UNION CUT CO.	Bone Stag	300.00
□2488	KA-BAR	Genuine Stag	250.00
□6488	KA-BAR	Bone Stag	250.00

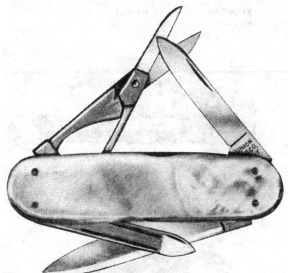

(LENGTH 3″ CLOSED)

PATTERN	STAMPING	HANDLE	MINT PRICE
☐7489	UNION CUT CO.	Genuine Pearl	200.00
☐7489	KA-BAR	Genuine Pearl	175.00

PHOTO SEE NO. 22100 (2 Blade Section)
(LENGTH 3½″ CLOSED)

PATTERN	STAMPING	HANDLE	MINT PRICE
☐24100	UNION CUT CO.	Genuine Stag	225.00
☐64100	UNION CUT CO.	Bone Stag	225.00

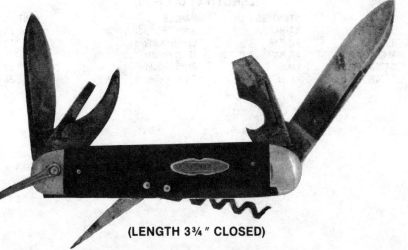

(LENGTH 3¾″ CLOSED)

PATTERN	STAMPING	HANDLE	MINT PRICE
☐66158	KA-BAR	Bone Stag	150.00

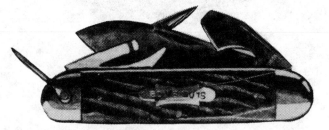

(LENGTH 3¼″ CLOSED)

PATTERN	STAMPING	HANDLE	MINT PRICE
☐24163	UNION CUT CO.	Genuine Stag	175.00
☐64163	UNION CUT CO.	Bone Stag	175.00
☐74163	UNION CUT CO.	Genuine Pearl	250.00

(LENGTH 4″ CLOSED)

PATTERN	STAMPING	HANDLE	MINT PRICE
☐64168	KA-BAR	Bone Stag	85.00

(LENGTH 4″ CLOSED)

PATTERN	STAMPING	HANDLE	MINT PRICE
☐54202	KA-BAR	Black Celluloid	90.00
☐T4202	KA-BAR	Cream Celluloid	120.00
☐M4202	KA-BAR	Metal Handles	110.00
☐54202	kabar	Black Celluloid	80.00
☐T4202	kabar	Cream Celluloid	80.00

KEEN KUTTER
ST. LOUIS, MISSOURI

The "Keen Kutter" was a brand of E. C. Simmons Hardware, and was used on tools as well as cutlery. The stamping was used beginning around 1870.

Simmons Hardware owned controlling interest in Walden Knife Company, and in 1905 at the Lewis & Clark Exposition in Portland, Oregon, an award was given Simmons for the *"Superior excellence of quality and finish of their Walden and Keen Kutter pocketknives".*

Winchester merged with Simmons Hardware and in 1923 moved the equipment of Walden Knife Company, who had been making Keen Kutter, to New Haven, Connecticut, and for the next 10 years Keen Kutter knives were made by Winchester.

Later, the Simmons Hardware and Winchester merger split, and in 1940, Shapleigh Hardware bought the assets (including the controlling interest in Walden Knife Company) of Simmons Hardware. All Simmons brands were continued by Shapleigh.

☐**K7WCCE—**(3⅛") Green celluloid handle, two blades, one large spear point and one pen, large blade full polished; nickel silver bolster, cap and shield; nickel silver lining **60.00**

☐**K7WCS—**(3⅛") Stag handle, as above . **60.00**

☐**K7WPC—**(3⅛") Pearl handle, two blades, one large spear point and one pen, full polished; nickel silver bolster, cap shield and lining **120.00**

☐**K013—**(2¼") Pearl handle, two blades, one pen and one nail file, full polished; nickel silver bolsters and lining **35.00**

☐**K013/S—**(2¼") Stag handle, two blades, one large pen and one nail file, full polished; nickel silver bolsters, shackle and lining . **50.00**

☐**K38 3/4—**(3¾") Stag handle, three blades, one large clip, one large spey point and one pen, half polished; nickel silver bolsters and shield; brass lining **175.00**

☐**K50—**(3⅜") Cocobola handle, glazed finish blades; nickel silver shield; polished steel bolster and cap; brass lining; two blades, one large spear point and one pen **45.00**

☐**K50K—**(3⅓") Red and black celluloid handle, two blades, one spear and one pen; glazed finish; steel caps and bolsters; crest shield; brass lining **65.00**

☐**K50 3/4K—**(3½") Red and black celluloid handle, two blades, one clip and one pen; glazed finish; steel caps and bolsters; crest shield; brass lining **65.00**

☐**K51 3/4—**(3⅜") Ebony handle, glazed finish blades; nickel silver shield; polished steel bolster and cap; brass lining, two blades, one large spear point and one pen **45.00**

☐**K53—**(3⅜") Stag handle, glazed finish blades; nickel silver shield; polished steel bolster and cap; brass lining; two blades, one large spear point and one pen **45.00**

☐**K53 3/4—**(3⅜") Stag handle, two blades, one large clip point and one pen; glazed finish blades; nickel silver shield; polished steel bolster and cap; brass lining **45.00**

☐**K080—**(3⅛") Pearl celluloid handle, two blades, one large spear point and one pen; large blade full polished; nickel silver tips and lining **60.00**

☐**K083T—**(3⅛") Pearl handle, two blades, one large spear point and one pen, full polished; nickel silver tips and lining **90.00**

☐**K094T—**(3¼") Pearl handle, two blades, one spear and one pen, full polished; nickel silver tips, shield and lining **70.00**

☐**K099T—**(3⅜") Pearl handle, two blades, one large spear point and one pen, full polished; nickel silver tips and lining **110.00**

☐**K0147 3/4**—MUSKRAT, (4") two large blades, full polished; nickel silver bolsters and lining. This knife is specially designed and constructed for skinning muskrats; the two long narrow, oval back blades are etched ''Muskrat'' **150.00**

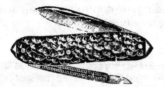

☐**K0151**—(3") Stag handle, two blades, one large spear pint and one long nail file, large blade full polished; nickel silver tips and lining **60.00**

☐**K0153**—(3") Stag handle, two blades, one large spear point and one long nail file, large blade full polished; nickel silver tips and lining **60.00**

☐**K153**—(3") Pearl handle, two blades, one large spear point and one long nail file, full polished; nickel silver tips and lining; full milled **70.00**

☐**K0195 3/4K**—(3⅜") Pearl blue celluloid handle, two blades, one large clip point and one small spey, large blade full polished; nickel silver bolsters and shield; nickel lining .. **40.00**

☐**K0195 3/4P**—(3⅜") Fancy red and black brilliant finish celluloid handle, two blades, one large clip point and one spey; large blade full polished; nickel silver bolsters, shield and lining **40.00**

☐**K0196**—(3⅜") Ebony handle, two blades, one large spear point and one pen, large blade full polished; nickel silver bolsters and shield; nickel lining **50.00**

☐**K0197 3/4K**—(3⅜") Red and black celluloid handle, two blades, one clip and one pen; large blade full polished; nickel silver bolsters and lining; crest shield **60.00**

☐**K0198**—(3⅜") Stag handle, two blades, one large spear point and one pen, large blade full polished; nickel silver bolsters and shield; nickel lining **50.00**

☐**K0198 3/4**—(3⅜") Stag handle, two blades, one large clip point and one small spey, large blade full polished; nickel silver bolsters and shield; nickel lining **40.00**

☐**K0207R**—(3") Stag handle, two blades, one large spear point and one pen, large blade full polished; nickel silver bolsters and lining. **30.00**

☐**K0109R**—(3") Pearl handle, two blades, one large spear point and one pen, full polished; nickel silver bolsters and lining **80.00**

☐**K0214**—(3") Stag handle, two blades, one large spear point and one pen, large blade full polished; nickel silver bolsters and shield; brass lining **30.00**

☐**K0214K**—(3") Red and black celluloid handle, two blades, one large spear point and one pen, large blade full polished; nickel silver bolsters and shield; brass lining **35.00**

☐**K0214TC**—(3") Pearl celluloid handle, two blades, one large spear point and one pen, largeblade full polished; nickel silver tips; brass lining **30.00**

☐**K0247**—(3⅞") Stag handle, two large blades, one spear and one clip point; spear blade full polished; nickel silver bolsters and shield; brass lining **100.00**

☐**K0256**—(3¼") Stag handle, two blades, one spear and one pen; large blade full polished; nickel silver lining and tips; crest shield .**45.00**

☐**K0258**—(3¼") Pearl handle, two blades, one large spear point and one pen, full polished; nickel silver tips, shield and lining **90.00**

☐**K264**—(3¼″) Stag handle, two blades, one large spear point and one pen, large blade full polished; nickel silver bolster, cap, shield and lining **35.00**

☐**K264 3/4**—(3¼″) Stag handle, two blades, one large clip point and one pen; large blade full polished; nickel silver bolster, cap, shield and lining **70.00**

☐**K0281T**—(3⅜″) Stag handle, two blades, one large spear piont and one pen, large blade full polished; nickel silver tips and shield; nickel lining **40.00**

☐**K309R**—(3″) Pearl handle, three blades, one large spear point, one pen and one curley nail file; full polished **80.00**

☐**K0333**—(3¼″) Stag handle, two blades, one large sheepfoot and one pen, large blade full polished; nickel silver bolsters and shield; nickel lining **80.00**

☐**K341**—(3¼″) Stag handle, three blades, one large spear point, one pen and one curley nail file; full polished; nickel silver tips, shield and lining **80.00**

☐**K343**—(3¼″) Pearl handle; nickel silver shield, tips and lining, three blades, one large spear point, one pen and one pick nail file, full polished; milled **70.00**

☐**K0348**—(3½″) Stag handle, two blades, one large clip and one pen, large blade full polished; nickel silver bolsters and shield; nickel lining **60.00**

☐**K356**—(3⅛″) Stag handle, four blades, one spear, two pens, and one pick file; blades full polished; nickel silver tips and shield; milled lining **90.00**

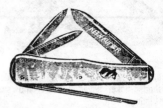

☐**K357**—(3⅛″) Pearl handle, four blades, one large spear point, two pen andone pick nail file, full polished; nickel silver tips and shield; nickel silver lining; full milled **120.00**

☐**K0388/S**—(2⅞″) Pearl handle, two blades, one large spear point and one pen, full polished; nickel silver tips, shield, shackle and lining **95.00**

☐**K443**—(3¼″) Pearl handle, four blades, one large spear point, two pens and one curley nail file, full polished; nickel silver tips, shield and lining **120.00**

☐**K0486**—(2⅞″) Stag handle, two blades, one large spear point and one pen, large blade full polished; nickel silver tips and lining **25.00**

☐**K0488**—(2⅞″) Pearl handle, two blades, one large spear point and one pen, full polished; nickel silver tips and lining **50.00**

☐**K0498**—(3″) Stag handle, two blades, one large sheepfoot point and one pen, large blade full polished; nickel silver rat tail bolsters and shield; nickel lining **50.00**

☐**K0499**—(3″) Pearl handle, two blades, one large sheepfoot point and one pen, full polished; nickel silver rat tail bolsters and lining . . . **90.00**

☐**K0529**—(2¾″) Pearl handle, two blades, one large spear point and one pen, full polished; long nickel silver bolsters; nickel silver lining **45.00**

☐**K0612R**—(3″) Pearl handle, two blades, one large spear point and one pen, full polished; long nickel silver bolsters; nickel silver lining **60.00**

☐**K0643**—(2¾″) Pearl handle, three blades, one large spear point, one pen and one pick nail file, full polished; nickel silver shield, shackle and lining; full milled **80.00**

☐**K0698**—(3½″) Stag handle, two blades, one large spear point and one pen, large blade full polished; nickel silver bolsters and shield; brass lining **80.00**

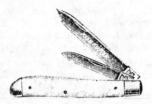

☐**K711**—(2¾″) Curved pearl handle, two blades, one large spear point and one pen, full polished; nickel silver bolster, cap and lining **90.00**

☐**K711G**—(2¾″) Gold celluloid handle, two blades, one large spear point and one pen; large blade full polished; nickel silver bolster, cap and shield; nickel silver lining **35.00**

☐**K711/SC**—(2¾″) Silver celluloid handle, two blades, one large spear point and one pen, large blade full polished; nickel silver bolster and cap; nickel silver lining **35.00**

☐**K713**—(2¾″) Stag handle, two blades, one arge spear point and one pen, large blade full polished; nickel silver bolster and cap; nickel silver lining **35.00**

☐**K713 3/4**—(2⅞″) Stag handle, two blades, one large clip and one pen; large blade full polished; nickel silver bolster cap and lining **35.00**

☐**K713 3/4A**—(3⅝″) Abalone (blue) celluloid handle, three blades, one large clip, one spey point and one patent leather punch; large clip blade full polished; nickel silver bolsters, shield and lining.................... **100.00**

☐**735 3/4A**—(3⅝″) Abalone (blue) celluloid handle, three blades, one large clip, one spey point and one patent leather punch; large lcip blade full polished; nickel silver bolsters, shield and lining **100.00**

☐**K735 3/4**—Red celluloid handle as above **100.00**

☐**K737 3/4**—(Red and white celluloid handle as above........................ **100.00**

☐**K738 3/4**—(3¾″) Stag handle, three blades, one large clip, one large spey point and one patent leather punch; large clip and large spear blade, full polished; nickel silver bolsters, shield and lining.................. **175.00**

☐**K0797**—(2⅞″) Stag handle, two blades, one large spear point and one pen, large blade full polished; nickel silver bolsters; nickel lining **30.00**

☐**K0798**—(2⅞″) Pearl handle, two blades, one large spear point and one pen, full polished; nickel silver bolsters and lining **50.00**

☐**K0799**—(2⅞″) Pearl celluloid handle, two blades, one spear and one pen; large blade full polished; nickel silver bolsters and lining . **40.00**

☐**K0814**—(3″) Nickel silver handle, two blades, one large spear point and one pen, full polished **30.00**

☐**K0815/S**—(3″) Nickel silver handle, two blades, one large spear point and one pen, both blades full polished; nickel silver shackle **30.00**

☐**K0878**—(3¾″) Stag handle, two blades, one large sheepfoot point and one pen; large blade full polished; nickel rat tail bolsters and shield; brass lining **50.00**

☐**K0883**—(3⅛″) Pearl handle, two blades, one large spear point and one curley nail file, full polished; nickel silver bolsters, shield and lining **110.00**

☐**K1704 1/4**—(3¾") Cocobola handle, one large spey blade, full polished; nickel bolster and lining **20.00**

☐**K1734 1/2**—(3½") Stag handle, one large spey blade, full polished; nickel silver bolster, cap, shield and lining **75.00**

☐**K01880A**—(3⅛") Abalone (blue) celluloid handle, two blades, one large spear point and one pen; large blade full polished; nickel silver bolsters, shield and lining **40.00**

☐**K01880R**—Iridescent celluloid handle as above **30.00**

☐**K01881**—(3½") Stag handle, two blades, one large spear point and one pen, large blade full polished; nickel silver bolsters, shield and lining **35.00**

☐**K01884**—(3⅛") Stag handle, two blades, one large spear point and one pen, large blade full polished; nickel silver bolsters, shield and lining **30.00**

☐**K02070M**—(3") Stag handle, two blades, one large spear point and one pen, large blade full polished; nickel silver bolsters and lining **30.00**

☐**K02071**—(3⅜") Stag handle, two blades, one large spear point and one pen, large blade full polished; nickel silver bolsters and shield; nickel lining **30.00**

☐**K02074**—(3⅜") Stag handle, two blades, one large spear point and one pen, large blade full polished; nickel silver bolsters, shield and lining **60.00**

☐**K02074L**—(3⅜") Varicolored brilliant finished celluloid handle, two blades, one large spear piont and one pen; large full polished; nickel silver bolsters, shield and lining **40.00**

☐**K02120**—(3⅜") White celluloid handle; etching on handle, two large blades, one spear and one eraser point; spear blade full polished; nickel silver lining; office knife **40.00**

☐**K02220**—(3⅜") White celluloid handle, etching on handle, two large blades, one spear and one eraser point; spear blade full polished; nickel silver lining **40.00**

☐**K02235N**—(3") Silvelour finish cellulloid handle, two blades, one large spear point and one pen; large blade full polished; nickel silver tips, shield and lining **80.00**

☐**K02237**—(3") Stag handle, two blades, one large spear point and one pen, large blade full polished; nickel silver tips and shield; nickel lining **45.00**

☐**K02238**—(3⅛") Pear celluloid handle, two blades, one large spear point and one pen; large blade full polished; nickel silver tips and lining **80.00**

☐**K02239**—(3") Pearl handle, two blades, one large spear point and one pen, full polished; nickel silver shield, tips and lining **95.00**

☐**K02423**—(3¾") Stag handle, two blades, one large spear point and one pen, large blade full polished; glazed blades; nickel silver bolster and shield; brass lining **50.00**

☐**K02436 3/4**—(3⅜") Black celluloid handle, two blades, one large clip and one pen; large blade full polished; nickel silver bolsters and shield; nickel lining **60.00**

☐**K02437 3/4**—(3⅜") Stag handle, two blades, one large clip and one pen; large blade full polished; nickel silver bolsters and shield; nickel lining **45.00**

☐**K02463**—(3") Pearl handle, two blades, one large spear point and one nail file, full polished; nickel silver bolsters, shield and lining . .**80.00**

☐**K02527**—(2⅝") Stag handle, two blades, one spear and one pen; large blade full polished; nickel silver bolsters and lining **30.00**

☐ **K02529**—(2¾") Pearl handle, two blades, one large spear point and one pen, full polished; long nickel silver bolsters; nickel silver lining **45.00**

☐ **K02529/S**—(2¾") Pearl handle, two blades, one large spear point and one pen, full polished; nickel silver bolsters, lining and shackle . **45.00**

☐ **K2720**—(3") Cocobolo handle, two blades, one large spear point and one pen, large blade full polished; nickel silver bolster, cap and shield; brass lining **35.00**

☐ **K2723**—(3") Stag handle, two blades, one large spear point and one pen, large blade full polished; nickel silver bolster, cap and shield; brass lining **35.00**

☐ **K02736**—(3") Smooth fibre handle, two blades, one large spear point and one pen, large blade full polished; nickel silver turned edge and lining **45.00**

☐ **K02878**—(3⅝") Stag handle, two blades, one large clip and one large spear; large spear blade full polished; nickel silver bolsters and shield; brass lining **60.00**

☐ **K02878 3/4**—(3⅝") Stag handle, two blades, one clip and one spear; clip blade full polished; nickel silver bolsters and shield; brass lining **75.00**

☐ **K3036T**—(3") Stag handle, three blades, one large spear point, one pen and one pick nail file on back, full polished; nickel silver tips, shield and lining **90.00**

☐ **K3037T**—(3") Pearl handle, nickel silver shield, tips and lining; three blades, one large spear point, one pen and one pick nail file, full polished; milled **70.00**

☐ **K3070J**—(3⅜") Green and black celluloid handle, three blades, one spear and two pens; large blade full polished; nickel silver bolsters, shield and lining **120.00**

☐ **K3070FK**—(3⅜") Red and black celluloid handle, three blades, one spear, one pen and one regular file; large bladel full polished; nickel silver bolsters, shield and lining **120.00**

☐ **K3070FL**—(3⅜") Red and green celluloid handle, three blades, one spear, one pen and one regular file; large blade full polished; nickel silver bolsters, shield and lining **100.00**

☐ **K3071F**—(3⅜") Stag handle, three blades, one spear, one pen and one regular nail file; large blade full polished; nickel silver bolsters, shield and lining **100.00**

☐ **K3071 1/4**—(3⅜") Stag handle, three blades, one large clip, one small spey and one pen, large blade full polished; nickel silver bolsters and shield; nickel lining **120.00**

☐ **K3071 1/2**—(3⅜") Stag handle, three blades, one clip, one sheepfoot and one pen; large blade full polished; nickel silver bolsters and lining; crest shield **120.00**

☐ **K3073**—(3¼") Pearl handle, three blades, one large spear point, one pen and one curley nail file, polished; nickel silver bolsters, shield and lining **150.00**

☐ **K3215 3/4G**—(3⅜") Gold celluloid handle, three blades, one large clip, one large sheepfoot and one pen; large clip blade full polished; nickel silver bolsters and shield; brass lining **120.00**

☐ **K3218 3/4**—(3⅜") Stag handle, three blades, one clip, one sheepfoot and one pen; large clip blade full polished; nickel silver bolsters and shield; brass lining **110.00**

☐ **K3278**—(3⅝") Stag handle, three large blades, one spear, one clip and one spey point; large spear blade full polished; nickel silver bolsters and shield; nickel silver lining . **120.00**

☐ **K3305RJ**—(3") Green and black brilliant finish celluloid handle, three blades, one large spear, one pen and one curley nail file; large blade full polished; nickel silver bolsters, shield and lining **90.00**

☐ **K3307R**—(3") Stag handle, three blades, one large spear point, on pen and one curley nail file, large blade full polished; nickel siver bolsters, shield and lining **120.00**

☐**K3310**—(3⅝″) Black celluloid handle, three blades, one large clip point, one small clip point and one pen, large blade full polished; nickel silver bolsters and shield; nickel lining . **120.00**

☐**K03311**—(3⅝″) Stag handle, two blades, one large clip point and one pen; large blade full polished; nickel silver bolsters, shield and lining **75.00**

☐**K3311 1/4**—(3⅝″) Stag handle, three blades, one large clip point, one small spey and one pen; large blade full polished; nickel silver bolsters, shield and lining **125.00**

☐**K3316**—(3⅝″) Stag handle, three blades, one large saber clip point; one small clip point and one pen, large blade full polished; nickel silver bolsters, shield and lining **160.00**

☐**K3317**—(3⅝″) Golden celluloid handle, three blades, one large saber clip pattern, one large clip point and one pen, large blade full polished; nickel silver bolsters; nickel lining **125.00**

☐**K0334**—(3¼″) Stag handle, two blades, one large spear point and one pen, large blade full polished; brass lining **50.00**

☐**K03342J**—(3¼″) Green and black brilliant finish celluloid handle, two blades, one large spear point and one pen; large blade full polished; brass lining **30.00**

☐**K03342K**—(3¼″) Red and black brilliant finish celluloid handle, two blades; one large spear point and one pen; large blade full polished; brass lining **30.00**

☐**K03344/S**—(3¼″) Nickel silver engine turned handle, two blades, one spear and one pen; full polished; skeleton trim; with shackle **35.00**

☐**K3430**—(4″) Genuine buffalo horn handle, three large blades, one clip, one sheepfoot and one spey; full polished; highly finished; nickel silver bolsters, shield and lining; full millled **125.00**

☐**K03433**—(4″) Stag handle, two large bldes, one clip and one spey, large clip blade full polished; nickel silver bolsters and shield; nickel lining **90.00**

☐**K3433**—(4″) Stag handle, one sheepfoot and one spey; large clip blade full polished; nickel silver bolsters and shield; nickel lining .**125.00**

☐**K3433 1/4**—(4″) Stag handle, three blades, one large clip point, one spey and one pen, large blade full polished; nickel silver bolsters, shield and lining **120.00**

☐**K03471**—(3⅜″) Stag handle, two blades, one large spear point and one pen, large blade full polished; nickel silver tips; brass lining . .**45.00**

☐**K3472**—(3⅝″) Stag handle, three blades, one large spear point, one pen and one file; large blade full polished; nickel silver tips and shield; brass lining **90.00**

☐**K3483**—(3⅛″) Pearl handle, three blades, one large spear point, one pen and one curley nail file, full polished; nickel silver tips, shield and lining **1209.00**

☐**K3527**—(3¼″) Stag handle, three blades, one large sheepfoot point, one pen and one nail file, large blade full polished; nickel silver rat tail bolsters and shield; nickel lining . . .**120.00**

☐**K3553**—(3⅜″) Stag handle, three blades, one large spear point, one large clip and one spey point; spear blade full polished; nickel silver bolsters and shield; nickel lining .**110.00**

☐**K3599T**—(3⅝″) Pearl handle, three blades, one large spear point and two pens, full polished; nickel silver tips and lining **150.00**

☐**K3619**—(3⅜″) Pear handle, three large blades, one spear, one clip and one spey point; full polished; nickel silver bolsters, shield and lining **175.00**

☐**K3681T**—(3⅜") Stag handle, three blades, one large spear point and two pens, large blade full polished; nickel silver tips and shield; nickel lining **120.00**

☐**K3698 3/4**—(3½") Stag handle, three blades, one large clip point and two pens, large blade full polished; nickel silver bolsters and shield; brass lining **120.00**

☐**K3705 1/4D**—(3¼") Red celluloid handle, three blades, one large clip, one spey and one pen, large blade full polished; nickel silver bolsters and shield; nickel lining **115.00**

☐**K03706**—(3¼") Stag handle, two blades, one large clip and one pen, large blade full polished; nickel silver bolsters and shield; nickel lining **40.00**

☐**K3706 1/2**—(3½") Stag handle, three blades, one long flat clip, one sheepfoot and one pen; large blade full polished; nickel silver bolsters and lining; crest shield **90.00**

☐**K03706 1/4**—(3¼") Stag handle, two large blades, one clip and one spey, large blade full polished; nickel silver bolsters and shield; nickel lining **40.00**

☐**K03707**—(3¼") Ebony handle, two blades, one clip and one pen; large blade full polished; nickel silver bolsters and lining; crest shield **40.00**

☐**K3708 1/4**—(3¼") Pearl handle, three blades, one large clip, one spey and one pen, full polished; nickel silver bolsters and shield; nickel lining **150.00**

☐**K3732**—(3½") Gold color celluloid handle, three large blades, one clip, one spear and one spey; large clip blade full polished; nickel silver bolsters and shield; nickel lining **90.00**

☐**K3733**—(3½") Stag handle, three large blades, one clip, one spear and one spey; large clip blade full polished; nickel silver bolsters, shield and lining **90.00**

☐**K3825**—(4") Black celluloid handle, three large blades, one clip, one sheepfoot and one spey, large blade full polished; nickel silver bolsters and shield; nickel lining **125.00**

☐**K3825H**—(4") Pearl celluloid handle, three large blades, one clip, one sheepfoot and one spey; large clip blade full polished; nickel silver bolsters, shield and lining **90.00**

☐**K3826**—(4") Red and white celluloid handle, three large blades, one clip, one sheepfoot and one spey, large blade full polished; nickel silver bolsters, shield and lining **110.00**

☐**K3828**—(4") Stag handle, three large blades, one clip, one sheepfoot and one spey, large blade full polished; nickel silver bolsters and shield; nickel lining **120.00**

☐**K3878 3/4**—(3⅝") Stag handle, three blades, one large clip, one large sheepfoot point and one pen, large blade full polished; nickel silver bolsters, shield and lining **140.00**

☐**K3908/S**—(2⅞") Pearl handle, three blades, one large spear point, one pen and one curley nail file, full polished; nickel silver tips, shield, shackle and lining **140.00**

☐**K4208**—(3¼") Pearl handle, four blades, one spear, two pens and one file; full polished; nickel silver bolsters and lining; crest shield **120.00**

☐**K4428**—(4") Stag handle, four blades, one large clip, one large sheepfoot, one large spey point and one pen, large blade full polished; nickel silver bolsters and shield; nickel lining **150.00**

☐**K04527**—(3¼") Stag handle, two blades, one large sheepfoot point and one pen, large blade full polished; nickel silver rat tail bolsters, shield and lining **110.00**

☐**K4527**—(3¾") Stag handle, four blades, one large sheepfoot point, two pens, and one nail file, large blade full polished; nickel silver rat tail bolsters and shield; nickel silver lining **120.00**

☐**K04529**—(3¼") Pearl handle, two blades, one large sheepfoot point and one pen, large blade full polished; nickel silver rat tail bolsters, shield and lining **120.00**

☐**K4843**—(2¾") Pearl handle, four blades, one large spear point, one pen, one nail scissor and one pick nail file, full polished; nickel silver shield and lining; full milled **110.00**

☐**K5328**—(3") Stag handle, two blades, one large spear point and one pen, large blade full polished; nickel silver bolster, cap and shield; brass lining **150.00**

☐**K5738/S**—(3⅛") Skeleton pearl handle, three blades, one spear, one pen and one flexible nail file, full polished; nickel silver shackle **60.00**

☐**K06256F**—(3¼") Stag handle, two blades, one large spear point and one curley nail file, full polished; nickel sivler tips, shield, shackle and lining **60.00**

☐**K6353**—(3½") Stag handle, four blades, one large spear blade, one can opener, one combination screw driver and bottle opener and one patent leather punch blade, large blade full polished;nickel silver bolsters and shield; brass lining, with steel center lining; nickel silver shackle **70.00**

☐**K6559**—(3⅝") Stag handle, four blades, one large spear blade, one can opener, one combination screw driver and bottle opener and one patent leather punch blade, large blade full polished; nickel silver bolsters and shield; brass lining, with steel center lining, nickel silver shackle **70.00**

☐**K07243**—(3¾") Stag handle, two large blades, one clip and one spey, large blade full polished; nickel silver bolsters and shield; nickel lining **90.00**

☐**K7433**—(3¾") Stag handle, three blades, one large spear, one large clip and one large spey; nickel silver bolsters and shield; nickel lining; large blade full polished **120.00**

☐**K7530J**—(3¼") Green and black brilliant finish celluloid handle, three blades, one large clip, one spey and one pen; large blade full polished; nickel silver bolsters, shield and lining **115.00**

☐**K7733**—(3⅛") Stag handle, two blades, one large spear point and one penm; large blade full polished; nickel silver bolster, cap and shield; brass lining **75.00**

☐**K7733 3/4**—(3⅛") Stag handle, two blades, one large clip and one pen; large blade full polished; nickel silver bolster, cap and shield; brass lining **75.00**

☐**K8464 1/4**—(3⅝") Ivory handle, etched ''Keen Kutter Kattle Knife'' on one side and Steer's Head on other, three large blades, one spear, one sheepfoot and one spey point, large spear blade full polished; nickel silver bolsters; nickel lining **140.00**

☐**K23628 3/4**—(3") Stag handle, two blades, one large clip and one pen, large blade full polished; nickel silver bolsters and shield; nickel lining **40.00**

☐**K27122**—(2⅞") Pearl celluloid handle, two blades, one large spear point and one pen; large blade full polished; nickel silver tips and lining **40.00**

☐**K27233 3/4**—(2¾") Stag handle, two blades, one large saber clip and one pen, large blade full polished; nickel silver bolster, cap and shield; brass lining **350.00**

☐**K32436 3/4**—(3⅜″) Black celluloid handle, three blades, one large clip, one pen and one nail file; large blade full polished; nickel silver bolsters and shield; nickel lining **90.00**

☐**K32437**—(3⅜″) Stag handle, three blades, one large spear point, one pen and one nail file, large blade full polished; nickel siver bolsters and shield; nickel lining **100.00**

☐**K33251**—(3¼″) Stag handle, three blades, one large spear point, one bottle decapper and one cork screw; spear blade full polished; nickel silver bolsters; shield and lining ..**50.00**

☐**K33253**—(3¼″) Pearl handle, three blades, one large spear point, one bottle decapper and one cork screw, full polished; nickel silver bolsters and lining **140.00**

☐**K33433**—(4″) Stag handle, three blades, one long flat clip, one sheepfoot and one pen; large blade full polished; nickel silver bolsters, shield and lining **125.00**

☐**K33720R**—(3¼″) Iridescent celluloid handle, three large blades, one spear, one sheepfoot and one spey point, large spear blade full polished; nickel silver bolsters, shield and lining **90.00**

☐**K33721**—Stag handle as above **90.00**

☐**K33732K**—(3½″) Red and black brilliant finish celluloid handle, three blades, one long flat narrow clip, one long spear point and one pen, clip blade full polished; nickel silver bolsters, shield and lining **90.00**

☐**K37334**—(3½″) Stag handle, three large blades, one clip, one spear and one spey point; clip blade full polished; nickel silver bolsters, shield and lining **90.00**

☐**K72286**—(3½″) Ebony handle, glazed finish blades, two blades, one spear point, one patent leather punch; steel bolster; nickel silver shield; brass lining **20.00**

☐**K72288 3/4**—(3½″) Stag handle, two blades, one clip point and one patent leather punch, glazed finish; steel bolster; nickel silver shield; brass lining **20.00**

☐**K72423**—(3¼″) Fibre handle, two blades, one large spear and one patent leather punch, large blade full polished; nickel silver bolsters and shield; brass lining **65.00**

☐**K72783**—(3½″) Stag handle, two blades, one spear and one punch; large blade full polished; nickel silver caps and bolsters; brass lining; crest shield **65.00**

☐**K72783 3/4**—(3½″) Stag handle, two blades, one large clip and one pen, large blade full polished; nickel silver boslter, cap and shield; brass lining **65.00**

☐**K73310 1/4R**—(3⅝″) Iridescent celluloid handle, three blades, one large clip, one spey and patent leather punch, large blade full polished; nickel silver bolstes and shield; nickel lining **150.00**

☐**K73311 1/4**—(3⅝″) Stag handle, three blades, one large clip, one spey and patent leather punch; nickel silver boslters and shield; nickel lining **50.00**

☐**K73433 1/4**—(4″) Stag handle, three blades, one large clip point, one spey and one patent leather punch, large blade full polished; nickel silver bolsters, shield and lining **140.00**

K73477 3/4—(3⅝″) White celluloid handle, etched "Keen Cutter Kattle Knife, with Steer's Head on handle, three large blades, one clip, one spey point and one patent leather punch; large blade full polished; nickel silver bolsters; nickel lining **140.00**

K73553 3/4—(3⅜″) Stag handle, three blades, one clip, one spey, and one punch; large blade full polished; nickel silver bolsters and lining; crest shield **90.00**

K73265G—(3″) Gold celluloid handle, three blades, one large spear point, one spey and one patent leather punch, large blade full polished; nickel silver bolsters and shield; nickel lining **90.00**

K73628—(3″) Stag handle, three blades, one large spear point, one spey and one patent leather punch, large blade full polished; nickel silver bolsters and shield; nickel lining . . **90.00**

K73706—(3¼″) Stag handle, three blades, one large clip, one pen and one patent leather punch, clip blade full polished; nickel silver bolsters and shield; nickel lining **110.00**

K73706 1/4—(3¼″) Stag handle, three blades, one large clip, one spey and one patent leather punch, clip blade full polished; nickel silver bolsters and shield; nickel lining . **110.00**

K73733—(3½″) Stag handle, three blades, one large clip, one large spey and one patent leather punch, large clip blade full polished; nickel silver bolsters, shield and lining . **130.00**

K73828—(4″) Stag handle, three blades, one large clip, one spey and patent leather punch, large blade full polished; nickel silver bolsters and shield; nickel silver lining **130.00**

K73845 1/4D—Red celluloid handle as above **150.00**

K73845 1/4L—(3⅞″) Varicolored brilliant finish celluloid handle, three blades, one large spear, one spey and one patent leather punch blade, large spear blade full polished; nickel silver bolsters, shield and lining **150.00**

K73848—(3½″) Stag handle, three blades, one large spear pint, one pen and one patent leather punch, large blade full polished; nickel silver bolsters, shield and lining **90.00**

K73848 1/4—(3½″) Stag handle, three blades, one large spear, one spey and one patent leather punch blade, large spear full polished; nickel silver bolsters, shield and lining **135.00**

K73875 3/4P—(3⅞″) Pearl blue celluloid handle, three blades, one large clip, one large spey and one patent leather punch; large clip blade full polished; nickel silver bolsters and shield; nickel silver lining **125.00**

K73878 1/4—(3⅜″) Stag handle, three blades, one spear, one spey and one punch, large blade full polished; nickel silver bolsters and lining; crest shield **125.00**

K73878 3/4—(3⅝″) Stag handle, three blades, one large clip, one large spey and one patent leather punch; large clip blade full polished; nickel silver bolsters and shield; nickel silver lining **125.00**

K74825E—f(4″) Pearl celluloid handle, four blades, one large clip, one large sheepfoot, one large spey and one patent leather punch blade; large clip blade full polished; nickel silver bolsters and shield; nickel lining **150.00**

K74828—(4″) Stag handle, four blades, one large clip, one large sheepfoot, one large spey and one patent leather punch blade, large clip blde full polished; nickel silver bolsters and shield; nickel lining **150.00**

KINFOLKS
LITTLE VALLEY, NEW YORK

Kinfolks was started in Little Valley, New York in 1927, with Tint Champlain (of Cattaraugus) as president. In 1929, Dean J. Case became president. The name "Kinfolks" was derived from the fact that all of the company's originators were cousins.

The firm produced mainly sheath knives, making many for the Armed Services during World War II. They also made knives marked Jean Case.

In the 1950's when Robeson hired Emerson Case as sales manager, he had or obtained control of the "Kinfolks" trademark. Robeson made a line of approximately 10 knives with the "Kinfolks" brand, and marketed them through the Robeson dealers. The patterns were usually tang stamped with green bone handles, and later when the handles were changed to the traditional strawberry bone, the Kinfolks tang stamp was dropped in favor of the name etched on the blade. Most of the knives made by Robeson with the Kinfolks name were pocketknives.

☐**1234**—PEN KNIFE (2¾") Lobster pattern, two blades, Hi Den scales, hand polished blades. A light and durable vest pocket knife **25.00**
☐**1234B**—Same as illustrated except with addition of bail........................**25.00**

☐**1267**—PEN KNIFE (2¾") Two blades, Hi Den scales, nickel silver tips, brass lining, hand polished blades **30.00**
☐**6267**—Same as illustrated except with bone stag scales......................**40.00**
☐**8267**—Same as illustrated except with imitation pearl scales. **30.00**

☐**4267**—PEN KNIFE (2¾") Two blades, genuine pearl scales, nickel silver tips, nickel silver lining, hand polished blades **85.00**
☐**5267**—Same as illustrated except with genuine stag scales and brass lining. **75.00**
☐**6109-L**—JACK KNIFE (4⅜") Lock blade, single clip blade, locks when knife is open. Blade is released for closing by pushing brass lock spring, bone stag scales, nickel silver bolster and cap, brass lining, hand polished blade **160.00**

☐**6209**—JACK KNIFE (4⅜") One large clip blade, one pen blade, bone stag scales, nickel silver bolster and cap, brass linings, hand polished blades......................**175.00**
☐**8209**—Same as illustrated except with imitation pearl scales. **160.00**

☐**6217-M**—MUSKRAT KNIFE (3¾") Two skinning blades, bone stag scales, nickel silver bolster, brass linings, hand polished blades **120.00**

☐**6223**—PEN KNIFE (2¾") Sleeve board pattern, two blades, bone stag scales, nickel silver bolsters, brass lining, hand polished blades **60.00**
☐**5223**—Same as illustrated except with genuine stag scales. **70.00**

☐**6265**—(2¾") Dog leg pattern, two blades, bone stag scales, nickel silver bolster and cap, brass linings, hand polished blades **50.00**
☐**8265**—Same as illustrated except with imitation pearl scales. **40.00**
☐**5265**—Same as illustrated except with genuine stag scales. **55.00**

☐**6292**—(5⅛") Hunter's pattern, heavy clip blade and large skinning blade, bone stag scales, nickel silver bolsters, brass lining, hand polished blades **175.00**

☐**6317**—(3¾") Stockman's pattern, skinning blade, sheep foot blade, spay blade, bone stag scales, nickel silver bolsters, brass linings, hand polished blades **150.00**
☐**5217**—Same as illustrated except genuine stag scales. **150.00**

☐**6317-P**—(3¾") Stockman's pattern, skinning blade, sheep foot blade, punch blade, bone stag scales, nickel silver bolsters, brass linings, hand polished blades **150.00**
☐**8317-P**—Same as illustrated except with imitation pearl scales................**150.00**

☐**3213**—FISHERMAN'S KNIFE (4¼") Stainless steel blades and springs, slitting and skinning blade, combination blade with hook disgorger, scaler teeth and cap lifter, hook sharpening stone inserted into scale of the knife and pin hole for straightening bent hooks at tip of bolster. Durable composition cream colored scales, nickel silver bolsters, brass linings, hand polished blades **30.00**

□**8223**—PEN KNIFE (2¾") Sleeve board pattern, two blades, imitation pearl scales, nickel silver bolsters, brass lining, hand polished blades **35.00**

□**8317**—(3¾") Stockman's pattern, skinning blade, sheep foot blade, spay blade, imitation pearl scales, nickel silver bolsters, brass linings, hand polished blades **90.00**
□**3317**—Same as illustrated except composition cream colored scales. **90.00**

□**8292**—(5⅛") Hunter's pattern, heavy clip blade and large skinning blade, imitation pearl scales, nickel silver bolsters, brass linings, hand polished blades **125.00**

□**06217**—(3¾") Serpentine pattern, two blades, bone stag scales, nickel silver bolsters, brass lining, hand polished blades **90.00**
□**08217**—Same as illustrated but with imitation pearl scales. **80.00**
□**03217**—Same as illustrated with cream colored composition scales. **80.00**

KISSING KRANE (ROBERT KLAAS COMPANY)
SOLINGEN OHLIGS, GERMANY

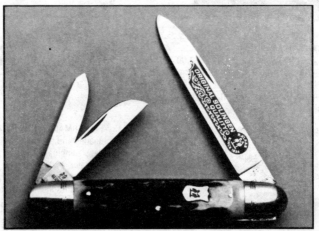

Robert Klass Kissing Crane, stag handled whittler. Imported exclusively by Star Sales of Knoxville, TN.
□ **Current Collector Value** **$55.00**

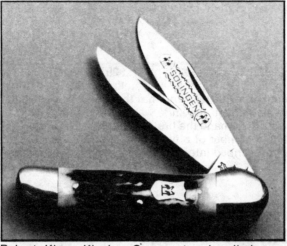

Robert Klass Kissing Crane, stag handled cop-
perhead. Imported exclusively by Star Sales of
Knoxville, TN.
☐ *Current Collector Value* **$48.00**

The Kissing Krane knife is produced by the Robert Klaas Company in Solingen Ohligs, Germany. The company was founded by Robert Klaas in 1834,
when he began making knives in the steel factories his wife's families had
managed since 1704. Around 1850, his multi-blade knives became quite
popular, and by 1880 Klaas went into full-time knife production. At one time
the company was importing cow horn from the United States as handle
material for some of its knives.

In 1972 Klaas began a dating system on its knives. It is explained below:
The first two numbers are the pattern number, the third number is the
number of blades, the fourth number is the handle material, and the remaining numbers are the Roman numeral keys for the year of manufacture.

The handle types are as follows:

1-Ivory type
2-Black Lifetime (composition)
3-Simulated Bone
4-Pearl type
5-Genuine Deer Stag

6-Yellow Lifetime (composition)
7-Mother of Pearl
8-Wood
9-Genuine Bone Stag
0-Red Lifetime (composition)

The Key to year of manufacture is:

XI-1972	XV-1976
XII-1973	XVI-1977
XIII-1974	XVII-1978
XIV-1975	etc.

An example of this is #2929XII. The first 29 would tell you that it is a small canoe pattern, the third numeral, a "2" tells you that the knife has 2 blades. The fourth number, a "9" tells you that the knife has bone handles, and the Roman numerals tell you the knife was made in 1973.

Kissing Krane also made the first NKC & DA knife, a three blade whittler, and have made a number of other commemoratives, including a stag handled lockback (described later in this book) and a three blade stag handled canoe.

KISSING KRANE LINEAGE

Peter Storsberg

Peter Daniel Pauls — Johanne Amalie Storsberg
(-1863)

Juliane Henriette Pauls — Friedrich Robt Klaas

Walter Klaas (1958-1912)	Ernst Klaas (1860-1916)	Max Klaas

Frida Klaas-Fritz Rontgen
(1882-1948)

Frank Rontgen (Pres.) present owner
(1911-   )

Hugo Schiesen
(1909-   )

Hans-Gerd Schiesen (export dept.)
(1935-   )

Ernst Jorgen Schiesen (purchasing and
home (1938-   )   sales)

KLICKER
ST. LOUIS, MISSOURI

Introduced in 1958 by Shapleigh Hardware, the brand consisted of eight different patterns: six jack-knife, one three blade stockman, and one four blade Swiss army knife. The knives were probably made by Camillus and were brass-lined, nickel silver, trimmed, and handled with synthetic handles of different colors. The knives were stamped Klicker.

LACKAWANNA CUTLERY COMPANY
NICHOLSON, PENNSYLVANIA

Started in 1915, Lackawanna was a major producer of the clear celluloid handled knives. It was destroyed by fire in 1923, but reopened only to go out of business seven years later, in 1930.

LANDERS, FRARY AND CLARK
NEW BRITTAN, CONNECTICUT

In 1930, LF&C made a special set of knives commemorating their 77th anniversary. There were sets of two knives, 3¼″ long, three blades each, with bone handles and nickel silver linings. The blades were etched "77th Anniversary, Universal, 1.00 Special". The knives normally retailed for $1.50. They were available for only 77 days.

Landers, Frary and Clark began with a partnership formed in 1842 between George Landers and Josiah Dewey to make cupboard catches. In 1883 Landers joined with Levi Smith to form the Landers and Smith Manufacturing Company

☐**0242**—(3⅜″) Stag handle, large spear and pen blades, half crocused finish; steel bolsters, brass lined 40.00

☐**2042**—(3⅜″) Stag handles, large sheepfoot and pen blades, half crocused finish; steel bolster, brass lined 40.00

☐**0244**—(3⅜″) Stag handle, large spear and pen blades, fine glazed finish; steel bolster, brass lined 50.00

☐**0244 3/4**—(3⅜″) Stag handles, large clip and pen blades, glazed finish; steel bolster, brass lined 40.00

☐**0245 3/4**—(3⅜″) Stag handle, large spear and pen blades, glazed finish; steel bolster, brass lined 45.00

☐**0245 3/4**—(3⅜″) Stag handle, large clip and pen blades, glazed finish; steel bolster, brass lined.........................45.00

☐**0247**—(3⅜″) Stag handle, large spear and pen blades, fine glazed finish; steel bolsters, brass lined.......................45.00

☐**0247**—(3⅜″) Stag handle, large sheepfoot and pen blades, fine glazed finish; steel bolsters, brass lined 45.00

☐**0247 3/4**—(3⅜″) Stag handle, large clip and pen blades, fine glazed finish; steel bolsters, brass lined 45.00

☐**00154**—(3¼″) Stag handle, large clip, spey blade and leather punch, half polished, nickel silver bolsters, nickel silver lined 95.00

☐**00155P**(3¼″) Stag handle, large spear, spey blade and leather punch, half polished; nickel silver bolsters, nickel silver lined 95.00

☐**00155 3/4**—(3¼″) Stag handle, large clip, spey blade and leather punch, half polished; nickel silver bolsters, nickel silver lined ..95.00

☐**01103**—(3¼″) Stag handles, easy opener, large spear blade, fine glazed finish; steel bolster, brass lined 40.00

☐**01637 5/8**—(3¾″) Stag handle, large sabre spear blade, half crocused finish; nickel silver bolsters, brass lined 90.00

☐**06150**—(3⅜″) Stag handle, large spear blade, glazed finish; steel bolster, steel lined 45.00

☐**06150 3/4**— Same as above except it has clip blade 45.00

☐**02103**—(3¼″) Stag handle, easy opener, large spear and pen blades, fine glazed finish; steel bolsters, brass lined **45.00**

☐**02204**—(3″) Stag handle, large weaver point and pen blades, glazed finish; steel bolster, steel lined **65.00**

☐**02266**—(3½″) Stag handle, easy opener, large spear and pen blades, half crocused finish; nickel silver bolster, brass lined . .**60.00**

☐**02472**—(3⅜″) Stag handle, easy opener, large spear and pen blades, half crocused finish; nickel silver bolsters, brass lined .**60.00**

☐**02650**—(3⅜″) Stag handle, large spear and pen blades, glazed finish; steel bolster, steel lined **50.00**

☐**02650 1/2**—(3⅜″) Stag handle, large spey and pen blades, glazed finish; steel bolster, steel lined **55.00**

☐**02650 3/4**—(3⅜″) Stag handle, large clip and pen blades, glazed finish; steel bolster, steel lined **50.00**

☐**03154**—(3¼″) Stag handle, large clip, spey and pen blades, half polished; nickel silver bolsters, nickel silver lined **95.00**

☐**03155**—(3¼″) Stag handle, large spear, spey and pen blades, half polished; nickel silver bolsters, nickel silver lined **115.00**

☐**03155 3/4**—(3¼″) Stag handle, large clip, spey and pen blades, half polished; nickel silver bolsters, nickel silver lined **95.00**

☐**2242**—(3⅜″) Cocobolo handle, large spear and pen blades, half crocused finish; nickel silver bolsters, brass lined **40.00**

☐**2243 3/4**—(3⅜″) Cocobolo handle, large clip and pen blades, half crocused finish, steel bolsters, brass lined **40.00**

☐**2244**—(3⅜″) Cocobolo handle, large spear and pen blades, fine glazed finish; steel bolster, brass lined **50.00**

☐**2244 3/4**—(3⅜″) Cocobolo handle, large clip and pen blades, glazed finish; steel bolster, brass lined **40.00**

☐**2247**—(3⅜″) Cocobolo handle, large spear and pen blades; fine glazed finish; steel bolster, brass lined **45.00**

☐**2247 3/4**—(3⅜″) Cocobolo handle, large clip and pen blades, fine glazed finish; steel bolsters, brass lined **45.00**

☐**3243**—(3⅜″) Ebonwood handle, large spear and pen blades, half crocused finish; steel bolsters, brass lined **40.00**

☐**3243 3/4**—(3⅜″) Ebonwood handle, large clip and pen blades, half crocused finish; steel bolsters, brass lined **40.00**

☐**3244**—(3⅜″) Ebonwood handle, large spear and pen blades, fine glazed finish; steel bolster, brass lined **50.00**

☐**3244 3/4**—(3⅜″) Ebonwood handle, large clip and pen blades, glazed finish; steel bolster, brass lined **40.00**

☐**3247**—(3⅜″) Ebonwood handle, large spear and pen blades, fine glazef finish; steel bolsters, brass lined **45.00**

☐**4085**—(3⅜″) Buffalo ivory handle, large sabre clip, pen blade and leather punch, half polished; nickel silver bolsters, nickel silver lined **120.00**

☐**8248G**—(3⅜″) Green ivory handle, large spear and pen blades, half polished; steel boslters, brass lined **45.00**

☐**8248 3/4G**—(3⅜″) Green ivory handle, large clip and pen blades, half polished; steel bolsters, brass lined **45.00**

☐**8248 R**—(3⅜″) Red ivory handle, large spear and pen blades, half polished; steel bolsters, brass lined **45.00**

☐**8248 3/4R**—(3⅜″) Red ivory handle, large clip and pen blades, half polished; steel bolsters, brass lined **45.00**

☐**8248S**—(3⅜″) Smoke pearl handle, large spear and pen blades, half polished; steel bolsters, brass lined **45.00**

☐**8248 3/4S**—(3⅜″) Smoke pearl handle, large clip and pen blades, half polished; steel bolsters, brass lined **45.00**

☐**8248Y**—(3⅜″) Gold ivory handle, large spear and pen blades, half polished; steel bolsters, brass lined **45.00**

☐**8248 3/4Y**—(3⅜″) Gold ivory handle, large clip and pen blades, half polished; steel bolsters, brass lined **45.00**

☐**22266**—(3½″) Cocobolo handle, easy opener, large spear and pen blades, half crocused finish; nickel silver bolster, brass lined **60.00**

☐**22472**—(3⅜″) Cocobolo handle, easy opener, large spear and pen blades, half crocused finish; nickel silver bolsters, brass lined .**60.00**

☐**31103**—(3¼″) Ebonized handle, easy opener, large spear blade, fine glazed finish; steel bolster, brass lined **40.00**

☐**31650**—(3⅜″) Ebonwood handle, large spear blade, glazed finish; steel bolster, steel lined
......................................**60.00**

☐**31650 3/4**—(3⅜″) Ebonwood handle, large clip blade, fine glazed finish; steel bolster, steel lined......................................**60.00**

☐**3266**—(3½″) Ebonwood handle, easy opener, large spear and pen blades, half crocused finish; nickel silver bolster, brass lined......................................**60.00**

☐**32472**—(3⅜″) Ebonwood handle, easy opener, large spear and pen blades, half crocused finish finish, nickel silver bolsters, brass lined......................................**60.00**

☐**32650**—(3⅜″) Ebonwood handle, large spear and pen blades, glazed finish; steel bolster, steel lined......................................**70.00**

☐**32650 1/2**—(3⅜″) Ebonwood handle, large spey and pen blades, glazed finish; steel bolster, steel lined......................................**70.00**

☐**32650 3/4**—(3⅜″) Ebonwood handle, large clip and pen blades; glazed finish; steel bolster, steel lined......................................**65.00**

☐**40154**—(3¼″) Buffalo ivory handle, large clip, spey blade and leather punch, half polished; nickel silver bolsters, nickel silver lined ...
......................................**100.00**

☐**80154Y**—(3¼″) Gold ivory handle, large clip, spey blade and leather punch, half polished; nickel silver bolsters, nickel silver lined ..**95.00**

☐**80155 3/4B**—(3¼″) Blue ivory handle, large clip, spey blade and leather punch, half polished; nickel silver bolsters, nickel silver lined
......................................**100.00**

☐**80155 3/4R**—(3¼″) Red ivory handle, large clip, spey blade and leather punch, half polished; nickel silver bolster, nickel silver lined ....
......................................**100.00**

☐**148**—(3″) Pearl handle, three blades, spear, pen, and small file, half polished; German silver bolsters, shielded, brass lined, spunk joints ...
......................................**110.00**

☐**194**—(3″) Pearl handle, three blades, spear, pen, and small file, half polished; brass lined
......................................**50.00**

☐**174X**—(2¾″) Pearl handle, two blades, spear and pen, half polished; German silver tips, brass lined....................**50.00**

☐**185**—(3⅜″) Pearl handle, three blades, spear pen and small file, full polished; German silver bolsters, shielded, brass lined.......**125.00**

☐**204**—(3¼″) Pearl handle, four blades, spear, two pens, and file, half polished; German silver bolsters, shielded, brass lined, sunk joints........................**100.00**

☐**273**—(2¾″) Stag handle, two blades, spear and pen, half polished; German silver tips; brass lined....................**30.00**

☐**277**—(3¼″) Pearl handle, three blades, spear, pen and small file, full polished; German silver tips, shielded, German silver lined; spunk joints........................**110.00**

☐**309**—(3″) Pearl handle, three blades, spear, pen and small file, full polished; German silver tips, shielded, German silver lined, sunk joints
......................................**125.00**

□320—(3¼″) Genuine Stag handle, three blades, spear, pen, and file, full polished; German silver tips, shielded, German sivler lined, sunk joints **75.00**

□321—(3¼″) Pearl handle, three blades, spear, pen and small file; German silver tips, shielded, German silver lined, extra highly finished throughout **120.00**

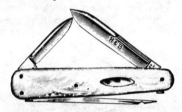

□325—(3⅛″) Pearl handle, three blades, spear, pen and flat file, full polished; German silver lined, sunk joints, shielded **60.00**

□327—(3⅜″) Pearl handle, three blades, wharncliffe, pen and flexible manicure file, full polished; German silver lined, German silver shields, sunk joints **75.00**

□337—(3″) Pearl handle, two blades, spear and pen, half polished; German silver tips, shielded, brass lined **50.00**

□346—(3¼″) Pearl handle, three blades, spear, pen, and flexible manicure file, full polished; German silver tips, shielded, German silver lined, sunk joints **75.00**

□360—(2¾″) Pearl handle, two blades, spear and pen, half polished; German silver lined, shielded **55.00**

□364—(2¾″) Pearl handle, two blades, spear and pen, half polished; brass lined, with shackle for use in attaching to watch chain . . . .
. . . . **55.00**

□**421**—(3¼") Genuine Stag handle, three blades, spear, pen and file, full polished; German silver tips, brass lined, sunk joints . . **70.00**

□**450**—(3⅜") Stag handle, three blades, spear, pen and file, half polished; brass lined **75.00**

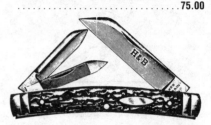

□**426**—(3") Pearl handle, two blades, spear and pen, half polished; German silver tips, brass lined **50.00**

□**454**—(3½") Pearl handle, three blades, spear, pen and small file, full polished; Geman silver lined, shielded, sunk joints **95.00**

□**443**—(3¼") Pearl handle, three blades, sheep foot, pen, and small file, full polished; German silver tips, shielded, brass lined, sunk joints **125.00**

□**499**—(2¾") Pearl handle, three blades, spear, pen and small file, full polished; German silver lined, shielded **80.00**

□**444**—(3¼") Genuine Stag handle, four blades, sheepfoot, two pens, and file, full polished; German silver tips, shielded, brass lined, full sunk joints **125.00**

□**507**—(3¼") Stag handle, three blades, spear, pen, and file, half polished; German silver tips, shielded, brass lined, sunk joints **75.00**

□**511**—(3") Stag handle, two blades, spear and pen, half polished; German silver tips, shielded, brass lined **30.00**

□**512**—(3⅛") Pearl handle, two blades, large spear, flat file, and scissors, full polished; German silver lined, shielded, sunk joints ... **75.00**

□**513**—(3") Stag handle, three blades, spear, pen and file, half polished; German silver tips, shielded, brass lined **50.00**

□**632**—(3⅛") Pearl handle, three blades, spear, pen, and long file, full polished; German sivler lined **65.00**

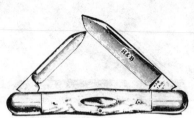

□**652**—(3⅜") Pearl handle, two blades, spear and pen, half polished; German silver bolsters, shielded, brass lined **50.00**

□**656**—(3") Antique Ivory handle, two blades, spear and pen, full polished; German silver lined **50.00**

□**658**—(3") Antique Ivory handle, two blades, spear and pen, full polished; German silver lined **50.00**

□**710**—(3") Fired gold steel scales, beautifully enameled handle, two blades, large pocket blade, small file blade, full polished **40.00**

☐**712**—(3″) Fired gold steel scales, beautifully enameled handle, three blades, large spear, small pen, and file, full polished **65.00**

☐**716**—(2¾″) Fired gold steel scales, beautifully enameled handle, four blades, large spear, two pens and file, full polished . . . **85.00**

☐**713**—(2¾″) Fired gold steel scales, beautifully enameled handle, four blades, large spear, two pen and file, full polished **65.00**

☐**717**—(3⅛″) Fired gold steel scales, beautifully enameled handle, three blades, large spear, small pen and French nail pick, full polished . . .
. . . . **50.00**

☐**718**—(3½″) Fired gold steel scales, beautifully enameled handle, four blades, large spear, two pens and file, full polished . . . **65.00**

☐**714**—(2⅜″) Fired gold steel scales, beautifully enameled handle, three blades, large spear, small pen and French nail pick, full polished . . .
. . . . **65.00**

☐**719**—(3¼″) Fired gold steel scales, beautifully enameled handle, four blades, large spear, two pens and file, full polished . . . **90.00**

☐**6201**—(3″) Pearl handle, two blades, spear and large file, full polished; German silver tips, German silver lined, knurled **60.00**

☐**715**—(2½″) Fired gold steel scales, beautifully enameled handle, four blades, large spear, two pens and file, full polished . . . **70.00**

LIBERTY KNIFE COMPANY
NEW HAVEN, CONN.

Filed a preliminary certificate of dissolution in December, 1925. It probably went out of business soon thereafter.

MAHER AND GROSH COMPANY
CLYDE, OHIO

Maher and Gross is probably the oldest mail order knife house in the United States. It began with an advertisement in the American Agriculturist in 1887, soon followed by ads in the Scientific American. During that time they moved quite a bit. In 1887 their address was 75 Summit St., Toledo, later moving to 34 Monroe Street, and then to 40 Monroe Street by 1883. In 1899 they moved to 75 A Street, Toledo, Ohio.

They are still in business today.

Many of their knives featured etched blades and Maher & Grosh's own tang stamp. Miller Brothers made many of their knives, with Schrade making their knives recently.

The company address is currently Clyde, Ohio.

☐CHANCEY DEPEWS PET (3") three pearl handles, three blades, one a file, german silver back and ends **45.00**

☐JACK KNIFE (4") Razor steel, wood handles, two blades **45.00**

☐TB. COLORADO STOCK KNIFE (4½") pearl Iscrew on handle, three blades, nickel silver linings and bolster, sheep foot, spay, and clip master blade **275.00**

☐*T COLORADO STOCK KNIFE same as above, but with pen blade instead of spay blade **275.00**

☐*09—(5") Stag handle, one blade, steel lined and steel bolstered. Same pattern as #119B
. . . . **300.00**

☐58—MONTANA MOUNTAINEER, (⅞") ebony handles, three blades, german silver ends . . . .
. . . . **100.00**

☐58—PEAR, (3⅞") pearl handle, three blades, brass linings, nickel-silver bolsters **250.00**

☐*69—(5") brass handles, one blade, same pattern as #119B **150.00**

☐**109**—(5⅜″) Bone stag handles, one blade, lockback **100.00**

☐**119B**—(5″) Wood handles, two blades, brass linings, german silver bolsters. This knife was carried by George Armstrong Custer, according to M & G's advertising **225.00**

☐**476**—(3½″) Pearl handles, four blades including scissors and nail file **80.00**

☐**492**—(4″) Pearl handles, three blades and a nail vile **175.00**

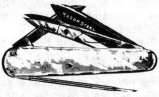

☐**190**—SKINNING KNIFE (4⅝″) Wood handles **65.00**

☐**209**—(6″) Bone handles, same as #109, but larger. Lanyard hole was available if desired at no extra charge **200.00**

☐***309**—(5″) Wood handles, two blades, one a large clip, one a large, long spear. Brass finish, brass linings, german silver bolsters. Same otherwise as #119B **225.00**

☐**493**—(3⅛″) Pearl handles, two cutting blades, scissor, and nail file **60.00**

☐**547**—(3⅜″) Pearl handles, two cutting blades, scissor, nail file, corkscrew **80.00**

☐**371**—(3⅜″) Pearl handle, three blades, nickel silver bolster and lining **95.00**

☐**4472**—(3⅝″) Pearl handles, three blades and a nail file **65.00**

☐**461**—(3⅝″) Pearl handles, four blades **110.00**

MARBLES ARMS AND MANUFACTURING COMPANY
GLADSTONE, MICHIGAN

Born in 1854, Webster Marbles became a timber surveyor and cruiser in his early manhood. During this time he saw a need, and filled it by inventing the waterproof matchbox and his safety pocket ax. He made these part-time until 1898, when he built a 64 square foot building.

He started full-time, advertising nationally in 1899, and was joined that year by F. H. Van Cleeve as a partner. He changed the name of his company from W. L. Marble, Gladstone, Michigan to "The Marble Safety Ax Company".

It soon grew into a 9,000 square foot building.

His first knife was introduced in 1901, The Ideal. In 1902 came the Dall DeWeese model.

Between 1903 and 1908 he started a line of pocketknives, most made by the Case brothers and a German company that made a switchblade.

In 1911 the name changed again to the Marbles Arms and Manufacturing Company and in that same year moved into a 30,000 square foot building. His knives were used by Teddy Roosevelt, the Peary Arctic Exposition and the Smithsonian Institution expeditions.

In the 1920s many of his patents ran out, and during World War II his knife designs were so far advanced that the government issued contracts to make knives that Marbles had previously had patented. At the war's end, the companies that had the tooling already made continued to make the knives for the general public. His ax line and folding knives were not re-introduced and the company dropped back to four patterns of sheath knives.

They are still in business today.

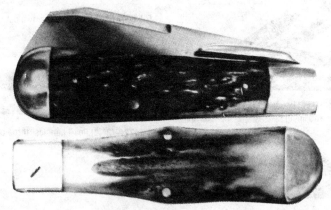

Both knives have stag handles, similar bolsters. A close look shows top Marble's to have end pins; bottom M.S.A. has none.

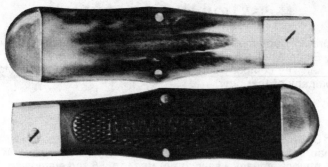

Two M.S.A. folders, both have no end pins and undercut modern-appearing bolsters.

Old-style "U" bolsters. (L) hard rubber, (R) stag.

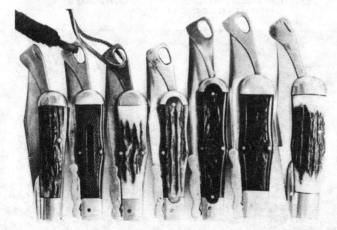

□ *Current Collector Value (Left to Right)* $350.00; 300.00; 350.00; 600.00; 450.00; 400.00; 300.00

Knives at each end are Marble's (made after 1920). Five folders in center are marked M.S.A. (of various types).

MASSILLION CUTLERY COMPANY,
MASSILLION, OHIO

Incorporated September 1925 for $25,000 to manufacture and deal in cutlery by Elson Whefler, John J. Smith, Glen T. Horn, Henry A. Back, and R. E. Dornacker. The company purchased the defunct Ohio Cutlery Manufacturing Company of that city.

MERIDEN CUTLERY COMPANY
MERIDEN, CONNECTICUT

Started by David Ropes and Julius Pratt, both of whom had run what John Russell had called the "Pratt Monopoly" in ivory handles for knives, the Meriden Cutlery Company was incorporated in 1855 and stamped its knives "Meriden Knife Co. Meriden Conn. USA."

MILLER BROTHERS COMPANY
MERIDEN, CONNECTICUT

Established in 1863 in Yalesville, Connecticut by William H. and George W. Miller. The company moved to Meriden, Connecticut prior to 1870. In 1870 George patented their screw on handles, one of the Miller Brothers knives most distinctive features. George was an innovative designer and registered cutlery patents as late as 1899.

In 1878 the brothers business failed, and it was reorganized. One of the new owners, Charles Rockwell, became a giant in the cutlery field, helping lobby the protective tariffs on cutlery in the 1890's through Congress. In 1926 they changed their name to the Miller Brothers Pen Company and had probably discontinued knives by this time.

NAGLE REBLADE KNIFE COMPANY
POUGHKEEPSIE, NEW YORK

One of the rarest knives, the famous Nagle Reblade made only 2 years.
☐ *Current Collector Value* **$2,500.00**

Operating only from 1912 until 1916, the Nagle Reblade knife is one of the most prized knives in knife collecting. Less than a dozen specimens are known to exist. The knives are unique in that they feature interchangeable blades that once assembled operated like any other pocketknife. Every blade was usually stamped on these knives. The only patterns known were bone handled tear drop jack, bone tear drop easy open, equal end, and black composition two blade, blade composition four blade, and a pearl two blade.

NAPANOCH KNIFE COMPANY
NAPANOCH, NEW YORK

The Napanoch Knife Company was founded at the site of the Duvall Rake Factory by William Horenbeek and Irving Carmen. The company was named Napanoch in 1905 and incorporated in 1909. It was sold to Winchester in 1919 or 1920, with Winchester hiring Carmen and a few of his former employees.

In 1921, four employees of Winchester bought the Napanoch site and started the Honk Falls Knife Company. That company operated until a fire in 1929 destroyed the factory. In the 1930's the company started again using the name Napanoch, but went out of business in 1939. Their knives were stamped "Napanoch Knife Co., Napanoch, New York U. S. A."

NEFT SAFETY HUNTING KNIFE

Manufacturer claimed the knife was dustproof and could be made waterproof. Series of eight interchangeable blades were available. The knife retailed for $3.75 and the additional blades were $1 each. Sales offices were at Newark, New York

Reported in one undocumented place that the knives were made by Boker, USA or Valley Forge.

NEVER DULL

Never Dull pocketknives were the brand of a major mail order house. At press time for this book the information of the owner of the "Never Dull" trademark had not been received from the U.S. Patent Office, or the U.S. Copyright Office.

The knives were made in the 1920's - 1930's, and were made on contract.

☐**G236**—(3¼") Rosewood handle, double swedged, steel bolster and lining **550.00**

☐**G250**—(3½") Stag and rosewood heavy pattern, swell polished brass lined, steel cap and bolster, German silver shield **90.00**

☐**G255**—(3⅜") Stained bone handle, one blade Barlow, heavy bolster **60.00**

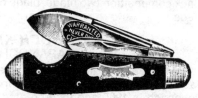

☐**G300**—(3⅝") Stag and rosewood handle, two blades, large blade crocused, g. s. cap, shield and bolster **70.00**

☐**G353**—(3⅝") Assorted stag and rosewood handle, gun stock pattern, brass lined, steel cap and bolster, German silver shield, large clip and medium blades crocuc polished **120.00**

☐**G358**—(3½") Assorted stag and rosewood handle, curved pattern, steel cap and bolster, German silver shield, brass lined **120.00**

☐**G387**—(3¾") Ebony and rosewood handle, heavy beveled blade, double swedged, crocused, steel bolster, German silver shield . . . **60.00**

☐G397—(4¼″) Assorted stag and rosewood handle, extra heavy spear, crocused, pen blade, German silver cap, bolster and shield, brass lining **60.00**

☐G1240—(3⅝″) Stag handle, beveled blades, German silver cap, bolster and shield, milled lining **120.00**

☐G1245—(3¼″) Mother of pearl, German silver shield, milled lining, fitted nail grooves, fluted back, four blades, full crocused . . **165.00**

☐G421—(4″) Stag handle, large clip, crocused, cattle and speying, cap and bolster, German silver shield, polished inside, brass lined . **80.00**

☐G424—(4½″) Assorted stag and rosewood handle, heavy steel bolster, German silver shield **55.00**

THE NEW YORK KNIFE COMPANY
WALDEN, NEW YORK

In its heyday, the New York Knife Company probably made the highest quality pocketknife of any American manufacturer. The fit, blade snap, bone jigging, etching, stamping and overall quality is a standard that is rarely equalled 100 years later.

The company began making knives at Mattewan, New York in the 1850's. In 1856 the town fathers of the town of Walden, New York offered the use of a factory in their town to the New York Knife Company. The company accepted, and the entire populace of Walden turned out in their wagons and horses to move the company to their town.

The president at the time of this move was Thomas W. Bradley. Under his management he built the New York Knife Company into the largest knife company in the U. S. by the time of death in 1879.

His son, Thomas J. Bradley took over the factory. A Civil War hero (he had won the Congressional Medal of Honor at Chancellorsville) Bradley maintained New York Knife as the premier cutlery company, and by the 1890's had amassed personal fortune from the knife factory. A close friend of

William McKinley, he served in Washington during McKinley's term, and in 1903 sold his interest in New York Knife to C. B. Fuller and J. E. Fuller. They ran the company until it went out of business in 1931. The building that housed the New York Knife Company was torn down in 1940.

The New York Knife Company's trademark was "Hammer Brand" with an arm and hammer. Almost all their knives had this etched on the blades. Tang stamps will be found with both the Hammer Brand and New York Knife Co. logos. A one blade folding hunter will sometimes have the Hammer Brand logo on the front and the New York Knife Co. stamped on the back of the tang. Some knives will have only the "New York Knife Co." logo.

The trademark was used in later years by Imperial Associated Knife Companies on a cheap line of knives. These knives will have patent numbers on a second blade and no New York Knife stampings. The bolsters will usually be crimped.

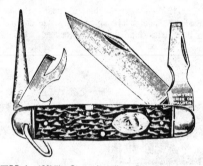

☐**BB-1**—(3⅜") Stag handle. Brass lining, nickel silver bolsters. One blade, screwdriver, leather punch, can and bottle opener. Ring in handle **150.00**

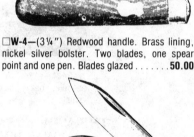

☐**W-4**—(3¼") Redwood handle. Brass lining, nickel silver bolster. Two blades, one spear point and one pen. Blades glazed **50.00**

☐**W-3**—(3⅞") Stag handle. Brass lining, nickel silver bolsters. One spear point blade, leather punch, can opener, screwdriver and bottle cap opener. Removable shackle **125.00**

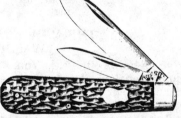

☐**W-S**—(3¼") Stag handle. Brass lining, nickel silver bolster. Two blades, one spear point and one pen. Blades glazed **90.00**

☐**W-6**—(3¼") Stag handle. Brass lining, nickel silver bolsters. Two blades, one spear and one pen. Blades glazed **65.00**

☐**187**—(5½") Large stag shaped handle. Brass lining, nickel silver bolsters. 4½" dirk blade. Lock back. Hole in handle for ring **550.00**

☐**100**—BUDDING KNIVES (3") Stag handle. Nickel silver bolster. Ivory budder. Length over all, 4¾". One blade **75.00**

☐**200**—(3¾") Ivoryshell handle, brass lining. Two-blade office knife **60.00**

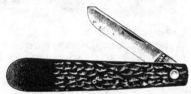

☐**102**—BUDDING KNIVES (4") Stag handle. Brass lining. One blade **100.00**

☐**104**—CORN KNIFE (3¼") Ivoryshell handle. One blade **45.00**

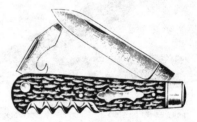

☐**379**—(3½") Stag handle. Brass lining, nickel silver bolster. One spear point blade, bottle cap opener and screwdriver blade, and corkscrew on back **75.00**

☐**127**—(3") Redwood handle . Steel lining and bolster. Nickel plated chain. One spear point blade **45.00**

☐**488**—(3¼") Stag handle. Brass lining, nickel silver bolsters. Has two blades, corkscrew, bottle opener and screwdriver . .**100.00**

☐**1101**—(3¼") Iron handle. Steel lining and bolster. One spear point blade **55.00**

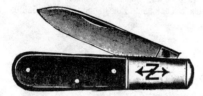

☐**1506**—(3½") Black Bone handle. Barlow pattern; steel lining and bolster. One spear point blade **125.00**

☐**1665**—(4½") Stag handle. Brass lining, nickel silver bolster. 3½" clip blade. Lock back **200.00**

☐**1750**—(3½") Redwood handle. Steel lining and bolster. One spear point blade ...**45.00**

☐**4018**—(4¾") Stag handle. Brass lining, nickel silver bolsters. One spear point blade **450.00**

☐**4225**—(3⅜") Stag handle. Brass lining, nickel silver bolsters. One blade, leather punch, can and bottle opener, screwdriver. Ring in handle **150.00**

☐**40426**—(3½") Genuine Stag handle. Brass lining, nickel silver bolsters. Four blades, two sheep foot and two pens **150.00**

NORMARK COMPANY
MINNEAPOLIS, MINNESOTA

Normark was the originator of the Rapala fishing lure, and from there they began production of Rapala fillet knives, and then into Normark Pocketknives.

The Minneapolis based firm was started by Ron Weber, current president of Normark, and Ray Ostrom, the current secretary-treasurer, in 1959.

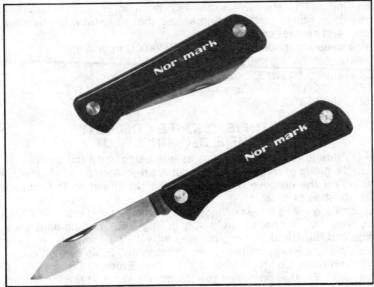

The Normark Big Swede.

The Presentation Big Swede.

Their line of cutlery have expanded much in recent years and now features three single blade folding knives that have movable handles for cleaning, and several sheath knives.

Their knives are made in Finland by Fiskars Corporation.

☐PRESENTATION HUNTING KNIFE **14.95**
☐PRESENTATION "BIG SWEDE" KNIFE **13.95**
☐PRESENTATION "LITTLE SWEDE" KNIFE **8.95**
☐PRESENTATION SWEDE 45 KNIFE **7.50**

NORTHFIELD KNIFE COMPANY
NORTHFIELD, CONNECTICUT

The Northfield Knife Company came into being when the town of Northfield lured a group of former Sheffield cutlers from their jobs in Waterville to Northfield for the purpose of setting up the Northfield Knife Company. It was established in 1858.

The company made an excellent grade of knives, most made by Sheffield cutlers who were recruited while still in England. The company paid for passage and furnished housing on their arrival. The company won awards at seven World's Fairs, including the Chicago and Paris exposition.

Northfield Knife Company was sold to Clark Brothers Cutlery, St. Louis, in 1919. Clark Brothers dropped the Northfield name, stamping the knives made there with their own logo.

The land and buildings were sold to the State of Connecticut. The state tore down the buildings and built a state park on the site.

Northfield at one time purchased many of the smaller knife factories in the area and combined them with Northfield. They bought American Knife Company of Thomaston, Connecticut in 1865. Excelsior Knife Company of Torrington, Connecticut was purchased in 1885. Their exhibition at the Pan American Exposition in 1901 contained over 1,000 different styles of knives.

Clark Brothers sold the company in 1929. (The plant was closed at that time).

NORTHHAMPTON CUTLERY COMPANY
NORTHHAMPTON, NEW YORK

Evolving from the Bay State Hardware Company that had entered cutlery manufacturing in 1868, the Northhampton Cutlery Company had set up a New York selling office by 1882 and set up a plating shop in 1890. Its knives were stamped "Northhampton Cutlery Co. USA.

OAK LEAF
ST. LOUIS, MISSOURI

"Oak Leaf", an E. C. Simmons Hardware brand was used on tools, knives, and other items. The pocketknife line consisted of 60 patterns, and was stamped on the tang with an oak leaf and "Oak Leaf" was etched on the master blade. The stamping was discontinued around 1915.

ONTARIO KNIFE COMPANY
FRANKLINVILLE, NEW YORK

The Ontario Knife Company did not enter the pocketknife business until 1971, only one year after being bought by Servotronics, Inc., although the company has made kitchen cutlery since 1889. The new line consists of 16 patterns and are made by the Queen Cutlery Co., also owned by Servotronics. The new line carry the "Old Hickory Logo."

PAL CUTLERY COMPANY
HOLYOKE, MASSACHUSETTS

Pal originated by the Mailmen Brothers who operated the Utica Drop Forge Tool Company. They sold the company to owners who became Utica Cutlery Company.

When the company sold, the brothers formed PAL Cutlery Company and did extensive government contracts during World War II.

The company for pocket knives was located in Holyoke, Massachusetts and was closed in 1953.

The company purchased the equipment of Remington in 1941.

PARKER KNIVES
CHATTANOOGA, TENNESSEE

Founded in 1975 and owned by James F. Parker, co-author of this book.

☐AMERICAN LOCKBACK WHITTLER, Bone .**45.00**
☐AMERICAN LOCKBACK WHITTLER, Pearl .**80.00**

☐APACHE TEARDROP (3⅞") Lockback, smooth bone **20.95**

☐BEAVERTAIL (3⅛") Smooth bone **20.95**

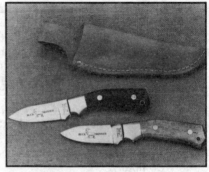

☐BIG CANNITTLER (3¾″) Smooth bone . . . **20.95**

☐BUCKSKINNER (7¼″) Wood **21.95**
☐BUCKSKINNER (7¼″) Bone **24.95**

☐CUB (3⅛″) Smooth bone **18.95**

☐LITTLE CANITTLER (2½″) Smooth bone . **17.95**

☐KING OF THE BEASTS **24.95**

☐SILVER FOX (3⅜″) Surgical steel handles **14.95**

☐SURVIVOR (3¾″) Linen micarta handle. .**14.95**

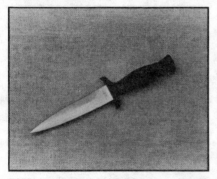

☐SMOKEY MOUNTAIN TOOTHPICK **22.95**

☐VIPER (3⅛″) Stainless steel handle **12.95**

☐K115—(4¼″) **28.95**

☐BUZZTAIL (3¼") **24.95**

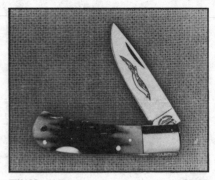

☐**K122**—(4") **27.95**

☐**K124**—(3½") 2 blades **22.95**

☐**K123**—(4") **31.95**

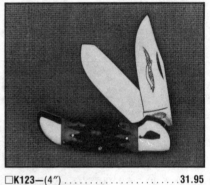

☐**K128**—(3½") **26.95**

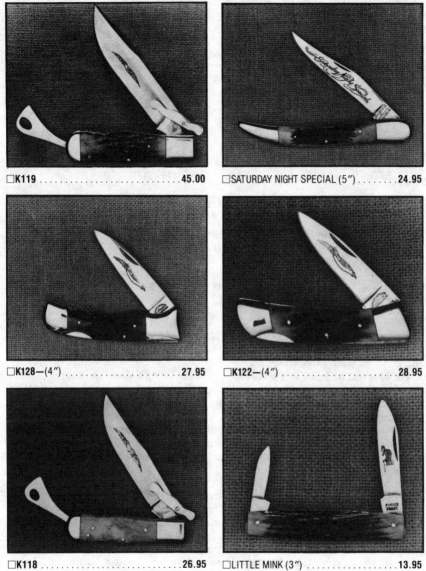

☐K119 . . . . **45.00**

☐SATURDAY NIGHT SPECIAL (5″) **24.95**

☐K128—(4″) **27.95**

☐K122—(4″) **28.95**

☐K118 . . . . **26.95**

☐LITTLE MINK (3″) **13.95**

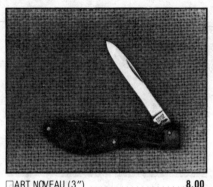

☐HITLER COPY KNIFE (3⅜")............8.00   ☐ART NOVEAU (3") 8.00

PLATTS BROTHERS
ANDOVER, NEW YORK

The Platts Brothers, Andover, New York company was started by Charlie, Joe, and Frank Platts who had sold their shares in C. Platts' Sons Cutlery to their brother H. N. in 1905.

They started the company in 1907, but only operated for a few years.

After the split of the brothers, they each worked in a variety of cutlery companies, including Thomaston, Eureka, W. R. Case and Remington.

PLATTS, C. AND SONS CUTLERY COMPANY
ELDRED, PENNSYLVANIA

Charles Platts began his apprenticeship as a cutler in Sheffield, England in 1854. He was 14 years old.

He worked at both Joseph Rodgers and George Woestenholms Cutlery Companies before leaving for the United States in 1864. Upon his arrival he went to work for the American Cutlery Company in Reynolds Bridge, Connecticut.

Northfield Knife Company hired Platts as superintendent in 1872, where he worked until 1893, when he was hired as superintendent of Cattaraugus. His son H. N. had worked for Cattaraugus for a couple of years, and with his move to Little Valley, New York, all of his sons (most trained cutlers by this time) moved with him. They all began work for Cattaraugus.

With five trained cutlers at his disposal, the idea of a family-owned business could not have been far from Platts' mind, and in 1896 he and his sons started the C. Platts & Sons Cutlery Company in Gowanda, New York making knives in the building that had been vacated when Schatt and Morgan had moved to Titusville, Pennsylvania.

Business boomed, and within a year they had moved to Eldred, Pennsylvania, doing contract work as well as developing their own "Keen Edge" brand.

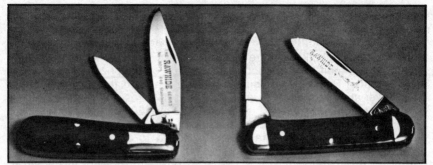

Two new introductions by Queen.
- *Current Collector Value: Wood handled canoe* **$18.00**
-                     *Wood handled barlow* 12.00

As the original foremen passed away, the others bought out their interests, until finally only two of the original families were in the business, the Mathews and Ericsons. Soon after Will Mathews and Ericson decided to begin making their blades of 440C steel. This hard steel has to have the nail mark cut by a milling machine instead of stamped, and the tang hole has to be drilled instead of punched.

At first their knives were stamped "Queen City" until 1945, when it changed to a large Q or a Q with a crown on top. Some of these knives were also stamped "stainless" on the tang, but in that time many consumers considered stainless steel unfit for pocketknife blades and would not buy them. Therefore Queen soon dropped this stamping "stainless", although the knives were still stainless and adopted instead "Queen Steel" to hide the fact that stainless steel was being used.

During the early '60's the company did away with all imprinting on the tang, instead etching "Queen Steel" on the master blade. In 1971 the company began again stamping their knives on the tang, using old dies they had on hand. In 1972, the 50th anniversary of Queen, a new stamping was used, a crown with Q with 1922 on one side and 1972 on the other and the dies were destroyed at the end of 1972.

In 1973, '74 and '75, Queen used a logo of the word Queen in script, Crown over the Q and a long pointed tail extending the length of the word "Queen".

In 1976 the stamping is a large Q with a crown on top, the long tail, and the number 76 over the tail. This was used only during 1976, and in 1977 a new die was made.

Queen still handles knives in genuine pearl (five patterns) although some dealers wait for as much as six months to get these knives. Bone was used in some patterns (the –52 2 blade stockman) up till 1975, but some of the other patterns had delrin handles as much as 10 years ago. The company now handles its knives 100% in delrin. The company also makes knives with slick black, smooth red, and smooth yellow handles.

Queen Cutlery was sold to Servotronics, Inc. in 1969. (This manufacturer of aerospace items, toys, and games also owns the Ontario Knive Company).

The factory still is in Titusville, Pennsylvania and the accounting and sales offices are in Franklinville, New York.

REMINGTON
BRIDGEPORT, CONNECTICUT

Excerpt from **Remington Pocketknives** *by Bruce Voyles, Copyright 1979.*

Remington pocketknives are among today's most collectible pocketknives. Any of their knives found in mint condition are prized possessions, and the Bullet Remington folding hunters are among the best collectors knives ever manufactured.

For a company that was in business a little over 20 years, they produced an enormous amount of knives. One catalog shows over 800 different patterns, and these were constantly being added to or discontinued. One source states that Remington made over 10,000 knives per day, and at the bottom of one catalog it states that the above knives were available in quantities of 25, 50 and 100 dozen per carton. Thus one carton alone might contain 1200 knives. Add to this the fact that every large wholesaler of the time from Belknap on down carried the Remington line and Remington advertised in almost every magazine, and you can then visualize the number of knives they made.

Most of their catalogs have instructions printed in three languages and no doubt there are still plenty of the old Remington knives in Brazil and other parts of South America.

The Story

The history of Remington goes back over 100 years before they entered the cutlery business, when Eliphalet Remington forged his first gun barrel in 1816. The business prospered, but was floundering when Remington died and passed the company on to his sons.

At this point enter Marcellus Hartley, the founder of Union Metallic Cartridge Company (started 1854). Hartley purchased the stock of the company and operated both companies independently of the other. At Hartley's death, his grandson, Marcellus Hartley Dodge, took over both companies. He was 20 years old.

His grandfather had combined the sales departments of both companies, but he wanted to consolidate the company under one name. He did, naming it the Remington Union Metallic Cartridge Company. The UMC. C. was the smaller of the two companies, and since the Remington trademark was better known, he soon dropped the Union Metallic Cartridge tag from the company name.

He did not want the name to be forgotten, and if you will notice most Remingtons will have UMC stamped inside the circle Remington logo. Even today, the U found stamped on the bottom of Remington rimfire ammunition is a remembrance of the Union Company.

The company prospered through World War I, but the war's end found Remington with some large manufacturing facilities but no government contracts. (Remington had made a huge number of bayonets during the war.)

The management decided to make cutlery, and made their first pocketknives, an R103 on February 9, 1920. The company expanded its knives in the 1920's, but with the coming of the depression in 1929 Remington was forced to sell controlling interest to E. I. DuPont Company, and the transaction was completed in 1933.

In the 1930's the government again began buying more war materiel, anticipating the coming global war, and Remington had dropped their pocketknife line completely by the start of World War II.

At the end of World War II the pocketknife line was not introduced and all of the cutlery equipment was sold to Pal Cutlery Company.

Pal also took a fair amount of Remington parts and transitions (knives with tangs stamped of both companies on the knife are not unheard of.)

PATTERN NUMBERS

Almost every Remington knife was stamped with pattern numbers. These were usually stamped on the reverse side of the tang, but sometimes they were inked on the back side of the tang, and on used knives stamped so the numbers will not be visible.

The company used a variety of stamping but the major breakdown of the stamping is the Circle Remington stamping and the straightline stamping. The straightline was the cheaper line, made more for sale as novelty items and little boys' knives. The Circle Remington stamping was usually used on better quality knives.

On the better quality knives the blades usually will be etched, the most common being "Remington, trade mark", "Remington Master Knife". Not quite as common are Remington etched "Great Western", "Remington Cattle Knife" and Remington Premium Stock Knife.

SHIELDS

Remington used a variety of shields, with the Bullet being the most famous. Knives with this shield are always the large hunting patterns. These knives will bring $75 in worn out condition. Another favorite shield with the collector is the acorn, which is usually found on knives having punch blades.

All things considered, Remington is probably the second most popular collector's knife ever made, and considering that Case, who is number one continued making knives for another 35 or 40 years, that says a lot for the type of knife Remington made.

Remington stamped pattern numbers on the reverse side of the tang, using an R before the pattern number to indicate a pocketknife and the last digit indicated the handle material. They were:

1-Redwood	5-Pyremite	9-Metal
2-Black	6-Genuine Stag	0-Buffalo Horn
3-Bone	7-Ivory or White Bone	Ch-after the numbers
4-Pearl	8-Cocobolo	means a chain
		attached

Three stampings were used by Remington: "Remington" stamped horizontally on the tang (this is called a "straightline"), "Remington" inside a circle with "Made in USA" around the outside and UMC also on the inside, and the "Remington" inside a circle with Made in USA around the outside without UMC. The circle was supposed to look like the end of a cartridge.

Remington's most sought after line is the knives with the shield in the shape of a bullet. These knives are scarce and command a top price.

Numbers RI-R2999 are jack knives, R-3000-R5999 are cattle, premium stock, farmers, mechanics and scout knives, and R6000 and R9999 are pen knives. Following are several patterns of Remingtons to be used as a general price guide.

POCKET KNIFE BLADES

| Remington two piece patented can opener | Long screw driver cap lifter | Sheep-foot blade | Spey blade | Budding blade | Spear blade | Sabre spear blade |

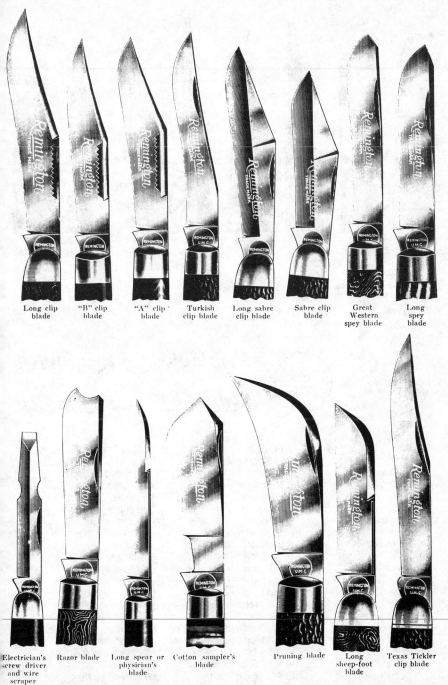

Long clip blade

"B" clip blade

"A" clip blade

Turkish clip blade

Long sabre clip blade

Sabre clip blade

Great Western spey blade

Long spey blade

Electrician's screw driver and wire scraper

Razor blade

Long spear or physician's blade

Cotton sampler's blade

Pruning blade

Long sheep-foot blade

Texas Tickler clip blade

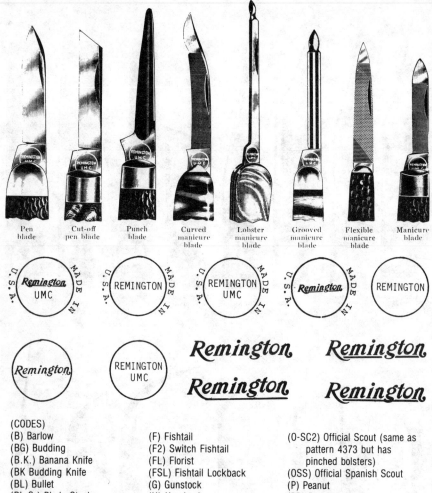

Pen blade | Cut-off pen blade | Punch blade | Curved manicure blade | Lobster manicure blade | Grooved manicure blade | Flexible manicure blade | Manicure blade

(CODES)

(B) Barlow	(F) Fishtail	(0-SC2) Official Scout (same as
(BG) Budding	(F2) Switch Fishtail	pattern 4373 but has
(B.K.) Banana Knife	(FL) Florist	pinched bolsters)
(BK Budding Knife	(FSL) Fishtail Lockback	(OSS) Official Spanish Scout
(BL) Bullet	(G) Gunstock	(P) Peanut
(BL.S.) Blade Stock	(H) Humback	(PR) Pruner
(BR) Bartenders	(H2) Humback 5 Blade	(R.B.) Round Bullet
(BU) Budder	(HA) Hawkbill	(R.S.) Regular Shield
(BG.K) Budding Knife	(L) Lobster	(S) Switch
(C) Cattle	(L.B.) Large Bullet	(SC) Scout
(CO) Congress	(L.C.) Large Cattle	(SS) Spanish Scout
(CO2) Congress 2 Blade	(L.K.) Leg Knife	(ST) Stock
(C.S.) Cotton Sampler	(L.W.) Lockback Whittler	(S.T. Standard Trapper
(D) Dogleg	(LO.W.) Lobster Whittler	(S.T.2) Standard Trapper with
(D.B.) Daddy Barlow	(M) Moose	HTT Shield
(D.G.) Dog Groomer	(MRB) Muskrat Round Bolsters	(T) Teardrop
(D.K.) Doctor's Knife	(MSB) Muskrat Square Blade	(TP) Toothpick
(E) Electrician	(O.G.S.) Official Girl Scout	(T.T.) Texas Toothpick
(E.E.) Equal End	(O.K.) Offician Knife	(W) Whittler
(E.O.) Easy Open	(O-SC) Official Scout	(W.B.) Worked Back

PATTERN NUMBERS THAT ARE UNNAMED ARE EITHER ONE OF THE FOLLOWING: JACKS, STOCKS, CATTLES OR PEN KNIVES.

PATTERN NO.	MINT PRICE	PATTERN NO.		MINT PRICE	PATTERN NO.		MINT PRICE
R-1	60.00	R-105		125.00	R-223	(T)	190.00
R-2	60.00	R-105A		125.00	R-225	(T)	160.00
R-2	75.00	R-105B		125.00	R-228	(T)	140.00
R-01	60.00	R-108ch		120.00	R-232	(T)	140.00
R-02	60.00	R-111		100.00	R-233	(T)	210.00
R-03	75.00	R-112		100.00	R-235	(T)	175.00
R-A1	60.00	R-113		135.00	R-238	(T)	140.00
R-C5	60.00	R-115		115.00	R-242	(E.O.)	185.00
R-C6	60.00	R-122		120.00	R-243	(E.O.)	220.00
R-C7	55.00	R-123		160.00	R-245	(E.O.)	185.00
R-C8	55.00	R-125		140.00	R-248	(E.O.)	160.00
R-C9	55.00	R-131		120.00	R-252	(T)	150.00
R-15 (L.K.)	100.00	R-132		120.00	R-253	(T)	200.00
R-015	75.00	R-133		160.00	R-255	(T)	175.00
R-17	45.00	R-135		140.00	R-258	(T)	150.00
R-21	80.00	R-141		120.00	R-262		125.00
R-21ch	100.00	R-142		120.00	R-263		175.00
R-22	80.00	R-143		160.00	R-265		150.00
R-23	100.00	R-145		140.00	R-272		140.00
		R-151		120.00	R-273		200.00
		R-152		120.00	R-275		160.00
		R-153		160.00	R-282		125.00
		R-155		140.00	R-283		185.00
R-23ch	110.00	R-155B		140.00	R-293	(S.T.)	250.00
R-25	80.00	R-155M		140.00	R-293	(S.T.2)	350.00
R-31	80.00	R-155Z		140.00	R-293	(L.B.)	1500.00
R-32	80.00	R-161		120.00	R-303		135.00
R-33	100.00	R-162		120.00	R-305		110.00
R-35	100.00	R-163		160.00	R-313		200.00
R-B040 (B)	75.00	R-165		140.00	R-315		125.00
R-041 (B)	74.00	R-171	(T)	140.00	R-322		160.00
R-B43 (B)	100.00	R-172	(T)	140.00	R-323		200.00
R-B44 (B)	100.00	R-173	(T)	200.00	R-325		175.00
R-B45 (B)	130.00	R-175	(T)	160.00	R-328		160.00
R-B44W (B)	75.00	R-181	(T)	160.00	R-333		175.00
R-B46 (B)	90.00	R-182	(T)	160.00	R-341		175.00
R-B47 (B)	130.00	R-183	(T)	200.00	R-342		175.00
R-51	80.00	R-185	(T)	165.00	R-343		225.00
R-71	75.00	R-191	(T)	150.00	R-352		150.00
R-72	85.00	R-192	(T)	150.00	R-353		200.00
R-73	110.00	R-193	(T)	200.00	R-355		175.00
R-75	95.00	R-195	(T)	175.00	R-358		150.00
R-81	75.00	R-201	(E.O.)	160.00	R-363		225.00
R-82	85.00	R-202	(E.O.)	160.00	R-365		175.00
R-83	110.00	R-203	(E.O.)	200.00	R-365		175.00
R-85	95.00	R-205	(E.O.)	180.00	R-372		160.00
R-C090	70.00	R-211	(E.O.)	150.00	R-373		200.00
R-C091	70.00	R-212	(E.O.)	150.00	R-375		180.00
R-91	100.00	R-213	(E.O.)	200.00	R-378		160.00
R-103	145.00	R-219	(E.O.)	100.00	R-383		200.00
R-103ch	160.00	R-222	(T)	140.00	R-391	(T)	135.00

PATTERN NO.		MINT PRICE	PATTERN NO.		MINT PRICE	PATTERN NO.		MINT PRICE
R-392	(T)	135.00	R-622		110.00	R-825		125.00
R-393	(T)	175.00	R-623		125.00	R-833		100.00
R-395	(T)	145.00	R-625		110.00	R-835		80.00
R-402	(E.O.)	150.00	R-633		100.00	R-843		100.00
R-403	(E.O.)	200.00	R-635		100.00	R-845		80.00
R-405	(E.O.)	175.00	R-635		130.00	R-853		100.00
R-410		150.00	R-643	(F)	135.00	R-855		80.00
R-412	(E.O.)	150.00	R-645	(F)	85.00	R-863		200.00
R-413	(E.O.)	200.00	R-645	(F2)	200.00	R-865		175.00
R-415	(E.O.)	175.00	R-653	(F)	150.00	R-873		80.00
R-423		140.00	R-655	(F)	85.00	R-874		80.00
R-432	(D.K.)	125.00	R-655	(S)	225.00	R-875		80.00
R-433	(D.K.)	165.00	R-662		250.00	R-881		100.00
R-435	(D.K.)	125.00	R-663		350.00	R-882		100.00
R-443	(D.K.)	175.00	R-668		300.00	R-883		135.00
R-444	(D.K.)	225.00	R-672	(D)	85.00	R-892	(E.O.)	150.00
R-453	(D.K.)	225.00	R-673	(D)	110.00	R-893	(E.O.)	200.00
R-455	(D.K.)	165.00	R-674	(D)	200.00	R-895	(E.O.)	175.00
R-463		150.00	R-675	(D)	85.00	R-901		145.00
R-465		125.00	R-677		85.00	R-913		225.00
R-473		165.00	R-679	(D)	85.00	R-921		80.00
R-475		125.00	R-682	(G)	200.00	R-932	(T.T.)	250.00
R-482		125.00	R-683	(G)	275.00	R-933	(T.T.)	225.00
R-483		160.00	R-684	(G)	325.00	R-935	(T.T.)	300.00
R-485		125.00	R-685	(G)	200.00	R-942	(T.T.)	250.00
R-488		125.00	R-693	(HA)	85.00	R-943	(T.T.)	300.00
R-493		165.00	R-698	(HA)	60.00	R-945	(T.T.)	250.00
R-495		125.00	R-703	(HA)	80.00	R-C953	(T.T.)	175.00
R-503		160.00	R-706	(HA)	60.00			
R-505		125.00	R-708	(HA)	60.00			
R-512		135.00	R-713	(HA)	125.00			
R-513		175.00	R-718	(HA)	100.00			
R-515		135.00	R-723	(HA)	110.00			
R-523		200.00	R-728	(HA)	85.00	R-953	(T.T.)	175.00
R-525		160.00	R-732		120.00	R-955	(T.T.)	200.00
R-551		125.00	R-733		160.00	R-962	(E.O.)	175.00
R-552		125.00	R-735		140.00	R-963	(E.O.)	225.00
R-553		160.00	R-738		120.00	R-965	(E.O.)	150.00
R-555		125.00	R-743		160.00	R-971	(C.S.)	125.00
R-563		150.00	R-745		140.00	R-982	(D)	65.00
R-572		125.00	R-753		160.00	R-983	(D)	100.00
R-573		160.00	R-755		140.00	R-985	(D)	65.00
R-575		125.00	R-756		130.00	R-992		80.00
R-583		150.00	R-763		160.00	R-993		110.00
R-585		125.00	R-772	(T)	165.00	R-995		80.00
R-590		150.00	R-773	(T)	200.00	R-1002		85.00
R-593		175.00	R-775	(T)	165.00	R-1003		125.00
R-595		150.00	R-783	(T)	200.00	R-1005		85.00
R-603		160.00	R-793		225.00	R-1012		150.00
R-605		135.00	R-803		100.00	R-1013		165.00
R-605		135.00	R-805		100.00	R-1022		250.00
R-609		150.00	R-C803		50.00	R-1023		300.00
R-613		200.00	R-813		225.00	R-1032		80.00
R-615		95.00	R-823		160.00	R-1033		125.00

PATTERN NO.	MINT PRICE	PATTERN NO.	MINT PRICE	PATTERN NO.	MINT PRICE
R-1035	80.00	R-1222	250.00	R-1409	100.00
R-1042	100.00	R-1223	175.00	R-1413	100.00
R-1043	135.00	R-1225W (L.C.)	175.00	R-1423	110.00
R-1045	100.00	R-1232	150.00	R-1437	130.00
R-1051	75.00	R-1233	190.00	R-1447	130.00
R-1053	90.00	R-1240 (D.B.)	200.00	R-1457	150.00
R-1055	90.00	R-1241 (D.B.)	200.00	R-1465 (BU)	160.00
R-1061	80.00	R-1242 (D.B.)	250.00	R-1477	130.00
R-1062	80.00	R-1243 (D.B.)	250.00	R-1483	130.00
R-1063	110.00			R-1485	110.00
R-1065W	80.00			R-1493	130.00
R-1071	80.00			R-1495	110.00
R-1072	80.00			R-1535 (FL)	100.00
R-1073	100.00			R-1545	100.00
R-1075	80.00			R-1555	130.00
R-1082	65.00	R-1253 (BL)	1000.00	R-1568	120.00
R-1083	85.00			R-1572	90.00
R-1085	60.00			R-1573	90.00
R-1092	65.00			R-1573ch	110.00
R-1093	85.00			R-1582	90.00
R-1102	75.00			R-1592	100.00
R-1103	100.00			R-1593	100.00
R-1112	75.00			R-1595	100.00
R-1113	110.00			R-1608 (B.K.)	50.00

PATTERN NO.	MINT PRICE
R-1263 (BL)	1200.00
R-1273 (BL)	2000.00
R-1283	80.00
R-1284	200.00
R-1285	75.00
R-1293	150.00
R-1295 (TP)	225.00
R-1303 (BL)	1200.00

PATTERN NO.	MINT PRICE
R-1613 (BL)	1500.00
R-1615	250.00
R-1615 (R.B.)	600.00
R-1622	100.00
R-1623	110.00
R-1623ch	115.00
R-1630L (D.B.)	350.00
R-1643	125.00
R-1644	200.00
R-1645	95.00
R-1653 (P)	125.00
R-1655	100.00
R-1668	150.00
R-1671 (BK)	70.00
R-1673 (BK)	90.00
R-1685	100.00
R-1687	100.00
R-1688 (BK)	100.00
R-1697 (BK)	100.00
R-1707 (BK)	100.00
R-1715 (BK)	70.00
R-1717 (BK)	100.00
R-1723	140.00
R-1751	85.00
R-1752	85.00
R-1753	100.00
R-1755	85.00
R-1763	125.00
R-1772	120.00
R-1773	125.00

PATTERN NO.	MINT PRICE
R-1123 (BL)	700.00
R-1128 (BL)	1400.00
R-1133	160.00
R-1143	165.00
R-1153	200.00
R-1163	200.00

PATTERN NO.	MINT PRICE
R-1306 (BL)	1000.00
R-1315	150.00
R-1323 (D)	90.00
R-1324 (D)	150.00
R-1325 (D)	80.00
R-1333	150.00
R-1343	200.00
R-1353	125.00
R-1363	150.00
R-1373	300.00
R-1379	85.00
R-1383	125.00
R-1383 (FSL)	200.00
R-1389	85.00
R-1399	85.00

PATTERN NO.	MINT PRICE
R-1173 (BL)	1500.00
R-1182	125.00
R-1183	170.00
R-1192	100.00
R-1193	120.00
R-1202	135.00
R-1203	150.00
R-1212	150.00
R-1213	250.00

PATTERN NO.	MINT PRICE	PATTERN NO.	MINT PRICE	PATTERN NO.	MINT PRICE
R-1782	110.00	R-3050Buf (ST)	225.00	R-3265	225.00
R-1783	125.00	R-3053 (ST)	190.00	R-3273 (C)	275.00
R-1785	100.00	R-3054 (ST)	300.00	R-3274 (C)	375.00
R-1803	100.00	R-3055 (ST)	200.00	R-3275 (C)	250.00
R-1823	110.00	R-3056 (ST)	300.00	R-3283	225.00
R-1825	125.00	R-3059 (ST)	200.00	R-3285	200.00
R-1833	140.00	R-3062 (ST)	200.00	R-3293	240.00
R-1853	90.00	R-3063 (ST)	250.00	R-3295	215.00
R-1855M	70.00	R-3064 (ST)	400.00	R-3302	375.00
R-1863	110.00	R-3065B (ST)	200.00	R-3303	375.00
R-1873	100.00	R-3065M (ST)	200.00	R-3305d	300.00
R-1882B	90.00	R-3065R (ST)	200.00	R-3312	300.00
R-1903	85.00	R-3070	250.00	R-3313	400.00
R-1905	80.00	R-3073	225.00	R-3315B	350.00
R-1913	120.00	R-3075	200.00	R-3322 (SC)	125.00
R-1915	100.00	R-3083 (ST)	250.00	R-S3333 (O-SC)	150.00
R-1962	100.00	R-3085 (ST)	200.00	R-3333 (SC)	125.00
R-1973 (E)	125.00	R-3093 (ST)	250.00	R-3335	150.00
R-1995 (BG)	110.00	R-3095 (ST)	175.00	R-3352	175.00
R-2043	65.00	R-3103 (ST)	200.00	R-3353	225.00
R-2045	65.00	R-3105 (ST)	175.00	R-3363	225.00
R-2053	65.00	R-3113	175.00	R-3372	150.00
R-2055	60.00	R-3115G	150.00	R-3373	200.00
R-2063	60.00	R-3115IW	150.00	R-3375	175.00
R-2065	55.00	R-3123 (M)	200.00	R-3382	175.00
R-2073	65.00	R-3133	325.00	R-3383	225.00
R-2075	55.00	R-3143 (BL.S.)	1000.00	R-3385S	200.00
R-2083	65.00	R-3153 (C)	225.00	R-3393	200.00
R-2085	55.00	R-3155 (C)	175.00	R-3395T	175.00
R-2093	75.00	R-3155b (C)	175.00	R-3403	250.00
R-2093	75.00	R-P (C)	175.00	R-3405J	225.00
R-2095	60.00	R-3163 (C)	225.00	R-3413	165.00
R-2103	75.00	R-3165T (C)	150.00	R-3414	300.00
R-2105MW	60.00	R-3173 (C)	225.00	R-3415	140.00
R-2111(elec) (E)	70.00	R-3183 (C)	225.00	R-3415H	140.00
R-2203	100.00	R-3185 (C)	150.00	R-3423	225.00
R-2205D	60.00	R-3193	225.00	R-3424 (W)	325.00
R-2213	60.00	R-3202	200.00	R-3425P (W)	165.00
R-2215M	60.00	R-3203	225.00	R-3432	140.00
R-2223	60.00	R-3212	200.00	R-3433	160.00
R-2303 (S)	250.00	R-3213	300.00	R-3435	140.00
R-2403 (S)	350.00	R-3215	250.00	R-3442	150.00
R-2503	60.00	R-3222	200.00	R-3443	160.00
R-2505B	60.00	R-3223	250.00	R-3445B	130.00
R-2505M	60.00	R-3225	225.00	R-3453 (W)	200.00
R-2505R	60.00	R-3232	200.00	R-3455 (W)	175.00
R-2603	65.00	R-3233	275.00	R-3463 (W)	275.00
R-2605B	65.00	R-3235	240.00	R-3465B (W)	225.00
R-3003	225.00	R-3242	275.00	R-3475K (W)	200.00
R-3005	185.00	R-3243	225.00	R-3475G (W)	200.00
R-3013	225.00	R-3245	250.00	R-3480	160.00
R-3015	185.00	R-3253	250.00	R-3483	190.00
R-3033	225.00	R-3255	225.00	R-3484	300.00
R-3035	185.00	R-3263	250.00	R-3485J	160.00

PATTERN NO.	MINT PRICE
R-3489	140.00
R-3493	175.00
R-3494	300.00
R-3495M	150.00
R-3499	130.00
R-3500	125.00
R-3503	165.00
R-3504	300.00
R-3505	125.00
R-3513 (W)	175.00
R-3514 (W)	300.00
R-3515 (W)	140.00
R-3520 (W)	135.00
R-3523 (W)	165.00
R-3524 (W)	300.00
R-3525 (W)	125.00
R-3533	170.00
R-3535	125.00
R-3545	140.00
R-3553 (ST)	225.00
R-3554 (ST)	350.00
R-3555G (ST)	200.00
R-3555IW (ST)	200.00
R-3563 (ST)	225.00
R-3565D (ST)	200.00
R-3573 (W)	145.00
R-3575	130.00
R-3580	130.00
R-3583	145.00
R-3585	130.00
R-3593	325.00
R-3595	300.00
R-3596	375.00
R-3600	125.00
R-3603	140.00
R-3604	250.00
R-3605	125.00
R-3613	140.00
R-3615	130.00
R-3620	130.00
R-3623	160.00
R-3625	135.00
R-3633	150.00
R-3635	135.00
R-3643	150.00
R-3644	225.00
R-3645	135.00
R-3653	160.00
R-3655	150.00
R-3665	300.00
R-3675	300.00
R-3683	225.00
R-3685	175.00
R-3693 (W)	500.00

PATTERN NO.	MINT PRICE
R-3695G	400.00
R-3700Buf	185.00
R-3703	200.00
R-3704	375.00
R-3705	185.00
R-3710Buf	200.00
R-3713	225.00
R-3714	375.00
R-3715F	185.00
R-3722 (W)	300.00
R-3723 (W)	500.00
R-3725	350.00
R-3732	350.00
R-3733	400.00
R-3735	350.00

PATTERN NO.	MINT PRICE
R-3843 (SC)	170.00
R-3853 (PR)	225.00
R-3855	200.00
R-3858	200.00
R-3863 (SC)	125.00
R-3870 (ST)	225.00
R-3873 (ST)	200.00
R-3874 (ST)	300.00
R-3875A (ST)	175.00
R-3883	200.00
R-3885	185.00
R-3893	140.00
R-3895	125.00
R-3903 (M)	140.00
R-3926	225.00
R-3932 (W)	425.00
R-3933 (W)	500.00
R-3935	425.00
R-3952	175.00
R-3953	225.00
R-3955	200.00
R-3962	165.00
R-3963	200.00
R-3965	165.00
R-3973 (ST)	200.00
R-3975 (ST)	175.00
R-3983 (W)	160.00
R-3985 (W)	125.00
R-3993 (ST)	200.00
R-3995 (ST)	160.00

PATTERN NO.	MINT PRICE
R-4003	165.00
R-4005	135.00
R-4013 (M)	200.00
R-4015 (M)	160.00
R-4023	160.00
R-4025	130.00
R-4033	125.00
R-4035	90.00
R-4043	160.00
R-4045	135.00
R-4053	165.00
R-4055	135.00
R-4063	175.00
R-4065	140.00
R-4073	175.00
R-4075	160.00
R-4083	175.00
R-4085	150.00
R-4093	165.00
R-4095	150.00
R-4103	150.00
R-4105	125.00
R-4113 (ST)	200.00
R-4114 (ST)	350.00
R-4123 (ST)	300.00
R-4124 (ST)	350.00
R-4133	160.00
R-4134	225.00
R-4135	165.00
R-4143	100.00
R-4144	250.00
R-4145	85.00
R-4163	175.00
R-4173	175.00
R-4175	175.00
R-4200	225.00
R-4203	175.00
R-4213	250.00
R-4223 (C)	175.00
R-4225	150.00
R-4233 (SC)	125.00
R-S4233 (0-SC2)	180.00
R-4234 (SC)	250.00

PATTERN NO.	MINT PRICE
R-4235 (SC)	175.00

PATTERN NO.	MINT PRICE

Pattern No.		Mint Price
R-4243	(BL)	800.00
R-4253		200.00
R-4263	(H)	300.00
R-4273	(H)	350.00
R-4274	(H)	200.00
R-4283	(H2)	1500.00
R-4293		125.00
R-4303		125.00
R-4313		175.00
R-4323	(O.G.S.)	75.00
R-4323	(ST)	250.00
R-4334	(BR)	200.00
R-4336	(BR)	175.00
R-4343		200.00
R-4345		250.00
R-4353	(R.G.)	1000.00

Pattern No.		Mint Price
R-4353	(BL)	1400.00
R-4363		300.00
R-4365		300.00
R-4373	(O.G.S.)	175.00
R-4375		150.00
R-4383		150.00
R-4384		325.00
R-4394		300.00
R-4403		125.00
R-4405		95.00
R-4413		140.00
R-4423		150.00
R-4425		130.00
R-4433	(W)	225.00
R-4443		125.00

Pattern No.		Mint Price
R-4466	(BL)	1800.00
R-4473		120.00
R-4483	(C)	250.00
R-4493		200.00
R-4495		100.00

PATTERN NO.		MINT PRICE
R-4495		150.00
R-4505		140.00
R-4506		200.00
R-4513		300.00
R-4523	(OSS)	200.00
R-4533	(SS)	200.00

Pattern No.		Mint Price
R-4548	(E)	120.00
R-4555		200.00
R-4563		170.00
R-4573		200.00
R-4583		175.00
R-4593	(MSB)	200.00
R-4593	(MRB)	225.00
R-4603		165.00
R-4605		130.00
R-4613		150.00
R-4623	(W)	175.00
R-4625	(W)	170.00
R-4633		100.00
R-4635G		95.00
R-4643		140.00
R-4679		115.00
R-4683		165.00
R-4685		135.00
R-4695		225.00
R-4702		130.00
R-4703	(M)	175.00
R-4713		150.00
R-4723	(O.G.S.)	75.00
R-4733	(D.G.)	175.00
R-4783	(SC)	150.00
R-4813		125.00
R-4815		100.00
R-4823		90.00
R-4825		90.00
R-4833		85.00
R-4835		85.00
R-4843		80.00
R-4845		80.00
R-4853		90.00
R-4855		85.00
R-4863		85.00
R-4865		80.00
R-6013		160.00
R-6014		225.00
R-6015		125.00
R-6023	(W)	200.00
R-6024	(W)	300.00

PATTERN NO.		MINT PRICE
R-6025		160.00
R-6032	(CO)	250.00
R-6033	(CO)	250.00
R-6034	(CO)	500.00
R-6043	(CO)	250.00
R-6053	(CO)	250.00
R-6063	(CO)	185.00
R-6073	(CO)	200.00
R-6083	(CO)	200.00
R-6093	(CO2)	125.00
R-6103		100.00
R-6104		175.00
R-6105		80.00
R-6113	(CO)	225.00
R-6123	(CO)	135.00
R-6133	(W)	250.00
R-6143		100.00
R-6145		80.00
R-6153		100.00
R-6155		75.00
R-6163		125.00
R-6175W	(O.K.)	100.00
R-6182		70.00
R-6183		90.00
R-6184		150.00
R-6185		90.00
R-6192		100.00
R-6193		125.00
R-6194		175.00
R-6195		100.00
R-6203		90.00
R-6204		160.00
R-6205		75.00
R-6213	(W)	125.00
R-6214		200.00
R-6515		100.00
R-6223	(W)	125.00
R-6224	(W)	175.00
R-6225	(W)	100.00
R-6233		125.00
R-6234		200.00
R-6235		100.00
R-6243	(L)	90.00
R-6244	(L)	100.00
R-6245	(L)	75.00
R-6249		65.00
R-6255	(L)	60.00
R-6259	(L)	60.00
R-6265	(W)	150.00
R-6275	(W)	350.00
R-6285	(W)	350.00
R-6295	(W)	350.00
R-6303		100.00
R-6313	(W)	225.00

PATTERN NO.	MINT PRICE	PATTERN NO.	MINT PRICE	PATTERN NO.	MINT PRICE
R-6323 (W)	225.00	R-6519	90.00	R-6733 (E.E.)	125.00
R-6325 (W)	190.00	R-6520 (W)	150.00	R-6735 (E.E.)	80.00
R-6330 (W)	125.00	R-6523 (W)	130.00	R-6744	90.00
R-6333 (W)	125.00	R-6524 (W)	225.00	R-6745F	90.00
R-6334 (W)	125.00	R-6533 (W)	230.00	R-6754 (W)	190.00
R-6335 (W)	170.00	R-6534 (W)	130.00	R-6755A (W)	135.00
R-6340Buf (W)	175.00	R-6535 (W)	130.00	R-6763 (W)	165.00
R-6340 (W)	175.00	R-6542	145.00	R-6764 (W)	275.00
R-6343 (W)	225.00	R-6543	200.00	R-6765A (W)	160.00
R-6344 (W)	325.00	R-6545	135.00	R-6773 (W)	250.00
R-6345T (W)	175.00	R-6554 (L)	65.00	R-6775 (W)	100.00
R-6350 (W)	200.00	R-6559	90.00	R-6781	100.00
R-6353 (W)	235.00	R-6563	100.00	R-6785 (O.K.)	100.00
R-6355G (W)	235.00	R-6565	90.00	R-6793	100.00
R-6362	90.00	R-6573	100.00	R-6795	85.00
R-6363	125.00	R-6575	75.00	R-6803 (W)	160.00
R-6365A (W)	90.00	R-6583	100.00	R-6805 (W)	160.00
R-6390 (W)	135.00	R-6585	80.00	R-6816 (L.W.)	1000.00
R-6393 (W)	275.00	R-6585	75.00	R-6823 (W)	400.00
R-6394 (W)	325.00	R-6593 (W)	135.00	R-6825 (W)	300.00
R-6395G (W)	135.00	R-6595 (W)	100.00	R-6834 (W)	500.00
R-6400 (W)	125.00	R-6603 (W)	125.00	R-6835 (W)	250.00
R-6403 (W)	125.00	R-6604 (W)	200.00	R-6836 (W)	300.00
R-6404 (W)	325.00	R-6605 (W)	100.00	R-6835	250.00
R-6405 (W)	175.00	R-6613 (W)	150.00	R-6843	50.00
R-6423	75.00	R-6615	125.00	R-6844	65.00
R-6424	100.00	R-6623	90.00	R-6845	40.00
R-6429	65.00	R-6624	160.00	R-6854	65.00
R-6433	75.00	R-6625	80.00	R-6859	50.00
R-6434	100.00	R-6633	90.00	R-6863	45.00
R-6439	65.00	R-6634	100.00	R-6864	60.00
R-6443	80.00	R-6635	90.00	R-6865	40.00
R-6444	90.00	R-6643	110.00	R-6872	40.00
R-6445	55.00	R-6644	160.00	R-6873	55.00
R-6448	55.00	R-6645	80.00	R-6874	100.00
R-6454 (L.W.)	165.00	R-6653	100.00	R-6875	40.00
R-6456 (L.W.)	140.00	R-6654	175.00	R-6883	160.00
R-6463	70.00	R-6655	85.00	R-6885	125.00
R-6464	90.00	R-6663	100.00	R-6893 (W)	185.00
R-6465	60.00	R-6664	200.00	R-6894 (W)	250.00
R-6463	75.00	R-6673 (CO)	124.00	R-6895 (W)	150.00
R-6464	120.00	R-6674 (CO)	250.00	R-6903	40.00
R-6465	75.00	R-6683 (CO)	130.00	R-6904	50.00
R-6473	90.00	R-6693 (CO)	175.00	R-6905	35.00
R-6474	120.00	R-6694 (CO)	225.00	R-6905	35.00
R-6483	100.00	R-6695 (CO)	125.00	R-6914	75.00
R-6484	100.00	R-6703	130.00	R-6919	40.00
R-6494	95.00	R-6704	175.00	R-6923	125.00
R-6495	55.00	R-6705Q	100.00	R-6924	175.00
R-6499	60.00	R-6713	130.00	R-6925	65.00
R-6504	100.00	R-6714	170.00	R-6933 (CO)	165.00
R-6505	65.00	R-6723 (W)	175.00	R-6934 (CO)	225.00
R-6513	75.00	R-6724 (W)	300.00	R-6949	75.00
R-6514	120.00	R-6725F (W)	125.00	R-6954 (W)	260.00

PATTERN NO.		MINT PRICE	PATTERN NO.	MINT PRICE	PATTERN NO.		MINT PRICE
R-6956	(W)	175.00	R-7090	100.00	R-7363		100.00
R-6964	(W)	240.00	R-7091	100.00	R-7364	(L)	140.00
R-6966	(W)	165.00	R-7094	100.00	R-7366		90.00
R-6973		200.00	R-G7099/1	100.00	R-7374		90.00
R-6974		400.00	R-/2	100.00	R-7375		90.00
R-6984	(W.B.)	550.00	R-/3	100.00	R-7384		90.00
R-6993		170.00	R-/4	100.00	R-7394	(L)	100.00
R-6994		250.00	R-/29	100.00	R-7396		60.00
R-6995		160.00	R-/30	100.00	R-7403		75.00
R-7003	(W)	250.00	R-/31	100.00	R-7404		110.00
R-7004	(W)	300.00	R-T7099	90.00	R-7414		110.00
R-7005	(W)	200.00	R-7103	75.00	R-7423		60.00
R-7023	(W)	100.00	R-7104	90.00	R-7425		95.00
R-7024	(W)	200.00	R-7114	(W)	100.00	R-7433	(W)	150.00
R-7026	(W)	100.00	R-7116	(W)	75.00	R-7443		70.00
R-7034	(W)	100.00	R-7120	80.00	R-7453		65.00
R-7044		75.00	R-7124	165.00	R-7463		75.00
R-7045		60.00	R-7126	100.00	R-7465		70.00
R-7039/5		75.00	R-7134	165.00	R-7473		75.00
R-/6		75.00	R-7144	250.00	R-7475		70.00
R-/7		75.00	R-7146	175.00	R-7483	(W)	200.00
R-/8		75.00	R-7153	150.00	R-7485	(W)	200.00
R-7044		90.00	R-7163	140.00	R-7493	(W)	310.00
R-G7049/21		75.00	R-7176	175.00	R-7495	(W)	275.00
R-/22		75.00	R-7183	(W)	250.00	R-7500Buf	(W)	130.00
R-/23		75.00	R-7196	(W)	225.00	R-7503	(W)	110.00
R-/24		75.00	R-7203	(W)	275.00	R-7513	(W)	160.00
R-G7054		90.00	R-7216	275.00	R-7526		120.00
R-G7059/17		75.00	R-7223	150.00	R-7536		110.00
R-/18		75.00	R-7224	200.00	R-7543		55.00
R-/19		75.00	R-7225	140.00	R-7544		80.00
R-/20		75.00	R-7233	80.00	R-7546		65.00
R-/39		75.00	R-7234	90.00	R-7554		100.00
R-/40		75.00	R-7236	75.00	R-7564		100.00
R-7064		75.00	R-7243	(W)	125.00	R-7566		65.00
R-7069/25		75.00	R-7244	(W)	300.00	R-7573		65.00
R-/26		75.00	R-7246	(W)	200.00	R-7574		90.00
R-/27		75.00	R-7254	80.00	R-7576		70.00
R-/28		75.00	R-7264	75.00	R-7584	(W)	200.00
R-7074		90.00	R-7274	75.00	R-7586	(W)	150.00
R-G7079/10		75.00	R-7284	(L)	80.00	R-7593		100.00
R-/11		75.00	R-7293	(W)	200.00	R-7594		175.00
R-/12		75.00	R-7284	100.00	R-7596		125.00
R-/35		75.00	R-7284-6	100.00	R-7603		100.00
R-/36		75.00	R-7293	(W)	200.00	R-7604		175.00
R-/37		75.00	R-7309	75.00	R-7606		150.00
R-7084		90.00	R-7319	75.00	R-7613		75.00
R-G7089/13		75.00	R-7324	90.00	R-7614		75.00
R-/14		75.00	R-7329	55.00	R-7623		70.00
R-/15		75.00	R-7335	40.00	R-7624		90.00
R-/16		75.00	R-7339	40.00	R-7633	(W)	160.00
R-/32		75.00	R-7343	65.00	R-7643		75.00
R-/33		75.00	R-7344	65.00	R-7645		75.00
R-/34		75.00	R-7353	80.00	R-7653	(W)	170.00

PATTERN NO.	MINT PRICE	PATTERN NO.	MINT PRICE	PATTERN NO.	MINT PRICE
R-7654 (W)	210.00	R-7785	120.00	R-7985	90.00
R-7663 (W)	175.00	R-7793	70.00	R-7993 (BR)	60.00
R-7664 (W)	250.00	R-7795	75.00	R-7995 (BR)	65.00
R-7674	75.00	R-7803	130.00	R-8003	65.00
R-7683	60.00	R-7805	150.00	R-8004	70.00
R-7684	90.00	R-7813	75.00	R-8013	55.00
R-7696 (W)	150.00	R-7814	110.00	R-8023 (W)	125.00
R-7706	80.00	R-7823	90.00	R-8039 (BR)	60.00
R-7713	55.00	R-7825	90.00	R-8044 (L)	90.00
R-7725 (BU.K)	55.00	R-7833	225.00	R-8055 (S)	100.00
R-7734	70.00	R-7853	60.00	R-8059 (BR)	60.00
R-7744	70.00	R-C7853	75.00	R-8063 (S)	150.00
R-7756	500.00	R-7854	60.00	R-8065 (S)	120.00
R-7766	500.00	R-7857	75.00	R-8069 (S)	120.00
R-7772	50.00	R-7863	75.00	R-9003ss	150.00
R-7773	60.00	R-7873	75.00		
R-7775	65.00	R-7895	60.00		
R-7783 (W)	90.00	R-7925	50.00		

ROBESON
PERRY, NEW YORK

Millard F. Robeson founded his factory in 1894, when he began making knives with 30 employees in Camillus, New York. He had been a cutlery salesman prior to this.

The following year, he bought into Rodchester Stamping Works, it becoming Robeson Rodchester Corporation. Five years later the business moved to Perry, New York.

In 1903, Robeson died, and the company went downhill until 1940, when Saul Frankel bought the bankrupt company.

The first thing he did was hire Emerson Case as general manager (see Case Family companies) who did such a good job that he was elected president in 1948.

Robeson was sold to Cutler Federal, Inc. in 1964, and the following year Case retired. Upon Case's retirement the company quit making their own knives, with Camillus making the knives on contract and the shipping continuing through the Perry offices.

In 1971 the Ontario Knife Company bought Robeson and made Robeson knives until 1977, when the trademark was dropped.

One of the most famous stampings of Robeson was the "Robeson Suredge Rochester." A popular line of Robeson knives among the collectors is the Pockeze line, identified by the "pocketeze" shield. Registered in 1914, this trademark meant that the backs of the blades were recessed below the handles of the knives, making them easy on the pocket.

Mastercraft was also a Robeson brand, also identified by the Mastercraft shield.

Some knives will be encountered with "Frozen Heat" etched on the blades; this process was developed in 1950 by Emerson Case.

Robeson knives will be found with a plastic coating on the blades. This was used on all knives wired to display boards to prevent rust. It was not used on regular production knives.

Robeson's older knives will be handled in green bone, followed later in brown bone, and the most recent bone they used was their famous strawberry bone. The strawberry bone is the reddest bone of any in knife collecting, and it makes one of the nicest cutlery handles. In the 1950's this bone handle was dropped in favor of a plastic handle the same color. The last Robeson knives had a darker delrin blade.

In their heyday Robeson also handled knives in Mother of Pearl, Genuine Stag, and the various composition handle materials. During World War II they were forced to use Rough Black handle material, due to the short supply of bone. Some Robeson knives will be found with a German stamping. These knives were made on contract in Germany.

The Robeson line used a six digit pattern number, broken down as follows:

First number—Handle material
Second number—Number of blades
Third number—Lining and bolsters
Remaining three numbers—Factory pattern number

Handle Material Keys *Lining and Bolsters Key*

1-Black Composition   1-Steel linings and bolster
2-Rosewood   2-Brass linings, nickel silver bolsters
3-Yellow Composition 3-Nickel silver lining and bolsters
4-White Composition   6-Brass lining and nickel silver bolsters
5-Metal, sometimes   9-Stainless steel or chrome plated
  Genuine Stag
6-Bone
7-Pearl
8-Swirl
9-Gun Metal

☐**4525**—STAINLESS STEEL SCISSOR KNIFE, two-bladed engine turned. German Import **20.00**

☐**4821**—SENATOR PEN KNIFE, German Import **35.00**

☐**4822**—JACK KNIFE **35.00**

☐**4833**—PREMIUM STOCK KNIFE, German Import **65.00**

☐**4864**—SWISS TYPE ARMY KNIFE, red celluloid, German Import **60.00**

☐**026319**—Father & Son set, contains No. 622026 and 622319, gift boxed **350.00**

☐**033750**—(4″) Metal handle, nickel silver lining and bolsters **50.00**

☐**126056**—(3¾″) Black pyralin handle, full mirror finished blades, nickel silver bolsters, brass lining **50.00**

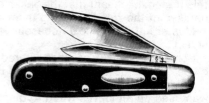

□**126240**—(3⅝″) Black pyralin handle, full mirror finished blades, nickel silver bolsters, brass lining **50.00**

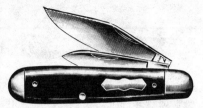

□**126636**—(3⅜″) Black pyralin handle, full mirror finished blades, nickel silver bolsters, brass lining **50.00**

□**128105**—(3″) Lifelong ebonized handle, black pyralin handle, nickel silver bolsters, nickel silver lining **30.00**

□**132433**—(3⅝″) Black pyralin handle, full mirror finished blades, nickel silver bolsters, brass lining **60.00**

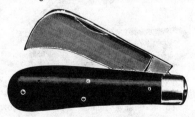

□**211007**—(4″) Rosewood handle, full mirror finished blades, nickel silver bolsters, steel lining **30.00**

□**211008**—(4″) Rosewood handle, full mirror finished blades, nickel silver bolsters, steel lining **35.00**

□**211035**—(3⅜″) Rosewood handle, steel bolsters, blades fine glazed, steel lining . **30.00**

□**222030**—(3½″) Walnut handle, brass lining **30.00**

□**222050**—(3⅞″) Rosewood handle, full mirror finished blades, nickel silver bolsters, brass lining **150.00**

□**322013**—Black pyralin handle, full mirror finished blades, nickel silver bolsters, brass lining **60.00**

2027—(3¾") Black pyralin handle, full mirror finished blades, nickel silver bolsters, brass lining **60.00**

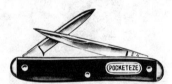

☐**322286**—(3⅜") Black pyralin handle, full mirror finished blades, nickel silver bolsters, brass lining **40.00**

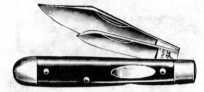

☐**323404**—(2¾") Black pyralin handle, full mirror finished blades, nickel silver bolsters, all joints sunk flush with handle **35.00**

☐**323404**—(2¾") Black pyralin handle, small serpentine pen knife, nickel silver bolster and lining **30.00**

☐**323480**—(3⅜") Black pyralin handle, full mirror finished blades, nickel silver bolsters **35.00**

☐**323617**—(2⅞") Black pyralin handle, full mirror finished blades, nickel silver bolsters, milled nickel silver linings, frictionless bronze bearing built into spring, never need oiling **40.00**

☐**323646**—(3") Black pyralin handle, full mirror finished blades, nickel silver bolsters . **35.00**

☐**323657**—(3⅜") Black pyralin handle, full mirror finished blades, nickel silver bolsters, milled nickel silver linings, frictionless bonze bearings built into spring, never needs oiling **45.00**

☐**323669**—(3½") Black pyraline handle, full mirror finished blades, nickel silver bolsters, milled nickel silver linings, frictionless bronze bearings built into spring, never needs oiling **65.00**

☐**323675**—(3″) Black pyralin handle, full mirror finished blades, nickel silver bolsters, all joints sunk flush with handle **40.00**

☐**323676**—(3″) Black pyralin handle, full mirror finished blades, nickel silver bolsters, milled nickel silver linings, frictionless bronze bearings builtinto spring, never needs oiling . . **45.00**

☐**323817**—(2⅞″) Black pyralin handle, full mirror finished blades, nickel silver bolsters, all joints sunk flush with handle **40.00**

☐**323826**—(3⅝″) Black pyralin handle, full mirror finished blades, nickel silver bolsters . . .
. . . . **35.00**

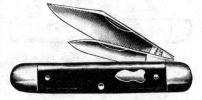

☐**323865**—(3¾″) Black pyralin handle, full mirror finished blades, nickel silver bolsters, brass lining **35.00**

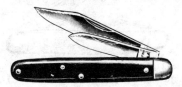

☐**326011**—(3″) Black pryalin handle, full mirror finished blades, nickel silver bolsters, brass lining **30.00**

☐**326015**—(3″) Black pyralin handle, full mirror finished blades, nickel silver bolsters, brass lining **40.00**

☐**326242**—(3⅝″) Black pyralin handle, full mirror finished blades, nickel silver bolsters, brass lining **50.00**

☐**333633**—(3⅝″) Black pyralin handle, full mirror finished blades, nickel silver bolsters, milled nickel silver linings, fricitonless bronze bearings built into spring, never needs oiling . .
. . . . **70.00**

☐**33750**—(4″) Metal handle, Premium Stock knife, nickel silver lining and bolsters . . . **80.00**

☐**421179**—(3⅜″) White pyralin handle, steel bolster, blades fine glazed, steel lining . . **70.00**

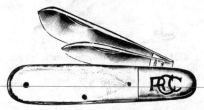

☐**421200**—(3⅜″) White pyralin handle, steel bolsters, blades fine glazed, steel lining . **80.00**

☐**422064**—(2¾") White pyralin handle, full mirror finished blades, nickel silver bolsters, brass lining **30.00**

☐**422174**—(3¾") White pyralin handle, full mirror finished blades, nickel silver bolsters, brass lining **40.00**

☐**422274**—(3¼") White pyralin handle, full mirror finished blades, nickel silver bolsters, brass lining **40.00**

☐**423405**—(3¼") White pyralin handle, full mirror finished blades, nickel silver trim, all joints sunk flush with handle **30.00**

☐**423480**—(3⅜") White pyralin handle full mirror finished blades, nickel silver trim, all joints sunk flush with handle **35.00**

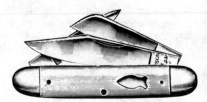

☐**432868**—(3⅜") White pyralin handle, full mirror finished blades, brass lining **45.00**

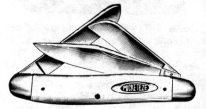

☐**433594**—(3⅞") White celluloid handle, full mirror finished blades, nickel silver bolsters, nickel silver lining **50.00**

☐**433595**—(3⅞") White pyralin handle, full mirror finished blades, nickel silver bolsters, nickel silver lining **50.00**

☐**433727**—(3⅝") White pyralin handle, full mirror finished blades, nickel silver lining **40.00**

□**511168**—(3⅜″) Bone handle, steel bolsters, blades fine glazed, steel lining **80.00**

□**511178**—(3⅜″) Bone stag handle, brass lining **55.00**

□**511179**—(3⅜″) Bone handle, steel bolsters, blades fine glazed, steel lining **90.00**

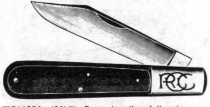

□**511224**—(3¾″) Bone handle, full mirror finished blades, nickel silver bolsters, steel lining **110.00**

□**512224**—(3¾″) Bone stag handle, brass lining **135.00**

□**512872**—(4″) Genuine stag handle, brass lining **135.00**

□**521168**—(3⅜″) Bone handle, steel bolsters, blades fine glazed, steel lining **100.00**

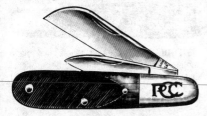

□**521178**—(3⅜″) Bone handle, steel bolsters, blades fine glazed, steel lining **100.00**

□**521179**—(3⅜″) Bone handle, steel bolsters, blade fine glazed, steel lining **100.00**

□**521199**—(3⅜″) Bone handle, steel bolsters, blade fine glazed, steel lining **70.00**

□**521199**—(3⅜″) Bone stag handle, brass lining **125.00**

□**522482**—(4½″) Genuine stag handle, brass lining **250.00**

□**523858**—(2⅞″) Genuine stag handle, nickel silver lining **50.00**

□**529003**—(2¾″) Chromium plated metal handle, blades, springs linings completely protected with durable lustrous chrome plating **25.00**

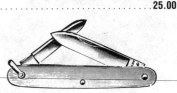

□**529007**—(2¾″) Chromium plated metal handle, blades, springs, linings completely protected with durable lustrous chrome plating **25.00**

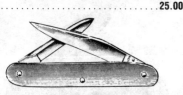

□**529404**—(2¾″) Chromium plated metal handle, blades, springs, linings completely protected with durable lustrous chrome plating **25.00**

□**529735**—(2½″) Chromium plated metal handle, blades, springs, linings completely protected with durable lustrouis chrome plating **25.00**

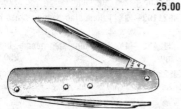

□**529740**—(2¾″) Chromium plated metal handle, blades, springs, linings completely protected with durable lustrous chrome plaing **25.00**

□**533167**—(3″) Genuine stag handle, nickel silver lining **110.00**

□**533278**—(3⅜″) Solid nickel silver handle, full mirror finished blade, nickel silver lining **30.00**

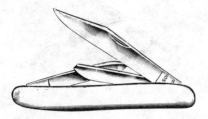

□**533729**—&3⅜″) Solid nickel silver handle, full mirror finished blade **50.00**

□**533750**—(4″) Solid nickel silver handle, full mirror finished blade, nickel silver bolsters**70.00**

□**539445**—(2¾″) Chromium plated metal handle, blades, springs, linings completely proteced with durable lustrous chrome plating ..**25.00**

□**612060**—(4⅛″) Bone stag handle, brass lining **80.00**

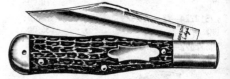

□**612118**—(5¼″) Bone stag handle, full mirror finished blade, nickel silver bolsters, brass lining **450.00**

□**612407**—(5″) Bone stag handle, brass lining **100.00**

□**612610**—(5″) Bone stag handle, lock blade hunting knife, full mirror finished blade, nickel silver bolsters, brass lining **200.00**

□**616407**—(5") Bone stag handle, full mirror finished blade, nickel silver bolsters, brass lining **120.00**

□**621105**—(3") Bone stag handle, full mirror finished blade, nickel silver bolsters, steel lining **40.00**

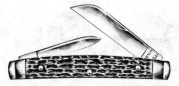

□**621177**—(3") Bone stag handle, full mirror finished blade, nickel silver bolsters, steel lining **50.00**

□**622001**—(3¼") Bone stag handle, full mirror finished blade, nickel silver bolsters, brass lining **65.00**

□**622003**—(2¾") Bone stag handle, full mirror finished blade, nickel silver bolsters, brass lining **50.00**

□**622013**—(3⅝") Bone stag handle, full mirror finished blade, nickel silver bolsters, brass lining **80.00**

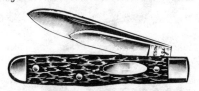

□**622020**—(3⅝") Bone stag handle, full mirror finished blade, nickel silver bolsters, brass lining **85.00**

□**622022**—(3⅝") Bone stag handle, full mirror finished blade, nickel silver bolsters, brass lining **70.00**

□**622026**—(3") Bone stag handle, full mirror finished blade, nickel silver bolsters, brass lining **45.00**

□**622027**—(3¾") Bone stag handle, full mirror finished blade, nickel silver bolsters, brass lining **120.00**

□**622037**—(4") Bone stag handle, full mirror finished blade, nickel silver bolsters, brass lining **130.00**

□**622048**—(2⅞") Bone stag handle, full mirror finished blade, nickel silver bolsters, brass lining **40.00**

□**622056**—(3¾") Bone stag handle, brass lining **75.00**
□**622061**—(4⅛") Bone stag handle, brass lining **95.00**

□**622062**—(4⅛") Bone stag handle, full mirror finished blade, nickel silver bolsters, brass lining **250.00**

□**622064**—(2¾") Bone stag handle, full mirror finished blade, nickel silver bolsters, brass lining **40.00**

□**622083**—(2¾") Bone stag handle, full mirror finished blade, nickel silver bolsters, brass lining **40.00**

□**622088**—(3¾") Bone stag handle, full mirror finished blade, nickel silver bolsters, brass lining **90.00**

□**622102**—(3¾") Bone stag handle, full mirror finished blade, nickel silver bolsters, brass lining **55.00**
□**622105**—(3") Bone stag handle, full mirror finished blade, nickel silver bolsters, steel lining **40.00**
□**622119**—(4½") Bone stag handle, full mirror finished blade, nickel silver bolsters, brass lining **100.00**

□**622119**—(4½") Bone stag handle, brass lining **100.00**

☐**622138**—(3¾") Bone stag handle, full mirror finished blade, nickel silver bolsters, brass lining **150.00**

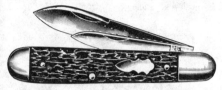

☐**622151**—(4½") Bone stag handle, full mirror finished blade, nickel silver bolsters, brass lining **100.00**

☐**622167**—(3") Bone stag handle, full mirror finished blade, nickel silver bolsters, brass lining **50.00**

☐**622177**—(3") Bone stag handle, full mirror finished blade, nickel silver bolsters, steel lining **50.00**

☐**622183**—(2¾") Bone stag handle, full mirror finished blade, nickel silver bolsters, brass lining **40.00**

☐**622187**—(4") Bone stag handle, full mirror finished blade, nickel silver bolsters, brass lining **150.00**

☐**622193**—(3¾") Bone stag handle, full mirror finished blade, nickel silver bolsters, brass lining **90.00**

☐**622195**—(3") Bone stag handle, full mirror finished blade, nickel silver bolsters, brass lining **150.00**

☐**622225**—(3⅝") Bone stag handle, full mirror finished blade, nickel silver bolsters, nickel silver lining **120.00**

☐**622253**—(3⅝") Bone stag handle, full mirror finished blade, nickel silver bolsters, brass lining **45.00**

☐**622295**—(3⅜") Bone stag handle, full mirror finished blade, nickel silver bolsters, brass lining **40.00**

☐**622229**—(2⅝″) Bone stag handle, full mirror finished blade, nickel silver bolsters, brass lining **30.00**

☐**622319**—(3″) Bone stag handle, full mirror finished blade, nickel silver bolsters, brass lining **40.00**

☐**622331**—(2⅝″) Bone stag handle, brass lining **85.00**

☐**622382**—(4⅛″) Bone stag handle, brass lining **150.00**

☐**622393**—(2¾″) Bone stag handle, full mirror finished blade, nickel silver bolsters, nickel silver lining **40.00**

☐**622457**—(4⅛″) Bone stag handle, full mirror finished blade, nickel silver bolsters, brass lining **100.00**

☐**622597**—(3⅞″) Bone stag handle, brass lining **60.00**

☐**633636**—(3½″) Bone stag handle, full mirror finished blade, nickel silver bolsters, brass lining **50.00**

☐**622841**—(3⅜″) Bone stag handle, full mirror finished blade, nickel silver bolsters, brass lining **70.00**

☐**623177**—(3″) Bone stag handle, nickel silver lining **55.00**

☐**623191**—(3¼″) Bone stag handle, full mirror finished blade, nickel silver bolsters, brass lining **50.00**

☐**623405**—(3¼″) Bone stag handle, full mirror finished blade, nickel silver trim, all joints suck flush with handle **50.00**

☐**623422**—(3⅝″) Bone stag handle, full mirror finished blade, nickel silver trim, all joints sunk flush with handle **75.00**

☐**623480**—(3⅜″) Bone stag handle, full mirror finished blade, nickel silver trim, all joints sunk flush with handle **55.00**

☐**623480**—(3⅜″) Bone stag handle, nickel silver lining **75.00**

☐**623500**—(3⅜″) Bone stag handle, full mirror finished blade, nickel silver trim, all joints sunk flush with handle **120.00**

☐**623501**—(3″) Bone stag handle, full mirror finished blade, nickel silver trim, all joints sunk flush with handle **50.00**

☐**623505**—(3¼″) Bone stag handle, full mirror finished blade, nickel silver trim, all joints sunk flush with handle **55.00**

☐**623671**—(3″) Bone stag handle, full mirror finished blade, nickel silver trim, all joints sunk flush with handle **40.00**

☐**623595**—(3⅞″) Bone stag handle, full mirror finished blade, nickel silver trim, all joints sunk flush with handle **85.00**

☐**623681**—(3″) Bone stag handle, full mirror finished blade, nickel silver bolsters, milled nickel silver linings, frictionless bronze bearings built into spring, never needs oiling .**40.00**

☐**623603**—(2¾″) Bone stag handle, full mirror finished blade, nickel silver bolsters, milled nickel silver linings frictionless bronze bearings built into spring, never needs oiling **40.00**

☐**623698**—(3⅝″) Bone stag handle, full mirror finished blade, nickel silver trim, all joints sunk flush with handle **45.00**

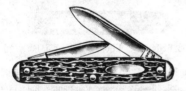

☐**623662**—(3¼″) Bone stag handle, full mirror finished blade, nickel silver bolsters, milled nickel silver linings, frictionless bronze bearings built into spring, never needs oiling .**40.00**

☐**623777**—&3⅝″) Bone stag handle, full mirror finished blade, nickel silver trim, all joints sunk flush with handle **40.00**

☐**623851**—(2¹¹⁄₁₆″) Bone stag handle, nickel silver lining **60.00**

☐**623667**—(3⅞″) Bone stag handle, full mirror finished blade, nickel silver trim, all joints sunk flush with handle **50.00**

☐**623858**—(2⅞″) Bone stag handle, full mirror finished blade, nickel trim, all joints sunk flush with handle **60.00**

☐**623875**—(3⅝″) Bone stag handle, woodcraft knife, full mirror finished blade, nickel silver trim, all joints sunk flush with handle **75.00**

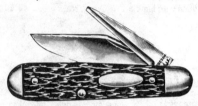

☐**626041**—(3¾″) full mirror finished blade, nickel silver bolsters, brass lining **55.00**

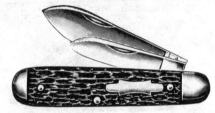

☐**626052**—(3¾″) Bone stag handle, full mirror finished blade, nickel silver bolsters, brass lining **65.00**

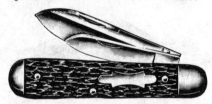

☐**626054**—(3¾″) Bone stag handle, full mirror finished blade, nickel silver bolsters, brass lining **55.00**

☐**626056**—(3¾″) Bone stag handle, full mirror finished blade, nickel silver bolster, brass lining **60.00**

☐**626094**—(3⅜″) Bone stag handle, full mirror blade, nickel silver bolsters, brass lining . **40.00**

☐**626104**—(3⅜″) Bone stag handle, full mirror finished blade, nickel silver bolsters, brass lining **45.00**

☐**626204**—(3⅜″) Bone stag handle, full mirror finished blade, nickel silver bolsters, brass lining **45.00**

☐**626240**—(3⅜″) Bone stag handle, full mirror finished blade, nickel silver bolsters, brass lining **55.00**

☐**626241**—(3⅜″) Bone stag handle, full mirror finished blade, nickel silver bolsters, brass lining **70.00**

☐**626242**—(3⅜″) Bone stag handle, full mirror finished blade, nickel silver bolsters, brass lining **70.00**

□**626331**—(2⅝″) Bone stag handle, full mirror finished blade, nickel silver bolsters, brass lining **40.00**

□**626636**—(3⅜″) Bone stag handle, full mirror finished blade, nickel silver bolsters, brass lining **50.00**

□**626637**—(3⅜″) Bone stag handle, full mirror finished blade, nickel silver bolsters, brass lining **55.00**

□**626765**—(3⅜″) Bone stag handle, full mirror finished blade, nickel silver bolsters, brass lining **40.00**

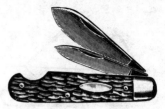

□**626766**—(3⅜″) Bone stag handle, full mirror finished blade, nickel silver bolsters, brass lining **75.00**

□**629005**—(3¼″) Bone stag handle, full mirror finished blade, nickel silver bolsters, stainless, nickel silver lining **55.00**

□**629675**—(3″) Bone stag handle, full mirror finished blade, nickel silver bolsters, nickel silver lining **75.00**

□**632102**—(3⅝″) Bone stag handle, full mirror finished blade, nickel silver bolsters, brass lining **120.00**

□**632167**—(3″) Bone stag handle, full mirror finished blade, nickel silver bolsters, brass lining **40.00**

☐**632225**—(3⅝″) Bone stag handle, full mirror finished blade, nickel silver bolsters, brass lining **80.00**

☐**632295**—(3⅝″)Bone stag handle, full mirror finished blade, brass lining **90.00**

☐**632319**—(3″) Bone stag handle, full mirror finished blade, nickel silver bolsters, brass lining **45.00**

☐**632596**—(3⅞″) as above **80.00**

☐**632750**—(4″) Bone stag handle, full mirror finished blade, nickel silver bolsters, brass lining **140.00**

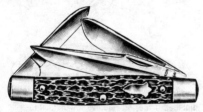

☐**632751**—(4″) Bone stag handle, full mirror finished blade, nickel silver bolsters, brass lining **140.00**

☐**632768**—(2½″) Bone stag handle, full mirror finished blade, nickel silver bolsters, brass lining **35.00**

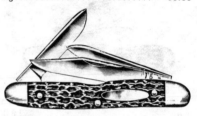

☐**632831**—(3⅜″) Bone stag handle, brass lining **65.00**

☐**632838**—(3⅜″) Horn pyralin handle, full mirror ifnished blade, nickel silver bolsters, brass lining **45.00**

☐**632868**—(3⅜″) Bone stag handle, full mirror finished blade, brass lining **65.00**

☐**632882**—(3⅝″) Bone stag handle, full mirror finished blade, nickel silver bolsters, brass lining **80.00**

□**633295**—(3⅜″) Bone stag handle, nickel silver lining **90.00**

□**6332295TC**—(3⅜″) Bone stag handle, nickel silver lining, large blade - flame edge **90.00**

□**633593**—(3⅞″) Bone stag handle, full mirror finished blade, nickel silver bolsters, nickel silver lining **80.00**

□**633594**—(3⅞″) Bone stag handle, full mirror finished blade, nickel silver bolsters, nickel silver lining **55.00**

□**633594**—(3⅞″) Bone stag handle, full mirror finished blade, nickel silver bolsters, nickel silver lining **55.00**

□**633594**—(3⅞″) Bone stag handle, nickel silver lining **95.00**

□**633594**—(3⅞″) Bone stag handle, nickel silver lining **115.00**

□**633595**—(3⅞″) Red pyralin handle, full mirror finished blade, nickel silver bolsters, nickel silver lining **60.00**

□**633596**—(3⅞″) Bone stag handle, nickel silver lining **115.00**

□**633662**—(3¼″) Bone stag handle, full mirror finished blade, milled nickel silver lining .**75.00**

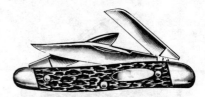

□**633670**—(3⅜″) Bone stag handle, full mirror finished blade, nickel silver bolsters, milled nickel silver linings, frictionless bronze bearings built into spring, never needs oiling **150.00**

□**633681**—(3″) Bone stag handle, full mirror finished blade, nickel silver bolsters, milled nickel silver linings, frictionless bearings built into spring, never needs oiling **95.00**

□**633727**—(3⅝″) Bone stag handle, full mirror finished blade, nickel silver lining **80.00**

□**633728**—(3⅜″) Bone stag handle, full mirror finished blade, nickel silver lining **80.00**

□**633750**—(4″) Bone stag handle, nickel silver lining and bolsters **75.00**

□**633830**—(3⅜″) Bone stag handle, full mirror finished blade, nickel silver lining **75.00**

□**633850**—(2⅝″) Bone stag handle, nickel silver lining **50.00**

□**633880**—(3⅝″) Bone stag handle, full mirror finished blade, nickel silver bolsters, nickel silver lining **90.00**

□**633865**—(3⅜″) Bone stag handle, full mirror finished blade, nickel silver lining **90.00**

□**633881**—(3⅝″) Bone stag handle, full mirror finished blade, nickel silver bolsters, nickel silver lining **110.00**

□**633866**—(3⅜″) Bone stag handle, full mirror finished blade, nickel silver bolsters, nickel silver lining **90.00**

□**633884**—(3⅝″) Bone stag handle, full mirror finished blade, nickel silver bolsters, nickel silver lining **110.00**

□**633875**—(3⅝″) Bone stag handle, Woodcraft knife — Pocket-Eze, nickel silver bolsters, nickel silver lining, milled **130.00**

□**633885**—(3⅝″) Bone stag handle, full mirror finished blade, nickel silver bolsters, nickel silver lining **110.00**

☐**633886**—(3⅝″) Bone stag handle, full mirror finished blade, nickel silver bolsters, nickel silver lining **110.00**

☐**642088**—(4⅛″) Bone stag handle, brass lining **160.00**

☐**642208**—(4⅛″) Bone stag handle, full mirror finished blade, nickel silver bolsters, brass lining **160.00**

☐**642214**—(3⅝″) Bone stag handle, full mirror finished blade, nickel silver bolsters, brass lining **140.00**

☐**643453**—(3½″) Bone stag handle, full mirror finished blade, nickel silver bolsters, nickel silver lining **90.00**

☐**643645**—(3⅝″) Bone stag handle, full mirror finished blade, nickel silver bolsters, nickel silver lining **90.00**

☐**643777**—(3⅜″) Bone stag handle, full mirror finished blade, nickel silver bolsters, nickel silver lining **90.00**

☐**723167**—(3″) Genuine pearl handle, nickel silver lining **50.00**

☐**723317**—(2⅞″) Genuine pearl handle, nickel silver lining **60.00**

☐**623681**—(3″) Pearl handle, full mirror finished blade, nickel silver bolsters, milled nickel silver linings **55.00**

☐**812118**—(5¼″) Maise pyralin handle, full mirror finished blade, nickel silver bolsters, brass lining **175.00**

☐**812872**—(4½″) Maize composition handle, brass lining **120.00**

☐**816407**—(5″) Red and white pyralin handle, full mirror finished blade, nickel silver bolsters, brass lining **75.00**

☐**822023**—(3¼″) Horn pyralin handle, full mirror finished blade, nickel silver bolsters, brass lining **40.00**

☐**822048f**—(2⅞″) Gold pyralin handle, full mirror finished blade, nickel silver bolsters, brass lining **40.00**

☐**822061**—(4⅛″) Maize composition handle, brass lining **65.00**

☐**822064**—(2¾″) Black pyralin handle, full mirror finished blade, nickel silver bolsters, brass lining **30.00**

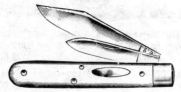

☐**822094**—(3⅜″) Miaze pyralin handle, full mirror finished blade, nickel silver bolsters, brass lining **40.00**

☐**822183**—(2¾″) Gold pyralin handle, full mirror finished blade, nickel silver bolsters, brass lining **40.00**

☐**822253**—(3⅝″) Maise pyralin handle, full mirror finished blade, nickel silver bolsters, brass lining **35.00**

☐**822295**—(3¾″) Horn pyralin handle, full mirror finished blade, nickel silver bolsters, brass lining **35.00**

☐**822319**—(3″) Russed pyralin handle, full mirror finished blade, nickel silver bolsters, brass lining **35.00**

☐**822355**—(3⅜″) Imitation pearl handle, brass lining **30.00**

☐**822393**—($2^{13}\%_{16}$″) Miaze composition handle, brass lining **50.00**

☐**822497**—(5″) Maise pyralin handle, fishing knife, full mirror finished blade, nickel silver bolsters, brass lining **100.00**

☐**822482**—(4½″) Maize composition handle, brass lining **175.00**

☐**822728**—(3⅜″) Maize pyralin handle, full mirror finished blade, nickel silver trim . .**60.00**

☐**822850**—(2¾″) Gold pyralin handle, full mirror finished blade, nickel silver bolsters, brass lining **35.00**

☐**822850**—(2¹¹⁄₁₆″) Imitation pearl handle, brass lining **30.00**

☐**832726**—(3⅜″) Miase pyralin handle, full mirror finished blade, brass lining **50.00**

☐**823505**—(3¼″) Gray mottled pyralin handle, full mirror finished blade, nickel silver trim, all joints sunk flush with handle **45.00**

☐**823724**—(3½″) Black pyralin handle, full mirror finished blade, nickel silver trim, all joints sunk flush with handle **60.00**

☐**823851**—(3¹¹⁄₁₆″) Maize composition handle, nickel silver lining **30.00**

☐**832838**—(3⅜″) Horn pyralin handle, full mirror finished blade, nickel silver bolsters .**80.00**

☐**823881**—(3⅝″) Miase pryalin handle, full miror finished blade, nickel silver trim, all joints sunk flush with handle **60.00**

☐**832883**—(3⅝″) Horn pyralin handle, full mirror finished blade, nickel silver bolsters, brass lining **80.00**

☐**833295**—((3¾″) Miaze composition handle, nickel silver lining **45.00**

☐**833594**—(3⅞″) Red pyralin handle, full mirror finished blade, nickel silver bolsters, nickel silver lining . . . .

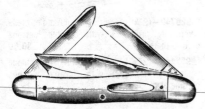

☐**832597**—(3⅞″) Maise celluloid handle, full mirror finished blade, nickel silver bolsters, brass lining **80.00**

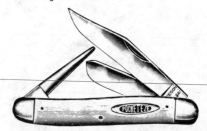

☐**833595**—(3⅞″) Red pyralin handle, full mirror finished blade, nickel silver bolsters, nickel silver lining **60.00**

☐**833850**—(2⅝″) Imitation pearl handle, nickel silver lining **40.00**

☐**833865**—(3⅜″) Maise pyralin handle, full mirror finished blade, nickel silver lining . **90.00**

☐**833867**—(3⅜″) Miase pyralin handle, full mirror finished blade, nickel silver bolsters, nickel silver lining **50.00**

☐**833880**—(3⅝″) Maise pyralin handle, full mirror finished blade, nickel silver bolsters, nickel silver lining **80.00**

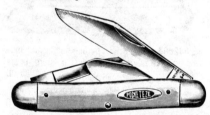

☐**833881**—(3⅝″) Miase pyralin handle, full mirror finished blade, nickel silver lining . **80.00**

☐**833887**—(3⅝″) Red pyralin handle, full mirror finished blade, nickel silver bolsters, nickel silver lining **80.00**

☐**922253**—(3⅜″) Brown "Shur Wood" handle, brass lining **40.00**

☐**922295**—(3⅜″) Brown "Shur Wood" handle, brass lining **40.00**

☐**922296TC**—(3⅜″) Brown "Shur Wood" handle, brass lining, large blade — Flame . . . **40.00**

☐**922295TC**—(3⅜″) Brown "Shur Wood" handle, brass lining, large blade — Flame . . . **40.00**

☐**922497**—(5″) Brown "Shur Wood" handle, brass lining **45.00**

☐**939004**—(2¾″) Fine gunmetal handle, blade completely protected with durable lustrous chrome plate **25.00**

☐**929007**—(2¾″) Fine gunmetal handle, blade completely protected with durable lustrous chrome plate **35.00**

☐**929404**—(2¾″) Fine gunmetal handle, blade completely protected with durable lustrous chrome plate **30.00**

☐**929735**—(2½″) Fine gunmetal handle, blade completely protected with durable lustrous chrome plate **35.00**

☐**929740**—(2¾″) Fine gunmetal handle, blade completely protected with durable lustrous chrome plate **30.00**

☐**939445**—(2¾″) Fine gunmetal handle, blade completely protected with durable lustrous chrome plate **35.00**

RODGERS, JOSEPH
SHEFFIELD, ENGLAND

The Joseph Rodgers dynasty of cutlery began in 1724, when John Rodgers began making knives in Holy Croft, Sheffield, England. He had three sons, one named Joseph, who continued the family business of making penknives. John lived until 1785, to the age of 84. But he had lived long enough to see his business move into larger surroundings at No. 6 Northfolk Street. Joseph died in 1821, the same year that the firm was made "Cutler to the Royal Family."

A book by Dr. A. Gatty, "Sheffield, Past and Present" gives an account of what happened: "In 1821 Mr. Stuart Wortley, the member of Parliament from Yorkshire and afterward created Lord Wharncliffe, undertook to present Mr. John Rodgers to the Prince Regent at Carlton House when he exhibited to the Prince a minute specimen of cutlery, and in return received the honour, by special appointment, of the firm being made cutlers to the Royal Family. The distinction thus conferred upon Messrs. Rodgers roused their energies as manufacturer, and they resolved, by the appliances of skill and labour, to produce the finest cutlery that could be made. They also opened a showroom, in which the articles they manufactured were exhibited to view; and as this proceeding had no precedent in the town, it caused for a while very serious inconvenience. Crowds came to inspect the novel display, who had no intention of purchasing anything they saw, but when the local curiosity abated, this room became the resort of all the visitors to the town, and it proved a very effective method of advertisement."

The John Rodgers in this story was the son of Joseph. He died in 1859 at the age of 80. John had no children, so he took into partnership his nephews, John, Jr. and Robert Newbold. John Jr. died in 1856, and Newbold took on some cousins as partners. They were George Joseph and Joseph. George Joseph died in 1866, leaving Joseph and Robert Newbold, who incorporated Joseph Rodgers as a Limited Company. The stock sold out in a few hours. Business boomed, and in 1882 they built a new factory, opened a London showroom in 1889, and by 1907 had over five acres of factories. In 1971 Rodgers bought IXL, Wostenholm, and in turn sold to Imperial Associated Companies in 1977.

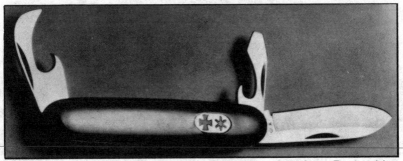

Rodgers lives again in the Regimental line imported from England by Imperial.

☐ *Current Collector Value: Life Guards* **$15.00**

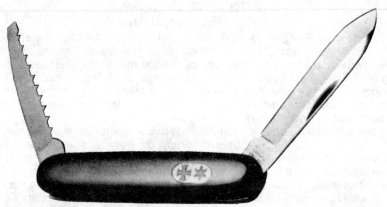

☐ *Current Collector Value: Scots Guards* $12.00

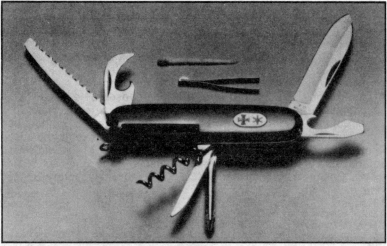

☐ *Current Collector Value: Grenadier Guards* $24.00

☐ *Current Collector Value: Cold Stream Guards* $15.00

THE SHOWROOMS

The Showrooms, first opened in 1821, boasted some cutlery wonders, including a 10 foot elephant tusk weighing 216 pounds, and several mounted heads of animals. Among the items of cutlery displayed were 12 pairs of minute scissors, so small that the whole 12 weighed less than one half grain, a one inch long knife with 57 blades, a knife with six prongs in the shape of the Rodgers trademark, with 144 blades, and the Norfolk sporting knife with 75 blades, each etched with hunting scenes, notable buildings and the faces of famous people. It was made for the 1851 exhibition and took two years to make. Also there was the year knife with a blade for each year, a pair of carvers five feet high, and many other cutlery items. From one of those showrooms was a pair of scissors about 2½ feet high now in the collection of Dr. Frank Forsyth and displayed at The National Knife Museum. A 10' x 4' display board wired full of Rodgers knives was in the possession of Mr. Hubert Lawell, but when his collection was stolen in 1978 the thieves took the knives along with them.

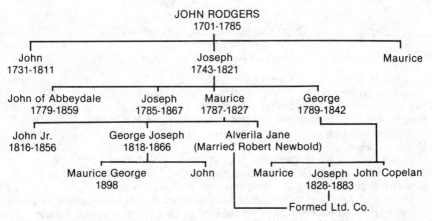

1850-*John of Abbeydale takes John Jr. and Robert Newbold as partners*
1856-*On death of John Jr., Newbold takes on as partners George Joseph and Joseph*
1866-*George Joseph dies*
1870-*Newbold and Joseph form Limited Co.*
1890-*Newbold retires, Maurice George and John take over*
1898-*Maurice dies, John assumes President*

RUSSELL COMPANY
TURNER FALLS, MASSACHUSETTS

John Russell was born in 1797 in Greenfield, Massachusetts. The son of a silversmith; he represented cotton speculators by going to Georgia to be closer to the actual trading. He lived there for 12 years and made a fortune. In 1830 he moved to Lancaster, Pennsylvania, where he married. Two years later he returned to Greenfield, Massachusetts.

JOHN RUSSELL CUTLERY COMPANY

GREEN RIVER WORKS

TURNERS FALLS, MASSACHUSETTS, U.S.A.

While in Massachusetts he came across a book by Zachariah Allen, *The Practical Tourist*. Allen, a Rhode Island manufacturer of clothes, described the cutlery operations in Sheffied, England in such a glowing manner that Russell decided to become a cutlery manufacturer. His first factory started making chisels on the banks of the Green River in Greenfield in 1834 when Russell was 37 years old.

In his factory he utilized the trip hammer, which had been used in industrial uses for years, but no one had used it before to make cutlery. His was the first factory to use steam power in Greenfield.

Making chisels and ax heads at first, he used the highest quality English steel, hoping to make up for the lack of skilled cutlers, which he did not have. Later phasing out the chisels and ax head manufacture, Russell began making kitchen cutlery.

In 1836 a flood washed away the Russell factory. Henry Clapp offered to become a partner, so that same year Clapp, John Russell and his brother Francis formed J. Russell & Co. The Russells were to manage the factory in exchange for Clapp providing $10,000 for seven years. Clapp was also to receive one-third of the profits.

The new factory they built was christened the "Green River Works" and soon the knives made there were carrying that trademark across America.

In 1837, John Russell's two brothers moved to New York for selling and purchasing, and Russell soon rose his wages to those higher than that in Sheffied. This guaranteed that any experienced cutler arriving in the United States would go straight to Russell for employment.

In the 1840's Russell began to make what he called ***"An American Hunting Knife"***. To do something "Up to Green River" meant that it was as good as could be made, and when a knife fight thrust was described as "Up to

Green River" it meant that the knife had been thrust in up to the hilt, until only the words Green River were showing. Between 1840 and 1860, over 60,000 dozen Russell Green River knives were sent to the Western trade. Soon the Sheffield cutler's were copying the words flooding the American market with their own "Green River" knives.

In 1868 a fire destroyed much of the factory, and the decision was made to move to Turner Falls, Massachusetts. At the time of the move the company was incorporated as the John Russell Manufacturing Company, by Russell, his nephew Charles, and Matthew Chapman. John Russell retired during the move to Turner Falls.

The new factory was the largest cutlery factory in the world at the time. The cost of the factory was more than expected, and the company went bankrupt in 1873. The reorganization took place soon thereafter, and at this point no members of the John Russell family chose to reinvest.

At the 1876 Philadelphia Exposition the Russell Company exhibited 150 types of cutlery and a five foot butcher knive with pictures of Greenfield and Turner Falls on the blade. The company also decided to become more active in the pocketknife trade, and by 1877 had over 400 different knives and had sold over 50,000 dozen.

"The History of the John Russell Company" stated that the first Barlow was invented by Obadiah Barlow, a Stannington Cutler in 1667 (the Sheffield Company reportedly went out of business in 1797). But regardless, we can from examining Sheffield records, almost certainly say that the Barlow knife was invented by a Sheffield cutler whose last name was Barlow.

A common referral to the Barlow is in Tom Sawyer, but since it was published in 1875, the Barlow referred to could not have been made by Russell, since they had not begun production of it in 1875.

The Barlow was the best selling knife of the Russell Company, and it became famous as selling for 15¢ for a one blade and 25¢ for the two blade. The rise in steel prices after World War I caused the company to raise the price on the Barlows, and many people thought they were getting a different knife. The cry was so loud that the company dropped the knives from production in the early '30's.

A columnist for the Louisville Courier Journal, Allen Trout, founded the Barlow Bobcats Club in the early '50's. To join you had to own an original Russell Barlow, and for a time the Russell Harrington Company was restoring Russell Barlows as a part of this interest for $1. (They do not do this today.)

In 1879 the Green River Works was sold, and in 1880 the company quit stamping their name on their knives, acid etching them instead.

In 1933 the Russell Company was bought by Harrington Cutlery Company, and in 1936 the company moved to Southbridge, Massachusetts..

The Russell Harrington Company still makes kitchen cutlery today, but it has not made pocketknives since 1930, except for a limited edition commemorative put out in 1973, probably by Schrade.

For anyone wanting a more detailed history of the John Russell Cutlery Company, we recommend *"The History of the John Russell Company"* available from the BETE PRESS, 45 Federal Street, Greenfield, Massachusetts 01301.

☐**No. 10**—BARLOW (3⅜″) Iron handle . **150.00**

☐**No. 20**—BARLOW (3⅜″) Cocobola handle ...
................................**150.00**

☐**No. 22**—BARLOW (3⅜″) Cocobola handle ...
................................**175.00**

☐**No. 60**—BARLOW (3⅜″) Bone handle **150.00**

☐**No. 62**—BARLOW (3⅜″) Bone handle **175.00**

☐**No. 68**—BARLOW (3⅜″) Bone handle **225.00**

☐**No. 600**—BARLOW (5″) Bone handle . **225.00**

☐**No. 601**—BARLOW (5″) Bone handle . **225.00**

☐**No. 6000**—BARLOW (5″) Bone handle **225.00**

☐**No. 6010**—BARLOW (5″) Bone handle **225.00**

SCHATT & MORGAN
TITUSVILLE, PENNSYLVANIA

From the bottom to the top, and back down again, the Schatt & Morgan Cutlery Company went from one of the largest cutlery companies of its time to end spawning a cutlery company still in business today. The machines they used so long ago are still turning out knives today, in the same building, by descendants of the same workers.

From the beginning Schatt & Morgan was a hit, and much of their enthusiasm was evident in the introduction of the 1911 catalog. It said:

"In placing this catalog before the trade we do so with a feeling of pardonable pride. Although comparatively young as knife manufacturers, we have already grown to be one of the largest and best known houses of the United States.

"There is a reason for this growth. It is not an accident, neither is it due to any chance. The product of the Schatt & Morgan Cutlery Co. has by its undoubted merit made the growth of the company rapid and easy.

"There is every reason for our cutlery to be the best on the market. The best materials our money can buy, the latest and most improved methods of manufacture, the most skilled workmen we can employ, and the most rigid inspection make the excellence of our product so superlative that it has grown in popularity every year. Sold under our UNCONDITIONAL GUARANTEE our cutlery must give satisfaction to all.

"This is the only brand that is sold under an unconditional guarantee. We know what is in our cutlery and we show our faith in it. We protect the retailer and the consumer from every defect incident to manufacture. If you are not selling our product send us a sample order today. Remember it is the cutlery that sells. If you find that it is not all we claim for it return it to us at our risk and expense."

Mr. Schatt and Mr. Morgan

Messrs. Schatt and Morgan were no pilgrims to the cutlery trade.

J. W. Schatt was born in New York City in 1856. He began working for a Philadelphia tinware business until he switched to working for the J. R. Torrery Razor Company. Obtaining a strong background in cutlery while at Torrery, he began discussing cutlery with his friend C. P. Morgan in New York City in 1895.

When you talked to C. P. Morgan about cutlery in 1895, he knew what you were talking about too. Born in Chicago, Illinois in 1862, he attended high school in his ancesteral home of Gowanda, New York, where both his father and grandfather had operated newspapers.

At the age of 19 he went to work for C. B. Barker Company, a dealer in sewing machine supplies. The Barker Company soon expanded into knife jobbing, buying knives from the Canastota Knife Company of Canastota, New York, stamping the knives with Barker's brand, "Howard Cutlery."

In 1888 Morgan left Barker to work for his brother Frank Morgan, proprietor of the Bayonne Knife Company, Bayonne, New Jersey. He worked there until 1895, when he and J. W. Schatt began discussing a cutlery business.

Though created in their minds in 1895, it was not until January 15, 1896, that the pair formed their first company, "The New York Cutlery Company." This was certainly unamusing to Col. Tom Bradley of the New York Knife Company, at the time one of the largest cutlery companies in the world. In Schatt & Morgan's offices at 53-55 Franklin Street, the New York Cutlery Company worked out fine until 1898 when they moved to Gowanda, New York. Although we don't know, it is probable that Schatt & Morgan were importing knives until 1898, and then with the Dingley Tariff of 1897 raising the cost of imported cutlery 98%, it forced them to find their own way to obtain knives. The obvious choice was to make them themselves.

And that is exactly what they did. They employed 33 men, utilizing drop forging on standard grade cutlery, and handforging their superior grade line.

The company was still named the New York Cutlery Company, but they stamped their trademark "S&M" crossed by an elongated "X". (A safe marked "New York Cutlery Co." is still in use at the Queen factory in Titusville.)

The company thrived and soon outgrew their Gowanda building, plus the rumor that businessmen in nearby Titusville offered all sorts of incentives if the company would move to Titusville, Pennsylvania. So the company moved in 1901, incorporating as the Schatt & Morgan Cutlery Company on January 1, 1902.

The Gowanda location still stands today. A building that once housed Schatt & Morgan and C. Platts & Sons cutlery today houses an appliance dealer.

Schatt was not too taken with the move, and a 1906 Special Edition of the Titusville Evening Courier stated Schatt still resided in Gowanda, New York although he continued "on the road" for Schatt & Morgan. It is possible that for a brief time the two partners operated both factories at the same time, Schatt overseeing the Gowanda operation and Morgan the Titusville. Morgan bought out Schatt in 1911. Schatt remained in Gowanda, opening an opera house in the 1920's, and becoming quite the fondly remembered figure. One Gowanda resident whose father used to fish with Schatt remembers him for his snow white hair and habit of wearing diamond stickpins.

He was well thought of. In the "Gowanda Rouges Gallery," a satirical look at the village's prominent businessmen, his entry read, "Crimes: Using his talents so vigorously that he has arrived at competency and independence before the rest of us have fairly started; although of a very kindly disposition he has been frequently known to "knife" his most intimate friends. Good looks, brains, and a handsome wife — what more can you ask from a mundane life?"

At the time of incorporation in 1902 the company listed $35,000 in capital stock, but it grew even faster now.

In 1906 the local paper bragged of their newly formed company, "The product of the Schatt & Morgan Cutlery Company has gained a national reputation for the superiority of workmanship and material used, and is such a quality that the company warrants every piece of cutlery made by them and this guarantee is given unconditionally. This guarantee applies to every knive made whether the price is 25¢ or $50 each."

And indeed Schatt & Morgan did have a nearly $50 knife. At a time when pearl handled four-blade worked back knives were selling for $3 each, the company made a special four blade #48182 Gold, with full polish and the handles, rivets, and linings of solid 14 karat gold. The cost on the knife was $45 each.

It was not until 1905 that the company began using high grade material, for as The Evening Courier related, "During the past year they have added an extensive line of very finely made and beautifully finished goods with genuine stag, pearl, gold and silver handles" . . . "And judging from the fact that their business has more than doubled during the past few months, they are putting this high grade of goods on the market most successfully."

The company issued its number 2 catalog in 1911, and in that same year C. P. Morgan bought out J. W. Schatt. Morgan also became active in local Titusville affairs, serving as school director, common council member and one term as Mayor.

The Beginning of the End

1922 was the beginning of the end for the company, with this statement in the 1922 American Cutler, "The Queen City Cutlery Co. of Titusville, Pa., manufacturers of pocketknives, has been incorporated with a capital stock of 25,000 dollars. The company regularly employs seventeen workers and claims to have orders in hand which will take its output for the next four months."

In that same year the Cutler also reported "The Schatt & Morgan Cutlery Company, manufacturers of pocketknives, has resumed operations at its Titusville, Penna. plant with a staff of about 60 men, about one-third of its usual organization."

According to a former sales manager at Queen, what was happening at this time was that five foremen at Schatt & Morgan were running extra parts after the shift, then assembling the parts with the Queen City tang marking. This moonlighting was looked upon calmly by the Schatt & Morgan Company, but when the Queen City mark began eating into S&M's sales, it was time to stop. The company fired all five foremen, and as you might imagine with most of the supervisory personnel being fired, it threw the plant into a turmoil.

The end result left the five foremen with full time to devote to their cutlery business, and Schatt & Morgan trying to run a factory of skilled workmen without any trained supervisory personnel. It was too much for Schatt & Morgan, and the company went under around 1930.

The irony of it all was that on August 31, 1932, Queen City Cutlery purchased the building, machinery and stock of the Schatt & Morgan Cutlery Company. They moved into the building, and it is where Queen Cutlery is today, still making fine pocketknives, such as their own brand and contract work for Bob White, Voyles Cutlery, Kabar, and others.

The S&M tradition of pearl handled knives is still carried on by Queen, making more than any American manufacturer.

THE KNIVES OF SCHATT & MORGAN

Schatt & Morgan made a tremendous variety of knives. While there are few manufacturers today that make over 100 different patterns, in 1911 Schatt & Morgan offered 597 different patterns of pocketknives, and this does not include 54 different patterns of straight razors. The introduction to the 1911 catalog states the company was capable of rolling out 3,500 knives per day, and since they did not make kitchen or hunting knives, almost all of the knives were pocketknives. This comes to 1,095,500 knives per year, based on the six day work week of the time.

In comparison with most companies, these knives are more scarce, since only Russell and the New York Company were popular collectors knives that were out of business earlier. Remington and Winchester weren't out of business and Case wasn't to drop the Case Tested XX stamping until 10 years in the future.

Every Schatt & Morgan knife had its own pattern number, but few were stamped on the knive. Each pattern was numbered in sequence, so there is no key number for number of blades, bolsters, etc. However, the suffixes can tell you something about the knife. They are:

½ = following the pattern number is a sheepfoot blade
¼ = clip blade
EO = Easy open pattern
JS = Swell center balloon pattern (most common seen Schatt)
CH = Chain
S = Equal end jackknife with pen blade on one end, master blade and a shorter blade on the opposite end.
B = Black Celluloid
W = White Celluloid
S = Shell Celluloid

The company used every conceivable variation of bolster, liner, including brass, nickel, silver, steel, Norway iron. The blades were either mirror polish overall, mirror polish on front of master blade only, and brushed finish overall. Etched blades will be found only on knives with an entire mirror polish.

All common styles of the day were used for shields, including bar, crest, and the double end type commonly found on Cattaraugus and New York Knife Company knives.

In general, the company used a key number for the handle material. They called bone "imitation stag." These are not hard and fast keys for the handle material, but in most instances they do fit. This will be the last number in the pattern number.

0 Cocobola
1 Genuine Mother of Pearl
2 Ebony
3 Ebony or stag
4 Cocobola
5 Rosewood, sometimes bone
6 Bone
7 Stag
8 Transparent celluloid, sometimes ebony
9 Stag

The Schatt & Morgan knives marked "Gowanda N.Y." are by far the rarest. Most will be found bearing an "S & M Titusville Pa," or "Schatt & Morgan, Titusville, PA." Schatt & Morgan was also a big contract knife maker, making "A Field of Progress," "Curtain & Clark, Kansas City, Mo." "M & L Hardware, Waco Tx" "Barnsley Brothers," and "Clauss, Freemont Ohio." In 1926 they also started "Dollar Knife Co", with the Titusville stamping.

The Queen section of Dewey Ferguson's *"Collecting Cattaraugas, Russell, Robeson & Queen Knives"* contains extensive illustrations of the Schatt & Morgan line.

In their day, Schatt & Morgan was one of the leading cutlery companies of the time, making some of the finest knives and what is today one of the nicest collectibles.

□**152 1/2**—(3⅝″) Ebony handle, half polished, German silver bolsters, brass lined **90.00**

□**156**—(3⅝″) Imitation stag handle, half polished, brass lined **100.00**

□**336 1/4**—(3¾″) Imitation stag handle, half polished, German silver bolsters, brass lined **50.00**

□**370**—(4″) Cocoa handle, half polished, German silver bolsters, brass lined **55.00**

□**370 1/4**—(4″) Cocoa handle, half polished, German silver bolsters, brass lined **55.00**

□**386**—(3⅝″) Imitation stag handle, half polished, German silver bolsters, brass lined **70.00**

□**396**—(4″) Imitation stag handle, half polished, brass lined **170.00**

□**1016**—(3⅝″) Imitation stag handle, half polished, brass lined **50.00**

□**1092EO**—(3¾") Ebony handle, half polished, German silver bolsters, brass lined **55.00**

□**1096**—(3¾") Imitation stag handle, half polished, German silver bolsters, brass lined **55.00**

□**1099**—(3⅝") Imitation stag handle, half polished, brass lined **60.00**

□**1126 1/2**—(3¾") Imitation stag handle, half polished, German silver bolsters, brass lined **65.00**

□**1136 1/4**—(3½") Imitation stag handle, half polished, brass lined **60.00**

□**1152**—(3⅝") Ebony handle, half polished, German silver bolsters, brass lined **50.00**

□**1166**—(3⅝") Imitation stag handle, half polished, German silver bolsters, brass lined **225.00**

□**1170**—(4") Cocoa handle, half polished, German silver bolsters, brass lined **65.00**

□**1206**—(4") Imitation stag handle, half polished, German silver bolsters, brass lined . . **60.00**

□**1396**—(4") Imitation stag handle, half polished, brass lined **50.00**

□**2036**—(3¾") Imitation stag handle, half polished, brass lined **55.00**

□**2066**—(3½") Imitation stag handle, half polished, German silver bolsters, brass lined, extra heavy blades **40.00**

□**2072 1/4**—(4") Ebony handle, half polished, German silver bolsters, brass lined **50.00**

□**2076 1/4**—(4") Imitation stag handle, half polished, brass lined **55.00**

□**2076 1/2**—(4") Imitation stag handle, half polished, German silver bolster, brass lined **55.00**

□**2156**—(3⅝") Imitation stag handle, half polished, brass lined **65.00**

□**2195**—(3⅝") Ebony handle, half polished, German silver bolsters, brass lined **50.00**

□**2356**—(4") Imitation stag handle, fine glaze finish, German silver bolsters, brass lined **65.00**

□**2357**—(4") Imitation stag handle, fine glaze finish, German silver bolster, brass lined . **65.00**

□**2700**—(4") Cocoa handle, half polished, German silver bolsters, brass lined **65.00**

□**2700 1/4**—(4") Cocoa handle, half polished, German silver bolsters, brass lined **65.00**

□**3096S**—(3⅝") Imitation stag handle, half polished, German silver bolster, brass lined **90.00**

□**3306**—(4") Imitation stag handle, half polished, German silver bolsters, brass lined **120.00**

□**3593**—(2½") Genuine stag handle, full polish, German silver lined **50.00**

□**3706**—(3⅞") Imitation stag handle, half polished, German silver bolster, brass lined . **90.00**

□**3766 1/4**—(4") Imitation stag handle, half polished, German silver bolsters, brass lined **100.00**

□**4126 1/2**—(3¾") Imitation stag handle, half polished, Norway iron bolster, brass lined **90.00**

□**4146 1/2**—(4") Imitation stag handle, half polished, Norway iron bolsters, brass lined **75.00**

□**4197**—(4½") Imitation stag handle, half polished, Norway iron bolster, brass lined **75.00**

□**4593**—(2½") Genuine stag handle, full polish, German silver lined **50.00**

□**4743**—(3") Genuine stag handle, full polish, German silver lined **50.00**

□**5016**—(3⅝") Imitation stag handle, glaze finish, Norway iron bolster, steel lined . . . **45.00**

□**5226**—(3⅝") Imitation stag handle, glaze finish, Norway iron bolsters, steel lined . . **60.00**

□**5286**—(3½") Imitation stag handle, glaze finish, Norway iron bolsters, steel lined . . **40.00**

☐**24143**—(3⅝″) Genuine stag handle, full polished, German silver bolsters, brass lined **45.00**

☐**34173**—(3⅝″) Genuine stag handle, full polished, Norway iron bolsters, brass lined .**70.00**

☐**34263**—(3⅜″) Genuine stag handle, full polish, brass lined **95.00**

☐**37153**—(3⅛″) Genuine stag handle, full polish, German silver lined **40.00**

☐**37193**—(3⅝″) Genuine stag handle, full polished, German silver lined **200.00**

☐**37203**—(3⅜″) Genuine stag handle, full polished, German silver lined **60.00**

☐**37283**—(3″) Genuine stag handle, full polish, German silver lined **45.00**

☐**44133**—(4″) Genuine stag handle, full polished, Norway iron bolsters, brass lined .**70.00**

☐**46163**—(3⅜″) Genuine stag handle, full polish, German silver lined **50.00**

☐**47283**—(3″) Genuine stag handle, full polish, German silver lined **50.00**

SCHRADE CUTLERY
WALDEN, NEW YORK

The Schrade Cat Paw.
☐ *Current Collector Value*.....................**$15.00**

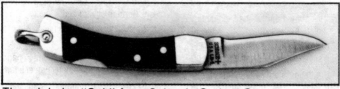

The mini size "Cub" from Schrade Cutlery Co.
☐ *Current Collector Value* **$19.95**

Louis, William and George Schrade incorporated the Schrade Cutlery Company in 1904 with George as President and J. Louis as Treasurer.

The former Walden Knife Company employee's first factory was a 30x70 foot building. It was expanded in 1911 and again in 1915 when Schrade bought out the Walden Cutlery Handle Company, a cooperative formed by New York Knife Company, Walden Knife Company and Schrade Cutlery to manufacture handle material for knives.

About this same time George left the company to market a shielding device he had invented. George Schrade Cutlery Company in Bridgeport, Connecticut, soon began making a switchblade knife he invented.

Louis became President upon George's departure, and converted the factory to mass production, opening a second factory under Joseph Schrade in Middletown, New York. Both companies made knives under government contracts during World War II.

Henry and Albert Baer of Ulster Knife Company bought Schrade in 1947, and in 1957 moved the production to Ellenville, New York closing the Walden factory. Most of the employees were maintained and for a time a bus from Ellenville to Walden ran every day to transport Schrade employees, the aisle cluttered with parts from the Walden factory.

The earliest stamping to be found on Schrade is the rarest. It is SCHRADE CUT CO. WALDEN, N.Y. GERMANY used about 1904. The next marking was a half moon circle SCHRADE CUT CO. marking over WALDEN, NY in a straight line. No record is found of how long this marking was used but due to the rarity of the marking today and from the type bone found on these Schrade Cut Co. circle markings, it is estimated that it was used until about World War I. The straight line Schrade Cut Co. marking was adopted after World War I and was used until World War II. Right after World War II the trademark was changed to SCHRADE-WALDEN NY. (Note that the **USA** was not included in the marking at that time). This SCHRADE-WALDEN NY marking was used until the early to mid 1950's. After that time the trademark or tang stamp was changed to SCHRADE WALDEN NY USA. This tang stamp was used until 1973 at which time it was changed to SCHRADE NY USA. Also, in the early 1970s they began using on the contract knives and limited edition knives the stamp of SW .CUT USA. This stamping usually appears on the rear of the tang.

Throughout the years Schrade used every conceivable handle material on knives, but one of their all-time favorites with collectors is their bone handles. Their knives that were made from 1920 to 1955 were handled with what collectors refer to a peachtree seed bone or peachseed bone, due to the fact that the bone looks like a cured cut peachseed. This bone was made for them by the old Rogers Bone Company which burned in 1956. This bone was colored with a medium tan to brown color. After that they made very few genuine bone handle knives, although there were some made. The red bone and especially the smooth tan bone handle Schrades are considered much rarer to collectors than the peachseed bone. Schrade did not produce any bone handle knives from about 1960 until 1978. In 1978 they produced several different genuine bone handle knives for Parker-Frost Cutlery on a contract basis. They made these knives with green, red and brown tones. These knives were discontinued by Parker-Frost Cutlery after about 6,000 each were made. They are today sought after both by Parker-Frost Eagle Brand collectors and by Schrade Collectors as they were marked Schrade on the rear of the tang.

Schrade has made knives for almost everyone, including such popular names as Diamond Edge, Hibbard, Spencer and Bartlett, L. L. Bean, Parker-Frost, and Buck.

Schrade is also one of the largest producers of commemorative knives, having made the following: Kentucky Rifle, Minuteman, Paul Revere, Liberty Bell, Will Rogers, Eagle Sets, 13 Colony Series, Service Series, Buffalo Bill, Custers Last Fight and many more.

Schrade is also the manufacturer of Uncle Henry and Old Timer knives. The Uncle Henry knife carries the guarantee that if the knife is lost in the first year of ownership it will be replaced. Uncle Henry knives are stainless steel.

The oldest Old Timer knife will be found with bone handles in a swell end pattern. All Old Timers are carbon steel.

PATTERN NUMBERS

SCHRADE HAD ITS OWN PATTERN NUMBER SYSTEM, BUT NOT EVERY SCHRADE KNIFE YOU SEE WILL BE STAMPED. We would advise you to become familiar with this system, since we will have a much expanded section on Schrade in next year's edition.

THE FIRST DIGIT-The number of blades in the knife.

1-1 Blade
2-2 Blades, both blades in one end
3-3 Blades, all 3 blades in one end
7-2 Blade Knife, 1 blade in each end
8-3 Blade Knife, 2 blades in one end and 1 blade in the other end
9-4 Blade Knife, 2 blades in each end

THE SECOND AND THIRD DIGITS-The factory pattern number.
For example 2011, the "01" will always mean an easy open.

THE LAST FIGURE-Handle material.

1-Cocobola
2-Ebony
3-Bone Stag
4-Celluloid
5-White Bone
6-Mother of Pearl
7-Stained Bone
8-Buffalo Horn
9-Miscellaneous

Whenever a handle material number ends with a 4 (celluloid), there will be an additional letter telling what kind of celluloid color it is. That listing is as follows: (Please remember these are celluloid colors, not natural material).

AC-Assorted Colors
AP-Abalone Pearl
B-Black
BLUE-Blue Pearl
BP-Black Pearl
BRNZ-Bronze
C-Cocobola
GL-Goldaleur
GP-Golden Pearl
B-Green Pearl
H-Black and White Striped
HORN-Horn

J-Red, White, Amber Striped
K-Brown Line Cream
M-Marine Pearl
MB-Mottled Blue
MR-Mottled Red
O-Onyx
P-Smoked Pearl
PP-Persian Pearl
S-Tortoise Shell
US-Red, White, Blue Striped
W-White
X-Mottled Green

If the last Handle digit is "9" Miscellaneous, it will be followed by letters revealing its handle material. These letters are natural materials.

BR-Solid Brass
GM-Gun Metal
GOLD-12K Gold Plated

GS-Genuine Stag
GSIL-Nickel Silver
SS-Sterling Silver

A fraction at the end of a number indicates the kind of blade that has been substituted for a spear blade. No fraction would indicate a spear blade.

¼-Spay Blade
½-Sheepfoot Blade

¾-Clip
⅞-Razor Point

Additional letters will also indicate the type of bolsters found on the knife. If the pattern illustrated in a catalog is a shadow pattern, the same pattern number followed by a "T" would indicate nickel silver tip bolsters.

The letter B would indicate the same knife with conventional bolsters (this applies only to patterns such as sleeveboards and senators which are made this way).

Additional letters reveal the following on numbers not ending in "9" or "4".

S-Special Combination or Finish
SS-Stainless Steel Blades and Springs
CH-Chain
EO-Easy Open (on a knife not usually made easy open)
LB-Leather Borer or Punch
SHACK-Shackle to attach knife to a watch chain
B-(As a prefix) Brass Linings in a knife usually made with Nickel Silver Linings
F-(As a prefix) Knife with a Nail File Blade usually made with Cutting Blades

The following are some of the current knives manufactured by Schrade Cutlery Company. Their older knives handled in genuine bone command prices of $50 to $200 and are very much sought after by collectors.

SCHRADE KNIVES
(CURRENT PRODUCTION)

☐**80T**—(4″) Staglon handle, large clip, sheepfoot, and spay blade, crocus polished . . . **16.00**

☐**180T**—(2¾″) Lockblade, staglon handle, one clip blade . . . **8.95**

☐**260T**—(5¼″) Staglon handle, one large clip one long skinning blade . . . **25.95**

☐**330T**—(3$\frac{5}{16}$″) Staglon handle, one clip blade, one pen blade . . . **10.00**

☐**340T**—(3$\frac{5}{16}$″) Staglon handle, one clip blade, one sheep foot blade, one pen blade . . . **14.00**

☐**510T**—(4¾″) Lockback, staglon handle, one large blade . . . **33.95**

☐**610T**—(4″) Staglon handle, one long California Clip blade, one sheepfoot blade, one spray blade . . . **17.00**

☐**770T**—MUSKRAT (4″) Staglon handle, two denticle California Clip blades . . . **13.95**

☐**940T**—TRAPPER (3⅞″) Staglon handle, one clup blade, one long spay blade . . . **14.95**

☐**1080T**—(2¾″) One clip blade, one pen blade, one sheepfoot blade . . . **12.95**

☐**1250T**—LOCKBACK FOLDING HUNTER (5¼″) One large clip blade . . . **22.95**

☐**1940T**—LOCKBACK TRAPPER (3⅞″) One long California Clip blade . . . **11.95**

☐**8580T**—(4⅝″) Staglon handle, one clip blade, one spay blade, one sheepfoot blade . . . **23.95**

☐**130T**—OLD-TIMER (8½″) Fixed blade . . .

☐**140T**—(8½″) Staglon handle . . . **35.00**

☐**150T**—DEERSLAYER (10½″) Staglon handle . . . **26.95**

☐**1520T**—SHARPFINGER (7¼″) Staglon handle . . . **17.95**

☐**1540T**—DROP POINT (7¼″) Staglon handle . . . **17.95**

☐**1560T**—LITTLE FINGER (6¾″) Staglon handle . . . **21.95**

☐**1650T**—WOODSMAN (9½″) Staglon handle . . . **31.95**

UNCLE HENRY

☐**LB-1**—Laminated wood handle . . . **19.95**
☐**LB-5**—Laminated wood handle . . . **29.95**
☐**LB-7**—BEAR PAW. Imitation stag handle **34.95**
☐**LB-8**—GRIZZLY. Imitation stag handle . **39.95**
☐**197UH**—CAT PAW (3$\frac{9}{16}$″) Imitation stag handle . . . **39.95**

☐**285UH**—PRO-TRAPPER (3⅞″) Imitation stag handle . . . **39.95**

☐**885UH**—KING RANCH (4″) Imitation stag handle . . . **14.95**

☐**897UH**—(3$\frac{9}{16}$″) Imitation stag handle **17.95**
☐**127UH**—(5¼″) Imitation stag handle . . **26.95**
☐**227UH**—(5¼″) Imitation stag handle . . **32.95**
☐**144UH**—(8½″) Imitation stag handle . . **44.95**
☐**153UH**—(9¼″) Imitation stag handle . . **37.95**
☐**171UH**—(10½″) Imitation stag handle . **44.95**

SCHRADE SCRIMSHAWS

☐**503SC**—(3⅞″) Scrimshawed delrin . . . **18.00**
☐**505SC**—(4″) Scrimshawed delrin . . . **21.00**
☐**506SC**—(3$\frac{7}{16}$″) Scrimshawed delrin . . **19.00**
☐**500SC**—(5¼″) Scrimshawed delrin . . . **28.95**
☐**508SC**—(5¼″) Scrimshawed delrin . . . **35.00**
☐**502SC**—(7¼″) Scrimshawed delrin . . . **25.00**
☐**507SC**—Scrimshawed delrin . . . **39.95**
☐**509SC**—(6¾″) Scrimshawed delrin . . . **30.00**

SCHRADE OPEN STOCK

☐**136**—(4$\frac{7}{16}$″) . . . **16.00**
☐**186**—(4$\frac{7}{16}$″) . . . **16.00**
☐**206**—(3$\frac{7}{16}$″) . . . **16.00**
☐**293**—(3⅞″) . . . **12.95**
☐**708**—(2¾″) . . . **11.95**
☐**787**—(4″) . . . **11.95**
☐**808**—(2¾″) . . . **11.95**
☐**834**—(3$\frac{5}{16}$″) . . . **11.95**
☐**835Y**—(3$\frac{5}{16}$″) . . . **13.95**
☐**863**—(3⅝″) *(discontinued)* . . . **12.50**
☐**881**—(4″) *(discontinued)* . . . **14.00**
☐**881Y**—(4″) . . . **14.95**
☐**896K**—(3$\frac{9}{16}$″) *(discontinued)* . . . **14.00**
☐**899**—(3$\frac{9}{16}$″) . . . **13.95**
☐**175RB**—(3¾″) . . . **11.95**
☐**778RB**—(2⅞″) . . . **15.95**
☐**825RB**—(3$\frac{9}{16}$″) . . . **16.95**

SCHRADE WALDEN POCKETKNIVES

☐C3-150—(4″) Bone stag, push button, light hunting type, slim clip blade, polished on one side; brass lining; nickel silver bolsters and caps **100.00**

☐C3-151—Assorted colors, celluloid handle **100.00**

☐C3-152—(4″) Celluloid assorted colors, push button; light hunting pattern; slim clip blade, polished on one side; nickel silver bolsters and caps **75.00**

☐C3-153—(4⅞″) Stag handle; push button; blade glazed finish; large clip; steel linings; steel bolsters; nickel silver folding guard **200.00**

☐C3-154—(4⅞″) Stag handle; push button; large clip blade; steel linings; steel bolsters **170.00**

☐C3-174—BUDDING KNIFE (6″) Imported cocabola wood handle, one carbon steel budding blade, 2⅛″ inches long; two compression rivets **30.00**

☐C3-186—PRUNING KNIFE (4⅞″) Cocobola handle, purning blade; steel lining; steel bolster **40.00**

☐C3-234—SERPENTINE JACKKNIFE (3⁵⁄₁₆″) K-Horn celluloid handle, two blades, clip and pen; large blade polished on one side; brass linings; nickel silver bolsters and shield . . .**45.00**

☐**C3-242**—EQUAL END JACKKNIFE (3⅛″) Bone stag handle, slim pattern; two blades; spear and pen; brass lining; nickel silver bosters and shield **75.00**

☐**C3-272**—SERPENTINE JACKKNIFE (2⅞″) two blades; clip and pen; large blade polished on one side; brass lining; nickel silver bolsters and shield **45.00**

☐**C3-272Y**—Yellow pyralin handle as above **45.00**

☐**C3-293**—STOCKMAN'S KNIFE (3⅞″) Bone stag handle, two blades; large half saber clip and large spey; nickel silver bolsters, caps and shields **75.00**

☐**C3-708**—SERPENTINE PENKNIFE (2¾″) Stag handle, two blades; clip and pen; large blade polished on one side; brass lining; nickel silver bolsters and shield **40.00**

☐**C3-708**—Yellow pyralin handle as above **40.00**

☐**C3-742**—(3⅜″) Bone stag handle, push button, two blades; spear and pen; brass lining **80.00**

☐**C3-745**—(2⅞″) Celluloid handle, assorted colors, push button; two blades; spear and pen; brass lining . . . .

☐**C3-746**—(2⅞″) Embossed stainless steel handle, ''Executive'' push button; two blades; pen and file; nickel silver lining **75.00**

☐**C3-750**—(3¾″) Celluloid handle, assorted colors, push button; two blades; clip and pen; large blade polished on one side **100.00**

☐**C3-766**—(3¹⁄₁₆″) Black celluloid handle, Wharncliffe pattern; two blades; clip and pen; large blade polished on one side; brass lining; nickel silver bolsters and shield **30.00**

☐**C3-744**—(3") Bone stag handle, Congress pattern; two blades; sheepfoot and pen; large blade polished on one side; brass lining; nickel silver bolsters **55.00**

☐**C3-787**—MUSKRAT SKINNING KNIFE (4") Bone stag handle, two blades, one side polished; nickel silver bolsters and shield; brass lining **75.00**

☐**C3-808**—(2¾") Stag handle, serpentine pattern, three blades; clip sheepfoot and pen; large blade polished on one side; brass lining, milled back; nickel silver bolsters and shield . . .**25.00**

☐**C3-808Y**—Yellow pyralin as above **25.00**

☐**3C-810**—(3⅛") Bone stag handle, Senaotr pattern; three blades; spear, sheepfoot and pen; large blade polished on one side; brass lining; nickel silver bolsters and shield **45.00**

☐**3C-820**—(2¾") Propwood handle, serpentine pattern, three blades; clip, pen and sheepfoot; large blade polished on one side; brass lining; nickel silver bolsters and shield **20.00**

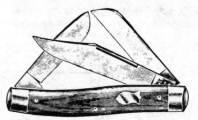

☐**3C-822**—PREMIUM STOCK KNIFE (4") Texas pattern, three blades; clip, spey and sheepfoot; large blade polished on one side; brass lining; nickel silver bolsters and shield **65.00**

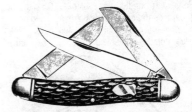

☐**3C-825**—WESTERNER (3⁹⁄₁₆") Bone stag handle, three stainless steel blades; clip, sheepfoot and spey; nickel silver bolsters and shield; large blade polished on one side; milled back; individually boxed **50.00**

☐**3C-834**—(3⁵⁄₁₆") Bone stag handle, serpentine pattern, three blades; clip, sheepfoot and pen; large blade polished on one side; brass lining; nickel silver bolsters and shield **35.00**

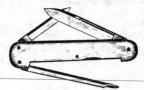

☐**3c-848**—THE COSMOPOLITAN (2¾") Marine pearl, shadow pattern handle, hand made, two blades, pen and rigid nail file; nickel silver lining **30.00**

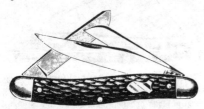

☐**3C-861**—SLIM PREMIUM STOCK KNIFE (4") Bone stag handle, three blades; Turkish clip, sheepfoot and spey; large blade polished on one side; nickel silver lining; milled back; nickel silver bolsters and shield **80.00**

☐**3C-881**—(4") Stag handle, premium stock Texas pattern, three blades; clip, spey and sheepfoot; large blade polished one side; brass lining; nickel silver bolsters and shield . . **80.00**

☐**C3-881Y**—Yellow pyralin handle as above . . .
. . . . **80.00**

☐**C3-890**—PREMIUM STOCK KNIFE (3½") Bone stag handle, three blades; clip, sheepfoot and spey; large blade polished on one side; brass lining; nickel silver bolsters and shield **50.00**

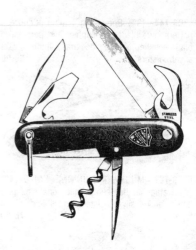

☐**C3-900**—FIELD & STREAM (3⅝") Unbreakable red handle; deep embossed shield; six stainless steel blades; spear master and small clip cutting blades, can opener, screwdriver-cap lifter, punch, corkscrew; rosette rivets; individually boxed **60.00**

☐**C3-906**—SPEARMASTER (3⁹⁄₁₆") Red cellulose handle, seven blades; small clip, can opener, screwdriver and cap lifter, punch, Phillips screwdriver and beer can opener; nickel silver linings; embossed and shielded shackle **60.00**

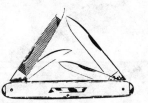

☐**C3-951**—PRESIDENT (2⅞") Marine pearl handle, four stainless steel blades; spear, pen, flexible manicure file and lance blade; nickel silver linings milled; nickel silver tips and shield; blades fully polished; individually boxed with purse **45.00**

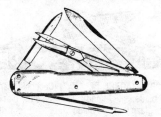

☐**C3-967**—MASTERPIECE (3") Mother of Pearl handle, manicure file, pen and spear pocket blades and scissors all stainless; nickel silver linings and tips; blades full polished; each knife packed with genuine leather purse; individually boxed **45.00**

☐**3C-973**—(3⅓") Bone stag handle, Congress pattern, four blades; two sheepfoot, two pen; brass lining; steel bolsters; nickel silver shield **125.00**

☐**C3-974**—(3") Bone stag handle, Congress pattern; four blades; two sheepfoot, and two pen blades; brass lining; nickel silver bolsters **125.00**

☐**C3-233S**—SERPENTINE JACKKNIFE (3⁵⁄₁₆") Stag handle, two blades; clip and pen; nickel silver bolsters and shield **60.00**

☐**3C-233Y**—Yellow pyralin handle as above **60.00**

☐**C3-709SHA**—ESQUIRE (3¹⁄₁₆") Stainless steel engine turned handle, one stainless steel spear blade and stainless flexible nail file; with shackle; large blade polished on one side; individually boxed with purse **25.00**

☐**C3-793SHA**—(2½") Solid marine pearl handle, Senator pattern, with shackle, two blades; spear and flexible nail file; large blade polished on one side; nickel silver lining; nickel silver tips and shackle **40.00**

☐**3C-809M**—"ESQUIRE" (2¾") Unbreakable marine pearl handle, A Country Gentleman's, hand made, three blades; clip, pen and file; large blade polished on one side; nickel silver shield; brass lining, milled back; nickel silver bolsters **22.00**

☐**C3-863S**—CARPENTER KNIFE (3⅝″) Stag handle, three blades; large clip; Kon-Kay ground, copying pen and small clip; large blade polished on one side; nickel silver bolsters and shield **65.00**

☐**C3-863Y**—Yellow pyralin handle as above . . .
. . . . **65.00**

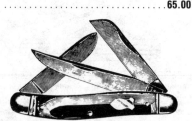

☐**C3-896K**—SLIM PREMIUM STOCK KNIFE (3⁹⁄₁₆″) K-Horn celluloid handle, three blades; clip, sheepfoot and spey; large blade polished on one side; brass lining; nickel silver bolsters and shield **40.00**

☐**C3-SS102**—(4¹¹⁄₁₆″) White celluloid handle, one stainless steel long blade; brass lining . . . .
. . . . **35.00**

☐**C3-SS105**—(5¾″) White celluloid handle, one stainless steel long blade; brass lining . . . .
. . . . **25.00**

☐**C3-SS700**—(4½″) Marine pearl handle, two stainless steel blades, extra long for sampling; brass lining; nickel silver bolsters **45.00**

☐**115S**—BARLOW KNIFE (3⅜″) Bone stag handle; one blade; steel lined; steel bolsters; black inside; glaze finished blade; one clip blade . . . .
. . . . **50.00**

☐**718**—(2¾″) RB; Gentleman's pen; staglon
. . . . **8.00**

☐**1091**—JACKKNIFE (3⅝″) Cocobola handle; one blade; steel lined; steel bolsters; black inside; glaze finished blade **60.00**

☐**2061 3/4**—JACKKNIFE (3⅝″) Cocobola handle; two blades; brass lined; nickel silver bolsters, caps and shield; cleaned inside; large blade crocus polished on one side **96.00**

☐**2062 3/4**—Ebony handle, as above **75.00**

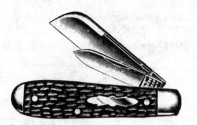

☐2063 1/2—JACK KNIFE (3⅝″) Bone stag handle, two blades; brass lined; nickel silver bolsters, caps and shield; cleaned inside; large blade crocus polished on one side **132.00**

☐2063 3/4—JACKKNIFE (3⅝″) Bone stag handle, two blades; brass lined; nickel silver bolsters, cap and shield; cleaned inside; large blade crocus polished on one side **110.00**

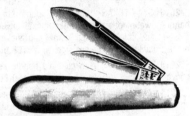

☐2069BR—JACKKNIFE (3⅝″) Solid brass composition handle, two blades; cleaned inside; large blade crocus polished on one side ..**96.00**

☐2069 3/4BR—as above; pen and clip pocket blades **96.00**

☐2071—JACKKNIFE (3⅝″) Cocobola handle, two blades; brass lined; nickel silver bolsters and shield; cleaned inside; large blade crocus polished on one side.................**96.00**

☐2071 3/4—JACKKNIFE (3⅝″) Cocobola handle, two blades; brass lined; nickel silver bolsters and shield; cleaned inside; large blade crocus polished on one side **96.00**

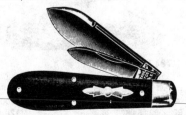

☐2072—JACKKNIFE (3⅝″) Ebony handle, two blades; brass lined; nickel silver bolsters and shield; cleaned inside; learge blade crocus polished on one side.................**96.00**

☐2072 3/4—JACKKNIFE (3⅝″) Ebony handle, two blades; brass lined; nickel sivler bolsters and shield; cleaned inside; large blade crocus polished on one side.................**96.00**

☐2073—JACKKNIFE (3⅝″) Bone stag handle, two blades; brass lined; nickel silver boslters and shield; cleaned inside; large blade crocus polished on one side...............**110.00**

☐2073 3/4—JACKKNIFE (3⅝″) Bone stag handle, two blades; brass lined; nickel silver bolsters and shield; cleaned inside; large blade crocus polished on one side **120.00**

☐2091—JACKKNIFE (3⅝″) Cocobola handle, two blades; steel lined; steel bolsters; nickel silver shield; cleaned inside; glaze finished blades **110.00**

☐2093—Bone stag handle as above ...**144.00**

☐2221—SERPENTINE JACKKNIFE (3¹⅝″) Cocobola handle, two blades; brass lined; nickel silver bolsters, caps and shield; cleaned inside; large blade crocus polished on one side .
...............................**96.00**

☐2222—Ebony handle as above **96.00**

☐2223—Bone stag handle as above ...**110.00**

☐2224 AC—Assorted celluloid handles as above...........................**80.00**

☐2224GP—Golden pearl pyralin handle as above...........................**80.00**

☐**226**—SERPENTINE JACKKNIFE (3½") Mother of Pearl handle, two blades; brass lined; nickel silver bolsters, caps and shield; cleaned inside; large blade crocus polished on one side **162.00**

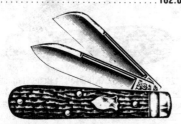

☐**2293**—CARPENTER'S KNIFE (3½") Bone stag handle, two large pocket blades; brass lined; steel rat bolsters; nickel silver shield; cleaned inside; spear pocket blade crocus polished on one side **162.00**

☐**2363**—JACKKNIFE (3½") Bone stag handle, two blades; brass lined; steel rat bolsters; nickel silver shield; cleaned inside; large blade crocus polished on one side **132.00**

☐**2392**—JACKKNIFE (3½") Ebony handle, two blades; brass lined; steel bolsters; nickel silver shield; black inside; glaze finished blades **96.00**

☐**2392**—Bone stag handle as above with leather punch and clip pocket blade **45.00**

☐**2393 3/4**—Bone stag handle as above . **50.00**

☐**2813**—TEXAS JACKKNIFE (4") Bone stag handle, two blades; pen and spear pocket blades; brass lined nickel silver bolsters and shield; cleaned inside; clip pocket blade crocus polished on one side **156.00**

☐**2813 3/4**—TEXAS JACKKNIFE Bone stag handle, two blades; brass lined nickel silver bolsters and shield; cleaned inside; clip pocket blade crocus polished on one side **156.00**

☐**2814 3/4G**—Green pearl celluloid handle as above **140.00**

☐**2814 3/4P**—Smoked pearl celluloid handle as above **140.00**

☐**2814 3/4 AC**—Assorted celluloid handle as above **140.00**

☐**7243B**—(3⅝") Bone stag handle, Sleeveboard pattern, pen and extra long spear pocket blades; brass lined; nickel silver bolsters and shield; cleaned inside; large blade crocus polished on one side **96.00**

☐**7243T**—(3⅜") Bone stag handle, Sleeveboard pattern, pen and extra long spear pocket blades; brass lined; nickel silver tips and shield; cleaned inside; large blade crocus polished on one side **120.00**

☐**7244HT**—Black and white pyralin handle as above **90.00**

☐**7326**—(÷⅜") Mother of Pearl handle, Sleeveboard pattern, two blades; brass lined; nickel sivler bolsters at one end; cleaned inside; large blade crocus polished on one side . **108.00**

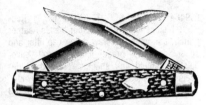

☐**7812**—TEXAS JACKKNIFE (4") Ebony handle, two large pocket blades; brass lined; nickel silver bolsters and shield; cleaned inside; clip pocket blade crocus polished on one side**190.00**

☐**7813**—Bone stag handle as above . . .**210.00**

☐**9113B**—(3⅜") Bone stag handle, Sleeveboard pattern, four blades; brass lined; nickel silver bolsters and shield; cleaned inside; large spear blade crocus polished on one side
. . . .**192.00**

☐**116B**—(3⅜") Mother of Pearl handle, Sleeveboard pattern, four blades; brass lined; nickel silver bolsters; cleaned inside; large spear blade crocus polished on one side **264.00**

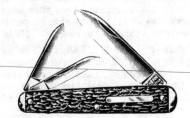

☐**8313B**—(3⅜") Bone stag handle, Sleeveboard pattern, three blades (two cutting pens and large spear pocket); brass lined; large nickel silver bolsters; cleaned inside; large blade crocus polished on one side **190.00**

☐**8313T**—(3⅜") Bone stag handle, Sleeveboard pattern, three blades (two cutting pens and large spear pocket); brass lined; nickel sivler tips and shield; cleaned inside; large blade crocus polished on one side **180.00**

☐**8316B**—(3⅜") Mother of Pearl handle, Sleeveboard pattern, three blades (two cutting pens and large spear pocket); brass lined; nickel silver tips and shield, cleaned inside; large blade crocus polished on one side .**250.00**

☐**8323**—(3⅜") Bone stag handle, Sleeveboard pattern, three blades; brass lined; nickel silver boslters at one end; nickel silver shield; cleaned inside; large blade crocus polished on one side .
. . . .**180.00**

☐**8324S**—Tortoise shell celluloid handle as above **150.00**

☐**8443**—AUTOMOBILE AND ELECTRICIAN'S KNIFE (3⅝") Stag handle, equal end pattern, three blades (leather punch, screw driver-wire scraper-file and spear pocket); brass lined; nickel silver bolsters and shield; cleaned inside; spear pocket blade crocus polished on one side
. . . .**192.00**

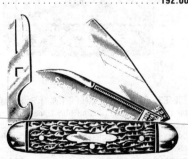

☐**8463**—AUTOMOBILE AND CAMPER'S KNIFE (3⅝") Bone stag handle, equal end pattern, three blades (screw driver-wire scraper-file, can opener-cap lifter and spear pocket); brass lined; nickel silver bolsters and shield; cleaned inside; spear pocket blade crocus polished on one side **168.00**

☐**8803**—PREMIUM STOCK KNIFE (4") Bone stag handle, three large pocket blades; brass lined; round end nickel silver bolsters and shield; cleaned inside; clip pocket blade crocus polished on one side **210.00**

☐**8813**—PREMIUM STOCK KNIFE (4") Bone stag handle, Texas pattern, three blades, brass lined; nickel silver bolsters and shield; cleaned inside; clip pocket blade crocus polished on one side **210.00**

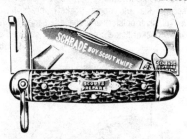

☐**9463**—BOY SCOUT KNIFE (3⅝") Bone stag handle, four blades (leather punch, can opener, screw driver-cap lifter and spear pocket); brass lined; nickel silver bolsters, shield and shackle; cleaned inside; spear pocket blade crocus polished on one side **144.00**

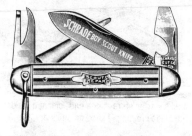

☐**9464US**—BOY SCOUT KNIFE (3⅝") Red-white-blue celluloid handle; four blades (leather punch, can opener, screw driver-cap lifter and spear pocket); brass lined; nickel silver bolsters, shield and shackle; cleaned inside; spear pocket blade crocus polished on one side **132.00**

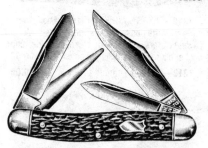

☐**9803LB**—PREMIUM STOCK KNIFE (4") Bone stag handle, four blades; brass lined; round end nickel silver bolsters and shield; cleaned inside; clip pocket blade crocus polished on one side **228.00**

☐**9466**—BOY SCOUT KNIFE (3⅝") Mother of Pearl handle, four blades (leather punch, can opener, screw driver-cap lifter and spear pocket); brass lined; nickel silver boslters, shield and shackle; cleaned inside; fancy milled edges on back of linings and centers; spear pocket blade full crocus polished **240.00**

☐**9603**—PREMIUM STOCK KNIFE (4") Bone stag handle, four blades; nickel silver lined, with full milled back; round end nickel silver bolster and shield; cleaned inside; clip pocket blade crocus polished on one side **270.00**

☐**9806**—PREMIUM STOCK KNIFE (4") Mother of Pearl handle, four blades; nickel silver lined, with full milled back; round end nickel silver bolsters and shield; cleaned inside; blades full crocus polished **225.00**

☐**S2393**—CAMPER'S KNIFE (3½″) Bone stag handle, two blades (can opener-cap lifter and large spear pocket); brass lined; steel boslters; nickel silver shield; cleaned inside; spear pocket blade crocus polished on one side**134.00**

☐**S9463**—BOY SCOIUT KNIFE WITHOUT SHACKLE (3⅝″) Bone stag handle, (or) Everybody's Companion, four blades (leather punch, can open screw driver-cap lifter and spear pocket); brass lined; nickel silver boslters and shield; cleaned inside; spear pocket blade crocus polished on one side **144.00**

POCKET KNIVES
SCHRADE
PUSH BUTTON

INSTRUCTIONS TO OPERATE
SCHRADE SAFETY PUSH BUTTON KNIVES

Important—To open or close—The button must be pressed.
NEVER USE FORCE. Use only one hand.
To Open. Unlock by pulling safety slide away from button, and the blade will open and lock in an open position.
To Close. Push the button and hold to release lock, then close blade with index finger and when it locks move safety slide toward button as far as it will go. In this condition the knife is *DOUBLE LOCKED* and cannot open while being carried in the pocket.
AUTHOR'S NOTE: (Federal law has prohibited owning, displaying, selling or possessing switchblades since 1957.)

☐**G1514J**—(4″) Red-White-Amber Striped Pyralin handle; same as above with guard on bolsters. **108.00**

☐**G1514K**—(4″) Brown Sined Cream Pyralin handle; same as above with guard on bolsters **108.00**

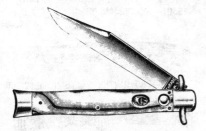

☐**1514AC**—SAFETY PUSH BUTTON KNIFE (4″) Assorted Pyralin handles, dagger type, slim clip blade; brass lined; nickel silver boslters without guard; nickel silver caps; cleaned inside; blade crocus polished on one side **108.00**

☐**1543 3/4**—SAFETY PUSH BUTTON KNIFE (4⅞″) Bone stag handle, large clip blade; steel lined; steel bolsters; cleaned inside; glaze finished blade **270.00**

☐**1553**—SAFETY PUSH BUTTON KNIFE (4¼″) Bone stag handle, large spear blade; steel lined; steel boslters; cleaned inside; glaze finished blade **180.00**

☐**1553 3/4**—SAFETY PUSH BUTTON KNIFE (4¼″) Bone stag handle, large clip blade; steel lined; steel bolsters; cleaned inside; glaze finished blade **180.00**

☐**1613 3/4**—SAFETY PUSH BUTTON KNIFE (4⅞″) Bone stag handle, large saber clip blade; steel lined, nickel silver bolsters; cleaned inside; blade one-half crocus polished on one side **330.00**

☐**6489W**—(3″) Engine turn jewelers design handle. The blades open automatically and there is no breaking of finger nails; blades are full crocus polished, 14K white gold top, oval signet for initials; brass lined; cleaned inside spring. Packed on in attractive individual box...**150.00**

SCHRADE SHEATH KNIVES

*(KNIVES IN CURRENT PRODUCTION)

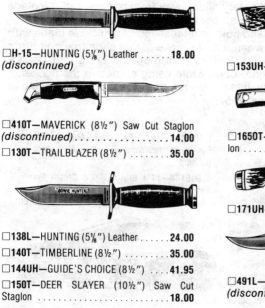

☐**H-15**—HUNTING (5⅛″) Leather ......**18.00** *(discontinued)*

☐**410T**—MAVERICK (8½″) Saw Cut Staglon *(discontinued)*.................**14.00**

☐**130T**—TRAILBLAZER (8½″) **35.00**

☐**138L**—HUNTING (5⅛″) Leather **24.00**

☐**140T**—TIMBERLINE (8½″) **35.00**

☐**144UH**—GUIDE'S CHOICE (8½″) **41.95**

☐**150T**—DEER SLAYER (10½″) Saw Cut Staglon **18.00**

☐**153UH**—GOLDEN SPIKE (5″) Staglon .**30.00**

☐**1650T**—WOODSMAN (9½″) Saw Cut Staglon **14.40**

☐**171UH**—PRO HUNTER (5⅝″) Staglon .**24.00**

☐**491L**—MODIFIED BOWIE (4½″) Leather *(discontinued)*.................**16.80**

☐491S—MODIFIED BOWIE (4½") Staglon *(discontinued)* **15.00**

☐497L—(4½") Leather *(discontinued)* **16.80**

☐498S—SKINNING KNIFE (5") Staglon *(discontinued)* **15.00**

☐499L—SKINNING KNIFE (4½") Leather **16.80**

☐499S—SKINNING KNIFE (4½") Staglon *(discontinued)* **15.00**

☐1540T—DROPPOINT (7¼") **17.95**

☐1560T—LITTLE FINGER (6¾") **21.95**

☐1520T—SHARPFINGER **17.95**

SCHRADE, GEORGE
BRIDGEPORT, CONNECTICUT

Invented by George Schrade

☐**6489W**—(3") Engine turn jewelers design handle. The blades open automatically and there is no breaking of finger nails, blades are full crocus polished, 14K white gold top, oval signet for initials; brass lined; cleaned inside spring. Packed one in attractive individual box **150.00**

George Schrade began his cutlery career when a local inventor brought a prototype of a switchblade knife into Schrade's machine shop and asked Schrade if it could be made. It could not. But Schrade was not one to let anything stump him, and a few months later he came out with his own design for a switchblade knife.

His first knife had a button set into the bolster, and when it was pushed the blade would spring open.

Schrade formed the "Press Button Knife Company" in 1893, operating from a small shop in New York City that employed 18 men. His production was not what he desired, for he was having a difficult time finding cutlers.

Enter Edward Whitehead, President of Walden Knife Company. He liked the knife and persuaded Schrade to move to Walden to set up his operation. As a part of the move, the Walden Knife Company bought an interest in the Press Button Knife Company and set up a factory for the press button, with George Schrade as superintendent.

Under Schrade the company made 12 patterns, ranging from a large folding hunter pattern to a ladies leg knife. He sold his patent to Walden (it had seven more years to run) in 1903 and moved across town to start his own company.

Schrade Cutlery Company was started by George Schrade in 1904, where he brought his brothers, J. Louis and William into the business. He devoted years to developing a good line of pocketknives, then in 1906 he developed an improved switchblade knife, incorporating an automatic spring and a lock on the blade, which had been a major criticism of the press button knife. The following year he changed the location of the button to the middle part of the handle adding a button lock.

Soon thereafter he invented an automatic shielding machine, and left Schrade Cutlery in 1910 to seek his fortune with his shield machine.

Thomas Turner & Company in Sheffield was impressed with Schrade's machine; however, the trade unions were not. Turner had contracted with the British navy for a hard rubber handled knife, but the cutlers were protesting since it was much harder to gouge the shield on the rubber than bone and wood.

Turner secretly set up a Schrade machine in a back room and began using it to pace the shields. But the cutlers were not to be fooled. When it was discovered further down the assembly line that the knife had been shielded with a machine, the cutlers walked out, returning only after the machine was removed.

With the outbreak of World War I, Schrade decided to stay in Germany, sure that the war would be over in a few months. He returned to the United States in 1916, after the German government had confiscated all of his raw material for use in the war effort.

That same year he began making still another style of switchblade, the Flylock. Most of these were made by the Challenge Cutlery Company, which later bought the rights to the knife from Schrade.

Soon he was making them again, under the George Schrade Cutlery Co. trademark, marking many of them "Presto". He supplied many of these to the United States Government during World War II.

It is believed that the company went out of business in the 1950's.

SEARS, HENRY AND SON, 1865

Farwell, Ozmun and Kerk Hardware Company of St. Paul, Minnesota used the Henry Sears brand, but information on the origin of the company is sketchy, possibly the hardware company bought an independent cutlery firm named Henry Sears and Son. Some Henry Sears knives have "Queen" stamped on a bolster of shield. (The Henry Sears, 1865 is, to this writer's knowledge, not related in any way to Queen Cutlery or Sears, Roebuck & Co.)

SHAPLEIGH HARDWARE
ST. LOUIS, MISSOURI

Shapleigh was a hardware company that has produced many collectable pocketknives, including Bridge Cutlery Company and Diamond Edge.

The hardware company was founded by A. F. Shapleigh in 1843, adopting the Diamond Edge logo in 1864. Made by Camillus and Schrade, the Diamond Edge was very popular. Shapleigh made over 600 patterns of pocketknives, including some Diamond Edge knives stamped Norvel Shapleigh (named for a Shapleigh Hardware company buyer, Sanders Norvel).

Shapleigh went out of business in 1960, making cutlery until that time.

The Diamond Edge trademark is currently used by Imperial Knife Associated Companies on one of their lines of cutlery and should not be confused with the older Diamond Edge knives.

☐**E101ST**—(3") Imitation bone stag; large spear and small pen blades; glazed finish; iron bolsters; brass lining **50.00**

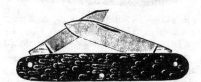

☐**E103ST**—(3⅛") Imitation bone stag; large spear and small pen blades; glazed finish; brass lining **50.00**

☐**E104C**—(4⅞") Striped celluloid handle; nickel silver bolsters; brass lining **50.00**

☐**E105PC**—(4⅞") Pearl celluloid handle; large clip blade; half polished **50.00**

☐**E201C**—(3¼") Celluloid lhandle; large clip and small pen blades; nickel silver shield and bolsters; brass lining **50.00**

☐**E102ST**—(3") Imitation bone stag; large spear and small pen blades; glazed finish; iron bolsters; brass lining **50.00**

☐**E202ST**—Bone stag handle as above except with iron bolsters **175.00**

☐**E205ST**—(3⅜") Bone stag handle; large spear and small pen blades; half polished; nickel silver shield; iron bolsters; brass lining . . . **180.00**

□**E206C**—(3") Celluloid handle; large clip and small pen blades; half polished; nickel silver shield; iron bolsters; brass lining **45.00**

□**E207ST**—(3⅜") Bone stag handle; large spear and small pen blades; half polished; nickel silver shield; iron bolsters; brass lining **90.00**

□**E208C**—(3⅜") Celluloid lhandle; large spear and small pen blades; half polished; nickel silver shield; iron bolsters; brass lining .. **90.00**

□**E211ST**—(3¼") Bone stag handle; large spear and small pen blades; half polished; nickel silver shield; iron bolsters; brass lining **60.00**

□**E212C**—(3¼") Celluloid handle; large spear and small pen blades; half polished; nickel silver shield; iron bolsters; brass lining .. **60.00**

□**E217PC**—(3¼") Pearl celluloid handle; large clip and small pen blades; half polished; nickel silver shield; nickel silver bolsters; brass lining **55.00**

□**E221PC**—(3¼") Pearl celluloid handle; large spear and small pen blades; half polished; nickel silver shield; nickel silver bolsters; brass lining **45.00**

□**E222PC**—(3¼") Pearl celluloid handle; large spear and small pen blades; half polished; nickel silver shield; nickel silver tips; brass lining **45.00**

□**1S440 3/4C**—(5") Fancy celluloid handle, large clip blade, half polished and etched; nickel silver bolsters, brass lining **160.00**

□**1S440 3/4CP**—(5") Celluloid pearl handle, sabre clip blade, half polished and etched; nickel silver bolsters; brass lining **150.00**

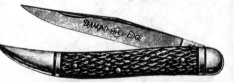

□**1S440 3/4S**—(5") Bone stag handle, large clip blade, half polished and etched; nickel silver bolsters; brass lining **160.00**

☐**1S441 3/4C**—(4¾″) Fancy celluloid handle; large clip blade, half polished; nickel silver bolsters; brass lining **150.00**

☐**1S442 3/4C**—(4″) Red celluloid handle, large clip blade; half polished and etched; nickel silver bolsters; brass lining **90.00**

☐**1S442 3/4S**—Bone stag handle as above **90.00**

☐**1S443 3/4S**—(4″) Bone stag handle; large clip blade; half polished and etched; nickel silver bolster; brass lining **75.00**

☐**1S445**—(4⅛″) Cocobola wood handle; large maize blade; glazed and etched; steel lining; steel bolster **60.00**

☐**1S447 3/4C**—(4″) Fancy celluloid handle; large sabre clip blade; half polished and etched; nickel silver bolster; brass lining **75.00**

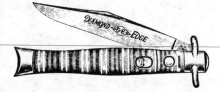

☐**1S448 3/4C**—(4″) Fancy celluloid handle; large clip blade; half polished and etched; nickel silver bolsters; brass lining **90.00**

☐**1S449 3/4C**—(4″) Fancy celluloid handle, large clip blade; half polished and etched; nickel silver bolsters; brass lining **90.00**

☐**1S621**—(3⅜″) Cocobola handle, large spear blade, glade glazed and etched; steel lining; steel bolster **40.00**

☐**1S621 3/4**—Cocobola handle; large clip blade as above **40.00**

☐**1S622ST**—(3⅜″) Bone stag handle; large spear blade; glazed finish blade; steel bolster; steel lining **70.00**

☐**1S662 3/4ST**—Bone stag handle; large clip blade as above **70.00**

☐**1S622 5/8ST**—Bone stag handle; large spey blade as above **70.00**

☐**S14ST**—(4⅞″) Bone stag handle; steel lining; steel bolsters; one large clip blade; glazed finish and etched **150.00**

☐**S15ST**—(4¼″) Bone stag handle; steel lining; steel bolsters; one large clip blade; glazed finish and etched **150.00**

☐**S101**—(4″) Cocobola wood handle; large pruning blade; glazed finish; steel bolsters; iron lining **60.00**

☐**S104**—(4″) Cocobola wood handle; large maize blade; glazed finish; steel bolsters; iron lining **60.00**

☐**S103 3/4**—(5") Bone stag handle; large clip blade; half polished and etched; nickel silver bolsters; brass lining **165.00**

☐**S104 3/4**—Celluloid pearl handle as above **165.00**

☐**S105**—(5") Bone stag handle; large spear blade; glazed finish and etched; steel bolsters, iron lining **130.00**

☐**S106 3/4**—(5") Bone stag handle; large clip blade; glazed finish and etched; steel bolsters, iron lining **130.00**

☐**S209**—(2¾") Bone stag handle; large spear and small pen blades; half polished and etched; nickel silver shield; nickel silver shield; brass lining **50.00**

☐**S210**—Fancy celluloid handle as above **45.00**

☐**S211**—(2⅞") Bone stag handle; large spear and small pen blades; half polished and etched; nickel silver shield; nickel silver bolsters; brass lining **110.00**

☐**S212C**—Fancy celluloid handle as above **100.00**

☐**S217 3/4**—(3") Bone stag handle; large clip and small pen blades; half polished and etched; nickel silver shield; nickel silver bolsters; brass lining **60.00**

☐**S218 3/4**—(3") Fancy celluloid handle; large clip and small pen blades; half polished and etched; nickel silver shield; nickel silver bolsters; brass lining **55.00**

☐**S231**—(3") Bone stag handle; large spear and small pen blades; half polished and etched; nickel silver bolsters; brass lining **50.00**

☐**S232**—Fancy celluloid handle as above **45.00**

☐**S233**—(3") Bone stag handle; large spear and small pen blades; half polished and etched; nickel silver shield; nickel silver bolsters; brass lining **50.00**

☐**S234**—Fancy celluloid handle as above **45.00**

☐**S235**—(3") Bone stag handle; large spear and small pen blades; half polished and etched; nickel silver shield; nickel silver bolsters; brass lining **55.00**

☐**S236**—Celluloid handle as above **45.00**

☐**S248**—(2¾") Celluloid pearl handle; large spear and small pen blades; half polished and etched; nickel silver bolsters; brass lining **50.00**

☐**S249**—(2¾") Celluloid pearl handle; large spear and small pen blades; half polished and etched; nickel silver bolsters; brass lining **50.00**

☐**S301 1/4**—(3¼") Bone stag handle; large clip; small spey and punch blades; half polished and etched; nickel silver shield; steel bolsters; brass lining **100.00**

☐**S302 3/4**—(3¼″) Bone stag handle; large clip, small spey and sheepfoot blades; half polished and etched; nickel silver shield; steel boslters; brass lining **100.00**

☐**S306 3/4**—(3¼″) Fancy celluloid handle; large clip, spey and sheepfoot blades; half polished and etched; nickel silver shield; steel bolsters; brass lining **90.00**

☐**S307 3/4**—(3⅜″) Fancy celluloid handle; large clip, small spey and pen blades; half polished and etched; nickel silver shield; steel bolsters; brass lining **90.00**

☐**S303 3/4**—(3¼″) Fancy celluloid handle; large clip, spey and sheepfoot blades; half polished and etched; nickel silver shield; steel bolsters; brass lining **90.00**

☐**S304 1/4**—(3⅜″) Bone stag handle; large spear, small spey and punch blades; half polished and etched; nickel silver shield; steel bolsters; brass lining **80.00**

☐**S308 1/4**—(3⅞″) Bone stag handle; large clip, small spey and punch blades; half polished and etched; nickel silver shield; nickel silver bolsters; nickel silver lining **125.00**

☐**S305 1/4**—(3⅜″) Fancy celluloid handle as above **65.00**

☐**S309 1/4**—(3⅞″) Celluloid pearl handle; large clip, small spey and punch blades; half polished and etched; nickel silver shield; nickel silver bolsters; nickel silver lining **100.00**

☐**S310 1/4**—(3⅝″) Bone stag handle; large spear, small spey and punch blades; half polished and etched; nickel silver shield; nickel silver bolsters; nickel silver lining **80.00**

☐**S311 1/4**—Celluloid handle as above ..**65.00**

☐**S405 1/4**—(3⅞″) Bone stag handle; large spear, punch, can opener and screw driver blades; half polished and etched; nickel silver shield; nickel silver bolsters, brass lining **75.00**

☐**2S272GS**—(4½″) Genuine stag handle; large spear and small pen blades, half polished and etched; nickel silver shield; nickel silver bolsters; brass lining **125.00**

☐**2S375C**—(3⅜″) Fancy celluloid handle; large spear and small pen blades; half polished and etched; nickel silver silver shield; nickel silver tips; brass lining **50.00**

☐**2S375S**—Bone stag handle as above ..**50.00**

☐**2S375CP**—Celluloid pearl handle as above ...
................................**35.00**

☐**2S376C**—(3⅞″) Fancy celluloid handle; large spear and small pen blades; half polished and etched; nickel silver shield; nickel silver bolsters; brass lining **50.00**

☐**2S276P**—Pearl handle as above **60.00**

☐**2S376S**—(3¾″) Bone stag handle; large spear and small pen blades; half polished and etched; nickel silver shield; nickel silver bolsters; brass lining **55.00**

☐**2S377W**—(3¾″) Celluloid handle; large ink eraser and small pen blades; half polished and etched; brass lining **550.00**

☐**2S380C**—(2¾″) Fancy celluloid handle; large spear and small pen blades; half polished and etched; nickel silver shield; nickel silver bolsters; brass lining **50.00**

☐**2S380ST**—Bone stag handle as above .**50.00**

☐**2S381**—(3⅛″) Celluloid handle; large clip and small pen blades; half polished and etched; nickel silver shield; nickel silver bolsters; brass lining **40.00**

☐**2½s371 3/4ST**—Bone stag handle as above .
................................**50.00**

☐**2S305C**—(3⅜″) Fancy celluloid handle; large spear and small pen blades; half polished and etched; nickel silver shield; nickel silver bolsters; brass lining **50.00**

☐**2S305P**—Pearl handle as above **60.00**

☐**2S305P**—Pearl handle as above **60.00**

☐**2S311 3/4C**—(3½") Fancy celluloid handle, large clip and small spey blades; half polished and etched; nickel silver shield; nickel silver bolsters; brass lining **60.00**

☐**2S311 3/4ST**—Bone stag handle as above **45.00**

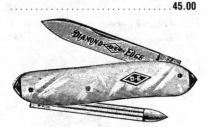

☐**2S312P**—(3") Pearl handle; large spear and nail file blades; half polished and etched; nickel silver shield; nickel silver tips; nickel silver lining **50.00**

☐**2S315P**—(2½") Pearl handle; large spear and nailfile blades; half polished and etched; nickel silver shield; brass lining **60.00**

☐**2S336 3/4C**—(3¼") Fancy celluloid handle; large clip and small pen blades; half polished and etched; nickel silver shield; nickel silver bolsters; brass lining **50.00**

☐**2S336 3/4S**—Bone stag handle as above **65.00**

☐**2S342C**—(3⅜") Fancy celluloid handle; large spear and small pen blades; half polished and etched; nickel silver shield; nickel silver bolsters; brass lining **60.00**

☐**2S362P**—(3") Pearl handle; large spear and flexible file blades; half polished and etched; nickel silver shield shackle; nickel silver tips; brass lining **60.00**

☐**2S382 3/4C**—(2⅞") Celluloid handle; large sabre clip and small pen blades; half polished and etched; nickel silver shield; nickel silver bolsters; brass lining **50.00**

☐**2S382 3/4ST**—Bone stag handle as above **50.00**

☐**2S383 3/4C**—(3⅜") Celluloid handle; large clip and small pen blades; half polished and etched; nickel silver shield; nickel silver bolsters; brass lining **40.00**

☐**2S383 3/4ST**—Bone stag handle as above **45.00**

☐**2S386C**—(3") Celluloid handle; large spear and small pen blades; half polished and etched; nickel silver shield; nickel silver bolsters; brass lining **75.00**

☐**2S386ST**—Bone stag handle as above . **75.00**

☐**2S404C**—(3") Celluloid handle; large spear and small pen blades; half polished and etched; nickel silver shield; nickel silver boslters; brass lining **100.00**

☐**2S404ST**—Bone stag handle as above **125.00**

☐**S417P**—(2¾") Pearl handle; large spear and small pen blades; half polished and etched; nickel silver shield; brass lining **60.00**

☐**2S432C**—(3") Celluloid handle; large spear and small pen blades; half polished and etched; nickel silver shield; brass lining **125.00**

☐**2S432ST**—Bone stag handle as above **150.00**

☐**2S443GS**—(3⅛") Nickel silver handle; ring opener; large spear and small pen blades; half polished and etched **40.00**

☐**2S447C**—(3½") Celluloid handle; large spear and small pen blades; half polished and etched; nickel silver shield; nickel silver bolsters; brass lining **60.00**

☐**2S447ST**—Bone stag handle; large spear and pen blades, half polished and etched; nickel silver shield; nickel silver bolsters; brass lining **70.00**

☐**2S447 3/4C**—(3½") Celluloid handle; large clip and small pen blades; half polished and etched; nickel silver shield; nickel silver bolsters; brass lining **65.00**

☐**2S447 3/4ST**—Bone stag handle as above **70.00**

☐**2S450C**—(3") Celluloid handle; large spear and small pen blades; half polished and etched; nickel silver shield; nickel silver bolsters; brass lining **90.00**

☐**2S450ST**—Bone stag handle as above . **90.00**

☐**2S457C**—(3⅛") Celluloid handle; large spear and small pen blades; glazed finish and etched; nickel sivler shield; steel bolsters, brass lining **60.00**

☐**2S457ST**—Bone stag handle as above **100.00**

☐**2S506C**—(2⅞″) Celluloid handle; large spear and small pen blades; half polished and etched; nickel silver shield; nickel silver bolsters; brass lining **50.00**

☐**2S506ST**—Bone stag handle as above . **50.00**

☐**2S514 1/2ST**—(3⅛″) Bone stag handle; large sheepfoot and small pen blades; half polished and etched; nickel silver shield; nickel silver bolsters; brass lining **50.00**

☐**2S520ST**—(3⅜″) Bone stag handle; large spear and small pen blades; half polished and etched; nickel silver shield; nickel silver bolsters; brass lining **55.00**

☐**2S 526 3/4 ST**—(4″) Bone stag handle; large clip and large spear blades; half polished and etched; nickel silver shield; nickel silver bolsters; brass lining **140.00**

☐**2S527 3/4C**—(4″) Celluloid handle; large clip and small spey blades; half polished and etched; nickel silver shield; nickel silver bolsters; brass lining **170.00**

☐**2S427 3/4ST**—Bone stag handle as above **170.00**

☐**2S528C**—(3″) Celluloid handle; large spear and small pen blades; half polished and etched; nickel silver shield; nickel silver bolsters; brass lining **40.00**

☐**2S528CP**—Bone stag handle as above . **45.00**

☐**2S534 3/4C**—(3¼″) Celluloid handle; large clip and small pen blades; half polished and etched; nickel silver shield; nickel silver bolsters; brass lining **40.00**

☐**2S535 3/4ST**—Bone stag handle as above **50.00**

☐**2S538C**—(3⅛″) Celluloid handle; large clip and small pen blades; half polished and etched; nickel silver shield; nickel silver bolsters; brass lining **50.00**

☐**2S539 3/4C**—(3½″) Celluloid handle; large clip and small pen blades; half polished and etched; nickel silver shield; nickel silver bolsters; brass lining **50.00**

☐**2S542C**—(3″) Celluloid handle; large spear and small pen blades; half polished and etched; nickel silver shield; nickel silver bolsters; brass lining **40.00**

☐**2S542ST**—Bone stag handle as above . **45.00**

☐**2S555P**—(2¼″) Pearl handle, large spear and nail file blades; half polished and etched; brass lining **60.00**

☐**2S546C**—(2⅞″) Celluloid handle; large spear and small pen blades; half polished and etched; nickel silver shield; nickel silver bolsters; brass lining **50.00**

☐**2S567C**—(3⅜″) Celluloid handle; large spear and small pen blades; half polished and etched; nickel silver shield; nickel silver bolsters; brass lining **40.00**

☐**2S467CP**—Celluloid pearl handle as above **40.00**

☐**2S467ST**—Bone stag handle as above . **45.00**

☐**2S580C**—(3⅜″) Celluloid handle; large spear and small pen blades; half polished and etched; nickel silver shield; steel bolsters; brass lining **50.00**

☐**2S580ST**—Bone stag handle as above . **55.00**

☐**2S580CEO**—(3⅜″) Celluloid handle; easy opener; large spear and small pen blades; half polished and etched; nickel silver shield; steel bolsters; brass lining **65.00**

☐**2S580SEO**—Bone stag handle; easy opener as above **65.00**

☐**2S580 3/4C**—(3⅜″) Celluloid handle; large clip and small pen blades; half polished and etched; nickel silver shield; steel bolsters; brass lining **50.00**

☐**2S580 3/4ST**—Bone stag handle as above **55.00**

☐**2S581C**—(3″) Celluloid handle; large spear and small pen blades; glazed finish and etched; nickel silver shield; steel bolsters, brass lining **40.00**

☐**2S581ST**—Bone stag handle as above . **50.00**

☐**2S586 3/4C**—(3⅛″) Celluloid handle; large clip and small pen blades; half polished and etched; nickel silver shield; nickel silver bolsters; brass lining **50.00**

☐**2S568 3/4ST**—Bone stag handle as above **60.00**

☐**2S587C**—(2⅞″) Celluloid handle; large spear and small pen blades; half polished and etched; nickel silver shield; brass lining **45.00**

☐**2S588 3/4C**—(3⅛″) Celluloid handle; large clip and small pen blades; half polished and etched; nickel silver shield; nickel silver bolsters; brass lining **45.00**

☐**2S618C**—(3⅜″) Celluloid handle; large spear and small pen blades; half polished and etched; nickel silver shield; nickel silver bolsters; brass lining **65.00**

☐**2S618S**—Bone stag handle as above . . **80.00**

☐**2S623C**—(3″) Celluloid handle; large clip and small pen blades; half polished and etched; nickel silver shield; nickel silver bolsters; brass lining **50.00**

☐**2S623CP**—Celluloid pearl handle as above **45.00**

☐**2S623ST**—Bone handle as above **55.00**

☐**2S623 3/4C**—(3″) Celluloid handle; large clip and small pen blades; half polished and etched; nickel silver shield; nickel silver bolsters; brass lining **50.00**

☐**2S623 3/4CP**—Celluloid pearl handle as above **60.00**

☐**2S623 3/4C**—(3½″) Bone stag handle as above **60.00**

☐**2S64 3/4C**—(3½″) Celluloid handle; large clip and small pen blades; half polished and etched; nickel silver shield; nickel silver bolsters; brass lining **45.00**

☐**2S624 3/4ST**—Bone stag handle as above **60.00**

☐**2S625C**—(4¼″) White celluloid handle; large spear blade; half polished and etched; nickel silver shield; nickel silver bolsters; brass lining **100.00**

☐**2S625ST**—Bone stag handle as above **175.00**

☐**2S655 3/4ST**—Bone stag handle; large clip and small pen blades; half polished and etched; nickel silver shield; nickel silver bolsters; brass lining **175.00**

☐**2S626 3/4C**—(3¼″) Celluloid handle; large clip and small pen blades; half polished and etched; nickel silver shield; nickel silver bolsters; brass lining **50.00**

☐**2S626 3/4ST**—Bone stag handle as above **60.00**

☐**2S627C**—(3¼″) Celluloid handle; large spear and small pen blades, half polished and etched; nickel silver shield; nickel silver bolsters; brass lining **50.00**

☐**3S20 5/8ST**—(3⅞″) Bone stag handle; large spey, small clip and sheepfoot blades; half polished and etched; nickel silver shield; nickel silver bolsters; brass lining **160.00**

☐**3S67 1/4C**—(3⅜″) Celluloid handle; large clip, small punch and spey blades; half polished and etched; nickel silver shield; nickel silver bolsters; brass lining **60.00**

☐**3S67 1/4ST**—Bone stag handle as above **80.00**

☐**3S67 3/4C**—(3⅜″) Celluloid handle; large clip, small pen and spey blades; half polished and etched; nickel silver shield; nickel silver bolsters; brass lining **80.00**

☐**3S67 3/4P**—Pearl handle as above . . **150.00**

☐**3S67 3/4ST**—Bone stag handle as above **110.00**

☐**3S76 3/4C**—(3⅜″) Celluloid handle; large clip, small pen and spey blades; half polished and etched; nickel silver shield; nickel silver bolsters; brass lining **70.00**

☐**3S76 3/4ST**—Bone stag handle as above **90.00**

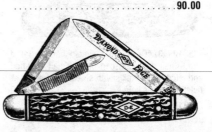

☐**3S103CP**—(3½″) Pearl celluloid handle; large spear, small pen and nail file blades; half polished and etched; nickel silver shield; nickel silver bolsters; brass lining **100.00**

☐**3S103ST**—Bone stag handle as above **125.00**

☐**3S193C**—(3⅜″) Fancy celluloid handle; large spear, small pen and nail file blades; half polished and etched; nickel silver bolsters; brass lining **50.00**

☐**3S193P**—Pearl handle as above **90.00**

☐**3S193ST**—Bone stag handle as above .**65.00**

☐**3S105P**—(3½″) Pearl handle; large spear, small pen and nail file blades; half polished and etched; nickel silver shield; nickel silver bolsters; brass lining **100.00**

☐**3S105ST**—Bone stag handle as above .**80.00**

☐**3S209C**—(3¼″) Fancy celluloid handle; large spear and two small pen blades; half polished and etched; nickel silver shield; nickel silver bolsters; brass lining **90.00**

☐**3S209P**—Pearl handle as above **200.00**

☐**3S209ST**—Bone stag handle as above **125.00**

☐**3S109 1/4C**—(3⅝″) Celluloid handle; large clip, small spey and punch blades; half polished and etched; nickel silver shield; nickel silver bolsters; brass lining **80.00**

☐**3S109 1/4ST**—Bone stag handle as above **100.00**

☐**3S220C**—(3⅛″) Celluloid handle; large spear and two small pen blades; half polished and etched; nickel silver shield; nickel silver bolsters; brass lining **50.00**

☐**3S220ST**—Bone stag handle as above .**65.00**

☐**3S109 3/4C**—(3⅝″) Celluloid handle; large clip, small spey and pen blades; half polished and etched; nickel silver shield; nickel silver bolsters; brass lining **110.00**

☐**3S109 3/4S**—Bone stag handle as above **130.00**

☐**3S253 1/4C**—(3¼") Celluloid handle; large clip, small pen and punch blades; half polished and etched; nickel silver shield; nickel silver bolsters; brass lining **75.00**

☐**3S253 1/4ST**—Bone stag handle as above **110.00**

☐**3S253 3/4C**—(3¼") Celluloid handle; large clip, small spey and pen blades; half polished and etched; nickel silver shield; nickel silver bolsters; brass lining **90.00**

☐**3S253 3/4P**—Pearl handle as above . **200.00**

☐**3S253 3/4ST**—Bone stag handle as above **125.00**

☐**3S261P**—(3") Pearl handle; one large spear, small pen and nail file blades; half polished and etched; nickel silver lining **50.00**

☐**3S275C**—(3⅜") Celluloid handle; large spear, small pen and nail file blades; half polished and etched; nickel silver shield; nickel silver bolsters; brass lining **50.00**

☐**3S275P**—Pearl handle as above **90.00**

☐**3S275ST**—Bone stag handle **60.00**

☐**3S311 1/4C**—(3½") Celluloid handle; large clip, small spey and punch blades; half polished and etched; nickel silver shield; nickel silver bolsters; brass lining **100.00**

☐**3S311 1/4ST**—Bone stag handle as above **125.00**

☐**3S311 3/4C**—(3½") Celluloid handle; large clip, small pen and spey blades; half polished and etched; nickel silver shield; nickel silver bolsters; brass lining **100.00**

☐**3S311 3/4T**—Bone stag handle as above **125.00**

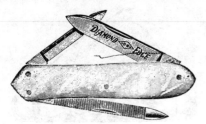

☐**3S354P**—(3″) Pearl handle; large spear; small pen and nail file blades; half polished and etched; nickel silver lining **50.00**

☐**3S355P**—(3″) Pearl handle; large spear; small pen and long file blades; full polished and etched; nickel silver lining **60.00**

☐**3S362P**—(3″) Pearl handle; large spear, small pen and long file blades; half polished and etched; nickel silver shield; nickel silver bolsters; brass lining **75.00**

☐**3S374P**—(3⅛″) Pearl handle; large spear, small pen and nail file blades; half polished and etched; nickel silver shield; nickel silver lining
. . . . **50.00**

☐**3S375C**—(3⅛″) Celluloid handle; large spear, small pen and large file blades; half polished and etched; nickel silver shield; nickel silver bolsters; brass lining **50.00**

☐**3S383 3/4C**—(3½″) Celluloid handle; large clip, small spey and sheepfoot blades; half polished and etched; nickel silver shield; nickel silver bolsters; brass lining **100.00**

☐**3S447 1/4ST**—(4″) Bone stag handle; large spey, small clip and punch blades; half polished and etched; nickel silver shield; nickel silver bolsters; brass lining **170.00**

☐**3S523 1/4C**—(4″) Celluloid handle; large clip, small spoey and punch blades; half polished and etched; nickel silver shield; nickel silver bolsters; brass lining **110.00**

☐**3S523 1/4ST**—Bone stag handle as above **140.00**

☐**3S523 3/4C**—(4″) Celluloid handle; large clip, small spey and pen blades; half polished and etched; nickel silver shield; nickel silver bolsters; brass lining **110.00**

☐**3S523 3/4ST**—Bone stag handle as above **140.00**

☐**3S525C**—(3⅛″) Celluloid handle; large spear, small spey and pen blades; half polished and etched; nickel silver shield; nickel silver boslters; brass lining **60.00**

☐**3S525ST**—Bone stag handle as above .**75.00**

☐**3S525 1/4C**—(3½″) Celluloid handle; large spear, small spey and punch blades; half polished and etched; nickel silver shield; nickel silver bolsters; brass lining **70.00**

☐**3S525 1/4ST**—Bone stag handle as above **90.00**

☐**3S529 3/4ST**—(3⅞″) Bone stag handle; large clip and two small spey blades; half polished and etched; nickel silver shield; milled back and linings; nickel silver bolsters; nickel silver lining **130.00**

☐**3S565 1/4C**—(3½″) Celluloid handle; large clip, small spey and punch blades; half polished and etched; nickel silver bolsters; brass lining **100.00**

☐**3S565 1/4ST**—Bone stag handle as above **125.00**

☐**3S565 3/4C**—(3⅜″) Celluloid handle; large clip and small pen and sheepfoot blades; half polished and etched; nickel silver shield; nickel silver bolsters; brass lining **60.00**

☐**3S565 3/4S**—Bone stag handle as above **90.00**

☐**3S568 1/4C**—(3½″) Celluloid handle; large clip, small spey and punch blades; half polished and etched; nickel silver bolsters; brass lining **100.00**

☐**3S568 1/4ST**—Bone stag handle as above **125.00**

☐**3S568 3/4C**—(3½") Celluloid handle; large clip, small spey and pen blades; half polished and etched; nickel silver bolsters; brass lining **70.00**

☐**3S568 3/4ST**—Bone stag handle as above **90.00**

☐**3S568 5/8CP**—(3½") Pearl celluloid handle; large clip, small spey and sheepfoot blades; half polished and etched; nickel silver shield; nickel silver bolstrs; brass lining **100.00**

☐**3S568 5/8S**—Bone stag handle as above **125.00**

☐**3S626 1/4S**—(3¼") Celluloid handle; large clip, small spey and punch blades; half polished and etched; nickel silver shield; nickel silver bolsters; brass lining **80.00**

☐**3S626 1/4S**—Bone stag handle as above **95.00**

☐**3S565 3/4C**—(3⅜") Celluloid handle; large clip and small pen sheepfoot blades; half polished and etched; nickel silver shield; nickel silver bolsters; brass lining **60.00**

☐**3S565 3/4S**—Bone stag handle as above **90.00**

☐**4S20 1/4ST**—(4") Bone stag handle; large clip, small spey, pen and punch blades; half polished and ethced; nickel silver shield; nickel silver bolsters; brass lining **150.00**

☐**4S20 3/4ST**—(4") Bone stag handle; large clip and sheepfoot, small pen and punch blades; half polished and etched; nickel silver shield; nickel silver bolsters; brass lining **150.00**

☐**4S31P**—(3") Pearl handle; large spear, two small pen and nail file blades; full polished and etched;nickel silver shield; nickel silver lining **150.00**

☐**4S66 1/2ST**—(3") Bone stag handle; large sheepfoot, tobacco, and towo small pen blades; glazed finish and etched, steel bolsters, brass lining **200.00**

☐**4S214 1/2ST**—(3½") Bone stag handle; one large sheepfoot, one tobacco and two small pen blades; half polished and etched; nickel silver shield; steel bolsters; brass lining **150.00**

☐**4S215 1/2S**—(3⅞″) Bone stag handle; one large sheepfoot, one tobacco and two small pen blades; half polished and etched; nickel silver shield; nickel silver bolsters; brass lining **200.00**

☐**4S375P**—(3⅛″) Pearl handle; large spear, two small pen and nail file blades; half polished and etched; nickel silver shield; nickel silver bolsters; brass lining **125.00**

☐**4S376P**—(3⅛″) Pearl handle; large spear, two small pen and nail file blades; half polished and etched; nickel silver shield; nickel silver bolsters; brass lining **150.00**

☐**4S376ST**—Bone stag handle as above . **80.00**

☐**4S275ST**—(3⅜″) Bone stag handle; large spear, sheepfoot and small pen and nail file blades; half polished and etched; nickel silver shield; nickel silver bolsters; brass lining **85.00**

☐**4S517S**—(4⅛″) Bone stag handle; large spear, punch, can opener and screw driver with combination cap lifter and can opener blades; half polished and etched; nickel silver shield; nickel silver bolsters; brass lining **75.00**

☐**4S518S**—(3⅜″) Bone stag handle; large spear, punch, screw driver and combination can opener and cap lifter blades; half polished and etched; nickel silver shield; nickel silver bolsters; brass lining **75.00**

☐**4S275 1/4ST**—(3⅜″) Bone stag handle; large spear, and spey, small pen and punch blades; half polished and etched; nickel silver shield; nickel silver bolsters; brass lining **125.00**

☐**4S519CP**—(2⅞″) Celluloid handle; large spear, two small pen and flexible file blades; half polished and etched; nickel silver shield; nickel silver bolsters; brass lining **65.00**

☐**4S374P**—(3⅛″) Pearl handle; large spear, two small pen and nail file blades; half polished and etched; nickel silver shield; brass lining **125.00**

☐**4S519S**—(2⅞″) Bone stag handle; large spear, two small pen and flexible blades; half polished and etched; nickel silver shield; nickel silver bolsters; nickel silver lining **70.00**

SMITH & WESSON

About 1974 Smith & Wesson introduced a series of knives designed by Blackie Collins. Of these knives there was only one pocketknife, the model 6060 folding hunter, a dropped point knife with German silver bolsters and Wessonwood handles. The knife is made of 440 stainless steel.

This line was discontinued in 1981, and Smith & Wesson introduced a new line of stainless steel folders.

SOUTHINGTON

Begun in 1867, the company also made squares, curry combs and bicycle parts. They dropped the manufacture of cutlery in 1905.

STAINLESS CUTLERY COMPANY

In 1821 a Frenchman named Berhiier found steel containing chromium could be made rust resistant. In 1915, Harry Brearley, an Englishman, discovered the exact proportion necessary to make steel stainless, and in 1924, W. D. Wallace of the Stainless Cutlery Company discovered how to temper and harden the steel so that it could be sharpened and resharpened.

He had spent five years of study in England, Germany, and the United States before his discovery, and in addition he developed a new style of polishing the stainless blades. His idea was readily adopted by Camillus Cutlery Company, which organized Stainless Cutlery Company as a branch of Camillus.

STANDARD KNIFE COMPANY

Originated in 1901 by Dean and Elliot Case, sons of Jean Case, they offered to pay the funeral expenses of anyone found dead with a Standard Knife in their pockets.

Elliot died from typhoid fever in 1903 and the company closed its doors thereafter.

SWANNER CUTLERY

Swanner Cutlery knives were made by Stan Swanner of Hamilton, Ohio. Two of his better known knives are the Swanner muskrat with genuine pearl handles, and the Ohio Valley River dirk with genuine stag handles.

He will be adding knives to this line in 1981 and '82.

SYRACUSE KNIFE COMPANY

Syracuse Knife was owned by Camillus and discontinued in the early 1930's. Most were handled in celluloid.

TAYLOR'S EYE WITNESS
SHEFFIELD, ENGLAND

In 1836 Taylor's Eye Witness began their company and they are still very active in the pocketknife business today. This company has done well in the business by acquiring other companies and trademarks and by continuing to reduce the number of styles of pocketknives produced to keep pace with current labor shortages in Sheffield. In 1948 Taylor's acquired Saynor, Cooke and Ridal. In 1951 Saynor was bought and they also bought Southern & Richardson.

Currently they produce very few pocketknives with natural handle material. All of the above company names and marks have been discontinued except Taylor's Eye Witness.

THOMAS TURNER
SHEFFIELD, ENGLAND

In 1871 Thomas Turner was the Master Cutler of the Sheffield Cutlers. At one time he became lord mayor of London. His company was reorganized in 1818, but went into receivership in July of 1932.

ULSTER KNIFE COMPANY
ELLENVILLE, NEW YORK

The Ulster Knife Company was formed by former Sheffield Cutlers in 1872, and bought by Dwight Devine & Sons in 1876. The company changed hands again in 1941, being bought by Henry and Albert Baer; and again in 1947, when it was brought into the fold of Imperial Knife Associated Companies, Inc.

Although Ulster currently uses plastic handles, in the past they used bone and most of the older handle materials. The stampings they have used are: "Ulster Knife Co.", "Ulster, Dwight Devine & Sons, U. S. A." and "Ulster, U. S. A."

Some "Old-Timer" knives will be found made by Ulster. Many of these were sold through an offer on a Prince Albert Tobacco tin and closely resemble the Schrade-Walden "Old-Timer", which is also a division of Imperial Knife Associated Companies.

UNION CUTLERY & HARDWARE COMPANY
UNIONVILLE, CONNECTICUT

Although we have only sketchy information on the founding of this company, its stockholders decided to liquidate the companies stock in September 1925, and in December 1925 the machinery of the company was sold at public auction.

UTICA CUTLERY COMPANY
UTICA, NEW YORK

Utica was formed by Samuel, Abraham and Joseph Mailmen in 1910. It became Utica Cutlery Company in 1929. The "Kutmaster" trademark was adopted in 1937, which would later replace all other Utica trademarks. Among the trademarks used by Utica were: Agatewood, American Maid, Featherweight, Seneca, Pocket Pard, and Pal. The company is still in business today.

VALLEY FORGE
NEWARK, NEW JERSEY

Valley Forge began cutlery production around 1892 in Newark, New Jersey, with Hermann Boker and Company coming into ownership of Valley Forge by 1916. The factory was used to produce both Boker, USA and Valley Forge knives.

The Valley Forge trademark was last used about 1950.

☐ **0868**—(3½″) Four blades, nickel silver bolster and shackle, stag handle **60.00**

☐ **0978GP**—(3⅛″) Three blades, nickel silver bolsters; three spring, gold celluloid handle **125.00**

☐ **438**—(3⅛″) Four blades, nickel silver bolsters and shackle, stag handle **50.00**

☐ **1443ABA**—(3¾″) Three blades, nickel silver bolsters, Abalonial pearl pyralin handle . **100.00**

☐ **1978**—(3½″) Three blades, nickel silver bolsters, stag handle **60.00**

☐ **2078**—(3¼″) Three blades, nickel silver tips, stag handle **85.00**

☐ **2078BP**—(3¼″) Three blades, nickel silver tips, black pearl pyralin handle **100.00**

☐ **2164**—(2⅝″) Three blades, nickel silver bolsters, pearl handle **125.00**

☐ **2273ABA**—(3″) Three blades, nickel silver bolsters, Abalonian pyralin handle **100.00**

☐**2583CABA**—(3¼") Three blades, nickel silver bolsters, Abalonian handle **90.00**

☐**3288ABA**—(3⅜") Three blades, nickel silver bolsters, Abalonian pearl pyralin handle ..**90.00**

☐**3008**—(3⅛") Three blades, nickel silver bolsters, stag handle **60.00**

VICTORY CUTLERY COMPANY
NEW HAVEN, CONNECTICUT

This company was incorporated in January 1925 with capital of $50,000 by B. N. Beard, William Munson and Charles Victory.

VAN CAMP HARDWARE & IRON COMPANY, INC.,
INDIANAPOLIS, INDIANA

Cortland Van Camp founded the company in 1876, buying knives on contract from Boker, Camillus, and Imperial, stamped with the Van Camp logo. The company is still in business but has discontinued the "Van Camp" pocketknife.

Some of the stampings used were: "Raola Cutlery," Van Camp" inside a circle, "Van Camp Hardware Company, Indianapolis," "Vanco, Indianapolis," "Van Camp, U. S. A.," "V Camp Germany," and "Van Camp H & I Co."

VOOS
(With arrow through the trademark)
NEW HAVEN, CONNECTICUT

This knife is common in a two blade bone handled jack. The knives were made by the New Haven Hardware Specialty Hardware Company of New Haven, Connecticut. The name was advertised as early as a December 1922 issue of the American Cutler.

VOSS CUTLERY COMPANY
SOLINGEN, GERMANY

Established in 1880, Voss Cutlery was the exclusive distributor for Hen & Rooster at that time. On many of the knives, the Hen & Rooster logo was stamped on the front with Voss Cutlery stamped in the reverse of the tang, but some of the newer knives had only "Voss Cutlery Co. Soligen Germany" stamped on the front with pattern numbers on the back of the tang.

This importing business was bought in the early 1970's by Cole National.

WABASH CUTLERY COMPANY
TERRA HAUTE, INDIANA

Established in 1921, the company primarily made celluloid handled knives, with a few others in the standard handle materials. It ceased production in 1935.

WALDEN KNIFE COMPANY
WALDEN, NEW YORK

The Walden Knife Company was formed by employees of the New York Knife Company. Different sections in the New York Knife Company would play baseball during lunch break, and during one of those games a fight broke out.

Owner Tom Bradley told the group that if they wanted to keep their jobs there would be no more baseball games.

The employees thought a lot of their baseball, so they immediately quit and started the Walden Co-Operative Knife Company in the early 1870's. In 1874 the company incorporated as the Walden Knife Company with a stock of $20,000. Until 1874 they had operated in rented rooms of the Rider Engine Company, but with their incorporation they purchased their own factory.

By 1893 the company employed 225 people and consisted of four buildings. E. C. Simmons Hardware Company began buying knives from Walden, and when George Weller, the principal stockholder in Walden Knife retired, the Simmons Company bought his stock and with it control of the company. Simmons made Walden Knife Company the home of the Keen Kutter knife, whose trademark is illustrated here.

Simmons replaced office personnel with employees from the home office in St. Louis, and added several more buildings by 1914. During World War I the company operated at full capacity making large knives for the Navy.

At the war's end Simmons was in rough financial shape and merged with Winchester Arms, which took over the knife manufacturing for Simmons. Walden closed its doors in 1927.

The Walden Knife Company made many knives, in a large variety of patterns. Most will be found stamped Walden Knife Co., Walden, N. Y. The Keen Kutter's made by Walden and those later made by Winchester are almost impossible to tell apart, for Winchester duplicated many of the Walden Knife patterns, including the 1920 folding hunter pattern (Volume One of the Official Price Guide to Pocketknives has a photograph of Walden and Winchester 1920's side by side.)

Walden Knives were top quality, and handled in bone, celluloid, pearl and most of the popular handle materials of the day.

E. WECK
NEW YORK, NEW YORK

Born in Solingen, Germany, he immigrated at the age of 15, where he began work with Pauls Brothers, cutlery importers in New York. He started his first retail shop in Lower Manhattan and when he began opening branch stores, he incorporated as Edward Weck & Sons, Inc.

The company had a razor plant in Brooklyn, a wholesale house and five retail stores. Upon his death in 1922 Albert H. Weck was made President. He had been in direct charge of the operation for several years.

WESTER BROTHERS KNIVES
SOLINGEN, GERMANY
by Ed Bruner

(This information originally appeared in the Blue Mill Blade, and our thanks go to Mr. Bruner for doing this article for this book.)

I have some Wester Brothers knives in my own collection and became interested in their history. The account which follows is the history of Wester Brothers. I wish to thank Mr. Herbert Wester, and his daughter, Barbara, for the help they gave a knife nut like me. They are kind and generous people.

A Mr. Butz was making cutlery and pocketknives in Solingen, Germany as early as 1832. He took in as an apprentice, August Wester, who not only became a master cutler, but married Butz's daughter, and they established the firm of Wester and Butz. The knives that they produced for the German and European market had Wester and Butz on one side of the tang and their trademark, an anchor, star, and arrow, on the other side. All blades were marked. Very few of these Wester and Butz knives are found in the United States.

Wester and Butz also made knives for the English market under such labels as "Tyler & Co.," "James Allen," "Caststeel IA," "Elberfield Cutlery Co." and "ZP. H. G." After England passed a law that all foreign products had to be stamped with the country of origin, these knives were no longer made for the English market. None of the above knives were stamped with Solingen or Germany or with any indication of the country in which they were manufactured. They do not, of course, have the anchor, star and arrow trademark.

August Wester, who was running the company in the 1880's, decided to establish an outlet for their pocketknives and cutlery in the United States rather than pay an importer. August Wester had five sons. The three oldest sons remained in the German factory working with their father. The two youngest, Max and Charles, were sent to the United States. With a Mr. Jacoby, they established the firm of Jacoby and Wester in New York in 1891. The knives made in Germany by Wester and Butz for the American market were marked "Jacoby & Wester" on one side of the tang, with the anchor, star and arrow trademark on the other side.

Eventually the Wester family bought Jacoby out and Wester Brothers, New York was formally established in 1902. Jacoby and Wester knives date from 1891-1902.

The knives with Wester Brothers, on one side of the tang and the anchor, star and arrow on the reverse side date from 1902 to about 1966. Wester

Brothers was the exclusive importer of knives produced by the Wester and Butz factory in Solingen. Their handle materials were genuine mother of pearl, genuine stag, bone stag, buffalo horn, gun metal, nickel silver, celluloid, and special alloys for their bartender knives. Ivory and tortoiseshell were not standard items for the American line as they had been for the European and English trade.

In the early period until about 1918, Wester Brothers carried under their label a few large two blade jackknives made for them in New England cutlery factories. After that their jackknives were produced in Germany. About 1915 the firm name was changed to Wester-Stone, and there were some knives made with this mark, but this was temporary and they soon went back to the original name.

Wester Brothers did more business in razors, barber shears, and manicure equipment than in pocketknives. In 1913 they imported 15,000 dozen straight razors and were the largest importer of razors in the United States. They also produced many advertising knives, especially for insurance companies and the beer companies, including Pabst and Schlitz. They made an outstanding line for Anheuser-Busch. Some of these latter knives are of pearl, with engraved bolsters, hand lettering on the pearl and a picture of Mr. Busch in a little peephole, and are among the most elaborate advertising knives ever made.

The early knives produced by Wester and Butz were handcrafted and of outstanding quality. They produced hundreds of models: a genuine stag handled 4½ inch whittler, a four inch lockback whittler, many four, three, and two blade knives, and even tiny ladies' purse knives. The steel was forged, and the heat treating was done by skilled workers in the Wester and Butz factory. The blades were not ground by machine as this produces too thick an edge, but were ground by hand to produce a thin cutting edge, yet the blades had enough metal stock so that they were strong.

Wester Brothers knives were expensive, yet they still sold many knives to the better hardware and sporting goods stores. However, they never sold to the big hardware jobbers as their knives cost too much.

The quality of the knives deteriorated somewhat in the post World War II period and the number of models in the line was drastically reduced. As the skilled grinders and workers died off, they could not be replaced. The recent knives of the past 20 years were simply not of the quality of the knives produced before 1939. The company eventually had to discontinue.

WESTERN CUTLERY COMPANY
BOLDER, COLORADO

Western States Cutlery Company was started by H. N. Platts, who during his time saw the origins of some of the most famous cutlery factories first hand, for at one time or the other he worked for most of them. For his story we must start with his father, Charles W. Platts. (A more detailed account of Charles Platts is included in this book.)

H. N. grew up in the knife factories, learning the cutler's art in the North-field Knife Company where his father was superintendent.

In 1891 he moved to Little Valley, New York where he started work for Cattaraugus. While there he met Debbie Case, who also worked for Cattaraugus. They married in 1892.

His father moved to Little Valley to be superintendent of Cattaraugus in 1893, bringing with him his other sons, most of them grown. Three years later they were all starting C. Platts & Sons Cutlery Company which they ran until Charles Platts died in 1900. At his death they changed the named and continued to operate the factory.

H. N., while selling on the road for C. Platts & Sons, would often be in contact with his brother-in-law, Russ Case. His wife was helping her brother with his jobbing operation in Bradford, and before long Russ and H. N. decided they would carry on the knife business better if they merged.

The Platts brothers sold out to H. N., who then merged with Russ Case to form W. R. Case & Sons in 1905.

Platts had grinders consumption from his years in the factories, and began to get worse in 1911. On the advice that a drier climate would held his condition, he moved to Boulder, Colorado, where he set up a jobbing operation.

The jobber was named Western State Cutlery and Manufacturing Company, handling Challenge, Clyde, Utica and Ureka brand knives.

Russ Case agreed to buy H. N.'s shares of W. R. Case & Sons when H. N. left Bradford, and as a partial payment Russ began stamping knives Western States Cutlery and trading them out with Platts.

While Platts had always wanted a factory, it was not until his son Harlow returned home from World War I that he began construction. It was in operation in the early '20's.

Platts retired in the 1940's, turning the factory over to Reg and Harlow, his sons.

After the deaths of Platts and his wife Debbie, Reg left the company. Harlow and his son Harvey reincorporated the company in 1950. They run the factory today.

The first trademark for Western was a tic tac toe board stating W Tested S, Trade SHARP Mark, C Temper G. This was used from 1911 to 1928.

The tang stampings were Western States Boulders, Colorado from 1911 until 1956, when the company dropped the States from its logo.

In the early 1970's, Western dropped their Western, Boulder, Colo. stamping and instead went to Western, U. S. A.

Tang stampings used by Western was "Western States, Boulder, Colo." from 1911 until 1950. From 1920 to 1938 the company used the "Western States, Sharp Cutlery" with the bleached buffalo head etching, and from 1920 until 1930 they used the Tested Sharp Temper inside a tic tac toe board etching. In 1950 the stamping was changed to "Western, Boulder, Colo." During the 1960's the stamping was changed to its current stamping, "Western, USA".

The company name was changed from Western States Cutlery Company to Western Cutlery Company in 1957.

WILBERT CUTLERY COMPANY

A new factory was built in 1979 in nearby Longmart, Colo., at which time the entire company moved there.

This company's knives appear in the 1900's editions of the Sears & Roebuck catalog, and resemble Schatt and Morgan knives. Some of the knives were handled in bone and mother of pearl.

☐**6L16831**—(3½") Rosewood handle; steel lining; iron bolster **50.00**

☐**6L16835**—(3⅜") Cocoa handle, equal end pocket knife, German silver bolster, caps and shield; brass lined; finished inside and out . . . .
. . . .**50.00**

☐**6L16837**—TEAMSTERS' KNIFE (3⅝") Cocoa handle; one large, heavy, finely tempered and ground spear blade and one pounch or swage blade with which holes can be bored in leather or wood; heavy German silver shield; full brass lined **50.00**

☐**6L16858**—(3¾") Ebony handle; hand fitting high grade knife; German silver bolsters, cap and shield; brass lining **80.00**

☐**6L16863**—MISSOURI FAVORITE (3¾") Ebony handle; has clip point saber blade, made of full 12-guage steel; long German silver bolsters, caps and shield; brass lining; finished inside and out **80.00**

☐**6L16878**—EASY OPENER POCKETKNIFE (3¾") White bone handle; 2¾ spear blade and one ¾ pen blade; polished bolsters and shield; brass lining; nicely polished. A well made, strong dependable knife **80.00**

☐**6L16888**—YANKEE BOY JACKNIFE (2⅔") Cocoa handle with polished brass rivets; one large clip blade, polished and swaged and a 2" pen blade; the blades are made of the best English steel, finely tempered and ground; brass lined; polished bolster; polished German silver shield **50.00**

☐**6L16807**—GENTLEMEN'S JACKKNIFE (3⅜") Stag handle; German silver bolsters, caps and shield; brass lining, throughly finished in every particular, inside and out **65.00**

☐**6L16913**—JACKKNIFE (3¾") Large 2¾" spear point blade, double swage, forge of the best 11-guage Wardlow English steel, and a 2" pen blade. The blades are hand ground and properly tempered. Full brass lined; German silver polished bolsters and cap; German silver polished bolsters and cap; German silver crest shield
. . . .**90.00**

☐**6L16934**—JACKKNIFE (3⅝") Stag handle, German silver boslters, caps and shield, grass lined, finely finished throughout **25.00**

☐**6L16939**—TEXAS TOOTHPICK (3⅞") Stag handle; clip point saber blade. While the blade is long and slim the peculiar shape makes it very strong and durable as well as an excellent whittler. German silver bolster and shield; brass lining; finely finished inside and out **70.00**

☐**6L16944**—CATTLEMAN'S KNIFE (4") Stag handle; saber clip point blade and speying blade 3" long from bolster. German silver bolsters and shield; brass lined, finely finished throughout
. . . .**150.00**

☐**6L16946**—(3¾") Stag handle, Swelled handle beauty; large 2¾" spear point blade, double swage, forged of the best 11-gauge Wardlow English steel, and a 2" pen blade; the blades are hand ground and property tempered. Full brass lined, German silver polished bolsters and cap; German silver crest shield **90.00**

☐**6L16949**—JACKKNIFE (4¼") Cocoa handle; two blade, double end; brass lined; German sivler bolster and shield, large 3¼" swaged spear blade and 2½" pen blade. A high grade, well finished, finely ground and tempered knife **50.00**

☐**6L16951P**—JACKKNIFE (3¾") Stag handle, new pattern; brass lined, 2⅞") spear point blade, fourged of 12-gauge Wardlow steel, and a small pen blade; two polished springs, fancy round end German silver boslters; German silver square end cap; stag handle inlaid with German silver crest shield **100.00**

☐**6L16990**—OLD FAITHFUL (4¼") Stag handle, large spear blade 3" long, forged of the finest 8-gauge Wardlow steel; small blade is forged of 13-gauge steel and is 2" long. The large blade of this knife is full ⅛" thick at the back; full brass lined; polished bolsters, finely tempered and hand ground **250.00**

☐**6L16997**—GLADIATOR DOUBLE (4¼") Stag handle, saber clip and spear point blades, length with spear blade open 7½"; German silver boslters and shield; brass lined and finely finished throughout **90.00**

☐**6L16998**—JACKKNIFE (3½") Polished buffalo horn handle, two blade buffalo horn, hollow bolster; brass lined; German silver bolsters and shield; largw swag clip blade and finely ground pen blade **70.00**

☐**6L17017**—JACKKNIFE (3⅜") Pear handle, two blade; one large jack balde for shittling and one small pen blade, full polished. A high class knife fitted with the finest quality pearl scales, heavy German silver bolsters, caps and shields, full German silver lined and polished **65.00**

☐**6L17149**—DAKOTA COWBOYS' KNIFE (3⅝") Fine stag handle, three blades; spear point sheepfoot and pen blade; German silver shield; heavy German silver polished boslters; full brass lined and finely finished inside and out. The steel used in these knives is extra heavy gauge and it is the very best English steel suitable for this purpose. The blades are tempered by electricity, insuring uniform temper from heel to point. The grinding, finish and cutler's work in this knife cannot be surpassed. This is an extra strong, heavy knife for the stockman, hunter or trapper, who requires a dependable knife **80.00**

WINCHESTER
NEW HAVEN, CONNECTICUT

After World War I, Winchester decided to expand into new fields to make up for the cutback in government arms contracts. Cutlery such as shears and kitchen knives could be made with modification of existing equipment, but pocketknives required special machines and experienced personnel. For this reason, Winchester bought two knife companies in 1919.

The first company bought was the Eagle Knife Company of New Haven, Connecticut, bought for $174,500. The Eagle Knife Company had made an economically priced knife, making many for the George Borgefeldt Company, a major cutlery importer. For a short time Winchester manufactured knives for Borgefeldt stamped with the Borgefeldt name, but this ended as soon as existing contracts ran out. The President of Eagle had invented and used machinery that allowed interchangeable components, blade blanked by pressed and automatic grindings. Winchester moved Eagle's equipment into their plant and hired almost the entire work force of Eagle.

The second company bought was the Napanoch Knife Company, which had made a higher quality knife than Eagle. With the skill of Napanoch cutlers and the modern production methods of Eagle, Winchester began to mass produce a high quality knife. However, they did run into some problems.

Winchester originally stamped blades out of Chrome-Vanadium steel, which was superior to Napanoch's hand forged blades, but the Chrome-Vananium steel could not be polished as well as the forged blade. The public preferred the high polish, so Winchester had to resume the inferior forged blades.

A second problem was that Germany had retooled after World War I and introduced low grade cutlery that was stiff competition for Winchester.

In 1922, Winchester and the Associated Simmons Hardware companies (E. C. Simmons) merged, with Winchester acting as the manufacturing end and Simmons as distributor.

At the time of the merger, Simmons owned controlling interest in the Walden Knife Company. The production of Walden knives was ended in 1923 and at that time all of Walden's equipment was moved from Walden, New York, to Winchester in New Haven, Connecticut. At the time of relocation, the value of items moved was something under $11,000. The Keen Kutter was a brand of Simmon's that Winchester also made for a time.

The exact date that Winchester quit pocketknife production is not known, but as of January 13, 1942 all commercial production was halted and Winchester turned to World War II arms manufacturing.

The pattern numbers used by Winchester are broken down as follows: first number, number of blades; second number, handle material; third number variations of the knifemaking processes.

Winchester used almost every common pattern, handle material and bolster.

There were two distinct lines of Winchester knives. The higher quality knives tend to have a logo on every blade while the lesser quality line tends to have the logo on only one blade, but there are some exceptions to this.

☐**2H2009P**—(3¾″) Celluloid handle. Jack pattern; spear and pen blades; steel bolster; brass lining **100.00**

☐**H1610P**—(4″) Cocobola handle, pruner pattern, pruner blade. Steel bolster; steel lining, black inside finish **70.00**

☐**2H2049P**—(3¼″) Celluloid handle; Senator pattern; spear and pen blades; shadow effect on handle; brass lining **80.00**

☐**2H1625P**—(3⅜″) Cocobola handle, steel lining and bolster. Black inside finish. Stabber pattern, spear blade **50.00**

☐**2H2123P**—(3⅜″) Fiber handle, straight Jack pattern, spear blade **50.00**

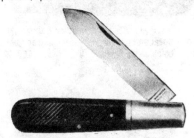

☐**H1701P**—(3½″) Bone handle. Barlow pattern, pruner blade. Steel bolster and lining. Black inside finish **175.00**

☐**H2609**—(3½″) Cocobola handle. Barlow pattern; clip and pen blades; steel bolster and lining; black inside finish **200.00**

☐**H2615**—(4″) Cocobola handle. Pruner pattern, pruner and saw blades; steel bolster; black inside finish **120.00**

☐**H2632P**—(3⅜″) Ebony handle. Light premium stock pattern, clip and pen blades; brass lining; nickel silver bolster; polished inside finish; crest shield **90.00**

☐**H2636P**—(3½″) Ebony handle; regular Jack pattern; spear and pen blades; brass lining; nickel silver bolster, cap and shield; glazed inside finish **120.00**

☐**H2638P**—(3½″) Ebony handle; serpentine Jack pattern; spear and pen blades; nickel silver bolster, cap and shield; brass lining; polished inside finish **175.00**

☐**H2701P**—(3½″) Bone handle; Barlow pattern; spear and pen blades; steel lining and bolster; black inside finish **200.00**

☐**H2943P**—(3¼″) Stag handle; sleeveboard pattern; spear and pen blades; nickel silver bolster, cap and crest shield; flush tang; polished inside finish **90.00**

☐**H2950P**—(3½″) Stag handle; regular Jack pattern; spear and pen blades; steel bolster and brass lining; nickel silver shield; glazed inside finish **150.00**

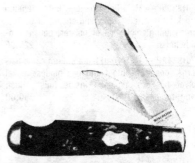

☐**H2953P**—(3½″) Stag handle, regular Jack pattern, spear and pen blades; brass lining; nickel silver bolster, cap and shield; easy opener; glazed inside finish **200.00**

☐**H2951P**—(3½″) Stag handle; regular Jack pattern; clip and punch blades; brass lining and steel bolster; nickel silver shield; glazed inside finish **135.00**

☐**H2956P**—(3½″) Stag handle, serpentine Jack pattern; spear and pen blades; nickel silver bolster, cap and shield; brass lining; polished inside finish **150.00**

☐**H2952P**—(3½″) Stag handle, regular Jack pattern, clip and pen blades; brass lining; nickel silver bolster, cap and shield; glazed inside finish **150.00**

☐**H2966P**—(3⅝″) Stag handle, equal end Jack pattern; spear and pen blades; nickel silver bolsters and shield; polished inside finish, flush tang; brass lining **175.00**

☐**H3305P**—(3⅜″) Pearl handle, light premium stock pattern; clip, spey and sheepfoot blades; brass lining; nickel silver bolster; polished inside finish **225.00**

☐**H3342P**—(3⅜″) Pearl handle, light cattle pattern; spear, sheepfoot and pen blades; nickel silver boslters; polished inside finish; flush tang; brass lining **250.00**

☐**H3361P**—CATTLE KNIFE (3⅝″) Pearl handle, spear, sheepfoot and pen blades; nickel silver bolsters; brass lining; flush tang; polished inside finish **250.00**

☐**H3646P**—CATTLE KNIFE (3⅝″) Ebony handle, spear, sheepfoot and punch blades; brass lining; nickel silver bolsters and shield; flush tang; polished inside finish **200.00**

☐**H3607P**—(4″) Ebony handle; heavy premium stock pattern; clip, spey and pen glades; brass lining; nickel silver bolsters; polished inside finish; nickel silver crest **225.00**

☐**H3941P**—(3⅜″) Stag handle, light premium stock pattern; clip, spey and sheepfoot blades; brass lining; nickel silver bolsters; polished inside finish; nickel silver crest shield . . . **175.00**

☐**H3942P**—(3¾″) Stag handle, light cattle pattern; spear, sheepfoot and pen blades; nickel silver bolsters and shield; polished inside finish; flush tang; brass lining **200.00**

☐**H4961P**—(4″) Stag handle, heavy premium stock pattern; clip, sheepfoot, spey and punch blades; brass lining; nickel silver bolster; polished inside finish; nickel silver crest shield **300.00**

☐**H3950P**—CATTLE KNIFE (3⅝″) Stag handle, sabre clip, sheepfoot and spey blades; nickel silver bolsters and shield; brass lining; flush tang; polished inside finish **225.00**

☐**H3952P**—CATTLE KNIFE (3⅝″) Stag handle, spear, spey and punch blades; nickel silver boslters and shield; brass lining; flush tang; polished inside finish **225.00**

☐**1050**—(5″) Abalone celluloid handle, one large sabre blade, glazed finish; steel bolster and cap; brass lining **300.00**

☐**1051**—(4⅜″) Red and black brilliant finish celluloid handle, one large clip blade, full polished; nickel silver bolster, cap and shield, brass lining **300.00**

☐**J3961P**—(4″) Stag handle, heavy premium stock patter; clip, spey and punch blades; brass lining; nickel silver bolsters; polished inside finish; nickel silver crest shield . . .**250.00**

☐**H4950P**—(3⅝″) Stag handle, scout pattern; spear and punch blades; has also can opener and cap lifter, screwdriver and shackle; brass lining; nickel silver bolster; polished inside; gimp shiedl with word ''Scout'' on handle **275.00**

☐**1060**—(4⅛″) Red and black brilliant finish celluloid handle, one large saber clip blade, full polished; nickel silver bolster and shield, brass lining **200.00**

☐**1201**—(3¼″) Nickel silver handle, satin finish, one large sheepfoot blade, full polished, threaded bolster and cap; brass lining, easy opener **175.00**

☐**1605**—(3½″) Cocobola handle, one large spear blade, glazed finish; steel bolster and lining **75.00**

☐**1608**—(3½″) Cocobola handle, one large spey blade, glazed finish; steel bolster and lining **75.00**

☐**1611**—(3¼″) Cocobola handle, one large sheepfoot saber blade, glazed finish; steel hollow bolster; steel lining **75.00**

☐**1613**—(3⅜″) Cocobola handle, one large spey blade, full polished; nickel silver boslter and lining **125.00**

☐**1632**—(3½″) Cocobola handle, one large clip blade, glazed finishe; steel bolster and lining **75.00**

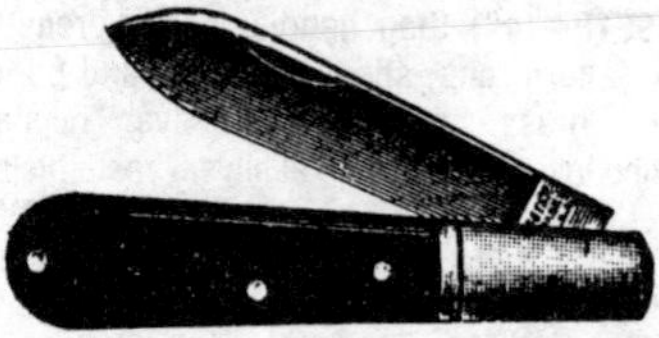

☐**1701**—(3½") Bone handle, one large spear blade, glazed finish; steel bolster and lining **200.00**

☐**1905**—(4¼") Stag handle, one large spear blade, full polished; nickel silver bolster, cap and shield; brass lining **275.00**

☐**1920**—(5¼") Stag handle, one large saber clip blade, glazed finish; nickel silver bolster, cap and shield; brass lining, Lanyard hole **1,000.00**

☐**1921**—(3½") Stag handle, one large clip blade, glazed finish; steel bolster and lining **125.00**

☐**1922**—(3⅜") Stag handle, one large spey blade; glazed finish; polished steel bolster; steel lining **125.00**

☐**1923**—(4⅛") Stag handle, one large saber clip blade, full polished; nickel silver bolster and shield; brass lining **200.00**

☐**1924**—(4¼") Stag handle, one large clip blade, full polished; nickel silver bolster, cap and shield; brass lining **300.00**

☐**1925**—(3½") Stag handle, one large spey blade, full polished; nickel silver bolster, cap, shield and lining **300.00**

☐**1936**—(5") Stag handle, one large saber clip blade, glazed finish; steel bolster and cap; brass lining **350.00**

☐**1937**—(3⅞") Stag handle, one large saber clip blade, full polished; nickel silver bolster, cap, shield and lining **150.00**

☐**1938**—(3½") Stag handle, one large spear blade, glazed finish; steel bolsters and lining **125.00**

☐**1950**—(6¾") Lockback, bone handles, nickel silver bolsters, brass lining, polished inside finish **1,200.00**

☐**2028**—(3⅜") Shell celluloid handle, two blades, one large spear and one pen; large blade full polished; nickel silver bolster, cap, shield and lining **150.00**

☐**2037**—(3") Red and black celluloid handle, two blades, one large spear and one pen, full polished; nickel silver tips and shield, brass lining **90.00**

☐**2038**—(3") Pearl celluloid handle, two blades, one large spear and one pen; large blade full polished; nickel silver tips; brass lining **150.00**

☐**2039**—(3") Red and black celluloid handle, two blades, one large spear and one pen; large blade full polished; nickel silver boslters and shield; brass lining **90.00**

☐**2051**—(3¼") Stag handle, two blades, one large sheepfoot and one pen; large blade full polished; nickel silver rat-tail bolsters, shield and lining **145.00**

☐**2052**—(2⅝") Pearl celluloid handle, two blades, one large spear and one pen; large blade full polished; nickel silver tips and lining **80.00**

☐**2053**—(2⅝") Green and red celluloid handle, two blades, one large spear and one pen; large blade full polished; nickel silver bolsters, shield and lining **120.00**

☐**2054**—(3¼") Green and black brilliant finish celluloid handle, two blades, one large spear and one pen; large blade full polished; brass lining **80.00**

☐**2055**—(3¼") Red and black brilliant finish celluloid handle **80.00**

☐**2057**—(3⅜") Varicolored brilliant finish celluloid handle, two blades, one large spear and one pen; large blade full polished; nickel silver bolsters, shield and lining **120.00**

☐**2058**—(3⅛") Abalone (blue) celluloid handle, two blades, one large spear and one pen; large blade full polished; nickel silver bolsters, shield and lining **90.00**

☐**2059**—(3⅛") Iridescent celluloid handle **90.00**

☐**2067**—(3⅜") Pearl celluloid handle, two blades, one large spear and one pen; large blade full polished; nickel silver tips and lining **110.00**

☐**2068**—(3⅜") Fancy red and black brilliant finish celluloid handle, two blades, one large clip and one pen; large blade full polished; nickel silver bolsters, shield and lining **175.00**

☐**2069**—(3⅛″) Pearl blue celluloid handle, two blades, one large spear and one pen; large blade full polished; nickel silver boslter, cap and shield; brass lining **150.00**

☐**2070**—(3½″) Varicolored brilliant finish celluloid handle, two blades, one large spear and one pen; large blade full polished; nickel silver boslteer, cap and shield, brass lining.... ....**150.00**

☐**2078**—(3³–₈″) Black celluloid handle, two blades, one large clip and one pen; clip blade full polished; nickel silver bolsters, shield and lining **110.00**

☐**2079**—(3⅜″) White celluloid handle, marked ''Office Knife'', two large blades, one spear and one eraser; spear blade full polished; shadow ends; nickel silver lining **100.00**

☐**2082**—(3⅛″) Pearl celluloid handle, two blades, one large spear and one pen; large blade full polished; nickel silver tips and lining **110.00**

☐**2083**—(3⅛″) Green celluloid handle, two blades, one large spear and one pen; large blade full polished; nickel silver bolster, cap, shield and lining..................**150.00**

☐**2084**—(3¼″) Blue celluloid handle, two large blades, one long clip and one spey; clip blade full polished; nickel silver bolsters, shield and lining **175.00**

☐**2085**—(3″) Varicolored brilliant finish celluloid handle, two blades, one large spear and one pen; large blade full polished; nickel silver bolster, cap and shield; brass lining **125.00**

☐**2086**—(2⅞″) Gray celluloid handle, two blades, one large spear and one pen; large blade full polished; nickel silver bolster, cap and lining......................**125.00**

☐**2087**—(3″) Shell celluloid handle, two blades, one large spear and one pen; large blade full polished; nickel silver bolster, cap and shield; brass lining **125.00**

☐**2088**—(3⅜″) Gray celluloid handle, two blades, one large spear and one pen; spear blade full polished; nickel silver tips, shields and lining **110.00**

☐**2089**—(3¾″) White celluloid handle, marked ''Office Knife'', two large blades, one spear and one eraser; spear blade full polished; shadow ends; nickel silver lining **100.00**

☐**2090**—(3″) Silvelour finish celluloid handle, two blades, one large spear and one pen; large blade full polished; nickel silver tips, shield and lining...............................**120.00**

☐**2094**—(3½″) Green and black brilliant finish celluloid handle, two blades, one large spear and one pen, glazed finish; steel bolster, cap and shield; brass lining **200.00**

☐**2098**—(3÷%►″) Green celluloid handle, two blades, one large clip and one pen; large blade full polished; nickel silver bolster, cap, shield and lining................**175.00**

☐**2099**—(3¾″) Shell celluloid handle, two blades, one large clip and one pen; large blade full polished; nickel silver bolster, cap and shield; brass lining **200.00**

☐**2106**—(3¼″) Abalone blue celluloid handle, two blades, one large spear and one patent leather punch blade; spear blade full polished; nickel silver bolster and shield; brass lining **150.00**

☐**2107**—(2¾″) Gold celluloid handle, two blades, one large spear and one pen; large blade full polished; nickel silver bolster, cap and lining......................**125.00**

☐**2109**—(2⅞″) Gold celluloid handle, two blades, one large spear and one pen; large blade full polished; nickel silver bolsters and lining **80.00**

☐**2110**—(3½″) Red and black celluloid handle, two blades, one large spear and one pen; large blade full polished; nickel silver bolster, cap and shield; brass lining **150.00**

☐**2111**—(3½″) Red and black celluloid ;handle, two blades, one large clip and one pen; large blade full polished; nickel silver bolster, cap and shield; brass lining **150.00**

☐**2112**—(3½″) Green and black celluloid handle, two baldes, one large clip and one patent leather punch blade; large blade full polished; nickel silver bolster, cap and shield, brass lining **150.00**

☐**2115**—(2⅞″) Pearl celluloid handle, two baldes, one large spear and one pen; large blade full polished; nickel silver bolsters and lining **150.00**

☐**2117**—(3⅛″) Black celluloid handle, two baldes, one large spear and one pen; large blade full polished; nickel silver bolster and shield; brass lining **125.00**

☐**2201**—(3¼″) Nickel silver skeleton handle, two blades, one large spear and one pen, full polished; flush rivets, shackle **60.00**

☐**2202**—(3″) Smooth fiber handle, two blades, one large spear and one pen; large blade full polished; nickel silver-turned edge **75.00**

☐**2204**—(3⅛″) Nickel silver skeleton handle with flush rivets, two blades, one large spear and one pen; full polished **70.00**

☐**2205**—(3½″) Nickel silver engine turned handle, two blades, one large spear and one pen, full polished; shackle **75.00**

☐**2215**—(3½″) Nickel silver handle, two blades, one large spear and one pen, full pollished **75.00**

☐**2306**—(2⅝″) Short Pearl handle, two blades, one large spear and one file; large blade full polished; long nickel silver bolsters and lining **90.00**

☐**2309**—(3″) Pearl handle, two blades, one large spear and one pen; full polished; nickel silver bolsters and lining **120.00**

☐**2316**—(3″) Pearl handle, two blades, one large spear and one file; large blade full polished; nickel silver bolsters, shield and lining **140.00**

☐**2338**—(3¼″) Pearl handle, two blades, one large spear and one curley nail file, full polished, nickel silver bolsters, shield and lining **150.00**

☐**2352**—(3⅛″) Pearl handle, two blades, one large spear and one pen; full polished; nickel silver bolster, cap, shield and lining **175.00**

☐**2361**—(2⅞″) Pearl handle, two blades, one large spear and one pen; full polished; nickel silver bolster, cap and lining **110.00**

☐**2369**—(2⅝″) Pearl handle, two blades, one large spear and one pen; full polished; nickel silver tips, shield and lining **90.00**

☐**2375**—(2⅝″) Pearl handle, two blades, one large spear and one file, full polished; nickel silver bolsters and lining; shackle **90.00**

☐**2376**—(3″) Pearl handle, two blades, one large spear and one pen; full polished; nickel silver bolsters and lining **120.00**

☐**2377**—(2⅝″) Pearl handle, two blades, one large spear and one pen; full polished; nickel silver bolsters and lining **150.00**

☐**2380**—(3¼″) Pearl handle, two blades, one large spear and one pen, full polished; nickel silver bolster, cap and lining **300.00**

☐**2603**—(3½″) Cocobola handle, two blades, one large clip and one pen; glazed finish; steel boslter and lining **150.00**

☐**2604**—(3⅜″) Cocobola handle, two blades, one large clip and one pen; glazed finish; steel bolster; nickel silver shield; brass lining **150.00**

☐**2605**—(3⅜″) Cocobola handle, two blades, one large spear and one pen, glazed finish; steel bolster and cap; nickel silver shield; brass lining **200.00**

☐**2606**—(3½″) Cocobola handle, two blades, one large spear and one pen; glazed finish; steel bolster and lining **150.00**

☐**2608**—(3½″) Cocobola handle, two blades, one large spear point and one pen, glazed finish; steel bolster and lining; shackle and chain **125.00**

☐**2608**—(3½″) Cocobola handle, two blades, one large spear point and one pen, glazed finish; steel bolster and lining; shackle and chain **125.00**

☐**2610**—(3⅜″) Cocobola handle, two blades, one large spey and one pen, glazed finish; steel bolster and lining **150.00**

□**2611**—(3″) Cocobola handle, two blades, one large spear and one pen; large blade full polished; nickel bolster, cap and shield; brass lining **125.00**

□**2612**—(3⅝″) Cocobola handle, two blades, one large spear and one pen; large blade full polished; polihed steel bolster and cap; nickel silver shield; brass lining **200.00**

□**2613**—(3⅝″) Cocobolo handle, two blades, one large spear and one pen; large blade full polished; polished steel bolster and cap; nickel silver shield; brass lining **200.00**

□**2614**—(3⅝″) Cocobolo handle, two blades, one large saber clip and one pen; large blade full polished; nickel silver bolster, cap and shield; brass lining **200.00**

□**2627**—(3¼″) Cocobolo handle, two blades, one large spear and one pen; large blade full polished; nickel silver bolster, cap and shield; brass lining **125.00**

□**2629**—(3½″) Ebony handle, two blades, one large clip and one pen; large blade full polished; nickel silver bolster, cap, shield and lining **175.00**

□**2630**—(3⅝″) Ebony handle, two blades, one large clip and one pen; large blade full polished; nickel silver bolster, cap, shield and lining **175.00**

□**2631**—(3¼″) Ebony handle, two blades, one large spear and one pen; large blade full polished; nickel silver boslters, shield and lining **90.00**

□**2633**—(3¼″) Ebony handle, two blades, one large clip and one pen; large blade full polished; nickel silver bolsters, shield and lining . **110.00**

□**2635**—(3½″) Cocobolo handle, two blades, one large spear and one pen; glazed finish; steel bolster; nickel silver shield; brass lining **150.00**

□**2636**—(3½″) Ebony handle, two blades, one large spear and one pen; large blade full polished; nickel sivler bolster, cap and shield; brass lining **200.00**

□**2638**—(3½″) Ebony handle, two blades, one large spear and one pen; large blade full polished; nickel silver bolster, cap and shield; brass lining **150.00**

□**2649**—(3¾″) Ebony handle, two blades, one large spear and one pen; large blade full polished; steel bolster and cap; nickel silver shield; brass lining **150.00**

□**2660**—(3½″) Ebony handle, two blades, one large spear and one punch blade; glazed finish; steel bolster; nickel silver shield; brass lining **150.00**

□**2661**—(3½″) Cocobolo handle, two blades, one large spear and one pen; glazed finish; steel cap and bolster; nickel silver shield; brass lining **150.00**

□**2662**—(3½″) Ebony handle, two blades, one large clip and one pen; glazed finish; steel bolster and cap; nickel silver shield; brass lining **150.00**

□**2665**—(3⅜″) Ebony handle, two blades, one large spear and one pen; large blade full polished; nickel silver bolster, cap, shield and lining **175.00**

□**2665**—(3⅜″) Ebony handle, two blades, one large spear and one pen; large blade full polished; nickel silver bolster, cap, shield and lining **175.00**

□**2702**—(3½″) Plain bone stag handle, two blades, one large spey and one pen, glazed finish; steel bolster and lining **250.00**

□**2703**—(3½″) Bone handle, two blades, one large clip and one pen, glazed finish; steel bolster and lining **250.00**

☐**2830**—(3¼″) Stag handle, two blades, one large spear point and one pen; large blade full polished; brass lining **70.00**

☐**2840**—(2″) Stag handle, two blades, one large spear and one pen; large blade full polished; nickel silver tips, and shield; brass lining **90.00**

☐**2841**—(3″) Stag handle, two blades, one large spear and one pen; large blade full polished; nickel silver bolsters and shield; brass lining **90.00**

☐**2842**—(3¼″) Stag handle, two blades, one large spear and one pen; large blade full polished; nickel silver bolsters, shield and lining **120.00**

☐**2843**—(3⅜″) Stag handle, two blades, one large spear and one pen; large blade full polished; nickel silver bolsters, shield and lining **150.00**

☐**2844**—(3¾″) Stag handle, two blades, one large clip and one pen; large blade full polished; polished steel boslter; nickel silver shield; brass lining **250.00**

☐**2845**—(3¾″) Stag handle, two blades, one large clip and one pen; large blade full polished; steel bolster and cap; nickel silver shield; brass lining **225.00**

☐**2846**—(3¼″) Stag handle, two large blades, one clip and one pen; large blade full polished; nickel silver bolsters, shield and lining .**125.00**

☐**2847**—(3¼″) Stag handle, two large blades, one clip and one spey; clip blade full polished; nickel silver bolsters, shield and lining .**150.00**

☐**2848**—(3½″) Stag handle, two blades, one large clip and one pen; full polished; polished steel bolster and cap; nickel silver shield; brass lining; 15 in. steel chain and shackle . . .**125.00**

☐**2849**—(3¼″) Stag handle, two blades, one large spear and one pen; large blade full polished; nickel silver bolster, cap and shield; brass lining **175.00**

☐**2850**—(3¾″) Stag handle, two blades, one large saber clip and one pen; large blade full polished; nickel silver bolster, cap and shield; brass lining **275.00**

☐**2853**—(3⅜″) Stag handle, two blades, one large saber clip and one pen; large blade full polished; nickel silver bolster, cap and shield; brass lining **200.00**

☐**2854**—(3¼″) Stag handle, two blades, one large spear and one pen; large blade full polished; nickel silver bolster, cap and shield; brass lining **150.00**

☐**2855**—(3¼″) Stag handle, two blades, one large spear and one patent leather punch blade; large blade full polished; nickel silver bolster, cap and shield, brass lining **150.00**

☐**2856**—(2⅞″) Stag handle, two blades, one large clip and one pen; large blade full polished; nickel silver bolster, cap and lining **100.00**

☐**2859**—(2⅞″) Stag handle, two blades, one large spear and one pen; large blade full polished; nickel silver bolsters and lining **80.00**

☐**2860**—(3¼″) Stag handle, two blades, one large spear and one pen; large blade full polished; nickel silver bolster, cap, shield and lining **150.00**

☐**2861**—(3¼″) Stag handle, two blades, one large clip and one pen; large blade full polished; nickel silver bolster, cap, shield and lining **150.00**

☐**2862**—(3⅜″) Stag handle, two blades, one large spear and one pen; large blade full polished; nickel silver bolsters, shield and lining **90.00**

☐**2863**—(3¼″) Stag handle, two blades, one large sheepfoot and one pen; large blade full polished; nickel silver bolsters. Shield and lining **145.00**

☐**2865**—(3½″) Stag handle, two large blades, one clip and one spear; spear blade full polished; nickel silver bolsters and shield; brass lining **300.00**

☐**2866**—(2⅞″) Stag handle, two blades, one large spear and one pen; large blade full polished; nickel silver tips and lining **80.00**

☐**2867**—(3⅜″) Stag handle, two blades, one large spear and one pen; large blade full polished; nickel silver tips and shield; brass lining **120.00**

☐**2868**—(3¼″) Stag handle, two blades, one large spear and one pen; large blade full polished; nickel silver bolsters and shield; brass lining **120.00**

☐**2869**—(3¾″) Stag handle, two large blades, one clip and one spey; clip blade full polished; nickel silver bolsters, shield and lining . **225.00**

☐**2870**—(3¾″) Stag handle, two blades, one large clip and one pen; large blade full polished; nickel silver bolster, cap, shield and lining **175.00**

☐**2872**—(3¼″) Stag handle, two blades, one large spear and one pen; large blade full polished; nickel silver bolsters, shield and lining **140.00**

☐**2874**—(3½″) Stag handle, two blades, one large clip and one patent leather punch blade; large blade full polished; nickel silver bolster, cap and shield; brass lining **150.00**

☐**2901**—(3½″) Stag handle, two blades, one large clip and one pen; glazed finish; steel bolster; nickel silver shield; brass lining **150.00**

☐**2902**—(2⅝″) Stag handle, two blades, one large spear and one pen; large blade full polished; nickel silver bolsters and lining **80.00**

☐**2903**—(3½″) Stag handle, two blades, one lage spear and one pen; large blade full polished; nickel silver bolsters and shield; brass lining **200.00**

☐**2904**—(3⅞″) Stag handle, two large blades, one saber clip and one spey; clip blde full polished; nickel silver bolster, cap, shield and lining **400.00**

☐**2905**—(4¼″) Stag handle, two blades, one large spear and one pen; large blade full polished; nickel silver bolster, cap and shield; brass lining **500.00**

☐**2907**—(4¼″) Stag handle, two blades, one large clip and one pen; large blade full polished; nickel silver bolster, cap and shield; brass lining **500.00**

☐**2908**—(3⅝″) Stag handle, two blades, one large flat clip and one pen; large blde full polished; nickel silver bolsters, shield and lining **160.00**

☐**2910**—(3″) Stag handle, two blades, one large spear and one French file, full polished; nickel silver tips, shield and lining **90.00**

☐**2911**—(3½″) Stag handle, two blades, one large spear and one pen; glazed finish; steel bolster and cap; nickel silver shield; brass lining **150.00**

☐**2914**—(3¼″) Stag handle, two large blades, one long clip and one spey; clip blde full polished; nickel silver boslters, shield and lining **175.00**

☐**2917**—(3″) Stag handle, two blades, one large spear and one pen; large blade full polished; nickel silver bolster, cap and shield; brass lining **125.00**

☐**2918**—(3⅜″) Stag handle, two blades, one large spear and one pen; spear blade full polished; nickel silver tips; shield and lining **150.00**

☐**2921**—(3½″) Stag handle, two blades, one large spear and one pen; large blade full polished; nickel silver boslters; octagon cap and shield; brass lining **275.00**

☐**2923**—(4″) Stag handle, two large blades, one clip and one spey; clip blade full polished; nickel silver boslters, shield and lining .**250.00**

☐**2924**—(3″) Stag handle, two blades, one large sheepfoot and one pen; large blade full polished; nickel silver rat-tail bolsters, shield and lining **120.00**

☐**2925**—(3⅛″) Stag handle, two blades, one large spear and one pen; large blade full polished; nickel silver bolster, cap, shield and lining **150.00**

☐**2928**—(4″) Stag handle, two blades, one large clip and one patent leather punch blade; clip blde full polished; nickel silver bolster, shield and lining **200.00**

☐**2930**—(3⅜″) Stag handle, two blades, one large spear and one pen; large blade full polished; steel bolster and cap; nickel silver shield; brass lining **200.00**

☐**2932**—(3¼″) Stag handle, two blades, one large sheepfoot and one pen; large blade full polished; nickel silver rat-tail bolsters, shield and lining **145.00**

☐**2933**—(3″) Stag handle, two blades, one large spear and one pen; large blade full polished; nickel silver tips, shield and lining **140.00**

☐**2934**—(3⅜″) Stag handle, two blades, one large spear and one pen; large blade full polished; nickel silver bolsters, shield and lining **90.00**

☐**2938**—(3¼″) Stag handle, two blades, one large spear and one pen; large blade full polished; nickel silver tips, shield and lining **140.00**

☐**2940**—(3⅜″) Stag handle, two blades, one large spear and one pen; large blade full polished; nickel silver bolster, cap, shield and lining **200.00**

☐**2943**—(3¾″) Stag handle, two blades, one large spear and one pen; large blade full polished; nickel silver bolsters, shield and lining **120.00**

☐**2945**—(3¼″) Stag handle, two blades, one large spear and one pen; large blade full polished; nickel silver tips, shield and lining **90.00**

☐**2948**—(3⅜″) Stag handle, two blades, one large spear and one pen; large blade full polished; nickel silver bolsters, shield and lining **110.00**

☐**2949**—(3½″) Stag handle, two blades, one large spear and one pen; glazed finish; steel bolster and cap; nickel silver shield; brass lining **150.00**

☐**2950**—(3½″) Stag handle, two blades, one large spear and one pen; glazed finish; steel bolster; nickel silver shield; brass lining **150.00**

☐**2951**—(3½″) Stag handle, two blades, one large clip and one punch blade, glazed finish; steel bolster; nickel silver shield; brass lining **150.00**

☐**2952**—(3½″) Stag handle, two blades, one large clip and one pen; large blade full polished; nickel silver bolster, cap and shield; brass lining **200.00**

☐**2954**—(3½″) Stag handle, two blades, one large spear and one pen; large blade full polished; nickel silver bolster, cap and shield; brass lining **200.00**

☐**2956**—(3½″) Stag handle, two blades, one large spear and one pen; large blade full polished; nickel silver bolster, cap and shield; brass lining **150.00**

☐**2958**—(3½″) Stag handle, two blades, one large clip and one pen; glazed finish; steel bolster and lining **150.00**

☐**2959**—(3⅜″) Stag handle, two blades, one large spear and one pen; glazed finish; steel bolster and cap, nickel silver shield; brass lining **200.00**

☐**2961**—(3⅜″) Stag handle, two blades, one large spey and one pen; glazed finish; steel bolster and lining **150.00**

☐**2962**—(2⅞″) Stag handle, two blades, one large spear and one pen; large blade full polished; nickel silver bolster, cap and lining . . . . .
. . . .**100.00**

☐**2963**—(3″) Stag handle, two blades, one large spear and one pen; large blade full polished; nickel silver bolsters, shield and lining
. . . .**120.00**

☐**2964**—(3⅜″) Stag handle, two blades, one large spear and one pen; large blade full polished; nickel silver bolster, cap and shield; brass lining **150.00**

☐**2966**—(3⅝″) Stag handle, two blades, one large spear and one pen; large blade full polished; steel bolster and cap; nickel silver shield; brass lining **275.00**

☐**2967**—(3⅞″) Stag handle, two large blades, one spear and one clip; spear blade full polished; nickel silver bolsters, shield and lining . . . .
. . . .**325.00**

☐**2969**—(3⅞″) Stag handle, two large blades, one clip and one spey; clip blade full polished; nickel silver bolsters, shield and lining . **300.00**

☐**2973**—(3⅝″) Stag handle, two blades, one large clip and one pen; clip blade full polished; nickel silver bolster and shield; brass lining . . .
. . . .**175.00**

☐**2974**—(3½″) Stag handle, two blades, one large clip and one pen; large blade fully polished; nickel silver bolster, cap and shield; brass lining **150.00**

☐**2976**—(4″) Stag handle, two blades, one large clip and one pen; large blade full polished; nickel silver bolsters, shield and lining . **200.00**

☐**2978**—(3½″) Stag handle, two blades, one large spear and one pen; large blade full polished; nickel silver bolster, cap, shield and lining **300.00**

☐**2980**—(3⅜″) Stag handle, two blades, one large clip and one pen; clip blade full polished; nickel silver bolsters and shield; brass lining **175.00**

☐**2981**—(3¼″) Stag handle, two blades, one large spear and one file; large blade full polished; nickel silver tips, shield and lining; shackle **90.00**

☐**2982**—(4″) Stag handle, two blades, one large spear and one pen; large blade full polished; nickel silver bolster, cap and shield; brass lining **300.00**

☐**2983**—(3½″) Stag handle, two blades, one large clip and one pen; glazed finish; steel bolster and lining; shackle and chain . . . **125.00**

☐**2988**—(4″) Stag handle, two blades, one large clip and one pen; large blade full polished; nickel silver bolster, cap and shield, brass lining **300.00**

☐**2990**—(2⅞″) Stag handle, two blades, one large saber clip and one pen; large blade full polished; nickel silver bolster, cap and shield; brass lining **125.00**

☐**2991**—(3⅝″) Stag handle, two large blades, one spear and one clip; spear blade full polished; nickel silver bolsters and shield; brass lining **300.00**

☐**2993**—(3⅞″) Stag handle, two blades, one large saber clip and one pen; large blade full polished; nickel silver bolster, cap, shield and lining **350.00**

☐**2994**—(3⅝″) Stag handle, two blades, one large spear and one pen; large blade full polished; steel bolster; nickel silver shield; brass lining **150.00**

☐**2995**—(3⅝″) Stag handle, two blades, one large spear and one pen; large blade full polished; steel boslter and cap; nickel silver shield; brass lining **200.00**

☐**2996**—(3¾″) Stag handle, two blades, one large sheepfoot and one pen; large blade full polished; nickel silver rat-tail bolsters and shield; brass lining **175.00**

☐**2997**—(3⅜″) Stag handle, two blades, one large clip and one pen; clip blade full polished; nickel silver bolsters, shield and lining . **160.00**

☐**2998**—(3½″) Stag handle, two blades, one large spear and one pen; glazed finish; steel boslter and lining **150.00**

☐**2999**—(3¼″) Stag handle, two blades, one large clip and one pen; large blade full polished; nickel silver bolster, candle end cap and shield; brass lining **200.00**

☐**3001**—(3½″) Gray celluloid handle, three blades, one large spear, one large spey and one patent leather punch blade; spear blade full polished; nickel silver bolsters, shield and lining **275.00**

☐**3002**—(3⅝″) Iridescent celluloid handle, three blades, one large flat clip, one large spey and one patent leather punch blade; clip blade full polished; nickel silver bolsters, shield and lining **250.00**

☐**3003**—(3½″) Golden celluloid handle, three large blades, one clip, one spear and one spey; clip blade full polished; nickel silver bolsters, shield and lining **250.00**

☐**3005**—(31⅝″) Black celluloid handle, three blades, one large flat clip, one small clip and one pen; flat clip blade full polished; nickel silver bolsters, shield and lining **200.00**

☐**3006**—(3⅜″) Black celluloid handle, three blades, one large clip, one pen and one file; clip blade full polished; nickel silver bolsters, shield and lining **150.00**

☐**300**—(4″) Black celluloid handle, three large blades, one clip, one sheepfoot and one spey; clip blade full polished; nickel silver bolsters, shield and lining **275.00**

WINCHESTER
CATTLE KNIFE

☐**3008**—(3⅝″) White celluloid handle, three large blades, one spear, one sheepfoot and one spey; spear blade full polished; steer's head on reverse side; nickel silver bolsters and lining **175.00**

☐**3009**—(3⅝″) White celluloid handle, three blades, one large flat clip, one large spey and one patent leather punch blade; clip blade full polished; steer's head on reverse side; nickel silve bolsters and lining **275.00**

☐**3010**—(3¾″) Abalone celluloid handle, three blades, one large clip, one large spey and one patent leather punch blade; clip blade full polished; three springs; nickel silver bolsters, shield and lining **325.00**

☐**3014**—(4″) Pearl gray celluloid handle, three large blades, one clip, one sheepfoot and one spey; clip blade full polished; nickel silver bolsters, shield and lining **275.00**

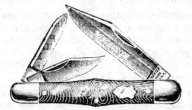

☐**3015**—(3⅝″) Golden celluloid handle, three blades, one large saber clip, one small clip and one pen; saber clip blade full polished; nickel silver bolsters, shield and lining **250.00**

☐**3016**—(3⅝″) Gray celluloid handle, three blades, one large flat clip, one large spey and one patent leather punch blade; clip blde full polished; nickel silver bolsters, shield and lining **300.00**

☐**3017**—(4″) Varicolored brilliant finish celluloid handle, three large blades, one clip, one sheepfoot and one spey; clip blade full polished; nickel silver bolsters, shield and lining **300.00**

☐**3018**—(4″) Red and white celluloid handle, three large blades, one clip, one sheepfoot and one spey; clip blade full polished; nickel silver bolsters, shield and lining **275.00**

☐**3019**—(3½″) Red celluloid handle, three blades, one large spear, one large spey and one patent leather punch blade; spear blade full polished; nickel silver bolsters, shield and lining **275.00**

☐**3020**—(3½″) Green and red celluloid handle, three blades, one large spear, one large spey and one patent leathe punch blade; spear blade full polished; nickel silver bolsters, shield and lining **275.00**

☐**3025**—(3½″) Abalone blue celluloid handle, three large blades, one clip, one spear and one spey; clip blade full polished; nickel silver bolsters, shield and lining **250.00**

☐**3026**—(3¼″) Iridescent celluloid handle, three large blades, one spear, one sheepfoot and one spey; spear blade full polished; nickel silver bolsters, shield and lining **250.00**

☐**3027**—(3¼″) Red cellulloid handle, three blades, one large clip, one spey and one pen; clip blade full polished; nickel silver bolsters, shield and lining **200.00**

☐**3044**—(3⅜″) Red and green celluloid handle, three blades, one large spear, one pen and one file; large blade full polished; nickel silver bolsters, shield and lining **200.00**

☐**3331**—(3⅛″) Pearl handle, three blades, one large spear, one pen and one pick file, full polished; nickel silver tips, shield and milled lining; sunk joints **200.00**

☐**3352**—(3½″) Pearl handle, shadow ends, three stainless blades, one large spear, one pen and one file, full polished; nickel silver lining **250.00**

☐**3533**—(2⅝″) Pearl handle, three stainless steel blades, one large spear, one pen and one French file, full polished; nickel silver tips and lining; shackle **150.00**

☐**3357**—(3¼″) Pearl handle, three blades, one large spear, one pen and one curley nail file; full polished; nickel silver tips, shield and lining **275.00**

3370—(3″) Pearl handle, shadow ends, three blades, one large spear, one pen and one French file, full polished; nickel silver milled lining shackle **200.00**

3371—(3″) Pearl handle, three blades, one large spear, one scissors and one French file, full polished; nickel silver milled lining . . **275.00**

3376—(4″) Pearl handle, three large blades, one clip, one sheepfoot and one spey, all blades full polished; nickel silver bolsters, shield and lining **275.00**

3377—(3¼″) Pearl handle, three blades, one large spear and two pens, full polished; nickel silver tips and lining **275.00**

3380—(2¾″) Shadow-end Pearlhandle, three blades, one large spear, one pen and one pick file; full polished; nickel silver milled lining and shield; shackle **150.00**

3381—(3⅛″) Pearl handle; skeleton, three blades, one large spear, one pen and one flexible file, full polished; shackle **200.00**

3382—(3″) Pearl handle, shadow ends, three blades, one large spear, one pen, and one French file, full polished; nickel silver milled lining **200.00**

3902—(3½″) Stag handle, three blades, one large clip and two pens; large blade full polished; nickel silver bolsters and shield; brass lining **300.00**

3028—(3¼″) Green and black celluloid handle, three blades, one large clip, one spey and one pen; clip blade full polished; nickel silver bolsters and lining **200.00**

3029—(3¼″) Red and black celluloid handle, three blades, one large clip, one large spey and one patent leather punch blade; clip blade full polished; nickel silver bolsters, shield and lining **200.00**

3030—(3⅜″) Abalone blue celluloid handle, three blades, one large clip, one large clip, one large spey and one pen; clip blade full polished; nickel silver bolsters, shield and lining . **200.00**

3031—(3⅜″) Gray celluloid handle, three blades, one large spear, one pen and one patent leather punch blade; spear blade full polished; nickel silver bolsters, shield and lining . **250.00**

3035—(3⅜″) Golden celluloid handle, three blades, one large clip, one large sheepfoot and one pen; clip blade full polished; nickel silver bolsters, shield and lining **175.00**

3041—(3″) Red and black celluloid handle, three blades, one large spear and two pens; large blade full polished; nickel silver bolsters, shield and lining **175.00**

3042—(3⅜″) Green and black celluloid handle, three blades, one large spear and two pens; large blade full polished; nickel silver bolsters, shield and lining **175.00**

3043—(3⅜″) Red and black celluloid handle, three blades, one large spear, one pen and one file; large blade full polished; nickel silver bolsters, shield and lining **200.00**

3903—(3¾″) Stag handle, three blades, one large clip, one large spey and one patent leather punch blade; clip blade full polished; three springs; nickel silver bolster, shield and lining **375.00**

3904—(3¾″) Stag handle, three blades, one large clip, one large spey and one pen; clip blade full polished; three springs; nickel silver bolsters, shield and lining **300.00**

3905—(3½″) Stag handle, three blades, one large spear, one large spey and one patent leather punch blade; spear blade full polished; nickel silver bolsters, shield and lining . **275.00**

3906—(4″) Stag handle, three large blades, one clip, one sheepfoot and one spey; clip blade full polished; nickel silver bolsters, shield and lining **300.00**

3907—(4″) Stag handle, three blades, one large clip, one large spey and one patent leather punch blade; clip blade full polished; nickel silver bolsters, shield and lining **350.00**

☐**3909**—(3⅜″) Stag handle, three blades, one large clip, one spey and one pen; clip blade full polished; nickel silver bolsters, shield and lining **240.00**

☐**3915**—(3½″) Stag handle, three blades, one large spear, one pen and one patent leather punch blade; spear blade full polished; nickel silver bolsters, shield and lining **250.00**

☐**3916**—(3½″) Stag handle, three blades, one large clip, one large spey and one patent leather punch blade; clip blade full polished; nickel silver bolsters, shield and lining **250.00**

☐**3917**—(3½″) Stag handle, three large blades, one clip, one spear and one spey; clip blade full polished; nickel silver bolsters, shield and lining **250.00**

☐**3924**—(3″) Stag handle, three blades, one large spear, one pen and one curley file; large blade full polished; nickel silver bolsters, shield and lining **200.00**

☐**3925**—(3⅜″) Stag handle, three blades, one large saber clip, one small clip and one pen; saber clip blade full polished; nickel silver bolsters, shield and lining **300.00**

☐**3927**—(3⅜″) Stag handle, three blades, one large spear, one pen and one file; large blade full polished; nickel silver bolsters, shield and lining **200.00**

☐**3928**—(4″) Stag handle, three large blades, one clip, one sheepfoot and one spey; clip blade full polished; nickel silver bolsters, shield and lining **300.00**

☐**3929**—(3¼″) Stag handle, three blades, one large sheepfoot, one pen and one file; large blade full polished; nickel silver rat-tail bolsters, shield and lining **275.00**

☐**3931**—(3⅛″) Stag handle, three blades, one large spear, one pen and one pick fule; full polished; nickel silver tips, shield and lining **125.00**

☐**3932**—(3⅜″) Stag handle, three blades, one large spear, one pen and one file; large blade full polished; nickel silver bolsters, shield and lining **175.00**

☐**3933**—(3⅜″) Stag handle, three blades, one large clip, one large sheepfoot and one pen; clip blade full polished; nickel silver bolsters, shield and lining **175.00**

☐**3936**—(3⅜″) Stag handle, three large blades, one spear, one clip and one spey; spear blade full polished; nickel silver bolsters, shield and lining **300.00**

☐**3938**—(3⅜″) Stag handle, three blades, one large spear and two pens; large blade full polished; nickel silver bolsters, shield and lining **175.00**

☐**3939**—(3⅜″) Stag handle, three blades, one large spear, one pen and one patent leather punch blade; large blade full polished; nickel silver bolsters, shield and lining **275.00**

☐**3924**—(3⅜″) Stag handle, three large blades, one spear, one sheepfoot and one spey; clip blade full polished; nickel silver bolsters, shield and lining **250.00**

☐**3944**—(3¼″) Stag handle, three blades, one large spear, one pen and one file; large blade full polished; nickel silver bolsters, shield and lining **300.00**

☐**3948**—(3¾″) Stag handle, three large blades, one clip, one sheepfoot and one spey; clip blde full polished; nickel silver bolsters, shield and lining **275.00**

☐**3950**—(3⅜″) Stag handle, three large blades, one flat clip, one sheepfoot and one spey; clip blade full polished; nickel silver bolsters, shield and lining **300.00**

☐**3951**—(3⅜″) Stag handle, three blades, one large spear, one large spey and one patent leather punch blade; spear blades full polished; nickel silver bolsters, shield and lining . **300.00**

☐**3952**—(3⅜″) Stag handle, three blades, one large clip, one large sheepfoot and one pen; clip blade full polished; nickel silver bolsters, shield and lining **325.00**

☐**3959**—(4″) Stag handle, three large blades, one clip, one sheepfoot and one spey; clip blade full polished; nickel silver bolsters, shield and lining **300.00**

☐**3960**—(4″) Stag handle, three blades, one long flat clip, one sheepfoot and one pen; clip blade full polished; nickel silver bolsters, shield and lining **300.00**

☐**3961**—(4″) Stag handle, three blades, one large clip, one large spey and one patent leather punch blade; clip blade full polished; nickel silver bolsters, shield and lining **300.00**

☐**3962**—(4") Genuine buffalo horn handle, three large blades, one long flat clip, one sheepfoot and one spey; full polished; crest shield; nickel silver round bolsters, shield and lining; full milled on front and back **300.00**

☐**3965**—(3¼") Stag handle, three large blades, one spear, one sheepfoot and one spey; spear blade full polished; nickel silver bolsters, shield and lining **200.00**

☐**3967**—(3¼") Stag handle, three blades, one large clip, one spey and one pen; clip blade full polished; nickel silver bolsters, shield and lining **200.00**

☐**3968**—(3¼") Stag handle, three blades, one large clip, one pen and one patent leather punch blade; clip blade full polished; nickel silver bolsters, shield and lining **275.00**

☐**3971**—(3⅝") Stag handle, three blades, one large clip, one spey and one pen; clip blade full polished; nickel silver bolsters, shield and lining **275.00**

☐**3972**—(3⅝") Stag handle, three blades, one large flat clip, one spey and one patent leather punch blade; large blade full polished; nickel silver bolsters, shield and lining **300.00**

☐**3973**—(3½") Stag handle, three large blades, one flat clip, one spear and one spey; clip blade full polished; nickel silver bolsters, shield and lining **250.00**

☐**3975**—(3⅜") Stag handle, three large blades, one large clip, one large spey and one patent leather punch blade; clip blade full polished; nickel silver bolsters, shield and lining **275.00**

☐**3977**—(3⅜") Stag handle, three blades, one large clip, one large sheepfoot and one pen; clip blade full polished; nickel silver bolsters, shield and lining **175.00**

☐**3978**—(3¼") Stag handle, three blades, one long, flat clip, one sheepfoot and one pen; clip blade full polished; nickel silver bolsters, shield and lining **150.00**

☐**3979**—(3⅝") Stag handle, three blades, one large flat clip, one large spey and one patent leather punch; clip blade full polished; nickel silver bolsters, shield and lining **300.00**

☐**3980**—(3") Stag handle, three blades, one large spear, one large spey and one pen; spear blade full polished; nickel silver bolsters, shield and lining **200.00**

☐**3991**—(3¼") Stag handle, three blades, one large spear and two pen; large blade full polished; nickel silver tips, shield and lining . . **175.00**

☐**3992**—(3⅜") Stag handle, three blades, one large spear and two pens, large blade full polished; nickel silver bolsters, shield and lining **250.00**

☐**3993**—(4") Stag handle, three blades, one large clip, one large spey and one pen; clip blade full polished; nickel silver bolsters, shield and lining **300.00**

☐**4001**—(4") Green celluloid handle, four blades, one large clip, one large sheepfoot, one large spey and one patent leather punch blade; clip blade full polished; nickel silver bolsters, shield and lining **400.00**

☐**4301**—(2¾") Shadow-end pearl handle, four blades, one large spear, one pen, one scissors and one pick file; full polished; nickel silver milled lining; crest shield **275.00**

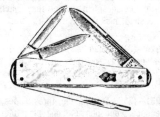

☐**4320**—(3¼") Flat pearl square edge handle, four blades, one large spear, two pens and one pick file, full polished; nickel silver tips and milled lining **200.00**

☐**4340**—(3¼") Pearl handle, four blades, one large spear, two pens and one file, full polished; nickel silver bolsters, shield and lining . **300.00**

☐**4341**—(3¼") Pearl handle, four blades, one large spear, two pens and one file, full polished; nickel silver tips, shield and lining **300.00**

☐**4910**—(4″) Stag handle, four blades, one large clip, one large sheepfoot, one large spey and one patent leather punch blade; clip blade full polished; nickel silver boslters, shield and lining **500.00**

☐**4918**—(3″) Stag handle, four blades, two large sheepfoot, one pen and one nail file; large blades full polished; nickel silver rat-tail bolsters, shield and lining **225.00**

☐**4920**—(3¼″) Stag handle, four blades, one large spear, two pens and one pick file, full polished; nickel silver tips, shield and milled lining **150.00**

☐**4930**—(3¼″) Stag handle, four blades, one large sheepfoot, two pens and one file; large blade full polished; nickel silver rat-tail bolsters, shield and lining. **275.00**

☐**4931**—(3½″) Stag handle, four blades, two large sheepfoot and two pens; large blades full polished; nickel silver rat-tail bolsters and shield; brass lining **325.00**

☐**4961**—(4″) Stag handle, four blades, one large clip, one large sheepfoot, one large spey and one patent leather punch blade; clip blade full polished; nickel silver bolsters, shield and lining **300.00**

☐**4962**—(4″) Stag handle, four blades, one large clip, one large sheepfoot, one large spey and one patent leather punch blade; clip blade full polished; nickel silver bolsters, shield and lining **500.00**

GEORGE WOSTENHOLM & SON CUTLERY COMPANY (I*XL)
SHEFFIELD, ENGLAND

The George Wostenholm family in cutlery dates back to 1745, when a George Wolstenholme (1717-   ) and his son Henry (-1803) ran a small cutlery business in Stannington, England. Henry was one of the first cutlers to use springs for pocketknives and in 1757 was granted the "Spring" trademark. Henry's son George made many changes in the company. He moved the business to nearby Sheffield, changed the name of the family from Wolstenholme to Wostenholm so it would be easier stamped on a blade tang, and was one of the first to concentrate cutlers in a factory. He named his son George and it was this third George Wostenholm who expanded the firm into world trade.

The company did not originate many of their trademarks. The Pipe Trademark, currently used only on razors and kitchen knives, dates to 1694 and is the oldest cutlery trademark in the Register of the Sheffield Cutler's Company. Wostenholm got the trademark in 1843. The Tally-ho trademark was listed in 1833 and obtained in 1860. I*XL, meaning "I excell," was granted in 1787 and acquired in 1826.

I*XL made some of the most collectible Bowie knives in the 1840's, but over the years has made almost every imaginable pattern of cutlery.

Among the earlier stampings were "I*XL George Wostenholm & Son LTD," and "I*XL George Wostenholm Celebrated, Sheffield, England." The current stamping is "I*XL George Wostenholm, Sheffield, England" with "Oil the Joints" stamped on the reverse of the tang.

In the mid seventies Schrade Cutlery bought IXL and in 1981 introduced a line of IXL knives.

COMMEMORATIVE AND LIMITED EDITION KNIVES
THE AMERICAN BICENTENNIAL SERIES

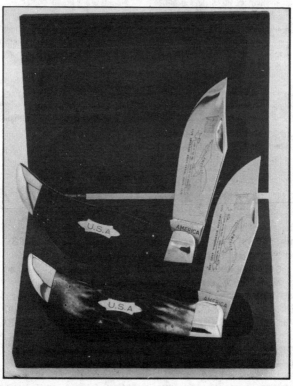

Handcrafted by Alcas Cutlery in New York for Parker-Frost Cutlery. Only 1,500 pair of these 5½ inch clasp knives were made. The first has wood handles and the other has beautiful genuine stag. The two flags etched on the blade depict the 1776 flag and the current 1976 flag. These knives were sold in serial numbered pairs. They are packed in a solid walnut gold leafed box. Serial number appears on the rear of tang. The knives retailed for $200-$400 per set depending on the serial numbers.

☐ *Current Collector Value* . . . . **$250.00/set of 2**

THE AMERICAN EAGLE BICENTENNIAL SERIES

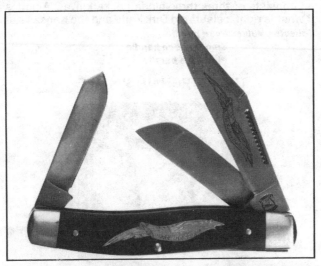

The Eagle series is a commemorative set of five knives honoring Patrick Henry, Nathan Hale, John Adams, Thomas Jefferson and George Washington. There were 12,000 sets of Eagle Commemorative Knives produced and over 10,000 of them have already been sold and are in the hands of collectors. Each knife is handcrafted, deluxe gift boxed with registration papers, serial numbered and has solid nickel silver bolsters. The linings are brass and the blades are 440 stainless.

146ices on these knives range from $200 to $500 per set with matching serial numbers and original display plaque.

☐ *Current Collector Value* . . . .**$175.00/set of 5**

THE AMERICAN LOCKBACK WHITTLER SERIES

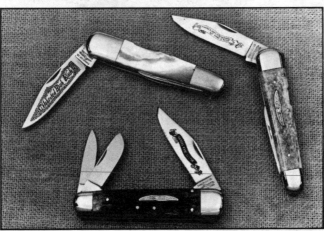

The American Lockback Whittler Series was manufactured by Parker Cutlery. The set consists of three three-blade pocketknives; America asks for nothing but what is right, celebrated Dirk knife and the Kansas Kane Cutter.

☐ **Current Collector Value: Pearl handle** $80.00
☐   **Smooth bone handle** 45.00
☐   **Pick bone handle** 45.00

THE ASTRONAUTS' KNIFE

The Case Astronauts' knife has been carried in all NASA flights since March 23, 1965 when one was carried in the survival kits of Major Virgil Grissom and Navy Commander John Young.

The blade is 13 gauge high carbon stainless steel and the handle is polypropylene (the lightest plastic that gives off no fumes). The polished edge will shave and the back of the blade has a row of saw teeth. The handle is attached by round brass rods and the handle is drilled for a lanyard. Case made 2,494 of these knives for sale to the public at $75 per knife, including display case. The knife was discontinued January 1, 1972, and has an 11 inch blade inside a display box that measures 2½"x8½"x20½". Naturally, the lower the serial number, the more valuable the knife.

☐ *Current Collector Value (Depending on Serial Numbers)* .... **$350.00 to $600.00**

THE AURUM SERIES

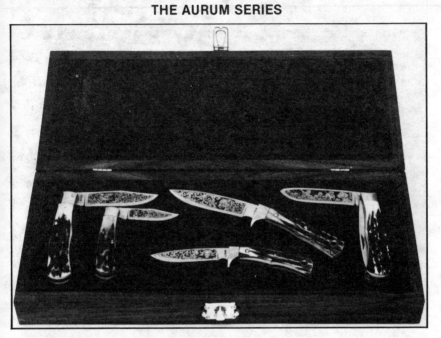

This S knife set consists of the following:

1. One-blade, 4½ inch with genuine stag handles
2. One-blade, 3¼ inch with genuine stag folder
3. Small sheath (comes with leather sheath)
4. Large sheath (comes with leather sheath)
5. Large two-blade genuine stag folder

☐ *Current Collector Value* .... **$350.00/set of 5**

THE BATTLE-AXE COMMEMORATIVE SERIES

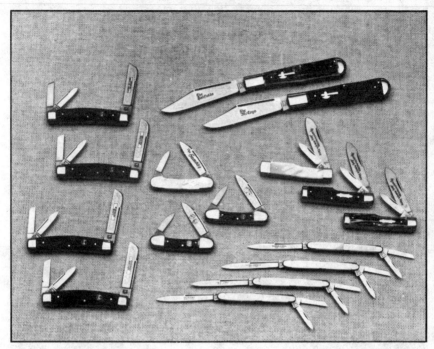

1. The Congress Whittlers
□ *Current Collector Value* ....$200.00/set of 4

2. The Gamblers
□ *Current Collector Value* ....$150.00/set of 3

3. The Hatfields and McCoys
□ *Current Collector Value* ....$150.00/set of 2

4. The Mountaineers
□ *Current Collector Value* ....$200.00/set of 3

5. World War II
□ *Current Collector Value* ....$200.00/set of 4

THE BATTLE AXE FOLDING HUNTER SERIES
(picture on following page)

This set of six one-blade pocketknives; Ohio Diplomat, Queen of Tennessee, Coal Miners Companion, King of Kentucky, King of Washington C.H. and Arkansas Picksticker is manufactured by Battle-Axe Knives.
□ *Current Collector Value* ....$200.00/set of 6

THE BATTLE AXE FOLDING HUNTER SERIES

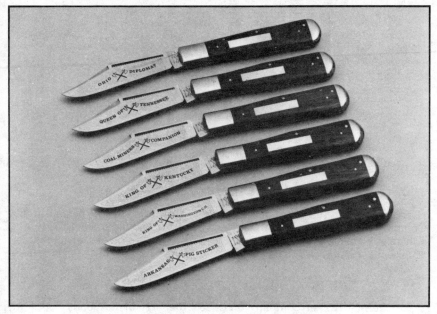

THE BIRD DOG WHITTLER

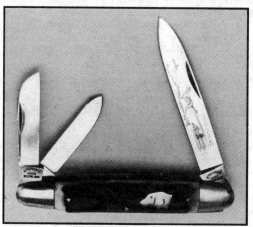

Made by Hoffritz, Germany, the Bird Dog Whittler is made on the 4½ inch whittler pattern used in the North South Whittler sets and the 1975 NKCA club knife. Only 1,000 were made, with stag handles, etched blade, and Dogshead shield. Retail on the knives was $75 for serial number 1-10, $60 for serial numbers 11-100, and $50 for serial numbers.

☐ *Current Collector Value* **$40.00**

THE BLACK BEAR SKINNER

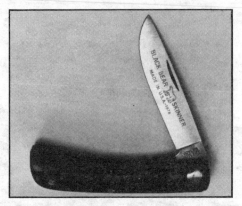

This knife was the second limited edition knife made by Voyles Cutlery Company. The blade is etched with a black bear and "Made in USA-1978". The knives are stainless steel. Only 600 of the knives were serial numbered.
☐ *Current Collector Value* **$18.00**

THE BOKER WISS 1971 COMMEMORATIVE

The German Boker company produced the first of its yearly series in 1971, commemorating the Boker U. S. A. and Wiss anniversary. The first knife were a three-bladed stockman with a black simulated handle, "Boker, Soligen, Germany," stamped on the tang, and "Premium Stock Knife #7474 L. T. D." etched on the master blade. The knives were not serial numbered, but there were 10,000 produced. The knife has two shields in the handle, one of the usual tree brand and the other saying "Wiss 1971." The original retail price was $12.95.
☐ *Current Collector Value* **$50.00**

THE BOKER WISS 1972 COMMEMORATIVE

12,000 of the 1972 Wiss were made, using a three-blade, round bolster pattern. The 3½ inch knife has "Tree Brand" in a gold emblem and "#7588 LTD" both etched on the master blade. The knife has black simulated handles with two gold shields in them, one with the "Tree Brand emblem" and the other with "1972 Wiss." The knife originally sold for $11.95. These knives do not have serial numbers.
☐ *Current Collector Value* **$45.00**

THE BOKER WISS 1973 COMMEMORATIVE

The 1973 Wiss is 3¾ inches long and a four-blade congress pattern. The knife has black simulated handles with two red shields; one with the "Tree Brand" and the other with "Wiss 1973." The master blade carries the etching "Tree Brand" and the number "5464 LTD." The large blade opposite the master blade carries the serial number on the tang, and there were 18,000 made. The knife comes in a plastic box stamped "Limited Edition, Collector's Item." The knife originally sold for $16.95.

☐ *Current Collector Value* **$40.00**

THE BOKER WISS 1974 COMMEMORATIVE

Boker made 18,000 of this four inch, three-blade, stock pattern, with square bolsters. The knife has black simulated handles with two gold shields, one with "Tree Brand" and the other with "1974 Wiss". The serial number is stamped on the tang of the spay blade opposite the master blade. The master blade is etched with the scene of an elk and a pine branch on either side of "Tree Brand Classic" with "6066 LTD." The knife comes in a green cardboard box. The knife originally sold for $19.95.

☐ *Current Collector Value* **$30.00**

THE BOKER 1975 LIMITED EDITION RIVERBOAT CLASSIC

"The Sternwheeler" Boker Tree Brand features superb quality, hand-created by master craftsmen. The deluxe penknife pattern with simulated pearl handle is Individually serial numbered. It has an engraved sternwheeler illustration, beautifully etched master blade, nickel silver bolsters and pins. Retail on this knife was $21.95.

☐ *Current Collector Value* **$30.00**

THE BOKER 1976 HERITAGE OF FREEDOM KNIFE

This five-inch folding hunter bicentennial knife is a continuation of Bokers yearly series started in 1972. 24,000 knives were manufactured.

☐ *Current Collector Value* **$40.00**

THE BOKER WISS 1977 COMMEMORATIVE

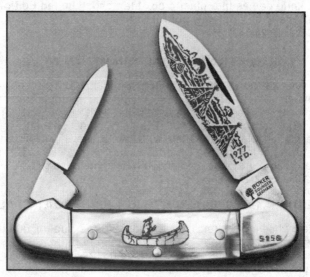

This knife was a two-bladed Canoe with cracked ice handles.
☐ *Current Collector Value* $35.00

THE BOKER BONE HANDLES

Boker, Solingen, in response to collector demand, reintroduced a series of bone handled knives in 1977. The knives were made in a quantity of 5,000 each, in five different patterns.
☐ *Current Collector Value* ....$100.00/set of 5

THE BOKER WISS 1978 COMMEMORATIVE

Bokers 1978 knife is a two-blade bone handled pattern trapper, honoring the Southern mountaineer. The knife is named the "Hillbilly."
☐ *Current Collector Value* $35.00

THE BOKER WISS 1979 COMMEMORATIVE

The 1979 edition of the Boker yearly knife was a five inch folding hunter lockback honoring the hardware industry. The knives have wood handles and an etched blade. Suggested retail on the knives was $52.95.
☐ *Current Collector Value* $50.00

THE BOKER WISS 1981 COMMEMORATIVE

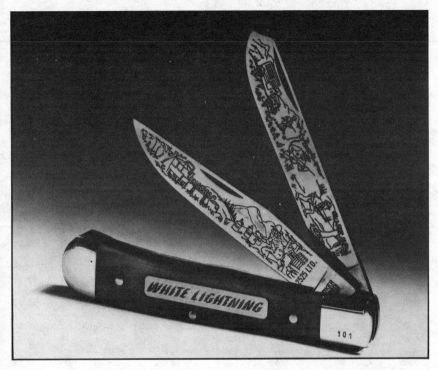

The 1981 edition by Boker "White Lightning" was released in limited edition.

☐ *Current Collector Value* **$45.00**

THE BOKER SPIRIT OF AMERICA SERIES

This series of 24 knives was first introduced in 1974 and a different knife was supposed to be introduced every three months until 1978. The original price was $12 each. The knives were as follows:

Knife #	Theme	Emblem & Legend	Pattern	Release Date	Current Collector Value
☐1770	Sweet Land of Liberty	Pilgrim & Map "Thirteen Colonies"	Stock Knife	May 1974	25.00
☐1771	One out of Many	American Eagle July 4, 1776	Stock Knife	July 1974	20.00
☐1772	Manifest Destiny	Spanish Mission "The Alamo"	Texas Jack	Sept. 1974	20.00
☐1773	Westward Ho	Conestoga Wagon "Prairie Schooner"	Equal End Jack	Dec. 1974	18.00

☐1774	The Melting Pot	Statue of Liberty "Statue of Liberty"	Large Stock	Feb. 1975	**18.00**
☐1775	Dixie	Confederate Soldier "Jonny Reb"	Congress	April 1975	**18.00**
☐1776	On to the Last Frontier	Head-on Locomotive "The Golden Spike"	Stock Knife	July 1975	**15.00**
☐1777	Old Wild West	Two: Cowboy & Indian "Sitting Bull & Buffalo Bill"	Trapper	Sept. 1975	**15.00**
☐1778	Rise to World Power	Sinking Battleship "Remember the Maine"	Swell End Jack	Nov. 1975	**15.00**
☐1779	War to End all Wars	Bibplane "Lafayette Escadrille"	Serpentine Jack	Feb. 1976	**15.00**
☐1880	Dawn of the Atomic Age	Atom "16, July 1945- Alamagordo"	Stock Knife	April 1976	**25.00**
☐1881	200 Years of Freedom	American Flag "July 4, 1776"	Stock Knife	July 4, 1776	**15.00**
☐1782	Birth of Southern Industry	Cotton Gin/ Cotton Gin	Congress Knife	End Aug. 1976	**15.00**
☐1783	Westward Expansion	Map of Louisiana Purchase/Louisiana Purchase	Trapper's Knife	End Oct. 1976	**15.00**
☐1784	Blazing the Trail	Lewis & Clark/ Lewis & Clark	Premium Stock	End Dec. 1976	**15.00**
☐1785	American Proclamation	Monroe Doctrine Scroll/Monroe Doctrine	Texas Jack	End Feb. 1977	**15.00**
☐1786	California Gold Rush	Panning for Gold at Sutters Mill/Sutters Mill	Premium Stock	End April 1977	**15.00**
☐1787	Bridging the Continent	Stage Coach/ Stage Coach	Premium Stock	End June 1977	**15.00**
☐1788	Modern Fuel	Oil Derrick/ Black Gold	Jack Knife	Mid Sept. 1977	**15.00**
☐1789	Continental Mail Service	Pony Express Rider/ Pony Express	Congress Knife	Begin. Nov. 1977	**15.00**
☐1790	Modern Energy	First Hydro Electric Plant/Hydro Electricity	Whittler	End Dec. 1977	**15.00**
☐1791	On to Oklahoma	Homesteaders/ The Sooners	Dogleg Jack	Mid Feb. 1978	**15.00**
☐1792	Revolution in Transportation	Henry Ford's Quadrocycle/Horseless Carriage	Premium Stock	Mid April 1978	**15.00**
☐1793	200 Million Americans	Map of Continental U. S. A./One Nation	Premium Stock	Mid June 1978	**15.00**

THE BONNIE AND CLYDE COMMEMORATIVE SERIES

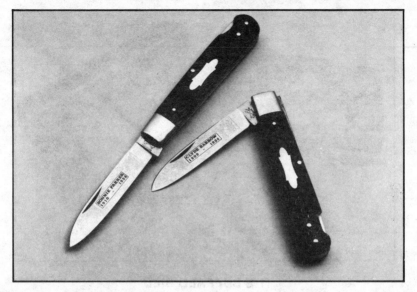

The Bonnie and Clyde lockbacks were a limited production run of 578 knives featuring bone handled lockbacks with gold etched blades. Battle Ax brand made the knives. They were released in April 1979.

☐ *Current Collector Value* . . . . **\$65.00/set of 2**

THE BUCK BICENTENNIAL

The Buck knife was a cased sheath knife with etched blade and a medallion. Original retail on the knives was \$200 each.

☐ *Current Collector Value* **\$225.00**

THE BUCK COLT
(picture on following page)

This limited edition colt was manufactured by Buck Knives.

☐ *Current Collector Value* **\$75.00**

THE BUCK COLT

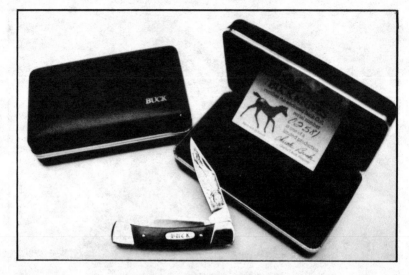

THE BUFFALO BILL

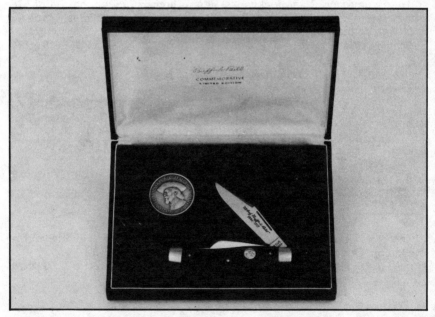

This 4 inch three-bladed stock knife was manufactured by Schrade and came packaged with a medallion in a satin lined gift box.
☐ *Current Collector Value* $25.00

THE BUFORD PUSSER

Commemorating the sheriff from "Walking Tall", the knives were made in a limited edition of 5,000. Based on The R1123 Remington Bullet pattern the knife has 440A carbon stainless steel blades, delrin handles, and a special large shield. The sharpening stick with each knife had a matching serial number.

☐ *Current Collector Value* **$40.00**

THE CAPTAIN'S ROOSTER

This 3⅝ inch, two-blade canoe has genuine fiery mother-of-pearl handles and a gold etched blade, only 1,200 serial numbered knives will be produced, made in Soligen, Germany.

☐ *Current Collector Value* **$65.00**

THE CASE BICENTENNIAL
(picture on following page)

Case made two knives for the bicentennial, a 5165 folding hunter with stag handles and a deep etched blade, and a unusual stainless steel hunting knife. Both knives came attractively boxed. 2,500 sheath knives were made and 10,000 of the folding hunters. Original retail on the knives was $200 on the sheath knife and $150 on the folding hunter.

☐ *Current Collector Value:* **Folding hunter knife** **$225.00**
☐   **Sheath knife** **$375.00**

THE CASE BICENTENNIAL

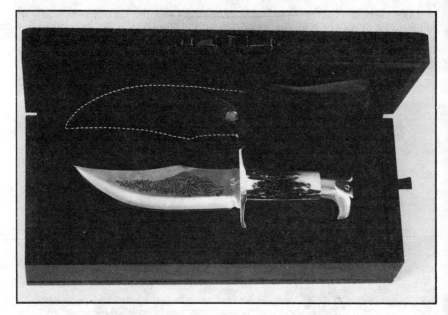

THE CASE FOUNDERS KNIFE

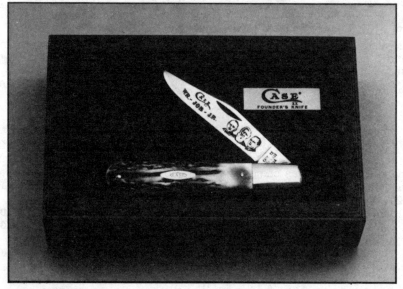

☐ *Current Collector Value* $100.00

THE CAS ▓▓▓▓▓▓▓▓▓▓ **SERIES**

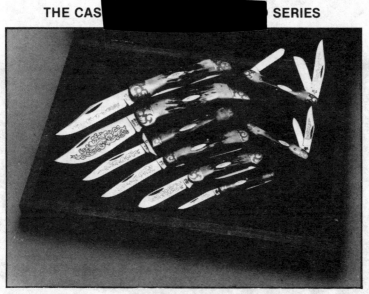

Case has released a limited edition (1,000) of their eight-knife three-dot engraved blade set.

☐ *Current Collector Value* . . . . **$500.00/set of 8**

THE CASE FOUR-DOT ENGRAVED SERIES

Case has also released a limited edition (1,000) of their seven-knife four-dot engraved blade set.

☐ *Current Collector Value* . . . . **$550.00/set of 7**

10,000 Moby Dicks were made by Case, featuring a scrimshaw on slick undyed bone, with engraved bolsters and attractive gift box. The suggested retail on the knife is $200.

☐ *Current Collector Value* $200.00

THE CASE-6165

Troy and Susan Dillingham created this customized Case knife in a limited edition of 750. Each knife is serial numbered, has a deep etched blade and engraved bolsters.

☐ *Current Collector Value: Etched only* . . . . $ 65.00
☐   *Gold plated deer* 85.00
☐   *Engraved bolsters* 105.00
☐   *Engraved bolsters, plated, and etched* 115.00

THE CASE-P172
(description on following page)

Originally made for the American Blade Jim Bowie sets, there was supposed to have been 500 of the knives made for distribution not in the sets. Each knife came with a sheath, African black wood handles and had a three dot stamping. They were only available through the California Lawman Gallery. Something went wrong with obtaining handle material and only 50 of the knives were made. The knives were advertised in the National Knife Collector Magazine at $75 each.

☐ *Current Collector Value* **$150.00**

THE CASE XX SMOKY MOUNTAIN TRAPPER SERIES

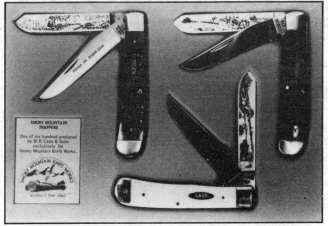

A front lock made by one hander W. T. Fuller.

To commemorate the heritage of the early trappers and settlers who carved a living out of the Great Smoky Mountains, Smoky Mountain Knife Works brings to you "THE SMOKY MOUNTAIN TRAPPERS."

THE SMOKY MOUNTAIN TRAPPERS are a special factory order, produced exclusively for Smoky Mountain Knife Works by W. R. Case & Sons. These are regular factory patterns, being the 6254, the 3254, and the 6254 SSP, with special factory etching and numbering. These are not available from W. R. Case & Sons. They are only available through Smoky Mountain Knife Works.

The total production on this exclusive series will only be 600 sets. Each set is handsomely displayed in a deluxe presentation case with the CASE logo on the inside and the outside of the case.

☐ *Current Collector Values: Serial numbers 1-10* . . . . **$200.00/set of 3**
☐ *Serial numbers 10-25* . . . . **$175.00/set of 3**
☐ *Serial numbers 25-100* . . . . **$150.00 set of 3**
☐ *Serial numbers 100-600* . . . . **$135.00/set of 3**

THE CAMILLUS 100 YEAR ANNIVERSARY

Camillus offers these two knives in individual boxes to honor the 100th anniversary of the company.

☐ *Current Collector Value* **$40.00/each**

THE COAL MINER

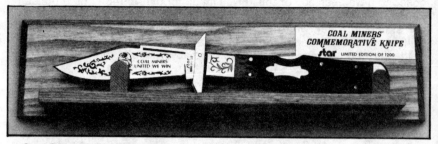

Star Sales imported this 5½ inch front lockback from Japan to honor the Coal Miners of America. The blade is etched "Coal Miners, United We Win." 1,200 of the knives were made.

☐ *Current Collector Value* 80.00

THE COAL MINERS SERIES

Boker made this set of three knives that comes in a special wood box that opens like a double sided tackle box. A medallion is set in the handles. These were not widely distributed and are not common.

☐ *Current Collector Value* .... $120.00/set of 3

THE COAL MINERS DOUGHTER SERIES

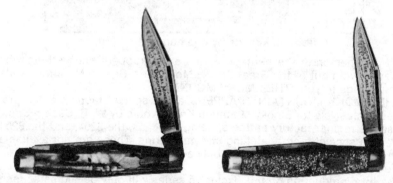

George Smith, of Hardin Wholesale, located in the coal mining country of West Virginia, had this pair of knives made on a contract with Fightin' Rooster. The knives are two-blade jackknives with Christmas tree and fancy composition handles. The blades all have a deep gold etching. One knife is etched "The Coal Miner" while the other carries, "The Coal Miners Doughter". The current retail on the knives is $65.

☐ *Current Collector Value* .... $65.00/set of 2

THE COLORADO FOLDING HUNTER

Hand assembled by Skip Bryan, the Colorado folding hunter features genuine stag handles, a rifle bullet shield, and a serial number. All parts were American made and assembled by Skip. The knives sold for $35 each.
☐ *Current Collector Value* **$60.00**
☐ *1978 Edition with white bone handles* **60.00**

THE CONQUEROR SERIES

This set of two one-blade pocketknives was manufactured by Battle-Axe Knives.
☐ *Current Collector Value* . . . . **$150.00/set of 2**

THE COTTONMOUTH

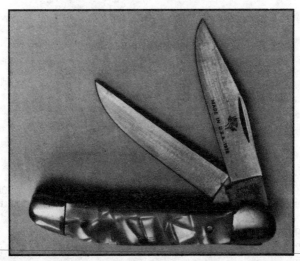

This knife is one of the first knives ever made on a copperhead pattern with stainless steel blades (1978). The handles are cracked ice, and the blade is etched and dated. Only 600 of the knives were made and serial numbered.
☐ *Current Collector Value* **$20.00**

THE COURTHOUSE WHITTLER SERIES

Commemorating the beginning of knife collecting, the courthouse whittlers were made exclusively for Parker-Frost by the Frank Buster Fightin' Rooster Cutlery Company. The set consists of two three-blade whittlers, with gold etched blades in an alligator leather type satin lined box. Handles are red and blue antique celluloid. 600 pairs were made. The set retailed for $100.

☐ *Current Collector Value* . . . . $125.00/set of 2

THE COVERED BRIDGE

The covered bridge was a knife made in a limited edition by Mrs. Dewey Ferguson, author of *The Romance of Collecting Case Knives.* The knives were made by Alcas, similar to the Case M1051L trailpacker, except it has a covered bridge picture stamped into the handle instead of the Case Emblem. It is tang stamped Lavonna's Cutlery.

☐ *Current Collector Value* $20.00

CUSTER'S LAST FIGHT

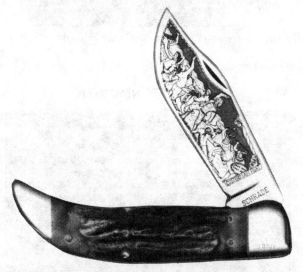

This knife is a companion piece to the Trail of Tears, issued at the same time. Some pairs are available in matching serial numbers. 1,200 of these knives were made, with a deep quality etch commemorating Custer's last fight. The handles are genuine stag. These knives were made for Parker-Frost. Suggested retail was $100.

☐ *Current Collector Value* $150.00

THE DAVY CROCKETT AND DANIEL BOONE SERIES

The Davy Crockett and Daniel Boone is a set of the Tennessee Kentucky series by Parker-Frost. The lockback knives are 5½ inches long, have a three color etching on their stainless steel blades and have genuine stag handles. Made by Robert Klaas, the knives were serial numbered in 1,000 pairs and packed in a satin lined display case. Suggested Retail was $130.
☐ *Current Collector Value* . . . . **$150.00/set of 2**

THE DEERSLAYER - (PARKER-FROST)

This knife is a one-blade stag handled lockback featuring a three color etched blade. 600 of the knives were made for Parker-Frost in 1977 in Solingen, Germany. Original retail on the knives was $45.
☐ *Current Collector Value* **$70.00**

THE DEERSLAYER - (RISNER)

1,200 of the knives were made in Japan through Star Sales. The knives have a photo etched blade and each knife is deep struck with a serial number. The interesting thing about this knife is the bolster shaped into the shape of a deer's head. The current retail is $30.
☐ *Current Collector Value* **$45.00**

THE DEERSLAYER - (STAR)
(picture on following page)

The Star deerslayer is a five inch clasp knife with a photo etched blade. 1,200 of the knives were serial numbered and released in 1976. These knives came in a wood box similar to the buffalo box by Case. The knives were later released unnumbered. The numbers on the limited edition knives were deep struck and the back of the master blade was etched with the statement that the knives were made especially for Parker-Frost Cutlery.
☐ *Current Collector Value* **$50.00**

THE DEERSLAYER - (STAR)

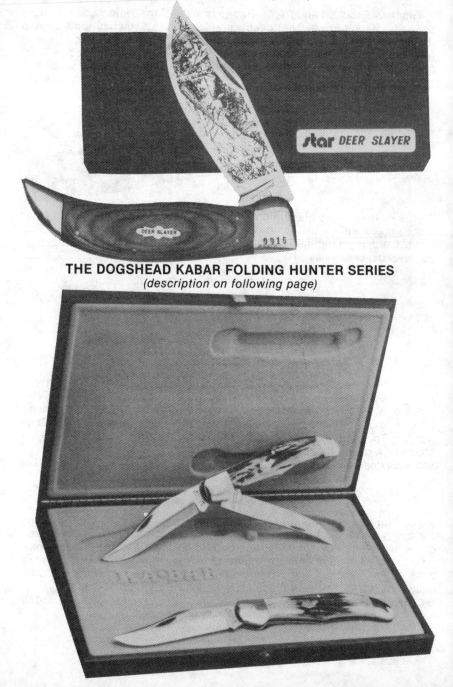

THE DOGSHEAD KABAR FOLDING HUNTER SERIES
(description on following page)

Some 10,000 pairs of these were released without serial numbers with a suggested retail of $150 per set.

☐ *Current Collector Value: Serial numbered* .... **$250.00/set of 2**

☐   *Non-serial numbered* .... **140.00/set of 2**

THE EAGLE BRAND SERIES

Probably the largest limited edition set to date is the Parker-Frost set of Eagle knives. This set consists of 22 knives, including 12 patterns of red, brown, and green bone. All knives are American made except a three blade four inch canoe made by Rodgers Wostenholm with Christmas tree handles. The set consists of three one-blade trappers with lock blades, the three-blade canoe, a two-blade folding hunter with scrimshaw scene handle, two sheath knives with scrimshaw scene handles, four three-blade stock knives, four two-blade trappers, four muskrats, a one-blade lockback, and a smaller three-blade stock, and a black handled peanut pattern. All the knives come in a leather covered salesman's sample case. Although the sets will be regular production, 2,000 sets of matching serial numbers were made. Suggested retail on the knives is $450.

☐ *Current Collector Value* .... **$500.00/set of 22**

THE FIGHTIN' BULLS SERIES
(picture on following page)

The Fightin' Bulls manufactured by Parker-Frost features two clasp knives; one with stag handles and the other with bone handles.

☐ *Current Collector Value* .... **$125.00/set of 2**

THE FIGHTIN' BULLS SERIES

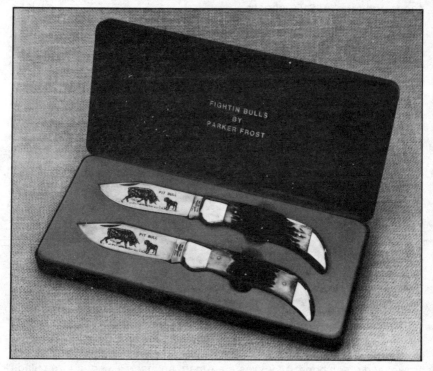

THE FIGHTIN' ROOSTER SERIES

Fightin' Rooster made a pair of five inch folding hunters with extra long bolsters and Christmas Tree handles and a gold etched blade. 600 pairs of these knives were made with an original retail of $80.

☐ *Current Collector Value* . . . . $100.00/set of 2

THE FIGHTIN' ROOSTER CANOE SERIES

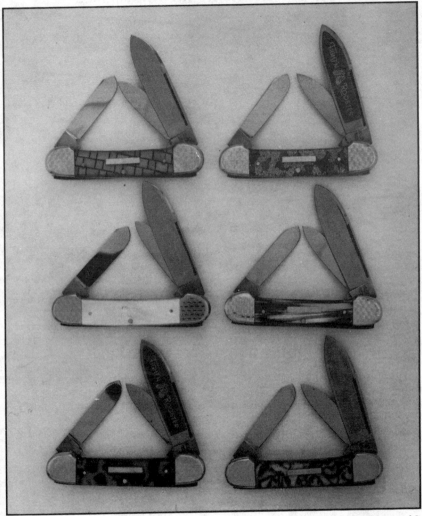

☐ *Current Collector Value* . . . . **$225.00/set of 6**

THE FIGHTIN' ROOSTER
DIXIE SWITCH AND HONKY TONK SERIES

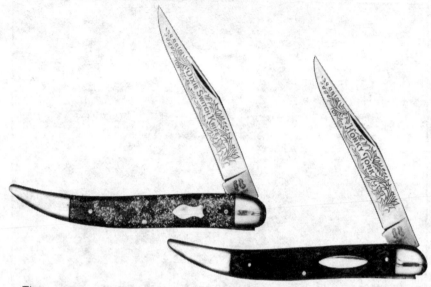

There were only 600 each of these knives made with Christmas tree or genuine bone stag handles.

☐ *Current Collector Value* . . . . $75.00/set of 2

THE FIGHTIN' ROOSTER PEANUTS SERIES

There were only 300 sets produced, four in each set with matching serial numbers. Four different handles, butter and molasses, pearl and black, red and black and Christmas. The set comes cased in a beautiful walnut presentation case.

☐ *Current Collector Value* . . . . $80.00/set of 4

THE FRANK BUSTER SERIES

The Frank Buster Cutlery Company offers regular edition set of some extremely well-made German knives in attractive handles and gold etched blades. Among those released were:

Name	Amount Made	# in Set	Style	Current Collector Value
☐ Country Gentlemen	400	3	Barlows	125.00
☐ Cock of the Walk	400	2	Folding Hunters	125.00
☐ King of the Woods	600	2	Gunstocks	100.00
☐ Black Diamond	1200	1	4" Stock Knife	30.00
☐ One Arm Dr's Knife	600	2	Dr's Knives	150.00

THE GENERAL

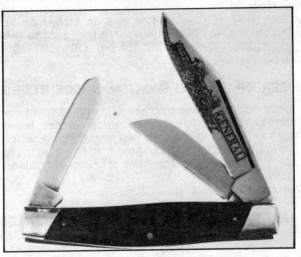

The Great Locomotive Chase was what the pursuit of the train "The General" was called during the Civil War, and Bowen Knife Company came out with a commemorative to honor this locomotive. Bowen made 1,200 of the 3⅝ inch, three-blade knives, and they sold for $20.

☐ *Current Collector Value* **$25.00**

THE GEORGE WASHINGTON VALLEY FORGE WHITTLER
(description on following page)

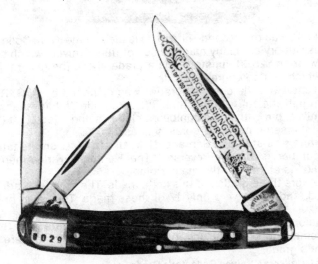

The George Washington Valley Forge whittler was made by Robert Klaas for J. Nielsen Mayer.

The four inch stag handled whittler has an etched blade and serial numbered. The pattern was discontinued by Klaas prior to 1940. Retail on the knives was #1 $100, #2-10 $75, #51-100 $70, #101-1200 $60.

☐ **Current Collector Value** **$45.00**

THE GERBER FOLDING SPORTSMAN BICENTENNIAL

Gerber's entry into the commemorative line is a limited edition of 200 folding hunter lockbacks, featuring an Aurum etched blade, engraved bolsters, stag handles, saddle leather belt sheath and a walnut presentation case. The knife is etched with the American Eagle on the back and the "Don't Tread on Me" snake on the front of the master blade. The knife retailed for $195.

☐ **Current Collector Value** **$300.00**

THE GRANDADDY BARLOW FOLDING HUNTER

This knife was the second knife to be issued by the Knife Collectors Club. Camillus Cutlery company made 12,000 of these knives, which sold for $20 and now bring $25.00. Illustrated is a grade above the general production knive, which has no engraved blade.

The Kentucky Rifle commemorative was designed by A. G. Russell and sold through the Knife Collectors Club. Schrade-Walden made 12,048 of these knives, but with some numbered blades being rejected at the factory, some of the serial numbers go as high as 15,000.

The knife was stamped Schrade, N. Y. U.S.A. CM-1 on the tang, and the serial number is on the reverse. "The Kentucky Rifle-America's Own, 1750-1880" is etched on the master blade.

There were three grades of this knife made. The premier grade was hand engraved, and there were only 17 of these made. They sold originally for $350-500.

Excelsior grade is etched, and sold for $60. There were 98 of these made.

The remaining knives, 11,933 of them, sold for $15 and were called the collector's grade.

☐ **Current Collector Value: Collector's Grade** . . . . **$ 55.00**
☐   **Excelsior Grade** **300.00**
☐   **Premier Grade** **1,200.00**

THE GRAND DAD'S OLD TIMER

There are four Grand Dad Old Timer Limited Editions manufactured. The Grand Dad Old Timer No. 1 is a four inch, three-blade stock with a diamond finish back spring and retails for $30.

The Grand Dad Old Timer No. 2 is a 3¼ inch stock with a diamond finish back spring and retails at $25. Grand Dad Old Timer No. 3 is the Sharpfinger as illustrated. Retail $25.

Grand Dad Old Timer No. 4 is the Barlow and retails for $25.

☐ *Current Collector Value* **$25.00**

THE GOOD GUYS AND BAD GUYS SERIES

These knives were really two different sets. The Good Guys were two 3½ inch gunstocks, featuring Bat Masterson on one knife and Wyatt Earp on the other. The Bad Guys were two-three inch mini canoes, featuring Billy the Kid and Jesse James. Both sets come in satin lined boxes and have genuine stag handles. They were made in Japan for Taylor Cutlery. The suggested retail on the sets was $79.98, but at the time of release you could buy both sets for $100.

☐ *Current Collector Value* . . . . **$45.00/set of 2**

THE GUNFIGHTERS SERIES I
THE EARPS
(picture on following page)

The Gunfighters Series I consists of three single-bladed pocketknives commemorating the three Earp brothers; Morgan, Virgil and Wyatt. This set was manufactured by, in a limited edition (1,000), by the Parker Cutlery Company.

☐ *Current Collector Value* . . . . **$80.00/set of 3**

THE GUNFIGHTER SERIES I

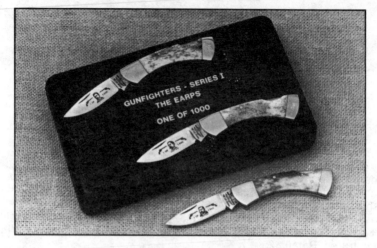

THE GUNFIGHTER SERIES II
THE CLANTONS

The Gunfighters Series II consists of three single-bladed pocketknives. The set was also manufactured by Parker Cutlery Company.

☐ *Current Collector Value* . . . . **$110.00/set of 3**

THE HICKEY SERIES

John Hickey of Louisville, Kentucky has made three notable sets in the commemorative field. His first two sets came in attractive wood boxes and featured a set of three folding hunters with relief handles. They generally bring $125 per set.

He has made several club knives for the various clubs, and made one series Statesman whittlers.

☐ *Current Collector Value* . . . . $150.00/set of 3

THE HENRY REPEATER SERIES

The Henry Repeater set was manufactured in limited quantities (600) by Bulldog Brand Knives.

☐ *Current Collector Value* . . . . $140.00/set of 2

THE INDIAN CANOE SERIES

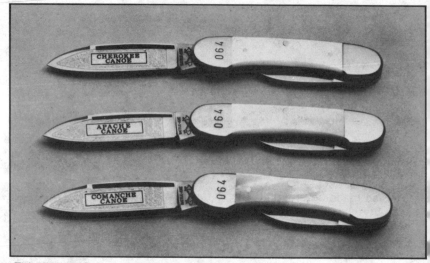

This Indian Canoe set consists of three two-blade pocketknives — The Cherokee, Apache and Comanche Canoes. This set was manufactured by Battle-Axe Knives.

☐ *Current Collector Value* . . . . **$160.00/set of 3**

THE JIM BOWIE

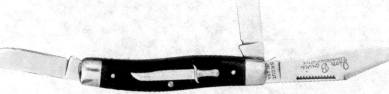

This three-blade pattern commemorative honoring Jim Bowie has a Bowie knife shield and "Jim Bowie Commemorative" etched on the master blade. The tang of the master blade is stamped, "S. W. Cut. JBI, U. S. A." The serial number is stamped on the inside liner. The knife comes in a wood-grained cardboard box. Schrade-Walden made 18,000 of this four inch knife. With an original retail of $20.

☐ *Current Collector Value* **$25.00**

THE KABAR BICENTENNIAL

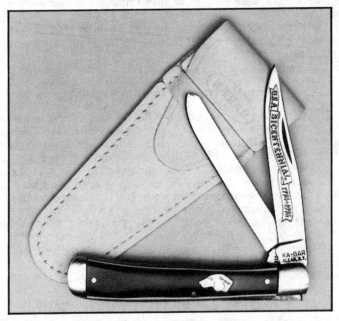

This trapper features red, white and blue celluloid handles, with one blade etched Union Cut. Co. (an early stamp of Kabar) and the other blade will carry the current Kabar logo.

7,500 Kabar Dogshead trappers were made and were originally priced from $30 to $100.

☐ *Current Collector Value* **$60.00**

THE KEENKUTTERS 100 YEAR ANNIVERSARY KNIFE

A three blade stock pattern with a California clip blade was the pattern chosen for the 1969 commemorative Keen Kutter issued for its 100th birthday. They made 6,000 of the knives selling originally for $10. The knives are 3½ inches long.

☐ *Current Collector Value* **$50.00**

THE KENTUCKY RIFLE

The Kentucky Rifle commemorative was designed by A. G. Russell and sold through the Knife Collectors Club. Schrade-Walden made 12,048 of these knives, but with some numbered blades being rejected at the factory, some of the serial numbers go as high as 15,000.

The knife was stamped Schrade, N. Y. U.S.A. CM-1 on the tang, and the serial number is on the reverse. "The Kentucky Rifle-America's Own, 1750-1880" is etched on the master blade.

There were three grades of this knife made. The premier grade was hand engraved, and there were only 17 of these made. They sold originally for $350-500.

Excelsior grade is etched, and sold for $60. There were 98 of these made.

The remaining knives, 11,933 of them, sold for $15 and were called the collector's grade.

☐ *Current Collector Value* **$60.00**

THE KISSING CRANE 140th ANNIVERSARY

To celebrate its 140th anniversary the Robert Klaas Company is offering a limited edition commemorative Kissing Crane knife. Only 5,000 will be produced, and each will have its own serial number stamped on the tang of the master blade for ease of identification, 3¾ inch closed size genuine bone handle congress style with four blades especially polished and the master blade hand etched to show the 140th year of the Klaas Factory. Each blade has the Kissing Crane emblem. The tang of the master blade is stamped with the actual serial number of that knife, which makes it truly the only one of its kind in the world. The handle has a 1½ inch shield with red enamel trim depicting the 140th year. Included with each knife is a convenient carrying pouch made of top grain leather stamped in gold leaf to commemorate the occasion.

☐ *Current Collector Value* **$45.00**

THE KISSING CRANE 145th ANNIVERSARY

A stag handled lockback. 2,000 knives were made with a retail of $75. Released in 1979, the knives come with a pine wall plaque. Made in Solingen, Germany and distributed by Star Sales, Knoxville, Tennessee.

☐ *Current Collector Value* **$50.00**

THE KNIFE GRINDING 1600 AD

This knife was made for the General Store, and has genuine mother of pearl handles and comes in a presentation box with a history of Solingen included. There were 2,000 of these made starting at $139.50 for serial number one ranging to $69.50 for the higher numbers. The knife is four inches long.

☐ *Current Collector Value* **$90.00**

THE LIBERTY BELL, PAUL REVERE AND MINUTEMAN SERIES

These knives were a three part series by Schrade, commemorating independence. 24,000 were made of each pattern. The knives are all 3⅝ inch stock patterns, and all come in acetate boxes with enclosed registration forms for the knives. All three sold for $12.50 when first issued. The Liberty Bell and Minuteman knives have black handles, and the Paul Revere has red handles. Each knife has a shield that the name is derived from. The Liberty Bell has a Liberty Bell shield, the Paul Revere has a Paul Revere figure on it for a shield, and the Minuteman has a Minuteman for a shield. The serial numbers for the knives are stamped on the inside liners.

☐ *Current Collector Value: Liberty Bell* $27.50
☐   *Paul Revere* $20.00
☐   *Minuteman* $20.00

THE LITTLE LOUIE

The Little Louie was a limited edition set of 1200 miniature Barlows. Only two inches long, the knives were handled in bone, rosewood, pearl and abalone. They were made in Japan for Parker Cutlery.

☐ *Current Collector Value* .... $50.00/set of 4

THE LONGHORN

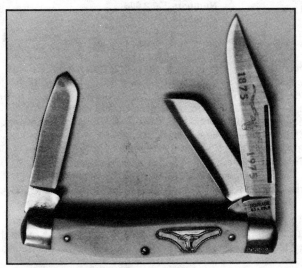

This knife is a three blade stockman from Schrade commemorating the saga of the transformation of the longhorn steers into today's prime beef herds. The knife was issued in 1975 and the number made is unknown. The original retail price was $15.

☐ *Current Collector Value* $35.00

THE LUGER

The third issue of the A. G. Russell Knife Collector's Club was the Luger, honoring the 75th anniversary of the Luger pistol. The single-blade knife was made in Germany and handled in genuine stag. The knife is etched with "Luger 1900-1974". 5,000 of the knives were made in three grades. Numbers 1-22 were the premier grade, featuring 14 karat gold bolsters and engraving. The knives sell for $390.

☐ *Current Collector Value:* **Numbers 23-275** $85.00
☐   **Numbers 300-2,000**........................ 45.00
☐   **Numbers 2,000-5,000** 40.00

THE MAC TOOLS KNIFE

Mac Tool of Washington Courthouse, Ohio has made two limited edition knives. The first in 1979 was a three-blade stock knife with antique brass cast handles commemorating the 40th anniversary of the company. 12,000 were made, and carry a collector's value of $40 each.

Then in the fall of 1979 Mac contracted with George Wostenholm, IXL to make 3,600 personal knives, serial numbered with white bone handles. These knives were three-blade canoes, and retailed for $50.

☐ *Current Collector Value*.......................................$70.00/each

THE MAKING OF THE FIRST FLAG BICENTENNIAL
(picture on following page)

This knife is a single-blade lockback with a folding guard and stag handles, much like the Case Cheetah. The knife commemorates the making of the First Flag and comes in a walnut box. The knives were made in Germany by the Robert Klaas Company and 3,000 were produced to reatil at $72 per knife.

☐ *Current Collector Value* $65.00

THE MAKING OF THE FIRST FLAG BICENTENNIAL

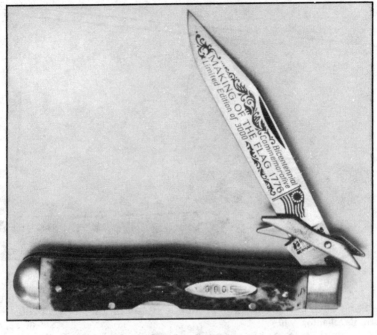

THE MARINER

The Mariner was manufactured in a limited edition (600) by the Smoky Mountain Knife Works.

☐ *Current Collector Value* **$50.00**

THE MASTER CUTLERS COLLECTION SERIES

The first set of this series is a set of two trappers, both with green bone Rogers cut handles. The knives manufactured by Queen Cutlery, are gift boxed and have matching serial numbers. Retail on the set was $50.

☐ *Current Collector Value* . . . . $65.00/set of 2

The second knife in this series is a single-blade Texas Toothpick with green bone handles. Suggested retail was $20 per knife, no gift box.

☐ *Current Collector Value* $30.00/each

THE NANTUCKET SLEIGHRIDE

Whaling inspired this companion piece to the Moby Dick. Made by Case, the knife is identical to the Moby Dick, except for a different scene on the handle and a red lining in the box. At this writing they had not been released, but the suggested retail is to be $200.

☐ *Current Collector Value* $200.00

THE NKC&DA COMMEMORATIVE WHITTLER
(picture on following page)

Introduced in 1975, Kissing Krane made 1,200 of these knives for members of the National Knife Collectors & Dealers Association. 4½ inches long, the knife is supposed to closely resemble the 5391 Case Whittler. The knife has stag handles, "NKC&DA" on the shield and master blade tang, the serial number on the bolster and one small blade, and the Kissing Krane logo on the other small blade. The blade is etched "National Knife Collectors, 1 of 1,200, 1975."

The knife sold to members for $12 but the price rose very quickly.

☐ *Current Collector Value* $700.00

THE NKC&DA COMMEMORATIVE WHITTLER

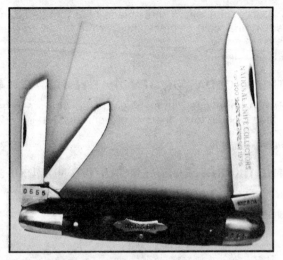

THE NKC&DA COMMEMORATIVE NUMBER 2

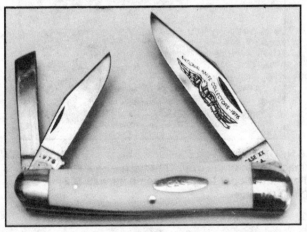

This knife is made by W. R. Case & Sons using an existing pattern (the 80 pattern whittler) with a discontinued handle material (white composition) that was never used on this pattern before. The knife has the pattern number "4380" and the NKC&DA name on it. The serial numbers are etched on the bolsters. 3,000 of the knives will be made and sold to NKC&DA members.

☐ *Current Collector Value* **$250.00**

THE NKC&DA COMMEMORATIVE NUMBER 3

The Third NKCA knife was a three-blade stag handled canoe made by Robert Klass. Original cost of these knives were $17.25 to members. 5,000 of the knives were made.

☐ *Current Collector Value* $150.00

THE NKC&DA COMMEMORATIVE NUMBER 4

The 1978 NKCA knife was a three-blade canoe with green bone handles made by Rodger Wostenholm division of Schrade Cutlery. 6,000 of these knives were made.

☐ *Current Collector Value* $100.00

THE NKC&DA COMMEMORATIVE NUMBER 5

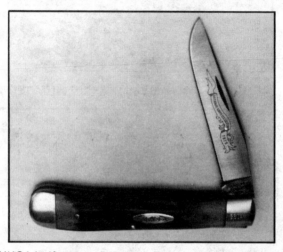

The 1979 NKCA knife was a 5154 ssp. This was the first time W. R. Case & Sons had made a one-blade trapper pattern with a stainless steel blade and stag handles. Initial cost to NKCA members was $22.

☐ *Current Collector Value* $60.00

THE NORTH SOUTH WHITTLER SERIES

Parker-Frost Cutlery had this series made up in Germany commemorating the Civil War, or War for Southern Independence as it is called in parts of the South. The set consists of four genuine stag handled whittlers. The two smaller knives are four inches long and have Johnny Reb etched on one knife and Billy Yank etched on the other knife. The two larger whittlers will be etched, one with Grant, and one with Lee. 1,500 of the sets were made, retailing at $220 to $300 per set depending on serial number. The set comes packaged in a deluxe satin and velvet lined display box.

☐ *Current Collector Value* . . . . **$250.00/set of 4**

THE OLD HICKORY

Old Hickory is the trademark of Ontario Knife Company, so it was only natural that they made an Andy Jackson Commemorative. The knife was made by Queen and has wood handles. Each knife comes individually boxed.

☐ *Current Collector Value* **$15.00**

THE OLYMPIC KNIFE

The Case Olympic knife was a limited edition of 1,000 knives, especially made for the 1980 winter olympics in Lake Placid, New York. The knife was on the '278 pattern, but featured sterling silver handles cast using the lost wax process by Shaw Liebowitz. Suggested retail on the knife was $300.
☐ *Current Collector Value* **$400.00**

THE ORIGINAL THIRTEEN COLONY SERIES
(description on following page)

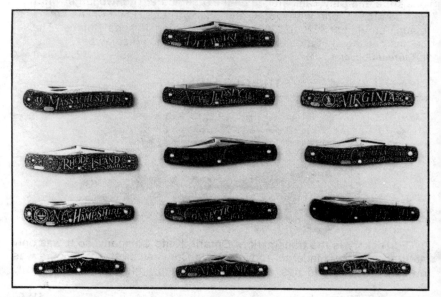

This set of 14 knives was issued beginning in March 1976, with a knife issued each month through the Bicentennial. Thirteen of the knives were issued honoring the 13 original colonies. These pewter, silver, brass and copper handled knives featured intricate artwork and a diamond finished backspring. The fourteenth knife honored the United States, and has a genuine stag handle folding hunter clasp knife with etched blade. Schrade-Walden manufactured the 3,000 sets for Parker-Frost Cutlery. The sets retailed for $449.35

☐ *Current Collector Value*.....................................$550.00/set of 14

THE PARKER-FROST INDIAN SERIES I AND II

1,200 sets of these knives were made commemorating Geronimo and Sitting Bull. Each set consists of four knives, two knives with bone handles and twoknives with country molasses handle. Blades are etched and made of surgical steel. Each set comes in a satin lined box. Suggested retail for the set is $70.

☐ *Current Collector Value: Series 1* ....$100.00/set of 4
☐   *Series 2* .... 90.00/set of 4

THE PARKER-FROST INDIAN SERIES III

A set of three bone handled surgical steel knives, two of the knives are folding lockbacks, and the third is a fixed blade made on the same pattern. All have bone handles and carry a matching serial number. The knives come in a satin lined box. 1,200 were made. Suggested retail was $80. They were released in October 1979.

☐ *Current Collector Value* . . . . **$80.00/set of 3**

THE PARKER-FROST INDIAN SERIES IV

The Indian Series IV was the fourth in the series released by Parker Cutlery. The knives were the same pattern as Indian Series III, but these honored Running Bear, Red Cloud and Chief Ocala of the Seminoles. 1,200 were made and retailed for $80.

☐ *Current Collector Value* . . . . **$80.00/set of 3**

THE PAUL KNIFE · GERBER 40th ANNIVERSARY

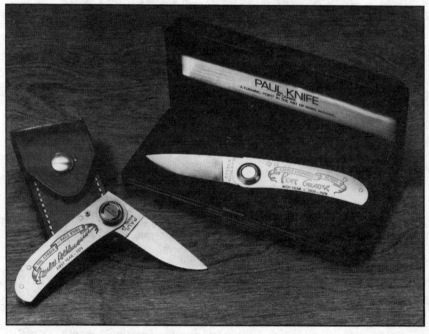

Made in 1979 by Gerber.

☐ *Current Collector Value* **$100.00**

THE PEARL PEANUT

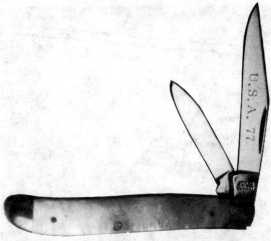

Voyles Cutlery's first limited edition knife is a peanut pattern with genuine pearl handles. The blade is etched "USA-77" and every knife is serial numbered. The knives were American made by Pennsylvania craftsmen. Original retail was $35 for serial #1 down to $22 for 101-600.

☐ *Current Collector Value: No.'s 1-100* $50.00
☐   *No.'s 101-600* 35.00

THE PLAINS SERIES

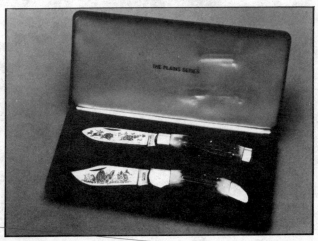

The Plains Series was a 1200 knife set made by Taylor Cutlery for Parker Cutlery and Smoky Mountain Knife Works. The set consisted of a one-blade five inch stag gunstock and a five inch stag handled clasp knife.

☐ *Current Collector Value* .... $75.00/set of 2

THE PLAINSMEN SERIES

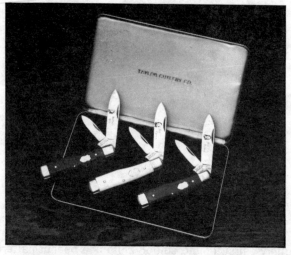

The Plainsmen series consists of three two-bladed pocketknives commemorating: Buffalo Bill, Kit Carson and Bill Hickok. This set was manufactured by Taylor Cutlery Company.

☐ *Current Collector Value* .... $50.00/set of 3

THE PRESIDENTS SERIES

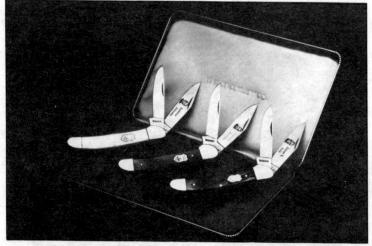

The President series consists of three two-bladed pocketknives commemorating: Andrew Johnson, Andrew Jackson and James K. Polk. The set was manufactured by the Taylor Cutlery Company.

☐ *Current Collector Value* .... $50.00/set of 3

THE PUMA

The Puma Commemorative Knife commemorates the founding of PUMA-WERK in Solingen, Germany in 1769. It is handmade from beginning to end and represents the ultimate in the art of knifemaking. The Super Keen Cutting Steel blade has been especially polished and hand etched to produce a magnificent oak leaf design that is delicate and artistic in appearance. The year of the birth of Puma has been etched and filled with gold. The reverse side of the blade is identically etched with the words "Puma Germany" and the exact serial number of each knife which is also filled with gold.

The back of the main spring and blade is finished with an artistic and functional non-slip pattern. Each bolster has been highly polished. The two bolsters nearest the blade have been engraved with a wreath and the year 1769 in the center. The two bolsters nearest the safety lock are engraved with the words "me fecit Solingen" which translates to "made in Solingen". The handle is made of the finest especially treated European stag horn.

The Puma Commemorative Knife is made in a very limited edition of only 1769 pieces with each knife having its own serial number which makes it the only one of its kind in the world. This is attested to by the registration certificate provided with each knife.

The Puma Commemorative Knife is truly a collector's prize in every sense of the word.

☐ *Current Collector Value* **$325.00**

THE QUEEN BICENTENNIAL
(picture on following page)

Queens offering was a one blade Daddy Barlow with a special Colonial flag shield. The knife was set into a pine block and originally sold for $15. 15,000 of the knives were made.

☐ *Current Collector Value* **$35.00**

THE QUEEN BICENTENNIAL

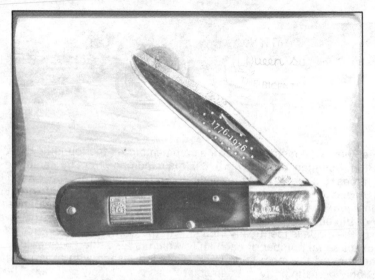

THE QUEEN DRAKE OIL WELL

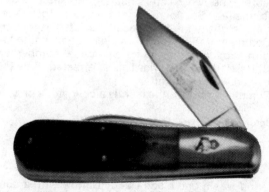

Queen's 50th anniversary was honored in 1972 by the introduction of 3,600 commemorative Barlows. The Drake oil well is etched on the master blade and the pen blade has the model number 139 stamped on it. The knife has the Drake oil well because the home of Queen Cutlery is Tidioute, Pennsylvania, the site of the first oil well in America. It is nicknamed the "Queen City". The 3⅜ inch knife sold for $15 in 1972.

☐ *Current Collector Value* **$35.00**

THE QUEEN TEXAS TOOTHPICK

Queen Cutlery made these green bone handle toothpicks from bone they had used in the 1950's. The pattern itself was already discontinued at the time. The knives carried the Q76 tang stamping. Although there was a limited number made (in the 1200 range), they were not serial numbered.

☐ *Current Collector Value* **$30.00**

THE ROBERT E. LEE

This stag handled big Coke bottle folding hunter was a limited edition of 1,250, released in October 1979. It had stag handles and was made in Japan for Taylor Cutlery.

☐ *Current Collector Value* **$45.00**

THE RUSSELL BARLOW REPRODUCTION
(picture on following page)

The Russell Harington Company of Southbridge, Massachusetts produced a commemorative of the Russell Barlow in 1974. The Russell Barlow was originally produced by the John Russell Company from 1875 until World War II. During that time it was one of the most popular knives manufactured.

12,000 commemoratives were produced with delrin handles and a commemorative etching on the blade. Otherwise the knife is a duplicate of the original Russell Barlow.

The first 2,000 were priced at $35, including a saddle-stitched leatherette pouch inside a wooden case. Numbers 2,001-10,000 are in a suede-lined pouch and sold for $25.

☐ *Current Collector Value:* . . . . *First 2,000* . . . .$ 50.00
☐ . . . . *No.'s 2,001-10,000* 40.00
☐ . . . . *No.'s under 100* 100.00-125.00

THE RUSSELL BARLOW REPRODUCTION

THE SCHRADE IXL SERIES
(description on following page)

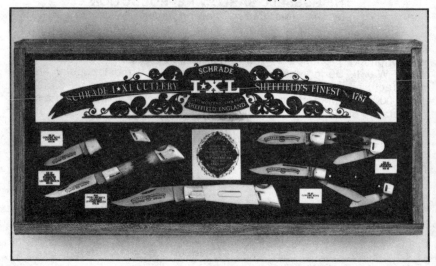

☐ *Current Collector Value:* **Small bone lockback** $50.00
☐   **Stag lockback** 75.00
☐   **Micarta lockback** 65.00
☐   **Stag canoe** 60.00
☐   **Bone stockman** 50.00

THE SCHRADE LIMITED EDITION LOVELESS HUNTER

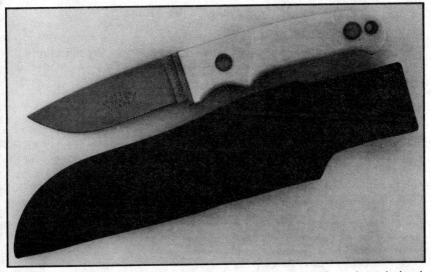

    This knife was personally designed by Bob Loveless, the acknowledged dean of custom knife-making and cutlered to his exacting specifications by Schrade, one of America's oldest makers of quality cutlery. The blade is of special high grade steel alloy for extra-holding hardness, resistant to corrosion and super resilient, custom ground, hand glazed and hand oilstone edged.

    The delrin handle guaranteed to last the life of the knife. The thumb groove grip provides extra control.

    The solid brass guard for added beauty and safety is custom fitted to blade and joined with solid brass escutcheons and fastened for life with tapered rivets.

    The top-grain steerhide sheath is wet molded for perfect fit and velvet action.

    The original retail price was $100.

☐ *Current Collector Value* $125.00

THE SCHRADE SCRIMSHAW

    These knives were made in a series, utilizing a Schrade Sharpfinger and a Schrade two blade folding hunter (1976). The knives come individually boxed with matching scenes in white delrin handles. They are among the most attractive of the commemoratives.

    The first series contained black sheaths.

☐ *Current Collector Value* $60.00

THE SHAW LEIBOWITZ SERIES

Shaw Liebowitz produce some very fine etched knives and planned a series of 10 knives on the Bicentennial theme. The knives were first introduced in 1974, and one knife pattern was introduced every three months thru 1976. 200 of each pattern was made.

The Bicentennial Series:
- ☐ 1. The Boston Tea Party etched on a Rigid Knife
- ☐ 2. The Ride of Paul Revere etched on a Gerber Knife
- ☐ 3. The Shot heard round the World etched on a Case Buffalo (P172)
- ☐ 4. The Declaration of Independence on a Westmark Western Knife
- ☐ 5. Washington Crossing the Delaware etched on an Olsen Model 503 hunting knife
- ☐ 6. John Paul Jones etched on a Case Sunfish (6250)
- ☐ 7. Winter at Valley Forge on a Gerber Sheath Knife
- ☐ 8. Patrick Henry on a Westmark Knife
- ☐ 9. The Victory at Yorktown on a Case Knife
- ☐10. Washington's Triumphant return to New York City on a Rigid Knife
- ☐*Current Collector Value (Depending on Serial #)* . . . . **$3,500.00-12,000.00/set of 10**

Shaw Leibowitz also produced a continuing series of wildlife knives, which began in 1974. 300 of each knife pattern is made, with numbers 1-15 (gold plating) retailing for $155 and numbers 16-300 retailing for $105.

The Wildlife Series:
- ☐ 1. Grizzly on a Gerber Lockback
- ☐ 2. Raccoon on a Schrade-Walden
- ☐ 3. Bobcat on a Case Canoe (62131)
- ☐ 4. Moose on a Case Moose (5275)
- ☐ 5. Squirrel on a Case 6380 Whittler
- ☐ 6. Deer on a Buck Esquire
- ☐ 7. Big Horn Sheep on a Case 6235½
- ☐ 8. Eagle on a Kabar Barlow
- ☐ 9. Elephant on Case 6250
- ☐10. Buffalo on Case P-172
- ☐*Current Collector Value (Depending on Serial #)* . . . . . . **$2,500.00-8,000.00/set of 10**

THE SMITH AND WESSON COMMEMORATIVE

This knife was a standard production Smith and Wesson folding hunter with a serial number and etched blade. The knives came with a leather pouch and less than 500 were made. Original retail was $100.

☐*Current Collector Value* **$100.00**

THE SMOKY MOUNTAIN TRAPPER SERIES

These knives were standard production Case trappers with a special factory etching and serial number. The knives were cased inside a satin lined box. 600 sets were made. Suggested retail was $150, but at the time of release you could buy three sets for $100 per set.

☐*Current Collector Value* . . . .**$115.00/set of 3**

THE SOUTHERN STYLE PART ONE AND TWO SERIES

These knives were made by Frank Buster's Fightin' Rooster Cutlery Company. The sets are two sets of two sodbuster patterns with antique celluloid handles and each set coming in a genuine leather display pouch. Only 300 pairs of each knife were made, all serial numbered, with two fightin' roosters inlaid into the handles (1978). Suggested retail for the pair is $45 per set. $90 for the complete set of four knives.

☐ *Current Collector Value* . . . . **$75.00/set of 2**

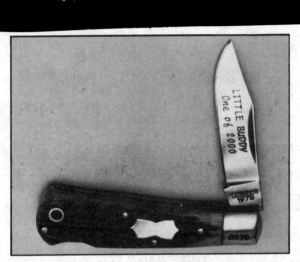

These knives are both bone handled stainless steel lockbacks made exclusively for the Hixon Knife Shop, owned by Charles Genella. The blades are stamped Genella on the tang and the year of manufacture stamped on the back. 2,400 of each knife were made.

☐ *Current Collector Value:* **No.1-10** . . . . **$35.00/set of 2**
☐   *others* . . . . **15.00/set of 2**

THE SPIRIT OF ST. LOUIS

Schrade-Walden made this knife to commemorate the first flight from New York to Paris by Lindbergh in the Spirit of St. Louis. The three blade stock pattern has "Keen Kutter Limited Edition" etched on the blade, and three special shields; one is of the airplane, one a Keen Kutter emblem, and on the back of the black handled knife, a shield bearing the date of the flight.

The knife is stamped "S. W. Cut. K74 U.S.A." and the serial number is stamped on the inside liner. When introduced in 1974, the knife sold for $20. There were 12,000 of the knives made, which currently retails for $25.

☐ *Current Collector Value* **$30.00**

THE STAR CANOE

This commemorative is a metal handled canoe made by Star Sales, and comes in a wood presentation box. 1776 of the knives were made and issue began in October of 1975. The high numbers retail for $35 and the low numbers (below 100) retail for $45.

☐ *Current Collector Value* **$35.00**

THE STONEWALL JACKSON

A stag handled Barlow made by Taylor Cutlery. 1,200 knives were made in 1979.

☐ *Current Collector Value* **$30.00**

THE SWAMP FOX

Made by Robert Klaas for Messer-Gullette, the knife is a slick bone lockback, with 2 color etched blades, stainless steel and a nickel silver inlay of a running fox. 1,200 were made. Suggested retail price was $65.

☐ *Current Collector Value* **$45.00**

THE TAYLOR CUTLERY BARLOW SERIES

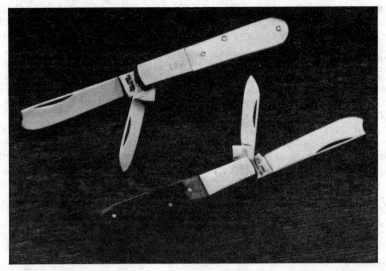

This Barlow knife series consists of two two-blade pocketknives and is manufactured by the Taylor Cutlery Company.

☐ *Current Collector Value* . . . . **$75.00/set of 2**

THE TAYLOR CUTLERY DOCTOR SERIES

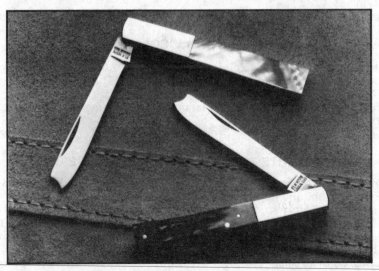

The One-Arm Doctor series consists of two one-blade pocketknives. These knives were manufactured by the Taylor Cutlery Company.

☐ *Current Collector Value* . . . . **$75.00/set of 2**

THE KENTUCKY BICENTENNIAL SERIES

The set of three knives commemorating the first settlement in Kentucky was made by W. R. Case in 1976. All the knives were the Case 2137SS pattern, but with a variety of handles. 30,000 of each of the three editions were made.

The first knife had green delrin handles and carried the pattern number G137. 35,299 of these knives were made, and were stamped with five dots. The serial numbers ran as follows 0000001-0015000, 0001-9999, J0001-J9999, and the most collectible of the green handled knives, S0001-S2001.

☐ *Current Collector Value* **$30.00/each**

A very few of the knives were stamped and given out when Case's South Bradford Plant opened in 1975. These were heat stamped into the handle Grand Opening: South Bradford Plant, and on the reverse side April 1975. A few of these have made their way into the collector's market and currently bring $100.

The second of the series had wood handles.

☐ *Current Collector Value* **$30.00/each**

The third of the series was stag handled, and stamped with a large serial number. There is a variation in these also. The knife will commonly be found stamped as follows:

Case XX
U. S. A.

☐ *Current Collector Value* **$35.00/each**

The rarer version, of which only 2,000 were made, will be stamped:

Case XX
Stainless

☐ *Current Collector Value* **$50.00/each**

THE KENTUCKY COLONEL

The Kentucky Colonel was introduced in 1973. 12,000 of the knives were made on a four inch, three blade stock pattern. The original price was $18.00.

Note: These knives were not serial numbered. The model #0001 appears on the back of the master blade.

☐ *Current Collector Value* **$30.00**

THE SALUTE TO KENTUCKY BY QUEEN SERIES

This 2 knife set consists of a small knife commemorating the 100th Kentucky Derby, and the large knife that commemorates the 200th birthday of the settling of Fort Harrod, Kentucky. Both knives have two blades, with the small knife being 2¾ inches long and the large one four inches long. You should make sure that the serial numbers on both knives match. The knives are boxed together in a plastic box. Issued in 1974.

☐ *Current Collector Value* .... **$45.00/set of 2**

THE TENNESSEE AND KENTUCKY BICENTENNIAL WHITTLER SERIES

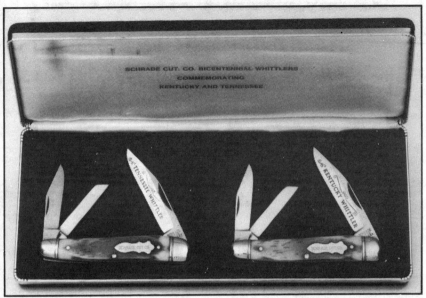

THE TENNESSEE AND KENTUCKY MUSKRATS SERIES

The Tennessee and Kentucky Muskrats were made by Fightin' Rooster. Frank Buster Cutlery Company for Parker-Frost Cutlery. 600 pair were made, 250 with red and gold celluloid, and 100 pair with genuine pearl handles. All knives have reverse gold etching and come in a satin lined box. Retail was $100 for the celluloid handled sets and $125 for the genuine pearl handled sets.

☐ *Current Collector Value: Celluloid Handles* . . . . **$110.00/set of 2**
☐   *Pearl Handles* . . . . **$175.00/set of 2**

THE TENNESSEAN, THE KENTUCKIAN, AND THE SOUTHERN BELL SERIES

300 sets of three knives available serial numbered 1-300-plus 300 pair of Kentuckian and Tennessean serial numbered 301-600. The frames and handle materials of these 3¾ inch Teardrop Jacks are Old Stock. The handles are beautiful metallic gold flake. The blades are gold etched and stamped with the "Fightin' Rooster" logo. Back of tang on master blade is marked Frank Buster Cutlery Co., Solingen, Germany. Serial number appears on small blade. Price per set of three - $120. Display frame optional - $10 each.

☐ *Current Collector Value* . . . . **$100.00/set of 3**

THE TENNESSEE AND KENTUCKY COPPERHEADS SERIES

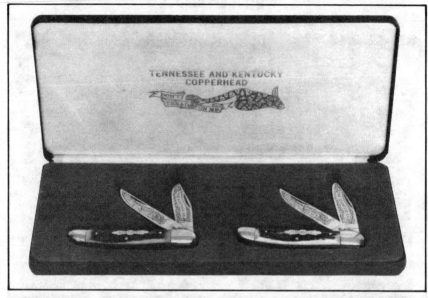

These knives are four inch two blade stag handled copperhead patterns, made in sets numbering up to 1200. Each set of knives is boxed in a satin lined presentation case. Suggested retail on the knives was $100. German made for Parker-Frost.

☐ *Current Collector Value* . . . . $125.00/set of 2

THE TENNESSEE AND KENTUCKY BICENTENNIAL
WHITTLER SERIES
(picture on following page)

Commemorating two of the greatest knife collecting states: Tennessee and Kentucky. These knives were made from all old parts except handles and handcrafted like knives were 50 years ago. All parts except handles and shields have been lying dormant in the Schrade factory for many years. (Schrade Cut Co. stamp not used since early 1950's.) 135 hand operations and 22 separate parts were used to make these knives.

☐ *Current Collector Value* . . . . $140.00/set of 2

THE TEXAS SPECIAL

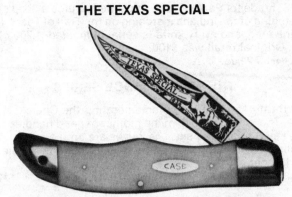

"The Texas Special" was conceived in the minds of two brothers, Bill and Buck Overall of Texas. They felt it was time someone came out with a serial numbered knife commemorating the Lone Star State. The etched blade has a longhorn steer, map of Texas and the year the battle of the Alamo was fought. They felt that these three things were Texas, making the knife unique.

The knife is a Case 4165 pattern. (To our knowledge, this knife and last year's NKC&DA knife are the only knives made by Case that have been serial numbered with white composition handles.)

W. R. Case & Sons manufactured the knife, which has white composition handles and a flat ground stainless steel blade with a full etching.

☐ *Current Collector Value: Serial numbers: 1-10* $150.00
☐   *10-50* 100.00
☐   *51-100* 80.00
☐   *101-1000* 70.00
☐   *1001-up* 60.00

THE TRAIL OF TEARS
(description on following page)

Made by Schrade for Parker-Frost, the knife features a deep etched blade with a full etching of the Indians marching on the Trail of Tears. Handles are thick genuine stag, and every knife is serial numbered. 1,200 of the knives were made. Original retail was $100.
☐ *Current Collector Value* **$150.00**

THE TRIBAL CANOE SERIES

Made by Battle Ax, they are commemorating the Cherokee, Comanche and Apache. The knives have genuine mother of pearl handles and come in a matching serial numbered set. The knives are on the mini-canoe pattern. Made in Solingen, Germany, suggested retail at the time of release in early 1979 was $120 per set.
☐ *Current Collector Value* . . . . **$120.00/set of 3**

THE TRIPLE CROWN SERIES

The Triple Crown collection was a special set of knives built on the '51 pattern case, only these featured the knife with rosewood handles. A special etch was on each blade, and a knife was made for each winner of the Triple Crown. The name of each winner was etched on the shield of each knife. There are 11 knives in the set, and were made by Case for Central Knife Exchange. 100 sets were made, with a suggested retail of $1,400 per set. The first 11 sets were given to the owners of the horses that had won the Triple Crown and the 12th set was given to Churchill Downs where it is on display until the next winner of the Triple Crown, at which time it will be given to the owner of the next Triple Crown winner.
☐ *Current Collector Value* . . . . **$1,100.00/set of 11**

THE U.S. ARMED FORCES SERVICE SERIES

This commemorative knife set, honors the 200th anniversary of the Army, Navy, and Marines. Each knife is serial-numbered. Only 8,000 sets were produced, all made in America with Hammer forged blades.

These sets originally sold for $45 and were packaged in a deluxe gift box.
☐ *Current Collector Value* . . . . **$36.00/set of 3**

THE VIRGINIA AND WEST VIRGINIA COPPERHEADS SERIES

The Virginia and West Virginia Copperheads were made by Taylor Cutlery in Japan. 600 sets were made of the stag handled copperheads. Suggested retail at the time of release (October 1979) was $70.
☐ *Current Collector Value* . . . . **$70.00/set of 2**

THE WALDEN VILLAGE KNIFE
(picture on following page)

Schrade made the Walden knife to commemorate the town that was the home of New York Knife Company, Walden Knife Company, and at one time, Schrade Cutlery Company. The knives were all serial numbered.
☐ *Current Collector Value* **$27.50**

THE WALDEN VILLAGE KNIFE

THE WHALING KNIFE

To commemorate the old-time whaling industry, Shaw Liebowitz etched and scrimshawed the Shrade-Loveless Hunter. A whaler, standing in his long boat, raises his harpoon to strike the great sperm whale who has surfaced before it sounds again, while an old salt strains on his oar trying to keep the boat from being swamped. The gold whalers and their boat rise against a black nickel sky as they ride on a chromate-blue wave. The scene is carried onto the handle as a whale overturns the boat in a typical scrimshaw technique on the ivory delrin.

Although the knife is a collector's item already, Shrade has further added to the unique quality of this edition by using ivory delrin handles instead of the standard maroon. The blade is 440C, the guard is brass, and a fitted steerhide sheath is included.

☐ *Current Collector Value* **$400.00**

THE WINCHESTER SERIES
(Not Authorized by Winchester)
(picture on following page)

The actual size of this knife is 5½ inches closed. It has bone stag handles, brass liners, deep gold leaf etching on front of blades and is made in Germany.

☐ *Current Collector Value* . . . . **$150.00/set of 2**

THE WINCHESTER SERIES

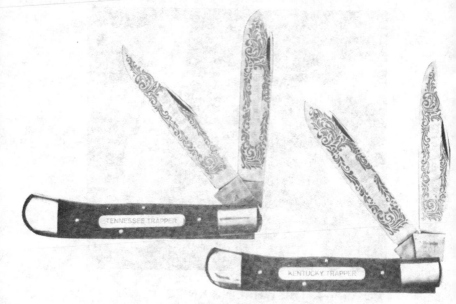

THE WISS WHITTLER

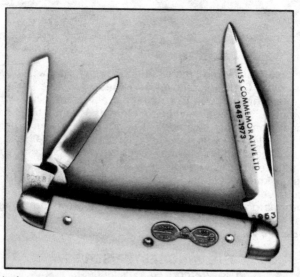

A three blade whittler pattern was chosen by Boker to commemorate 125 years of business by Wiss Cutlery. 24,000 of the knives were made. The blade is etched "Wiss Commemorative 1848-1973" with the serial number stamped on the master blade tang. A special shield is set into the white handles, two circles with a triangle overlapping both. One circle pictures a

KNIFE MANUFACTURERS OF THE WORLD

The following is a concentrated effort to list every known knife manufacturer in the world and to give a "price range" for each one's knives.

Many of these manufacturers made a wide variety of different patterns of knives. This is the reason this section lists a low and high value. **Example:** A-1 NOVELTY CUTLERY (1st listing) made small penknives that sell for $10 but their folding hunters sell for $120.

The prices listed are for mint condition knives.

HOW TO USE THIS SECTION

This is one of the hardest parts of this book to communicate to the new collector. What makes it so hard is the fact that many of the brands or makers listed manufactured anywhere from a few to several hundred different patterns of knives.

The Novelty Cutlery Company is a good example of this. In their old catalogs, they show around 150 patterns of knives. Many of their smaller penknives in mint condition will retail from $12 to $15, whereas the bigger whittler styles and folding hunter knives will bring in the $125 to $150 range in mint condition.

For the above reasons and after considerable thought, we have listed a price range on the knives from the low dollar to the high dollar *IN MINT CONDITION.* A knife in excellent condition will be worth 50% less than these figures and a knife in good to very good condition will be worth 40 to 75% below these figures. Remember too: JUST BECAUSE IT IS SHINY DOESN'T MEAN IT'S MINT.

We also ask the help of collectors in making this guide more complete. If there are any knife brands you have that are not listed here, a note of description and what you consider its value would be appreciated. Just send them to James F. Parker, 6928 Lee Highway, Chattanooga, Tennessee. 37421 or J. Bruce Voyles, P. O. Box 21127, Chattanooga, Tennessee 37421.

Also, if you have questions about specific knives, the author will be happy to answer them. A self-addressed stamped envelope will always be appreciated for the reply.

Please note in this guide if a knife is listed and only one knife of that name is made, we will have only one price. Sheffield in this guide will mean Sheffield, England, and Solingen will mean Solingen, Germany even though in some instances, the country is left out.

NOTE: THE FOLLOWING PRICES ARE LISTED IN DOLLARS ONLY FOR KNIVES IN MINT CONDITION. FOR LESSER GRADES: NEAR MINT-75% OF MINT PRICE, EXCELLENT-50% OF MINT PRICE, GOOD-VERY GOOD-25% OF MINT PRICE.

NAME	RANGE	
A-1 Novelty Cutlery		
Canton, OH	$10	$120
A. A. Fischer Co.		
NY	—	15
A. C. Penn		
New York, NY	15	60
A. C., U.S.A.	10	25
A. E. Mergott & Co.		
Newark, NJ	3	45
A. F. Bannister & Co.	15	—
A Field & Co., U.S.A.	6	90
A. Field & Co., Germany	6	35
A. Fisher		
Solingen, Germany	6	20
A. Friest & Co.		
Solingen, Germany	4	20
A. J. Jordan		
Sheffield, England	5	60
A. J. Jordan,Germany	6	25
A. J. Westersson		
Eskiltuna	4	15
A&A Mfg. Co.		
Solingen	10	100
A&K, Germany	6	25
AKC, Germany	3	25
A. Kastor Bros.		
New York, NY	15	100
A. Kastor Bros., Germany	8	25
A. L. S. N.	6	15
A. M. Implement		
Company, Germany	6	10
A.C		
Nashville, TN	25	75
A. P. Cp.		
New York, NY	12	25
A.P.S., Germany	5	24
A. Tillen & Company	15	30
A. W. Bradshaw &		
Sons, Germany	8	30
A. W. Flint & Co.		
Sheffield, England	50	150
A. W. Wadsworth & Sons		
Germany	10	65
A. W. Walker & Sons		
Germany	5	25
A. W. Walker & Sons		
Austria	5	25
A. Wingen		
Solingen, Germany	7	22

NAME	RANGE	
Acco, Atlanta, GA	5	22
Ack Cutlery Co.		
Freemont, OH	25	60
Adams & Bros.	30	90
Adams & Sons	30	90
Adolph Blaich		
San Francisco, CA	15	165
Adolphuis Cutlery Co.		
Sheffield, England	7	65
Aerial Mfg. Co.		
Marionette, WI	4	110
Akron Cutlery Co.		
Akron, OH	25	65
Alamo, Japan	2	6
Albertson Co.		
Kane, PA	30	50
Alcoso, Solingen	5	20
Alxoso Salinger		
Solingen, Germany	6	10
Alexander		
Sheffield, England	35	200
Alex Fraser & Co.		
Sheffield, England	15	50
Alford Williams		
Sheffield, England	15	75
Alfred Field & Co.		
Sheffield, England	10	—
Alfred & Son		
Celebrated Cutlery	63	185
J. Allen & Son	10	250
Allen Cutlery Co.		
Newburgh, NY	15	65
AllenBach		
Ivanswok, Germany	8	22
Allman, Germany	6	15
Aloise, Germany	6	15
Alpha, England		
Cutlery to His Majesty	15	35
Altenbach,		
Swans Work, Germany	3	25
Ambassador, U.S.A.	2	6
American Ace, U.S.A.	12	25
American Best		
New York	12	25
American Cutlery Co., U.S.A.	15	35
American Cutlery Co.		
Germany	8	20
American Cutlery Co.		
Japan	4	10

NAME	RANGE		NAME	RANGE	
American Import Co.			**B. T. Co.**		
Germany (Arrow Brand)			New Haven, CT	10	25
U.S.A.	10	25	**B. & T. Implement**		
American Knife Co.			Cutlery Co.	15	25
Plymouth, MA	65	95	**Badger State Knife Co.**		
American Knife Co.			Germany	8	15
Winstead, CT	20	45	**Baker,** New York, NY	8	35
American Knife Co.			**Baldwin Cutlery Co.**		
Japan	6	15	Tidioute, PA	15	95
American Knife Co.			**Baldwin Cutlery Co.**		
Germany	12	20	New Orleans, LA	35	150
American Knife Co.			**Banner Cutlery Co.**		
Thomaston, CT	20	60	Germany	12	25
American Shear &			**Banner Knife Co.**	12	25
Knife Co., U.S.A.	25	75	**A. F. Bannister & Co.**		
American Shirt Co. U.S.A.	7	—	New Jersey	3	45
Ames Cutlery Co.	90	—	**Barhep**		
Amico, Japan	3	5	Solingen, Germany	6	10
Anheuser Busch, Germany	20	125	**Barnsif Bros.**		
Antelope, Germany	6	10	Sheffield, England	25	55
Anton Wigen Jr.			**Barnsley Bros.,** U.S.A.	5	15
Germany	8	15	**Baron**		
Ardobo Cutlery Co.			Solingen, Germany	8	25
Germany	10	25	**Barrett & Sons 63-64**		
Argyle Cutlery Co.			Picadilly, England	15	35
(Brown Bros.)	15	35	**Barry & Co.** Germany	6	15
Aribis, Havana	12	—	**Barrett & Sons**	6	65
Armstrong Cutlery Co. U.S.A.	8	15	**Barlett Tool Co.**		
Armstrong Cutlery Co.			Newark, NY	15	65
Germany	6	12	**Barton Bros.**		
Arnex (stainless)			Sheffield, England	15	95
Solingen, Germany	4	10	**Bassett**		
Arrow Brand Knife Co.	5	25	Derby, CT	8	25
Art Knife Co.			**Bastian Bros. Co.**		
Nicholson, PA	25	—	Rochester, NY	25	65
Ashley	6	16	**Bates & Bacon**	25	150
Atco, Japan	2	5	**Battle Ax Cutlery Co.**	45	75
Atenback			**Bay Ridge Works**		
Swanswork, Germany	10	50	Solingen, Germany	10	20
Atlantic Cutlery Co.			**Bayonne Cutlery**		
Germany	12	25	Bayonne, NJ	10	75
Autopoint			**Bayridge Works,** Germany	5	30
Chicago, IL	3	8	**Bay State,** Worcester, MA	30	175
Axel Nielsson			**Beaver Cutlery Co.**		
Swedish Steel	15	—	Beaver Falls, PA	35	175
B&B, St. Paul, MN	15	35	**Belknap Hwde. Co.**	20	400
B. K. Cutlery Co.			**Belmont Knife Co.**	15	35
Cleveland, OH	8	15	**Benedict Warren**		
			Davidson & Co.	20	150

NAME	RANGE	
Bering-Cortes		
Hdwe. Co.	15	35
Berkshire Cutlery Co.	20	85
Bertram		
(Hen & Rooster)	40	250
Besteel Warranted	10	25
Best English Cutlery	8	125
Beta Bos'n, Germany	6	10
Betz Biffman, Germany	3	15
W. W. Bingham		
Cleveland, OH	15	175
Big Horn, Italy	4	10
Binghamton Cutlery Co.	15	100
Bison, Japan	2	4
Blake & Lamb		
Utica, NY	25	200
Blandula Cutlery Co.		
Germany	5	20
Blish, Mize &		
Stillman Hdwe. Co.	20	150
Blue Grass Belknap Hdwe.		
Louisville, KY	15	100
Blue Ribbon	15	25
Bohler Star	8	15
Bohler Stahl	8	15
Boker, U.S.A.	10	100
Boker		
Solingen, Germany	10	175
Bon Knife Co.	3	15
Bonsa		
Solingen, Germany	4	25
Bonser Inc.		
Germany	6	10
Bontgen & Sabin		
Solingen, Germany	15	35
Booth Bros.		
Sussex, NY	35	200
Borneff, Germany	3	10
Bostwick Braun Co.		
Toledo, OH	25	150
Bowen Knife Co.		
Atlanta, GA	20	110
Bower Dist. Co.	7	25
Bower Implement Co.	7	25
Bowman Cutlery Co.		
Germany	15	25
Brach, Germany	10	25
Branda P.R. Patento	4	15
Brantford Cutlery Co.	20	150

NAME	RANGE	
Briddell, Charles D. Inc.	15	25
J. Bunger & Sons		
Celebrated Cutlery	30	150
Bridge Cutlery Co.		
St. Louis, MO	65	200
Bridgeport Gun &		
Implement Co.		
Bridgeport, CT	40	65
Bristol Line, Germany	6	25
Brighton Cutlery Works	18	25
Brit Nife		
St. Louis, MO	15	30
Broch & Koch	15	35
Brooklyn Knife Co.		
New York	25	45
Brooks Cutlery Co.		
Morristown, TN	45	105
Brooks & Brooks		
Sheffield, England	40	125
Brooks & Crooks		
Sheffield, England	4	200
Brown Bros., Germany	12	25
Brown-Camp Hdwe. Co.		
St. Louis, MO	30	200
Brown Shoe Co.		
St. Louis, MO	15	75
Browning, USA	15	60
Browning, Germany	10	18
E. Bruckmann	15	125
Buck Creek, Solingen	10	25
Buck, El-Cajon, CA	7	45
Buffalo Cutlery Co.	35	160
Buhl & Sons Co.		
Detroit, MI	15	65
R. Bunting & Sons		
Sheffield	75	500
Burkinshaw Knife Co.		
Pepperell, MA	35	300
Frank Buster Cutlery Co.	10	1000
Butler Bros.		
Chicago, IL	15	85
Butler & Co.		
Sheffield, England	15	45
Cam, Germany	6	10
C.B.S., Solingen, Germany	15	25
C. Bertram (Acorn Emblem)	40	250
C. F. Wotherts		
Solingen	15	35

NAME	RANGE	
C. J. & Co.		
Sheffield, England	40	65
C. K. Co., Germany	10	35
C. & X., Sheffield, England	12	25
Caldwell Cutlery Co.		
Philadelphia, PA	15	100
Caldwell Mfg. Co.		
Indianapolis, IN	35	65
Cambridge Cutlery Co.	45	75
Camco, U.S.A.	1	15
Camden Cutlery Co., Germany	25	100
Camillus Cutlery Co.		
Camillus, NY	8	110
Camillus, New York, NY	5	25
Camp Buddy, USA	8	25
Camp King	8	25
Cameron Knife Co.	15	35
Canastota Knife Co.	15	65
Candco, Switzerland	6	15
Canton Cutlery Co.	15	120
Capital Cutlery Co.		
Indianapolis, IN	35	300
Carl Wusthof, Solingen	15	45
C C C (Barlow), U.S.A.	45	90
Carrier Cutlery Co.		
Elmira, NY	35	250
Carters (Hen & Rooster)		
Scottsville, KY	40	200
Carter Blade Master		
Cleveland, OH	15	35
Car-Von S.P. Co., Canton OH	15	90
Case Bros., Little Valley, NY	50	1000
Case Bros. Cutlery Co.	50	1000
Case Bros., Springville, NY	75	1200
Case Bros., Little Valley, NY	40	1000
Case MFG.	50	800
Case Cutlery Co.	50	500
Catskill Knife Co., New York	12	85
Ceb Muller, Germany	3	12
Centaur, Germany	4	10
Centennial Mills		
Solingen, Germany	15	45
Central Cutlery Co.	40	130
Challenge Cutlery Co.		
Bridgeport, CT	15	150
Chalmers & Murray	35	70
Champion	25	45
Chapman (Hand-Forged)	35	60
Charlton, Sheffield, England	15	65

NAME	RANGE	
Chicago Pocket Knife Co.	25	125
Chipaway Cutlery Co.	35	400
John Chatillion & Son	35	200
Charles Langbein, New York	65	100
Chero-Cola Co.	35	70
Christians		
Solingen, Germany	20	150
Cix Christy	3	18
Clark Bros.		
Kansas City, MO	15	60
Clark & Carriers Mfg. Co.		
Nontour Falls, NY	35	75
Clark Cutlery	15	45
Clauberg Cutlery Co.		
Germany	8	18
Clauss, Freemont, OH	15	65
Clay-Andover, New York	15	60
Clay Cutlery Co.		
Andover, NY	30	200
Claysen & Son, Germany	10	35
Clearcut Co., U.S.A.	12	30
Clements Cutlery		
Sheffield, England	8	60
Cleveland Cutlery		
Germany	35	60
Cleveland Cutlery Co.		
Japan	4	8
Clover Brand, Syracruse, NY	15	25
Clyde Cutlery Co.		
Clyde, OH	12	60
Coast Cutlery Co.		
Portland, OR	25	125
Coca Cola		
Germany (original)	35	75
Coca Cola		
USA stamped on tang		
(original)	35	75
Coca Cola		
USA stamped on tang		
(Repro.)	.50¢	1
Cofwanoe Works		
Philadelphia, PA	60	90
Cohelle Coin	30	90
Cold Finger	6	15
Coleman Cutlery Co.		
Titusville, PA	15	60
Coles, New York	8	50
Colonial, Providence, RI	2	12
Colonial Cutlery Co.	15	65

NAME	RANGE		NAME	RANGE	
Colonial Knife Co.	10	35	Dance Cutlery Co.		
Colonial Knife Co., U.S.A.	6	16	Germany	10	26
Colt, Germany	30	45	Dart. U.S.A.	3	20
Colt (Arms Co.)	50	250	Dasco, Rockford, IL	6	15
Colt (Imperial), U.S.A.	4	12	Dawes & Ball		
Columbia Knife Co., New York	45	60	Sheffield, England	65	125
Commander			De Boer & Bach	15	35
Little Valley, NY	65	95	Decora, Germany	5	15
Conn Cutlery Co.	15	65	Deherd (Ohilg, Solingen)	5	15
Contents, Germany	6	10	Wenger Delemont, Switzerland	5	20
Continental Cutlery Co.			Delmar Cutlery Co.	15	65
New York	15	60	Delta, Germany	8	20
Continental Cutlery Co.			Delux	6	15
Sheffield, England	12	60	Depend-on-me-Cutlery Co.,		
Continental Cutlery Co.			New York	7	35
Kansas City, MO.	25	65	Diamond Knife Co., Germany . . .	15	—
Cook Bros.	75	125	Diamond Edge Val-Test		
Copper Bros.	8	18	Chicago, IL	10	175
Coppel, Germany	6	15	Dickinson		
Cora, Germany	6	15	Sheffield, England	15	80
Corlis Cutlery, Germany	20	35	Dictator	10	20
Cornwall Knife Co., New York	15	20	Dincer, A.		
Corsan Denton			Kaiserlauntern, Germany	12	70
Burkdeki & Co.			E. Dirlam, Solingen	15	35
New York, NY	15	300	Diston Steel 1840-1944	7	35
Craftsman (Sears), U.S.A.	3	25	Dixie Knife	30	60
Crandall			Dixon Cutlery Co., U.S.A.	15	65
Bradford, PA	75	500	Dixon Cutlery, U.S.A.	15	65
Cresent Cutlery Co.	15	25	Dixon Cutlery Co., Germany	8	25
Croisdale Leeds	35	85	J. Dixon Cutlery Co.		
Crown Cutlery Co., New York	15	65	Germany	8	25
Crown Cutlery Co.			Dodson, Chicago, IL	15	100
Austria	5	15	Dollar Cutlery Co.		
Crown Cutlery Co.			Atlanta, GA	15	100
Prussia	5	15	Dolmetach,		
Crucibal Brand, U.S.A.	25	65	Zurich, Sweden	5	20
Crucibal Knife Co., New York	20	100	Dolphin Cutlery Co.		
Curtin & Clark Cutlery Co.			New York, NY	15	35
Kansas City, MO	25	110	Domar Cutlery Co.		
Culf & Kay			Oklahoma City, OK	10	30
Sheffield, England	65	90	H. Dorwal, Germany	5	15
Curley Bros., New York	10	75	Double Cola, U.S.A.	3	22
Cumberland Cutlery Co.	15	65	Douglas, Brockton, MA.	15	36
Cussin & Fern, U.S.A.	25	75	Drake Hdwe. Co., U.S.A.	15	60
D.S.K., Boston, MA	12	25	H. A. Dreer		
Dahlia, Germany	6	15	Philadelphia, PA	35	75
Dan Quallo Specialty Co.			Dreitium, Germany	8	15
Knoxville, TN	6	15	Driezack, Germany	4	12
			Dresden, Germany	4	12

NAME	RANGE	
Droeschers (Arrow Brand)	6	10
Duane Cutlery Co.		
Germany	6	10
Dukes, Father of Barlows	35	65
E. Dulon		
Solingen, Germany	4	25
G. Dunbar, Germany	4	25
J. Dunlap & Co.		
Solingen, Germany	12	18
Dunn Bros.		
Providence, RI	6	25
Duro-Edge		
Utica, NY	5	10
Dwight Devine & Sons	20	100
Edward Tryon Co.		
Philadelphia, PA	20	150
E.AA.		
Solingen, Germany	5	10
E. F. & Co.	65	90
Eagle	20	35
Eagle Cutlery Co.	65	300
Eagle Knife Co., U.S.A.	30	300
Eagle Pencil Co.	5	15
Eagleton Knife Co.	20	125
Eal K. Co., Germany	15	60
Eder & Co., Germany	25	65
Edgar Cutlery Co.		
Germany	8	25
Edge, Germany	4	14
Edge Master, U.S.A.	8	20
Edirlam		
Solingen, Germany	5	15
Edulon		
Solingen, Germany	5	15
Edward Barnes & Sons	65	400
Edward K. Tryon Co.		
Philadelphia, PA	20	150
Edward Weck	15	35
Edward Weck & Sons		
New York	15	50
Edward Zinn, Germany	5	15
Edithwerks		
Solingen, Germany	15	35
E. F. & S.		
(Enos Furness on blade)	65	200
J. Eicher Ohligar		
Germany	15	65
Eig, Germany	4	15
Eig, Italy	4	15

NAME	RANGE	
Eig, Japan	2	6
Elberfield Cutlery Co., U.S.A.	20	200
Elder & Co., Germany	10	25
Electric Cutlery Co.		
Newark, NJ	30	120
Electric Cutlery Co.		
Walden, NY	30	200
Elephant Mark	Info Wtd.	—
El Gallo, Germany	5	12
Elgin AM Mfg. Co., U.S.A.	6	25
Eliksch Kadison, Germany	3	7
Ellenville Knife Co., U.S.A.	15	100
Elliot Cutlery Corp.		
Czechoslovakia	4	15
Elliot Cutlery Corp.		
Germany	8	25
Wm. Elliott & Co.		
England	65	95
I. Ellis & Sons Ltd.		
England	125	200
Eloise, Germany	6	35
Elyte	4	15
E. Moulin		
Greenville, IL	15	65
Emmon Hawkins Hardware	15	100
Empire Knife Co.		
Winsted, CT	30	300
Empire, Winsted, CT	30	300
Emrod Co., Germany	4	15
Wm. Enders Mfg. Co., U.S.A.	15	125
Enderses	10	40
Endmon	4	25
Engelswerk, Germany	3	20
English Cutlery Co.	15	65
John Engstrom, Sweden	4	15
Enterprise Cutlery Co.		
St. Louis, MO	25	75
Enterprise Cutlery Co.		
Germany	15	35
Erber, Germany	5	15
Erma Finedge		
Astoso, Germany	15	25
Ern, Solingen, Germany	5	20
Ern, Stainless Steel	5	15
Frieder Ern & Co., Weyer	10	25
Ernand Esser	5	25
Ernst Gerlereg, Germany	15	65
Ervin C. T. Co., Germany	15	50
Esinco Stainless	3	10

NAME	RANGE	
Essem Co.	10	20
Essex Cutlery Co.	50	125
Etched P. Lo, New York	15	65
Everkeen	25	65
Eversharp Cutlery, U.S.A.	25	60
E. Wild & Sons	15	65
W. H. Everts, Germany	10	20
Excelsior Knife Co.	35	125
Executove, U.S.A.	6	35
E. B. Extra		
(Hartford Cutlery Co.)	25	75
B. J. Eyre & Co.		
Germany	15	35
Eye Brand, Germany	7	45
F. & K.		
Solingen, Germany	6	15
F. & L.,		
Celebrated Cutlery Co.	75	125
E. Faber, Germany	6	25
Fabico, Germany	3	15
Fabico, Japan	2	7
Fabyan Knife Co.		
New York	12	60
Fairmont Cutlery Co.		
New York	15	45
Fairplay Bros.	5	100
Falcon Knife Co.	15	35
Farwell Ozmun Kirk & Co.	35	65
Faulkhiner & Co.		
Germany	10	20
Favorite Knife Co.		
Germany	4	25
Fayetteville Knife Co.	12	30
Federal Knife Co.		
Syracuse, NY	15	40
Feinstahl, Germany	4	15
Joseph Feist, Germany	25	65
G. Felix	8	15
E. Felsenheldmaker		
New York	35	65
Thomas Fenton	14	20
Fidelity Knife Co.		
New York	5	35
A Field & Co., Prussia	20	75
A Field & Co., (Progress)	15	90
A Field & Co. (Criterion)		
Germany	15	45
Alfred Field & Co.		
Germany	15	30

NAME	RANGE	
Marshall Field & Co.		
Germany	15	60
Fife Cutlery Co.		
(Hen & Rooster), Germany	40	150
Fightin' Rooster Cutlery Co.		
Solingen, Germany	10	1000
Fillmore Cutlery Co.	10	60
Finstahl	5	15
Flenef	5	100
Fletcher Hwde. Co.		
Detroit, MI	20	65
Floraworks Cutlery Co.		
Germany	5	15
Flosa, Germany	25	65
Floyd & Bohr Co.		
Louisville, KY	35	125
Flylock Knife Co.		
Bridgeport, CT., U.S.A.	25	120
Fords' Medley, England	10	95
W. F. Ford (Shepards &		
Dudley) NY	35	125
Forged Steel	15	30
Forest Master (Colonial)	4	15
Foster Bros. & Chatillon Co.		
Fulton, NY	15	65
Fox Cutlery Co.	30	65
France & Russie	10	15
Frank Mills & Co.,		
Ltd. England	8	85
Frank Owen Hdwe. Co.	15	35
Frankfurth Hdwe. Co.	30	50
Frary, Germany	5	25
Alex Fraser & Co.		
England	15	35
Fred Biffor		
Chicago, IL	5	65
Frederick Reynolds		
England	35	125
Fried, Herber ABR Sohn		
Solingen, Germany	15	65
Friedman Lauterjang		
Celebrated Cutlery	45	165
Frieds Ern & Co.		
Solingen, Germany	15	50
Frost Cutlery Co., Japan	10	35
Fulton, New York	25	60
Fulton, U.S.A.	25	60
Fulton Cutlery Works	45	115

NAME	RANGE	
G. Butler & Co.		
Sheffield, England	15	65
G. C. Co., Italy	4	15
G. J. Eyre Co., Germany	12	35
G.R.C. Co. (Golden Rule Cutlery Co.) Chicago, IL	20	125
G.W. & H. Hdwe. Co.		
St. Louis, MO	30	65
Gambill Stores	4	15
Garantie	5	10
Garantie (Stahl)	15	35
Garden City Cutlery Co.	25	60
Garland Cutlery Co.		
Germany	10	25
Gateway Cutlery Co.	5	25
Gebr. Stamm Tidax		
Germany	12	35
Gelbros Co., Germany	12	40
H.W. Geler's E-Z-Cutter	25	60
Gellman Bros.		
Minneapolis, MN	15	60
General, Chicago, IL	15	30
Geneva Cutlery Co.		
Geneva, NY	25	60
George Schrade Knife Co.		
U.S.A.	30	150
Gerber, Germany	20	35
Gerber, U.S.A.	20	150
Gerbr Hopre, Germany	10	15
Gerlach, Poland	8	20
Ernst Gerleg, Germany	15	50
Germania Cutlery Co.	10	25
Germo Mfg. Co.		
Germany	5	18
Gerson Co., Germany	6	18
Ges. Co., Japan	1	4
Gesco, Japan	1	4
Gesco, Ireland	2	7
Gets. Razor Knife		
Chicago, IL	4	25
Giant Grip	15	65
Gibberson & Co.		
Scotland	6	15
Gilbert Saville Works		
Sheffield, England	60	150
Git's Razor Nife		
Chicago, IL	6	15
Gladstone	15	50
Gladstone Co.	15	50
Glasner & Barzen		
Germany	10	30
Globrismen, Germany	8	15
Golden Rule Cutlery Co.		
Chicago, IL	20	150
Glen Fall Cutlery Co.		
England	15	60
Globe Cutlery Co., Germany	10	30
Gold Seal	18	40
Gold Top	10	30
Goodell Co.		
Antrim, NH	60	90
Gottlieb		
Solingen, Germany	12	20
Grace Bros., Graef & Schmidt, Germany	25	75
Grand Leader, Germany	15	30
G. Grebory	10	20
Green & Thompson	1830	2500
Theo. M. Green		
Oklahoma City, OK	5	60
Griffon Cutlery Works		
Bridgeport, CT	30	125
Griffon Worchester		
Germany	10	30
Grove Mfg. Co.		
Chicago, IL	25	75
Guttman, Germany	15	35
Gussstahl, Germany	12	60
Gust. Melcher, Solingen	10	20
H&B Mfg.		
New Britain, CT	25	200
H&J King 856 Warranted	75	95
H & L Mfg. Co.		
Bridgeport, CT	15	75
H. S. C. Co	25	75
H.M.C. & D	35	—
H. C. Long & Co.		
Sheffield, England	65	150
Haag, Otto		
Solingen, Germany	5	15
Hacket-Walter Gates	65	95
Gust Haker	5	18
Hall	15	35
Hall, Randall & Co.		
Germany	5	15
Hamilton Knife Co.		
St. Louis, MO	35	65
Hammer Brand (New York Knife Co.)	15	450

NAME	RANGE	
Hammer Brand		
(Imperial)	3	20
G. Hannes Fahr	3	10
Hancock, George & Sons		
Celebrated Cutlery	25	115
Harris Bros. & Son		
Chicago, IL	10	150
Harrison Bros. & Howsen		
Sheffield, England	10	150
Hart Cutlery Co., New York	20	200
Hart Kopt & Co.		
Solingen, Germany	15	65
Hartford Cutlery Co.	10	150
Harveyn Bros., Germany	5	15
Hatch Cutlery Co.		
Bridgeport, CT	10	200
Hatch Cutlery Co.		
Milwaukee, WI	10	150
Harukswort, I. E.	10	15
Hawthorne Cutlery Co.		
Germany	25	60
Hay Market	20	60
Hayward	15	30
Heathcote, England	25	60
Heinr Boker Baumuswerk		
Solingen, Germany	10	200
Heinz, Germany	3	15
Heller Bros. Co.		
Newark, NJ	25	60
Hendingtan & Son Eshilstuna		
Sweden	3	15
Henry Branascond & Sons		
Sheffield, England	30	75
Henckels International		
Germany	5	30
Henry Hudson & Sons	5	200
Henry Sears 1865	30	250
Henkel & Joyce		
Hardware Co.	15	85
Henry Seymour Sure Co.,		
New York	5	100
Herder & Co., Germany	10	35
Herder, Rich A.		
Solingen, Germany	12	65
A. Hermes, Germany	10	35
Hermitage Cutlery	8	25
Herms, Germany	10	35
T. Hessen Bruch & Co.	15	35

NAME	RANGE	
Hibbard, Spencer, & Bartlett		
Chicago, IL	10	350
Hickory	4	200
Highcarbon Steel, U.S.A.	10	150
Higler & Sons	15	75
Hike Cutlery Co.		
Solingen, Germany	10	35
Hill Bros.	20	60
Hindnburg Sehneid		
Solingen, Germany	15	60
Hit, U.S.A.	20	60
H. Howsen & Sons	60	90
I. Hoffman, Germany	15	35
Hoffritz, Germany	7	45
Johns, Holler & Co.	65	400
Holley Mfg. Co.		
Lakeville, CT	10	500
Hollinger		
Fremont, OH	10	150
Hollingsworth, Kane, PA	10	200
J. Holmes		
Sheffield, England	50	90
Holub, Sycamore, IL	15	35
Home	15	35
Honk Falls		
Napanoch, NY	35	900
Horizont, Germany	14	28
Hornis Cutlery Co.	20	60
Howard Bros., Germany	15	75
Howes Cutlery Co.	50	135
Hubertus, Germany	20	50
Hudson Knife Co.	10	60
Hunason & Backley Co. U.S.A.	5	55
Hugal 7 Works, Germany	10	50
Humphreys		
Sheffield, England	8	20
Hunter Cutlery Co.		
Germany	15	75
Hunkill Hunter	65	90
H. Ville Knife Co.	65	90
I. N. C. Co.	5	15
I. B. Y., Germany	55	15
I. K. Co., U.S.A.	3	8
I. S. Set	15	75
Ibbotson & Sons		300
Ibberson	7	125
Ideal, U.S.A.	3	10
IKCO, U.S.A.	2	15
Illo Cutlery Co., Germany	3	15

NAME	RANGE	
Imperial Knife Co.	2	75
Imperial Knife Co.		
Providence, RI	2	75
Imperial, Mexico	1	3
Imperial, Germany	6	26
Indiana Cutlery Co.	36	75
Inter, Italy	3	10
Intrinsic John Milner & Co.		
Sheffield	15	35
Iowan Co.		
Cedar Rapids, IA	40	85
Ipany, Spain	3	15
Iroka, Germany	7	10
Iroquois, U.S.A.	2	12
Iroquois Cutlery Co.		
Utica, NY	3	25
Iros, Keen, NY	8	45
Irving Cutlery Co.		
Germany	4	15
Issac Milner, Sheffield	25	60
Ivy, Germany	5	15
Jack Knife		
Ben, Chicago, IL	25	150
Jackmaster, U.S.A.	20	60
Jackoby & Webster		
Germany	20	200
Jackson, Fremont, OH	15	65
Jaeger Bros.		
Marinette, WI	10	125
James Nillward & Co.	5	15
Janker Works	8	35
Jean Case		
Little Valley, NY	20	300
Jensen-King Byrd Co.		
Spokane, WA	50	110
Jet Knife Corp., U.S.A.	12	65
Jet-Aire Knife Corp.	12	65
Jim Bowie (German Eye)	12	65
Jim Dandy	20	150
John Catillion & Son		
New York, NY	25	300
John Newton, Sheffield	15	200
John Petty & Son		
Sheffield	15	125
John Primble,		
Belknap Hardware	10	500
John Primble,		
India Steel Works	30	800
John Pritziaff Knife Co.	15	50
John Watts	10	30

NAME	RANGE	
John Wilton, Sheffield	45	125
Jonathan Crooks, England	10	200
Jones & Son, Germany	5	15
Jordan, St. Louis, MO	10	65
Joseph Allen & Sons	10	250
Joseph Elliott, Sheffield	15	75
Joseph H. Rodgers &		
Sons Cutlery	5	1000
Judson Cutlery Co.		
New York	20	40
Julanco, Germany	5	35
Justus Bierholff		
Solingen	40	80
J. W. James, Sheffield	65	250
K&B Cutlery Co. New York	15	55
K&B Cutlery Co. Germany	5	35
K&B Hardware Co.		
Cincinnati, OH	15	150
K. C. Seelbe, Germany	10	15
K & Co.		
Solingen, Germany	8	35
K. I. E., Sweden	3	15
Ka-Bar, U.S.A.	10	600
Kabar, U.S.A.	10	300
Kamp Cutlery Co.		
Germany	5	15
Kamp Huaser		
Plumacher, Germany	15	60
Kampfe Bros., New York	10	20
Kamphaus	10	20
Kan-Der, Germany	15	35
Kane Cutlery Co., Kane, PA	65	300
Kane, Germany	25	65
A. Kastor & Bros.		
Germany	15	75
N. Kastor, Germany	15	75
Kaufmann		
Solingen, Germany	4	30
C. F. Kayser, Germany	8	125
Keeneredge, C. M. McClung		
& Co., Knoxville, TN	10	125
Keene, New York	15	65
Keenite, Boston, MA	15	65
Keen Kutter, E C		
Simmons Hardware	15	500
Keen Cutter		
(Valtest) Chicago, IL	15	35
Keinoritter, Germany	5	15
Kellin & Co., Germany	15	65

NAME	RANGE	
Kendall, Winsted, CT	4	25
R. Kelley & Sons		
Liverpool, England	25	75
Kent	4	35
H. Keschner, Germany	5	20
Kenwell Mfg. Co.		
Olean, NY	15	150
Keystone Cutlery	35	200
Kinfolks		
Little Valley, NY	40	300
Kings Quality, U.S.A.	4	10
King Cutlery Co.		
Germany	15	30
Kingston, U.S.A.	8	30
Kirkan & Co., Germany	5	15
Klicker, U.S.A.	20	40
Kissing Krane	6	175
Klostermeier Bros.		
Atchison, KS	35	75
G. Knauth, My.	10	25
Aug Knecht, Germany	10	30
Knickerbocker Cutlery Co.	10	100
F. A. Koch & Co., New York	15	200
F. A. Koch & Co.		
Germany	10	30
H. & J. W. King	15	40
Koeller & Schmitz		
Cutlery Co.	30	60
Koester & Sons	15	60
Hugo Koller, Germany	12	35
Korien, Germany	5	15
Korten Schert, Germany	10	30
Kortehn & Schere	10	30
J. Kowill		
Sheffield, England	50	95
Fred Kroner Hdwe.	10	50
Kruse Hardware		
Cincinnati, OH	35	150
R. C. Kruschil		
Duluth, MN	40	60
Krusius Cutlery, Germany	8	60
Kunde & al		
Remscherd, Germany	55	95
Kutmaster, U.S.A.	3	35
Kutwell, Olean, NY	50	300
Kwik Cut, U.S.A.	15	60
L. F. & C.		
New Britain, CT	10	150
L. F. & C., U.S.A.	10	150

NAME	RANGE	
LCA Hardware, Omaha, NE	25	60
LK Co.		
New Britain, CT	5	15
LL Bean Inc.		
Freeport, MA	10	150
LLH Co.		
Cleveland, OH	5	15
L. K. Co.		
New Britain, CT	5	15
Labelle	15	60
Lackawanna Cutlery		
Nicholson, PA	40	200
Lafayette Cutlery Co.		
Germany	5	65
Laclide Simmons,		
Germany	5	30
Lakeside Cutlery	40	400
Lamson and Goodnow		
Mfg. Co.	15	150
Landers Frary & Clark	35	75
Landwerk, Solingen	4	10
Langstaff Hardware Co.		
Prussia	15	60
Latoma, Italy	4	8
Lalli Bros.		
Celebrated Cutlery	35	200
Charles Land, Sheffield	60	80
Law Brothers	5	100
Lawton Cutlery Co.	12	60
Layman Cutlery Co.	15	75
Leader, U.S.A.	5	20
Lee Hardware Co.		
Salina, KS	25	75
LeBalkanique	3	15
Legal, U.S.A.	15	60
Lehenberg, Solingen	12	20
Lenox Cutlery Co., Germany	10	20
Leonard	59	10
Levering Knife Co.		
U.S.A.	10	45
Lewis Muray	5	15
Liberty Knife Co., U.S.A.	25	60
Lignam Mfg. Co.		
Chicago, IL	12	25
Lincoln Novelty Co.	5	40
C. R. Linden Weyer		
Solingen	20	60
Lion Cutlery Co.		
Sheffield	5	15

NAME	RANGE		NAME	RANGE	
Lipic, U.S.A.	3	10	Garantito Mantellalo	5	15
H. Lipscomp & Co.			Marx & Cos		
Nashville, TN	15	75	Celebrated Cutlery	75	225
Lipchutz	30	90	Marx, Germany	5	35
Lish, Germany	5	10	Henry Mason	10	35
Little Valley Cutlery			Mason & Sons	5	100
Association, New York	65	150	Massuer, Germany	20	60
Lockwood Bros.			Mayer, Germany	5	15
Sheffield, England	25	175	C. M. McClung & Co.	15	100
H. G. Long & Co.,			McIntosh Heather		
Sheffield	15	65	Cleaveland, OH	20	150
Lott & Schmitt, New York	25	75	McNitor Knife Co.	5	20
Lublim, Germany	7	20	Meehan, Germany	3	10
Luhdt Co., Solingen	4	15	Gust, Melcher	10	25
Lubot Co.	5	20	Melka, Germany	5	20
Lugrosse, Germany	5	100	Mercator,		
Luna Werk, Germany	15	75	Solingen, Germany	3	15
Lut Oates	12	75	Metrose Cutlery Co.		
Lux, Solingen	4	15	Germany	35	65
Luxrite, Hollywood, CA	15	60	J. E. Mergott Co.		
LVK Assn.	65	150	Newark, NY	30	60
Lyon Cutlery Co.	15	60	Meriden Cutlery Co.	25	150
M. B. Co.	25	125	Merrimac Cutlery Co.	40	70
M. C. Co.	15	30	Messerviy's	5	25
M. F. & S., England	60	135	Metropolitan Cutlery Co.		
MS Y, England	5	15	Germany	4	10
M. Mocal, Inc.	10	35	Mill Mfg. Co.	35	90
M. Mocal, Inc., Germany	8	15	Miller Bros., U.S.A.	30	400
Madden & Sons			Miller Bros., Germany	15	60
Sheffield	25	65	Issac Milner, Sheffield	20	60
Magnetic Cutlery Co.	15	35	Millwards	5	20
Maher & Grosh			Mitsubashi, Japan	3	100
Toledo, OH	40	300	Blish Mize &		
Maher & Grosh, Prussia	30	175	Sellimar Hardware Co.	15	150
Majector Cutlery Co.			M. Mocal, Inc.	5	15
Germany	12	20	Monroe Cutlery Co.	35	60
Manhattan Knife Co., U.S.A.	10	20	Moore-Handley Hardware Co.		
Maniago, Italy	4	15	Birmingham, Al	20	200
Manos Cutlery Co.	5	15	Montgomery Ward & Co.		
I. Manson, Sheffield	10	35	U.S.A.	4	55
Mantua Cutlery	5	15	Monumental Cutlery Co.		
Mantria	5	15	Sheffield	15	30
Mappin Bros., Sheffield	65	200	Moore House & Wells Co.	10	30
Marbles, Gladstone, MI	75	2000	Moorman, U.S.A.	5	15
Mariel Co., New York	8	15	W. H. Morley & Sons	10	55
Marshel Bros.	25	60	Morris Cutlery Co.	15	175
Marshall Wells Hdwe. Co.	50	1000	W. G. Mosher	10	25
Martin Bros., Sheffield	60	90	Moslery Cutlery Cp.	15	65
Marsh Bros., Sheffield	45	400			

NAME	RANGE		NAME	RANGE	
J. T. Mount & Co.			**Northhampton Cutlery**		
Newark, NJ	35	75	Company	25	200
E. Moulin, Greenville, IL	12	20	**Norvell Shapleigh**		
Mumbley Peg, Camillus	50	95	St. Louis, MO	15	400
Murcott, Germany	5	25	**Norwich Cutlery Co.**	15	60
R. Murphy, Boston, MD	15	25	**Novelty Cutlery Co.**		
Mutual Cutlery Co.			Canton, OH	10	150
Canton, OH	15	50	**NOX & ALL Cutlery Co.**	5	100
N. C. Co., Canton, OH	5	75	**O.N.B.**, Sheffield	5	55
N. Y. Knife Co.			**O.N.B.**, Germany	5	55
Walden, NY	25	1000	**O.N.B. Cutlery Works**		
Nagbaur, U.S.A.	15	55	Germany	5	55
Nagle Reblade Knife Co.	200	1100	**O.V.B.**	10	100
Nana, Solingen, Germany	5	15	**Oakland Cutlery Company**	5	15
Bafhelier, Anantes	Info wanted		**Ohio Cutlery Company**	20	200
Napanoch Knife Co.	30	1000	**Ohio Cut. Co.**		
National Cutlery Works			Massillon, OH	20	200
Germany	15	75	**Oklahoma City Hardware**		
National Silver Co.			Oklahoma City, OK	25	65
New York	10	30	**Olbos**, Germany	5	8
Naucatuck Cutlery	30	125	**Olcut**, Olean, NY	45	300
Needham Bros., Sheffield	60	300	**Old Cutlery**		
Neft Safety Knife	65	95	Olean, NY	15	125
Nelson Knife Co.	15	35	**Old American Knife**, U.S.A.	10	35
Neo Sho Products	4	30	**Old Hickory**		
Never Dull, U.S.A.	12	40	(Ontario Knife Company)	4	12
New Britton	8	30	**Old Timer**		
New England Knife Co.	15	75	(Schrade Walden)	5	100
New Port Cutlery Company			**Obon**, New York, U.S.A.	25	125
Germany	12	18	**Olscut**, Germany	6	15
New Century Cutlery			**Olsen Knife Co.**		
Company	8	14	Howard City, MI	6	45
Newton Premier			**Omega**, Germany	5	15
Sheffield	10	25	**Omar**, Japan	2	5
New York Knife Company			**Omar**, Germany	5	15
Walden, NY	25	1000	**Omar**, Pakistan	2	7
Axel Nielsson			**O'Neill & Thomson**	6	16
Swedish Steel	3	15	**Ontario Knife Company**		
William Nicholson			(Tru-edge)	3	10
Sheffield	6	150	**Oppenreimer**, Italy	4	8
Nifty Knife Company	4	10	**Osborne, Keene & Co.**, U.S.A.	15	60
Nippes & Plumacher			**The Ostdiek Company**		
Germany	15	65	Minneapolis, MN	25	45
Noberis Cutlery, Germany	15	30	**Otto Haag**		
N. American,			Solingen, Germany	10	35
Wichita, KS	10	55	**O. Barnett Tool Co.**		
Norsharp	10	35	Newark, NY, U.S.A.	15	65
Northfield Knife Co., U.S.A.	15	85	**O. D. Gray & Co.**	30	500

NAME	RANGE	
Oval Cutlery Co.		
Sheffield	15	75
Overland	5	100
Owe Cutlery		
Sheffield, England	—	—
P.K., Solingen, Germany	4	15
Pacific Hardware Steel Co.	15	75
Pal Blade Co., U.S.A.	15	90
Pal Cutlery Co., U.S.A.	15	90
Pal Cutlery		
Plattsburg, NY	15	90
Palace Cutlery Co.	25	30
Palmett Cutlery Co.	20	35
Palalto Cutlery Co.		
Germany	5	15
Papes Thiebes Cutlery Co.	10	200
Parker Cutlery Co.	10	900
Parker-Frost	10	200
Wm. & J. Parker		400
Pinzer Messa	4	10
L. Pondo	15	65
Parision Novelty Co.	2	8
Paris Bead, Chicago, IL	15	25
Edward Parker & Sons	20	65
W. H. Parker, Sheffield	65	135
Pastian Bros. Company	5	18
Pauls Bros. Cutlery		
Germany	15	35
Paxton & Gallagher, U.S.A.	15	65
Peal Ranton	5	15
Peerless	5	15
Penn Cutlery Co.		
Tidioute, PA	10	150
Pennsylvania Knife Co.	35	200
Pepsi Cola	15	30
Peres, Germany	5	14
Permisso	3	35
Peters Bros.		
Celebrated Cutlery	50	165
Petters Cutlery Company		
Chicago, IL	25	85
Phoenix Knife Co.		
Phoenix, NY	10	135
Pic, Germany	3	8
PIC, Japan	2	5
Pine Knot, U.S.A.	35	300
Pine Knot		
James W. Price	45	400

NAME	RANGE	
C. Platts & Sons		
Andover, NY	40	800
Platts Bros.		
Andover, NY	40	800
Platts Bros., Union, NY	75	800
Pop Cutlery Co.		
Camillus, NY	5	20
Poor Boy	5	100
Pottery		
Hoy Hardware Co.	35	65
Powell Bros.	15	60
Power Kraft	5	10
C. Pradel	15	60
Pradel, France	15	60
Pratt & Co., London	70	110
Premier, Germany	3	10
Premier Cutlery Co.		
New York	4	15
Prentiss Knife Co.	10	45
M. Pressman & Co., New York	15	150
Press Button Knife Co.		
Walden, NY	35	150
Presto		
(George Schrade)	30	150
Pribyl Bros.	14	30
H. C. Price Co.		
Solingen	15	45
Primble, U.S.A.	20	75
J. Pritxloff Hardware Co.		
Milwaukee, WI	35	75
Produx, Sheffield	10	25
Providence Cutlery Co.	15	65
Puma, Germany	25	900
Putman Cutlery Co.	50	75
Q. C. Mfg. Co.		
Massillon, OH	15	75
QCCC	12	300
Q & Crown (Queen)	7	200
Large Q	7	150
Queen, U.S.A.	3	15
Queen City	20	250
Queen City		
Titusville, PA	10	250
Queen Steel		
Titusville, PA	10	110
Quick Point		
St. Louis, MO	25	75
Quick Point		
(Winchester stamped on		
back of tang)	50	75

NAME	RANGE	
Quick Point		
(Remington stamped on back of tang)	50	75
Quick-Kut, Inc.		
Freemont, OH	10	35
R. C. Co.		
Rochester, NY	25	400
R. I. Knife Co.	15	35
R. J. & R. S. Co.		
Germany	14	35
Race Bros.		
Celebrated Cutlery	50	200
Rainbow		
Providence, RI	5	15
Rand, Germany	4	15
Chas. R. Randall		
Germany	15	35
Raola Cutlery	4	10
Rather & Co., Germany	12	40
Tom Ray Cutlery Co.		
Kansas City, MO	35	200
Rawsom Bros.		
Sheffield	65	150
Red Devil S. Co., U.S.A.	15	60
Regent, St. Louis, MO	10	30
Rec-nor Co.		
Boston, MA	15	30
Reichert Bros.		
Reliance Cutlery Co.		
Germany	45	90
Remington, U.S.A.	20	2000
Remington, Germany	15	45
T. Renshaw & Son		
Sheffield	75	1500
Resistant		
(made by Lf&C)	35	—
Rev-O-Nov	45	75
Richards, U.S.A.	35	60
Richards, Sheffield	60	150
Richards & Conover Hardware		
U.S.A.	15	35
Richartz & Sons LTD		
Germany	12	40
Richmond Cutlery Co.	5	100
William Reid Rich's		
Celebrated Cutlery	40	175
R. J. Richter, Germany	4	15
Ring Cutlery, Japan	—	5
Rivington Works	15	65

NAME	RANGE	
Rizzaro Estilato, Milan, Italy	35	75
Roberts & Johnson & Rand		
St. Louis, MO	15	75
Robertson Bros. & Co.		
Louisville, KY	15	300
Robeson, Germany	25	75
Robeson, Rochester, NY	15	400
Robeson, Suredge	10	125
Robeson, Pocketeze	25	400
Robeson Cutlery		
Rochester, NY	10	400
Robinson Bros. & Co.		
Louisville, KY.	15	300
Rodgers Cutlery		
Sheffield	40	1000
Rodgers Cutlery		
Hartford, CT	15	30
Romo, Germany	5	15
Romo, Japan	1	6
J. Rosenbaulm	15	35
I. H. S. Rose & Co.	15	60
T. Ross & Son	30	60
Royce Brand, U.S.A	5	10
Royce Cutlery Co.	15	35
Royal Cutlery Co.	10	25
Royal Oak	15	45
Rugers Knife Co.		
Germany	15	50
Russell, U.S.A.	60	700
S&A, New York	12	55
S&A, New York, Made in Germany	8	30
S. B. Co	10	20
S & Co	5	15
S & L & Co.	5	15
S & M, Titusville, PA	20	300
S & M, Gowanda, NY	20	300
S. M. E., Solingen	5	10
SMCL, Solingen	5	10
S. P. Co., Centaur, NY	15	30
St. Lawrence Cutlery		
St. Louis, MO	25	75
STA SHARP, U.S.A.	15	30
STT Co., Louisville, KY	6	15
Sabatier, Rue st. France	15	35
Sabre, Japan	1	7
Sabre, Germany	4	12
Sabre American Knife Co.		
Germany	5	15

NAME	RANGE	
Salem	25	50
S. Salem	25	50
Salns, Torrence, CA	15	60
Salnor, Cook & Pidal	15	60
Sam L. Buckley & Son	10	35
Samco, Nashville, TN	15	30
Sands	10	40
Sanders Mfg. Co., Nashville, TN	35	85
Sarazento	5	15
Savoy Cutlery Co.		
Germany	5	25
Saxonia Cutlery Co.		
Germany	15	35
Saynor, Cook & Ridal	25	60
Sceptre	5	15
Schatt & Morgan		
Cutlery Co.		
Gowanda, NY	20	400
Carl Schlieper		
(German Eye) Germany	6	45
Schmachtenberg Bros.		
Germany	10	35
Schmidts Holmac Brand		
Germany	10	25
J. A. Schmidt & Doehne		
Germany	30	65
Schmidt & Ziegler		
(bull) Germany	10	75
Scholfield, Germany	8	20
Schrade Cutlery Co.		
Walden, NY	20	1000
Schrade-Walden		
Walden, NY	5	200
Seaboard Steel Co.		
France	3	15
Henry Sears Co.		
Prussia	15	65
Seco Works		
New Orange, NJ	15	35
E. Semco	5	10
F. Sem. Co.	5	15
Seneca Cutlery Co.	10	50
H. Seymour Cutlery Co.	15	55
Shapleigh Hardware Co.	10	350
Sharpkutter XX Cutlery Co.	15	55
Sheffield Steel	5	15
F. W. Sheldon & Co.		
Germany	4	25

NAME	RANGE	
Sheldon, Sheffield	15	35
Shumatic Cutlery Co.	20	75
Shur Snap (Colonial)	15	20
Sizeker		
Manstealed, Germany	10	15
Sliberstein Laporte & Co.	35	65
Simmons Hardware Co.		
Germany	20	300
Simmons Hardware		
St. Louis, MO	25	300
Simmons Warden White Co.		
Dayton, OH	15	75
C. F. Simon, Solingen	5	20
Singleton & Preistman		
Sheffield	50	150
Six Steel Edge Cutlery Co.		
Germany	5	20
Skiffman, Germany	4	15
Skilstuna, Germany	15	35
Skumbe & Son		
Dresden, Germany	10	U5
Slash-Charles Roberts &		
Sons & Co., Sheffield	25	75
H. M. Slater LTD, Sheffield	15	120
John II & Sons	10	35
Small Bros. Inc., Germany	10	25
Smith Bros. Hardware Co.		
Columbus, OH	35	75
J. P. Snow * Co., Chicago	25	65
Solidus	10	20
Solingen, Germany	4	15
Sootia, Sheffield	15	35
Southern & Richardson		
Sheffield	5	25
Southington Cutlery Co.		
England	25	200
Spear Cutlery Co., Germany	10	25
Spartts, England	35	90
Spring Cutlery Co.		
Sheffield	15	125
Springer, Japan	4	15
Stahl, Germany	5	15
Stainless Cutlery Co., U.S.A.	15	95
Stainless Cutlery Co.		
Germany	10	25
Standard Cutlery Co., U.S.A.	50	200
Standard Cutlery Co.		
Germany	5	25

NAME	RANGE	
Standard Cutlery Co.		
Division of Case	65	400
Sta-Sharp	20	150
Steelton Cutlery Works		
Germany	15	25
F. Sterling	5	25
Stellar, Japan	2	5
Stenton	5	15
Stercy	3	15
Stilletto Cutlery Co.		
New York	15	400
Otto Stoll	5	15
Streamline (etched)	15	35
Stocker & Co., Germany	5	25
Strauss Bros. & Co.		
Germany	12	25
Stringer, Philadelphia, PA	35	85
Sturdy, U.S.A.	10	35
Sudag, U.S.A.	5	23
Superior Cutlery	15	65
Supple Hardware Co.	10	35
Supreme, U.S.A.	—	—
J. H. Sutcliffe & Co.	10	125
Swan Works, Germany	5	35
Swank	7	15
Swank, Stainless	7	15
J. M. Swift	15	35
Sword (Camillus)	5	35
Syracuse Knife Co., U.S.A.	10	25
TIC	2	8
Tammen, Germany	5	12
Tarry	15	45
Taylor Cutlery Co.		
Kingsport, TN (made in Japan)	5	100
Taylor's Eye Witness		
Sheffield	10	35
Tell, Germany	5	100
Tellin & Co.	8	40
Thomas Wilton, Sheffield	15	75
Tink Hardware Co.		
Quincy, IL	35	75
Terrier Cutlery	15	75
C. Sarry Theirs	10	25
Pape Thiebis, Germany	10	150
Thomas Mfg. Co.		
Dayton, OH	15	150
Thomaston Knife Co.	15	35
J. H. Thompson Cutlery Ltd.		
Sheffield	30	200

NAME	RANGE	
Thompson, Germany	5	15
Thornton, U.S.A.	3	9
G. Tieman, New York	15	65
Tidioute Cutlery Co.		
Tidioute, PA	15	200
Tiger Cutlery	15	35
A. Tilles & Co.		
Philadelphia, PA	35	75
A. Tilles & Co.	35	75
Tima	3	10
Tip Top	25	40
Toledo Cutlery Co., Germany	15	35
Toothill	5	15
Torrey	20	70
Towika, Germany	3	10
Towika, Ireland	2	8
Townley, Kansas City, MO	35	75
S. Trakert	5	15
Trinton Cutlery Co.	15	30
Trout Hardward Co.		
Chicago, IL	25	50
Thomas Turner & Co.		
Sheffield, England	15	175
Trout Hardware Co.		
Chicago, IL	5	20
Twentieth Century Cutlery	10	35
Twenty Grand, U.S.A.	15	40
Two Eagles	10	45
U. C. Co., U.S.A.	15	75
U. D. Co., U.S.A.	5	15
U. K. Co., U.S.A.	46	115
U. K. & R. Co., Germany	75	200
N. U. Co., New York	10	70
U. S. Knife Co.	20	85
Ulery, U.S.A.	5	15
Ulrich, Germany	4	15
Ulster Knife Co.	3	75
Ulster, Ellenville, NY	15	65
Ulster, Dwight Devine &		
Sons, U.S.A.	30	250
Uncle Henry (Schrade-Walden) Walden, NY	12	30
Union Cutlery Co.		
Olean, NY	25	2500
Union Cutlery Co.		
Tidioute, PA	25	1500
Union Knife Co.		
Newgatuck Co.	25	300

NAME	RANGE	
Union Razor Co.		
Tidioute, PA	50	800
Union Knife Works	25	300
United, Grand Rapids, MI	5	25
United, Germany	3	10
Universal Knife Co.		
New Britain, CT	15	35
Utica Co., Czechoslovakia	12	35
Utica Cutlery Co.		
Utica, NY	10	150
Utica Knife Co., U.S.A.	10	150
V. K. Cutlery Co., Germany	5	15
Valley Falls Cutlery Co.	15	75
Valley Forge Cutlery Co.	20	95
Valor, Germany	3	15
Valor, Japan	3	15
Vanco, Indianapolis, IN	5	35
Van Camp, U.S.A.	3	100
Van Camp H & I Co., U.S.A.	15	300
Van Camp		
Indianapolis, IN	15	300
Van Camp, Germany	10	30
Vernider, St. Paul, MN	5	25
Veritable Pradel	12	20
Victor	5	20
Victorinox, Switzerland		
(Swiss army knives)	4	25
Vignos Cut. Co.	15	125
Viking, U.S.A.	5	15
H. Ville Knife Co.	15	65
Vive Knife Works, Germany	5	15
Volort Cutlery Co., Sheffield	5	15
Vom Cleff & Co., Germany	10	135
Voos, U.S.A.	25	40
Voos Cutlery Co., Germany	5	25
Voos Cutlery Co., Germany		
(Hen & Rooster)	40	200
Voyles Cutlery	20	50
Vulcan Knife Co., Germany	5	30
Vulcan & Tellin & Co.	10	35
Vulcan, Sheffield	15	75
W & A Co., Providence, RI	15	65
W & H Co., Newark, NJ	10	35
W R B Co., Terre Haute, IN	35	75
W RR, Sheffield	10	40
W & W, Germany	5	15
Wabash Cutlery Co.		
Terre Haute, IN	35	200
Wade Bros Celebrated Cutlery	15	1000

NAME	RANGE	
Wade & Butcher, Germany	20	70
Wade & Butcher, Sheffield	20	1000
Wadsworth, Germany	5	40
Wadsworth & Sons, Austria	10	45
Wahl Wagner, Solingen	5	15
Wait Co., U.S.A.	5	30
Walden Knife Co.,		
Walden, NY	35	400
Walker Cutlery Works, Germany	5	35
Walkill River Works		
Walden, NY	35	200
Wall Bros., Sheffield	35	150
Wallace Bros.	35	60
Walt Co., U.S.A.	5	16
Watter Bros.	10	30
Watter Bros. Cutlery, Germany	10	30
Waltham Cutlery, U.S.A.	5	25
Waltham Cutlery, Germany	5	15
Wandy, Italy	4	10
Ward Bros.	5	35
Wards, U.S.A.	5	35
Wardlon Cutlery Co.		
Walden, NY	25	85
W & W Walter Warrington		
Sheffield	15	65
Warren, Baker, OR	5	25
Warren Bros.,		
Soffolk Works, England	35	150
Warwick Knife Co., NY	151	200
Washington Cutlery Co.		
Milwaukee, WI	15	75
Washington Cutlery, Germany	151	60
Watauga (H. G.		
Liscomb, Nashville, TN)	15	75
Waterville Cutlery Co.		
Waterville CT	15	85
John Watts, Sheffield	15	30
Webster, Sycamore Works		
U.S.A.	10	35
Webster Cutlery Co., Germany	5	15
Weck, N.Y.	15	65
Wedgeway Cutlery Co.	14	35
Weed & Co., Buffalo	35	75
Wherwolf Cutlery Works		
Germany	10	120
G. Weiland, New York	5	25
Marshall Wells		
Hardware Co.	35	125

NAME	RANGE		NAME	RANGE	
H. C. Wentworth & Son			**Whittingslowe**	15	75
Germany	5	35	**Whittlecraft** (By		
Weske Cutlery Co.			Cattaragus)	45	90
Sandusky, OH	15	35	**Wilbert Cutlery Co.**		
Westaco, Boulder, CO	30	60	Chicago, IL	15	75
Wester, B. C.	5	35	**E. Wilds & Sons**	15	75
Wester Bros., Germany	35	250	**H. Y. Wilkinson Cutlery Co.**	10	35
Wester Stone, Inc., U.S.A.	15	115	**Wilson Celebrated Cutlery Co.**	40	175
Western, Boulder, CO	50	500	**Wilson Cutlery Co.**	35	75
Western Cutlery Co., Germany	5	30	**Henry Wilton**, Germany	5	35
Western Shear Co.	15	65	**John Wilton**, Sheffield	35	75
Western States			**Thomas Wilton**, Sheffield	35	75
Boulder, CO	10	150	**Wade Wingfield**, Sheffield	5	35
Weyles	10	150	**A. Wingen**, Solingen	5	15
A. J. Westersson,			**Wismar Cutlery**, Germany	5	25
Esdiktuna	5	15	**Wisman Cutlery Co.**		
Weterson Co., Germany	5	35	Germany	15	35
Wheatly, Sheffield	15	65	**Wismar**	5	20
White House	5	25			

GENERAL SHARPENING

A knife should be kept sufficiently sharp to do the work for which it is intended. When possible, always cut in direction away from body. When this can't be done, keep body, particularly hand and fingers, in the clear. Avoid jerking motions, sudden strains or other movements causing a loss of balance.

KNIFE BLADE — ANGLE of 10° to 15°

SHARPENING STONE

SHARPENING STONE

HOW TO SHARPEN—Hold back of blade up from stone at angle of 10 to 15 degrees as shown in illustration above. Stroke cutting edge against stone in direction of arrows from heel to point of blade (as though to cut a thin slice of stone), alternating first on one side of blade and then the other. Use a good quality stone such as **CASE'S 6" Oil Stone.** A fine light oil should be applied to the stone since this will produce the sharpest possible edge if smooth even strokes are used. To obtain an extremely keen edge, finish sharpening on **CASE'S Arkansas Stone.**

The stone should be wiped clean of excess oil after each use. This waste oil will carry away with it the fine steel grindings which, if not removed, would soon clog the pores of the stone.

DO NOT use a coarse emery wheel or grindstone. Furthermore, improper use of steel disc sharpeners or electric sharpeners may damage even the finest knife blade.

DO NOT lay the blade flat on the sharpening stone. It will thin and scar the sides of the blade, and will produce a paper-thin edge which will not stand up in use or remain sharp.

DO NOT lay the blade at too steep an angle as the edge will be too blunt for maximum cutting efficiency.